PostScript® by Example

Henry McGilton
Mary Campione

 Addison-Wesley Publishing Company.

Reading, Massachusetts • Menlo Park, California • New York
Don Mills, Ontario • Wokingham, England • Amsterdam
Bonn • Sydney • Singapore • Tokyo • Madrid • San Juan
Paris • Seoul • Milan • Mexico City • Taipei

Library of Congress Cataloging in Publication Data

McGilton, Henry.
    PostScript by Example / Henry McGilton. Mary Campione.
      p. cm.
    Includes bibliographical references and index.
    ISBN 0-201-63228-4
    1. PostScript (Computer program language)   I. Campione, Mary.
  II. Title.
  QA76.73.P67M34   1992
  006.6'6--dc20   92–19743
                                                      CIP

Many of the designations used by manufacturers and sellers to distinguish their products are claimed as trademarks. Where these designations appear in this book, and Addison-Wesley were aware of a trademark claim, the designations have been printed in initial capital letters or all capital letters.

The authors and publishers have taken care in preparation of this book, but make no expressed or implied warranty of any kind and assume no responsibility for errors or omissions. No liability is assumed for incidental or consequential damages in connection with or arising out of the use of the information or programs contained herein.

Sponsoring Editor ...... David Rogelberg
Project Editor .... Joanne Clapp Fullagar
Cover Design .... Trish Sinsigalli LaPointe
Cover Art .... Donald Craig
Production .... Set in eleven-point Palatino and Optima
                                  by Henry McGilton at Trilithon Software.

6 7 8 9 1011 MA   01 00 99 98
6th Printing December 1998

strangeness of the numbers for the moment—you'll soon see how to make the units more manageable.

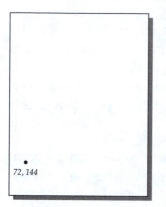

```
%!PS                          %    PostScript "Magic Number"
72 144 moveto                 %    set initial point
306 648 lineto                %    add line segment
540 144 lineto                %    add another line segment
closepath                     %    finish the shape
stroke                        %    paint the path
showpage                      %    display page
```

moveto *establishes the current point.*

Notice the PostScript *comment* introduced by the percent (%) sign. All characters from the percent sign to end of line are ignored.

The next instruction draws a line *to* a specific place, in this case, to position (306, 648). But from where will the line be drawn? It will be drawn from the current point set by the **moveto** operation.

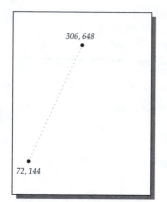

```
%!PS                          %    PostScript "Magic Number"
72 144 moveto                 %    set initial point
306 648 lineto                %    add line segment
540 144 lineto
closepath
stroke
showpage                      %    display page
```

lineto *adds a line segment to the current path.*

306 648 lineto is an instruction to draw a straight line segment from the current point to position (306, 648)[†] on the page.

Saying "**lineto** draws a line" is a little imprecise. **lineto** doesn't in fact draw anything. All **lineto** or any other path operator does is add a path segment to the current path. These operators establish a path to be used for stroking, filling, or clipping, if indeed they

---

† Again, the units are $1/72$ inch, so this point is at (4¼ inches, 9 inches).

get used for any of those purposes at all.† Nothing is actually drawn—in the sense of paint being applied to the paper or screen—until you supply specific instructions to do so.

The current point is initially undefined. If you were to delete the **moveto** instruction from this example program (or comment it out by placing a percent sign at the beginning of the line), you would get your first PostScript error. Any error-reporting mechanism you have in place would return a message telling you there was a **nocurrentpoint** error.

Having added the first straight line segment to the current path, the current point is left at the end of the line segment just added. **540 144 lineto** adds another straight line segment from the current point to position (540, 144); that's 7½ inches, 2 inches on the page. Once again, the current point is left at the end of the line segment just added to the current path.

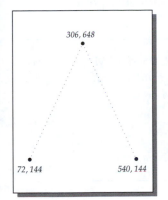

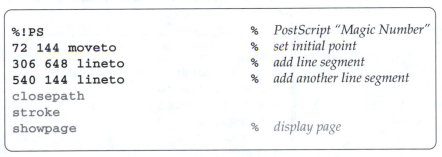

```
%!PS                  %   PostScript "Magic Number"
72 144 moveto         %   set initial point
306 648 lineto        %   add line segment
540 144 lineto        %   add another line segment
closepath
stroke
showpage              %   display page
```

lineto adds a second line segment to the current path.

Now you have two line segments of the triangle added to the current path. The next part of the program is interesting. Instead of drawing a third line back to the starting point, you finish the path using **closepath**, a new operator.

---

† You might, for instance, establish a path just to find out how big it is.

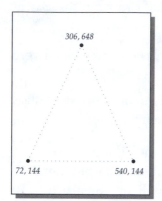

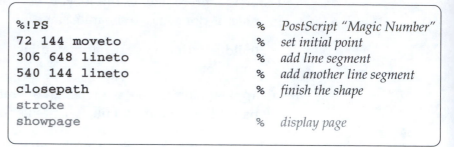

```
%!PS            %  PostScript "Magic Number"
72 144 moveto   %  set initial point
306 648 lineto  %  add line segment
540 144 lineto  %  add another line segment
closepath       %  finish the shape
stroke
showpage        %  display page
```

closepath *completes the shape.*

You could draw the final line using another **lineto**. But as you shall see later, potential problems exist when you close a shape with explicit path operators. This example uses **closepath** to do what its name implies—to ensure that the final point and the initial point are connected correctly by drawing a line from the current point to the initial point of the path.[†]

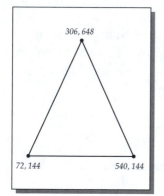

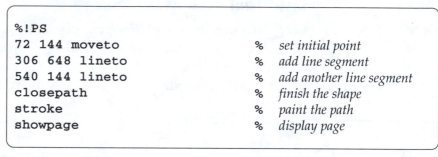

```
%!PS
72 144 moveto   %  set initial point
306 648 lineto  %  add line segment
540 144 lineto  %  add another line segment
closepath       %  finish the shape
stroke          %  paint the path
showpage        %  display page
```

stroke *paints the outline of the path.*

As you just read, nothing gets printed until you explicitly ask to apply paint. This example uses **stroke** to do the drawing. **stroke** applies ink to draw along the current path. Finally, **showpage** prints the page on the printing device. Nothing prints if you omit **showpage**—the printer blinks its lights for a while and then nothing happens. Omitting **showpage** is a common mistake made by PostScript experts and beginners alike, so if your PostScript program doesn't print, first ask yourself, "did I put **showpage** at the end of the program?"

---

† More precisely, to the initial point of the current *subpath*.

From the preceding example you see that drawing PostScript graphics is done in two separate stages:

- ❑ build a path using operators you just learned, such as **moveto** and **lineto**

- ❑ apply paint to the path using operators like **stroke**, which paints the outline, and **fill**, which fills the interior of a path

This two-step process is a simple view of the situation. You can create elaborate paths and perform complex computations to determine how, when, and where paths will be constructed. In addition to straight lines, you can use arcs and curves to construct paths. Arcs (to draw arcs and circles) and curves (specifically Bézier curves) are discussed in Chapter 7. You can build complex illustrations with only a small set of simple graphics operators.

Basic Text—Show a Message

Sticking to the philosophy of minimal theorizing, let's jump right into our second PostScript program. Here's a simple program to image text on the page. Suppose you wish to print the string **PostScript!** very large across the page.

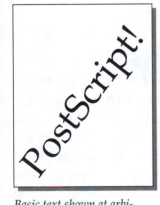

Basic text shown at arbitrary angle.

```
%!PS
/Palatino-Roman findfont      %   find required font
162 scalefont                 %   scale font to required size
setfont                       %   set as current font
108 36 moveto                 %   set current point
52 rotate                     %   rotate coordinate system
(PostScript!) show            %   image title on page
showpage                      %   display page
```

Again, let's examine this program line by line. You're already familiar with **%!PS**—the PostScript magic number. The next three lines set a current font for printing text. Setting the current font is in fact three separate operations, namely, find the font you want to use (Palatino-Roman in this case) from the system, scale it to the specified size, and set the scaled font as the current font.

```
%!PS
/Palatino-Roman findfont          %   find required font
162 scalefont                     %   scale font to required size
setfont                           %   set as current font
108 36 moveto                     %   set current point
52 rotate                         %   rotate coordinate system
(PostScript!) show                %   image title on page
showpage                          %   display page
```

These three lines of PostScript make 162-point Palatino-Roman the current font—the font in which the text appears. The current font remains in effect until you change it to something else.

Having set the current font, you want to image some text in that font somewhere on the page. Where? At the current point. So the next line uses a PostScript operator you learned in the triangle example on page 10. **moveto** sets the current point on the page. The lower-left point of the baseline of the first character shown appears at this point. The line **(PostScript!) show** paints the indicated string of text on the page.

```
%!PS
/Palatino-Roman findfont          %   find required font
162 scalefont                     %   scale font to required size
setfont                           %   set as current font
108 36 moveto                     %   set current point
52 rotate                         %   rotate coordinate system
(PostScript!) show                %   image title on page
showpage                          %   display page
```

After the string of text is added to the current path, the current point is moved to the end of the string, and is now ready for more text (or graphics) to be placed into the path. Finally, **showpage** renders the text to the page or the screen. When working with text, you don't need a **stroke** or **fill** to paint the path created by **show**. The **show** operator does both steps:

❑   constructs the path made up of characters

❑   paints the path

You can get a lot fancier with text, and you'll see examples of some of these fancy operations in Chapter 3.

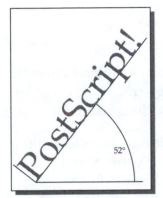

PostScript can rotate text to arbitrary angles.

Notice that the **rotate** line in the example code has been left out of the explanation so far. You want to paint the string of text across the page from bottom-left to upper-right. Without **rotate**, the line of text would image horizontally across the page and would fall off the edge. To rotate the text up and across the page you need to slide in the **rotate** operation so the text will be painted at an angle on the page. The value to rotate is 52°, which happens to be the angle whose arctangent is 11 inches divided by 8½ inches.

Rotating text at arbitrary angles is a major strength of PostScript and that sets it apart from other page description languages and text display systems. You'll see a little more about rotations in *Transformations* on pages 20–27 in this chapter, and a more detailed discussion in Chapter 4.

In the example a font is located, scaled, and set in a series of operations involving **findfont**, **scalefont**, and **setfont**. Setting the current font is a two-part process: decide which font you want (Palatino, Lithos, Charlemagne, Ah'Mose), then decide what kind of transformation you want. PostScript Level 2 and Display PostScript added a "convenience operator" to find, scale, and set the font all at once, for very real performance reasons. The new operator is **selectfont**, shown in the next example.

In this example you use **selectfont** to find Palatino-Roman, scale it to 162 points large, and set that scaled font as the current font in the graphics state. In fact, in PostScript Level 2, both **findfont** and **selectfont** are special cases of a more general **findresource** operator that deals with general resource management.

```
%!PS
/Palatino-Roman 162 selectfont  %  set required font and size
108 36 moveto                   %  set current point
52 rotate                       %  rotate coordinate system
(PostScript!) show              %  image title on page
showpage                        %  display page
```

Same text scaled using **selectfont**.

Our examples of text showed text imaged in the preset black color. But text, just like any other PostScript graphical object, can be painted with color, or shades of gray, and patterns in PostScript Level 2. This example is the same as the original text example on page 14, with the addition of a line to set the "color" of the text, a shade of gray, prior to **show**.

```
%!PS
/Palatino-Roman findfont        %  find required font
162 scalefont                   %  scale font to required size
setfont                         %  set as current font
108 36 moveto                   %  set current point
52 rotate                       %  rotate coordinate system
0.50 setgray                    %  set medium gray color
(PostScript!) show              %  image title on page
showpage                        %  display page
```

Text can be imaged in gray or color.

Basic PostScript Syntax

Examples so far have been very simple. You've seen a few basic PostScript operators. **moveto** and **lineto** set the current point and add line segments to the current path. **stroke** paints the outline of a path and **show** images text on the page. **showpage** prints the assembled page image on the printing or display device. In addition to illustrating basic PostScript operators, the examples have introduced fundamentals of PostScript syntax. Now you'll see a few basic syntactical notions of PostScript before continuing with the show and tell. More details of the PostScript language can be found in Chapter 5.

A PostScript file should start with the **%!PS** characters. **%!PS** is a magic number to tell printer management software this is a PostScript file and not just some other kind of text file. In theory a simple **%!** is enough.

PostScript has many more conventions. You will see constructs like **%!PS-Adobe-3.0** and even more complicated constructs like **%!PS-Adobe-3.0 EPSF-2.0**. For now, just take on faith that PostScript files should always begin with the **%!PS** characters.

PostScript is what is known as a *postfix* language, meaning all PostScript operators follow their arguments. For example, the basic syntax of **moveto** is

x y `moveto`

where x and y are the coordinates of the place to which you wish to move the current point. In general, the syntax of a given **PostScript_operator** is

arg_1 arg_2 arg_3 . . . arg_n `PostScript_operator`

where arg_1, arg_2, arg_3,... arg_n are arguments for that specific operator. When you write

`100 200 moveto`

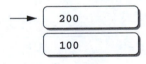

(x, y) coordinate pair pushed onto stack.

the two coordinate values, $x = 100$ and $y = 200$, are pushed onto a *stack*. Chapter 5 discusses stacks in detail. **moveto** removes (pops) these two numbers from the stack and sets the current point to that (x, y) position.

All PostScript operators behave in this way—they consume operands from the operand stack. Some operators may return values to the operand stack; this is one way short-term intermediate results of calculations can be passed between sections of a PostScript program.

Take some time to understand the stack mechanisms. PostScript provides three different stacks, the *operand* stack being the one you use the most. PostScript provides great control over the operand

Contents

Acknowledgments

To Richard Campione

黄
彩 *and*
閃 Sandra Jane Wong

In The Beginning...

Adobe Systems made everything possible by creating PostScript in the first place. Adobe staff members (too numerous to mention) answered many questions over long periods. Ross Jeynes and Carl Orthlieb supplied vital information to break mental logjams, while Ken Lunde and Paul Haahr supplied critical insights into composite fonts and multiple master fonts.

The Book Design...

Teri Fujimoto was the principal guide for a book design that started several years ago with a completely different project and has stood the test of time.

Creating and debugging more than seven hundred PostScript pictures would have been impossible without PostScript interpreters to display on computer screens.

Many thanks to L. Peter Deutsch of Aladdin Enterprises (Menlo Park, California) and to the Free Software Foundation for **Ghostscript**, a PostScript-compatible interpreter and viewer used to create and debug many PostScript diagrams during the early stages of writing. An extra-special thank-you to Ali Ozer of NeXT for YAP (Yet Another Previewer) bundled with NeXT systems. Without Ghostscript and YAP, developing PostScript examples would have been orders of magnitude more difficult. Aeons ago (by computer industry timescales) Ned Batchelder and Trevor Darrell created **psfig**, a nifty utility that greatly eased the job of injecting vast numbers of (correctly scaled) PostScript figures into this document.

EPS images on pages 3–7, 103–106 are from the ClickArt® series© 1984–1992, all rights reserved, T/Maker Company, Mountain

View, California. Maureen Stone of Xerox PARC provided the color gamut diagram appearing on page 505 and in plate XV. The film gamut was measured by Alan Paeth.

A special mention to our many reviewers, contributors, and supporters ...

Chuck Bigelow of Bigelow and Holmes provided early insights on the nature of multiple master fonts; Mister Arlen Britton of Minneapolis College of Art and Design; Dick Dunn of Eklektix provided much moral support over years of E-mail conversations; Marjolein Hoekstra of Encore Software, 's-Gravenhage; Ken Fromm and Sterling Hutto of Vivid Publishing Corporation; Bob Goodenough, Consulting Philosopher, for support, counselling, and many interesting hours designing Agora for Entrepreneurs; Ian Kemmish of 5D Solutions did a sterling detailed proofreading job as well as performing as special "guest lecturer" on PostScript Level 2 color; Ray Liere provided the initial encouraging boost, seemingly years ago, to get started in the first place; Liam Quin of SoftQuad, Toronto; Glenn Reid of Right Brain Software provided much help and inspiration over the years; Tom Rokicki of Radical Eye ($\sqrt{i}$) Software was the fastest technical reviewer in the West; Chris Sears and Dan Sears; Nathan Shedroff of Vivid Publishing Corporation for advice on design. Rob Francis, Vivienne Aldred, and Suni Munshani of Trirex Systems; Derek Penn of JP Morgan.

Thanks to the staff of Addison-Wesley for (lots of) patience ...

Dave Rogelberg, Joanne Clapp-Fullagar, and Amy Cheng of Addison-Wesley West; Vicki Hochstedler of Addison-Wesley East for wizard production management; Tana Schimberg for wizard copy editing, and Rita Siglain for wizard proof editing. A round of applause goes to Peter Greis at Graphics Express for last-minute crisis management and being the calm at the center of the storm.

Writing a book takes lots of sustenance ...

Pearl's Seafood Restaurant and Caffe Verona in Palo Alto and Hotel Sofitel in Foster City, unwittingly provided the milieu for the design, discussion, fisticuffs, reasoned debate and so forth, of this book, fueled by 248 crab cake dinners at Pearl's restaurant and 196 pasta dinners at Caffe Verona, accompanied by 628 bottles of premium California Chardonnay.

Preface

"What is the use of a book,"
thought Alice, "without pictures or conversations?"

Lewis Carroll—*Alice's Adventures in Wonderland*

Characters drawn with a PostScript program consisting of Bézier curves.

PostScript has become an established part of worldwide graphics, design, publishing, and printing. If you want to know more—or even a little—about PostScript, read on. The theme of this book is to advise instead of pontificate, to show *by example* rather than explain.

A conviction that books about graphics really ought to contain more than five pictures, and the famous Doctor Samuel Johnson's statement "Example is always more efficacious than precept," led to this guided tour through PostScript.

If you're a PostScript novice wondering what all the fuss is about, or a user dealing with day-to-day practicalities of printing and publishing, this book is for you. If you're an application programmer wondering "where do I start?" and need hints and tips about issues of good, better, and other kinds of PostScript programming, this book is also for you.

About PostScript

PostScript is first and foremost a powerful *graphics* language whose goal is to provide application programmers with both a printer-independent and a computer-system-independent means to describe integrated text and graphics destined for printed pages and computer display screens. To meet these needs, PostScript evolved as a graphical page description language backed by a full-featured, interpreted, programming language.

For the most part PostScript is not intended to be hand-written. The intent, really, is to have PostScript printer files generated by application software such as desktop publishing programs and other software packages that produce hard copy. In reality, a working knowledge of PostScript and its place in the real world of printers and displays will help you.

If you'd like to experiment with this powerful language, you'll find beginning and intermediate-level examples of PostScript code you can change around to suit your own needs. Application users dealing with day-to-day issues (printer specific-code, Encapsulated PostScript, structured PostScript, downloading fonts, debugging PostScript programs, and printers with mass storage capabilities), you can find material to point you in the right direction.

About This Book

This book approaches PostScript from a practical viewpoint of "here's some PostScript code and here's what you see on the printer." We cover many PostScript graphics and text operators in detail. The subset of PostScript in this book should get you started in PostScript programming and provide you the springboard to help you explore the remainder.

This book is not a full-fledged PostScript reference manual containing a complete guide to the nuts and bolts of the language. The full-blown reference book already exists—the *PostScript Language Reference Manual*, Second Edition—written by Adobe Systems.[†] Commonly known as "The Red Book," the *PostScript Language Reference Manual* contains a detailed description of the syntax and semantics of PostScript.

---

† If you don't already have a copy of the *PostScript Language Reference Manual*, Second Edition, run out immediately and get one. See Appendix A for references.

You can view this book as two collections of topics—the basics, and the not-so-basics. The basics introduces basic notions of PostScript—points, lines, text, curves, arcs, and images. All these text and graphical objects are composed using PostScript ready-made objects such as fonts and pattern fills. The not-so-basics describes tools for building your own fonts, patterns, and forms, delves into color and halftones, and deals with system issues such as printers, printing, and document structure.

Collection 1—the Basics

The basics includes Chapter 1 through Chapter 9. Chapter 1, *Introducing PostScript*, starts with a brief "show and tell" of PostScript graphics, text, and transforms, an overview of PostScript imaging model, plus color and patterns, and includes a discussion of what you need to get started creating your own PostScript programs.

Basic graphics and text.

Chapters 2, 3, and 4 describe the most basic PostScript graphics and text facilities. In Chapter 2 you will read about the current point, adding line segments to the current path, plus PostScript Level 2 and Display PostScript rectangle operators.

Chapter 3 introduces showing text and selecting fonts, covers variations on facilities for showing text, covers methods to obtain precise widths and heights of character strings, and describes effects you can obtain using character paths as outlines to paint or as regions with which to clip.

Chapter 4 describes in detail transformations you can perform when rendering text, graphics, and sampled images. Chapter 4 introduces the *Current Transformation Matrix*, or CTM, and shows you many examples of manipulating the CTM, and their effects on resultant images.

Chapter 5 covers basic ideas of the PostScript language and its execution model—stacks, dictionaries, and procedures. The last part of Chapter 5 contains a detailed discussion of some of the more useful and most commonly used PostScript operators— you'll find an overview of the workings of PostScript arithmetic, string, array, and control operators.

PostScript shapes drawn through a clipping area.

Chapters 6 through 8 cover the remainder of PostScript analytical graphics capabilities. Chapter 6 describes line weights and line styles, Chapter 7 describes arcs and, by extension, circles and ellipses. Chapter 7 also covers **arcto** and its Display PostScript variations. The latter part of Chapter 7 describes Bézier curves—cubic curves that lend so much power to PostScript's ability to describe æsthetically pleasing letterforms.

Chapter 8 describes PostScript clipping facilities—the ability to establish a path as an area to which other text and graphical shapes may be "clipped."

Chapter 9 rounds out the first collection of topics with images—sampled images or bitmaps that might be obtained from scanning photographs or from using pixel painting software. Chapter 9 discusses issues of rendering images as well as image masks as stencils through which color may be applied.

Collection 2—Build Your Own

Chapters 10 through 14 comprise the second collection. Think of this collection as "do-it-yourself-PostScript." These chapters describe tools for building fonts, patterns, and forms.

User-defined PostScript font.

Chapter 10 leads you through the basic details of creating your own user-defined font, known as a PostScript Type 3 font. You will see how to construct a Type 3 font and how to create a derived font. *Composite Fonts* in Chapter 10 discusses the details of PostScript Level 2 composite fonts—fonts capable of supporting huge character sets as are needed, for example, in Asian languages such as Chinese and Japanese. Finally, *Multiple Master Fonts* in Chapter 10 provides an overview of Adobe Systems' new technology of multiple master, or interpolated, fonts.

Chapter 11 discusses PostScript Level 2 patterns—regular self-contained graphical objects used to "tile" an area of the page. Chapter 11 shows you how to create a pattern from scratch, how to use the pattern you created, and discusses various fields necessary in a pattern dictionary.

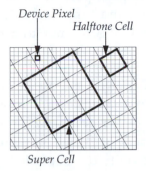

Device Pixel

Halftone Cell

Super Cell

Chapter 12 covers PostScript Level 2 forms—self-contained graphical shapes that can be painted multiple times on one page or repeated one or more times across multiple pages. Chapter 12 covers creating and using forms.

Chapter 13 discusses the related topics of color and halftones. Adobe made significant advancements in color specification and halftone screens in PostScript Level 2. Chapter 13 first covers the main color models and PostScript Level 2 color spaces. The topic then turns to halftones, covering screen angles, frequencies, and spot functions.

The final chapter might be roughly labeled "PostScript for people who just want to get on with the job.[†] Chapter 14 discusses details of dealing with real printers. You can read about obtaining lists of fonts from your printer, downloading fonts, and error handling. Issues of cooperative printing discuss how PostScript documents are (or should be) generated. Chapter 14 talks about PostScript's *Document Structuring Conventions* and *Encapsulated PostScript*.

The appendix lists some books you might read on PostScript, graphics, and typography issues.

Some Conventions

`Bold Courier` font represents PostScript code in the source listings of examples, while **Bold Optima** represents PostScript operators inline in text.

Going Metric—the whole nine yards.

Throughout this book, we use inches as the main unit. As North America inches its way into the metric system, we are somewhat limited in the use of *Systeme Internationale*, so we stick with what's widely supported. In addition, there are precisely 72 PostScript units to an inch, so rounding issues aren't evident.

---

† Thanks to Tim O'Reilly for this practical viewpoint of PostScript.

For the same reason we use inches as the units of measurement, we use Good Ol' U.S. "standard letter paper"—8½ by 11 inches—in examples. The world of computer support in North America revolves around this format of paper, and support for ISO paper sizes—A4 and such—is hard to find. We try not to let assumptions about paper sizes creep into the discussion.

Because this book covers PostScript Level 2 as well as PostScript Level 1, some examples will run only on PostScript Level 2 devices. When you see code samples with this PostScript Level 2 logo () it's a signal that either the code example will run only on PostScript Level 2 devices, or that you can modify the example to run on PostScript Level 1 devices.

1 Introducing PostScript

And the first rude sketch that the world had seen
    Was joy to his mighty heart.
Till the Devil whispered behind the leaves,
    "It's pretty, but is it Art?"

Rudyard Kipling—*The Conundrum of the Workshops*

Effects with PostScript clipping and opaque imaging model.

You have probably seen illustrations like the one on the left and wondered how they were created. If the pictures were created any time since 1985, chances are they were created using application software capable of generating *PostScript*. If you're a beginning PostScript programmer or a graphics designer, read on, to see how to produce pictures like this, and much more.

First off though, just what *is* PostScript? PostScript is a powerful *graphics language*—PostScript describes how text and graphical objects shall be integrated and laid out on a sheet of paper or on a computer display screen.

Of course, you don't usually write PostScript programs yourself—you employ publishing software, illustration packages, CAD software, report generators, and software packages that act as go-betweens, to interpret what you need and generate PostScript for you. In principle, PostScript is intended primarily as intermediary between page layout or graphics software and display devices—users shouldn't need to worry about details of how printing is actually done. In practice, a working knowledge of PostScript is a major asset when you use applications that generate PostScript and printers that understand PostScript.

1

Levels of PostScript

This book introduces *PostScript Level 2* in addition to "regular" PostScript (Level 1). Many of the examples will run fine on PostScript printers that have been around for the past seven years or so. Many more examples will run only on PostScript Level 2 devices, which started trickling onto the market around the end of 1991. By now you have no doubt heard the terms *PostScript Level 1*, *PostScript Level 2*, and *Display PostScript* bandied around. What are all these levels and what do they mean to you?

Apple LaserWriter IINTX is a popular PostScript printer.

PostScript has been a fact of personal computer-based printing since 1985, when Adobe Systems and Apple Computer cooperated to bring Apple LaserWriters to market. From small beginnings, PostScript grew to a position of importance in every facet of publishing and graphics design. PostScript brought high quality graphics and scalable font technology to low resolution printing devices at moderate prices and effectively fueled the "Desktop Publishing" business. The flavor of PostScript popular in Apple laser printers since 1985 is what has become known as PostScript Level 1—the "original" PostScript.

Over the first seven years of its life, in practical everyday use, PostScript was extended and enhanced in several ways. Various manufacturers created products in cooperation with Adobe to serve special needs of the market. For instance, QMS Corporation created a color laser printer, and the version of PostScript for that printer was extended to cater to new color models and color images. As another example, Apple manufactured the Laser-Writer IINTX-J specifically to meet the needs of the Japanese marketplace, using a PostScript enhancement called composite fonts.

PostScript was originally used to drive printers. Adobe Systems and NeXT Incorporated cooperated in producing a version of PostScript to drive computer displays. Enhancements to support displays include multiple contexts, higher performance, shared memory, hit detection for input devices, and so on. The display version of PostScript is, of course, called Display PostScript. NeXT computers and Silicon Graphics have adopted Display PostScript as the imaging model for their computer systems.

In 1990, Adobe Systems held a major developers' conference where they announced PostScript Level 2 (existing PostScript implementations being designated as PostScript Level 1). PostScript Level 2 represents both a consolidation of piecemeal extensions added over the years plus new features that enrich the language and cater to the Display PostScript marketplace.

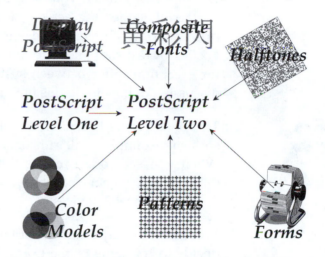

PostScript evolution from Level 1 to Level 2.

Evolution of PostScript from Level 1 to Level 2 comprises many enhancements. Major extensions include device-independent color models and operators to support new color printers. New halftones produce improved and more accurate color separations. Composite fonts support Asian marketplaces where character sets are very large. Composite fonts existed prior to Level 2 in printers specifically targeted to Japan. PostScript Level 2 pattern color spaces support device-independent pattern filling—previous pattern-filling methods using halftone screens or fonts were unsatisfactory. An important addition is *Display PostScript*—the move from a pure printer language to the same language and imaging model for computer display screens. Many performance enhancements and new operators support displays.

Tools You Need to Explore PostScript

Tools you need to explore PostScript are fairly accessible. First you need a personal computer—Macintosh, NeXT, IBM personal computer or equivalent. On this computer you need a simple text editing facility; nothing fancy, just a means to produce text in a file. Finally, you need a means to interpret and display PostScript, either the screen of your computer or a PostScript printer to which you send the text file. Details for creating PostScript text files and shipping them to a PostScript interpreter for execution differ between systems, and you'll find a detailed discussion of how to do this in the next few pages.

PostScript Level 2 logo.

This book covers PostScript Level 2 as well as PostScript Level 1, so some examples will run only on PostScript Level 2 devices. When you see code samples with this PostScript Level 2 logo () it's a signal that the code example will run only on PostScript Level 2 devices.

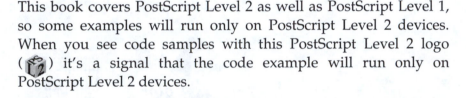

You will see many examples of PostScript code in this book. If you decide to try some of the examples, you will need to type them into your computer and send them to your PostScript printer or display device. How you actually get your PostScript program typed into a file and shipped to a printer depends on the computer system you're using. You must address two separate issues:

❑ creating files of plain ungarnished ASCII text (the PostScript code you wish to send to your printer)

❑ shipping that unembroidered ASCII file to your printer

First of all, no matter which computer system you use, you need a means to type plain ASCII text into a file so the text has absolutely *no* structuring information—no changes of size, no changes of font, no page layout—just plain old unadulterated ASCII text. This is probably the most important issue, because the PostScript interpreter in your printer or display just wants to see ASCII text.

Second, you need to transmit the PostScript code to the printer so the PostScript interpreter can run it. PostScript printers are sophisticated devices, and your computer must handle the two-way communications protocol with the PostScript printer. Think of your PostScript printer as another computer attached to the host computer *via* some kind of communication channel. You can't treat the PostScript printer as just a "dumb" printer—you must ensure correct interaction between the host computer and the printer. That said, let's look at some of the main systems out there to see what you need to get PostScript code typed in and shipped to your printer. Chapter 14 contains more detail about font downloading and system-related issues.

PostScript Examples on Macintosh

Macintosh has a highly structured view of the world—the notion of plain ASCII (reminiscent of mainframe days) is almost entirely passé. Fortunately, there's an escape hatch. Macintosh systems usually come with a utility called TeachText—a bare bones editor with which you can enter text without formatting information. Enter the PostScript code using TeachText. Type the PostScript code lines the way you see them in the example code blocks, and remember to use RETURN characters at ends of lines. You can omit PostScript comments that start with the % character (but you must type the first **%!PS** line in each case). When you have typed your PostScript example using TeachText, save the file.

If you choose to use your favorite word processor to create your PostScript code, life gets a little more complicated. When you save the file, you must save as ASCII text with line breaks in the correct places. Using MacWrite, for example, you can elect to save the file as text only (no formatting codes) with line breaks. The problem with this approach is that the creating program can't open the text file again. If you double-click on the text file you'll get the standard message telling you the application is missing or busy. You can, however, explicitly open this text file from within TeachText, which is a good reason for using TeachText in the first place.

Now you want to ship your PostScript code to your printer. This discussion assumes your PostScript printer is connected to your Macintosh through an AppleTalk connection, although the story is much the same for serial or EtherTalk connections. Don't use **Print** from the TeachText **File** menu—you'll print the text you see on the screen, which is not what you want. You want the text in the file you created to be shipped to your PostScript printer so the interpreter can execute the PostScript and produce great pictures.

To get PostScript from a Macintosh text file to a PostScript printer you need a *downloader*. A downloader is a utility to ship PostScript code or fonts to a PostScript printer. A downloader utility usually appears on every font diskette you buy with Adobe Type 1 fonts. The utility is called, surprisingly, Downloader. At the time of writing, we were using Downloader version 5.0.1. and version 5.0.4. Alternatively, Macintosh System 7 supplies a PostScript download utility on the More Tidbits disk. Start the downloader utility by double-clicking on its icon. Select **Down-Load PostScript File** from the **File** menu. A panel appears so you can select the file you wish to download.

PostScript Examples on UNIX Systems

There are many flavors of UNIX systems in the world, but just about every flavor has **vi** (the visual editor that comes with BSD-based systems and "modern" System V-based systems) or **Emacs**, or possibly both **vi** and **Emacs**, as well as other kinds of editors. You could use the basic **ed** UNIX editor, but if you get that desperate, you might as well give up on UNIX altogether and switch to DOS. UNIX-based editors lend themselves more readily toward creating basic ASCII text files.[†]

Some UNIX systems supply visual mouse driven editors. NeXT computers, for instance, come with a mouse driven editor called Edit, which is very well integrated with the rest of the system. If you use one of these mouse driven visual editors, make sure an end-of-line character is placed after the last line in the file;

---

† For a thorough treatment of the UNIX **ed**, **ex**, and **vi** editors, consult *Introducing the UNIX System* or *Introducing UNIX System V*, both by Henry McGilton and Rachel Morgan, published by McGraw-Hill.

otherwise the PostScript interpreter will not recognize the last line of the file. Also, make sure your editor is saving the file as plain ASCII and not as Rich Text Format (RTF).

Some modern UNIX systems provide interactive PostScript viewers so that you can check your PostScript examples on the screen prior to printing. On NeXT systems, for example, there's a utility called YAP for creating and debugging PostScript, and Preview for paging through PostScript documents. On Sun systems, PageView is useful for creating and debugging PostScript code.

To get your PostScript programs to the printer on UNIX systems, use the system line printer spooler. The very name—line printer spooler—indicates just how old the concept is. Berkeley-based UNIX systems call the spooler **lpr**. System V-based UNIX systems call the spooler **lp**. In any event, the spooler queues a print job and another utility handles the communications between the printer and the host computer.[†]

PostScript Examples on PC

Creating PostScript examples on PC-based systems differs depending on which level of DOS you have. If you have DOS-5.0, you're in luck because DOS-5.0 supplies edit—an editor with which you can edit plain ASCII text in a reasonable fashion. If you're still using DOS-3.x, you need to find a reasonable editor. Better yet, upgrade to DOS-5.0. If you insist on using a word processor, make sure you save the file in plain ASCII with line breaks in the right places. Microsoft Windows comes with an editor called Notepad which is very similar in function to DOS-5.0 edit. You can also use Word for Windows and save your file as **Text + Breaks**.

To print your PostScript examples on a PC, you need a communication utility between your PC and the PostScript printer. Adobe supplies utilities to assist you. The utility called psdown

---

† Line printer utilities are covered in *Introducing the UNIX System* or *Introducing UNIX System V*, both by Henry McGilton and Rachel Morgan, published by McGraw-Hill.

(PostScript Download) is designed for use with printers attached to serial (com:) ports. The utility called pcsend is designed for use with printers attached to parallel (lpt:) ports. Choose the one that fits your configuration. pcsend doesn't work with ept:-style parallel ports; it works only with lpt:-style parallel ports. If you have an ept: device, you will almost certainly get a font and PostScript downloader as part of the installation package for the device. For use in Windows there's a utility called windown.

If you're creating PostScript on a PC, there's always the temptation to use **print** or **copy** to ship the PostScript files to the printer. This usually doesn't work, because there's more to getting PostScript files to print than just sending bytes down a wire. PostScript printers have a job control protocol that you must obey. PostScript printers communicating across serial channels often use Control-D characters as "end-of-job" indicators, so the next temptation for PC users is to place Control-D characters in PostScript files to ensure that the serial communications protocol works. Placing Control-D characters in PostScript files, however, eventually leads to all kinds of problems for just about everybody, including the originator of the file. Here's a golden rule for PC users who create PostScript files:

> Do not put Control-D characters in PostScript files. Use a downloader utility or a print manager instead.

While you're at it, do not put Control-Z characters in PostScript files either. Control characters in PostScript files confuse other application software and are considered antisocial activities in the PostScript programming community.

Error Handling in PostScript Printers

PostScript printers are truly wonderful devices, but they suffer from one minor personality defect. If your PostScript code contains any errors, as you might get from simple typing errors, the printer will blink for a while and you get nothing. Just at the time you most need help diagnosing what was wrong with the PostScript code you wrote, the printer emulates the "strong, silent" type and says absolutely nothing about what went wrong.

To diagnose errors in PostScript programs you need an error handler—a file of PostScript code that you download to your PostScript printer to trap errors and give you some indication of the problem. The error handler prints some minimal information about the state of the PostScript operand stack, and, most important, prints the page as it was before the error happened. Make sure you obtain an error handler.

The Adobe Downloader on Macintosh systems reports PostScript errors. You'll get a message from the printer telling you what the problem was. Adobes' download utilities on PC systems also tell you the error message that came back from the printer. On UNIX systems you're not so lucky because of the asynchronous nature of the spooling software. You need to download an error handler to your printer. If you can't find an error handler handy at your local installation, or you can't get one from a friend, Chapter 14 shows you how to create and download a minimal error handler that will point out the reason for the failure and the PostScript instruction causing the problem.

Most PostScript errors are fairly trivial to diagnose and can be determined from very little information. The error and the PostScript instruction causing the error are usually enough to point you in the right direction. Probably the most common mistake is an error of omission rather than of commission— remember to put a **showpage** at the point in your PostScript program where you want to display the page image. Remember the **showpage**! Even "experts" trip over this one.

Now you know what you need to get started, so get a glass of champagne, turn on your computer, warm up the printer, start your text editor, and let's begin.

Basic Graphics—A Triangle

Here is your first hands-on PostScript program. Let's start with a very simple PostScript program that produces visible results—a program to draw a triangle in the middle of a page—as you see in the miniature page in the margin. Here is the PostScript program to draw the picture you see on the left. You need only enter the **boldtext** from this code example. The percent (**%**) signs and all the text following them to the end of line are PostScript comments and you don't need to type them.

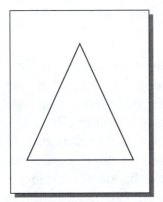

Basic shape drawn by minimal PostScript program.

```
%!PS              %  PostScript "magic number"
72 144 moveto     %  set initial point
306 648 lineto    %  add line segment
540 144 lineto    %  add another line segment
closepath         %  finish the shape
stroke            %  paint the path
showpage          %  display page
```

Now, if you send this PostScript program to your printer or display device, you should see the outline triangle appear on the sheet of paper as shown.[†] This PostScript program is pretty simple, but it gives you something to look at. Let's pull this program apart into its constituent pieces.

Every PostScript program starts with **%!**—known as a "magic number" in computer jargon. Strictly speaking, **%** signals the start of a PostScript comment, but the very first line of a PostScript program starting with **%!PS** is special and is explained in more detail in *Basic PostScript Syntax* on pages 17–20 in this chapter.

The second line of the program is the first real line of PostScript code—an instruction to position the pen on the page. **72 144 moveto** is an instruction to move to position (72, 144) on the page.[‡] In PostScript terminology, **moveto** establishes the position of the current point. Think of PostScript drawing with an invisible "pen" of infinitesimal thickness. **moveto** places this pen at the specified place. 72 and 144 are PostScript units that are $\frac{1}{72}$ inch, so you're placing the pen at the position (1 inch, 2 inches). Ignore the

---

† If you skipped *Tools You Need to Explore PostScript* on pages 4–9 in this chapter, take a look at it now to see how to create PostScript and ship it to your printer.

‡ More correctly, in "user space," which you get to later in this book.

stack, and you need to become comfortable with using the stack to be facile programming PostScript.

Speaking of operands, what is the syntax of operands? Numbers can be integers or reals. Integers are numbers like **306** and **648** as you've already seen. Reals contain decimal points and are numbers like **0.25** and **3.1415926**. *Basic Text—Show a Message* on page 14 in this chapter imaged the string **(PostScript!)** on the page. Strings are enclosed in (and) characters. (and) are not a part of the string, but serve to delimit the string.

Some of the preceding examples contained syntax like

```
/Palatino-Roman findfont
```

where a name is preceded by a slash character. The slash introduces a *literal name*. That is, the name is placed on the operand stack as a literal instead of being searched for and executed as an operator. You'll see more examples of literal names.

As a final introduction to the syntax, the percent (%) sign introduces a PostScript comment. All characters from the % to the end of the line are ignored. So a line starting with the % character is a comment line. Every line of code is commented in the example on the next page. Each comment is introduced with a percent (%) sign and all characters to the end of each line are ignored.

This next example also contains your first encounter with **setgray**—the PostScript operator to set the "color" of a fill in shades of gray. The gray color model is explained in detail in *Gray Color Model* on pages 488–491 in Chapter 13.

You'll see more informal examples of PostScript syntax in this chapter and later chapters. Chapter 5 contains a discussion of the PostScript execution model, its use of stacks, and dictionaries in which objects can be defined. The latter part of Chapter 5 contains detailed discussions of various classes of PostScript operators.

Every line in this PostScript program is commented.

```
%!PS
306 396 270 0 360 arc        %  draw a circle
closepath                    %  finish circle
gsave                        %  remember graphics state
    0.50 setgray             %  medium gray shade
    fill                     %  fill circle
grestore                     %  restore graphics state
72 setlinewidth              %  fat line width
stroke                       %  paint outline of circle
/Palatino-Bold findfont      %  find a font
360 scalefont                %  make letters large
setfont                      %  set current font
96 275 moveto                %  position current point
(PS) false charpath          %  get character path
gsave                        %  remember graphics state
    18 setlinewidth          %  fat line width
    stroke                   %  paint outline of characters
grestore                     %  restore graphics state
1.0 setgray                  %  white color
fill                         %  fill character outlines
showpage                     %  display page
```

Transformations

Throughout this chapter, we've ignored details to make your first taste of PostScript palatable. Now, let's peel a layer of the onion and investigate PostScript *user space*. At this point many layers of the onion will remain untouched. User space is a completely device independent coordinate system. Hark back once more to the original triangle example, shown on the next page.

Each number in the code—**72**, **144**, **306**, **648**, **540**—is a coordinate in user space units. User space is pliable—you can stretch, rotate, and move it relative to the physical page. PostScript takes care of details of transforming ideal user space coordinates into physical units used by specific devices.

```
%!PS
72 144 moveto          %   set initial point
306 648 lineto         %   add line segment
540 144 lineto         %   add another line segment
closepath              %   finish the shape
stroke                 %   paint the path
showpage               %   display page
```

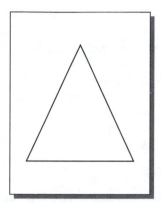

Original basic shape drawn by minimal PostScript program.

Seventy-two PostScript units in one inch.

Before delving into the next example, let's make life a little easier. You may have noticed that the coordinates in the examples so far were a bit odd—**504 576 moveto**, for example.

The PostScript user coordinate system contains 72 units per inch. Coordinates in previous examples are contrived—they are inches converted to PostScript units. Let's define a PostScript function to do that work for us. After all, what are computers for? Numbers will be easier to work with.

The next example is the triangle example from page 10 where we now introduce a *procedure definition* that multiplies its operand by 72, thus converting inches to PostScript user space coordinates. In this next example, the line reading

```
/inch { 72 mul } def
```

defines a procedure to convert inches to PostScript units. Note the use of the form **/inch** while defining the procedure. The **/inch** is another example of a literal name. The name is being defined at this point and you don't want the PostScript interpreter to try to execute this name before it's defined, hence the / to make it literal. **/inch** is the name of the procedure you're defining. {**72 mul**} is the procedure body—this is what executes when you use the form **1 inch**. **def** defines **inch** as a name that can be looked up.

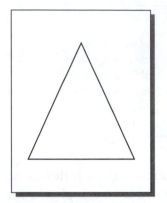

Basic triangle using inches as units of measurement.

```
%!PS
/inch { 72 mul } def         %  define inch procedure
1 inch 2 inch moveto         %  set initial point
4.25 inch 9 inch lineto      %  add line segment
7.5 inch 2 inch lineto       %  add another line segment
closepath                    %  finish the shape
stroke                       %  paint the path
showpage                     %  display page
```

Now you can use units you're familiar with—at least if you live in North America—instead of funny looking numbers. For example, to move the current point to the center of an 8½-by-11-inch sheet of paper, you would use

```
4.25 inch 5.5 inch moveto
```

You'll encounter more procedures as you read through more examples, and Chapter 5 defines procedures in detail.

Of course, inches look equally funny to the other five billion people who use the metric system. If you prefer to work in centimeters,[†] you could change your code as in this example:

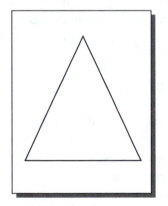

Basic triangle using centimeters as units of measurement.

```
%!PS
/cm { 28.35 mul } def        %  define cm procedure
2 cm 5 cm moveto             %  set initial point
11 cm 24 cm lineto           %  add line segment
20 cm 5 cm lineto            %  add another line segment
closepath                    %  finish the shape
stroke                       %  paint the path
showpage                     %  display page
```

---

† Or maybe "centimetres," depending where you live.

PostScript standard units are $1/72$ inch. PostScript units are close to printer's "points." A point is one of the standard units of measurement in the typesetting and printing business. The precise definition of point differs from country to country. PostScript units differ from printer's points by such a small amount that it's *usually* not worth quibbling over the difference.

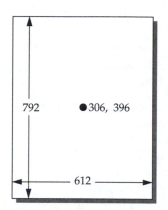

792   ● 306, 396

612

Size and center of U. S. standard letter paper in PostScript units.

Inches, centimeters, and occasionally other units such as barleycorns are used throughout this book—for *illustrative purposes*. But instead of sticking to your everyday inches, cubits, centimeters, pipeés, or whatever, think in PostScript units as much as possible. For example, the middle of an 8½-by-11-inch sheet of paper is at (306, 396) in PostScript units. The quick round numbers (300, 400) are very close to the middle—you're off by two percent horizontally and one percent vertically.

Similarly, the middle of an A4 sheet of paper is at (14.85 cm, 10.5 cm) which is (298, 421) in PostScript units. If you use the quick rounded off values (300, 420), you're off by one percent horizontally and a fifth of a percent vertically. A sheet of A4 paper is 595 PostScript units wide and 842 PostScript units high. An 8½-by-11-inch sheet of paper is 612 PostScript units wide and 792 PostScript units high. Now having dealt with centimeters, inches, and the most basic procedures, let's move on with the discussion on transformations, beginning with translating.

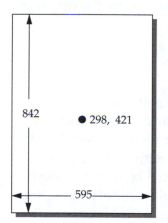

842   ● 298, 421

595

Size and center of ISO A4 paper in PostScript units.

Translating the Origin of the Coordinate System

The next example is another simple program to draw a two-inch radius circle in the center of a page. You can use one of two basic techniques to set the center of the circle:

❑   move the current point to the center of the page, or

❑   translate the origin of user space to the center of the page

You're already an expert at moving the current point about in user space, so let's use the second method and examine how to translate the origin of user space. You use the PostScript **translate** operator to provide the coordinates at which you would like the origin placed. This program uses **translate** to draw a circle at the center of the page.

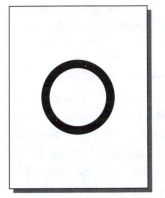

```
%!PS
/inch { 72 mul } def          %  define inch procedure
4.25 inch 5.5 inch translate  %  origin to center of page
0 0 2 inch 0 360 arc          %  draw a circle
closepath                     %  finish the shape
0.5 inch setlinewidth         %  set a fat line
stroke                        %  stroke the path
showpage                      %  display page
```

Basic circle drawn as a full 360° arc.

This program contains three operators with which you are not yet familiar—**translate**, **arc**, and **setlinewidth**. Let's explore these operators. As mentioned previously, **translate** moves the origin of user space. In the circle example, the line

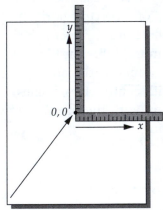

```
4.25 inch 5.5 inch translate
```

moves the origin of user space from its current location (the bottom left corner of the page) to the center of an 8½-by-11-inch sheet of paper. The picture illustrates the effect of this **translate**. All coordinates in subsequent operations are relative to the new origin in user space. Moving the origin is often convenient so you can work with manageable numbers or write modular code and place objects in their own coordinate system. *Translating the Origin* on page 147 in Chapter 4 discusses **translate** in more detail.

translate repositions the origin of the user coordinate system.

Introducing Arcs and Circles

arc draws arcs of circles. A circle is simply an arc circumscribed 360°, so **arc** can draw complete circles as well. **arc** requires five arguments—the (x, y) coordinates of the center of the circle, the *radius*, and the two *angles* between which the arc will be traced. The general syntax for **arc** is

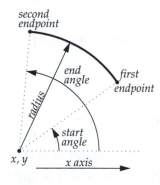

second endpoint

end angle

first endpoint

radius

start angle

x, y   x axis

*Parameters of **arc**.*

x_{center} y_{center} *radius*   *angle$_{start}$*   *angle$_{end}$*   **arc**

where x_{center} and y_{center} define the center of the arc. x and y are both zero in the example because the origin of user space was translated to the exact location for the center of the circle. *radius* is the radius of the arc; an arbitrary choice of two inches. *angle$_{start}$* and *angle$_{end}$* are the start and end angles between which the arc is traced. Angles of 0° and 360° plot a complete circle.

Also notice the **closepath** after drawing the complete 360° arc. **closepath** after **arc** is important when stroking a complete circle with a fat line width. Without the **closepath**, there can be a "notch" at the zero degree position which isn't stroked. You can learn more about **arc** in Chapter 7, *Arcs and Curves*. The example introduces another small twist to illustrate the effect of setting a fat line width prior to the **stroke**, using **setlinewidth**.

Scaling the Coordinate System

Suppose you really want an ellipse and not a circle. You can draw ellipses with a simple addition to the circle program. Here's the previous circle program with a single line of PostScript added.

Circle in scaled coordinate system draws an ellipse.

```
%!PS
/inch { 72 mul } def          % define inch procedure
4.25 inch 5.5 inch translate  % origin to center of page
1 2 scale                     % scale y axis of user space
0 0 2 inch 0 360 arc          % draw an ellipse
closepath                     % finish the shape
0.5 inch setlinewidth         % set fat line width
stroke                        % stroke the path
showpage                      % display page
```

The additional line in the preceding code fragment introduces the PostScript **scale** operator, which changes the proportion of the x axis, the y axis, or both x and y axes of user space. In this example, **scale** squashes what was a circle into an ellipse. The general syntax of **scale** is

$$S_x \quad S_y \quad \texttt{scale}$$

where S_x and S_y are the scale factors for the x coordinate and the y coordinate, respectively. The line

```
1 2 scale
```

makes a unit in the y direction twice as large as before. Notice how vertical units are twice as long as horizontal units. Even the "rulers" are stretched. The x axis is unchanged. The effect of **scale** is that the ellipse is twice as tall (8 inches), where the width of the ellipse is the same as the circle (4 inches).

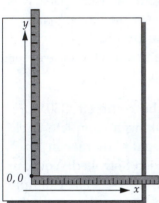

*Effect of **scale** on the coordinate system rulers.*

Notice also how the stroked line width is scaled along with the circle. Scaling lines in a non-uniform coordinate system is perfectly consistent with PostScript transformations, although it may not be exactly what you want. You can avoid this by scaling for **arc** and unscaling for **stroke**. You'll see details of **scale** in *Scaling the Coordinate System* on pages 150–153 in Chapter 4.

Rotating the Coordinate System

Now that you've seen **translate** and **scale** in action, the final transformation you can apply is to rotate the coordinate system about its origin using the **rotate** operator. You already saw **rotate** used in *Basic Text—Show a Message* on page 14 in this chapter.

Ellipse in rotated coordinate system.

```
%!PS
/inch { 72 mul } def              %   define inch procedure
4.25 inch 5.5 inch translate      %   origin to center of page
45 rotate                         %   rotate image by 45°
1 2 scale                         %   scale y axis of user space
0 0 2 inch 0 360 arc              %   draw an ellipse
closepath                         %   finish the shape
0.5 inch setlinewidth             %   set fat line width
stroke                            %   stroke the path
showpage                          %   display page
```

Let's take a look at what happens to user space in relation to the physical page when the user coordinate system is rotated about its origin using **30 rotate**.

Part of the first quadrant, which usually corresponds to a physical page, is no longer visible and part of the fourth quadrant is now visible. This is often the source of some confusion about **rotate**— you can lose partial or even entire objects this way. Keep in mind you are rotating user space about its origin. You are not rotating paths or objects about their origins. Of course, you can rotate objects about their origins, but to do so is a bit more complicated than just using a single **rotate** as shown here. Rotations are covered in more detail in *Rotating the Coordinate System* on pages 153–155 in Chapter 4.

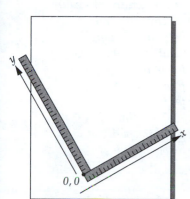

User space rotated about its origin.

Another important concept is the order in which user space is transformed with **translate**, **scale**, and **rotate**. Experiment with the many permutations, but a rotated, scaled coordinate system is different from a scaled and rotated one, just as a translated, rotated coordinate system is different from a rotated, translated one. There's more discussion of this issue in *Order of Transformations* on pages 158–160 in Chapter 4.

Creating Paths

PostScript is built on a foundation of a few simple but powerful ideas. You will see some of these ideas, such as stacks, dictionaries, and graphics states in later chapters. For now, one of the principal concepts in the PostScript imaging model is that of a *path*. A path doesn't actually generate any image. Rather, a path establishes a set of points or an area that can be stroked, filled, or used as a clipping region. A path is established in a device-independent user coordinate system using PostScript graphics operators that move to specific coordinates and draw straight lines, arcs, and curves. The next figure illustrates a page with the outline of a path established using **moveto** and **lineto** operators.

A path established using **lineto** *operators.*

```
%!PS
/inch { 72 mul } def            %   define inch procedure
1 inch 1 inch moveto            %   set current point
7.5 inch 1 inch lineto          %   bottom of rectangle
7.5 inch 10 inch lineto         %   right side of rectangle
1 inch 10 inch lineto           %   top of rectangle
closepath                       %   finish the shape
1.0 inch setlinewidth           %   fat line width
1 setlinejoin                   %   rounded line joins
stroke                          %   paint the path
showpage                        %   display page
```

Notice a small twist in this example—the **setlinejoin** instruction. **setlinejoin** controls the way lines are joined when they meet at corners. A value of **1** for line join means *rounded* line joins.

Another noteworthy item is that stroking a path clears the path out of the graphics state. The current path is cleared after a **stroke** or a **fill**. You will see the importance of this in the example on page 30 in this chapter, where you need to save the current path to both fill and stroke the path.

This example stroked the path using the preset color of black. You can change the color or shade of gray, and in PostScript Level 2, you can even use patterns to paint the path.

Filling Paths

An established path can be *filled* instead of stroked—its interior is painted with a specified color. The path in the next picture is filled with 50 percent gray. This path is only filled, not stroked. This picture illustrates that painting (filling) the interior of a path is independent of painting (stroking) its outline.

A path filled with medium gray shade.

```
%!PS
/inch { 72 mul } def          %   define inch procedure
1 inch 1 inch moveto          %   set current point
7.5 inch 1 inch lineto        %   bottom of rectangle
7.5 inch 10 inch lineto       %   right side of rectangle
1 inch 10 inch lineto         %   top of rectangle
closepath                     %   finish the shape
0.50 setgray                  %   medium gray color
fill                          %   paint the shape
showpage                      %   display page
```

This example establishes the same path as in the previous example. But it sets the current color where the previous example set the line width and line join. And this code example fills the path instead of stroking it. Just as with stroking, filling clears the current path. The use of **closepath** in this example is redundant— a path is closed automatically before it is filled.

As with stroking, filling would use the preset color black, but this example uses a 50 percent (medium) shade of gray. You can fill with color, and in PostScript Level 2, the "color" can be a pattern.

Stroking and Filling Paths

An established path can be both filled and stroked—its interior can be painted with one color and its border can be painted with a different color. The path in this next picture is filled with 50 percent gray and stroked with a fat black line.

Once again, this example introduces a small twist. The **2 setlinejoin** operation sets a beveled line join—the lines are beveled off where they meet at corners.

A path both filled and stroked.

```
%!PS
/inch { 72 mul } def          %    define inch procedure
1 inch 1 inch moveto          %    set current point
7.5 inch 1 inch lineto        %    bottom of rectangle
7.5 inch 10 inch lineto       %    right side of rectangle
1 inch 10 inch lineto         %    top of rectangle
closepath                     %    finish the shape
gsave                         %    remember graphics state
    0.50 setgray              %    medium gray color
    fill                      %    paint the shape
grestore                      %    restore old graphics state
1.0 inch setlinewidth         %    fat line width
2 setlinejoin                 %    beveled line joins
stroke                        %    paint the path
showpage                      %    display page
```

You saw in the previous two examples that either a **stroke** or a **fill** applied to a path clears the path after the operation. What if you wish to both fill and stroke a path? One way is to generate the path twice—generate the path and fill it, then generate the path again and stroke it. However, if you actually do this (and some applications have been known to do just that), your PostScript file will be twice as big as it needs to be.

A more economical method is to use **gsave** and **grestore** to remember the current *graphics state*. The graphics state is a collection of parameters that affect how paths are painted and text is shown. The current path is a part of the graphics state, as are other parameters such as line width, line join, color, current font, and so on. Using graphics states, you generate a path once, remember the path, fill it, restore the remembered path, then stroke it. Read more about graphics states in *Graphics States and the Graphics State Stack* on page 42 in this chapter.

Disconnected Subpaths

A path does not have to be contiguous. A path can be constructed of several *disconnected subpaths*. This figure is composed of three separate subpaths. The small rectangle is one subpath. The circle is another subpath. The shape in the upper-right is the third subpath; it's the same rectangle drawn in a rotated coordinate system. All three subpaths were filled and stroked in one **fill** and **stroke** operation.

Disconnected subpaths filled with a pattern.

```
%!PS
/inch { 72 mul } def                  %   define inch procedure
                                      %   draw circle
3.75 inch 6.00 inch 2 inch 0 360 arc
closepath                             %   finish circle
0.5 inch 0.5 inch moveto              %   start new subpath
2 inch 0 rlineto                      %   bottom of rectangle
0 3 inch rlineto                      %   right side of rectangle
-2 inch 0 rlineto                     %   top of rectangle
closepath                             %   finish rectangle
6.5 inch 7 inch moveto                %   start new subpath
40 rotate                             %   rotate coordinate system
2 inch 0 rlineto                      %   bottom of rectangle
0 3 inch rlineto                      %   right side of rectangle
-2 inch 0 rlineto                     %   top of rectangle
closepath                             %   finish rectangle
gsave                                 %   remember graphics state
    AstroidLeaf setpattern            %   fancy pattern fill
    fill                              %   fill with pattern
grestore                              %   restore graphics state
0.25 inch setlinewidth                %   fat line width
stroke                                %   paint the path
showpage                              %   display page
```

The current path contains three disconnected subpaths when the **gsave** is encountered. **gsave**, **grestore**, **stroke**, and **fill** operate at once on all the subpaths. Note another twist in this example—the use of **setpattern** to define a fancy patterned fill instead of a color or a shade of gray. Patterns are capabilities of PostScript Level 2. **setpattern** means this example will work only on PostScript Level

2 systems. You can run this example on a PostScript Level 1
printer if you change the **setpattern** line to using a shade of gray,
or a color. You will see how to define your own patterns in
Chapter 11, where, on pages 458–461, you will also find the definitions for this fancy pattern.

Any given PostScript interpreter imposes a limit on the number of
elements in a path. 1500 elements is a common limit. You should
ensure that your PostScript programs don't approach such limits.

Opaque Paint

Another key component of the PostScript imaging model is
opaque paint. This means that paint laid down on top of
existing paint completely obscures the existing paint. This
diagram shows a light gray ellipse, partially obscured by a dark
gray rectangle, in turn partially obscured by a patterned circle.

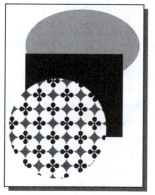

*Opaque paint imaging
model. Newly created
objects obscure those
created earlier.*

```
%!PS
/inch { 72 mul } def                    %  define inch procedure
gsave                                   %  remember graphics state
    4.75 inch 8.5 inch translate
    2 1.25 scale                        %  scale for elliptical path
    0 0 1.75 inch 0 360 arc             %  draw ellipse
    closepath                           %  finish ellipse
    0.75 setgray fill                   %  fill ellipse with light gray
grestore                                %  restore graphics state
1.25 inch 3 inch moveto                 %  set current point
6 inch 0 rlineto                        %  bottom of rectangle
0 5 inch rlineto                        %  right side of rectangle
-6 inch 0 rlineto                       %  top of rectangle
closepath                               %  finish the shape
0.25 setgray fill                       %  fill with dark gray
                                        %  draw circle
3.25 inch 3.5 inch 3 inch 0 360 arc
closepath                               %  finish circle
AstroidLeaf setpattern                  %  fancy pattern fill
fill                                    %  fill with pattern
showpage                                %  display page
```

The light gray ellipse was painted first, the dark gray rectangle was painted second, and the patterned circle painted last. The shapes overlap each other in the order in which they were created. Once again, this example will work only on PostScript Level 2 systems because of **setpattern**. You can run this example on a PostScript Level 1 printer if you change **setpattern** to either **setgray** or one of the variations of **setcolor**.

PostScript opaque imaging is easy to deal with when you really want sections of images to overlap each other. In such cases you can simply forget about sections of the image that are "underneath" since the painting model guarantees they will be covered up by whatever comes later.

Overlapping paths need to be handled with clipping.

PostScript imaging model becomes a little more difficult when sections of images mutually intersect each other, such as this Japanese crest, or certain kinds of heavily self-intersecting Islamic patterns. In such cases you need to be somewhat more clever using clipping, dealt with in Chapter 8.

Some computer vendors have introduced new operators that bend the opaque imaging model a little. NeXT computers, for example, introduced the notion of *compositing* and *dissolving*—using semi-transparent paint. Neither of these features are a part of the "official" PostScript language, although they may sometimes appear to be so. Compositing and dissolving are useful features on screen displays for user interface effects, but they may not make as much sense on printers.

Clipping with Paths

Another powerful feature of PostScript is the ability to use a path as a *clipping region*, instead of filling or stroking it. Using a path as a clipping region eases the task of computing endpoints of lines, which would be onerous if the clipping region were a complicated path. This figure shows multiple strings of text clipped through an elliptical path.

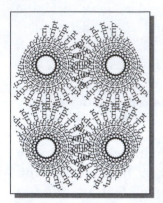

Strings of text clipped through an elliptical path.

```
%!PS
/inch { 72 mul } def                        % define inch procedure
matrix currentmatrix                        % save transformation matrix
4.25 inch 5.5 inch translate                % origin to center of page
1.5 2 scale                                 % set scale factor
0 0 2.75 inch                               % center and radius of ellipse
0 360 arc closepath                         % draw ellipse
clip                                        % use as clipping path
newpath                                     % start a new path
setmatrix                                   % restore matrix
/Palatino-Roman findfont                    % find required font
36 scalefont                                % scale to required size
setfont                                     % set current font
/CircleText {                               % define procedure
    gsave                                   % remember graphics state
    translate                               % move coordinate system
    24 {                                    % do 24 times
        0.5 inch 0 moveto                   % set current point
        (PostScript) show                   % show string
        15 rotate                           % rotate coordinate system
    } repeat                                % end of loop
    grestore                                % restore graphics state
} def                                       % end of procedure definition
2.125 inch 7.75 inch CircleText             % upper left fan
6.375 inch 7.75 inch CircleText             % upper right fan
2.125 inch 2.75 inch CircleText             % lower left fan
6.375 inch 2.75 inch CircleText             % lower right fan
showpage                                    % display page
```

This example first established an elliptical path. Instead of filling or stroking this path as before, you clip with it. **clip** establishes the elliptical path as the current clipping path. Paint applied on the page from now on shows up only if the paint lies inside the clipping region. PostScript takes care of the details of ensuring that text appears only inside the elliptical clipping region.

Notice the **newpath** right after the **clip** operator. Unlike **stroke** and **fill**, **clip** does not clear the current path, so a new path must be set explicitly if it is required.

Integrated Text and Graphics

Text is a major strength that sets PostScript apart from other page description languages. PostScript integrates text much more closely into the graphics model than previous page description languages. Text may be stroked, filled, rotated, scaled, and used as clipping regions, just like any other graphical object.

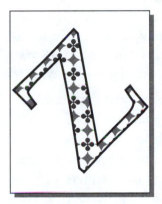

Rotated, filled, and stroked character outline.

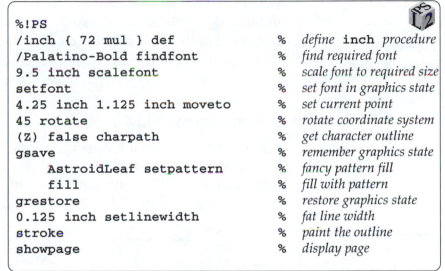

```
%!PS
/inch { 72 mul } def                % define inch procedure
/Palatino-Bold findfont             % find required font
9.5 inch scalefont                  % scale font to required size
setfont                             % set font in graphics state
4.25 inch 1.125 inch moveto         % set current point
45 rotate                           % rotate coordinate system
(Z) false charpath                  % get character outline
gsave                               % remember graphics state
    AstroidLeaf setpattern          % fancy pattern fill
    fill                            % fill with pattern
grestore                            % restore graphics state
0.125 inch setlinewidth             % fat line width
stroke                              % paint the outline
showpage                            % display page
```

You can stroke and fill the outline of a character just as easily as you can stroke and fill a graphic object such as a line or box. The line reading **(Z) false charpath** turns the outline of the large character into a path. You can then treat this path as you would any other path from previous examples.

The basic operations of displaying text are somewhat specialized due to the nature of letterforms, but shapes of characters are described in terms of PostScript graphic operators. PostScript fonts are stored as outlines. Instead of representing characters as bitmaps, PostScript defines characters from a font with operations such as moves, lines, and curves. You can take advantage of this graphical description of text to get special effects. *Special Effects Using Character Paths* on page 129 in Chapter 3 describes just a few of the effects you can obtain using character paths.

Text around a path.

In accordance with the PostScript philosophy that "text characters are graphics," you can create elaborate effects with text, such as laying text along arbitrary paths.

The picture modifies one of the examples from the *PostScript Language Tutorial and Cookbook*—the Adobe "Blue Book"—to accomplish that task. This example shows text set around an ellipse. You could set text along any path such as a Bézier curve or series of line segments. Many of today's sophisticated "desktop publishing" applications contain tools to manipulate text in these fashions. For the basic code of this example, consult the *PostScript Language Tutorial and Cookbook*, published by Addison-Wesley.

Images and Image Masks

PostScript provides a means to include bitmap images in your programs. Art from pixel paint programs or scanners can be integrated into a PostScript program easily. Using PostScript, you can create a page complete with graphics, bitmaps, and text.

Bitmap image

```
%!PS
/bufstr 128 string def          %   temporary buffer
0 144 translate                 %   move origin
0.56 dup scale                  %   scale to fit
1023 799 scale                  %   scale image to user space
1023 799 1                      %   width, height, depth
[1023 0 0 -799 0 799]           %   image transformation matrix
{ currentfile bufstr readhexstring pop }
          . . .
          . . .                 %   image data omitted
          . . .
image                           %   render image
showpage                        %   display page
```

Data for the image is included directly in the PostScript file and, in PostScript Level 2, can come from various filters, including data compression filters. The bitmap data is omitted for brevity. You can read more details about images in Chapter 9.

The bitmap data you paint onto the display or printing surface can also be used as an image mask to control where color gets applied to the printing surface. Instead of painting the actual bits on the display surface, an image mask acts as a stencil through which the current color is "poured." Once more, you can read about image masks in Chapter 9.

Bitmap image as mask.

```
%!PS
0 0 moveto                          %   set current point
8.5 inch 0 rlineto                  %   bottom of rectangle
0 11 inch rlineto                   %   right side
-8.5 inch 0 rlineto                 %   top
closepath                           %   finish shape
0.9 setgray fill                    %   fill with light gray
0.0 setgray                         %   restore to black
/bufstr 128 string def              %   temporary buffer
0 144 translate                     %   move origin
0.56 dup scale                      %   scale to fit
1023 799 scale                      %   scale image to user space
1023 799 false                      %   width, height, paint black
[1023 0 0 -799 0 799]               %   image transformation matrix
{ currentfile bufstr readhexstring pop }
                    · · ·
                    · · ·           %   image data omitted
                    · · ·
imagemask                           %   render image
showpage                            %   display page
```

Color and Patterns

So far you've seen examples using various shades of gray to fill areas and paint paths. There's a good reason for this parsimony—color is expensive. But right from the beginning, PostScript had color capabilities as part of the imaging model. The first versions of PostScript supported the RGB (Red, Green, Blue) model of color, as well as the HSB (Hue, Saturation, Brightness) color model. PostScript printers without color capabilities simulate colors with halftones—you get grays when you ask for color.

PostScript Level 2 supports these two color models, plus the more sophisticated CMYK (Cyan, Magenta, Yellow, Black) and CIE color models used in the printing industry. Here's an example to draw a beginning skier's circle in the center of the page.

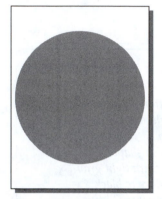

Beginning skier's "green" circle. See color plate I.

```
%!PS
/inch { 72 mul } def          %   define inch procedure
4.25 inch 5.5 inch            %   (x, y) coordinates of center
4.0 inch 0 360 arc            %   4 inch circle
closepath                     %   finish circle
0.0 1.0 0.0 setrgbcolor       %   beginner's green
fill                          %   fill circle
showpage                      %   display page
```

Of course, this "green" circle comes out as gray here. PostScript simulates color with gray shades on printers that print only black and white. Plate I shows the results of this code in color.

In addition to color models, PostScript Level 2 supports *pattern color spaces*, or *patterns* for short. Support for patterns in PostScript Level 1 was somewhat limited because the notion of pattern spaces was not well understood. PostScript Level 2 pattern color spaces give you the ability to define complicated patterns that can be used as if they were colors. The different parts of the patterns themselves can be colored.[†]

Once again, you can run this example on a PostScript Level 1 printer by changing the pattern to gray or color. Alternatively, patterns can be defined as uncolored patterns, whose color components are specified at the time the patterns are used. In this way, a given pattern template can be used in many different places, with different color schemes each time.

---

† The definition for the AstroidLeaf pattern can be found in Chapter 11 on pages 458–461.

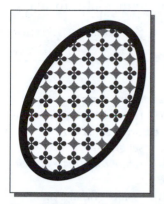

Pattern fill in PostScript Level 2.

```
%!PS
/inch { 72 mul } def              %  define inch procedure
/DrawEllipse {                    %  stack = x y xr yr
    matrix currentmatrix          %  remember CTM
    5 3 roll translate            %  translate coordinate system
    3 1 roll scale                %  scale coordinate system
    0 0 1 0 360 arc closepath %   draw circle
    setmatrix                     %  restore CTM
} def
-30 rotate                        %  rotate coordinate system
1 inch 7 inch 3 inch 5 inch DrawEllipse
gsave                             %  remember graphics state
    AstroidLeaf setpattern        %  fancy pattern fill
    fill                          %  fill with pattern
grestore                          %  restore graphics state
0.5 inch setlinewidth             %  fat line width
stroke                            %  paint the path
showpage                          %  display page
```

Fonts

One of the major contributions of PostScript to the publishing world was its sophisticated capability to define and use *outline fonts*. Until PostScript appeared in the marketplace, the "font problem" plagued designers and users of page description languages alike. The most fundamental problem was that the technology of outline fonts was neither well-defined nor well-developed. Indeed, not so long ago, industry "experts" were saying scan conversion from outlines to bitmaps was not possible.

Prior to PostScript, page description systems stored character shapes as *bitmaps*. Storing fonts as bitmaps meant users could get only a certain number of fonts at certain predefined sizes. Some amount of scaling could be applied to obtain intermediate sizes, but the results were less than satisfactory. Obtaining characters at fractional point sizes and arbitrary rotations and transformations was nearly impossible. PostScript overcame all these problems in one fell swoop with its capabilities to define letterforms as sequences of graphical operations.

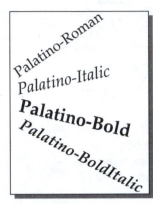

Text at arbitrary rotations.

```
%!PS
/inch { 72 mul } def                    %   define inch procedure
gsave                                   %   remember graphics state
   /Palatino-Roman findfont 64 scalefont setfont
   0.5 inch 7 inch translate            %   set origin
   34 rotate                            %   rotate coordinate system
   0 0 moveto (Palatino-Roman) show
grestore                                %   restore graphics state
gsave                                   %   remember graphics state
   /Palatino-Italic findfont 72 scalefont setfont
   0.5 inch 6 inch translate            %   set origin
   11 rotate                            %   rotate coordinate system
   0 0 moveto (Palatino-Italic) show
grestore                                %   restore graphics state
gsave                                   %   remember graphics state
   /Palatino-Bold findfont 80 scalefont setfont
   0.5 inch 5 inch translate            %   set origin
   -13 rotate                           %   rotate coordinate system
   0 0 moveto (Palatino-Bold) show
grestore                                %   restore graphics state
gsave                                   %   remember graphics state
   /Palatino-BoldItalic findfont 68 scalefont setfont
   0.5 inch 4 inch translate            %   set origin
   -28 rotate                           %   rotate coordinate system
   0 0 moveto (Palatino-BoldItalic) show
grestore                                %   restore graphics state
showpage                                %   display page
```

This example shows PostScript fonts used to set text at arbitrary angles and sizes across the page. This is a simple example of PostScript power in handling text.

Halftones

Halftones form an important part of PostScript imaging models. Halftones are needed for three distinct areas. First, PostScript uses its halftone machinery to simulate gray scales on printers and display devices that deal only with black and white, or with limited gray levels. When you ask for a 50 percent (medium) gray using **setgray**, PostScript forms the gray shade using halftone cells if the device itself doesn't directly support continuous gray tones.

Halftones to simulate gray levels.

```
%!PS
/inch { 72 mul } def               % define inch procedure
0.25 inch 0.5 inch translate       % position origin
0 1 9 {                            % count rows of squares
   0 1 7 {                         % count columns of squares
     gsave                         % remember graphics state
                                   % position origin
        dup inch 2 index inch translate
        0 0 moveto                 % set current point
        1 inch 0 rlineto           % bottom of square
        0 1 inch rlineto           % right side of square
        -1 inch 0 rlineto          % top of square
        closepath                  % finish square
                                   % compute gray
        1 index 8 mul 1 index add 80 div setgray
        fill                       % fill square
     grestore                      % recall saved graphics state
     pop                           % remove spare number
   } for                           % end for loop
   pop                             % remove spare number
} for                              % end for loop
showpage                           % display page
```

Second, PostScript uses halftones to simulate color on devices that don't directly support color. You can set color on black and white (or grayscale) devices, but you get shades of gray. Finally, halftones find major use in color separations. Read about color, color separations, and halftone issues in Chapter 13.

Forms

PostScript Level 2 introduced the notion of forms—objects imaged multiple times on a single page, or singly on multiple pages. Typical forms are company logos, overhead slide presentations, and traditional forms a bureaucrat will have you fill out instead of getting something done. Forms are cached and significantly improve performance by reducing transmission time, interpretation time, and imaging time. Here's an example use of forms. This is probably what Johannes Gutenberg's business presentation to the Archbishop of Mainz might have looked like.

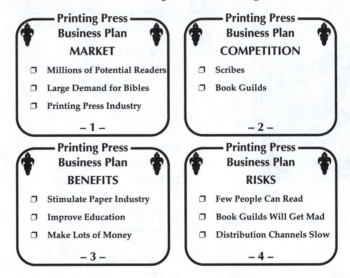

This form implements the "master objects" for an overhead slide presentation. The borders, decorations, and titles are fixed from one form to the next. For each page of the presentation, you "fill in the form" and place other objects on the page. But the master objects are imaged once and cached for reuse on each page.

Graphics States and the Graphics State Stack

The PostScript execution model revolves around the use of four stacks. These four stacks are discussed in more detail in Chapter 5, but for the moment you need to concentrate on the *graphics state stack*, and, by implication, the graphics state.

At any time, the graphics state contains a collection of parameters that affect the final appearance of graphical operations. The graphics state contains two major collections of data:

❏ the current path—the path you have drawn so far using graphics operators such as **moveto** and **lineto**. The current path includes the current point.

❏ attributes that affect the appearance of the shapes you draw. The most pervasive of these attributes is the Current Transformation Matrix, or CTM. Other attributes include current color, line width, line joins, dashed line style, and others you will read about in future chapters.

The graphics state stack provides a means to remember and recall the graphics state. A common situation in which to remember the graphics state is when you have drawn a path and you wish to both stroke and fill the path. Remember, either **stroke** or **fill** automatically clears the current path. Refer to the examples in *Stroking and Filling Paths* on page 29 in this chapter.

To remember the graphics state for later recall, use **gsave** to push the current graphics state onto the top of the graphics state stack. To recall the most recently saved graphics state, use **grestore** to pop the top element off the graphics state stack and back into the current graphics state.

Some of the examples you saw earlier (starting on page 29) contained code constructs like this next example, to draw the large filled circle in the middle of the page.

The key code elements in this following example are the **gsave** and **grestore** operators. Prior to **gsave**, the graphics state contained the current path—the circle **arc** created, the current color (assumed black, since it wasn't changed), the current line width, and other components of the graphics state.

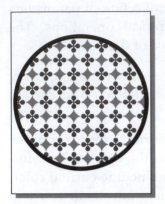

Fill and stroke the same shape using the graphics state stack.

```
%!PS
/inch { 72 mul } def            % define inch procedure
4.25 inch 5.5 inch              % in middle of the page
4 inch                          % four inch radius
0 360 arc                       % draw a circle
closepath                       % finish circle
gsave                           % remember graphics state
    AstroidLeaf setpattern      % fancy pattern fill
    fill                        % fill with pattern
grestore                        % recall graphics state
0.25 inch setlinewidth          % fat line width
stroke                          % paint the outline
showpage                        % display page
```

gsave pushes the current graphics state onto the top of the graphics state stack. You change the current color in the current graphics state to a pattern fill using **setpattern**. Then you can **fill** the circle with the "color" just established. Note that **setpattern** is a PostScript Level 2 operator.

grestore pops the previous graphics state off the top of the graphics state stack; the graphics state reverts to what it was prior to the **gsave**. The only change to the graphics state now is setting a different line weight; the current color reverts to black.

Writing Your Own PostScript

Applications

PostScript Program

PostScript Printer

Applications

PostScript Printer

At some point you might wonder why you would ever want to confront PostScript in the raw. After all, doesn't your page layout or graphics application generate PostScript for you? You read earlier that PostScript is intended as an intermediary between a computer application program and a PostScript printing device or display device. This illustration shows the general idea of how PostScript is supposed to fit into the world.

You use a graphics or page layout application on your computer. When the time comes to print the output, the application converts its images into a PostScript program that is transmitted to a

PostScript printer. This is the most general scenario, as they say in the Pentagon, and, in fact, probably 90 percent or more of all PostScript is used in precisely this fashion—as a silent invisible worker who does the job and never intrudes.

In this less-than-ideal world, however, practical issues of PostScript do intrude. PostScript generated from applications running on computer systems other than your own model may have been written to different assumptions. Sometimes, different PostScript programs don't cooperate. You may have to deal with issues such as fonts being different between systems. In such cases, a working knowledge of PostScript nuts and bolts can be immensely helpful in dealing with day-to-day printing issues.

This book, then, acquaints you with some of the less-than-ideal details of the somewhat imperfect world in which we all live. With that, we conclude your introduction to basic PostScript. Read on to see many more examples of PostScript code and pictures. *Per PostScript ad Astra*, or something.

2 Paths and Painting

They built a tower to shiver the sky
  And wrench the stars apart.
Till the Devil grunted behind the bricks,
  "It's striking, but is it Art?"

Rudyard Kipling—*The Conundrum of the Workshops*

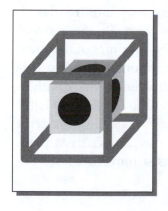

Now you've had a lightning-fast tour of basic PostScript notions, you're ready to delve into PostScript graphics in greater detail. Although this chapter discusses basic PostScript graphics—lines and rectangles—a major strength of PostScript is that there is little differentiation between graphics and text. Text characters are themselves graphical objects drawn using combinations of graphical operators introduced in this chapter and in Chapter 7.

This chapter, as its title implies, concentrates on two basic notions of PostScript—constructing paths and painting them. This chapter focuses mainly on lines and rectangles, with emphasis on the PostScript painting model. Here you will read about setting the current point, drawing lines, and drawing rectangles with PostScript Level 2 and Display PostScript rectangle operators. Additionally, this chapter covers parameters of the graphics state that you can change to affect the appearance of lines—widths, joins, caps, and dashed line styles, among others.

The PostScript Painting Model

All PostScript text, graphics, and images are controlled by a device-independent and resolution-independent coordinate system known as the *user coordinate system*. This user coordinate system works in terms of 72 units to the inch or approximately 28.35 units to the centimeter. PostScript units are very close to traditional printers' points, and while PostScript literature refers to "PostScript units," common usage has them as "PostScript points." While PostScript units are not exactly equal to traditional printers' points, the difference is so small you *usually* needn't worry about it. All user space coordinates are represented by floating point numbers.

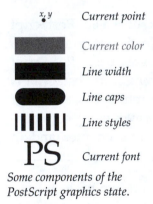

Current point

Current color

Line width

Line caps

Line styles

Current font

Some components of the PostScript graphics state.

The PostScript graphics state is a collection of parameters that affect what graphics will look like when they are rendered. PostScript programs establish parameters such as the current color in the graphics state. Parameters of the graphics state affect the execution of all subsequent graphics operations, but not previous operations. Once you establish a parameter in the graphics state, it remains set to that value until such time as you explicitly change it with another PostScript operator. Part of the PostScript graphics state is the notion of a current point and a current path. This following PostScript fragment first uses **moveto** to set the current point to (1 inch, 1 inch).

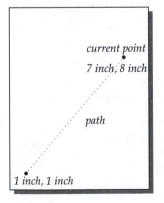

current point

7 inch, 8 inch

path

1 inch, 1 inch

```
%!PS
/inch { 72 mul } def        %   define inch procedure
1 inch 1 inch moveto        %   set current point
7 inch 8 inch lineto        %   etch line segment
```

Then **lineto** adds a line segment from the previously set current point to the specified coordinates, in this case (7 inch, 8 inch). The current point is left at the end of the line segment just added. Once again, be aware that the current point starts out undefined, so you must set the current point prior to operations such as **lineto** or **curveto** that draw from the current point to another point.

The current path may be constructed from a series of disconnected subpaths. Each subpath may be constructed from a series of straight lines, circular arcs, and Bézier curves. A subpath is a sequence of operations commencing with a **moveto** and ending with either an explicit or implicit **closepath**. Once you have constructed the path, you can **stroke** it (paint its outline), **fill** it (paint the area enclosed by the path), or **clip** with it (use the path as a clipping region). **stroke** and **fill** leave the current point and the current path undefined in the graphics state. The PostScript painting model is very simple in concept, and is very intuitive. To build a PostScript image, you do the following:

- ❏ construct a path
- ❏ adjust visual effects (width, color, dashes, and so on)
- ❏ apply paint

Complicated pictures involve many iterations of the preceding steps. Let's go through the steps with a concrete example. The first example on page 10 in Chapter 1 illustrated the process of drawing a triangle. The next simplest PostScript program ever is a basic square. Let's draw a six-inch blue square[†] in the middle of the page. To draw a square you need four line segments.

This example introduces a couple of new notions. One twist is the **rlineto** operators. **rlineto** requires the current point to be defined, and requires two operands: the x and y coordinates for the endpoint of the line. Where **lineto** specifies the absolute position of the end of the line, **rlineto** specifies its coordinates relative to the current point. As with **lineto**, the current point is left at the endpoint of the line just drawn. The syntax of **rlineto** is

$$\delta x \quad \delta y \quad \texttt{rlineto}$$

where δx and δy are offsets from the current point. In addition to **rlineto** for drawing lines relative to the current point, PostScript also provides **rmoveto** for moving to a new coordinate relative to

† Skiers will recognize this symbol as marking intermediate ski slopes.

the current point, and **rcurveto** for drawing Bézier curves relative to the current point.

Plate II has the color version.

```
%!PS
/inch { 72 mul } def          %   define inch procedure
newpath                        %   initialize path
1.25 inch 2.5 inch moveto      %   set current point
6 inch 0 rlineto               %   bottom of square
0 6 inch rlineto               %   right side of square
-6 inch 0 rlineto              %   top of square
closepath                      %   close the shape
0.0 0.0 1.0 setrgbcolor        %   set color blue
fill                           %   paint the shape
showpage                       %   display page
```

Paths, of course, can be a lot more complex than just the straight lines you've seen so far. You can continue your path by appending arcs and curves to the current path. Chapter 7 talks about arcs and circles, while Chapter 7.5 covers Bézier curves. Leave this example as it is—a simple square.

newpath is the other new idea in the example. **stroke** and **fill** clear the current path and the current point, but other operators, most notably **clip**, leave the current path defined. If you wish to start with a clean slate, you must explicitly clear the current path with **newpath**. The first path drawn in user space is implicitly initialized, so you don't need a **newpath** at the very start, but you do for subsequent paths.[†]

Some operators require a current point before you use them. The current point must be defined prior to adding line or curve segments to the current path, or before you show text. Some operators (such as **arc**) don't need a predefined current point.

---

† Get into the habit of starting genuine new paths with **newpath** so your PostScript code is robust in the face of future modifications.

Closing a Path

PostScript has the concepts of *open* and *closed* paths. A path (more correctly, a subpath) is closed if it has been explicitly closed with the **closepath** operator. **closepath** explicitly closes a path by drawing a straight line segment from the last point of the subpath to the first point of the subpath. A subpath is open if it has not been explicitly closed, even if the final point of the subpath is congruent with the initial point.

The very first example you saw in *Basic Graphics—A Triangle* on page 9 in Chapter 1 showed how to draw a triangle using **moveto** to set the current point, two **lineto** instructions to add line segments to the current path, followed by **closepath** to finish the shape by connecting the final point to its initial point.

Here is the picture and code again to refresh your memory. The code is much the same except for two items: numbers were converted to inches to make life easier, and the bottom leg of the triangle is drawn using an explicit **lineto** instead of **closepath**.

Basic triangle example.

```
%!PS
/inch { 72 mul } def          %   define inch procedure
1 inch 2 inch moveto          %   set initial point
4.25 inch 9 inch lineto       %   add line segment
7.5 inch 2 inch lineto        %   add another line segment
1 inch 2 inch lineto          %   add final segment
stroke                        %   paint the path
showpage                      %   display page
```

This triangle looks fine, doesn't it? But there's a snag you'll see by stroking the triangle with a fat line. Let's draw the shape again, using **setlinewidth** to make the stroked line fatter. You encountered **setlinewidth** in previous examples.

```
%!PS
/inch { 72 mul } def              % define inch procedure
1 inch 2 inch moveto              % set initial point
4.25 inch 9 inch lineto           % add line segment
7.5 inch 2 inch lineto            % add another line segment
1 inch 2 inch lineto              % add last line segment
1.0 inch setlinewidth            % fat line width
stroke                            % paint the path
showpage                          % display page
```

Triangle without explicit **closepath**.

There's an ugly "notch" where the start of the shape joins the end of the shape. There's a good reason for this appearance—the start and end of the shape really aren't joined at all. The first two lines of the shape were drawn from the current point to a second point. Those lines are joined, and the PostScript interpreter "knows" those lines are connected.

But the endpoint of the third line doesn't really join the initial point—the two points are in the same place only by coincidence, and the interpreter doesn't "know" this. The lines are just lying there unconnected.

The way to make start points and end points join properly is to use **closepath**—the glue that keeps elements of the path together as a unit so the interpreter can do the right thing. What happens is the same as if the object weren't really a triangular shape but three lines randomly drawn in space. The ends of the lines are treated as ends of lines, not as intersections of lines.

The next picture shows the same shape using **closepath** instead of the final **lineto**. This small example illustrates the importance of using **closepath**. The only time you shouldn't use **closepath** is when you make a conscious decision not to! Get in the habit now, and avoid hours of debugging in the future.

```
%!PS
/inch { 72 mul } def              % define inch procedure
1 inch 2 inch moveto              % set initial point
4.25 inch 9 inch lineto           % add line segment
7.5 inch 2 inch lineto            % add another line segment
closepath                         % complete the path
1.0 inch setlinewidth             % fat line width
stroke                            % paint the path
showpage                          % display page
```

Triangle with explicit **closepath**.

Stroking the Outline of a Path

Painting the outline of a path with **stroke** uses the current path and the current graphics state to paint a line of the specified line width, color, style, and so on, along the path.

Let's draw a simple square using a series of lines. Later in this chapter you will see specific operators to deal with rectangles in single operations. You will stroke the square with a one-inch-wide line using a 50 percent gray shade, and beveled line joins.

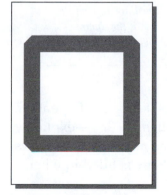

```
%!PS
/inch { 72 mul } def              % define inch procedure
1.25 inch 2.5 inch moveto         % set current point
6 inch 0 rlineto                  % bottom of square
0 6 inch rlineto                  % right side of square
-6 inch 0 rlineto                 % top of square
closepath                         % finish the square
1.0 inch setlinewidth             % fat line width
2 setlinejoin                     % beveled line joins
0.5 setgray                       % medium gray shade
stroke                            % paint the square outline
showpage                          % display page
```

Stroking outline of a path.

The actual path you establish using any graphics operators runs along the middle of the line width as shown. This issue will become clearer after you see the next few examples.

A side-effect of **stroke** is an implicit **newpath** operation following the application of paint to the path, obliterating the path. If you wish to retain the path for use after the **stroke** operation, remember to use **gsave** and **grestore**.

Filling the Interior of a Path

Filling the interior of a path using **fill** differs from **stroke** in that **fill** fills the area enclosed by the path rather than painting along the path. Here is the same square as in the example on stroking, but this time the square is filled instead of stroked.

Filling interior of a path.

```
%!PS
/inch { 72 mul } def              %   define inch procedure
1.25 inch 2.5 inch moveto         %   set current point
6 inch 0 rlineto                  %   bottom of square
0 6 inch rlineto                  %   right side of square
-6 inch 0 rlineto                 %   top of square
closepath                         %   finish the square
0.5 setgray                       %   medium gray shade
fill                              %   paint the square
showpage                          %   display page
```

If the path is not closed, **fill** implicitly closes it for you. In general, you should not rely on hidden features such as this—explicitly close paths when you want them closed. The next example draws only two lines of a triangle, but the entire shape is filled in when a **fill** operator is encountered.

```
%!PS
/inch { 72 mul } def          %   define inch procedure
1 inch 2 inch moveto          %   set current point
4.25 inch 9 inch lineto       %   left side of triangle
7.5 inch 2 inch lineto        %   right side of triangle
0.5 setgray                   %   medium gray shade
fill                          %   paint the shape
showpage                      %   display page
```

fill *implicitly closes paths.*

stroke does not implicitly close paths for you. Why do **stroke** and **fill** behave differently? This point has caused confusion. **stroke** does not implicitly close paths so you can draw unconnected paths. If **stroke** implicitly closed paths, you could never have an open shape. Good PostScript programming practice suggests that you close paths explicitly, not rely on your memory as to which operators close paths and which do not.

Following is the same example, but the triangle is stroked after it is filled. **fill** acts as if the shape were closed, but **stroke** paints only the parts of the path that were explicitly drawn.

```
%!PS
/inch { 72 mul } def          %   define inch procedure
1 inch 2 inch moveto          %   set current point
4.25 inch 9 inch lineto       %   left side of triangle
7.5 inch 2 inch lineto        %   right side of triangle
gsave                         %   remember graphics state
    0.5 setgray               %   medium gray shade
    fill                      %   paint the shape
grestore                      %   restore graphics state
0.5 inch setlinewidth         %   fat line width
stroke                        %   paint the path
showpage                      %   display page
```

stroke *does not implicitly close paths.*

As with **stroke**, **fill** performs a **newpath** upon completion of the painting operation. To retain the path after a **fill** you should use the **gsave** and **grestore** operators.

Rules for Filling Intersecting Subpaths

The *PostScript Language Reference Manual* states "**fill** fills disjoint subpaths." What does this mean? Here's a page with a couple of filled squares. The two subpaths are separate—that is, disjoint—and don't intersect each other.

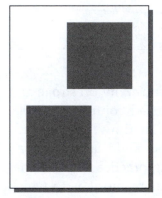

Two shapes—no intersection.

```
%!PS
/inch { 72 mul } def          % define inch procedure
/width 4 inch def             % define width of rectangle
/height 4 inch def            % define height of rectangle
1 inch 1 inch moveto          % set current point
width 0 rlineto               % bottom of rectangle
0 height rlineto              % right side
width neg 0 rlineto           % top
closepath                     % close the path
7.5 inch 10 inch moveto       % set current point
width neg 0 rlineto           % top of rectangle
0 height neg rlineto          % left side
width 0 rlineto               % bottom
closepath                     % close the path
0.50 setgray fill             % fill with medium gray
showpage                      % display page
```

So far so good. Nothing particularly weird about this simple example. However, filling becomes slightly complicated when you wish to fill subpaths that intersect themselves, because you get involved in the question of what is "inside" of the path and what is "outside." Let's complicate things a little by making the squares into rectangles so they intersect.

Intersecting shapes.

```
%!PS
/inch { 72 mul } def          %   define inch procedure
/width 4 inch def             %   define width of rectangle
/height 7 inch def            %   define height of rectangle
1 inch 1 inch moveto          %   set current point
width 0 rlineto               %   bottom of rectangle
0 height rlineto              %   right side
width neg 0 rlineto           %   top
closepath                     %   close the path
7.5 inch 10 inch moveto       %   set current point
width neg 0 rlineto           %   top of rectangle
0 height neg rlineto          %   left side
width 0 rlineto               %   bottom
closepath                     %   close the path
0.50 setgray                  %   set fill shade
fill                          %   fill the shapes
showpage                      %   display page
```

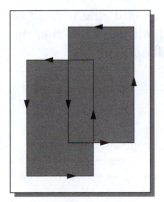

Winding number rule with both rectangles drawn counterclockwise.

Notice from the preceding examples that both subpaths were drawn in a counterclockwise direction, as shown here. They are drawn this way to illustrate a PostScript rule for deciding what's inside and what's outside a shape. The rule employed in this particular case is known as the *winding number rule* and is one of two rules PostScript can use. The other rule, known as the *even-odd rule*, is discussed a little later.

The next picture draws the second rectangle's path clockwise instead of counterclockwise. Here's a different interpretation—the winding number rule considers the intersections of the rectangles "outside" the shape, so they aren't filled.

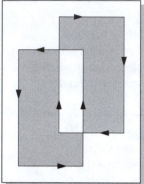

Winding number rule with one rectangle drawn in each direction.

```
%!PS
/inch { 72 mul } def          %  define inch procedure
/width 4 inch def             %  define width of rectangle
/height 7 inch def            %  define height of rectangle
1 inch 1 inch moveto          %  set current point
width 0 rlineto               %  bottom of rectangle
0 height rlineto              %  right side
width neg 0 rlineto           %  top
closepath                     %  close the path
7.5 inch 10 inch moveto       %  set current point
0 height neg rlineto          %  right side of rectangle
width neg 0 rlineto           %  bottom
0 height rlineto              %  left side
closepath                     %  close the path
0.50 setgray                  %  set fill shade
fill                          %  fill the shapes
showpage                      %  display page
```

Finally, you see the picture from before with both paths drawn counterclockwise. This version uses the even-odd rule instead of relying on the standard winding number filling rule. Note that the **eofill** operator is used instead of the plain **fill** operator.

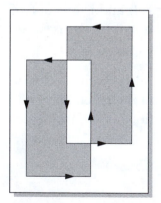

Even-odd rule with both rectangles drawn counter-clockwise.

```
%!PS
/inch { 72 mul } def          %  define inch procedure
/width 4 inch def             %  define width of rectangle
/height 7 inch def            %  define height of rectangle
1 inch 1 inch moveto          %  set current point
width 0 rlineto               %  bottom of rectangle
0 height rlineto              %  right side
width neg 0 rlineto           %  top
closepath                     %  close the path
7.5 inch 10 inch moveto       %  set current point
0 height neg rlineto          %  right side of rectangle
width neg 0 rlineto           %  bottom
0 height rlineto              %  left side
closepath                     %  close the path
0.50 setgray eofill           %  fill with medium gray
showpage                      %  display page
```

Filling Rules

One very important aspect of PostScript is the pair of rules **fill** uses to determine what parts of a path are "inside" a shape and what parts are "outside." PostScript uses a standard rule known as the *non-zero winding number rule*, or, more simply, the *winding number rule*, to determine what parts of a shape are inside and outside. The rules are important only when you create complex self-intersecting shapes. Most reasonable shapes are intuitive as to what's inside and what's outside.

Inside and outside decisions.

The winding number rule determines if a point is inside or outside a path by drawing a line from that point to infinity. You start with a count of zero and add one every time the line crosses a path segment going from left to right. Subtract one every time the line crosses a path segment going from right to left. After you have counted all the path crossings, a result of zero means that the point is outside the path. A result of other than zero means the point is inside the path. To see this in action, let's fill a rectangle. First, let's define a rectangle procedure that will be used in more examples. This rectangle procedure is called **widdershins**—so called because it draws paths in the *counterclockwise* direction.

```
%!PS
/widdershins {                  %   stack = x  y  width  height
    4 2 roll moveto             %   set current point
    1 index 0 rlineto           %   bottom of rectangle
    0 exch rlineto              %   right side
    neg 0 rlineto               %   top of rectangle
    closepath                   %   finish shape
} def
```

Now let's use **widdershins** to construct a filled rectangle (actually, a square because the sides are the same length).

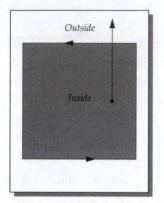

Winding number filling rule.

```
%!PS
/inch { 72 mul } def                        %  define inch procedure
                                            %  draw rectangle
0.75 inch 2 inch 7 inch 7 inch widdershins
currentgray                                 %  remember gray shade
0.50 setgray                                %  medium gray color
fill                                        %  fill rectangle
setgray                                     %  revert to previous gray
2 setlinewidth                              %  fatter line width
                                            %  draw rectangle
0.75 inch 2 inch 7 inch 7 inch widdershins
stroke                                      %  paint outline
showpage                                    %  display page
```

This is easy. Notice the arrow crosses one path going from right to left, so the final count is −1. The point indicated is inside so that part of the path is filled. Now let's see what happens when you draw a shape with a rectangle inside another rectangle.

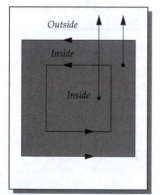

Winding number filling rule—doing the "wrong" thing.

```
%!PS
/inch { 72 mul } def                        %  define inch procedure
                                            %  outer rectangle
0.75 inch 2 inch 7 inch 7 inch widdershins
                                            %  inner rectangle
2.25 inch 3.5 inch 4 inch 4 inch widdershins
currentgray                                 %  remember gray shade
0.50 setgray                                %  medium gray color
fill                                        %  fill rectangle
setgray                                     %  restore previous gray
2 setlinewidth                              %  fatter line width
                                            %  outer rectangle
0.75 inch 2 inch 7 inch 7 inch widdershins
stroke                                      %  paint outline
                                            %  inner rectangle
2.25 inch 3.5 inch 4 inch 4 inch widdershins
stroke                                      %  paint outline
showpage                                    %  display page
```

You see the winding number rule doesn't always do the "right" thing. You would like the area inside the inner rectangle not to be filled. But according to the winding number rule, both areas are inside the path, because the winding number count at the end of the exercise is non-zero.

You get around this problem in one of two ways. The first method is to use a different fill rule, the *even-odd fill rule*. The even-odd fill rule uses the same trick of drawing a line from a point to infinity. But the even-odd rule counts the number of crossings it makes. If the line makes an odd number of crossings, the point is inside the path. If the line makes an even number of crossings, the point is outside the path. Here is the same shape drawn using the even-odd fill rule.

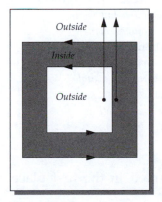

Even-odd filling rule.

```
%!PS
/inch { 72 mul } def               %   define inch procedure
                                   %   outer rectangle
0.75 inch 2 inch 7 inch 7 inch widdershins
                                   %   inner rectangle
2.25 inch 3.5 inch 4 inch 4 inch widdershins
currentgray                        %   remember gray shade
0.50 setgray                       %   medium gray color
eofill                             %   fill rectangle
setgray                            %   restore previous gray
2 setlinewidth                     %   fatter line width
                                   %   outer rectangle
0.75 inch 2 inch 7 inch 7 inch widdershins
stroke                             %   paint outline
                                   %   inner rectangle
2.25 inch 3.5 inch 4 inch 4 inch widdershins
stroke                             %   paint outline
showpage                           %   display page
```

The even-odd fill rule is not as flexible as the winding number rule in most cases. A somewhat better way to deal with the issue described is to draw the shape you want with paths going in different directions so as to use the winding number rule to its advantage. To use the winding number rule in this case, you need to define another procedure to draw the path in the reverse direction. Let's define a procedure called **deasil**—so called because it draws paths in the *clockwise* direction.

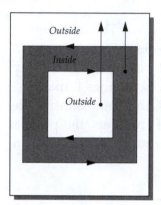

Winding number filling rule—doing the "right" thing.

```
%!PS
/inch { 72 mul } def                    %   define inch procedure
                                        %   outer rectangle
0.75 inch 2 inch 7 inch 7 inch widdershins
                                        %   inner rectangle
2.25 inch 3.5 inch 4 inch 4 inch deasil
currentgray                             %   remember gray shade
0.50 setgray                            %   medium gray color
fill                                    %   fill rectangle
setgray                                 %   restore previous gray
2 setlinewidth                          %   fatter line width
                                        %   outer rectangle
0.75 inch 2 inch 7 inch 7 inch widdershins
stroke                                  %   paint outline
                                        %   inner rectangle
2.25 inch 3.5 inch 4 inch 4 inch deasil
stroke                                  %   paint outline
showpage                                %   display page
```

Now you see you get the results you wanted in the first place. Here's the definition of **deasil**.

```
%!PS
/deasil {                               %   x y width height
        4 2 roll moveto                 %   set current point
        dup 0 exch rlineto              %   left side of rectangle
        exch 0 rlineto                  %   top of rectangle
        neg 0 exch rlineto              %   right side of rectangle
        closepath                       %   finish shape
} def
```

That's it for filling rules. They are fairly easy to deal with.

A Small Efficiency Hint

You'll notice in the examples we used an interesting construct to change the gray scale from black to gray and to black again. Here is the sequence to refresh your memory.

```
currentgray              % remember gray shade
0.50 setgray             % medium gray color
fill                     % fill rectangle
setgray                  % restore previous gray
```

Instead of using **gsave** and **grestore** just to remember the gray scale, these examples use **currentgray** to get the value of the current gray level onto the operand stack. After **fill**, **setgray** uses the value from the stack. Use short sequences like this to save the overhead of **gsave** and **grestore** when you change only one or two elements of the graphics state.

Order of Filling and Stroking Paths

Suppose you want a square with a solid black fat border and filled with 50 percent gray. The order in which you **stroke** and **fill** the square is significant, because you get different results depending on whether you **stroke** first or **fill** first. The first example draws a square by filling first and stroking second.

Fill first and stroke second.

```
%!PS
/inch { 72 mul } def           % define inch procedure
1.25 inch 2.5 inch moveto      % set current point
6 inch 0 rlineto               % bottom of square
0 6 inch rlineto               % right side of square
-6 inch 0 rlineto              % top of square
closepath                      % finish the square
gsave                          % remember graphics state
   0.50 setgray fill           % fill with medium gray
grestore                       % restore graphics state
1.0 inch setlinewidth stroke   % stroke with fat line
showpage                       % display page
```

This second example strokes first and fills second.

Stroke first and fill second.

```
%!PS
/inch { 72 mul } def              %   define inch procedure
1.25 inch 2.5 inch moveto         %   set current point
6 inch 0 rlineto                  %   bottom of square
0 6 inch rlineto                  %   right side of square
-6 inch 0 rlineto                 %   top of square
closepath                         %   finish the square
gsave                             %   remember graphics state
    1.0 inch setlinewidth         %   fat line width
    stroke                        %   paint the path
grestore                          %   restore graphics state
0.50 setgray                      %   medium gray shade
fill                              %   fill the shape
showpage                          %   display page
```

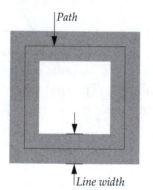

Path

Line width

The only difference in the code is the order of stroking and filling the box. The following diagram illustrates what happens.

The middle solid line is the path you establish when you construct a figure. The fat gray line represents where the line is stroked in relation to the path. The path is an abstract infinitesimally thin line. When you stroke the path, the line width extends either side of the path—not all outside or all inside.

Note that line width is relevant only for a **stroke** on a path—the line extends half the specified line width either side of the constructed path. Filling only extends to the path and does not extend beyond the path.

Notice that **gsave** and **grestore** retain the current path. This enables us to use the same path for both **stroke** and **fill** without having to go through the effort of drawing the path twice.

Rectangle Operators

Display PostScript introduced new operators specifically to deal with rectangles, since drawing rectangular areas was found to be a very common operation in graphics packages and window systems. These rectangle operators were then made a part of PostScript Level 2. The new rectangle operators are **rectstroke**, **rectfill**, and **rectclip**. The new rectangle operators are more compact and perform significantly better for several reasons:

❑ algorithms to implement the rectangle operators are highly optimized

❑ rectangle operators can deal with a list of rectangles in one operation

❑ rectangle lists can be in one of two representations: "numarray" or "numstring." Both representations are very compact and require less transmission time to the physical device, or, in Display PostScript systems, less communication time between the client application and the PostScript interpreter.

Besides obvious performance gains, these operators also encourage writing code that is easier to read, maintain, and reuse, on both the client side and the PostScript side. All rectangle operators accept their parameters in a variety of ways. In particular, you can supply a whole array of position-size pairs to render multiple rectangles in one operation. For now, the simplest form of the various rectangle operators is

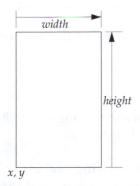

$$x \quad y \quad width \quad height \quad \begin{array}{l} \texttt{rectstroke} \\ \texttt{rectfill} \\ \texttt{rectclip} \end{array}$$

(x, y) is the coordinate of one corner of the rectangle, *width* is the width of the rectangle, and *height* is the height. Each rectangle defined in this way has sides parallel to the current axes of user space. In this particular illustration, (x, y) happens to be the coordinate of the lower-left corner of the rectangle, with *width* and *height* being positive, so that the upper-right corner of the rectangle is at $(x + width, y + height)$.

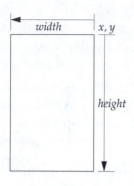

Note (x, y) is the coordinate of one corner of the rectangle. But the syntax of the rectangle operators didn't specify which corner. This slight vagueness comes about because *width* or *height* or both can be negative. This picture shows that (x, y) is the coordinate of the upper-right corner of the rectangle. Both *width* and *height* are negative, so the lower-left corner is at $(x - width, y - height)$.

As a final note, all the rectangle operators perform an implicit **closepath**. The next two sections discuss operators for stroking and filling rectangles. Clipping with rectangles is discussed in detail in *Clipping with Rectangles* on pages 327–328 in Chapter 8.

Stroking Rectangles

Let's start our discussion on rectangle operators by looking at **rectstroke**. You use **rectstroke** to define and stroke a rectangular path in one compact operation. The simplest form of **rectstroke** expects four operands and strokes one rectangle. Let's draw a stroked rectangle on the page.

Simple stroked rectangle.

```
%!PS
/inch { 72 mul } def          %  define inch procedure
1 inch 1 inch                 %  lower-left corner
6 inch 8 inch                 %  width and height
rectstroke                    %  stroke the path
showpage                      %  display page
```

As you saw in the introductory section, the general form of **rectstroke** is

x y *width*   *height*   **rectstroke**

where (x, y) is the coordinate of one corner of the rectangle, *width* is the width of the rectangle, and *height* is the height.

You'll remember from previous examples of drawing and stroking paths that you could set up the path, change attributes of the graphics state (such as line width), then actually **stroke**.

When you use **rectstroke**, you see that the position and size of the rectangle plus the operator are given in one fell swoop. You must modify attributes within the graphics state to affect the new rectangle before executing **rectstroke**. You can see this effect by using **rectstroke** to stroke a rectangle with a fat gray line.

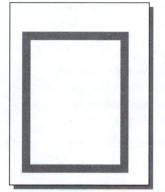

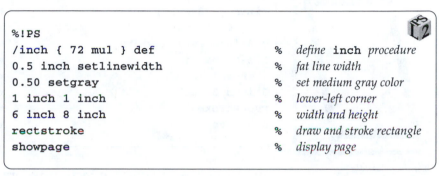

```
%!PS
/inch { 72 mul } def              %   define inch procedure
0.5 inch setlinewidth             %   fat line width
0.50 setgray                      %   set medium gray color
1 inch 1 inch                     %   lower-left corner
6 inch 8 inch                     %   width and height
rectstroke                        %   draw and stroke rectangle
showpage                          %   display page
```

Simple stroked rectangle—
fatter line.

This example illustrates that you should set up elements of the graphics state before you execute **rectstroke**. The fat line width and the medium gray shade were set up prior to stroking the rectangle. Were you so inclined, you could write the code like this

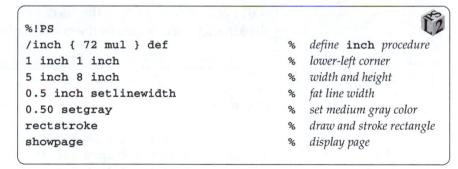

```
%!PS
/inch { 72 mul } def              %   define inch procedure
1 inch 1 inch                     %   lower-left corner
5 inch 8 inch                     %   width and height
0.5 inch setlinewidth             %   fat line width
0.50 setgray                      %   set medium gray color
rectstroke                        %   draw and stroke rectangle
showpage                          %   display page
```

But this style of coding is confusing. The operation (draw rectangle) is separated from its parameters (position and size) by code to set parameters of the graphics state. Separating elements of code in this fashion invites misunderstanding.

Continuing with this story, you alter other elements of the graphics state in the same fashion—change the graphics state, then perform the rectangle operation. Here, for instance, is a rectangle with a fat line width, round line joins, sheared 12° by changing the CTM with **concat** prior to **rectstroke**

Sheared rectangle.

```
%!PS
/inch { 72 mul } def                    %   define inch procedure
[ 1  0  12 sin  1  0  0 ] concat        %   shear transformation
0.5 inch setlinewidth                   %   fat line width
1 setlinejoin                           %   round line join
1 inch 1 inch                           %   lower-left corner
5 inch 8 inch                           %   width and height
rectstroke                              %   draw and stroke rectangle
showpage                                %   display page
```

You haven't seen **concat** in action before—it is covered in more detail in *Shear Transformations* on pages 160–165 in Chapter 4.

Stroking Multiple Rectangles

The previous example of **rectstroke** is simple and shows just one rectangle. You can stroke an entire set of rectangles by supplying a list of position-size pairs in the form of a *numarray*. Let's see this by stroking four rectangles in the corners of the page.

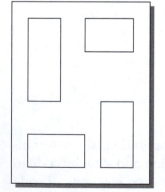

Stroking multiple rectangles in one operation.

```
%!PS
/inch { 72 mul } def                              %   define inch procedure
[                                                 %   start numarray
  1.0 inch 1.0 inch 3.5 inch 2.0 inch  %   lower-left rectangle
  5.5 inch 1.0 inch 2.0 inch 4.0 inch  %   lower right rectangle
  4.5 inch 8.0 inch 3.0 inch 2.0 inch  %   upper-right rectangle
  1.0 inch 5.0 inch 2.0 inch 5.0 inch  %   upper left rectangle
]                                                 %   end numarray
rectstroke                                        %   stroke the path
showpage                                          %   display page
```

This *numarray* representation provides significant performance gains, especially for display applications. The general form of the *numarray* representation is

[*rect*$_1$ *rect*$_2$ *rect*$_3$ . . .]   `rectstroke`

where each *rect*$_n$ consists of an *x*, *y*, *width*, and *height* quartet defined previously.

Stroking Rectangles with a Matrix

You can achieve interesting stroked effects using **rectstroke** in one of its variant forms that accepts a *matrix*—that is, a CTM—as an operand in addition to the position-size pairs.

Rectangle stroked with matrix operand.

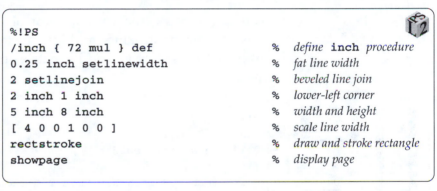

```
%!PS
/inch { 72 mul } def          % define inch procedure
0.25 inch setlinewidth        % fat line width
2 setlinejoin                 % beveled line join
2 inch 1 inch                 % lower-left corner
5 inch 8 inch                 % width and height
[ 4 0 0 1 0 0 ]               % scale line width
rectstroke                    % draw and stroke rectangle
showpage                      % display page
```

The simple form of **rectstroke** with a *matrix* operand looks like this

x   *y*   *width*   *height*   *matrix*   `rectstroke`

matrix is a regular transformation matrix. But, note carefully

> The *matrix* operand does not affect the path. The *matrix* operand affects only elements of the graphics state— such as the line width, as you just saw—after the path has been drawn.

Let's embellish the previous example a little to illustrate this effect. You can combine the CTM from the preceding shear example and the matrix from the example above to produce a sheared rectangle with fat scaled lines.

Rectangle stroked with matrix operand.

```
%!PS
/inch { 72 mul } def                    %  define inch procedure
[ 1 0 12 sin 1 0 0 ] concat             %  set up for shear
0.25 inch setlinewidth                  %  fat line width
2 setlinejoin                           %  beveled line join
1 inch 1 inch                           %  lower-left corner
5 inch 8 inch                           %  width and height
[ 4 0 0 1 0 0 ]                         %  scale line width
rectstroke                              %  draw and stroke rectangle
showpage                                %  display page
```

You can also use the variant form of **rectstroke** with a matrix operand when stroking multiple rectangles. Let's revisit our example from before and add a matrix operand to the story.

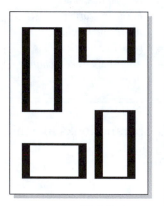

```
%!PS
/inch { 72 mul } def                        %  define inch procedure
0.125 inch setlinewidth                     %  fat line width
[                                           %  start numarray
  1.0 inch 1.0 inch 3.5 inch 2.0 inch       %  lower-left rectangle
  5.5 inch 1.0 inch 2.0 inch 4.0 inch       %  lower right rectangle
  4.5 inch 8.0 inch 3.0 inch 2.0 inch       %  upper-right rectangle
  1.0 inch 5.0 inch 2.0 inch 5.0 inch       %  upper left rectangle
]                                           %  end numarray
[ 4 0 0 1 0 0 ]                             %  scale line width
rectstroke                                  %  stroke the path
showpage                                    %  display page
```

Notes on Stroking Rectangles

You may have noticed that using **rectstroke** for several rectangles is not as flexible as using a loop with one **rectstroke** inside, or doing boxes by hand. You cannot modify the graphics state for each rectangle within a single **rectstroke** operator. Each rectangle has the same linewidth, the same rotation, the same scale—the same graphics state. Size and position are the only changes you can make in a single **rectstroke** operation. Keep this in mind when designing your PostScript code. Group rectangles that share the same properties and render them at the same time.

Filling Rectangles

Now you've seen **rectstroke** in action, let's visit **rectfill**, which fills rectangles instead of stroking them.

rectfill is somewhat simpler to describe than **rectstroke** because **rectfill** doesn't have a form where you supply a *matrix* operand in the process of constructing the rectangle.

Other than its name being different, **rectfill** is much the same as **rectstroke**. Let's use the original example from the discussion on **rectstroke**, but this time let's fill the rectangle with 50 percent gray instead of stroking it.

Simple filled rectangle.

```
%!PS
/inch { 72 mul } def          %   define inch procedure
0.5 setgray                   %   set medium gray
1 inch 1 inch                 %   lower-left corner
6 inch 8 inch                 %   width and height
rectfill                      %   paint the area
showpage                      %   display page
```

Now you have a 6-by-8-inch rectangle filled with gray. This example spelled out each portion of the **rectfill** example, but in real life you can think of **rectfill** as a common cliché and simply write the whole thing out on one line.

```
%!PS
/inch { 72 mul } def                        %   define inch procedure
0.5 setgray                                 %   set medium gray
1 inch 1 inch 6 inch 8 inch rectfill %      fill a rectangle
showpage                                    %   display page
```

Of course, you can combine **rectfill** with **rectstroke** to produce rectangles that are filled and stroked. Here's a sheared rectangle, filled with 75 percent gray and stroked with a fat scaled line.

Simple filled and stroked rectangle with shear.

```
%!PS
/inch { 72 mul } def                %   define inch procedure
[ 1 0 12 sin 1 0 0 ] concat         %   set up for shear
0.5 setgray                         %   set medium gray
1 inch 1 inch                       %   lower-left corner
5 inch 8 inch                       %   width and height
rectfill                            %   paint the area
0.0 setgray                         %   set black color
0.125 inch setlinewidth             %   fat line width
1 inch 1 inch                       %   lower-left corner
5 inch 8 inch                       %   width and height
[ 1 0 0 3 0 0 ]                     %   scale line weight
rectstroke                          %   paint the path
showpage                            %   display page
```

Filling Multiple Rectangles

rectfill accepts an array of numbers as an operand, just like **rectstroke**. You can produce a series of filled boxes with this code

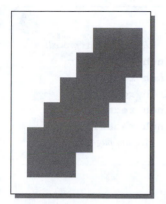

```
%!PS
/inch { 72 mul } def                          %   define inch procedure
0.5 setgray                                   %   set medium gray
[                                             %   start numarray
    1 inch 1.0 inch 3 inch 3 inch             %   rectangle descriptions
    2 inch 2.5 inch 3 inch 3 inch
    3 inch 4.0 inch 3 inch 3 inch
    4 inch 5.5 inch 3 inch 3 inch
    5 inch 7.0 inch 3 inch 3 inch
]                                             %   end of numarray
rectfill                                      %   paint the area
showpage                                      %   display page
```

*Multiple rectangles filled in
one operation.*

Now you have drawn five rectangles using a *numarray* argument
to **rectfill**. You could draw the five rectangles equally well and get
the same picture using this code.

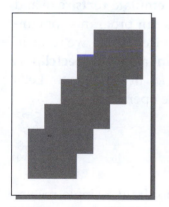

```
%!PS
/inch { 72 mul } def                       %   define inch procedure
0.5 setgray                                %   set medium gray
1 inch 1.0 inch 3 inch 3 inch rectfill
2 inch 2.5 inch 3 inch 3 inch rectfill
3 inch 4.0 inch 3 inch 3 inch rectfill
4 inch 5.5 inch 3 inch 3 inch rectfill
5 inch 7.0 inch 3 inch 3 inch rectfill
showpage                                   %   display page
```

*Multiple rectangles filled in
multiple operations.*

Either code segment yields the same picture. Now, a series of
filled squares all the same color is not very interesting. Let's
modify our example such that each box is a different color. Note
that you can't modify the graphics state within a *numarray* parameter to a **rectstroke** or **rectfill** operator. You achieve this modification only with the second code segment, which uses one **rectfill**
per rectangle. However, the modification is extremely easy, and
you end up with the following:

```
%!PS
/inch { 72 mul } def                    %   define inch procedure
0.1 setgray 1 inch 1.0 inch 3 inch 3 inch rectfill
0.3 setgray 2 inch 2.5 inch 3 inch 3 inch rectfill
0.5 setgray 3 inch 4.0 inch 3 inch 3 inch rectfill
0.7 setgray 4 inch 5.5 inch 3 inch 3 inch rectfill
0.9 setgray 5 inch 7.0 inch 3 inch 3 inch rectfill
showpage                                %   display page
```

Multiple rectangles filled in multiple operations.

Emulating Level 2 Rectangle Operators

Two PostScript Level 2 rectangle operators—**rectstroke** and **rectfill**—were introduced in *Stroking Rectangles* and *Filling Rectangles*. All the examples in *Stroking Rectangles* and *Filling Rectangles* will run only on PostScript Level 2 devices because of the presence of those two operators. You can emulate **rectstroke** and **rectfill** on Level 1 devices, enabling you to run programs containing those operators on any PostScript device. While we're at it, let's throw in the emulation for **rectclip** as well. **rectclip** is covered in detail in *Clipping with Rectangles* in Chapter 8. Let's start with the simplest form of the rectangle operators:

```
                        rectstroke
 x  y  width   height   rectfill
                        rectclip
```

Let's define a procedure called **DrawBox** to draw a single rectangle. Arguments to **DrawBox** are the *x*, *y*, *width* and *height* values for a single rectangle, the same arguments for the simple form of the rectangle operators.

If both width and height have the same sign, **DrawBox** draws the rectangle counterclockwise. Otherwise **DrawBox** draws the rectangle clockwise.

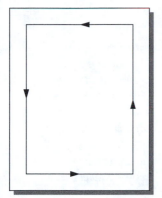

```
%!PS
/DrawBox {                          %   stack = x y width height
    4 2 roll moveto                 %   move to x, y
    1 index 0 rlineto               %   bottom edge
    0 exch rlineto                  %   right edge
    neg 0 rlineto                   %   top edge
    closepath                       %   close rectangle
} def
```

DrawBox would be sufficient emulation if the rectangle operators did not accept a *numarray* argument to describe multiple rectangles. But life is never easy and emulation of **rectstroke**, **rectfill**, and **rectclip** must handle arguments for describing either a single rectangle or multiple rectangles. Here's a procedure to help process *numarray* arguments.

```
%!PS
/DoNumArray {                             %   stack = numarray
   /numarray exch def
   0                                      %   start with first element
   4                                      %   increment by four elements
   numarray length 1 sub                  %   until no more elements
   {
       numarray exch 4 getinterval        %   get x, y, width, height
       aload pop DrawBox                  %   draw rectangle
   } for                                  %   loop through numarray
} def
```

DoNumArray loops through the numarray four elements at a time, drawing the path for the corresponding rectangle. Now we're ready to write the emulation procedures themselves. Let's start with **rectfill**, which is easier than **rectstroke** because it does not accept a transformation matrix like **rectstroke**.

```
%!PS
/rectfill {
    gsave                               %    save graphics state
    newpath                             %    clear current path
    dup type /arraytype eq {            %    is operand an array
        DoNumArray                      %    if so, process numarray
    } {                                 %    else
        DrawBox                         %    draw single rectangle
    } ifelse
    fill                                %    fill everything
    grestore                            %    restore graphics state
} def
```

This emulation of **rectfill** checks the type of its operand. If the operand is a numarray, then multiple rectangles are drawn with **DoNumArray**. If the operand is not a numarray, then **rectfill** calls **DrawBox** directly. After all the rectangle paths are drawn, they are filled. Here's a program to test the emulation of **rectfill**.

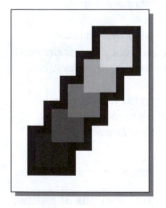

```
%!PS
/inch { 72 mul } def                    %    define inch procedure
[                                       %    fill five black rectangles
    1 inch 1.0 inch 3 inch 3 inch
    2 inch 2.5 inch 3 inch 3 inch
    3 inch 4.0 inch 3 inch 3 inch
    4 inch 5.5 inch 3 inch 3 inch
    5 inch 7.0 inch 3 inch 3 inch
] rectfill

                                        %    fill five gray rectangles
0.1 setgray 1.5 inch 1.5 inch 2 inch 2 inch rectfill
0.3 setgray 2.5 inch 3.0 inch 2 inch 2 inch rectfill
0.5 setgray 3.5 inch 4.5 inch 2 inch 2 inch rectfill
0.7 setgray 4.5 inch 6.0 inch 2 inch 2 inch rectfill
0.9 setgray 5.5 inch 7.5 inch 2 inch 2 inch rectfill
showpage                                %    display page
```

The picture shows several rectangles drawn using the emulation of **rectfill**. Seems easy enough; however, this emulation procedure has a subtle bug. Here's a PostScript program illustrating the bug.

```
%!PS
/inch { 72 mul } def              %   define inch procedure
[
    1 inch 8 inch 4 inch -7 inch  %   first rectangle
    3.5 inch 3 inch 4 inch 7 inch %   second rectangle
] rectfill                        %   fill rectangles
showpage                          %   display page
```

The first rectangle is drawn clockwise because its width and height have different signs. The second rectangle is drawn counterclockwise because the width and height have the same sign. According to the winding number rule, the intersection of these two rectangles is outside the shape. Therefore, the intersection of the rectangles is not filled. Here's the same picture run on a Level 2 device using the real **rectfill**.

```
%!PS
/inch { 72 mul } def              %   define inch procedure
[
    1 inch 8 inch 4 inch -7 inch  %   first rectangle
    3.5 inch 3 inch 4 inch 7 inch %   second rectangle
] rectfill                        %   fill rectangles
showpage                          %   display page
```

This points out a feature of PostScript Level 2 rectangle operators that is not clear in the *PostScript Language Reference Manual, Second Edition*—each rectangle stroked or filled is a separate rectangle. They are not components of the same path. So our emulation must fill each rectangle separately to produce the same results as the "real" **rectfill**. Here's a better version of the emulation procedures. **DrawBox** doesn't need to be changed, so let's look first at **DoNumArray**.

```
%!PS
/DoNumArray {                              %  stack = numarray procedure
    /proc exch def                         %  remember procedure
    /numarray exch def                     %  remember numarray
    0                                      %  start with first element
    4                                      %  increment by four elements
    numarray length 1 sub                  %  until no more elements
    {
        numarray exch 4 getinterval        %  get x, y, width, height
        aload pop
        { proc } exec                      %  execute the procedure
    } for                                  %  loop through numarray
} def
```

DoNumArray requires one more operand—the procedure to perform after the path for each rectangle is drawn. This procedure should contain **fill**, **stroke**, or **clip** depending on which emulation procedure calls **DrawBox**. Instead of a bunch of stack flagellations to get the operands in the right position on the stack at the right time, the arguments to **DoNumArray** are defined in temporary variables. Now **rectfill** looks like this:

```
%!PS
/rectfill {
    gsave                                  %  save graphics state
    newpath                                %  clear current path
    dup type /arraytype eq {               %  multiple rectangles
        { gsave DrawBox fill grestore } DoNumArray
    } {
        DrawBox fill                       %  draw single rectangle
    } ifelse
    grestore                               %  restore graphics state
} def
```

Now **fill** is called for each individual rectangle of *numarray*, and the emulation procedure is a true emulation of **rectfill**. Here's the preceding example again to prove the new emulation procedures work properly with rectangles drawn in different directions.

```
%!PS
/inch { 72 mul } def              %    define inch procedure
                                  %    fill two black rectangles
[
    1 inch 8 inch 4 inch -7 inch
    3.5 inch 3 inch 4 inch 7 inch
] rectfill
showpage                          %    display page
```

Now that you've worked out the bugs, you can write the emulation procedure for **rectstroke**.

```
%!PS
/rectstroke {                     %    define rectstroke procedure
gsave                             %    save graphics state
  newpath                         %    start new path
  dup                             %    copy top of stack
  type /arraytype eq {            %    if it's an array
    dup                           %    make a copy
    length 6 eq {                 %    and if it's six elements
      1 index                     %    get the element below
      type /arraytype eq {        %    if it's an array
                                  %    multiple rects with matrix
        exch
        { gsave DrawBox dup concat stroke grestore }
        DoNumArray pop
                                  %    one rect with matrix
      } {
        gsave
        5 1 roll DrawBox concat stroke
        grestore
      } ifelse
    } {                           %    multiple rects, no matrix
      { gsave DrawBox stroke grestore } DoNumArray
    } ifelse
  } {                             %    one rect, no matrix
  DrawBox stroke
  } ifelse
grestore                          %    restore graphics state
} def
```

rectstroke accepts a matrix operand that is concatenated to the CTM after the path is drawn but before the path is stroked.

This emulation of **rectstroke** handles four possible forms:

x y width height `rectstroke`
x y width height [*matrix*] `rectstroke`
[*numarray*] `rectstroke`
[*numarray*] [*matrix*] `rectstroke`

Here's a small program to test (although not exhaustively) the emulation of **rectstroke**.

```
%!PS
/inch { 72 mul } def                    %   define inch procedure
0.1 setgray                             %   new color
1.5 inch 1.5 inch 2 inch 2 inch         %   x, y, width, height
[ 20 0 0 5 0 0 ] rectstroke             %   stroke it
0.3 setgray                             %   new color
2.5 inch 3.0 inch 2 inch 2 inch         %   x, y, width, height
[ 20 0 0 5 0 0 ] rectstroke             %   stroke it
0.5 setgray                             %   new color
3.5 inch 4.5 inch 2 inch 2 inch         %   x, y, width, height
[ 20 0 0 5 0 0 ] rectstroke             %   stroke it
0.7 setgray                             %   new color
4.5 inch 6.0 inch 2 inch 2 inch         %   x, y, width, height
[ 20 0 0 5 0 0 ] rectstroke             %   stroke it
0.9 setgray                             %   new color
5.5 inch 7.5 inch 2 inch 2 inch         %   x, y, width, height
[ 20 0 0 5 0 0 ] rectstroke             %   stroke it
showpage                                %   display page
```

For completeness, here's an emulation of **rectclip**. See *Clipping with Rectangles* on pages 327–328 in Chapter 8 for more information about clipping with rectangles.

```
%!PS
/rectclip {
    newpath                            %   start new path
    dup type /arraytype eq {
        { DrawBox } DoNumArray clip    %   multiple rectangles
    } {
        DrawBox clip                   %   single rectangle
    } ifelse
    newpath
} def
```

Note that in the emulation of **rectclip**, the path for every rectangle is drawn, then **clip** is executed. This ensures that the clipping region is the intersection of all rectangles and is consistent with **rectclip**. As Brian Kernighan of UNIX fame once said,

"This code is not robust in the face of all possible inputs."

These emulation procedures make assumptions and are susceptible to problems if not called properly. For example, if **rectstroke** finds a six element-array on top of the stack, **rectstroke** assumes the array is a matrix operand and concatenates it with the CTM. While this is a reasonable assumption, problems can arise when **rectstroke** is called with the wrong operands.

These emulations of **rectstroke**, **rectfill**, and **rectclip** are also incomplete because they don't support *numstring* arguments. *Numstring* arguments are used primarily with Display PostScript and are intended to be generated from applications. You probably don't want to generate *numstring* arguments when writing PostScript by hand.

User Paths

User Paths are features of Display PostScript and PostScript Level 2. A user path is a self-contained description of a path in user space. A user path is passed to new (PostScript Level 2) path construction and rendering operators. The new operators are

ustroke, **ufill**, and **ueofill**, corresponding to the standard **stroke**, **fill**, and **eofill** operators. User paths can provide a mechanism for drawing with less overhead in the PostScript interpreter, because paths can be encoded for brevity and cached for efficient redrawing. User paths are fairly advanced features of PostScript and you can, if you wish, skip this section and move on to the next chapter on first reading.

Operators in a user path are executed as if **systemdict** were the current dictionary. For example, even if you defined your private version of **lineto** in the current dictionary, a **lineto** in the context of a user path will come from the system dictionary. **systemdict** is the part of the PostScript interpreter where operators (among other things) are defined. For more information regarding **systemdict** and dictionaries in general see *Dictionaries* in Chapter 5.

There are additional restrictions on what you can do inside a user path. First, all operands must be literals only—integers or reals. Second, name aliases aren't allowed. Third, you can't use either **arcto** or **charpath** inside a user path, because both leave data on the operand stack, and you can't **pop** inside a user path to remove values from the operand stack. You can use the new **arct** operator in lieu of **arcto**, because **arct** doesn't leave any values on the operand stack. Last, you must ensure that the bounding box of your user path is correct. You will get a **rangecheck** error if the user path exceeds the bounding box.

Let's take a look at a user path. Recall the example of the intermediate skier's blue square on page 50 in this chapter.

See plate II for the color version.

```
%!PS
/inch { 72 mul } def                    %   define inch procedure
newpath                                 %   initialize path
1.25 inch 2.5 inch moveto               %   set current point
6 inch 0 rlineto                        %   bottom of square
0 6 inch rlineto                        %   right side of square
-6 inch 0 rlineto                       %   top of square
closepath                               %   close the shape
0.0 0.0 1.0 setrgbcolor                 %   set color blue
fill                                    %   paint the shape
showpage                                %   display page
```

Let's rewrite this example as a user path. The first thing to go has to be all those **inch** names. You can't do any name lookup from within a user path; this is why user paths are really intended to be generated by application software and not necessarily to be written by people.

Intermediate skier's square drawn with user path.

```
%!PS
0.0 0.0 1.0 setrgbcolor                 %   set color blue
{
    90 180 522 612 setbbox              %   bounding box
    90 180 moveto                       %   set current point
    432 0 rlineto                       %   bottom of square
    0 432 rlineto                       %   right side of square
    -432 0 rlineto                      %   top of square
    closepath                           %   close the shape
} ufill                                 %   paint the shape
showpage                                %   display page
```

This example looks different from the previous example. First of all, you don't need the **newpath**—a user path operation performs an implicit **newpath** for you. You'll see in a moment that a user path operation also performs implicit **gsave** and **grestore** brackets around the operation.

The other item to note in this example is the new **setbbox** line at the start of the user path. This operator informs the user path operators of the bounding box to come. A bounding box is a rectangle that fully encloses the path. **setbbox** is required in a user path. You must ensure that the bounding box of your user path is correct. You will get a **rangecheck** error if the user path exceeds the bounding box.

The **setrgbcolor** instruction had to be done before **ufill**. You can't use operators such as **setrgbcolor** inside a user path. You could have written the code like this but just as in rectangle operations, this sort of coding is hard to follow:

```
%!PS
{
    90 180 522 612 setbbox        %   bounding box
    90 180 moveto                 %   set current point
    432 0 rlineto                 %   bottom of square
    0 432 rlineto                 %   right side of square
    -432 0 rlineto                %   top of square
    closepath                     %   close the shape
}                                 %   paint the shape
0.0 0.0 1.0 setrgbcolor           %   set color blue
ufill                             %   paint the shape
showpage                          %   display page
```

The next thing you can do is give the user path procedure a name so you can refer to it over and over. Here is another cut at a user path example, but this time using the beginning skier's green circle. An additional piece of code is inserted to **stroke** the circle as well as **fill** it.

Novice circle filled and stroked with user paths.

```
%!PS
/inch { 72 mul } def              % define inch procedure
/novice {                         % define beginner's procedure
    54 144 558 648 setbbox        % bounding box
    306 396 252 0 360 arc         % draw circle
    closepath                     % close the shape
} cvlit def
0.0 0.0 1.0 setrgbcolor           % set color blue
novice ufill                      % fill circle
0.0 setgray                       % black stroke
0.5 inch setlinewidth             % fat line width
novice ustroke                    % paint path
showpage                          % display page
```

This example changes the previous example from an in-line procedure to a defined procedure. This example contains some interesting points. The first and most important is the presence of the **cvlit** prior to **def** to define **novice**. Why is the **cvlit** there? Well, consider what **ufill** wants to see on the stack. It wants to see an executable procedure that will generate a path. Without the **cvlit**, the PostScript interpreter would execute **novice** when its name was mentioned. The effect of executing **novice** would be to generate some interpreter instructions and some moves, but then there would be nothing on the stack for **ufill** to consume. You would get a **typecheck** error from the interpreter. So **cvlit** converts the **novice** procedure to an array that is placed on the stack when its name is mentioned. An alternative method to achieve the same effect is to omit the **cvlit** and use **load** instead.

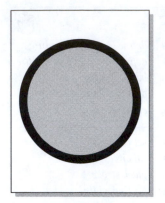

Novice circle filled and stroked with user paths.

```
%!PS
/inch { 72 mul } def                    %   define inch procedure
/novice {                               %   define beginner's procedure
    54 144 558 648 setbbox              %   bounding box
    306 396 252 0 360 arc              %   draw circle
    closepath                          %   close the shape
} def
0.0 0.0 1.0 setrgbcolor                %   set color blue
/novice load ufill                      %   fill circle
0.0 setgray                            %   black stroke
0.5 inch setlinewidth                  %   fat line width
/novice load ustroke                    %   paint path
showpage                               %   display page
```

One essential aspect of user paths is they can be *cached*. To cache your user path, insert a **ucache** operator at the very start of the user path procedure. If **ucache** is present it must be the first operator in the procedure, right before **setbbox**.

ustroke has a variant form where it can have a matrix as an operand, just as for **rectstroke**. **ustroke** may need a matrix to undo the effects of scaling prior to stroking a path. To show this in action let's look at the familiar example of an ellipse stroked with a fat line. This example doesn't do the "right" thing.

Ellipse drawn with user path—line width scaled.

```
%!PS
/inch { 72 mul } def                    %   define inch procedure
4.25 inch 5.5 inch translate            %   origin to middle of page
1 2 scale                              %   scale for ellipse
0.5 inch setlinewidth                  %   fat line width
{
    -144 -288 144 288 setbbox          %   bounding box
    0 0 144 0 360 arc                  %   draw ellipse
    closepath                          %   close the shape
}
ustroke                                %   paint path
showpage                               %   display page
```

The ellipse has been stroked with a fat line that changes width as you move around the path. This effect is a natural consequence of PostScript transformations. But if what you really want is a line of the same weight around the path, you need more shenanigans for use with **ustroke**. Let's construct a suitable matrix operand to work with **ustroke**.

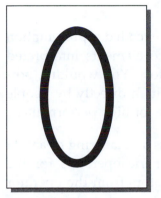

Ellipse drawn with user path—line width not scaled.

```
%!PS
/inch { 72 mul } def                        % define inch procedure
1 2 matrix scale                            % get a scale matrix
matrix invertmatrix                         % compute inverse transform
/inverse exch def                           % define for later
4.25 inch 5.5 inch translate                % origin to middle of page
1 2 scale                                   % now scale for ellipse
0.5 inch setlinewidth                       % fat line width
{
    -144 -288 144 288 setbbox               % bounding box
    0 0 144 0 360 arc                       % draw ellipse
    closepath                               % close the shape
} inverse ustroke                           % paint path
showpage                                    % display page
```

This code computes a transformation matrix containing only scale factors, then saves the inverse of that matrix in a variable called **inverse**. The code then proceeds just as before, but the **ustroke** line changes to use **inverse** as another operand. You can read more about using transformation operators with matrix operands in Chapter 4.

Operators in User Paths

User paths can contain only a restricted set of operators. They are regular path construction operators you've used already and will see in later chapters. **moveto** and **rmoveto** set the current point. **lineto** and **rlineto** add line segments to the current path. **curveto** and **rcurveto** add Bézier curve segments to the current path. **arc** and **arcn** draw arcs of circles. **arct** is a variation on **arcto** specifically designed for user paths. **arcto** and **arct** are discussed at length in Chapter 7. **closepath** closes a shape. The only unusual operators are **ucache** and **setbbox**, which you just learned. That's it—those are all the operators allowed in user paths. Any other operator gives rise to errors from the PostScript interpreter.

Encoded User Paths

User paths may be *encoded* for brevity. An encoded representation of a user path consists of an array of two elements interpreted directly by the user path rendering operators. You wouldn't normally expect encoded user paths to be written directly by people but to be generated by application software for high performance.

The first element of an encoded user path is a data string or a data array. This string or array contains numeric operands for the second element, the operator string. Operators from the operator string consume numbers in sequence from the first string or array. The operator string contains one encoded operator per character. The table at the top of page 88 shows the operator codes.

ENCODED USER PATH OPERATORS			
CODE	OPERATOR	CODE	OPERATOR
0	**setbbox**	6	**rcurveto**
1	**moveto**	7	**arc**
2	**rmoveto**	8	**arcn**
3	**lineto**	9	**arct**[†]
4	**rlineto**	10	**closepath**
5	**curveto**	11	**ucache**
$n > 32$	repeat the next operator $n - 32$ times		

[†]   The new **arct** operator behaves like **arcto** but doesn't leave any data on the operand stack. **arct** is roughly equivalent to **arcto pop pop pop pop**.

Let's see one very small example of encoded user paths in action, since anything larger would be an exercise in mental flagellation. Let's modify the green circle example from page 85.

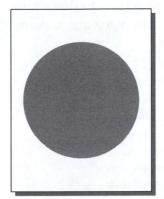

Encoded user path.

```
%!PS
0.0 1.0 0.0 setrgbcolor        %    set color green
[                              %    start outer array
    [                          %    start inner array
       54 144 558 648          %    bounding box
       306 396 252 0 360       %    draw circle
    ]                          %    end inner array
    <00070a>                   %    setbbox, arc, closepath
]                              %    end outer array
ufill                          %    fill circle
showpage                       %    display page
```

The first element of the two element array is an array consisting of the operands for the **setbbox** and **arc** operators. The second element is a string coded as a hexadecimal string. The three numbers are the codes for **setbbox**, **arc**, and **closepath**. You can see you don't want to do too much of this by hand—you need your application software to generate the numbers for you.

Final Words on User Paths

That's about all there is on user paths unless you're getting heavily into writing applications that require user paths. Here are a few other user path operators of note: **upath** makes the current path from the graphics state into a user path; **uappend** interprets the specified user path and appends the result to the current path in the graphics state; **ustrokepath** performs the equivalent of **strokepath** but uses the specified user path as the shape.

Hit Detection

Closely related to the various filling methods is a series of operators added to support Display PostScript. These operators are used for *hit detection*, usually for determining if a locator device such as a mouse is in a specific place on the display surface. For example, **infill** determines if a specified point in user space would be painted by a **fill** of the current path. Display PostScript and

PostScript Level 2 support several of these operators to determine if points are within specified areas. Here is one very quick example of how **infill** works.

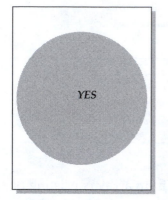

YES

Hit detected inside user path.

```
%!PS
/inch { 72 mul } def                    %    define inch procedure
/Palatino-Italic findfont               %    choose font
48 scalefont                            %    set font size
setfont                                 %    establish current font
4.25 inch 5.5 inch                      %    center of circle
3.5 inch 0 360 arc                      %    draw circle
closepath                               %    finish the shape
0.50 setgray                            %    medium gray
fill                                    %    fill the outline
4.25 inch 5.5 inch                      %    center of circle
3.5 inch 0 360 arc                      %    draw circle again
closepath                               %    finish the shape
0.00 setgray                            %    back to black
4.25 inch 2 inch infill {               %    test point in circle
    4.00 inch 5.5 inch moveto (YES) show
}
{
    4.00 inch 5.5 inch moveto (NO) show
} ifelse
showpage                                %    display page
```

The point at (4.25 inch, 2 inch) is inside the circle, so the true branch of the **ifelse** gets executed to place the word *YES* in the center of the circle. These operators are mentioned here for completeness but are not otherwise discussed as they are very specific to display-oriented systems.

3 Text

The Moving Finger writes; and having writ,
Moves on: nor all your Piety nor Wit
    Shall lure it back to cancel half a Line,
Nor all your Tears wash out a Word of it.

Ohmar Khayyám—*The Rubáiyát*

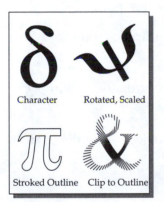

Character   Rotated, Scaled

Stroked Outline   Clip to Outline

Text operates exactly like any other graphical object.

One of the major strengths of PostScript is its close integration of graphical objects with text—or maybe its close integration of text with graphics? The very symmetry of the question is an indication of past difficulties of the problem. A smooth mix of text and graphics has been an elusive goal of many graphics systems, composition systems, and page description languages. Many such integration efforts have been only moderately successful. Melding graphical objects and textual data is a highly desirable goal, but text and graphics are radically different animals, with radically different characteristics requiring different viewpoints.

Although integrating text and graphics is a difficult task, PostScript appears to be one of the more successful integrations of text and graphics to date. Whatever the case, PostScript will likely provide new insights for even better future developments.

Showing Text

Enough philosophy. *Basic Text—Show a Message* on page 14 in Chapter 1 showed a simple PostScript program to write **PostScript!** diagonally across the page. Here is the example again, to refresh your memory. The example was changed from its first incarnation so that units are in inches instead of PostScript points.

Text imaged at an arbitrary angle.

```
%!PS
/inch { 72 mul } def          %  define inch procedure
/Palatino-Roman findfont      %  find required font
2.25 inch scalefont           %  scale font to required size
setfont                       %  set as current font
1.5 inch 0.5 inch moveto      %  set current point
52 rotate                     %  rotate coordinate system
(PostScript!) show            %  image title on page
showpage                      %  display page
```

This example illustrates the simplest way to render text into the current path using **show**. The example illustrates the basic notion of displaying (showing) text. PostScript text is treated in a manner very similar to the way graphical objects are treated:

❑ you must establish a current font in the graphics state[†]

❑ text is placed at the current point

❑ text is drawn relative to the user space coordinate system

❑ text is painted in the current color

❑ text is transformed—just like graphical objects—by the CTM

Finding, Scaling, and Setting a Font

Let's dissect the preceding piece of PostScript code. Setting a font into the graphics state is done in three parts:

❑ find the font you want

❑ scale or otherwise transform the font you just found to the size and orientation you wish

---

[†] This is true in most implementations. However, some display systems establish a preset font at startup time. This is a fruitful source of non-portable PostScript code and upside-down text.

❏   set that transformed font into the graphics state

The first part of the code reading

```
/Palatino-Roman findfont
```

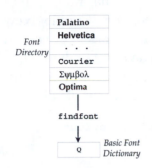

From font directory to basic font dictionary.

finds the specified font. All resident fonts in a PostScript printer or display device live in the *font directory*. **findfont** looks in the font directory for the font you asked for.[†] Definitions of PostScript fonts reside in *font dictionaries*. **findfont** places the font dictionary on the operand stack, where subsequent font operators can make modifications. Dictionaries are discussed in Chapter 5 and the specifics of creating PostScript fonts are covered in Chapter 10.

The font dictionary retrieved by **findfont** is placed on the operand stack and set up so characters from that font render at a size of one PostScript unit (that is, $1/72$ inch). Such characters will be so small as to be unreadable without a good magnifying glass, so the next operation is to transform the font to the size you want. The next part of the code in our example

```
2.0 inch scalefont
```

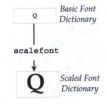

Scaling a font dictionary.

scales the font so characters are two inches high. By far the most common way to obtain the desired size of characters is to use **scalefont** to scale the font. **scalefont** is not the only way to transform the font, however. Later you will see **makefont**—a more general way to transform a font. Finally, you establish the transformed font into the current graphics state with **setfont**.

setfont establishes the current font, to be used in subsequent operations dealing with text (such as **show**) until you change it again with another **setfont**, **makefont**, or **selectfont**.

---

† Some printers can store fonts on mass storage devices like disks. In such systems, **findfont** locates the font from the storage device and installs it in the font directory.

Setting the scaled font in the graphics state.

Notice the name of the font, **Palatino-Roman**. You can't always tell easily from the "real world" name of the font what the name of the font in the PostScript interpreter will be. For example, New Century Schoolbook, in its regular plain face, is called **NewCenturySchlbk-Roman** in the printer. The basic **findfont** code sequence on page 92 is a common cliché. It's spelled out in excruciating detail, but normally you'd write something simple like

```
/Palatino-Roman findfont 2.0 inch scalefont setfont
```

Basic Notions of show

The simplest thing you do with text—once you have a font established—is show a string of characters. The line of code reading **1.5 inch 1.0 inch moveto** establishes the current point. The current point is the origin from which text is laid on the page using **show**. **52 rotate** turns user space 52° about its origin.

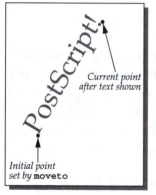

Current point before and after showing text.

```
%!PS
/inch { 72 mul } def          %   define inch procedure
/Palatino-Roman findfont      %   find required font
2.25 inch scalefont           %   scale font to required size
setfont                       %   set as current font
1.5 inch 0.5 inch moveto      %   set current point
52 rotate                     %   rotate coordinate system
(PostScript!) show            %   image title on page
showpage                      %   display page
```

Finally, the line reading **(PostScript!) show** places the indicated string of text into the current path. **show** expects a string of text on top of the operand stack. After the string of text is rendered, the current point is moved to the end of the string. The current point is now at a position ready for more text (or graphical objects) to be placed into the path. The way in which **show** works is quite "natural." You could just as easily use two or three **show** instructions and write the preceding code sequence as

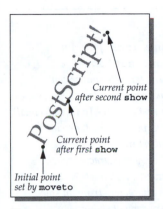

How current point moves
when showing text in mul-
tiple stages.

```
%!PS
/inch { 72 mul } def            %   define inch procedure
/Palatino-Roman findfont        %   find required font
2.25 inch scalefont             %   scale font to required size
setfont                         %   set as current font
1.5 inch 0.5 inch moveto        %   set current point
52 rotate                       %   rotate coordinate system
(Post) show                     %   image half of title
(Script!) show                  %   image other half of title
showpage                        %   display page
```

Under normal circumstances you don't need to stroke or fill text. **show** paints text in the current color. *Special Effects Using Character Paths* on pages 129—132 in this chapter discusses special effects you can perform when you stroke the character outline, clip to a character outline, or fill with a pattern.

One of the most common mistakes made when showing text is to forget to find and set a font into the graphics state. If you try to show text without having first set a font, you will get an **invalid-font** error.

Showing Text from Strings

Examples of showing text so far have used **show** with an explicit string operand, using lines like

```
(PostScript) show
```

but **show** just expects any string of characters on top of the operand stack. This next example illustrates this feature and also shows several interesting stack manipulations, which you can read more about in Chapter 5. This example defines a procedure to perform the various conversions on an integer. The remainder of the example prints the results of the conversions.

Q

10#81

8#121

16#51

Results of character conversions.

```
%!PS
/inch { 72 mul } def                  %   define inch procedure
/Palatino-Roman findfont 1 inch scalefont setfont
/CharCodes {                          %   character code conversion
    dup                              %   make copy of code
    16 (    ) cvrs                    %   convert in radix 16 (hexadecimal)
    1 index                          %   get copy of character code
    8 (    ) cvrs                     %   convert in radix 8 (octal)
    2 index                          %   get copy of character code
    (    ) cvs                        %   convert in decimal
    ( )                              %   one-character string on stack
    dup                              %   make copy of string
    6 -1 roll                        %   character code to op of stack
    0 exch put                       %   put code into string
} def                                %   end of procedure definition
81 CharCodes                         %   decimal value for Q
2.5 inch 8.5 inch moveto             %   set current point
show                                 %   show character
2.5 inch 6.5 inch moveto             %   set current point
(10#) show show                      %   show decimal value
2.5 inch 4.5 inch moveto             %   set current point
(8#) show show                       %   show octal value
2.5 inch 2.5 inch moveto             %   set current point
(16#) show show                      %   show hexadecimal value
showpage                             %   display page
```

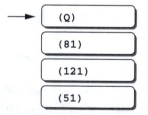

(Q)

(81)

(121)

(51)

Stack contents after call to **CharCodes**.

The interesting parts of this example are the instructions to convert numbers to strings. **cvs** converts numbers to their decimal string representation. Decimal is so common you use it most of the time. When you need conversion in another radix, you use **cvrs** to specify the radix as well as the number. The stack manipulations shown convert the integer to its ASCII character value and to its octal (radix 8), decimal, and hexadecimal (radix 16) values. The operand stack ends up looking like the picture, with the character strings ready to show.

Notice the use of **cvrs** to convert the octal and hexadecimal strings, where plain old **cvs** was good enough for decimal. Both **cvrs** and **cvs** accept a number and a string as operands, with **cvrs** requiring an extra number—the radix. The converted number ends up in the string supplied.

Selecting Fonts in PostScript Level 2

Setting a transformed font into the graphics state requires **findfont** to obtain the required font from the font directory, **scalefont** (or **makefont**, described on page 98), followed by **setfont** to place the transformed font into the graphics state. This sequence usually uses a code fragment like the following:

font name `findfont`   *point size* `scalefont`   `setfont`

This code sequence is such a cliché that PostScript Level 2 and Display PostScript introduced an operator specifically to act as a shorthand for this sequence. The new operator is **selectfont**, and you use it like this.

Font selected using **selectfont**.

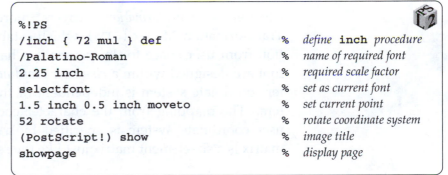

```
%!PS
/inch { 72 mul } def        %   define inch procedure
/Palatino-Roman             %   name of required font
2.25 inch                   %   required scale factor
selectfont                  %   set as current font
1.5 inch 0.5 inch moveto    %   set current point
52 rotate                   %   rotate coordinate system
(PostScript!) show          %   image title
showpage                    %   display page
```

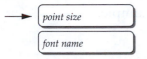

Stack contents before call to **selectfont**.

selectfont has two different forms. Here is the simpler form:

font name   *point size*   `selectfont`

selectfont can also accept a *matrix* instead of a single scale factor as an operand. If you supply **selectfont** with a matrix operand, it applies the transformation indicated by that matrix. Chapter 4 discusses transformations by way of matrices in detail. This form of **selectfont** is also pretty straightforward.

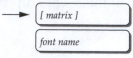

font name   [*matrix*]   `selectfont`

Stack contents before call to **selectfont**.

You will see this aspect of **selectfont** using a character transformation matrix in the next section, which discusses **makefont**.

Transforming a Font Using a Matrix

So far you've seen the simplest use of characters from a font using **scalefont** to scale fonts uniformly. You've also seen **selectfont** used the simple way, with allusions to it's ability to accept a transformation matrix instead of a single scale factor as an operand.

This section discusses **makefont**, which uses a matrix operand to transform a font, instead of a simple scale factor. Recall that PostScript fonts represent a character designed to fit into one unit of the user coordinate system, $1/72$ inch.

Chapter 4, *Transformations*, covers more about the Current Transformation Matrix (CTM), which establishes the transformation from user space to device space. Characters in a PostScript font are designed within a *character coordinate system*. The character coordinate system is independent of the user coordinate system. The mapping from the character coordinate system to the user coordinate system is specified by a *font matrix*. The font matrix is a six-element matrix just like the regular CTM.

In Chapter 4 you'll see that an operation such as **2 3 scale** is a shorthand notation for the more general case of changing the CTM by doing **[2 0 0 3 0 0] concat**. Similarly, **72 scalefont** is shorthand for the more general case of **[72 0 0 72 0 0] makefont**. Let's see **makefont** in action with a simple example.

```
%!PS
/inch { 72 mul } def                % define inch procedure
/ZapfChancery-MediumItalic findfont % find desired font
[ 10 inch 0 0 10 inch 0 0 ] makefont % scale it large
setfont                             % set font in graphics state
-0.5 3 inch moveto                  % set current point
(Q) show                            % image the character
showpage                            % display page
```

Character imaged large in proportional scaling.

This example uses **makefont** with uniform scaling—x and y scale factors are equal. You get non-uniform scaling by changing elements of the font matrix. Let's make the character short and fat.

```
%!PS
/inch { 72 mul } def                % define inch procedure
/ZapfChancery-MediumItalic findfont % find desired font
[ 10 inch 0 0 5 inch 0 0 ] makefont % scale it short and fat
setfont                             % set font in graphics state
-0.5 inch 4 inch moveto             % set current point
(Q) show                            % image the character
showpage                            % display page
```

Non-uniform scaling with **makefont**.

This matrix has the x scale factor at 10 inches, but the y scale factor is only 5 inches. The character comes out short and fat.

Showing Characters by Name

The **show** operator has many variations—all of which use an integer character code to find the character to be displayed. Without going into fine details of the way PostScript fonts are constructed, this is how you could display the "serpent"[†] character from the Sonata font in PostScript Level 1.

---

† Cleo Huggins, who designed Sonata, informs us that this character is actually a German Polka clef.

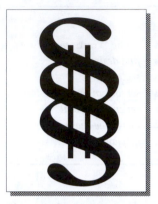

Showing the serpent character.

```
%!PS
/inch { 72 mul } def                % define inch procedure
/Sonata findfont                    % find required font
8 inch scalefont                    % scale font to required size
setfont                             % set as current font
2.25 inch 1.5 inch moveto           % set current point
($) show                            % image serpent character
showpage                            % display page
```

Notice the character code for "serpent" is the **$** sign—it vaguely connotes the image of the serpent. You could also use the **(\044)** construct to get the ASCII numerical code for the serpent. More information about ASCII character codes is contained in *Composite Data Types* on page 188. Other forms of **show** covered later in this chapter, beginning on page 101, behave in much the same way.

PostScript Level 2 introduced a new operator called **glyphshow**, which enables you to obtain the character by name instead of by character code. You use **glyphshow** like **show**, except you use the name of the character.

Showing the treble clef character by name.

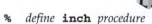

```
%!PS
/inch { 72 mul } def                % define inch procedure
/Sonata 6 inch selectfont           % find and scale Sonata font
2 inch 2.75 inch moveto             % set current point
/trebleclef glyphshow               % image trebleclef character
showpage                            % display page
```

glyphshow can operate only with base fonts. You can't use **glyphshow** with a composite font, because the top level font of a composite font contains only references to other fonts. You can, of course, use **glyphshow** with the base fonts of a composite font. Composite fonts are described in detail in *Composite Fonts* on pages 416–429 in Chapter 10. This example uses PostScript Level 2 **selectfont** since the program was already contaminated with PostScript Level 2 operators by **glyphshow**.

PostScript Level 2 Font Resources

PostScript Level 2 introduced the notion of named *resources*. PostScript Level 1 fonts (and other kinds of objects) reside in printer memory (or possibly on mass storage devices such as disks). Experience with PostScript Level 1 led to a more general model of resources.

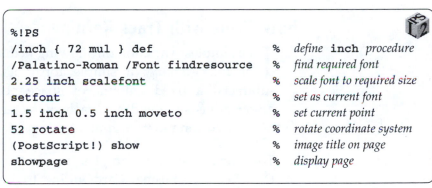

```
%!PS
/inch { 72 mul } def                    %  define inch procedure
/Palatino-Roman /Font findresource      %  find required font
2.25 inch scalefont                     %  scale font to required size
setfont                                 %  set as current font
1.5 inch 0.5 inch moveto                %  set current point
52 rotate                               %  rotate coordinate system
(PostScript!) show                      %  image title on page
showpage                                %  display page
```

This example isn't so different from the example on page 92. **findfont** is replaced by the more general **findresource**. Where **findfont** needs the name of the font as an operand, **findresource** needs two operands—the name of the thing you want and the category within which the named thing will be found. Resources cover many different categories of objects, but some of the more important from the everyday PostScript user's viewpoint are fonts, patterns, and forms.

Varieties of Showing Text

As well as the basic **show** you read about earlier in this chapter, PostScript provides several variants of **show** designed to give you fine control over placement of characters. Facilities for fine-tuning the placement of characters start from simple track kerning all the way up to a mechanism to show characters under control of a procedure for each character.

In general, calculations for accurate placement of characters should be performed in your application code and done in PostScript only in the most special cases. WYSIWYG applications that deal with placing characters must maintain parallel data structures reflecting character metrics of PostScript fonts. Such calculations are more efficient when performed in the application.

Show String with Track Kerning

The simplest variation on showing text is **ashow**, used primarily for *track kerning*, a simple form of kerning that adds (or subtracts) a fixed amount of space between every character. **ashow** adjusts the width of each character (in both x and y directions) according to its arguments.

The next several examples use two PostScript procedures, **DrawRect** and **BusinessCardOutline**, to draw the outline of a business card with a drop shadow. The business card is 3½ inches wide by 2 inches high. Here are PostScript procedure definitions for **BusinessCardOutline** and **DrawRect**. If you have a Level 2 device, you can substitute **rectfill** and **rectstroke** for **DrawRect fill** and **DrawRect stroke**, respectively. Here is the procedure definition of **DrawRect**.

```
/inch { 72 mul } def            % define inch procedure
/DrawRect {                     % stack = x y width height
    4 2 roll moveto             % set current point
    1 index 0 rlineto           % bottom edge
    0 exch rlineto              % right edge
    neg 0 rlineto               % top edge
    closepath                   % finish shape
} def
```

And here is the procedure definition for **BusinessCardOutline**, with an example call showing the image it draws.

```
%!PS
/BusinessCardOutline {
   0.66666 setgray                           %   light gray shade
   8 -8 3.5 inch 2.0 inch DrawRect fill      %   draw drop shadow
   1 setgray                                 %   white
   0 0 3.5 inch 2.0 inch DrawRect fill       %   draw white card
   0 setgray                                 %   black
   1 setlinewidth                            %   thin line
   0 0 3.5 inch 2.0 inch DrawRect stroke     %   stroke outline
} def
BusinessCardOutline                          %   image the card
showpage                                     %   display page
```

Here is the first draft of a business card for the terribly, terribly, upper-crust and extremely well-known ski resort at...um...uh...

```
%!PS
/inch { 72 mul } def                              %   define inch procedure
BusinessCardOutline                               %   draw business card
/Optima findfont 36 scalefont setfont             %   set font for name
0.25 inch 0.75 inch moveto                        %   set current point
(LAKEWOOD) show                                   %   display name
/Optima findfont 28 scalefont setfont             %   set font for caption
0.25 inch 0.25 inch moveto                        %   set current point
(Ski Resort) show                                 %   display caption
showpage                                          %   display page
```

The caption "Ski Resort" is much shorter than the name "LAKE-WOOD". "Ski Resort" is set in a smaller font. Graphic designers use track kerning to achieve special text effects when designing business cards or letterheads. In this case, the customer wants the card to look like the next picture, where "Ski Resort" spreads out to occupy the same width as "LAKEWOOD". The new business card uses track kerning to achieve the desired effect. Here's the PostScript code to generate the text on the business card.

```
%!PS
/inch { 72 mul } def                        %  define inch procedure
BusinessCardOutline                         %  draw business card
/Optima findfont 36 scalefont setfont %  set font for name
0.25 inch 0.75 inch moveto                  %  set current point
(LAKEWOOD) show                             %  display the name
/Optima findfont 28 scalefont setfont %  set font for caption
0.25 inch 0.25 inch moveto                  %  set current point
9.8 0 (Ski Resort) ashow                     %  kern caption
showpage                                    %  display page
```

The line of interest in this PostScript program reads

```
9.8 0 (Ski Resort) ashow
```

and introduces **ashow**. The general syntax of **ashow** is

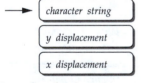

State of stack prior to invocation of **ashow**.

δx δy (*character string*) **ashow**

where δx is the width displacement for *every* character in the string, and δy is the height displacement for *every* character in the string. *character string* is the string you want shown. In the preceding example, $\delta x = 9.8$ and $\delta y = 0$ tell **ashow** to add 9.8 units of space to the width of each character and to not adjust the vertical spacing of the text, effectively adding 9.8 PostScript units of space between each character of "Ski Resort". A value of 0 for δy is typical for "Western" character sets.

Of course, there is a slight snag with this program. Whence came 9.8 points to leave between each character? Well, first, the job was done the hard way by measuring the width of the character strings and performing the appropriate arithmetic. "LAKEWOOD" at 36 points measures 206 points, while "Ski Resort" at 28 points measures 118 points. But, of course, this works only for these character strings in these specific fonts at these specific point sizes. A much better way to go about this exercise is to use the **stringwidth** function and let PostScript do the work.

```
%!PS
/inch { 72 mul } def                        % define inch procedure
BusinessCardOutline                         % draw business card
/Optima findfont 36 scalefont setfont       % set font for name
0.25 inch 0.75 inch moveto                  % set current point
(LAKEWOOD) show                             % display the name
(LAKEWOOD) stringwidth pop                   % get width of name
/Optima findfont 28 scalefont setfont        % set font for caption
0.25 inch 0.25 inch moveto                   % set current point
(Ski Resort) stringwidth pop                 % get width of caption
sub                                          % total extra space
(Ski Resort) length 1 sub div 0              % per character space
(Ski Resort) ashow                           % kern caption
showpage                                     % display page
```

stringwidth is described in more detail in *Precise Widths and Heights of Strings* on page 122 in this chapter.

You are not limited to adding space between characters. You can also subtract space by using negative numbers as the operands to **ashow**—or, for that matter, to any of the variations of **show**. You can use negative width displacements to force a larger word or phrase to take up less space, as in the next business card. Here is the PostScript code that generated the text effects you see in the business card for an imaginary *nouvelle cuisine* restaurant:

```
%!PS
/inch { 72 mul } def                        % define inch procedure
BusinessCardOutline                         % draw outline
/Palatino-Roman findfont                    % set current font
36 scalefont setfont
0.25 inch 0.75 inch moveto                   % set current point
(CHEZ) show                                  % display first line
/Times-Roman findfont                        % set new font
30 scalefont setfont
0.25 inch 0.25 inch moveto                   % reset current point
-2 0 (PIERRE) ashow                          % display second line
showpage                                     % display page
```

The instruction of interest is

```
-2 0 (PIERRE) ashow
```

The negative number for the first operand tells **ashow** to subtract two units of space from the width of each character. Now the longer word PIERRE requires the same amount of horizontal space as the smaller word CHEZ. In general, you should be careful using negative width adjustments. You can create interesting designs with them, but as the space between the characters decreases so does the legibility of the text. Incidentally, wide spaces between characters decrease legibility in the same way.

Show String with Specific Character Control

Track kerning may not be appropriate for all applications, so PostScript provides several other methods of controlling inter-character spacing. The next method of controlling space between characters is **widthshow**, which provides a different level of control from that of **ashow**. You can use **widthshow** to make the "LAKEWOOD" logo more æsthetically pleasing. By adjusting the width of one character, you can spruce up an otherwise plain word. This example typesets the Os so they overlap a tiny bit.

```
%!PS
/inch { 72 mul } def                      %  define inch procedure
BusinessCardOutline                       %  draw business card
/Optima findfont                          %  set current font
36 scalefont setfont
0.25 inch 0.75 inch moveto                %  set current point
-13 0 79 (LAKEWO) widthshow               %  adjust width of letter "O"
(OD) show
/Optima findfont                          %  set new font
28 scalefont setfont
0.25 inch 0.25 inch moveto                %  reset current point
8 0 (Ski Resort) ashow                    %  show second line of text
showpage                                  %  display page
```

Where **ashow** injects a set amount of space between every character, **widthshow** provides for altering the inter-character spacing for every occurrence of a specific character. The line of interest in this program is

```
-13 0 79 (LAKEWO) widthshow
```

In this example, **widthshow** subtracts 13 units of space from the width of the first "O". Now the second "O" overlaps the first a little bit. Notice the "WO" combination is displayed separately from the "OD" combination. Had you displayed all letters together with the first **widthshow**, the width of the second "O" would have been adjusted as well, and the letter "D" would have appeared on top of it—not the effect you wanted.

The mysterious number "79" is the ASCII code for the letter "O". In real life, this kind of PostScript code would be generated by your page layout application and you wouldn't need to worry about the values of the characters. Now the word "LAKEWOOD" is shorter—the **ashow** instruction was changed so "Ski Resort" is the same length again. The general syntax of **widthshow** is

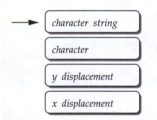

δx δy *character* (*character string*) **widthshow**

State of stack prior to invocation of **widthshow**.

where δx and δy are the width displacements in the x and y directions, respectively, of *character*—the integer code of the specific character you wish to control. And, of course, *character string* is the string you wish to show. This example demonstrates that **widthshow** adjusts the width for one character and modifies the widths for all occurrences of that particular letter in the string.

This particular example could also be handled with **xyshow** or **xshow**. **xyshow**, **xshow**, and **yshow** are covered in *Show String Using x and y Widths* on pages 115–118.

Track Kerning and Specific Character Control

Getting more sophisticated, let's now look at **awidthshow**, which combines the specific control of **widthshow** with the track kerning capabilities of **ashow**. **awidthshow** adjusts the inter-character spacing of all characters in the string, as well as defining the change in spacing for specific characters.

The next business card touting unusual experiences uses **awidthshow** to place the company motto under the line on the card. The other words are set with "vanilla" **show** instructions.

```
%!PS
/inch { 72 mul } def            % define inch procedure
BusinessCardOutline             % draw outline
/Optima-Bold findfont           % set current font
36 scalefont setfont
0.25 inch 1.5 inch moveto       % set current point
(P) show                        % show large capital "P"
/Optima findfont                % set new font
24 scalefont setfont
(lanetary) show                 % show rest of word
/Optima-Bold findfont           % set current font
36 scalefont setfont
0.25 inch 1.125 inch moveto     % set current point
(T) show                        % show large capital "T"
/Optima findfont                % set new font
24 scalefont setfont
(ravel) show                    % show rest of word
0 setgray                       % draw underline
2 setlinewidth
0.25 inch 1.00 inch moveto
3.0 inch 0 inch rlineto
stroke
/Optima findfont                % set new font
10 scalefont setfont
0.22 inch 0.75 inch moveto      % set current point
                                % typeset motto
8 0 32 4 0 (An Unworldly Experience!) awidthshow
showpage                        % display page
```

Let's step through this example. "Planetary" and "Travel" each require two different fonts—one for the large first character and one for the rest of the word. So you must use two **show** operators for each word, changing the current font each time. The large capital letter at the beginning of each word is set in 36-point type. The remainder of each word is typeset in 24-point type immediately following the capital letter, relying on the position of the current point from the initial **show**. Next, a horizontal line is drawn across the card. So far, this is fairly straightforward. Then comes the instruction reading

```
8 0 32 4 0 (An Unworldly Experience!) awidthshow
```

What do all those numbers mean? The general syntax of **awidthshow** is

$$c_x \ c_y \ character \ \delta x \ \delta y \quad (character \ string) \quad \textbf{awidthshow}$$

The first three numbers are equivalent to the operands required by **widthshow**. In the example, the x width adjustment is 8, the y width adjustment is 0, and 32 is the decimal value of the character you wish to adjust by these amounts (32 is the decimal equivalent of the space character). In English, you wish to separate words by eight extra units of space.

The next two operands are equivalent to the operands required by **ashow**. The x width adjustment is 4 and the y width adjustment is 0. These adjustments are applied to every character in the phrase "An Unworldly Experience", and produces the "spacy" effect you see in the motto on the business card.

Note that the width of the space character is adjusted twice in the preceding example. First the width of the space is explicitly adjusted by eight units by the first three operands. Then the width of the space is implicitly adjusted by four units (along with all the other characters) by the fourth and fifth operands.

---

character string

y displacement

x displacement

character

y displacement

x displacement

State of stack prior to invocation of **awidthshow**.

Show String Under Procedural Control

The most elaborate method of controlling inter-character spacing is with either **kshow**, which works with regular base fonts, or **cshow**, which also works with base fonts, although it is intended for use with composite fonts. **kshow** generates an error if used with a composite font. **kshow** has been around since PostScript Level 1. **cshow** arrived with the advent of composite fonts in PostScript Level 2. **kshow** and **cshow** provide the most control over placement of characters in the string and, because of this, are the slowest methods. Using **kshow** or **cshow**, a procedure is executed for every character in the string. The procedure controls the placement of that character.

kshow

kshow could be used for pair kerning, where the inter-character spacing is altered on a character pair basis, but you can put **kshow** to other interesting uses—for instance, to modify the current graphics state for each character. This PostScript program uses **kshow** to change the shade of gray for each character in the string—a kind of Cheshire Cat effect.

*Disappearing characters using **kshow**.*

```
%!PS
/inch { 72 mul } def                    %   define inch procedure
/Palatino-BoldItalic findfont           %   choose font
2.5 inch scalefont setfont
/gray 0.1 def                           %   gray for second character
1.125 inch 0.875 inch moveto            %   set current point
52 rotate                               %   turn coordinate system
{ pop pop                               %   pop characters off stack
    gray setgray                        %   change gray shade
    /gray gray 0.1 add def              %   increment for next time
} (fading out) kshow                     %   show string
showpage                                %   display page
```

Looking up kern pairs in tables requires too much time when rendering a PostScript image. Instead, applications compute character positions from kern tables. For PostScript Level 2 an application generates **xyshow**, **xshow**, or **yshow** instructions. For Level 1, an application generates combinations of **show** and **rmoveto**. The general syntax of **kshow** is

{ *procedure* } (*character string*) **kshow**

The first character is positioned at the current point. Then **kshow** calls *procedure* before showing each remaining character in *character string*. If the number of characters in the string is *n*, **kshow** calls *procedure* $n - 1$ times. When *procedure* is called, the stack contains two values—the integer code of the character just set and the integer code of the next character to be set.

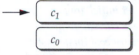

State of stack prior to each invocation of **kshow**.

The picture shows the state of the stack each time **kshow** calls *procedure*. Theoretically, *procedure* looks up both characters in a kerning table and adjusts the position of the character to be shown according to the values found. But in this example, the characters passed to *procedure* are not used and are popped off the stack. Let's look closer at the rest of *procedure* in the example. The two lines following the two **pop** instructions set the gray shade for the character to be shown and increment the gray shade ready for the next character. Note that *procedure* is not called before the first character in the string is shown.

Let's modify the preceding example and reverse the colors so it "fades in." In this program, the gray shade starts at white and subsequent shades are decremented.

Not quite right appearing characters using **kshow**.

```
%!PS
/inch { 72 mul } def              %   inch definition
/Palatino-BoldItalic findfont     %   choose font
2.5 inch scalefont setfont
/gray 0.9 def                     %   gray for second character
1.125 inch 0.875 inch moveto      %   set current point
52 rotate                         %   turn coordinate system
{ pop pop                         %   pop characters off stack
    gray setgray                  %   change gray shade
    /gray gray 0.1 sub def        %   increment for next time
} (fading in!) kshow              %   show string
showpage                          %   display page
```

This program has a small problem. The first character is black, but you want it to be white. This points out a feature of **kshow**—*procedure* is not called before showing the first character in the string. The first character is placed at the current point. So the letter "f" is black, the preset color in the current graphics state. The fix is simple; add a **setgray** at the beginning of the program.

*Better appearing characters using **kshow**.*

```
%!PS
/inch { 72 mul } def                    %   inch definition
/Palatino-BoldItalic findfont           %   choose font
2.5 inch scalefont setfont
/gray 0.9 def                           %   gray for second character
1.0 setgray                             %   set initial gray
1.125 inch 0.875 inch moveto            %   set current point
52 rotate                               %   turn coordinate system
{ pop pop                               %   pop characters off stack
    gray setgray                        %   change gray shade
    /gray gray 0.1 sub def              %   increment for next time
} (fading in!) kshow                     %   show string
showpage                                %   display page
```

cshow

cshow is analogous to **kshow** but has two major differences. **cshow** is designed to work with composite fonts (but also works with base fonts). **kshow** will raise an **invalidfont** error if used with a composite font. And **cshow** isn't really intended for pair kerning; instead of passing two characters to be kerned to *procedure*, **cshow** pushes the character along with its *x* and *y* displacements. The syntax of **cshow** is the same as for **kshow**:

    { *procedure* }   (*characterstring*)   cshow

The *PostScript Language Reference Manual*, Second Edition, says that **cshow** calls *procedure* "once for each operation of the font mapping algorithm." Let's ignore the whole ugly issue of font mapping algorithms for now and just say **cshow** calls *procedure* once for every "useful" character in the string. What does "useful" mean? For composite fonts, the string must choose the base font of the composite font. Useful characters are characters you want imaged, not characters that choose the base font.

When *procedure* is called, the stack contains three values:

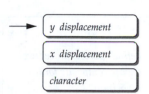

State of stack prior to each invocation of **cshow**.

❑ the integer value of the selected character

❑ the *y* displacement in the character coordinate system

❑ the *x* displacement in the character coordinate system

The picture shows the state of the stack each time *procedure* is called. To use **cshow**, you need a composite font. Let's borrow **Super-Palatino** from *Building a New Composite Font* in Chapter 10. Instead of using **ZapfDingbats** as one of the base fonts, let's use the music font **Sonata**. Here's the listing for the composite font used in the next example.

```
%!PS
12 dict                            %   create font dictionary
begin                              %   put on dictionary stack
    /FontName /Super-Palatino def  %   name of font
    /FontType 0 def                %   0 = composite font
    /WMode 0 def                   %   0 = horizontal writing mode
    /FontMatrix matrix def         %   dummy matrix
    /Encoding [ 0 1 2 3 4 ] def    %   simple encoding—five fonts
    /FMapType 3 def                %   3 = escape mapping
    /EscChar 255 def               %   use 255 as escape character
    /FDepVector [                  %   define descendant fonts
        /Palatino-Roman findfont
        /Palatino-Italic findfont
        /Palatino-Bold findfont
        /Palatino-BoldItalic findfont
        /Sonata findfont
    ] def                          %   descendant fonts
    FontName                       %   name of font on stack
    currentdict                    %   current dictionary on stack
end                                %   pop font from dictionary stack
definefont                         %   define the font
pop                                %   remove font dictionary
```

Let's watch **cshow** in action. In this program, the *procedure* operand of **cshow** displays the character, then displays the name of the character. The character string to be displayed is **Beethoven**.

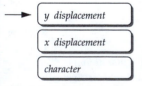

𝄡	cclef
♪	eighthnoteup
♪	eighthnoteup
𝄻	tablature
𝅗𝅥	halfnoteup
.	naturalharmonic
∨	wedgedown
♪	eighthnoteup
♮	natural

Music and prose using composite fonts and **cshow**.

```
%!PS
/inch { 72 mul } def                    % define inch procedure
/Super-Palatino 0.75 inch selectfont %  choose composite font
/top 9.5 inch def                       % y position
{    pop pop                            % pop displacements
    /char exch def                      % define character
    0.5 inch top moveto                 % set current point
    ( ) dup 0 char put show             % show character
    currentfont                         % remember current font
        dup /Encoding get               % get encoding array
        char get 100 string cvs         % get name of character
        /Palatino-Roman 0.75 inch selectfont
        1.75 inch top moveto            % set current point
        show                            % show character name
    setfont                             % restore font
    /top top 1.0 inch sub def           % update y position
} (\377\004Beethoven) cshow             % cshow Beethoven
showpage                                % display page
```

Let's look at a couple of interesting details in this program. First, set **Super-Palatino** to be the current font. This is a composite font, so the string shown by **cshow** must choose a base font from the composite font. The numbers **\377\004** in **(\377\004Beethoven)** choose the fourth base font, **Sonata**.

Now let's look at *procedure*, which **cshow** executes for each character in the string. Arguments to *procedure* are the width and height of the character and its eight-bit character code. *procedure* doesn't need width and height so it pops them from the stack. *procedure* needs the character several times so it stores the integer value of the character in a variable. Then *procedure* sets the current point and shows the character in the current font, **Sonata**, chosen with the **\377\004** sequence in the string. Notice *procedure* explicitly shows the character. **cshow** differs from other variations of **show** in that it doesn't show the characters for you; you are responsible for that. Now let's walk through the section of code reading

y displacement
x displacement
character

State of stack prior to each invocation of **cshow**.

```
currentfont                            %   remember current font
    dup /Encoding get                  %   get encoding array
    char get 100 string cvs            %   get name of character
    /Palatino-Roman 0.75 inch selectfont
    1.75 inch top moveto               %   set current point
    show                               %   show character name
setfont                                %   restore font
```

This section of code displays the name of the character. The first line is **currentfont**. *procedure* needs the current font for two reasons—first, to get the name of the character from **/Encoding**, and second, to change the font so the name of the character is set in Palatino instead of Sonata. So *procedure* has to remember the font and restore it later. Within *procedure*, the current font is the base font chosen, not the root composite font. In the example, the current base font is Sonata. **rootfont** obtains the root composite font—the ancestor of the selected base font. The root composite font is the font last selected by **setfont** or **selectfont**. The root font is **Super-Palatino** in this example.

procedure looks in the font dictionary for **/Encoding**, retrieves the name of the character, and converts it to a string. Then *procedure* shows the character name in a different font, taking care to reset the font afterwards. Finally, *procedure* moves the y position for the next character.

Show String Using x and y Widths

Display PostScript added new text operators to optimize simultaneous track and pair kerning with justification. These operators—**xyshow**, **xshow**, and **yshow**—were added to PostScript Level 2 for completeness. This section looks closely at **xyshow**, from which you can deduce the operation of **xshow** and **yshow**.

Like **show**, **xyshow** shows a string of characters. However, the origin of each character is determined individually from (x, y) displacements provided in the second operand. Here's the first six notes from "The Entertainer" by Scott Joplin. The music notes are characters from the Sonata font and are displayed using **xyshow**.

Scott Joplin could have used **xyshow**.

```
%!PS
/inch { 72 mul } def                    %   define inch procedure
/Sonata 1.8 inch selectfont             %   choose font
0.28 inch 7.05 inch moveto              %   set current point
(|) show                                %   show barline at beginning
7.77 inch 7.05 inch moveto              %   set current point
(|) show                                %   show barline at end
/Sonata 1.5 inch selectfont             %   choose font
0.29 inch 5.5 inch moveto               %   set current point
(=====) show                            %   show stave
0.4 inch 5.5 inch moveto                %   set current point
(&C)[ 80 54 80 -54 ] xyshow             %   treble clef and time signature
(eQeQqq)                                %   characters to show
[ 65 67 75 -67 65 67                    %   displacements
75 -67 50 67 0 0 ]
xyshow                                  %   show music notes
showpage                                %   display page
```

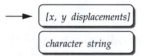

State of stack prior to invo-
cation of **xyshow**.

This program uses "vanilla" **show** instructions to set the stave. Then it uses two instances of **xyshow**, first to show the treble clef and time signature, and again to set the music notes on the stave. Let's look at **xyshow** in detail. The syntax of **xyshow** is

(*character string*) [$\delta x_1 \, \delta y_1 \, \delta x_2 \, \delta y_2 \ldots$] xyshow

where *character string* is the character string to be displayed, and the second operand is an array of (x, y) displacements. One pair of displacements should be included for each character in the character string, including the last one. If there aren't enough displacements in the second operand, a **rangecheck** error is raised.

xyshow places the first character at the current point, (x_0, y_0). The picture shows the placement of the first music note. To get the current point in the correct position, the treble clef and time signature are shown first. They are shown in white; we don't need them for this illustration.

Initial
Point

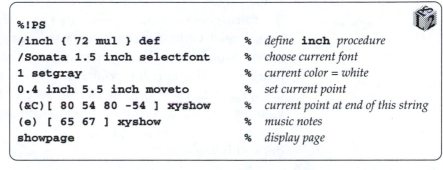

```
%!PS
/inch { 72 mul } def              %   define inch procedure
/Sonata 1.5 inch selectfont       %   choose current font
1 setgray                         %   current color = white
0.4 inch 5.5 inch moveto          %   set current point
(&C)[ 80 54 80 -54 ] xyshow       %   current point at end of this string
(e) [ 65 67 ] xyshow              %   music notes
showpage                          %   display page
```

Then **xyshow** moves the current point to $(x_0+\delta x_1, y_0+\delta y_1)$, where it positions the second character.

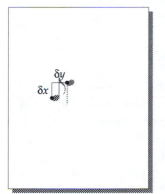

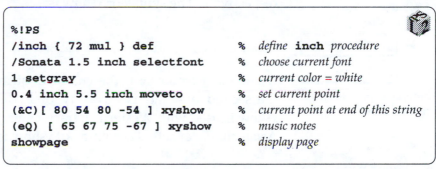

```
%!PS
/inch { 72 mul } def              %   define inch procedure
/Sonata 1.5 inch selectfont       %   choose current font
1 setgray                         %   current color = white
0.4 inch 5.5 inch moveto          %   set current point
(&C)[ 80 54 80 -54 ] xyshow       %   current point at end of this string
(eQ) [ 65 67 75 -67 ] xyshow      %   music notes
showpage                          %   display page
```

δx and δy replace the width and height of the characters defined in the font. δx and δy are not added to the character width and height. You can think of δx_1 as the width of the first character, and δy_1 as the height of the first character.

Final
Point

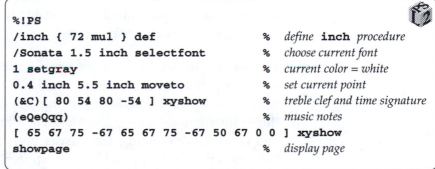

```
%!PS
/inch { 72 mul } def                              %   define inch procedure
/Sonata 1.5 inch selectfont                       %   choose current font
1 setgray                                         %   current color = white
0.4 inch 5.5 inch moveto                          %   set current point
(&C)[ 80 54 80 -54 ] xyshow                       %   treble clef and time signature
(eQeQqq)                                          %   music notes
[ 65 67 75 -67 65 67 75 -67 50 67 0 0 ] xyshow
showpage                                          %   display page
```

If the origin of the second character is (x_1, y_1), **xyshow** positions the third character at $(x_1 + \delta x_2, y_1 + \delta y_2)$. Each character is positioned relative to the character just before it, until all characters are positioned and all displacement pairs are exhausted. The final location of the current point is $(x_{n-1} + \delta x_n, y_{n-1} + \delta y_n)$, where (x_{n-1}, y_{n-1}) is the position of the last character. Note that the values provided to **xyshow** are the width and height of the characters, and are not added to the width and height of the characters defined in the font.

xshow and **yshow** behave similarly to **xyshow**, except that the position of each character is displaced in only the x or y direction, respectively. The syntax of **xshow** is

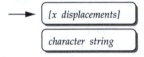

State of stack prior to invocation of **xshow**.

(*character string*) [$\delta x_1 \, \delta x_2 \dots$] **xshow**

where *character string* is the character string to be displayed, and the second operand is an array of x displacements. Typically, **xshow** is used with Western character sets, and **yshow** is used with Asian character sets. The syntax of **yshow** is

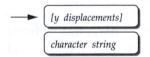

State of stack prior to invocation of **yshow**.

(*character string*) [$\delta y_1 \, \delta y_2 \dots$] **yshow**

where *character string* is the character string to be displayed, and the second operand is an array of y displacements.

For both **xshow** and **yshow**, each character in the character string, including the last character, should have one displacement value. If the second operand doesn't contain enough displacement values, a **rangecheck** error is raised.

xyshow, **xshow**, and **yshow** are Display PostScript and PostScript Level 2 operators. They provide significant performance improvements over other methods of kerning and tracking text. In general, these instructions are generated by application software. As you've seen, calculating the displacements of each character is tedious and is best handled by a computer.

Justification Operations

PostScript provides various operators to create and operate on string data types. These operators are discussed in Chapter 5—*PostScript Language*. Now you get to read about **stringwidth**, which you encountered briefly in the example on page 105 in this chapter. At first, **stringwidth** looks like another string operator, but in fact it is not so much a string operator as a facility for measuring widths of text strings. **stringwidth** is a slight misnomer. **stringwidth** returns the displacement that would occur were you to show a string in the current font.

stringwidth returns two values—the x and y *displacement* of the string. This leads to much confusion among PostScript programmers. People imagine that the height of a character or string can be obtained by examining the y displacement that **stringwidth** returns. Unfortunately, this is not what **stringwidth** does.

You will see some simple uses for **stringwidth**. These are simple because, as you will see later, **stringwidth** does not do a perfect job of computing the displacements of strings for you. But you can use **stringwidth** quite effectively most of the time. Obvious uses of **stringwidth** are to center a string of text about a given point or align the right end of a string of text to a given point. Aligning the left end of a string to a given point is trivial, because this is done by **moveto** followed by **show**.

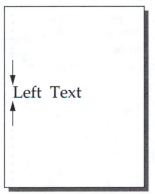

Left justified text.

```
%!PS
/inch { 72 mul } def            % define inch procedure
/Palatino-Roman findfont        % obtain font
1 inch scalefont                % scale font to required size
setfont                         % set into graphics state
0.5 inch 5.5 inch moveto        % set current point
(Left Text) show                % show the string
showpage                        % display page
```

Well, left aligned text is trivial. However, here is where **stringwidth** comes into its own in centering some text about the center of the page. Let's define a procedure called **center_show**:

```
/center_show {                        %   stack = x y   ( string )
    dup                               %   make copy of string
    stringwidth pop 2 div             %   compute half string width
    4 -1 roll exch sub                %   decrement x position
    3 -1 roll moveto                  %   set current point
    show                              %   image string
} def
```

Here's **center_show** in action.

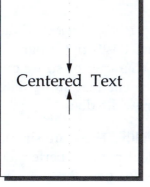

Centered text.

```
%!PS
/inch { 72 mul } def                  %   define inch procedure
/Palatino-Roman findfont              %   obtain font
1 inch scalefont                      %   scale font to required size
setfont                               %   set into graphics state
4.25 inch 5.5 inch                    %   current point
(Centered Text) center_show           %   show in middle of page
showpage                              %   display page
```

Finally, you can define another procedure called **right_show**, whose job is to align the right end of a string to a specific point.

```
/right_show {                         %   stack = x y   ( string )
    dup                               %   make copy of string
    stringwidth pop                   %   compute string width
    4 -1 roll exch sub                %   decrement x position
    3 -1 roll moveto                  %   set current point
    show                              %   display the string
} def
```

And here is **right_show** in action:

Right aligned text.

```
%!PS
/inch { 72 mul } def                    % define inch procedure
/Palatino-Roman findfont                % obtain font
1 inch scalefont                        % scale font to required size
setfont                                 % set into graphics state
8 inch 5.5 inch                         % current point
(Right Text) right_show                 % show string at right of page
showpage                                % display page
```

Notice every **stringwidth** in the preceding examples was followed by **pop** to discard the y component of the result. This combination of **stringwidth** followed by **pop** is a common cliché when dealing with "Western" character sets. Western (left-to-right characters) are generally written horizontally and do not have a vertical (y) displacement. But Asian character sets like Japanese or Chinese can be written vertically. In these characters, **stringwidth** returns different results altogether.

Accumulating Widths of Strings in Different Fonts

A frequently asked question about PostScript programming is how to concatenate character strings from different fonts. For example, people often use *italics* for emphasis, as in this next example—a quote from "The Conversations of Northcote."

The second line of the quote is typeset in two different fonts and, therefore, must be set using multiple **show** instructions. In PostScript you can't have a single character string comprised of more than one font—PostScript and its graphics and text operators don't work that way. A character string is simply a character string, with no particular interpretation placed on it, until such time as you want it to be the operand for any of the operators that deal with the font machinery. At that time, the contents of the string are treated quite differently.

> ...all the pith is
> in the *PostScript*.
>
> *William Hazlitt*

Accumulating widths in different fonts.

```
%!PS
/inch { 72 mul } def                   %   define inch procedure
/Palatino-Roman findfont               %   choose regular font
1 inch scalefont setfont
0.25 inch 7.5 inch moveto              %   set current point
(...all the pith is) show              %   show text
                                       %   set current point
0.25 inch 7.5 inch 1.25 inch sub moveto
(   in the ) show                      %   show text
/Palatino-Italic findfont              %   choose italic font
1 inch scalefont setfont
(PostScript.) show                     %   show text
/Palatino-Italic findfont              %   choose italic smaller font
48 scalefont setfont
4.0 inch 5.0 inch moveto               %   set current point
(William Hazlitt) show                 %   show text
showpage                               %   display page
```

The answer, of course, is that you *can* do this job, but you need to write appropriate PostScript procedures to do so. Application writers may well stop to think whether their application code should be doing these complex computations in PostScript.

Precise Widths and Heights of Strings

The approaches for centering and right-aligning strings using **stringwidth**, described in preceding examples, give reasonably accurate results as long as you aren't too fastidious. To obtain the precise height and width of a character (or a string) you must use another approach, **pathbbox.** Here you see **pathbbox** used to obtain information about text. A complete discussion on **pathbbox** appears in *Obtaining Path Bounding Box* on pages 331–334.

To show why you would need some precise measuring tools, let's look at an example that doesn't work. One popular approach to plotting graphical data with multiple data sets on the same plot is to use *markers*—different shaped characters—for each data set. Let's draw a "cross hair" at a point on our page and use a character from the Zapf Dingbats font as a marker; that way, you'll see the intent. Assume there's a data point at $x = 2$ inch and $y = 4$ inch. Draw a cross hair at that point and show a rosette from the Zapf Dingbats font at that point.

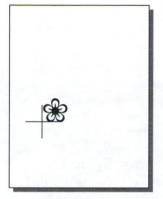

Marker—not in correct position.

```
%!PS
/inch { 72 mul } def              %   define inch procedure
2 inch 4 inch translate           %   set origin
-1 inch 0 moveto                  %   draw horizontal cross hair
2 inch 0 rlineto
0 -1 inch moveto                  %   draw horizontal cross hair
0 2 inch rlineto stroke           %   stroke the path
/ZapfDingbats findfont            %   obtain font
2 inch scalefont                  %   scale font to required size
setfont                           %   set into graphics state
0 0 moveto (\140) show            %   image the rosette
showpage                          %   display page
```

The rosette is definitely not at the point you want it to be—it's off to one side of the cross hair. Let's use **center_show** instead of **show** to position the rosette in the correct horizontal place.

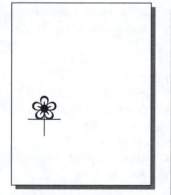

Marker—in correct horizontal position.

```
%!PS
/inch { 72 mul } def              %   define inch procedure
2 inch 4 inch translate           %   set origin
-1 inch 0 moveto                  %   draw horizontal cross hair
2 inch 0 rlineto
0 -1 inch moveto                  %   draw horizontal cross hair
0 2 inch rlineto stroke           %   stroke the path
/ZapfDingbats findfont            %   obtain font
2 inch scalefont                  %   scale font to required size
setfont                           %   set into graphics state
0 0 (\140) center_show            %   center rosette horizontally
showpage                          %   display page
```

That approach only gets the rosette in position horizontally—it doesn't solve the vertical positioning. And, as you saw in the preceding example, **stringwidth** used with Western character sets provides only the x displacement. The y value is provided, but for Western character sets y is zero. You need the y displacement. Here is the first approximation of a PostScript procedure to compute the height of a string.

ur_x, ur_y

ll_x, ll_y

Bounding box of characters.

```
/stringheight {
  gsave                              %   push graphics state
    newpath                          %   clear current path
    0 0 moveto                       %   set current point
    (PostScript!) false charpath     %   get path
    flattenpath                      %   flatten path
    pathbbox                         %   stack = llx lly urx ury
    exch pop                         %   stack = llx lly ury
    exch sub                         %   stack = llx (ury −lly)
    exch pop                         %   stack = (ury −lly)
  grestore                           %   pop graphics state
} def
```

Here is how you would use this procedure:

Height of string—not quite right.

```
%!PS
/inch { 72 mul } def                 %   define inch procedure
1 inch 5.5 inch moveto               %   draw horizontal base line
7.5 inch 5.5 inch lineto
stroke
/Palatino-Roman findfont             %   obtain font
1 inch scalefont                     %   scale font to required size
setfont                              %   set into graphics state
(PostScript!) stringheight           %   compute height
2 div 5.5 inch exch sub              %   x position
1.5 inch exch moveto                 %   set current point
(PostScript!) show                   %   show the string
showpage                             %   display page
```

The earlier **stringheight** is a first approximation. It is likely to fail in general because of limits on the number of elements in a path when you use **flattenpath**. Characters in PostScript fonts are programs. Long strings can exceed the limit on the number of points in a path. So the next (more complex but more robust) shot at measuring string height is to pull the string apart one character at a time, keeping maximum and minimum values, until the entire string is done. Here's the next cut at measuring height. Define a **charheight** procedure to measure the height of *one* character and return ll_y and ur_y on the stack. This isn't much different from the procedure for measuring the height of an entire string.

```
/charheight {                    %    string of one character
    gsave                        %    push graphics state
        newpath                  %    clear current path
        0 0 moveto               %    set current point
        false charpath           %    get path
        flattenpath              %    flatten path
        pathbbox                 %    stack = ll_x  ll_y  ur_x  ur_y
        exch pop                 %    stack = ll_x  ll_y  ur_y
        3 -1 roll pop            %    stack = ll_y  ur_y
    grestore                     %    push graphics state
} def
```

You can use this procedure right now, using the previous example to place a marker at a specified position. Let's print a page with cross hairs and the rosette centered in the page, with procedures from previous examples.

The character is centered both vertically and horizontally on the cross hairs. Now that you have a **charheight** procedure to measure the height of one character, you can create a **stringheight** procedure to work through an entire string, one character at a time, to accumulate the extreme values for ll_y and ur_y.

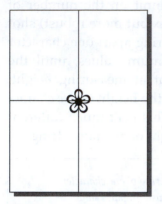

Marker—correctly centered.

```
%!PS
/inch { 72 mul } def                        %   define inch procedure
4.25 inch 0 moveto                          %   vertical cross hair
0 11 inch rlineto
0 5.5 inch moveto                           %   horizontal cross hair
8.5 inch 0 rlineto
stroke                                      %   stroke the cross hairs
/ZapfDingbats findfont                      %   obtain font
2 inch scalefont                            %   scale font to required size
setfont                                     %   set into graphics state
                                            %   compute x position
(\140) dup stringwidth pop 2 div 4.25 inch exch sub
                                            %   compute y position
5.5 inch 2 index charheight exch pop 2 div sub
moveto                                      %   set current point
show                                        %   show the character
showpage                                    %   display page
```

```
/stringheight {                             %   string
    /lly 0.0 def                            %   initial value of height_min
    /ury 0.0 def                            %   initial value of height_max
    {                                       %   work through string
        ( ) dup 0 4 -1 roll put             %   create one-character string
        charheight                          %   measure its height
        dup ury gt {                        %   if ur_y > height_max
            /ury exch def                   %   update with new value
        } {
            pop                             %   else discard ur_y
        } ifelse
        dup lly lt {                        %   if ll_y < height_min
            /lly exch def                   %   update with new value
        } {
            pop                             %   else discard lly
        } ifelse
    } forall                                %   work through string
} def
```

The next example shows how you might use the new **stringheight** procedure. This example sets white text on a black box. The width of the black box is the width of the string, and the height of the box is the height of the string. As you can see, the results aren't quite what you'd want. The height of the box is correct, but the origin of the box is incorrect. The height of the string includes ascenders and descenders, but the baseline of the string (and thus of the box) does not include descenders; the box is out of position.

Gutenberg

```
%!PS
/inch { 72 mul } def              %   define inch procedure
/Palatino-Roman findfont          %   choose font
2 inch scalefont setfont
/str (Gutenberg) def              %   define string
/w str stringwidth pop def        %   define width
/h str stringheight def           %   define height
0.75 inch 5.5 inch moveto         %   position current point
0 h rlineto                       %   draw rectangle
w 0 rlineto
0 h neg rlineto
closepath fill                    %   fill rectangle
1.0 setgray                       %   white color
0.75 inch 5.5 inch moveto         %   set current point
str show                          %   show string
showpage                          %   display page
```

You could "fix" the problem by eliminating the lower-case characters and displaying the string in all upper case. The font size and *x* position of the title were adjusted due to the larger word.

GUTENBERG

```
%!PS
/inch { 72 mul } def                       % define inch procedure
/Palatino-Roman findfont                   % choose font
1.5 inch scalefont setfont
/str (GUTENBERG) def                       % define string
/w str stringwidth pop def                 % define width
/h str stringheight def                    % define height
0.75 inch 6.5 inch moveto                  % position current point
0 h rlineto                                % draw rectangle
w 0 rlineto
0 h neg rlineto
closepath fill                             % fill rectangle
1 setgray                                  % choose gray tone
0.75 inch 6.5 inch moveto                  % set current point
str show                                   % show string
showpage                                   % display page
```

Of course, you can't display all upper-case characters just because your procedure doesn't work right. A better way to solve the problem is to calculate the lowest point of the character string and position the box there. Here's a small procedure, **descender**, to do just that. This procedure is very similar to **stringheight**.

```
/descender {                               % stack = string
    /lly 0.0 def                           % initial value of height_min
    /ury 0.0 def                           % initial value of height_max
    {                                      % work through string
        ( ) dup 0 4 -1 roll put            % create one-character string
        charheight                         % measure its height
        pop                                % remove ury
        dup lly lt {                       % if ll_y < height_min
            /lly exch def                  % update with new value
        } {
            pop                            % else discard ll_y
        } ifelse
    } forall                               % work through string
    lly                                    % return lowest descender
} def
```

Now you can fix the problem rather than side-stepping it, and the black box is positioned correctly.

```
%!PS
/inch { 72 mul } def            % define inch procedure
/Palatino-Roman findfont        % choose font
2 inch scalefont setfont
/str (Gutenberg) def            % define string
/w str stringwidth pop def      % define width
/h str stringheight def         % define height
0.75 inch                       % x position
6.0 inch str descender add      % adjust y
moveto                          % set current point
0 h rlineto                     % draw rectangle
w 0 rlineto
0 h neg rlineto
closepath fill                  % fill rectangle
1 setgray                       % choose gray tone
0.75 inch 6.0 inch moveto       % set current point
str show                        % show string
showpage                        % display page
```

Special Effects Using Character Paths

You've probably seen special effects like the large letter on the left and wondered how they were done. Effects like these are obtained using the capabilities of **charpath**. You met **charpath** in the examples in *Precise Widths and Heights of Strings* beginning on page 122 in this chapter.

Remember, a character in a PostScript font is a PostScript graphics program, like any other PostScript graphic, which means you can use the same graphics machinery with character paths as you can with any other kind of graphical image. Were you to execute the following PostScript code, you would simply get the large letter Z you see in the picture to the left.

```
%!PS
/inch { 72 mul } def                       %   dreaded inch procedure
/ZapfChancery-MediumItalic findfont        %   select the desired font
10 inch scalefont                          %   scale to fit page
setfont                                    %   set font in graphics state
0.5 inch 3 inch moveto                     %   set current point
(Z)                                        %   string to image
0.0 setgray                                %   set black color
show                                       %   image the character
showpage                                   %   display page
```

But if you use **charpath** and **stroke** instead of **show**, you can do many interesting things. Let's look at some code using **charpath**. Instead of getting the completely filled letter, you end up with a character outline.

```
%!PS
/inch { 72 mul } def                       %   dreaded inch procedure
/ZapfChancery-MediumItalic findfont        %   find required font
10 inch scalefont                          %   scale it to fit page
setfont                                    %   set font in graphics state
0.5 inch 3 inch moveto                     %   set current point
(Z) false charpath                         %   obtain character path
0.0 setgray                                %   set black color
8 setlinewidth                             %   set fat line width
stroke                                     %   paint the path
showpage                                   %   display page
```

Instead of **show**, this example uses **charpath** to get the character outline. What does **charpath** actually do? **charpath** returns a path, which is the character outline. That outline can be stroked, filled, or—as you will soon see—used to clip. Now you get to the code that created the special effects shown on page 129. The code follows the previous example, using different line weights.

```
%!PS
/inch { 72 mul } def                          %   dreaded inch procedure
/ZapfChancery-MediumItalic findfont %   find required font
10 inch scalefont                             %   scale to fit page
setfont                                       %   set font into graphics state
0.5 inch 3 inch moveto                        %   set current point
(Z) false charpath                            %   obtain character path
gsave                                         %   push graphics state
    24 setlinewidth                           %   set fat line width
    0.0 setgray                               %   set black color
    stroke                                    %   paint the path
grestore                                      %   pop graphics state
16 setlinewidth                               %   set narrower line width
1.0 setgray                                   %   set white color
stroke                                        %   paint the path
0.5 inch 3 inch moveto                        %   set current point
(Z)                                           %   character to image
0.0 setgray                                   %   set black color
show                                          %   image the character
showpage                                      %   display page
```

As always, remember to build images in layers, starting on the bottom and working toward the top. This picture shows the preceding example split into its constituent layers. We added a gray background so that you can see the white component.

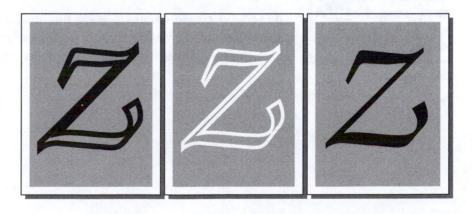

A Final Note About charpath

The syntax for **charpath** is

Boolean `charpath`

Throughout this book you've always seen **charpath** used with a **false** operand. What does *Boolean* indicate? Set *Boolean* to **false** when the current font is designed to be filled rather than stroked. Set *Boolean* to **true** when the current font is a *stroked font*. *Boolean* has nothing to do with whether or not *you* are going to stroke or fill the returned path. *Boolean* indicates the **/PaintType** of the font. Most fonts these days are filled fonts rather than stroked fonts. As a matter of fact, we haven't been able to get our hands on the only stroked font that we know of—the original Adobe Courier. Generally speaking, you will always use **false charpath**.

Clipping with Character Paths

The other major use of **charpath** is clipping. Using character outlines for clipping, you can create eye-damaging "op art" effects like the one here.

This piece of "op art" is created in four separate phases. The first phase is simple—establish a font in the graphics state and show the letter "**S**" a foot high.

The second phase creates a wide line and a dashed pattern, then paints that path, creating a set of bars over the letter shape. Phase one is the next section of code with its attendant picture.

Op-art text.

```
%!PS
/inch { 72 mul } def          %   define inch procedure
/Palatino-Bold findfont       %   set required font
12 inch scalefont setfont
1 inch 1 inch moveto (S) show %   display the character
showpage                      %   display page
```

Here is phase two. It creates a dashed pattern to paint the gray bars up the middle of the page.

```
%!PS
/inch { 72 mul } def          %   define inch procedure
/Palatino-Bold findfont       %   set required font
12 inch scalefont setfont
1 inch 1 inch moveto (S) show %   display the character
4.25 inch 0 moveto            %   set current point
0 11 inch rlineto             %   add line segment
8 inch setlinewidth           %   set fat line width
[ 0.5 inch 0.5 inch ] 0 setdash %   set dashed line
0.50 setgray                  %   medium gray color
stroke                        %   paint the bars
showpage                      %   display page
```

The third part places the large letter again using **charpath**, to get the outline of the foot-high "**S**" for use as a clip path. The fourth and final phase draws the same line with a fat line width and the same dash pattern but strokes in lighter gray. The lighter gray bars are now painted only in the area enabled as a stencil by the character's clipping path. Next are the third and fourth phases shown without the distraction of the first two phases.

Particularly important in this example is the **newpath** operator before drawing the dashed line for the second time. In the absence of **newpath**, the straight line drawn up the page is added to the outline of the clip path, and the result is strange and ugly.

```
%!PS
/inch { 72 mul } def              %   define inch procedure
/Palatino-Bold findfont           %   set required font
12 inch scalefont setfont
1 inch 1 inch moveto              %   set current point
(S) false charpath clip           %   make clipping path
newpath                           %   start new path—important!
4.25 inch 0 moveto                %   set current point
0 11 inch rlineto                 %   add line segment
8 inch setlinewidth               %   set fat line width
[ 0.5 inch 0.5 inch ] 0 setdash   %   set dashed line
0.75 setgray                      %   light gray color
stroke                            %   paint the bars through the letter
showpage                          %   display page
```

Finally, here is the complete code for this picture.

Op-art text.

```
%!PS
/inch { 72 mul } def                        %   define inch procedure
/Palatino-Bold findfont                     %   set required font
12 inch scalefont setfont
1 inch 1 inch moveto (S) show               %   display the character
4.25 inch 0 moveto                          %   set current point
0 11 inch rlineto                           %   add line segment
8 inch setlinewidth                         %   set fat line width
[ 0.5 inch 0.5 inch ] 0 setdash             %   set dashed line
0.50 setgray stroke                         %   stroke with medium gray
1 inch 1 inch moveto                        %   set current point
(S) false charpath clip                     %   make clipping path
newpath                                     %   start new path—important!
4.25 inch 0 moveto                          %   set current point
0 11 inch rlineto                           %   add line segment
8 inch setlinewidth                         %   set fat line width
[ 0.5 inch 0.5 inch ] 0 setdash             %   set dashed line
0.75 setgray stroke                         %   stroke with light gray
showpage                                    %   display page
```

Stroking Character Paths

Y ou just saw how to use a character outline as a clipping region with the help of **charpath**. You can use **charpath** for other "interesting" effects such as this hollow character.

```
%!PS
/inch { 72 mul } def                    %   define inch procedure
/Palatino-Roman findfont                %   choose large font
13.5 inch scalefont setfont
0.25 inch 0.75 inch moveto              %   set current point
0.75 inch setlinewidth                  %   fat line width
(P) false charpath                      %   get outline for "P"
stroke                                  %   stroke outline
showpage                                %   display page
```

Stroking outline of a character.

This program uses a combination of **setlinewidth**, **charpath**, and **stroke**. The character outline is stroked with a fat line width, giving the illusion of a hollow character. Suppose, however, instead of showing a character stroked with a fat black line, you wanted to show a background image through the outline of the shape resulting from the character stroked with a fat line. Enter **strokepath**, which replaces the current path with a new path consisting of the outline of the shape you would get if you were to **stroke** the current path. What does this mean? This example demonstrates.

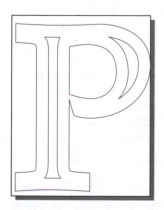

This program chooses a font, sets the current point and fat line width, and gets the character outline for the letter "P". Instead of stroking the path at this point, **strokepath** replaces the current path with the outline of the shape. The picture shows the path returned by **strokepath**. **clip** establishes the shape outline as a clipping region. **newpath** resets the current path in the graphics state. Without **newpath**, the final image would include the shape outline from **strokepath**. Finally, the program draws a simple starburst, which shows through the outline of the character.

Clipping to what would be stroked path.

```
%!PS
/inch { 72 mul } def                    %  define inch procedure
/Palatino-Roman findfont                %  choose large font
13.5 inch scalefont setfont
0.25 inch 0.75 inch moveto              %  set current point
0.75 inch setlinewidth                  %  set fat linewidth
(P) false charpath                      %  get character outline
strokepath                              %  replace path
clip                                    %  clip to character outline
newpath                                 %  newpath
1 setlinewidth                          %  smaller linewidth
5.25 inch 7.5 inch translate            %  upper right of page
180 {                                   %  repeat
  0 0 moveto 10 inch 0 lineto          %  draw line
  2 rotate                              %  rotate
} repeat                                %  loop again
stroke                                  %  stroke starburst
showpage                                %  display page
```

In PostScript Level 1, prior to the advent of patterns, **strokepath** was frequently used to tile shape outlines with repeating patterns. PostScript Level 2 patterns make the job easier. Now you just **stroke** the character outline with a pattern like this:

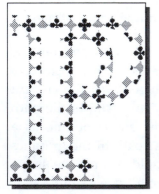

Outline of character stroked with a pattern.

```
%!PS                                                           PS
                                                               L2
/inch { 72 mul } def                    %  define inch procedure
/Palatino-Bold findfont                 %  set font in graphics state
13.5 inch scalefont setfont
0.25 inch 0.75 inch moveto              %  set current point
0.75 inch setlinewidth                  %  rotate coordinate system
(P) false charpath                      %  get character outline
AstroidLeaf setpattern                  %  fancy pattern fill
stroke                                  %  stroke with pattern
showpage                                %  display page
```

There is a limit on the number of points in a path. As with **charpath**, **strokepath** can exceed those limits if the string of characters is long. In this case, process each character of the string separately.

Obtaining Paths from Character Paths

PostScript Level 1 **pathforall** after **charpath** raised **invalidaccess**. These restrictions were in response to pressure from font manufacturers wishing to protect their intellectual property—the detailed design of their font outlines. Of course, restrictions serve as a challenge to certain people and so years of effort went into finding ways around the access restrictions and in cracking the encryption schemes Adobe had built into Type 1 fonts.

Pseudo-perspective letters drawn using **pathforall**.

Access restrictions on **pathforall** after **charpath** were removed when PostScript Level 2 came along, primarily because Adobe gained a landmark court ruling that font programs can enjoy copyright protection. And combined with publishing the format of Type 1 fonts, the need for access restrictions went away.

Why do you actually want to access paths? Well, among other things, you can do transformations—such as perspective transformations—that aren't possible with the straight affine transformations available through plugging values into the CTM.

Text Setting

PostScript has the programming and computational capability to do text justification, if you care to write PostScript programs complex enough. In fact, several writers have demonstrated PostScript to do quite out-of-the-ordinary text justification tasks. But using PostScript for truly sophisticated paragraph building algorithms is too much a *tour de force*. When you address issues like full justification *versus* ragged-right and ragged-left text setting, drop capitals, large capitals, hung capitals, several kinds of kerning, hanging punctuation, intelligent dictionary-driven and rule-based hyphenation, control of rivers and ladders, control of widow and orphan lines, and so on—you're clearly much better off doing the work in your application.

Adobe Font Metric (AFM) files are the repository from which your application obtains data on character widths, kerning pairs, composite characters, writing directions, and master designs for multiple master fonts. Applications need AFM data to perform computations for line breaking and paragraph building to generate "good" PostScript code to make the marks on the page. Adobe Systems supply code to parse AFM files so applications can manage character metrics data consistently.

Underlining Text

Typewriters, dot matrix printers, and letter quality printers generally did not have the capability to *switch typefaces* and so would use artifacts such as UPPERCASE and underlining for emphasis. Using underlining for emphasis is considered passé in the world of typography. Good typography uses different *typefaces* or different *weights* of type to emphasize things.

If your application absolutely <u>must</u> have underlining, consider adding options for continuous underlining, underlining words only (not the spaces between words), and not underlining descenders. Such options will, of course, complicate your application. Here is some example code illustrating how to underline text. This code is simple because it's for illustration only. This code has several potential pitfalls that you as an application writer must watch for. First the code, then the caveats.

Example of underlined text.

```
%!PS
/inch { 72 mul } def              %  define inch procedure
/Palatino-Roman findfont          %  find required font
1.125 inch scalefont              %  scale font to required size
setfont                           %  make it current font
52 rotate                         %  rotate for angled text
96 0 moveto                       %  set initial point
(Buy ) show                       %  show first part of string
(special eggs) UnderLineString    %  show string to be underlined
( Today) show                     %  show rest of text
showpage                          %  display page
```

That's the code to show text with underlining. The definition of

UnderLineString appears at the top of page 140. The premise of this code is simple. To underline some text you must show the strings in parts, which you probably do anyway.

First you need to obtain **/UnderlinePosition** and **/UnderlineThickness** from the **/FontInfo** dictionary of the current font. Both **/UnderlinePosition** and **/UnderlineThickness** are defined in the character coordinate system, so you must adjust them by the font scale factor—that's the function of the **dtransform** in the code.

Showing text with underlining is a four-part process. This underlining procedure is called with a string to be underlined, and the current point is assumed to be positioned at the correct place. Record the current point—the position at which underlining will start. Then show the text you wish underlined and record the current point again—the point at which underlining will stop. Then set the current point to the end position you recorded and draw a line to the start position. Then set the line width to the thickness obtained from **/FontInfo** and stroke the line. The last part is to set the current point to the end point you recorded, ready for more text that might be imaged.

As stated, this code is simple and contains assumptions application writers should not make. First, perform all positioning calculations in your application and not in your PostScript driver code. Get **/UnderlinePosition** and **/UnderlineThickness** from the AFM files for the font. Don't assume there's a **/FontInfo** dictionary— some fonts don't have one. Even if there is a **/FontInfo** dictionary, don't assume it contains **/UnderlinePosition** and **/UnderlineThickness** keys—some fonts get these wrong. Even if the thickness and position keys exist in **/FontInfo**, there's no guarantee the values are sensible—some fonts get them wrong also.

```
%!PS
/UnderLineString {                      % define underlining procedure
    currentfont dup                     % get current font dictionary
    /FontMatrix get                     % get current font matrix
    exch                                % font dictionary on top
    /FontInfo get dup                   % get font information dictionary
    /UnderlinePosition get              % get underline position
    exch                                % font info dictionary on top
    /UnderlineThickness get             % get stroke width
    3 -1 roll dtransform                % scale position and thickness
    /UnderThick exch def                % define for later
    /UnderPos exch def                  % define for later
    currentpoint                        % get current point
    pop                                 % don't need y coordinate
    /Start_x exch def                   % remember x coordinate
    show                                % show string to be underlined
    currentpoint                        % get current point
    /End_y exch def                     % remember x coordinate
    /End_x exch def                     % remember x coordinate
    0 UnderPos rmoveto                  % set start of line
    Start_x End_x sub 0 rlineto         % draw line
    currentlinewidth                    % remember current line width
    UnderThick setlinewidth             % set line width for underlining
    stroke                              % stroke the line
    setlinewidth                        % restore previous line width
    End_x End_y moveto                  % position for rest of string
} def
```

Strikethrough Text

Strikethrough is widely used in the legal profession to indicate that a part of a legal document was deleted. You can use the same approach for strikethrough text as you use for underlining. But note that the **FontInfo** dictionary, even assuming there is one, has no keys for strikethrough position or strikethrough thickness. You can use the **UnderlineThickness** value from **FontInfo** to determine the thickness of the strikethrough lines. To determine the position of the strikethrough lines, use the position of the dash.

Superscripts and Subscripts

Super^{scripts} and sub$_{\text{scripts}}$ are widely used for setting mathematical expressions such as $a^2 + b^2$. If your application is supposed to deal with mathematical typography, you have many more layout issues to think about than simple superscripts and subscripts. But at times your application must deal with superscripts and subscripts in line with ordinary text.

The typographically correct way to do superscripts and subscripts is to use fonts especially designed for the purpose. While you might accommodate superscripts and subscripts simply by using smaller type sizes, the best mathematical typography uses "expert" character sets with characters designed for this purpose. Look at Adobe Garamond Expert as a good example of a character set with special characters.

You may not have access to any of the "expert" character sets, and then you have to make do with what's available. A good method to provide superscripts and subscripts is to use non-uniform scaling. Adobe recommend using a scaling of 0.65 in the x coordinate and 0.6 in the y coordinate.

Given you can scale characters to the apparently correct size using a font transformation matrix, your next concern is adjusting the text baseline to set the superscripts or subscripts. The next example is very simple showing a superscript and a subscript.

If you're writing applications to created and edit equations, make sure you obtain rules for mathematical typesetting from authorities on this subject. Start with the American Mathematical Society and then go to the Government Printing Office. Rules for typesetting equations vary from one source to the next, and everybody has a different opinion on how they should be done. This example uses Adobes' suggestions for transforming the font, and uses rules of thumb for adjusting the baselines for the superscript and subscript. Opinions vary widely on the "correct" values. This example moves the baseline up 0.4 of an em for the superscript, and down 0.25 of an em for the subscript. Notice that letters in equations are set in Italic type, except for certain symbols such as **sin** and **abs**, but numbers revert to their Roman typeface.

Superscript and subscript.

```
%!PS
/Palatino-Italic findfont          % find italic font
300 scalefont                      % scale to required size
setfont                            % scale to required size
200 500 moveto                     % set current point
(a) show                           % show italic character
/Palatino-Roman findfont           % find Roman font
                                   % transform
[ 300 0.65 mul 0 0 300 0.6 mul 0 0 ] makefont
setfont                            % make current font
0 120 rmoveto                      % adjust baseline for superscript
(2) show                           % show superscript
/Palatino-Italic findfont          % find italic font
300 scalefont                      % scale to required size
setfont                            % scale to required size
200 200 moveto                     % set current point
(a) show                           % show italic character
/Palatino-Roman findfont           % find Roman font
                                   % transform
[ 300 0.65 mul 0 0 300 0.6 mul 0 0 ] makefont
setfont                            % make current font
0 -75 rmoveto                      % adjust baseline for subscript
(2) show                           % show subscript
showpage                           % display page
```

4 Transformations

The brief run through transformations on pages 20–27 of Chapter 1 illustrated basic PostScript operations for transforming the user coordinate system. This chapter expands on the theme, with particular attention to the PostScript Current Transformation Matrix, known as the CTM for short. You've already seen three "convenience" operators for transforming user coordinates to device space. The basic operations are **translate** (to move the origin of user space to a new place), **scale** (to stretch or shrink coordinates), and **rotate** (to turn the coordinate system around its origin). This picture shows a cube drawn by transforming the coordinate system with shear transformations, which you will encounter on pages 160–165 in this chapter.

What's actually going on when you use transformation operators? You transform from *user space* to *device space*. User space, also known as the user coordinate system, is an ideal coordinate system. User space is, for all practical purposes, an infinite plane on which you can move around with as fine a precision as you need. User space may well look like the picture at the left.

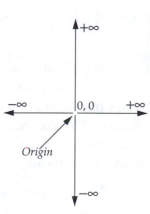

User space is an ideal infinite plane.

Device space, on the other hand, may not be so cooperative. For one, device space is usually limited in size. Popular paper sizes are United States "standard" 8½-by-11-inch letter paper and ISO standard A4 at 210 mm by 297 mm. Then the resolution of the devices differs. A computer screen with a resolution of 93 dots per inch, for example, can position points only to pixels—every 0.0107 inch in this case. A 300-dot-per-inch laser printer, as another example, can position dots every 0.00333 inch. 300 dots per inch may sound pretty good, but it's not good enough for first class typography. Device spaces with coarse resolution create problems of positioning lines precisely and also create problems obtaining lines of equal thickness. Various techniques exist to overcome these problems, and these topics are covered in *Accurate Positioning* on pages 173–179 later in this chapter.

In addition to being a less-than-ideal infinite plane, device space may be oriented differently from user space and possibly be at a different scale factor than user space. But device space is usually a physical sheet of paper or a computer screen. By convention, PostScript places the origin of user space at the lower-left corner of device space, as in the picture. The rest of this chapter describes how to manipulate the transformations between ideal PostScript user space and the device spaces of the real world.

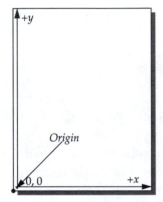

Origin at lower-left corner of device space.

Current Transformation Matrix

You've heard about the Current Transformation Matrix. Now you get to see it in more detail. The CTM is a six-element matrix with which PostScript performs all mappings from user space to device space. The CTM looks like this.

$$\left[\begin{array}{cccccc} a & b & c & d & T_x & T_y \end{array}\right]$$

To see what the CTM is all about you need a smidgeon of two-dimensional graphics and matrix arithmetic. Stick with this because it's important to effective use of PostScript transformation capabilities—the discussion doesn't get *too* esoteric. To take into account translation, scaling, and rotation, a transformation of a point x_{user}, y_{user} can be described with a pair of linear equations,

$$x_{device} = a \cdot x_{user} + b \cdot y_{user} + T_x$$

$$y_{device} = c \cdot x_{user} + d \cdot y_{user} + T_y$$

where the a, b, c, and d coefficients represent scaling and rotation factors, and T_x and T_y are translation components. All these factors can be combined into a single three-by-three matrix.

$$\begin{pmatrix} a & b & 0 \\ c & d & 0 \\ T_x & T_y & 1 \end{pmatrix}$$

Then the transformation of the point at (x_{user}, y_{user}) into (x_{device}, y_{device}) is described by a multiplication of two matrices.

$$\begin{bmatrix} x_{device} & y_{device} & 1 \end{bmatrix} = \begin{bmatrix} x_{user} & y_{user} & 1 \end{bmatrix} \cdot \begin{bmatrix} a & b & 0 \\ c & d & 0 \\ T_x & T_y & 1 \end{bmatrix}$$

The three-by-three matrix by which x, y coordinates are transformed is the CTM. So you can rewrite the equation.

$$\begin{bmatrix} x_{device} & y_{device} & 1 \end{bmatrix} = \text{CTM} \cdot \begin{bmatrix} x_{user} & y_{user} & 1 \end{bmatrix}$$

Notice the transformation matrix is a nine-element (three-by-three) matrix and the (x, y) pairs have an extra element added. These extra elements are needed to make the rules of matrix arithmetic work. The extra column in each matrix always has the same constant values. PostScript matrices leave out the constant elements and represent the CTM as one six-element vector.

$$\begin{bmatrix} a & b & c & d & T_x & T_y \end{bmatrix}$$

But whenever you need to think of which elements of the CTM affect x and which elements affect y, rewrite the matrix (on paper) so it looks this way.

$$\begin{pmatrix} a & b \\ c & d \\ T_x & T_y \end{pmatrix}$$

Then you can see more easily how elements in the first column affect x and elements in the second column affect y.

As already mentioned, device space may well be oriented differently from user space, and at a different scaling. If you write a program to print the CTM for your specific printer, you may get results like those shown in the next picture. Here is some PostScript code to discover the CTM for our laser printer—an Apple LaserWriter IIg. The code is a little fancy just to display elements of the CTM in matrix format.

```
4.16667     0.0

0.0        -4.16667

-1280.0     1650.5
```

Results of printing the CTM.

```
%!PS
/inch { 72 mul } def                        %   define inch procedure
/Courier-Bold findfont 36 scalefont setfont
/x_pos [ 1 inch 5 inch 1 inch 5 inch 1 inch 5 inch ] def
/y_pos [ 7 inch 7 inch 5 inch 5 inch 3 inch 3 inch ] def
0 1 5 {                                     %   start for loop
    /counter exch def                       %   save loop variable
    matrix currentmatrix                    %   get CTM
    counter get                             %   get required element
    100 string cvs                          %   convert to string
    x_pos counter get                       %   get x coordinate
    y_pos counter get                       %   get y coordinate
    moveto                                  %   set current point
    show                                    %   image converted string
} for                                       %   end for loop
showpage                                    %   display page
```

You see from the numbers that the CTM for the Apple LaserWriter IIg has this form:

$$\begin{bmatrix} 4.16667 & 0.0 \\ 0.0 & -4.16667 \\ -1280.0 & 1650.5 \end{bmatrix}$$

At this point, be aware you're treading into the shaky area of *device dependence*. When writing application software, do *not* wire details of specific printers into code. Use *PostScript Printer Description Files* (PPD files) instead to obtain information about characteristics and capabilities of specific printers.

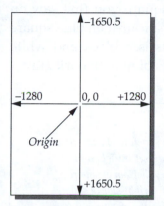

−1650.5

−1280   0, 0   +1280

Origin

+1650.5

Device space for a Laser-Writer IIg.

Both x and y scale factors are 4.16667, but you'll notice the y scale factor is negative, meaning the y coordinate is flipped. The CTM's job is to ensure that your pictures come out the right way up. Also, notice the values of T_x and T_y. Device space looks like the picture at left, and the initial CTM maps the origin of user space to the lower-left corner of device space. Device space for the Apple LaserWriter IIg is also scaled to four times that of user space.

Now that you're bored to tears with theory, let's go on to some practical applications of the CTM and you'll see how different transformations affect specific elements. The next three sections cover the basic transformations of **translate**, **scale**, and **rotate**. You'll see some tricks you can play with the CTM to provide shear transformations and projections.

One of the principal reasons for the transformation concept is so you can think of each object on the drawing surface as being in its own miniature coordinate system. Thinking of objects as living in their own miniature coordinate systems leads to a good style of PostScript programming, whether you're creating your own raw PostScript or generating PostScript from within your application. In fact, fonts, images, patterns, and forms all use their own coordinate systems which get transformed into the user coordinate system. By thinking of all objects in their own coordinate systems, you can achieve very modular and compact PostScript programs.

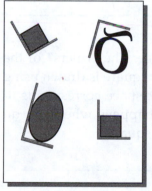

Objects in independent coordinate systems.

Translating the Origin

The first and simplest transformation is *translate*—a fancy word for linear displacement in either the x direction, the y direction, or both x and y directions at once. Translation means the origin of the coordinate system is moved by a specified amount in x and y. You reposition the origin of the coordinate system with **translate**, whose general format is

T_x T_y `translate`

where T_x and T_y are the amounts to translate in the x direction and the y direction, respectively. Here's a variation on the example of the intermediate skier's blue square you first saw on page 50 in Chapter 2. This example draws a four-inch blue square in the middle of the page. Of course, this is a black and white page, so the PostScript interpreter simulates blue with dark gray.

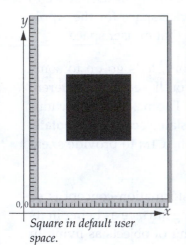

```
%!PS
/inch { 72 mul } def              % define inch procedure
2.25 inch 3.5 inch moveto         % set initial point
4 inch 0 rlineto                  % bottom of square
0 4 inch rlineto                  % right side of square
-4 inch 0 rlineto                 % top of square
closepath                         % close the shape
0.0 0.0 1.0 setrgbcolor           % set color blue
fill                              % paint the shape
showpage                          % display page
```

Square in default user space.

There's the square in the middle of the page. The "rulers" of the coordinate system are along the page. This square is drawn using the default coordinates—the origin of user space corresponds to 0,0 on the physical page. Now see what happens when you do **2 inch 2 inch translate** prior to drawing the square.

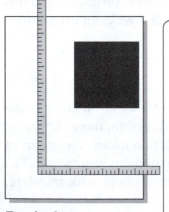

```
%!PS
/inch { 72 mul } def              % define inch procedure
2 inch 2 inch translate           % translate coordinate system
2.25 inch 3.5 inch moveto         % set initial point
4 inch 0 rlineto                  % bottom of square
0 4 inch rlineto                  % right side of square
-4 inch 0 rlineto                 % top of square
closepath                         % close the shape
0.0 0.0 1.0 setrgbcolor           % set color blue
fill                              % paint the shape
showpage                          % display page
```

Translated user space.

The origin of the entire coordinate system has moved over and up. All coordinates will now be relative to this new origin, until another **translate** moves the origin to a new point.

The mathematics of translation means that a point at (x, y) translated by (T_x, T_y) moves that point to $(x + T_x, y + T_y)$. You can write the translation equation

$$x_{new} = x_{original} + T_x$$

$$y_{new} = y_{original} + T_y$$

where T_x and T_y are the x and y translation distances. In terms of the CTM, T_x T_y **translate** actually generates a matrix like this:

$$\begin{bmatrix} 1 & 0 & 0 & 1 & T_{original\ x} + T_x & T_{original\ y} + T_y \end{bmatrix}$$

Translation moves the origin of the coordinate system to a new origin. Further translations move the origin relative to the new origin, and so on. Let's translate another inch in both x and y.

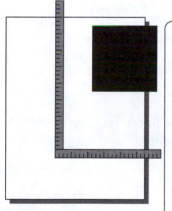

Further translated user space.

```
%!PS
/inch { 72 mul } def              %   define inch procedure
1 inch 1 inch translate           %   translate coordinate system
2.25 inch 3.5 inch moveto         %   set initial point
4 inch 0 rlineto                  %   bottom of square
0 4 inch rlineto                  %   right side of square
-4 inch 0 rlineto                 %   top of square
closepath                         %   close the shape
0.0 0.0 1.0 setrgbcolor           %   set color blue
fill                              %   paint the shape
showpage                          %   display page
```

You see the origin has moved up and over a little more, to the point where the square is drawn partially "off the page." Were this a real page on a real printer, the square would in fact be chopped[†] off by the edge of the paper.

---

† *clipped*, in graphics lingo.

Scaling the Coordinate System

The next simple transformation to user space is *scaling*, which means x and y coordinates are scaled (squeezed or stretched) by specified factors. Scale the coordinate system using **scale**, whose general form is

$$S_x \quad S_y \quad \texttt{scale}$$

where S_x and S_y are the amounts by which to multiply the x and y coordinates, respectively. Here's our square in the page again with the "rulers" shown, using the default coordinate system.

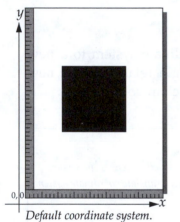

Default coordinate system.

```
%!PS
/inch { 72 mul } def              %   define inch procedure
2.25 inch 3.5 inch moveto         %   set initial point
4 inch 0 rlineto                  %   bottom of square
0 4 inch rlineto                  %   right side of square
-4 inch 0 rlineto                 %   top of square
closepath                         %   close the shape
0.0 0.0 1.0 setrgbcolor           %   set color blue
fill                              %   paint the shape
showpage                          %   display page
```

Now you can transform (scale) the square into a rectangle using a **0.75 1.25 scale** operation. Let's see an example.

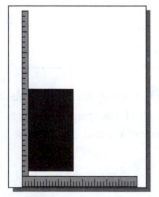

Scaled (and translated) coordinate system.

```
%!PS
/inch { 72 mul } def              %   define inch procedure
1 inch 1 inch translate           %   translate to correct position
0.75 1.25 scale                   %   scale coordinate system
0 0 moveto                        %   set initial point
4 inch 0 rlineto                  %   bottom of square
0 4 inch rlineto                  %   right side of square
-4 inch 0 rlineto                 %   top of square
closepath                         %   close the shape
0.0 setgray fill                  %   fill with black
showpage                          %   display page
```

This example also did a **translate** before the **scale**. Why? Because you want the box to appear at position (1 inch, 1 inch). Had you drawn the picture as in the previous unscaled example using **moveto** to set the current point, the coordinates of **moveto** would have been scaled also, so **moveto** would have moved to (0.75 inch, 1.25 inch). The mathematics of scaling are

$$x_{new} = x_{original} \times S_x$$

$$y_{new} = y_{original} \times S_y$$

where S_x and S_y are the x and y scale factors. In terms of the CTM, S_x S_y **scale** generates a matrix like this.

$$\left[S_x\ 0\ 0\ S_y\ 0\ 0 \right]$$

Using Scaling to Flip and Flop the Coordinate System

Of course, you can use **scale** to change more than just the proportions of the coordinate system. You can also change the orientation of the coordinate system. Here's the treble clef character from the Sonata font.

Treble clef from Sonata font.

```
%!PS                                    %   define inch procedure
/inch { 72 mul } def                    %   define inch procedure
/Sonata findfont                        %   find Sonata font
6 inch scalefont                        %   make large size
setfont                                 %   make current font
2.5 inch 2.625 inch moveto              %   set current point
/trebleclef glyphshow                   %   image character by name
showpage                                %   display page
```

An item of interest in this code is the use of **glyphshow** to image the character by name instead of by character code. **glyphshow** is a PostScript Level 2 feature to access characters by their names instead of by their character codes. **glyphshow** is useful in cases like this where the character codes don't have a very close correlation with the names of the characters. Now let's place this same character in four different places on the page. Each instance uses the same scale factor, but some of the scale factors are made negative, which has the effect of flipping the coordinate vertically or flopping it horizontally.

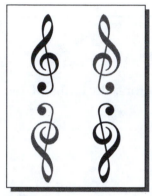

Treble clefs flipped and flopped using negative scaling.

```
%!PS
/inch { 72 mul } def                            % define inch procedure
/Sonata findfont                                % find Sonata font
5.5 inch scalefont                              % make large size
setfont                                         % make current font
/ScaleFactor 0.5 def                            % scale for all four instances
gsave                                           % remember graphics state
    1.5 inch 6.75 inch translate                % upper left clef
    ScaleFactor ScaleFactor scale               % +x and +y
    0.25 setgray                                % dark gray
    0 0 moveto                                  % set current point
    /trebleclef glyphshow                       % image character by name
grestore                                        % restore graphics state
gsave                                           % remember graphics state
    7 inch 6.75 inch translate                  % upper right instance
    ScaleFactor neg ScaleFactor scale           % −x and +y
    0.50 setgray                                % medium gray
    0 0 moveto                                  % set current point
    /trebleclef glyphshow                       % image character by name
grestore                                        % restore graphics state
gsave                                           % remember graphics state
    1.5 inch 4 inch translate                   % lower left instance
    ScaleFactor ScaleFactor neg scale           % +x and −y
    0.50 setgray                                % medium gray
    0 0 moveto                                  % set current point
    /trebleclef glyphshow                       % image character by name
grestore                                        % restore graphics state
gsave                                           % remember graphics state
    7 inch 4 inch translate                     % lower right instance
    ScaleFactor neg ScaleFactor neg scale       % −x and −y
    0.25 setgray                                % dark gray
    0 0 moveto                                  % set current point
    /trebleclef glyphshow                       % image character by name
grestore                                        % restore graphics state
showpage                                        % display page
```

Rotating the Coordinate System

The final transformation[†] on a PostScript diagram is *rotation*. Rotation involves rotating the entire coordinate system around its origin by a specified angle. **rotate**'s general format is

angle   **rotate**

where *angle* is the number of *degrees* to rotate the coordinate system. This picture shows what happens to the coordinate system when you rotate.

angle rotate

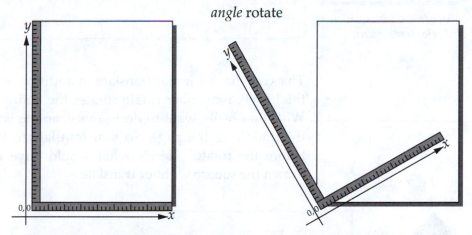

Let's transform the intermediate skier's blue square into an advanced skier's black diamond. One obvious way to build a diamond is to simply draw four lines composing the sides of the diamond. This method requires that you calculate each point on the diamond separately and would probably take several iterations to get a balanced diamond shape.

Another way to turn the square into a diamond is to **rotate** the coordinate system by 45° and draw the square in the rotated coordinate system. This seems like an indirect approach, but coordinate system transformations obtain the results easily.

---

† in terms of convenience operators.

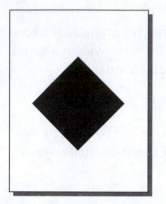

*Square drawn with rotation
(and prior translation).*

```
%!PS
/inch { 72 mul } def              % define inch procedure
4.25 inch 2.5 inch translate      % translate to correct position
45 rotate                         % rotate coordinate system
0 0 moveto                        % set initial point
4 inch 0 rlineto                  % bottom of square
0 4 inch rlineto                  % right side of square
-4 inch 0 rlineto                 % top of square
closepath                         % close the shape
0.0 setgray                       % set black
fill                              % paint the shape
showpage                          % display page
```

This code has an initial **translate** in addition to the **rotate**. Why is this? Well, remember **rotate** rotates the entire coordinate system. What you really want to do in this example is rotate the object in the middle of the page. So you **translate** to the correct position before the **rotate**. Here's what would have happened if you'd drawn the square without **translate**.

Square with rotation only.

```
%!PS
/inch { 72 mul } def              % define inch procedure
45 rotate                         % rotate coordinate system
4.25 inch 2.5 inch moveto         % set initial point
4 inch 0 rlineto                  % bottom of square
0 4 inch rlineto                  % right side of square
-4 inch 0 rlineto                 % top of square
closepath                         % close the shape
0.0 setgray                       % set black
fill                              % paint the shape
showpage                          % display page
```

The diamond is drawn partially off the "page," because all measurements are relative to the origin of the rotated coordinate system. By translating to the desired position first and then rotating, you achieve the effect of rotating just the object you want to draw.

Look at the mathematics of rotation and you find that while translation and scaling affect x and y positions independently, rotation affects both x and y positions simultaneously.

$$x_{new} = x_{original} \times \cos \theta - y_{original} \times \sin \theta$$

$$y_{new} = x_{original} \times \sin \theta + y_{original} \times \cos \theta$$

where θ is the angle of rotation. Let's see an example.

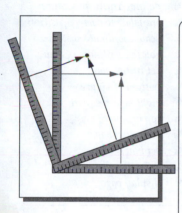

```
%!PS
/inch { 72 mul } def          %   define inch procedure
2 inch 2 inch translate       %   move origin
4.25 inch 5.5 inch            %   center of circle
0.125 inch 0 360 arc          %   draw circle
closepath                     %   finish the shape
0.50 setgray                  %   medium gray
fill                          %   fill the outline
20 rotate                     %   rotate coordinate system
4.25 inch 5.5 inch            %   center of circle
0.125 inch 0 360 arc          %   draw circle again
closepath                     %   finish the shape
0.00 setgray                  %   back to black
fill                          %   fill the outline
showpage                      %   display page
```

This picture shows a ⅛ inch dot drawn on the page, followed by the same dot on the page after a 20° rotation. If you plug the numbers into the preceding equations you see the following:

$$x_{new} = 4.25 \text{ inch} \times \cos 20° - 5.5 \text{ inch} \times \sin 20° = 2.1 \text{ inch}$$

$$y_{new} = 4.25 \text{ inch} \times \sin 20° + 5.5 \text{ inch} \times \cos 20° = 6.6 \text{ inch}$$

Combined Transformations

You used **rotate** to draw the expert skier's diamond, but it shouldn't be just a square rotated 45°—it ought to be tall and slender. You get this shape using **scale** and **rotate**, and **translate** to get the shape into the correct position on the page.

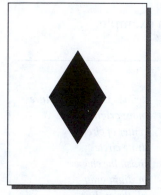

Square in translated, scaled, rotated coordinate system.

```
%!PS
/inch { 72 mul } def              %   define inch procedure
4.25 inch 2.5 inch translate      %   translate to correct position
0.625 1 scale                     %   scale coordinate system
45 rotate                         %   rotate coordinate system
0 0 moveto                        %   set initial point
4 inch 0 rlineto                  %   bottom of square
0 4 inch rlineto                  %   right side of square
-4 inch 0 rlineto                 %   top of square
closepath                         %   close the shape
0.0 setgray                       %   set black
fill                              %   paint the shape
showpage                          %   display page
```

Now you have a thinner diamond that looks about right. The x scale factor of 0.625 (⅝) was found by trial and lots of error. Let's look at the x, y position in space and apply all three transformations—**translate**, **scale**, and **rotate**—to that point.

$$x_{new} = (x_{original} \times \cos \theta - y_{original} \times \sin \theta) \times S_x + T_x$$

$$y_{new} = (x_{original} \times \sin \theta + y_{original} \times \cos \theta) \times S_y + T_y$$

Let's embellish the example to draw the last symbol in the series (the dreaded double diamond) to mark places where only the crazy go. This code uses a **draw_diamond** procedure.

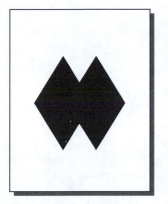

"Experts Only."

```
%!PS
/inch { 72 mul } def                  %   define inch procedure
3.25 inch 2.5 inch translate          %   translate to correct position
draw_diamond                          %   draw a diamond
2.0 inch 0 inch translate             %   translate so to overlap
draw_diamond                          %   draw another diamond
showpage                              %   display page
```

To get a double diamond, the code was changed to define a procedure to draw one diamond, then **translate** to the correct position to make the diamonds overlap. Here's **draw_diamond**.

```
%!PS
/inch { 72 mul } def              %   define inch procedure
/draw_diamond {                   %   define diamond drawing procedure
  gsave                           %   save graphics state
    0.625 1 scale                 %   shrink five eighths in x
    45 rotate                     %   rotate 45°
    0 0 moveto                    %   set initial point
    4 inch 0 rlineto              %   draw bottom of square
    0 4 inch rlineto              %   draw right side of square
    -4 inch 0 rlineto             %   draw top of square
    closepath                     %   finish the shape
    0.0 setgray fill              %   set black color
  grestore                        %   restore graphics state
} def                             %   end diamond drawing procedure
```

Note the **gsave** and **grestore** pair inside the procedure. These enable you to draw a scaled and rotated square in its own coordinate system without affecting transformations that may have been applied elsewhere. PostScript procedures are discussed in *Procedure Definitions* on pages 209–213 in Chapter 5.

Here's a useful trick to draw equilateral triangles with a minimum of line drawing, using **translate** and **rotate** to do the work for you.

Triangle drawn by translating and rotating coordinate system.

```
%!PS
/inch { 72 mul } def                    % define inch procedure
1.25 inch 2.5 inch translate            % translate to initial point
newpath                                 % start a new path
0 0 moveto                              % set current point
6 inch 0 rlineto                        % add line segment
6 inch 0 translate                      % translate to that point
120 rotate                             % rotate coordinate system
6 inch 0 rlineto                        % add another line segment
closepath                              % close the shape
1.0 inch setlinewidth                   % set fat line width
stroke                                 % paint the path
showpage                               % display page
```

Using **rotate**, you draw the second line in the rotated coordinate system without trigonometry to compute the endpoint of the second line.

Order of Transformations

The order in which you transform the coordinate system is very important. In mathematical jargon, transformations are not commutative. **rotate** followed by **translate** has a different effect than **translate** followed by **rotate**. Let's see an example.

rotate *before* **translate**. *Objects rotated off page.*

```
%!PS
/inch { 72 mul } def                    % define inch procedure
30 rotate                              % rotate about origin
2.25 inch 3.5 inch translate            % move origin
4 inch DrawSquare                       % four-inch square
0.0 0.0 1.0 setrgbcolor                 % set blue color
fill                                   % fill shape
showpage                               % display page
```

The initial **30 rotate** rotated the entire coordinate system about its origin. As a result, the square was rotated partially off the page. That's fine if that's what you want. But let's apply the transformations in the other order.

translate *before* **rotate**.
Objects rotated about their origin.

```
%!PS
/inch { 72 mul } def              %  define inch procedure
2.25 inch 3.5 inch translate      %  move origin
30 rotate                         %  rotate about origin
4 inch DrawSquare                 %  four-inch square
0.0 0.0 1.0 setrgbcolor           %  set blue color
fill                              %  fill shape
showpage                          %  display page
```

Once again, you have rotated the coordinate system about its origin, but this time the origin was translated before the rotation. The effect of this **rotate** after **translate** was that you actually rotated the square about its origin.

The same effect applies to **scale**. Scaling prior to translation clearly affects the distance by which the origin is translated.

scale *before* **translate**.
Translation distance scaled as well as object.

```
%!PS
/inch { 72 mul } def              %  define inch procedure
1 0.5 scale                       %  scale
2.25 inch 3.5 inch translate      %  move origin
4 inch DrawSquare                 %  four-inch square
0.0 0.0 1.0 setrgbcolor           %  set blue color
fill                              %  fill shape
showpage                          %  display page
```

After **scale** took effect, **translate** moved the origin only half the distance as in the previous example. And of course now the "square" has been squashed into a rectangle.

```
%!PS
/inch { 72 mul } def                  %   define inch procedure
2.25 inch 3.5 inch translate          %   move origin
1 0.5 scale                           %   scale
4 inch DrawSquare                     %   four-inch square
0.0 0.0 1.0 setrgbcolor               %   set blue color
fill                                  %   fill shape
showpage                              %   display page
```

translate *before* **scale**. *Translation distance correct and object only scaled.*

This example shows the same "square" as in the preceding example, except **translate** moved the origin to the required position before **scale** took effect.

Shear Transformations

Previous examples showed how to **translate**, **scale**, and **rotate**. The discussion on matrix arithmetic on pages 144–147 in this chapter discussed the CTM (Current Transformation Matrix) and how **translate**, **scale**, and **rotate** change elements in the CTM. But **translate**, **scale**, and **rotate** are really "convenience" operators that do common operations on the CTM. These operators are simplified versions of a more general way to alter the CTM by direct matrix manipulation. When you need to perform operations that can't be done using any of the "convenience" operators, you must use the more general **concat** operator to change the CTM. The most common operation discussed here is known as *shear* or *tilt*. Let's start with a simple example—a four-inch medium gray square a little off to the side of the page. This example uses a **square** procedure defined in the following section of code. You'll see this **square** a lot in this chapter so you might as well have a procedure definition for it.

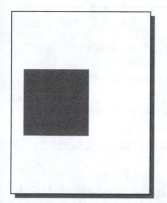

```
%!PS
/inch { 72 mul } def              %   define inch procedure
0.75 inch 3.5 inch translate      %   set origin
4 inch square                     %   draw square
0.5 setgray fill                  %   fill with medium gray
showpage                          %   display page
```

Square in standard preset coordinate system.

The square needs to be drawn off to the side because the tilt operation will shift the top-right corner point of the square over.

Here's the definition for **square**.

→ | side

Top of operand stack when **square** *is called.*

```
%!PS
/inch { 72 mul } def              %   define inch procedure
/square {                         %   stack = side
   0 0 moveto                     %   set current point
   dup 0 rlineto                  %   bottom of square
   dup 0 exch rlineto             %   right side of square
   neg 0 rlineto                  %   top of square
   closepath                      %   finish the shape
} def                             %   define procedure
```

There's no specific PostScript operation to tilt a figure—to transform its coordinates in one dimension only. You might like to see operators called **xtilt** and **ytilt**, so you could write

angle   **xtilt**

to tilt a shape *angle* degrees in the x direction only. But **translate**, **scale**, and **rotate** operate on both x and y dimensions at the same time. To operate on one dimension only, you need to supply a matrix with the correct numbers plugged in, then change the CTM using **concat**. Let's assume there is an **xtilt** operator and draw the same "square," tilted to the right at an angle of 45°. To make this change, add one line to the code.

Square drawn in shear.

```
%!PS
/inch { 72 mul } def              %  define inch procedure
0.5 inch 3.5 inch translate       %  set origin
45 xtilt                          %  want 45° tilt
4 inch square
0.5 setgray fill                  %  fill with medium gray
showpage                          %  display page
```

The work is done by **xtilt** in the code. Here is the procedure defini-tion for **xtilt**.

→ *angle*

Top of operand stack when **xtilt** *is called.*

```
/xtilt {                          %  stack = angle
    [ 1 0                         %  push mark, 1, 0
    4 -1 roll                     %  angle to top of stack
    sin                           %  take sine of angle
    1 0 0 ]                       %  add rest of matrix
    concat                        %  concatenate with CTM
} def                             %  end of definition
```

Recall the form of the CTM from previous discussions.

$$\left[a\ b\ c\ d\ T_x\ T_y \right]$$

Elements of the CTM affect x and y coordinates in this fashion.

$$x_{new} = a \cdot x_{original} + c \cdot y_{original} + T_x$$

$$y_{new} = b \cdot x_{original} + d \cdot y_{original} + T_y$$

The a, c, and T_x elements affect the x coordinate. By changing the c element of the matrix, you can affect the x coordinate without affecting the y coordinate. What you're actually doing here is "scaling" in the x direction only—you're "scaling" x as a function of y. To shear along the x axis, alter the element of the CTM that changes x as a function of y. This means changing the c element.

Changing the *a* element would scale only *x* because you would be changing *x* as a function of *x*. Similarly, to shear along the *y* axis, you alter the element of the CTM that changes *y* as a function of *x*. This means changing the *b* element. Changing the *d* element would scale only *y*. The **concat** operator concatenates (multiplies) its matrix operand with the CTM to produce a new CTM. For example, instead of scaling by using **2 2 scale**, you could do the same job less concisely by **[2 0 0 2 0 0] concat**.

The "square" on page 162 doesn't look quite correct, even though it's four inches wide and four inches high. You can make the "square" look more correct by scaling it in the *y* dimension.

Sheared and scaled square.

```
%!PS
/inch { 72 mul } def              %   define inch procedure
0.5 inch 3.5 inch translate       %   set origin
1 0.75 scale                      %   scale in y only
45 xtilt                          %   shear in x only
4 inch square
0.5 setgray fill                  %   fill with medium gray
showpage                          %   display page
```

You can use tilting to draw a square with a "shadow" behind it. Shadows are a very common effect in illustration.

Notice that the shadow part of the drawing is laid down first. The PostScript opaque paint imaging model demands that the piece of the drawing in front be placed down last. Notice also the convenience of this model. You don't have to compute where the shadow falls in relation to the upright square. You just draw the shadow and then draw the other square right over it.

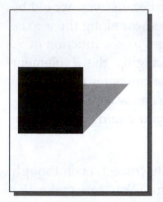

Shadow using shear.

```
%!PS
/inch { 72 mul } def                    % define inch procedure
gsave                                   % push graphics state
  0.5 inch 3.5 inch translate           % set origin
  1 0.75 scale                          % scale in y only
  45 xtilt                              % want 45° tilt
  4 inch square
  0.75 setgray fill                     % fill with lighter gray
grestore                                % pop graphics state
0.5 inch 3.5 inch translate             % set origin
4 inch square
0.0 setgray fill                        % fill with black
showpage                                % display page
```

Just as you can shear in the x axis, you can shear along the y axis. Here's the "square" again, tilted upward at an angle of 45°.

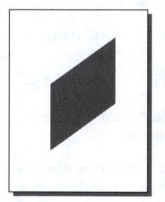

Shear along the y axis.

```
%!PS
/inch { 72 mul } def                    % define inch procedure
2.5 inch 2.5 inch translate             % set origin
45 ytilt                                % want 45° tilt
4 inch square
0.5 setgray fill                        % fill with medium gray
showpage                                % display page
```

And here's the definition for **ytilt**.

```
/ytilt {                                % stack = angle
    [ 1                                 % push mark, 1
    3 -1 roll                           % angle to top of stack
    sin                                 % take sine of angle
    0 1 0 0 ]                           % add rest of matrix
    concat                              % concatenate with CTM
} def                                   % end of definition
```

Parallel Projections

Using the capabilities for shear just described, you can do some more fun things, namely, various forms of *projections*. You use projections when you want to see a three-dimensional view of a solid object on a two-dimensional surface such as a sheet of printer paper or your computer screen. Here is how to use **square** (defined on page 161) to draw a cube.

Basic cube drawn using shear transformations.

```
%!PS
/inch { 72 mul } def                        %   define inch procedure
/side 4 inch def                            %   size of side
/y_shear { 30 sin } def                     %   shear angle for isometric
4.25 inch 1 inch translate                  %   set origin
gsave                                       %   remember graphics state
    [ 1 y_shear 0 1 0 0 ] concat
  side square 0.50 setgray fill             %   medium gray right side
grestore                                    %   restore graphics state
gsave                                       %   remember graphics state
    [ -1 y_shear 0 1 0 0 ] concat
  side square 0.00 setgray fill             %   black left side
grestore                                    %   restore graphics state
gsave                                       %   remember graphics state
  0 side translate
    [ 1 y_shear -1 y_shear 0 0 ] concat
  side square 0.90 setgray fill             %   light gray top
grestore                                    %   restore graphics state
showpage                                    %   display page
```

People who do drafting for a living define various projections to better visualize solid objects. You're probably familiar with isometric projection—a widely used form of projection. The preceding example used shear transformations to draw a simple isometric cube.[†]

[†] Notice the **gsave** and **grestore** in the code. They encapsulate changes to the CTM, as opposed to saving the current path as you saw in many previous examples.

This was the simplest "cube" you could draw. It doesn't look so great—it's too fat in the x direction. In addition to shearing along the y axis, you can improve the appearance of the cube by squashing it a little along the x axis. A reasonable value by which to squash x is in fact scaling by the cosine of the shear angle. The next example revamps this one a little, and the example immediately following adds more of the same.

Basic cube using shear with squashing.

```
%!PS
/inch { 72 mul } def              %   define inch procedure
/side 4 inch def                  %   size of side
/x_squash { 30 cos } def          %   squash the x dimension
/y_shear { 30 sin } def
4.25 inch 1 inch translate        %   set origin
gsave                             %   remember graphics state
    [ x_squash y_shear 0 1 0 0 ] concat
  side square 0.50 setgray fill   %   medium gray right side
grestore                          %   restore graphics state
gsave                             %   remember graphics state
    [ x_squash neg y_shear 0 1 0 0 ] concat
  side square 0.00 setgray fill   %   black left side
grestore                          %   restore graphics state
gsave                             %   remember graphics state
  0 side translate
    [ x_squash y_shear x_squash neg y_shear 0 0 ] concat
  side square 0.90 setgray fill   %   light gray top
grestore                          %   restore graphics state
showpage                          %   display page
```

Now you've squashed the cube so it doesn't look too fat. Having established the appropriate shear transform, you can draw as if you were drawing on a perfectly regular coordinate system. For instance, the second of the two examples on the previous page has a "hole" in the top of the cube—you almost get the effect of a round hole in a square peg, but not quite...

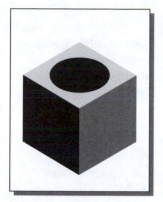

Circles are transformed by shear as well.

```
%!PS
/inch { 72 mul } def                    %   define inch procedure
/side 4 inch def                        %   size of side
/x_squash { 30 cos } def
/y_shear { 30 sin } def
4.25 inch 1 inch translate              %   set origin
gsave                                   %   remember graphics state
    [ x_squash y_shear 0 1 0 0 ] concat
  side square 0.50 setgray fill         %   medium gray right side
grestore                                %   restore graphics state
gsave                                   %   remember graphics state
    [ x_squash neg y_shear 0 1 0 0 ] concat
  side square 0.00 setgray fill         %   black left side
grestore                                %   restore graphics state
gsave                                   %   remember graphics state
  0 side translate
    [ x_squash y_shear x_squash neg y_shear 0 0 ] concat
  side square 0.90 setgray fill         %   light gray top
  side 2 div side 2 div                 %   center of circle
  1.5 inch                              %   radius
  0 360 arc                             %   complete 360° arc
  closepath                             %   finish the shape
  0.0 setgray fill                      %   fill with black
grestore                                %   restore graphics state
showpage                                %   display page
```

Isometric projections are usually done using an angle of 30°. But you can choose any angle you like. By choosing a different angle, you alter the viewpoint from which you look at the object. Let's change the angle to 10° so you're looking at the object from a much flatter viewpoint.

Flatter shear angle to change viewpoint.

```
%!PS
/inch { 72 mul } def              % define inch procedure
/side 4 inch def                  % size of side
/x_squash { 10 cos } def          % different tilt angle
/y_shear { 10 sin } def           % different tilt angle
4.25 inch 1 inch translate        % set origin
gsave                             % remember graphics state
    [ x_squash y_shear 0 1 0 0 ] concat
  side square 0.50 setgray fill   % medium gray right side
grestore                          % restore graphics state
gsave                             % remember graphics state
    [ x_squash neg y_shear 0 1 0 0 ] concat
  side square 0.00 setgray fill   % black left side
grestore                          % restore graphics state
gsave                             % remember graphics state
  0 side translate
    [ x_squash y_shear x_squash neg y_shear 0 0 ] concat
  side square 0.90 setgray fill       % light gray top
  side 2 div side 2 div 1.5 inch 0 360 arc
  closepath
  0.0 setgray fill
grestore                          % restore graphics state
showpage                          % display page
```

Now that you have your basic shear angle factors defined, you can use simple PostScript transformations to show the object in different orientations.

Preceding examples were "bird's eye" views of the cube—you see the shape looking from above. Now you get the "worm's eye" viewpoint—looking at the shape from slightly underneath.

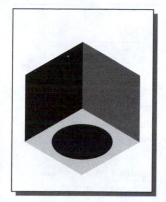

Flipped shear example.

```
%!PS
/inch { 72 mul } def                    %   define inch procedure
/side 4 inch def                        %   size of side
/x_squash { 30 cos } def
/y_shear { 30 sin } def
4.25 inch 9 inch translate              %   translate for upside down
1 -1 scale                              %   flip entire picture
gsave                                   %   remember graphics state
    [ x_squash y_shear 0 1 0 0 ] concat
  side square 0.50 setgray fill         %   medium gray right side
grestore                                %   restore graphics state
gsave                                   %   remember graphics state
    [ x_squash neg y_shear 0 1 0 0 ] concat
  side square 0.00 setgray fill         %   black left side
grestore                                %   restore graphics state
gsave                                   %   remember graphics state
  0 side translate
    [ x_squash y_shear x_squash neg y_shear 0 0 ] concat
  side square 0.90 setgray fill         %   light gray top
  side 2 div side 2 div 1.5 inch 0 360 arc
  closepath                             %   finish the shape
  0.0 setgray fill
grestore                                %   restore graphics state
showpage                                %   display page
```

In the same way, you can use standard PostScript transformation to swivel the object around for a different view, using **rotate**. The example at the top of page 170 illustrates a rotation of the coordinate system prior to the other transformations.

Isometric projection is just one type of projection in a large class of projections belonging to what are called *axonometric projections*. Such projections are also called *parallel projections*, because parallel lines remain parallel after transformation. These projections are also sometimes called *infinite perspective projections*, because a perspective projection, with its "vanishing point" at infinity, is the same as a parallel projection.

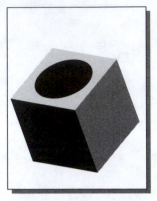

Shear works with rotation also.

```
%!PS
/inch { 72 mul } def                      % define inch procedure
/side 4 inch def                          % size of side
/x_squash { 30 cos } def
/y_shear { 30 sin } def
5.5 inch 1 inch translate                 % set origin
20 rotate                                 % swivel it around
gsave                                     % remember graphics state
    [ x_squash y_shear 0 1 0 0 ] concat
  side square 0.50 setgray fill           % medium gray right side
grestore                                  % restore graphics state
gsave                                     % remember graphics state
    [ x_squash neg y_shear 0 1 0 0 ] concat
  side square 0.00 setgray fill           % black left side
grestore                                  % restore graphics state
gsave                                     % remember graphics state
  0 side translate
    [ x_squash y_shear x_squash neg y_shear 0 0 ] concat
  side square 0.90 setgray fill           % light gray top
  side 2 div side 2 div 1.5 inch 0 360 arc
  closepath                               % finish the shape
  0.0 setgray fill
grestore                                  % restore graphics state
showpage                                  % display page
```

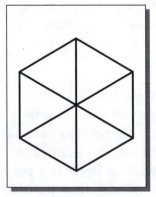

Wireframe cube to create eyestrain.

Straight isometric projection suffers when lines at the "back" of an object line up with lines at the "front" of an object, creating difficulty separating the lines from one another. The classic example of this is in a wire frame view of a cube, where the lines at the "back" are not hidden.

To overcome some visual limitations of straight isometric projection, you can use two other useful projections—namely, *dimetric projection* and *trimetric projection*. Where isometric uses one angle only (30°) for the projection, dimetric uses two different angles for different sides of the picture, and trimetric projection uses three different angles for different sides of the picture.

Here is our cube drawn using dimetric projection. To get dimetric projection you need to define two sets of angles—one set for the left side of the cube and the other set for the right side.

Cube imaged using dimetric projection.

```
%!PS
/inch { 72 mul } def                            %   define inch procedure
/side 4 inch def                                %   size of side
/left_y_shear { 10 sin } def
/left_x_squash { 10 cos } def
/right_y_shear { 25 sin } def
/right_x_squash { 25 cos } def
4.25 inch 2 inch translate                      %   set origin
                                                %   right side of cube
gsave                                           %   remember graphics state
    [ right_x_squash right_y_shear 0 1 0 0 ] concat
  side square 0.50 setgray fill                 %   medium gray right side
grestore                                        %   restore graphics state
                                                %   left side of cube
gsave                                           %   remember graphics state
    [ left_x_squash neg left_y_shear 0 1 0 0 ] concat
  side square 0.00 setgray fill                 %   black left side
grestore                                        %   restore graphics state
0 side translate
                                                %   top of cube
gsave                                           %   remember graphics state
  [ right_x_squash  right_y_shear
       left_x_squash neg left_y_shear 0 0 ] concat
  side square 0.90 setgray fill                 %   light gray top
grestore                                        %   restore graphics state
showpage                                        %   display page
```

Once more, you need to play around with the "squash" factors to achieve pleasing results.

Transformations Applied to Matrix

Up to now, examples of **translate**, **scale**, and **rotate** have operated on the CTM right away. You can use variant forms of the transformation operators where the last operand is a *matrix*.

T_x T_y *matrix*   `translate`
S_x S_y *matrix*   `scale`
angle   *matrix*   `rotate`

These variants of the transformation operators don't affect the CTM directly. Instead, the *matrix* operand is concatenated with the results of the transformation and the resultant matrix is pushed back onto the operand stack. Where does the *matrix* come from and what does it look like? You push an *identity matrix* onto the operand stack with the **matrix** operator. An identity matrix has **1**s on the principal diagonal, and **0**s elsewhere. You saw **matrix** used in the example of user paths on page 87 in Chapter 2 to obtain a scale matrix. A PostScript identity matrix looks like [1 0 0 1 0 0].

Then the results of applying a transformation operation on a matrix operand looks as in the next three diagrams.

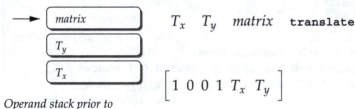

T_x T_y *matrix*   `translate`

$$\begin{bmatrix} 1 & 0 & 0 & 1 & T_x & T_y \end{bmatrix}$$

Operand stack prior to **translate**.

Results of applying **translate** *to a matrix operand.*

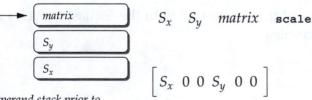

S_x S_y *matrix*   `scale`

$$\begin{bmatrix} S_x & 0 & 0 & S_y & 0 & 0 \end{bmatrix}$$

Operand stack prior to **scale**.

Results of applying **scale** *to a matrix operand.*

angle   *matrix*   `rotate`

$$\Big[\cos angle \quad \sin angle \quad -\sin angle \quad \cos angle \quad 0 \quad 0 \Big]$$

*Results of applying **rotate** to a matrix operand.*

Operand stack prior to **rotate**.

Accurate Positioning

You read at the start of this chapter that user space is an ideal, everywhere-dense coordinate system on an infinite plane. However, device space brings you into direct contact with the boring reality of a space where pixels can be positioned only at discrete intervals. On high resolution devices, such as typesetters with resolutions of up to 5000 dots per inch, you don't notice problems in positioning because the resolution of the device is better than the spatial resolution of your eyes. But on lower resolution devices,[†] problems arise in the accuracy of positioning points and in variations in the thickness of lines.

So far you've seen transformations such as **translate**, **scale**, and **rotate** for transforming user space coordinates to device space, using the CTM as the go-between. Related tools are **transform** and **itransform**—PostScript facilities to transform points between user space coordinates and device space coordinates. These operations were provided to solve a problem that arises on low resolution devices. This problem manifests itself when you draw a series of regularly spaced lines, like a grid. You frequently see lines of different thicknesses. This effect comes about because of the PostScript rules for deciding which pixels to paint.

---

† Less than 600 dots per inch is considered "low resolution" in the typesetting business.

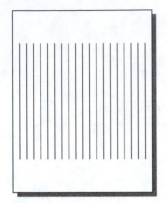

Unequal width lines because of positioning.

```
%!PS
/inch { 72 mul } def              % define inch procedure
1 1 20 {
    8.5 inch 20 div mul           % x coordinate
    dup                           % save for drawing line
    1 inch                        % y coordinate
    moveto                        % set current point
    9 inch lineto                 % add line segment
    0.24 setlinewidth             % one pixel line at 300 dpi
} for
stroke                            % paint the path
showpage                          % display page
```

On high resolution devices such as imagesetters, this effect is not as important because the pixels are so small that additional pixels are imperceptible. But on low resolution devices such as laser printers this effect is distinctive, and on even lower resolution devices like display screens, the effect is significant. The effect shows up in particular when you have regularly spaced lines like the picture. The fact that some lines are one unit wide and some are two units wide really jumps out at you. Another problem crops up when you draw lines at shallow angles—you get a "twisted rope" effect.

This next picture shows a path in user space. For this example you have to imagine this path is exactly one pixel wide in *device space*.

One pixel line in user space.

```
%!PS
/inch { 72 mul } def              % define inch procedure
4.25 inch 2 inch moveto           % set current point
0 4.5 inch rlineto                % add line segment
X setlinewidth                    % one pixel line width
stroke                            % paint the path
showpage                          % display page
```

x **setlinewidth** in the example is an instruction to set the line width to a value such that the line is precisely one device pixel wide. The next picture shows the same line superimposed on a grid of device pixels. The path just happens to lie precisely down the center of a column of pixels. The area painted by the path extends to the edge of the pixel column but doesn't overlap in any way. The line drawn is exactly one device pixel wide.

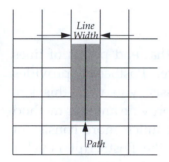

```
%!PS
/inch { 72 mul } def                    %    define inch procedure
4.25 inch 2 inch moveto                 %    set current point
0 4.5 inch rlineto                      %    add line segment
x setlinewidth                          %    one pixel line width
stroke                                  %    paint the path
showpage                                %    display page
```

One-pixel line relative to device space.

What happens if the center of the path doesn't lie precisely down the center of the pixel column but is off to one side? What happens is that the area painted by the path touches two lines of pixels, so you get a two-pixel-wide line instead of the one-pixel-wide line you expected.

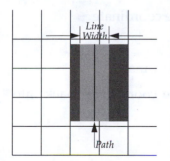

```
%!PS
/inch { 72 mul } def                    %    define inch procedure
4.25 inch 2 inch moveto                 %    set current point
0 4.5 inch rlineto                      %    add line segment
x setlinewidth                          %    one pixel line width
stroke                                  %    paint the path
showpage                                %    display page
```

Two-pixel line in device space because of path position.

The light gray illustrates the path you asked for. The dark gray shows the pixels that get painted. The same thing happens when the center of the path lies precisely on the boundary between two lines of pixels. Once again, the area painted by the path touches two lines of pixels and you end up with a two-pixel-wide line.

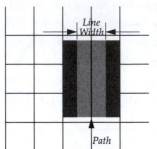

```
%!PS
/inch { 72 mul } def              %  define inch procedure
4.25 inch 2 inch moveto           %  set current point
0 4.5 inch rlineto                %  add line segment
x setlinewidth                    %  one pixel line width
stroke                            %  paint the path
showpage                          %  display page
```

Two-pixel line in device space—path on pixel boundary.

To solve this problem, you must ensure that end points of lines are uniformly adjusted in device space. PostScript provides **transform** and **itransform** operators to assist you with this job. PostScript Level 2 and Display PostScript provide another method called *stroke adjustment* to do the job in a much more consistent and convenient manner. First you'll see the PostScript Level 1 approach using **transform** and **itransform**.

There are as many approaches to stroke adjustment as there are application programmers writing software and authors writing books. Adjusting endpoints of lines goes like the following:

❏ use **transform** to convert user space coordinates to device space coordinates

❏ subtract ¼ pixel from each device space coordinate

❏ round to the nearest whole device pixel

❏ add ¼ pixel to the new device space coordinate

❏ use **itransform** to convert device space coordinates back into user space coordinates

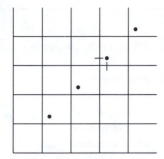

Pixel locations adjusted.

The result is to adjust every point to lie ¼ pixel from the lower left of the pixel boundary. This process sounds complicated, but it's actually simple. Here's how you'd define two procedures called **m** and **l** to do **moveto** and **lineto** using the new method.

```
%!PS
/m {                                   %    stack = x, y
    transform                          %    user space to device space
    0.25 sub round 0.25 add exch %    y to ¼ pixel point
    0.25 sub round 0.25 add exch %    x to ¼ pixel point
    itransform                         %    device space back to user space
    moveto                             %    set current point
} def
/l {                                   %    stack = x, y
    transform                          %    user space to device space
    0.25 sub round 0.25 add exch %    y to ¼ pixel point
    0.25 sub round 0.25 add exch %    x to ¼ pixel point
    itransform                         %    device space back to user space
    lineto                             %    add line segment
} def
```

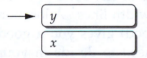

Operand stack prior to **transform**.

transform expects an *x*, *y* user space coordinate pair on the stack. **transform** replaces the user space coordinate pair with the corresponding coordinates in device space. For instance, our Apple LaserWriter IIg reports that user space point (1 inch, 1 inch) is actually (–975.0, 1350.5) in device space coordinates. **itransform** performs the inverse process, replacing device space coordinates with their corresponding user space coordinates.

You can define similar procedures for **curveto**, and also for **rmoveto**, **rlineto**, and **rcurveto**. Note for **curveto** and **rcurveto** you need to adjust only the end points. You don't normally need to adjust the intermediate control points of curves.

Now here's your earlier grid of lines example using the procedures you just defined.

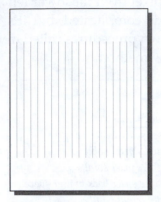

Equal width lines because of stroke adjustment.

```
%!PS
/inch { 72 mul } def                    % define inch procedure
1 1 20 {
    8.5 inch 20 div mul                 % x coordinate
    dup                                 % save for drawing line
    1 inch                              % y coordinate
    m                                   % set current point
    9 inch l                            % add line segment
    0.24 setlinewidth                   % one pixel line at 300 dpi
} for
stroke                                  % paint the path
showpage                                % display page
```

Why position points at ¼-pixel boundaries? The answer is simple but subtle. If you adjust endpoints to pixel boundaries, all lines you draw will be of even width, because you'll guarantee that a path will touch at least one pixel on either side of it. On the other hand, if you adjust endpoints to the middle of pixels, all lines you draw will be of odd width. You'll guarantee that a path would touch the pixel midpoint you choose, plus at least one pixel on either side of it, so you'll always get odd width lines. A location ¼-pixel in (or ¾-pixel would be just as good) gives you a good mix of even and odd line widths. You need to decide in your application whether to go for pixel boundaries, pixel middles, or ¼-pixel locations.

PostScript Level 2 and Display PostScript added automatic stroke adjustment. Use **setstrokeadjust** to turn stroke adjustment on or off. Display PostScript has stroke adjustment on by default, so there's no need to turn it off unless you're doing something special, such as a demonstration of why you need stroke adjustment. To set stroke adjustment, use

Boolean `setstrokeadjust`

where **true** turns stroke adjustment on and **false** turns stroke adjustment off. Here's the preceding example using stroke adjust:

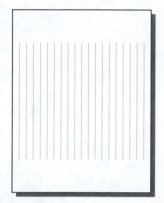

Equal width lines because of stroke adjustment.

```
%!PS
/inch { 72 mul } def              %   define inch procedure
true setstrokeadjust              %   turn on stroke adjustment
1 1 20 {
    8.5 inch 20 div mul           %   x coordinate
    dup                           %   save for drawing line
    1 inch                        %   y coordinate
    moveto                        %   set current point
    9 inch lineto                 %   add line segment
    0.24 setlinewidth             %   one pixel line at 300 dpi
} for
stroke                            %   paint the path
showpage                          %   display page
```

This time, you just use **setstrokeadjust** and the PostScript interpreter takes care of accurately aligning coordinates for you.

5 PostScript Language

If any one anything lacks
He'll find it all ready in **stacks**,
   If he'll only look in
     on the resident Djinn
Number seventy, Simmery Axe.

Gilbert and Sullivan—*The Sorcerer*

The Tower of Hanoi is often used as an analogy for a stack.

So far you've learned PostScript the way people learn natural languages. You learn enough words to get by. Then you learn more complicated phrases and sentences—just enough to communicate with others. Inherent in these phrases is the structure and vocabulary of the language. But you don't learn the nuts and bolts explicitly until you study the language. Then you learn about parts you'd taken for granted until now.

Earlier chapters introduced basic graphics and text operators to get you interested in PostScript, to show what you can accomplish, and to meet basic needs. You've learned the basics, you have the feel of the language, and you're communicating in PostScript. Now it's time for some nuts and bolts. The first three chapters, *Introducing PostScript*, *Paths and Painting*, and *Text*, described the PostScript imaging model—the ideas of paths and opaque paint. This chapter is a grab bag of information about the PostScript language. You'll learn about PostScript stacks, dictionaries, and procedures, to mention a few.

Language, to a large extent, shapes the speaker's thinking habits. Programming languages are no different in this regard. If your programming background is C or Pascal, try to put aside ingrained habits and not write "PostScript that looks like Pascal" (or C, or whatever). A friend, Dan Sears, made this comment: "Nothing is more painful to read than C written with a local accent." So, use the stack to its full advantage as a temporary storage area—get used to drawing mayhem sketches of the stack as you move data on and off it. Use the dictionary mechanism described in this chapter. Use **save** and **restore** to manage memory. Use **forall** as an efficient means to deal with aggregates. If you're an application programmer new to PostScript, spend time learning its basic concepts—stacks and dictionaries. Study other PostScript programs and try to determine what makes them "good" (or "bad" for that matter) and *experiment*.

PostScript differs from other popular programming languages in two very important ways. First, PostScript is *interpreted*. What does this mean? An interpreted language reads and executes its input stream "on the fly"—there's no "compile" or "link" or "load" phase as in languages such as C or FORTRAN. Interpreted languages can be extremely flexible. You can dynamically change the behavior of a program while it's executing.

PS ♥ { Honk! } if

PostScript is a postfix language.

The other major difference between PostScript and popular programming languages such as C and FORTRAN is that PostScript is a *postfix* language. What does this mean? Consider an expression in C or FORTRAN to compute the Euclidean distance between two points, a and b. The formula is $\sqrt{a^2 + b^2}$. In C or FORTRAN the expression would look something like **sqrt(a*a+b*b)**. The notation used in languages such as C or FORTRAN is known as *infix* notation, meaning operators such as **+** (add) and ***** (multiply) are in between their operands.[†] Another notation you could use is known as *prefix*, or *Polish* notation. Prefix notation has some analog with English and Romance languages where you put the verb first in a sentence. In Romance languages you say "*fetch* the groceries." Using prefix notation you'd write $\sqrt{a^2 + b^2}$ as **sqrt + * a a * b b**.

---

† When you use functions such as **sqrt** you get a little functional notation as well, but that doesn't affect the basic ideas discussed here.

PostScript is *postfix* or *reverse Polish* notation—the opposite of prefix or Polish notation. PostScript as a language is more like Japanese where verbs appear at the end of sentences. Anybody who uses a Hewlett-Packard™ calculator is already familiar with reverse Polish notation. In PostScript you write $\sqrt{a^2 + b^2}$ as

```
a a mul b b mul add sqrt
```

You'll notice immediately that PostScript spells out its operators as **add** and **mul** instead of using symbols like + and *.

Stacks

Regardless of notation, any programming system must store intermediate results during calculations. Most modern programming languages store intermediate results using an artifact known as a *stack*. A stack is a data structure plus a set of rules governing the way data can be added to or removed from that structure. An analogy for stacks is the disks on the Tower of Hanoi on page 181. In the Tower of Hanoi, you can add disks to the top of the tower only, and you can remove disks from the top of the tower only. To get at lower disks you must remove disks from the top of the tower. PostScript stacks operate in much the same manner as the tower; you can add data to the top of the stack only, and you can remove data from the top of the stack only. Unlike the tower, though, PostScript provides "convenience" operators to access elements lower down the stack without removing elements from the top.

Programming languages like C or FORTRAN generally hide the stack machinery from you. Interpreted languages like PostScript (and reverse Polish notation calculators) provide access and control of the stack. Let's see the stack in action as you code PostScript to compute the Euclidean distance between two points—$d = \sqrt{x^2 + y^2}$. Or, in PostScript,

```
x x mul y y mul add sqrt
```

Here's the state of the stack as the PostScript interpreter scans and processes the first three tokens. The tokens are listed above the stack in the illustrations. The stack pictures indicate the state of the stack after the token is processed, and the arrow points to the top of the stack in each case.

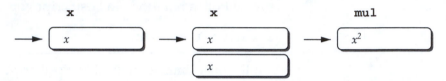

After **x x mul**, the top element of the stack contains x^2. Continuing with the next three tokens to process y, the sequence looks like

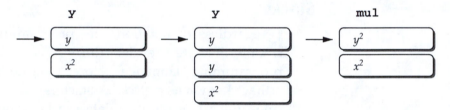

Now the top two elements of the stack contain x^2 and y^2. Finally, the PostScript interpreter processes **add** and **sqrt** to leave the stack looking like

You see from the above sequences of stack manipulation that the stack is a very efficient data structure. You use few stack elements, even though you apparently performed numerous operations.

This short introduction to stacks showed operands being pushed onto a stack and removed from a stack. The stack in question in the PostScript interpreter is the operand stack. The execution environment of a PostScript program in fact includes four stacks:

❑ *operand stack*—the stack you'll read most about in this chapter. The operand stack is used as a storage area by nearly all PostScript operators.

❏ *dictionary stack*—used primarily to establish *naming contexts* where objects can be defined by name and found automatically by name-lookup mechanisms. Dictionaries are described in detail on pages 198–208 of this chapter.

❏ *graphics state stack*—saves and restores the current graphics state. You've already seen the flavor of the graphics state stack in *Graphics States and the Graphics State Stack* on page 42 in Chapter 1.

❏ *execution stack*—executable procedures are placed on the execution stack at the time they are referenced. The interpreter runs whatever is on top of the execution stack. In general, execution of a PostScript program happens invisibly. You hardly ever need to know about the execution stack except when you are writing some wild and crazy error handling routines. If you're digging that deep into the PostScript language you certainly don't need our help.

PostScript Operand Stack

Without going into precise details of the format of data on the operand stack, suffice it to say that the operand stack is composed of a set of heterogeneous elements. One rule relative to accessing data elements is that data must always be added to the top of the stack. When you place a value on the stack, you *push* the value onto the stack, in the jargon of computer programming.

```
→  10
```

Starting with an empty stack, suppose the PostScript input stream contains just the number **10**. The number appears in a cell of the stack as shown. The arrow indicates the current top of the stack.

```
→  (Thailand)
   10
```

Suppose the next thing in the input stream is the string **(Thailand)**. The original top element of the stack (the value **10**) was *pushed* down to make room for a new top element—the string **(Thailand)**.

You can remove data only from the top of the stack. You *pop* the stack to remove an element from its top. You rarely need to explicitly pop the stack. PostScript operators usually pop the stack implicitly as part of the operation. For example, **moveto** expects to find two numbers, (x, y) coordinates, on the stack. **moveto** removes the two elements from the stack and sets the current point to the indicated position.

PostScript operators generally expect to find their operands on the operand stack. Operators pop elements from the stack, perform the indicated operation, and push any results back onto the stack. The stack grows and shrinks as data is pushed and popped. For example, **mul** (multiply) requires two operands. **mul** takes the top two elements off the stack, multiplies them, and pushes the result back onto the stack.

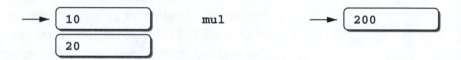

You use the operand stack to pass data values to PostScript operators and to user-defined procedures. You will read more about procedures later in this chapter.

Types of Data and Basic Syntax

Now you come to a very important area of PostScript: *data types*. The examples above showed the stack with numbers, strings, and such being pushed and popped. One of the key strengths of PostScript is that an element of the stack can be any data type. If your input stream were to look like this, the stack would contain the elements shown on the left.

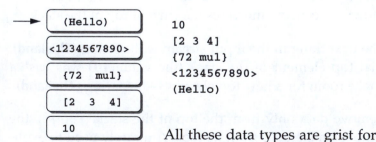

```
10                   %   number object
[2 3 4]              %   array object
{72 mul}             %   executable array object
<1234567890>         %   hexadecimal string
(Hello)              %   character string
```

All these data types are grist for the mill—or at least grist for the stack. Notice that the first objects encountered in the input stream are lower on the stack than later objects. This is because of the *last-in-first-out* nature of stacks. You can divide the types of data that can be pushed onto the stack into two broad classes—*simple data objects* and *composite data objects*. You need to understand the differences between the two classes of objects because their behavior differs in certain operations.

Simple Data Types

Simple data objects include familiar numbers such as integer, real, and Boolean. The numbers **7821** and **–1** are integers. The numbers **2.71828** and **–3.1415926** are real values. Real values can be written in exponential notation, as in **2.99793e10**. You represent based numbers by prefixing the number with a radix and a **#** sign. For example, **8#377** is the octal representation for the decimal number 255, and **16#3e8** is the hexadecimal representation for decimal 1000. The names **true** and **false** are Boolean values. Other kinds of simple data types include **mark** objects.

When you push a simple object such as an integer value on the operand stack, you can imagine for all intents and purposes the stack element contains the actual value. If your input stream contains the following values, the stack contains the values shown.

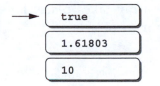

10	%	*integer value*
1.61803	%	*real value*
true	%	*Boolean value*

Composite Data Types

Composite objects include strings, arrays, dictionaries, and procedures, among many other data types. A string object is a series of characters enclosed in (and) delimiters. For example, **(Mozzarella)** is a string object. Another form of string is a hexadecimal string, which is written between < and > delimiters, so that **<0123456789ABCDEF>** gives you eight characters containing sixteen hexadecimal quartets.

Character strings delimited by (and) characters need a means to place the (and) characters themselves within the string, among many other kinds of characters. The cleanest way to include (and) characters within strings is to escape them using the \ character. So the construct (\(\)) is actually a character string containing the characters (). Using the backslash escape sequence, you can place non-printing characters into character strings. The sequence \nnn introduces a character whose code is the octal (base eight) number represented by nnn in the ASCII character set. You could write (\041) instead of writing (!), for instance. You can get the space character into a string by writing (\040) and so on.

PostScript *dictionaries* are a very powerful form of composite object. A dictionary is a collection of *key-value* pairs—a table of keys[†] and values associated with those keys. You'll read about them in *Dictionaries* on pages 193–208 in this chapter.

PostScript *arrays* come in two slightly different flavors. Which flavor you get depends on the syntax you use to construct the array. Constructing an array whose elements are enclosed within [and] signs gets you a regular array of data elements. Constructing an array whose elements are enclosed within { and } signs gets you an *executable array*. The difference between them is the time at which interpretation of objects within the array takes place. For example, the following code shows regular array objects.

Arrays on operand stack.

```
[ 8 0 0 8 ]                            %   four-element array
[ 2 2 mul    3 3 mul    4 4 mul ]      %   three-element array
[ 1 inch    2 inch    3 inch ]         %   three-element array
```

The next examples show the behavior of the PostScript interpreter while it's reading an array. The values stored in the array are simple numbers but can be the results of computations performed (interpreted) while the array is being scanned. Here is the same example coded two different ways, both ways showing that arrays can be filled with the results of computations.

---

† Keys are usually literal names, but they can in fact be any kind of PostScript object.

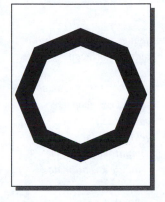

```
%!PS
/inch { 72 mul } def                        %   define inch procedure
/radius 3.5 inch def                         %   radius of octagon
/coordinates [                               %   define coordinates array
     [  45 cos radius mul    45 sin radius mul ]
     [  90 cos radius mul    90 sin radius mul ]
     [ 135 cos radius mul   135 sin radius mul ]
     [ 180 cos radius mul   180 sin radius mul ]
     [ 225 cos radius mul   225 sin radius mul ]
     [ 270 cos radius mul   270 sin radius mul ]
     [ 315 cos radius mul   315 sin radius mul ]
     [ 360 cos radius mul   360 sin radius mul ]
] def                                        %   end of coordinates definition
4.25 inch 5.5 inch translate                 %   origin to center of page
coordinates 0 get aload pop moveto           %   set current point
coordinates 1 get aload pop lineto           %   add line segments
coordinates 2 get aload pop lineto
coordinates 3 get aload pop lineto
coordinates 4 get aload pop lineto
coordinates 5 get aload pop lineto
coordinates 6 get aload pop lineto
coordinates 7 get aload pop lineto
closepath                                    %   finish shape
1 inch setlinewidth                          %   fat line width
stroke                                       %   paint outline
showpage                                     %   display page
```

The inner arrays of coordinates contain the results of multiplications and trigonometric functions. The definition of the array of coordinates is followed by code to extract the coordinates and draw the octagonal shape. The next example defines the array of coordinates in a different fashion.

```
%!PS
/inch { 72 mul } def                          % define inch procedure
/radius 3.5 inch def                          % radius of octagon
/angle 360 8 div def
/coordinates [                                % define coordinates array
    1 1 8 {                                    % start for loop
        [                                      % push mark object
            exch                               % get loop variable
            angle mul dup                      % compute correct angle
            cos radius mul                     % compute x coordinate
            exch                               % swap for y coordinate
            sin radius mul                     % compute y coordinate
        ]
    } for                                      % end for loop
] def                                          % end of coordinates array
4.25 inch 5.5 inch translate                  % origin to center of page
coordinates 0 get aloaad pop moveto           % set current point
coordinates 1 get aloaad pop lineto           % add line segments
coordinates 2 get aloaad pop lineto
coordinates 3 get aloaad pop lineto
coordinates 4 get aloaad pop lineto
coordinates 5 get aloaad pop lineto
coordinates 6 get aloaad pop lineto
coordinates 7 get aloaad pop lineto
closepath                                      % finish shape
1 inch setlinewidth                            % fat line width
stroke                                         % paint outline
showpage                                       % display page
```

This example illustrates that the computation filling the array can be a PostScript procedure—a **for** loop in this case. Notice especially the sequence

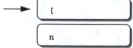

*Operand stack before **exch**.*

```
[
  exch
```

The starting bracket for an array is a **mark** object—a fully fledged PostScript object so you can perform stack operations on it. Here, the mark is exchanged with the loop variable *n*.

However, there's a major snag in this approach. The snag is not immediately obvious. The snag in this process is that every time you call on the **coordinates** procedure, a new array is allocated in PostScript virtual memory, where it remains even after its value is used. Virtual memory is covered in the next subsection.

You've seen many examples of executable arrays in the form of { **72 mul** } in definitions of **inch**. Executable arrays are also known as PostScript *procedures*. You can read more about executable arrays in *Procedure Definitions* on page 209 in this chapter. For now, the main difference between arrays and executable arrays is that the contents of an executable array are not interpreted (executed) while they're being scanned.

Composite Objects and Virtual Memory

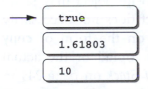

Simple objects on operand stack.

When simple objects are pushed on the operand stack, think of the actual value of the object appearing on the stack. The picture shows the state of the operand stack after three simple values have been read in. However, when you push a composite object onto the stack, what actually gets pushed is not the object itself, but a reference to the object. "But," you ask, "if the operand stack contains only references to composite objects, where are the actual values of the objects?" Good thing you asked.

Values of composite objects (as well as many other kinds of objects) are allocated from a large amorphous mass of memory known as *virtual memory*—called VM for short. When a composite object is created, memory is allocated in VM and a reference to that memory is pushed onto the stack. The actual value of the object is stored in virtual memory. In standard programming terms, you could say that a *pointer* to the object gets pushed onto the stack. The pointer-to-object analogy is all right for a while, but don't get caught up in pointer notions, because the PostScript interpreter isn't required to actually work that way. If your input stream contains the composite objects below, the stack contains references to the values of each object in VM as shown in the next picture.

```
(Mozzarella)                          %   string object
<0123456789ABCDEF>                    %   hex string object
[ 12 0 0 12 0 0 ]                     %   array object
```

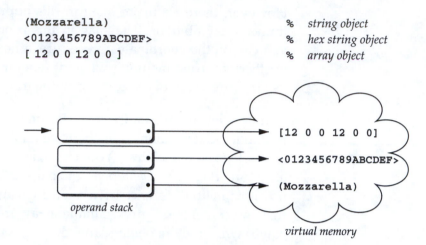

Composite objects on operand stack.

One reason you must know about composite objects being stored in VM is that references to the same composite object may share the actual data. Copying a composite object does not necessarily copy the value of the object. Depending on the form of **copy** operation you use, either the reference is copied or the actual value is copied. See *Copy Top n Elements of Stack* on page 244 in this chapter for a more detailed discussion of this subject.

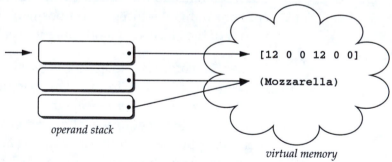

Duplicate composite objects on operand stack.

Virtual memory complicates the lives of PostScript programmers and applications developers. The PostScript interpreter implicitly allocates virtual memory when composite objects appear in the input stream. Many operators (such as **array** or **dict**) also implicitly allocate composite objects in VM. The PostScript interpreter allocates virtual memory "behind your back," but you, as a

PostScript programmer, are responsible for recycling virtual memory—giving memory back to the interpreter for reuse. If you ignore issues of VM, your PostScript programs may run out of VM, in which case the PostScript interpreter raises a **VMerror**. For more information on managing memory in PostScript programs see *Virtual Memory* on pages 224–229 in this chapter.

Dictionaries

At the heart of the PostScript language is the support for dictionaries. A PostScript dictionary is a composite object and is somewhat like the language dictionaries you're used to in everyday life. Suppose you want to know what **inch** means. You look it up in your favorite dictionary. The word **inch** is the *key* you use to locate definitions in the dictionary. Your favorite dictionary probably tells you an inch is three barleycorns or something silly like "an inch is $1/36$ of a yard," so you look up **yard**, and of course it'll tell you a yard is 36 inches.

PostScript uses the same scheme as regular dictionaries. The key is what you give to the PostScript interpreter when you want to find something in a dictionary. Associated with each key is its meaning, called the *value* in the PostScript language. PostScript dictionaries are *associative* lookup tables. PostScript dictionaries are said to contain *key-value pairs*. Keys in a PostScript dictionary are the names of objects. Values in the dictionary are the values of objects—numbers, strings, arrays, procedures. The value of a composite object in a dictionary is actually a reference to the object, just as it is when you create a composite object on the stack. Unlike regular dictionaries, keys and definitions in a PostScript dictionary have to lead to something sensible; otherwise, you get errors from the PostScript interpreter.

Just as the basic PostScript language uses a stack for operands, the dictionary mechanism uses a stack for dictionaries. You'll get to the dictionary stack a little later. For now, let's investigate how you can create dictionaries and operate on their keys and values.

Executable Names and Literal Names

To get a good understanding of dictionaries, you need to be aware that PostScript defines two different types of names. One kind of name is known as a *literal name*. Literal names begin with the / character. A name beginning with / indicates this name is the key used to define or look things up in a dictionary. You've already seen the ubiquitous **/inch** procedure. When you see **/inch**, you know this is a literal name that will have some value associated with it. You've also seen examples of **findfont** or **selectfont** where the parameter to the operator was a literal name—the name of the font such as **/Palatino-Roman** or **/Optima**.

The other kind of PostScript name is an *executable name*. Executable names are everything else except numbers. You can think of numbers as a special case of an executable name—the value of 10, for example, is the number itself. Executable names are just names in the token stream. When you see the name **inch** on its own, without a preceding /, you know this is an executable name. When the PostScript interpreter sees an executable, it searches for that name in the dictionaries on the dictionary stack. When the executable name is found somewhere in the dictionary stack, the value associated with that name is executed. What "executed" means depends on the value. Literal values—numbers, arrays, strings—are pushed on the stack. If the name is an operator or a procedure, the operator or procedure is executed if possible. For more information about the operation of the dictionary stack, see *How the Dictionary Stack Works* starting on page 200 in this chapter.

Creating a Dictionary

What's involved in making your own dictionaries? You create a dictionary using **dict**. When you create a dictionary you supply one piece of information—the maximum number of objects you will put into this dictionary. Here's a PostScript code fragment to create a dictionary.

```
%!PS
10 dict                                        %    create ten-element dictionary
```

*Operand stack after a **dict** instruction.*

This code fragment creates a dictionary object with enough room for ten key-value pairs. The dictionary object is created in VM, with a reference to the dictionary on the operand stack. In this picture, pretend, for the sake of argument, that the dictionary is actually on the operand stack.

Once you have created a dictionary, what can you do with it? You put things into it using **put**. You get things out of it using **get**. You can also place this dictionary on the dictionary stack using **begin**. For now, let's look at **put** and **get**.

Storing and Retrieving Entries in Dictionaries

The preceding example created a ten-entry dictionary. Let's see how to define entries in this dictionary. You place key-value pairs into a dictionary using **put**. Taking a merciful break from **/inch** we'll define a couple of other names in this dictionary, such as **/pi**.

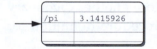

*Dictionary on operand stack after defining **pi**.*

```
%!PS
10 dict                              %    create ten-element dictionary
dup                                  %    duplicate dictionary for later use
/pi 3.1415926 put                    %    put value of π  into it
```

Why the **dup**? **put** removes the object into which values are being put. **dup** is a PostScript operator to duplicate the top element of the stack. Without **dup**, your carefully created dictionary would disappear from the operand stack and you'd never get it back. This process works because the dictionary itself is not on the operand stack—only a reference to the dictionary is on the stack. **dup** ensures there are two references to the dictionary on the top of the operand stack.

put stores the specified value into the dictionary under *key*, then removes the data item and the topmost reference to the dictionary. But there's still a reference to the dictionary on top of the operand stack because of the previous **dup** instruction. You can use that reference for further operations on that dictionary. Now let's define another value in the dictionary.

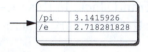

Dictionary on operand stack after defining **e**.

```
%!PS
10 dict                  %   create ten-element dictionary
dup                      %   duplicate dictionary for later use
/pi 3.1415926 put        %   put value of π into it
dup                      %   duplicate dictionary for later use
/e 2.718281828 put       %   put value of e into it
```

Once again, **dup** ensures that the dictionary remains accessible after **put**. Here is the syntax of **put** relative to dictionaries.[†]

dictionary   key   value **put**

The types of data stored in dictionaries are not limited to plain numbers. You can store any kind of PostScript object (simple or composite) in a dictionary. You can even store another dictionary in a dictionary. Here's how to store the procedure definition for centimeters (**cm**) in your dictionary.

---

† **put** can be used with strings and arrays, too.

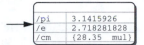

*Dictionary on operand
stack after defining* **cm**.

```
%!PS
10 dict                          %   create ten-element dictionary
dup                              %   duplicate dictionary for later use
/pi 3.1415926 put                %   put value of π into it
dup                              %   duplicate dictionary for later use
/e 2.718281828 put               %   put value of e into it
dup                              %   duplicate dictionary for later use
/cm { 28.35 mul } put            %   put value of cm into it
```

Having placed values in a dictionary, you need a means to get them out again. You extract values from dictionaries using **get**. Continuing with your dictionary on the operand stack, you can retrieve the value of **pi** as shown in the next example.

*Top of operand stack after
call to* **get**.

3.1415926

```
%!PS
10 dict                          %   create ten-element dictionary
dup                              %   duplicate dictionary for later use
/pi 3.1415926 put                %   put value of π into it
dup                              %   duplicate dictionary for later use
/e 2.718281828 put               %   put value of e into it
dup                              %   duplicate dictionary for later use
/cm { 28.35 mul } put            %   put value of cm into it
dup                              %   duplicate dictionary for later use
/pi get                          %   retrieve value of π
```

Using **put** and **get** to store values in dictionaries and retrieve values from dictionaries gets pretty clumsy because you have to keep track of where the dictionaries are on the operand stack. For that reason, PostScript provides another and more automatic way to deal with dictionaries and definitions—the dictionary stack.

Using the Dictionary Stack

The PostScript mechanism for making dictionaries "automatic" is the dictionary stack. Let's create another dictionary and push it onto the dictionary stack. You place a dictionary on the dictionary stack using **begin**. You remove a dictionary from the dictionary stack using **end**.

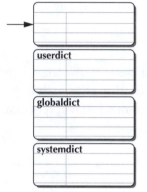

PostScript Level 2 dictionary stack after **10 dict begin** *instruction.*

```
%!PS
10 dict                    %   create ten-element dictionary
begin                      %   push onto dictionary stack
```

The picture now shows the dictionary stack instead of the operand stack. In addition to the dictionary you just created at the top of the dictionary stack, there are three other dictionaries. Where did these dictionaries come from? Any PostScript Level 2 job starts off with the dictionary stack containing three dictionaries.[†] These dictionaries are called **systemdict**, **globaldict**, and **userdict**. **systemdict** contains the names of all the PostScript operators. **globaldict** and **userdict** are writable dictionaries into which you can store objects.

The dictionary at the top of the dictionary stack is known as the current dictionary. **userdict** is at the top of the dictionary stack to start; it is the current dictionary. **userdict** contains several definitions, mostly related to page sizes.

Definitions in Dictionaries

Now you've created a dictionary and placed it on the top of the dictionary stack. How do you define and retrieve keys and values in it without using **put** and **get**? By using **def**, of which you've seen many examples. Here's a very basic definition.

---

† PostScript Level 1 jobs start with just two dictionaries on the dictionary stack— **systemdict** and **userdict**. **globaldict** doesn't exist in PostScript Level 1.

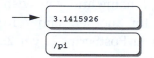

Contents of operand stack prior to def.

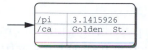

Dictionary on operand stack after pi and ca have been defined.

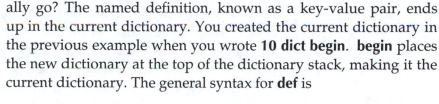

Operand stack before def is executed.

```
/pi  3.1415926  def
```

The operand stack looks like the picture in the margin just before **def** is parsed. But remember, a PostScript data object can be any data type. So you could write

```
/ca (Golden St.) def
```

to define a string with value **Golden St.** and whose name is **ca**.

When you define a named object, where does the definition actually go? The named definition, known as a key-value pair, ends up in the current dictionary. You created the current dictionary in the previous example when you wrote **10 dict begin**. **begin** places the new dictionary at the top of the dictionary stack, making it the current dictionary. The general syntax for **def** is

*key   value   **def***

where *key* is a name object and *value* is any PostScript object, including numbers, Boolean values, strings, arrays, executable arrays, or even dictionaries.

What's the point of defining PostScript objects by name? While the operand stack is a convenient way to store short-term values and intermediate results of computations, it's not necessarily convenient for storing data in the global sense, or for long-term storage. You would have great problems remembering where things are on the stack. So PostScript provides a means to define things by name, analogous to the way you define variables in other programming languages.

Undefining a Definition

PostScript Level 2 introduced **undef**—an instruction to remove a key-value pair from a dictionary. In PostScript Level 1, you can't really "undefine" a name. You can remove the dictionary containing that name from the dictionary stack, and you can then recover the VM used by that dictionary with **restore**. But this is convoluted—what if you're finished using a name and you wish to use that name's slot in the dictionary for another name? In PostScript Level 1, you can't. But you can in PostScript Level 2. You **undef** a name in a dictionary using syntax like this.

dictionary   name   **undef**

Operand stack before **undef** *is executed.*

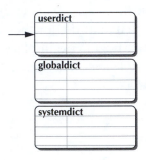

PostScript Level 2 dictionary stack at beginning of job.

How the Dictionary Stack Works

So you know how to create dictionaries, put things into them, refer to those things, and set the current dictionary. What's actually going on with the dictionary stack? As the PostScript interpreter processes its input stream (a series of tokens) the interpreter executes each token in turn. Exactly what does execution of a token mean? That depends on the type of token. To execute a numeric token such as **1.618034**, the interpreter pushes it onto the operand stack. To execute a name object, like **/ZapfChancery-MediumItalic**, the interpreter simply pushes it onto the operand stack. Basically, literal objects—objects that are themselves a value—are executed by being pushed onto the operand stack.

To process executable names (objects that are names of values) the PostScript interpreter looks them up in the dictionary stack. **mul**, **moveto**, **true**, and our own definition **DrawEllipse** are examples of executable names. When an executable name is encountered in the input stream, the PostScript interpreter searches the dictionary stack for the name, from the top down. The interpreter uses the first definition encountered for that key and executes its value. Let's watch the dictionary stack in action.

Here's a PostScript dictionary containing numbers and procedures for drawing circles.

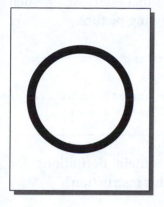

```
%!PS
/inch { 72 mul } def              % define inch procedure
/Circle 10 dict def               % define dictionary
Circle begin                      % current dictionary
    /radius 3 inch def            % define circle radius
    /linewidth 0.5 inch def       % define linewidth
    /Draw {                       % stack = x y
        linewidth setlinewidth    % set line width
        radius 0 360 arc stroke   % describe circle
    } def                         % define Draw procedure
end                               % remove current dictionary
Circle begin                      % current dictionary
    4.25 inch 5.5 inch Draw       % draw circle
end                               % remove current dictionary
showpage                          % display page
```

And here's another dictionary to draw rectangles.

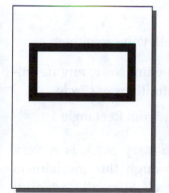

```
%!PS
/inch { 72 mul } def              % define inch procedure
/Rectangle 10 dict def            % define dictionary
Rectangle begin                   % current dictionary
    /linewidth 0.5 inch def       % define linewidth
    /width 6 inch def             % width of rectangle
    /height 3 inch def            % height of rectangle
    /Draw {                       % stack = x y
        linewidth setlinewidth    % set line width
        moveto width 0 rlineto    % bottom edge
        0 height rlineto          % right edge
        width neg 0 rlineto       % top edge
        closepath                 % finish shape
        stroke                    % draw shape
    } def                         % define Draw procedure
end                               % remove current dictionary
Rectangle begin                   % current dictionary
    1.25 inch 5.5 inch Draw       % draw rectangle
end                               % remove current dictionary
showpage                          % display page
```

Suppose you put both dictionaries on the dictionary stack such that the dictionary stack looks like the following picture.

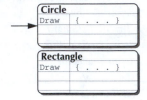

```
%!PS
Rectangle begin                    %    current dictionary
Circle begin                       %    current dictionary
```

Notice that **Circle** and **Rectangle** both contain definitions for **Draw**. What will happen when you issue this instruction?

```
4.25 inch 5.5 inch Draw
```

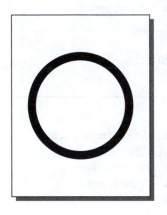

Will a circle or a rectangle be imaged on the page when **Draw** is executed? The picture tells you the answer—a circle is imaged. **Circle** is above **Rectangle** on the dictionary stack. The PostScript interpreter searches the dictionary stack from the top down looking for **Draw**. The interpreter finds the first definition for **Draw**, which is **Circle**.

Suppose you really wanted a rectangle. Well, you can either:

❑ put **Rectangle** on the dictionary stack again. Now, any definitions in **Rectangle** override the same definitions in **Circle**

❑ use **get** to retrieve the definition directly from **Rectangle**

The concept of dictionaries and the dictionary stack is a very powerful and flexible data structure. Through this mechanism you can redefine the PostScript language itself. Since all PostScript operators are simply definitions in **systemdict**, the operators are subject to being overridden as easily as are your definitions.

The following segment of PostScript creates a definition for **lineto** in the current dictionary. As long as that dictionary remains on the top of the stack, the definition for **lineto** you see in the code segment has precedence over **lineto** from **systemdict**.

Hello World!

```
%!PS
/inch { 72 mul } def                % define inch procedure
/Palatino-Roman findfont            % choose font
1 inch scalefont setfont
/lineto {                           % redefine lineto
    moveto (Hello World!) show
} def
1.25 inch 5.5 inch lineto           % call lineto
showpage                            % display page
```

You should be careful when redefining parts of the PostScript language; this is a fruitful source of bugs. Of course, you are responsible for keeping track of the objects you define and possible collisions with other definitions.

Test Name Defined in Dictionary

known tests whether a specific name is *known* in a specified dictionary. Here's a short example. When you can't remember where **diskonline** is defined you can write a little PostScript program to ask the interpreter if **diskonline** is known in a specific dictionary.

diskonline not in systemdict

Message to show **diskonline** *is not in* **systemdict**.

```
%!PS
/inch { 72 mul } def                % define inch procedure
/Palatino-Roman findfont            % find required font
42 scalefont                        % scale to required size
setfont                             % set in graphics state
systemdict                          % systemdict to stack
/diskonline known {                 % look for name
    0.5 inch 5.5 inch moveto        % set current point
    (diskonline in systemdict)      % affirmative message
    show                            % show message
} {
    0.5 inch 5.5 inch moveto        % set current point
    (diskonline not in systemdict)  % negatory message
    show                            % show message
} ifelse                            % end of conditional
showpage                            % display page
```

Well, **diskonline** is not in **systemdict**, so maybe you should try looking in **statusdict** instead.

Message to show diskon-line is in statusdict.

```
%!PS
/inch { 72 mul } def                      % define inch procedure
/Palatino-Roman findfont                  % find required font
42 scalefont                              % scale to required size
setfont                                   % set in graphics state
statusdict                                % statusdict to stack
/diskonline known {                       % look for name
    0.5 inch 5.5 inch moveto              % set current point
    (diskonline in statusdict)            % affirmative message
    show                                  % show message
} {
    0.5 inch 5.5 inch moveto              % set current point
    (diskonline not in statusdict)        % negatory message
    show                                  % show message
} ifelse                                  % end of conditional
showpage                                  % display page
```

Trying every possible dictionary in this way could be quite time consuming. A better way to inquire where a particular thing is defined would be to use **where**, described in *Test Name on Dictionary Stack* starting on page 207 in this chapter.

Using **known** in this way is a portable and version-independent way to ask for the existence of interpreter features. For example, **filenameforall** first appeared in version 42 of the PostScript interpreter. But testing the version number of the interpreter would not be a recommended way to ask such questions.

A common error in programming for **known** is omitting the name of the dictionary. For instance, you might think you could find out where **diskonline** is defined like this.

```
%!PS
/inch { 72 mul } def                            %   define inch procedure
/Palatino-Roman findfont                        %   find required font
42 scalefont                                    %   scale to required size
setfont                                         %   set in graphics state
/diskonline known {                             %   look for name—error here
    0.5 inch 5.5 inch moveto                     %   set current point
    (diskonline in statusdict)                   %   affirmative message
    show                                         %   show message
} {
    0.5 inch 5.5 inch moveto                     %   set current point
    (diskonline not in statusdict)               %   negatory message
    show                                         %   show message
} ifelse                                         %   end of conditional
showpage                                         %   display page
```

This is incorrect because **known** needs two operands—a dictionary and a name. Instead of something sensible, you get a **stackunderflow** error message.

Using forall to Traverse Dictionaries

forall is a polymorphic operator that can be applied to strings, arrays, and dictionaries, and whose behavior differs depending on the object to which it is applied. Here you see **forall** applied to dictionaries. The use of **forall** with strings and arrays is covered in *Using forall to Traverse Strings* on pages 256–256 in this chapter.

The basic syntax is the same as for string and array data types

dictionary   procedure   `forall`

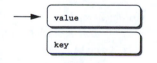

Operand stack after each iteration of **forall**.

forall works through a dictionary, one key-value pair at a time. On each iteration, **forall** pushes the key and value onto the operand stack and executes *procedure*—the second operand to **forall**. The next two code samples illustrate the use of **forall** to traverse a dictionary. First you need a dictionary full of stuff, so let's define a dictionary called **WeirdUnits**, whose contents are mostly familiar (and maybe unfamiliar) units expressed in terms of PostScript user space units. Here's the definition of this dictionary and all the key-value pairs in it.

```
/WeirdUnits 14 dict def              %   define weird units dictionary
WeirdUnits begin                     %   put on dictionary stack
        /Pi      3.141592653 def     %   good old π
        /G       9.80665 def         %   acceleration due to G
        /BakersDozen       13 def
        /AU      149597871 def       %   astronomical unit in Km
        /Radian      57.2957795 def  %   degrees per radian
        /Year      365.24219879 def  %   days in year
        /Inch      72 def            %   PostScript units in inch
        /Foot      12 Inch mul def   %   PostScript units in foot
        /Yard      3 Foot mul def    %   PostScript units in yard
        /Mile      1760 Yard mul def %   PostScript units in mile
        /Barleycorn       Inch 3 div def %  PostScript units in barleycorn
        /BoardFoot      144 Inch dup dup mul mul mul def
        /Fathom      6 Foot mul def  %   PostScript units in fathom
        /Furlong      220 Yard mul def %  PostScript units in furlong
end                                  %   pop from dictionary stack
```

Now the dictionary is full of definitions. Let's use **forall** to work through the key-value pairs one at a time and print them out.

```
BoardFoot  53747712
AU   149597871
Year   365.242
Furlong   570240
Foot   864
Radian   57.1235
Inch   72
Yard   2592
Pi   3.14159
Mile   4561920
Barleycorn   24.0
BakersDozen   13
G   9.80665
Fathom   5184
```

```
%!PS
/inch { 72 mul } def                 %   define inch procedure
/Palatino-Roman findfont             %   choose font
48 scalefont setfont
/top 10 inch def                     %   position of top line
WeirdUnits                           %   place on operand stack
{                                    %   start forall loop
    exch                             %   name on top
    100 string cvs                   %   convert name to string
    1 inch top moveto show           %   image name
    (        ) show                  %   add some space
    100 string cvs show              %   show converted value
    /top top 54 sub def              %   decrement line position
} forall                             %   end forall loop
showpage                             %   display page
```

Note that the order in which **forall** printed out the keys is not the same as the order in which you place the keys into the dictionary. In general, you can't assume any ordering of keys in dictionaries.

Chapter 14 contains another example of **forall** used to print a list of fonts in your printer.

Test Name on Dictionary Stack

If you just want to find out if a name is known somewhere, in any dictionary on the dictionary stack, use **where** instead. Here's an example to test if **execform** exists anywhere.

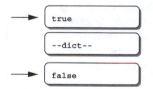

It's not there

```
%!PS
/inch { 72 mul } def            %   define inch procedure
/Palatino-Italic findfont       %   choose font
1 inch scalefont setfont
2.0 inch 5.5 inch moveto        %   set current point
/execform where                 %   look for execform
{                               %   true part
    (It's there) show           %   tell the world
    pop                         %   remove dictionary
} {                             %   false part
    (It's not there) show       %   tell the world
} ifelse                        %   end if statement
showpage                        %   display page
```

If the specified name exists in some dictionary on the dictionary stack, **where** places two things on the operand stack—the dictionary in which the key was found and a **true** value.

```
→  true
   --dict--
→  false
```

If the specified name is not found in any dictionary on the dictionary stack, **where** places only a **false** value on the operand stack.

There's a small problem—how do you find the name of the dictionary put on the operand stack? You can't, in general, find the name of a dictionary. You can circumvent this somewhat by defining, in all of your user-defined dictionaries, a key-value pair like the one in the following code listing.

```
/DictName (WeirdUnits) def
```

Then, just ask for **DictName** when you want the dictionary's name. Of course, this works only with dictionaries you define, not dictionaries such as **systemdict**, defined by others.

PostScript Level 2 Dictionary Constructors

PostScript Level 2 introduced a new "convenience" syntax for quickly and concisely creating a dictionary and filling that dictionary with key-value pairs. The new syntax uses << and >> to mark the start and end of a dictionary you construct "on the fly." The << places a **mark** object on the operand stack. Here's an example of dictionary constructors in action. PostScript Level 2 **image** can accept a dictionary instead of a collection of parameters as an operand to describe the image. Here is how you could use **image** in conjunction with PostScript Level 2 dictionary constructors.

```
%!PS
/inch { 72 mul } def                     %   define inch procedure
/temp 16 string def                      %   string for temporary results
1.25 inch 2.5 inch translate             %   set origin
6 inch 6 inch scale                      %   scale image large
<<                                       %   start dictionary
    /ImageType 1                         %   required
    /Width 64                            %   bits per scan line
    /Height 64                           %   number of scan lines
    /BitsPerComponent 1                  %   depth of image
    /ImageMatrix [ 64 0 0 64 0 0 ]       %   image matrix
    /DataSource { currentfile temp readhexstring pop }
    /Decode [ 0 1 ]                      %   transfer function
>>                                       %   end dictionary
image                                    %   image operation
FFFFFFFFFFFFFFFF FFFFFFFFFFFFFFFF        %   lines of data
FFFFFFF3FFFFFFFF FFFFFFF81FFFFFFF

          . . .
    28 lines of data omitted
          . . .

FFFFFFF83FFFFFFF FFFFFFF87FFFFFFF
FFFFFFFCFFFFFFFF FFFFFFFFFFFFFFFF
showpage                                 %   display page
```

The set of key-value pairs within the **<<** and **>>** create a transient dictionary which **image** uses as its control parameters. Notice that the key-value pairs within the dictionary are simply stated. Don't make the mistake of writing the code using **def** as shown in the following example.

```
%!PS
/inch { 72 mul } def                    %   define inch procedure
/temp 16 string def                     %   string for temporary results
1.25 inch 2.5 inch translate            %   set origin
6 inch 6 inch scale                     %   scale image large
<<
   /ImageType 1 def                     %   required
   /Width 64 def                        %   bits per scan line
   /Height 64 def                       %   number of scan lines
   /BitsPerComponent 1 def              %   depth of image
   /ImageMatrix [ 64 0 0 64 0 0 ] def   %   image matrix
   /DataSource { currentfile temp readhexstring pop } def
   /Decode [ 0 1 ] def                  %   transfer function
>>
image                                   %   image operation
FFFFFFFFFFFFFFFF FFFFFFFFFFFFFFFF       %   lines of data
FFFFFFF3FFFFFFFF FFFFFFF81FFFFFFF
                  . . .
  28 lines of data omitted
                  . . .
FFFFFFF83FFFFFFF FFFFFFF87FFFFFFF
FFFFFFFCFFFFFFFF FFFFFFFFFFFFFFFF
showpage                                %   display page
```

This code will just define the key-value pairs in the current dictionary—the one on the top of the dictionary stack—instead of in the constructed dictionary. You will get error reports from the PostScript interpreter but they won't be very obvious.

Procedure Definitions

Throughout this book you have seen many examples of procedures. In PostScript, { and } denote an executable array or a procedure. Here is an example of a procedure stored in the current dictionary as a key-value pair.

```
/barleycorn { 24 mul } def
```

The next example shows that a procedure doesn't have to have a name at all. All the loop operators such as **for** and **repeat** require a PostScript procedure as one of their operands. The procedure is built on the fly, used, and discarded.

```
%!PS
/inch { 72 mul } def                 % define inch procedure
4.25 inch 5.5 inch translate         % center of page
24                                   % number of times to repeat
{                                    % start procedure
    0 0 moveto                       % set current point
    4 inch 0 rlineto                 % draw line
    15 rotate                        % rotate
} repeat                             % loop
stroke                               % stroke starburst
showpage                             % display page
```

PostScript doesn't distinguish procedure definitions in a dictionary from definitions of numbers or strings. PostScript just puts keys and values of any type into a dictionary. People make artificial distinctions between numbers and procedures because it's conceptually easier. Here is a procedure to draw an isosceles triangle, with an example of its use.

```
/inch { 72 mul } def                 % define inch procedure
/triangle {                          % define triangle proc
    moveto                           % set current point
    6 inch 0 rlineto                 % one side
    120 rotate                       % rotate
    6 inch 0 rlineto                 % second side
    closepath                        % finish shape
} def
0.5 inch setlinewidth                % set line width
1.25 inch 3.5 inch                   % lower-left corner of triangle
triangle stroke                      % right side up triangle
showpage                             % display page
```

This program uses the triangle procedure just defined to draw a figure resembling the Star of David.

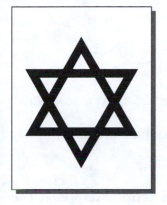

```
%!PS
/inch { 72 mul } def              %  define inch procedure
0.5 inch setlinewidth             %  set line width
gsave                             %  save graphics state
    1.25 inch 3.5 inch            %  lower-left corner of triangle
    triangle stroke               %  right side up triangle
grestore                          %  restore graphics state
0 11 inch translate               %  translate to upper left corner
1 -1 scale                        %  invert coordinate system
gsave                             %  save graphics state
    1.25 inch 4 inch              %  lower-left corner of triangle
    triangle stroke               %  upside down triangle
grestore                          %  restore graphics state
showpage                          %  display page
```

Notice the { and } construct in the preceding example for procedure definition of both **inch** and **triangle**. What do the curly braces actually do? { introduces an executable object—a procedure. Procedures are built on the operand stack. Watch the stack as the PostScript interpreter processes the procedure definition for **inch**. Let's begin with the first three tokens—{, **72**, and **mul**.

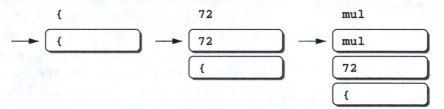

Each token is pushed onto the operand stack—even **mul**. { switches the interpreter to *deferred execution mode*—input tokens are not executed at this time but are pushed one by one onto the operand stack. } ends deferred execution mode and creates an executable array containing all the objects on the stack down to {. Here is the state of the stack and VM after } is processed.

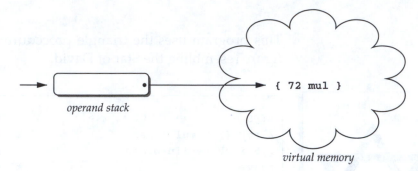

operand stack

virtual memory

State of VM and operand stack after procedure definition is complete.

Had you tried to define this sequence without the braces

```
/inch   72   mul   def
```

the result is a **typecheck** error from the PostScript interpreter. The interpreter executes **mul** as soon as the token is encountered because the interpreter is not in deferred execution mode. So **mul** tries to use a name object (**/inch**) as one of its operands.

Passing Values to Procedures

moveto *expects x and y coordinates on the operand stack.*

You've seen many times how PostScript operators consume their operands from the operand stack. For example, **moveto** expects the top two elements of the operand stack to contain the x and y values to which to set the current point. User-defined procedures often require operands and consume their operands from the stack just as PostScript operators do. One procedure that requires operands is the **triangle** procedure introduced on page 211. **triangle**'s operands indicate the position of the lower-left corner of the triangle. Other examples are the **square** procedure defined on page 161 in Chapter 4 and the **inch** procedure defined on practically every page in this book. The following example uses **triangle** to draw these rotating triangles.

```
%!PS
/inch { 72 mul } def                        %   define inch procedure
4.25 inch 5.5 inch translate                %   move to center of page
0.4 0.4 scale                               %   smaller size
8 {                                         %   8 triangles
    0.25 inch setlinewidth                  %   set line width
    gsave                                   %   save graphics state
        1.25 inch 3.5 inch                  %   operands for triangle
        triangle stroke                     %   draw the triangle
    grestore                                %   restore graphics state
    45 rotate                               %   rotate a bit
} repeat                                     %   keep going
showpage                                     %   display page
```

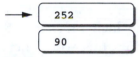

Operand stack before **triangle** *is executed.*

Just before the call to **triangle** this program pushes **1.25 inch** and **3.5 inch** onto the operand stack, effectively passing those values to **triangle**. The values are used by **triangle** to determine the lower-left corner of the shape. **triangle** removes its arguments from the stack with **moveto**.

Returning Values from Procedures

PostScript operators push their results onto the operand stack. Frequently, user-defined procedures return results as well. User-defined procedures behave like PostScript operators and push their results onto the operand stack. **inch** is an example of a procedure that returns results—a number expressed as PostScript points—to the operand stack.

| 306 |

Operand stack after **inch** *is executed.*

The picture illustrates the operand stack just after **4.25 inch** is executed. The result ($4.25 \times 72 = 306$) is pushed on the stack by **mul** within **inch**.

Binding

Throughout this book you've seen many examples of **def** used to define procedures, as in the by now canonical **/inch**.

```
/inch { 72 mul } def                % define inch procedure
```

This section now introduces the issue of *early binding*, the **bind** operator, and some pitfalls relative to **bind**.

Every time **inch** is called, the PostScript interpreter pushes the value **72** onto the operand stack. Then it must look up the name **mul** by searching down the dictionary stack until it eventually finds **mul** defined as an operator in **systemdict**. Even though PostScript is highly optimized for efficient name lookup, the process consumes lots of time if the interpreter has to look up the name **mul** every time you want to use **inch**. You can make this process more efficient by using **bind** on the **inch** procedure to bypass the name lookup machinery. How does this work? Let's change the way **inch** is defined just a little.

```
/inch { 72 mul } bind def          % define inch procedure
```

What's the **bind** for? What happens is that at the time this procedure is *defined*, the name **mul** is located in **systemdict**, and a direct reference to the definition of **mul** is plugged into the **inch** procedure definition. Now, every time **inch** is used, the name lookup step is bypassed, and the program runs faster. Correctly used in PostScript programs with many procedure definitions, **bind** can have a substantial effect on the overall performace of a PostScript program.

The snare lies in the phrase "correctly used." There are many ways to misuse **bind**, and when PostScript programmers trip over any of these, programs fail mysteriously. To appreciate the pitfalls of **bind**, let's first look at an example which works by coincidence, maybe. This simple program draws a ray of lines around a circle.

```
%!PS
/inch { 72 mul } def                    %  define inch procedure
/inner 3 inch def                       %  inner radius
/outer 4 inch def                       %  outer radius
4.25 inch 5.5 inch translate            %  origin to center of page
0.25 inch setlinewidth                  %  fat line width
0 15 345 {                              %  start for loop
    /index exch def                     %  save angle
    index cos inner mul index sin inner mul moveto
    index cos outer mul index sin outer mul lineto
} for                                   %  end for loop
stroke                                  %  paint outline
showpage                                %  display page
```

Although this example looks a little contrived, it is actually a scaled down version of a real-life program which worked fine for a long time until one day it was run on a different system with different preset behavior... The simplicity is for illustration, not as an example of how you should do things.

The gaping hole in this program is the **index** variable within the **for** loop to keep track of the current angle. **index** happens to be a predefined PostScript operator, defined in **systemdict**. This example works in this case, but purely by coincidence, because you're free, in principle, to name variables anything you like.

Let's try to make this program more "efficient" by binding the procedure definitions. This example places **bind** operators in the definition of **inch** and at the end of the **for** loop. You can apply **bind** to *any* executable procedure, not just procedures that are the subject of **def**. Now that the **for** procedure is bound, the interpreter has bypassed the name lookup scheme by placing inside the loop direct references to **exch**, **def**, **cos**, **sin**, **mul**, **moveto**, **lineto**, and, most unfortunately, to **index**—a predefined PostScript operator in **systemdict**.

```
%!PS
/inch { 72 mul } bind def                    %  define inch procedure
/inner 3 inch def                            %  inner radius
/outer 4 inch def                            %  outer radius
4.25 inch 5.5 inch translate                 %  origin to center of page
0.25 inch setlinewidth                       %  fat line width
0 15 345 {                                   %  start for loop
     /index exch def                         %  save angle
     index cos inner mul index sin inner mul moveto
     index cos outer mul index sin outer mul lineto
} bind for                                   %  end for loop
stroke                                       %  paint outline
showpage                                     %  display page
```

What happens when you run this procedure? You get a message from the PostScript interpreter:

```
%%[ Error: stackunderflow; OffendingCommand: index ]%%
```

Because of the **bind**, the name **index** in the **for** loop is replaced by a direct reference to the PostScript operator in **systemdict**. **index** expects to see at least one number on the operand stack. In this case there are none, and the program fails. Had there been numbers on the operand stack, the program might have executed to completion, but produced erroneous results by coincidence.

But didn't we just say that in principle you can call definitions anything you like, even names of system operators? Well, yes, but this is where the definition *versus* execution model bites you. **bind** is applied at the time the procedure is *defined*. The **/index exch def** line happens when the procedure is *executed*, some time later. By that time, **bind** has already taken effect and the program fails. Let's now fix this problem by renaming the variable.

```
%!PS
/inch { 72 mul } bind def          %   define inch procedure
/inner 3 inch def                  %   inner radius
/outer 4 inch def                  %   outer radius
4.25 inch 5.5 inch translate       %   origin to center of page
0.25 inch setlinewidth             %   fat line width
0 15 345 {                         %   start for loop
    /angle exch def                %   save angle
    angle cos inner mul angle sin inner mul moveto
    angle cos outer mul angle sin outer mul lineto
} bind for                         %   end for loop
stroke                             %   paint outline
showpage                           %   display page
```

Now that **index** has been renamed as **angle**, the code works.

If you absolutely *must* play games like this with names of PostScript operators, make sure you predefine names you expect to use, so that binding doesn't inadvertently bind those names to names defined in some other dictionary.

PostScript experts debate at length on the merits and otherwise of **bind**. As we said, the example from above worked fine for years, before being run on a PostScript interpreter which automatically applied **bind** as standard behavior (known as "autobind"). Then the program failed. Some experts encourage you to use **bind** wherever possible. Other experts deplore the use of **bind**. Ironically, had the authors of the original program used **bind** in the first place, they would have found this subtle bug—redefinition of a PostScript operator name—right away, instead of somebody else finding and fixing it years later.

Immediately Evaluated Names

The preceding section described the method to bind a procedure so names of operators within the procedure are bound to operators, bypassing name lookup. This section discusses another form of binding. Early in its life,† PostScript gained another kind of literal syntax specifically, *immediately evaluated names*. An immediately evaluated name is indicated by a double slash (*//*). *//* tells the PostScript interpreter to look up the value of the name and immediately substitute its value there and then. When do you use immediately evaluated names? Think of them as loosely analogous to named constants in other languages. If you program in C, for example, you might write something like this:

```
#define  boxwidth    inch(6)
#define  boxheight   inch(8)
DrawBox()
{
     body of function for drawing box
}
```

In PostScript, you define names somewhat differently. Let's first look at the definition of a procedure to draw a box and then you'll see this procedure definition in use.

```
/boxwidth    6 inch  def          %  define width of box
/boxheight   8 inch  def          %  define height of box
/DrawBox {                        %  define box drawing procedure
  0 0 moveto                      %  set current point
  //boxwidth 0 lineto             %  bottom of box
  //boxwidth //boxheight lineto   %  right side of box
  0 //boxheight lineto            %  top of box
  closepath                       %  close the shape
} bind def                        %  define the procedure
```

This is the definition of **DrawBox**—it contains immediately evaluated names **//boxwidth** and **//boxheight**. Let's see it used to actually draw a box.

---

† in all Adobe PostScript interpreters since ROM revision 25.0. Most modern PostScript interpreters should have this feature by now.

```
%!PS
/inch { 72 mul } def                    % define inch procedure
1 inch 1 inch translate                 % set origin
DrawBox                                 % establish the path
gsave                                   % push graphics state
  0.50 setgray fill                     % fill with medium gray
grestore                                % pop graphics state
0.25 inch setlinewidth                  % wide line width
1 setlinecap                            % round line cap
1 setlinejoin                           % round line join
[ 0.5 inch 0.75 inch ] 0 setdash        % dashed line pattern
stroke                                  % paint the path with dashes
showpage                                % display page
```

Here you see the difference between what happens when you use immediately evaluated names as opposed to plain names in a procedure definition. Here is your procedure definition using immediately evaluated name syntax.

```
/boxwidth  6 inch def
/boxheight 8 inch def
/DrawBox {                              % start of definition
  0 0 moveto                            % set current point
  //boxwidth 0 lineto                   % bottom of box
  //boxwidth //boxheight lineto         % right side of box
  0 //boxheight lineto                  % top of box
  closepath                            % complete the shape
} def                                   % end of definition
```

Here's what your procedure looks like—in terms of syntactic elements—right before **bind** and **def** are applied. Names have been substituted prior to **bind** and **def.**

```
/DrawBox {
    0 0 moveto
    432 0 lineto
    432 576 lineto
    0 576 lineto
    closepath
} bind def
```

The values of **boxwidth** and **boxheight** have been substituted directly into the body of the procedure prior to definition—these values are now constant and will not be changed by any further redefinition of **boxwidth**, **boxheight**, or **inch**. When this procedure is subsequently executed, it will run faster because the PostScript interpreter doesn't need to look up the names and evaluate them on the fly. Instead, it uses the substituted values.

The next pair of code examples shows the same procedure but uses plain names instead of immediately evaluated names. Once more, here's the procedure definition, but not using immediately evaluated name syntax.

```
/boxwidth    6 inch   def
/boxheight   8 inch   def
DrawBox {
   0 0 moveto
   boxwidth 0 lineto
   boxwidth boxheight lineto
   0 boxheight lineto
   closepath
} bind def
```

And here's the stream of syntactic elements that will be defined for **DrawBox**. Names are not substituted prior to **bind** and **def**.

```
/boxwidth    6 inch   def
/boxheight   8 inch   def
DrawBox {
    0 0 moveto
    boxwidth 0 lineto
    boxwidth boxheight lineto
    0 boxheight lineto
    closepath
} bind def
```

The procedure body contains names that will be looked up and evaluated at the time the procedure is executed, not at the time the procedure is defined. This means you could redefine **boxwidth** or **boxheight**, or even redefine **inch**, and get completely different results in the future.

When can you *not* use immediately evaluated names? Consider this code which attempts to be clever.

```
%!PS
/drawbox {                          %   width    height
  2 dict begin                      %   start temporary dictionary
    /height exch def                %   define height of box
    /width exch def                 %   define width of box
    0 0 moveto                      %   set current point
    //width 0 lineto                %   WILL NOT WORK
    //width //height lineto         %   WILL NOT WORK
    0 //height lineto               %   WILL NOT WORK
    closepath                       %   complete the shape
  end                               %   pop temporary dictionary
} def                               %   end of definition
gsave                               %   push graphics state
  2 inch 2 inch translate           %   set origin
  3 inch 5 inch drawbox             %   establish the path
  fill                              %   fill the shape
grestore                            %   push graphics state
showpage                            %   display page
```

Unfortunately, this code doesn't work. You will get a message from the PostScript interpreter that **width** is undefined. What is wrong with the code? Well, the PostScript interpreter reads the body of the procedure and looks up **width** as soon as it is encountered. But **width** has not yet been defined because the **def** statement has not yet been executed.

Statements inside the definition of a procedure body aren't executed because the interpreter is in deferred execution mode. A worse situation might occur if the values are already defined in some other dictionary. In either case, you get an error message from the interpreter, or incorrect results.

Stack Manipulation versus Defined Objects

In *Thinking in PostScript*, Glenn Reid states, "Trust the stack," meaning you should use the stack for short-term storage instead of defining things in variables unnecessarily. On the next page is a fragment from the PostScript prolog of a drawing application. This fragment is a procedure to draw ellipses.

This piece of the prolog first defines a dictionary just for **DrawEllipse** variables. Of itself, that's not such a bad idea, because you should keep variable definitions local to procedures instead of relying on **userdict** to hold everything. But as you shall see, this procedure misuses dictionaries and local definitions.

DrawEllipse is called with five parameters on the stack—the (x, y) coordinates of the center of the ellipse, the width and height of the ellipse, and the angle by which to rotate the ellipse.

The first thing **DrawEllipse** does is define all its parameters in variables. What does **DrawEllipse** do with these variables? It immediately puts them back on the stack so they can be used as parameters to **translate**, **scale**, and **rotate**. In other words, this procedure took its parameters off the operand stack, defined them in variables, then put the contents of the variables back on the stack right away. To do this work, the procedure needs a dictionary, which must be placed on the dictionary stack with **begin**, and later removed with **end**.

```
%!PS
/EllipseDict 6 dict def              %   define dictionary
/DrawEllipse {                       %   stack = x  y  width height angle
  EllipseDict begin                  %   place on dictionary stack
     /angle exch def                 %   define rotation angle
     /height exch def                %   define height of ellipse
     /width exch def                 %   define width of ellipse
     /y exch def                     %   define y coordinate of center
     /x exch def                     %   define x coordinate of center
     /mtx matrix currentmatrix def   %   save current CTM
     x y translate                   %   origin to center of ellipse
     angle rotate                    %   rotate coordinate system
     width height scale              %   scale for ellipse
     0 0 1 0 360 arc                 %   draw in scaled system
     closepath                       %   finish shape
     mtx setmatrix                   %   restore original CTM
  end                                %   remove from dictionary stack
} def                                %   end of definition
```

Timing tests on a NextStation showed this procedure executing in 1.6 milliseconds per invocation. The second cut at **DrawEllipse** manipulates the stack directly.

```
%!PS
/DrawEllipse {                       %   stack = x  y  width height angle
     matrix currentmatrix           %   save current CTM
     6 1 roll translate             %   origin to center of ellipse
     rotate                         %   rotate coordinate system
     scale                          %   scale coordinate system
     0 0 1 0 360 arc                %   draw circle in scaled system
     closepath                      %   finish shape
     setmatrix                      %   restore original CTM
} def
```

The variables went away, so there's no longer any need for the dictionary to hold the variables. This version of the procedure executes in 1 millisecond, for a 40 percent gain in performance.

Virtual Memory

You read in *Composite Objects and Virtual Memory* on pages 191–193 in this chapter that composite objects (strings, arrays, dictionaries...) are stored in virtual memory. The PostScript interpreter allocates virtual memory when you create composite objects. Even though you didn't allocate the virtual memory, and may not even be aware virtual memory has been allocated, you are responsible for returning it to the interpreter for reuse.

PostScript Level 2 supports two types of virtual memory—Local VM and Global VM. PostScript Level 1 supports only one type of virtual memory—called simply VM in PostScript Level 1 literature, which later became Local VM in PostScript Level 2.

Generally speaking, composite objects that exist only within the framework of some structure, say pages or PostScript jobs, should be stored in Local VM. Typically, this is just about everything in a PostScript program. Use Global VM for objects that persist across such structural boundaries. Resources such as fonts or patterns are good candidates for storage in Global VM. Less memory is required when you store large resources once in Global VM and share them between pages or PostScript programs, and less time is spent swapping large amounts of data into and out of memory.

If you want to store objects in Global VM you must explicitly change the VM allocation mode of the interpreter. Use **setglobal** to indicate whether composite objects are allocated in Local VM or Global VM. The general form of **setglobal** is

Boolean `setglobal`

where *Boolean* is either **true** or **false**. **true** tells the PostScript interpreter to store composite objects in Global VM. **false** tells the PostScript interpreter to store composite objects in Local VM. The preset allocation mode of the PostScript interpreter is Local, and thus the preset value of **setglobal** is **false**. A program can change the VM allocation mode whenever it needs to.

Even though you have little control over when and how much virtual memory is allocated, you do have control over when memory

---

→ `true`

State of stack prior to call to **setglobal**.

is reclaimed. PostScript provides two methods for reclaiming virtual memory. The first method is *active*—you issue **save** and **restore** instructions. The second method is *passive* and is available only in PostScript Level 2—the PostScript interpreter periodically rummages through virtual memory reclaiming unreferenced memory. This is known as *garbage collection*. **save** and **restore** reclaim memory only from Local VM. Garbage collection reclaims memory from both Local and Global VM. Conserve memory even when you have a garbage collection facility; garbage collection is an expensive operation.

Reclaiming Virtual Memory with Save and Restore

This next PostScript program displays a string on the page. When the PostScript interpreter encounters the string (**PostScript!**), several bytes of Local VM are allocated, the characters are stored in those bytes, and a reference to the string is pushed onto the operand stack.

```
%!PS
/inch { 72 mul } def                       %   define inch procedure
/Palatino-Roman findfont                   %   set current font
2.25 inch scalefont setfont
1.5 inch 0.5 inch moveto                    %   set current point
52 rotate                                   %   rotate coordinate system
(PostScript!) show                          %   display temporary string
showpage                                    %   display page
```

This picture at the top of the next page shows the state of the operand stack and virtual memory just after the interpreter processes (**PostScript!**).

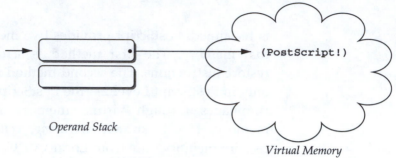

Reference to composite object.

Then **show** displays the string and removes its reference from the stack. At this point, the actual string is still stored in Local VM, but the stack no longer references the string.

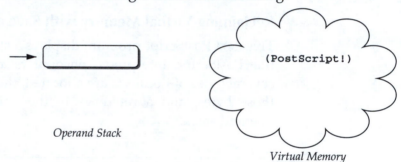

Composite object stranded in VM.

Local VM is used, but isn't needed. The PostScript program should reclaim that memory for future use. You can force the PostScript interpreter to reclaim unreferenced objects, such as this string, in Local VM, using a combination of **save** and **restore**.

```
%!PS
/inch { 72 mul } def                  %   define inch procedure
save                                  %   save state
    /Palatino-Roman findfont          %   set current font
    2.25 inch scalefont setfont
    1.5 inch 0.5 inch moveto          %   set current point
    52 rotate                         %   rotate user space
    (PostScript!) show                %   display temporary string
    showpage                          %   display page
restore                               %   restore state
```

save takes a snapshot of the current state of Local VM and saves the current graphics state in the manner of **gsave**. **save** returns a *save object* to the operand stack. **restore** resets VM (and, incidentally, the graphics state) back to the state in the save object—the state prior to **save**. **restore** discards all objects in Local VM created since **save** and reclaims the memory used by those objects.

This example is a bit simplistic. You certainly don't want to sprinkle **save** and **restore** pairs around every occurrence of temporary composite objects in your PostScript program. **save** and **restore** are computationally expensive operations. Generally, you should bracket logical structures, such as pages or included Encapsulated PostScript images, with **save** and **restore**. That's usually enough to prevent **VMerror** and, at the same time, maintain good performance. An added benefit of this approach is a modular PostScript program. **save** and **restore** pairs can be nested to some finite limit determined by the implementation of your interpreter.

restore also resets the values of composite objects that existed before **save**, with the notable exception of string elements. This exception is a source of some confusion. This next example exploits this "feature" of **save** and **restore** to invent a new type of cheese unlikely to become very popular in Italian cooking.

Parmesanla

```
%!PS
/inch { 72 mul } def              %  define inch procedure
/String (Mozzarella) def          %  define string object
/Array [ 2 0 0 2 0 0 ] def        %  define array
save                              %  save virtual memory
  String 0 (Parmesan) putinterval %  modify string object
  Array 0 [ 1 0 0 1 0 0 ] putinterval %  modify array
restore                           %  restore virtual memory
/Palatino-Italic findfont         %  choose font
0.75 inch scalefont setfont
0.75 inch 5.5 inch moveto         %  set current point
Array concat                      %  modify CTM
String show                       %  display string
showpage                          %  display page
```

This example creates two composite objects—a string and an array. Then it saves virtual memory, modifies both the string and the array, then restores virtual memory to its state just prior to the save. Remember **restore** operates slightly differently with string objects—rather than showing **Mozzarella** as you would expect, the example displays **Parmesanla**, a new breed of cheese, You can tell that the array is restored to its original state—it is concatenated with the CTM and characters are double height. Keep this in mind when using **save** and **restore**. At one point in PostScript history, Adobe claimed this feature was a "bug" and not to rely on its continued existence in future interpreters. However, Adobe have recanted and have stated that this behavior is henceforth a standard part of the PostScript language.[†]

restore raises an error when objects in VM are still referenced, as in this program.

```
%!PS
save                             %  save virtual memory
    /String (Mozzarella) def     %  create string
    String                       %  push reference to string
exch                             %  put save object on top
restore                          %  restore virtual memory
```

When you run this program, you get an **invalidrestore** error message from the interpreter because the operand stack contains a reference to **String** when **restore** is executed.

The Garbage Collector

The second method for reclaiming VM is through the garbage collector. The garbage collector is available only in PostScript Level 2 implementations and reclaims memory from both Local VM and from Global VM. To reclaim memory, the garbage collector

---

† Re-inforcing the folklore that a "feature" is just a "bug" dressed in a blue suit.

periodically searches through Local and Global VM and reclaims memory for objects no longer referenced by any PostScript program. The only way to reclaim memory in Global VM is with the garbage collector. You can't force reclamation of Global VM using **save** and **restore** as you can with Local VM.

You are responsible for "un-referencing" objects your PostScript program no longer requires, so the garbage collector can reclaim memory. Use PostScript Level 2 **undef** to explicitly dereference named objects you no longer need in Global VM. Temporary objects such as the string **(PostScript!)** in the earlier example have no remaining references once popped from the stack, and you needn't worry about them when they are stored in Global VM.

Control Flow—Overview

PostScript, like other programming languages, provides control structures to control the execution of sections of a PostScript program. PostScript provides loop control constructs and conditional execution constructs. To facilitate the conditional execution operators, PostScript also provides a set of relational operators to test relations between operands.

In addition to the "normal" set of looping and conditional operators, PostScript also supplies **forall**—a unique polymorphic operator that operates on aggregate objects such as arrays, strings, or dictionaries, regardless of their types. You saw an example of traversing a dictionary using **forall** on page 206 earlier in this chapter, and later, on page 256, you'll see an example of **forall** used to traverse strings.

Control Flow—Loops

A programming construct common to many programming languages is the loop. Loops provide ways to repeat an operation or series of operations several times. PostScript provides several flavors of loops described in this chapter. All PostScript loop constructs look more or less the same. They have, at a minimum, a *loop body*—a PostScript procedure executed repeatedly until some termination condition is satisfied and the loop stops. The four PostScript loop forms range from simple to complex in their operations.

loop is simplest. **loop** has no conditions or counters to terminate it. You must ensure you exit from the loop by testing some condition within the loop body.

repeat is a more controlled form that uses a simple counter to determine how many times to repeat the loop body.

for supplies a more general way of controlling the operation of a procedure body as well as providing the value of a control variable that may be used within the procedure body.

forall was already mentioned and illustrated on page 206 earlier in this chapter.

PostScript loops are described in detail in following subsections.

Simple Loop

The first kind of loop is the simplest. **loop** performs the procedure until the procedure executes an **exit** or a **stop**. Here is the general format of **loop**.

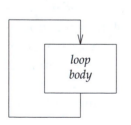

```
    {
        .  .  .
        loop body
        .  .  .
    } loop
```

If neither an **exit** nor **stop** are encountered, you are in an undesirable form of loop—the infinite loop. An infinite loop can be terminated only with an interrupt signal from the terminal (in an interactive environment) or by switching the printer off. Obviously, you must use **loop** carefully to avoid infinite loops.

Other programming languages provide a **while** loop that executes while a certain condition is true. PostScript does not have a **while** loop, but you can fake one with **loop**.

```
/whileloop {                    %   stack = test procedure
    /proc exch def              %   remember procedure
    /test exch def              %   remember test
    {                           %   start loop
        test                    %   perform the test
        { proc }                %   if true—exec procedure
        { exit }                %   else exit loop
        ifelse                  %   end of if
    } loop                      %   forever
} def
```

The next example uses **whileloop** to draw a bunch of filled triangles. The loop continues while the gray shade is "less than" white; that is, while **currentgray** is less than 1.

```
%!PS
/inch { 72 mul } def                    %   define inch procedure
/triangle {                             %   stack = llx lly
    moveto                              %   set current point
    3 inch 0 rlineto                    %   first side
    120 rotate 3 inch 0 rlineto         %   second side
    closepath                           %   finish shape
} def                                   %   define triangle procedure
4.25 inch 5.5 inch translate            %   center of page
{ currentgray 1 lt }                    %   while gray less than 1
{
    0.875 inch 0.875 inch               %   lower-left corner
    gsave triangle fill grestore        %   fill triangle
    currentgray 0.125 add setgray       %   update gray
    45 rotate                           %   turn user space
} whileloop                             %   loopty loop
showpage                                %   display page
```

You can get into an infinite loop with this example, if you aren't careful. If you change the test like this, the loop will run forever.

```
{ currentgray 1 le }
```

setgray prevents the current gray level from ever exceeding 1. So **currentgray** will always be less than or equal to 1 and the loop will continue forever.

Repeat Loop

repeat is another simple loop operator. **repeat** executes the loop body a specified number of times. As with **loop**, **repeat** requires an executable code segment as its operand. The **repeat** loop's syntax is as follows:

count {
    . . .
    loop body
    . . .
} **repeat**

Use **repeat** when you know how many times you want some code executed; that number is unrelated to the code within the loop body. This PostScript program repeats 10 times, drawing a flattened "card" for each iteration of the loop. Each card is drawn in a different shade of gray.

```
%!PS
/inch { 72 mul } def                  %   define inch procedure
1.25 inch 0.75 inch translate         %   position origin
0.1                                   %   initial value for gray
10 {                                  %   start loop
    dup                               %   need copy of gray value
    6 inch 0.75 inch                  %   width and height
    DrawCard                          %   draw card
    0.1 add                           %   increment gray value
    0 1 inch translate                %   translate origin again
} repeat                              %   end loop
pop                                   %   remove extraneous gray value
```

Having seen the loop in action, here's **DrawCard**.

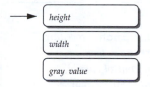

*State of stack prior to each invocation of **DrawCard**.*

```
%!PS
/DrawCard {                                    %  grayscale width height
    2 dict begin                               %  temporary dictionary
    /height exch def                           %  remember height
    /width exch def                            %  remember width
    newpath                                    %  clear current path
    width 2 div 0 moveto                       %  set current point
    width 0 width height 0.25 inch arcto
    width height 0 height 0.25 inch arcto
    0 height 0 0 0.25 inch arcto
    0 0 width 0 0.25 inch arcto
    closepath                                  %  finish the shape
    16 { pop } repeat                          %  clear debris from stack
    gsave                                      %  remember graphics state
      setgray                                  %  gray value off stack
      fill                                     %  fill with gray value
    grestore                                   %  recall graphics state
    4 setlinewidth stroke                      %  paint the path
    end                                        %  pop temporary dictionary
} def
```

DrawCard is called with three parameters—the gray value with which to fill the card, and the width and height of the card. Notice the width and height are defined as variables, but the gray value was left on the stack. Width and height are used several times, and leaving them on the stack would require cumbersome stack manipulation. But the gray value is used only once, so you can take its value straight off the stack.

For Loop

The PostScript **for** loop is the most general "standard" loop control construct—"standard" in this context because **forall**, described later, is more general than loop constructs found in other languages. You could simulate **for** loops using **repeat** and keeping track of your own control variable, but **for** is convenient and does a lot of the work behind the scenes. Here's a **for** loop to draw nine shaded rectangles up the middle of the page.

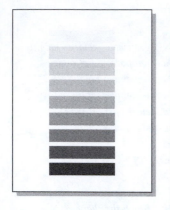

```
%!PS
/inch { 72 mul } def            %  define inch procedure
1 1 9 {                         %  start for loop
    dup                         %  copy control variable
    1 inch mul                  %  compute y position
    2.25 inch exch              %  set x position
    moveto                      %  set current point
    4 inch 0 rlineto            %  bottom of rectangle
    0 0.75 inch rlineto         %  right side
    -4 inch 0 rlineto           %  top
    closepath                   %  finish the shape
    0.1 mul setgray             %  set gray based on control variable
    fill                        %  fill the rectangle
} for                           %  end for loop
showpage                        %  display page
```

This example uses a **for** loop because the control variable is needed as a multiplier in the loop in two different places—once to calculate the location of the rectangle and once to calculate the shade of gray. A **repeat** loop is not appropriate in this example because you'd have to keep track of your own control variable.

Here's the general format of **for**.

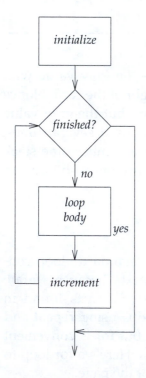

> *initial_value   increment   final_value   {*
>   . . .
>   *loop body*
>   . . .
> *}* **for**

Internally, the PostScript interpreter keeps a control variable for the loop. In the *initialize* phase, the interpreter sets the control variable to *initial_value*. In the *finished?* phase, the interpreter compares the control variable with *final_value* to see if the loop should finish. The test used depends on whether *increment* is positive or negative. If the control variable is increasing (*increment* is positive) the loop terminates when the control variable is greater than *final_value*. If the control variable is decreasing (*increment* is negative) the loop terminates when the control variable is less than *final_value*. In both cases the loop is executed when the control variable is equal to *final_value*.

The next example is a **for** loop to draw a fan of cards. The code is long enough that you need to see it in short sections. Here is the code that actually loops around calling the **DrawCard** procedure (defined on page 233) to draw the cards, one at a time.

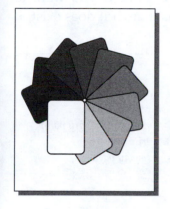

```
%!PS
/inch { 72 mul } def              %   define inch procedure
4.25 inch 5.5 inch translate      %   origin to middle of page
150 rotate                        %   initial rotation
1 1 10 {                          %   loop 10 times
    0.1 mul                       %   multiply to get gray scale value
    -33 rotate                    %   rotate each new card 33°
    2.25 inch 3.25 inch           %   width and height
    DrawCard                      %   draw shape—see following
} for
showpage                          %   display page
```

The **for** loop calls **DrawCard** for each iteration. The variable element is the gray scale with which each card is filled. The gray value is obtained by multiplying the **for** loop's control variable by 0.1 to get ten shades of gray ranging from dark gray (0.1) at the beginning to white (1.0) at the end.

Control Flow—Conditionals

Where the PostScript loop control operators described above execute a procedure body repeatedly, the conditional operators described here execute a procedure body only if a specific condition is true (or false). There are only two conditional operators, and they look much alike.

if takes a Boolean value from the stack and executes a procedure if the Boolean is **true**.

ifelse also takes a Boolean value from the stack, but it executes one procedure if the Boolean is **true**, and a different procedure if the Boolean is **false**.

The next few pages describe **if** and **ifelse** in more detail.

Simple Conditional

if is the simple conditional execution operator. Here is a very simple practical application for **if**. Suppose you want to determine if **filenameforall** exists in this version of your printer. You want to print a string of text stating **filenameforall** is there if it does exist.

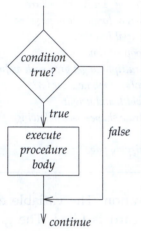

```
%!PS
systemdict /filenameforall known {     %  check in systemdict
   /Courier-Bold findfont 14 scalefont setfont
   144 144 moveto                       %  move to arbitrary point
   (filenameforall is there) show       %  print message
   showpage                             %  display page
} if
```

The general syntax of **if** is

Boolean_value   { procedure body } **if**

Two Way Conditional

The simple **if** executes a procedure if a condition is true. PostScript also provides the equivalent of *if–then–else* constructs from other languages. **ifelse** executes one procedure if a condition is true, and a different procedure if the condition is false.

The general syntax of **ifelse** looks like this.

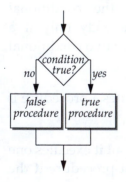

Boolean value   { true procedure body }   { false procedure body } **ifelse**

Let's enhance the previous example to use **ifelse**.

filenameforall is there

```
%!PS
/inch { 72 mul } def                        %   define inch procedure
/Palatino-Roman findfont                    %   find the required font
48 scalefont                                %   scale it to required size
setfont                                     %   set current font
systemdict /filenameforall known {          %   see if it's in systemdict
   0.25 inch 5.5 inch moveto                %   set current point ready
   (filenameforall is there) show           %   do this if it's there
} {
   0.25 inch 5.5 inch moveto                %   set current point ready
   (filenameforall is not there) show %     do this if it's not there
} ifelse
showpage                                    %   display page
```

Stack Manipulation Operators

This chapter so far has introduced basic concepts of the PostScript language—stacks, dictionaries, procedures, and the PostScript execution model. Operators such as **add** and **mul** *implicitly* manipulate the stack in the sense of removing elements, performing calculations, and returning results to the top of the stack. Other operators such as **moveto** and **lineto** also implicitly manipulate the stack. They remove elements but don't return results to the stack—their "results" are changes to the graphics state.

In addition to a rich set of operators to implicitly manipulate the operand stack, PostScript provides a set of operators to explicitly operate on the stack. These operators provide great convenience for short-term rearrangement of elements of the stack.

Remove Top Element from Stack

pop is about the simplest operator for operating on the stack. **pop** removes the topmost element from the operand stack.

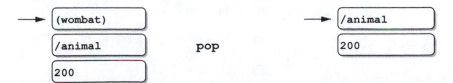

Why would you use **pop**? For a simple instance, **arcto** leaves four items of data on the stack.[†] Suppose you use **arcto** to draw a straight line connected by an arc.

```
%!PS
/inch { 72 mul } def              %  define inch procedure
2 inch 8 inch moveto              %  set current point
8 inch 5.5 inch                   %  corner point
4 inch 2 inch                     %  end point
2 inch arcto                      %  radius and draw arc
gsave                             %  push graphics state
    0.50 setgray                  %  medium gray color
    fill                          %  fill shape
grestore                          %  recall graphics state
0.125 inch setlinewidth           %  fat line width
stroke                            %  paint the outline
showpage                          %  display page
```

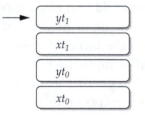

When **arcto** has completed, four extraneous values are left on the stack—the coordinates of the two tangent points.[‡] You can use **pop** to remove the extraneous items after the arc and line segments are drawn. You could write

pop pop pop pop

or, you could also be clever and do the trick this way:

4 { pop } repeat

This technique using **repeat** way is slightly more concise but doesn't save much execution time.

PostScript has no **push** operator. Objects are pushed onto the stack implicitly as they are encountered in the input stream.

---

† **arcto**, is discussed in detail in *Connect Arc to Path Segment* starting on page 296 in Chapter 7.

‡ **arct**, designed for user paths, does not leave values on the stack.

Exchange Top Two Elements of Stack

One of the most widely used stack manipulation operators is **exch**, which **exch**anges the top two elements of the stack.

A typical use for **exch** is when a procedure's arguments are passed on the stack and the procedure defines these values as local variables. You'll often see code fragments like the following:

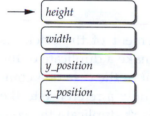

State of stack on entry to **Draw_Box** *procedure.*

```
/Draw_Box {              %  x_position y_position width height
    /height exch def      %  define height
    /width exch def       %  define width
    /y exch def           %  define y coordinate
    /x exch def           %  define x coordinate
    . . .
    rest of procedure body
    . . .
} def
```

In this example, **def** expects a value on the top of the stack with a name object below it. **exch** swaps the arguments to **def** to the correct order—the order in which variables are defined is reversed from the order the operands are on the stack.

Duplicate Top Element of Stack

dup (duplicate) makes a copy of the top element of the stack and pushes the copy onto the stack so the topmost two elements of the stack contain the same data value.

Using our old $\sqrt{a^2 + b^2}$ formula as an example, the original PostScript code was

```
a a mul b b mul add sqrt
```

but you could write the PostScript equally well as

```
a dup mul b dup mul add sqrt
```

Saying "**dup** makes a copy of the top element of the stack" is slightly misleading. To be sure, **dup** does make a duplicate of the top element of the stack. But remember that in the case of a composite object, the top of the stack contains only a reference to the object and not the object itself. So **dup** doesn't duplicate the contents of a composite object; it duplicates only the reference. You must use **copy** to copy the value of a composite object.

Rotate Top *n* Elements of Stack

roll rotates a specified number of elements of the stack a specified number of positions. Here is a picture showing what happens after a **4 1 roll** operation.

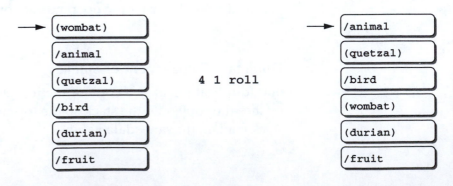

The top four elements of the stack "rotated" upwards. What's a good use for **roll**? A typical use is when stack elements are not in the order in which they're needed. Consider an ellipse procedure. You might call **Draw_Ellipse** something like this.

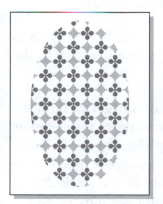

```
%!PS
/inch { 72 mul } def              %   define inch procedure
4.25 inch 5.5 inch                %   x center, y center
3 inch 5 inch                     %   x radius, y radius
Draw_Ellipse                      %   draw the ellipse
AstroidLeaf setpattern            %   fancy pattern
fill                              %   fill the shape
showpage                          %   display page
```

But at the time you call **Draw_Ellipse**, its parameters are on the stack in the wrong order—the *x* and *y* radii are on the top of the stack and the coordinates of the center are underneath. The first thing the procedure wants to do is **translate** to the specified (x, y) coordinates. So you use **roll** to get the stack elements in the correct order. **Draw_Ellipse** might look something like this.

| y radius |
| x radius |
| y center |
| x center |

Operands for
Draw_Ellipse.

```
/Draw_Ellipse {                   %   x center  y center  x radius  y radius
    /m matrix currentmatrix def
    4 2 roll                      %   bring x center, y center to top
    translate                     %   set origin to that position
    1 index div 1 exch scale
    0 0 3 -1 roll                 %   bring radius to top
    0 360 arc
    m setmatrix
} def
```

Draw_Ellipse contains two instances of **roll**. The first **roll** rotates the top four elements of the stack by two positions to bring the (x, y) coordinates of the center of the ellipse to the top. The second **roll** brings the radius to the top of the stack so the center coordinates and radius **arc** are in the correct order.

The general format of **roll** is

number_of_elements   number_of_positions   `roll`

where *number_of_elements* is the number of elements you wish to rotate (*number_of_elements* was 4 in the example above).

number_of_positions is the amount (in stack elements) you wish to rotate the number of elements (*number_of_positions* was 1 in the example above).

number_of_positions can be either a positive or a negative number. If *number_of_positions* is positive, the effect is to move the elements of the stack upward, with the existing top element of the stack moving down to the bottom position. If *number_of_positions* is negative, the effect is to move the elements of the stack downward, with the existing bottom element of the set moving to the top of the stack. Here is our example of weird fruits, animals, and birds again, with **4 −1 roll** as the operation this time.

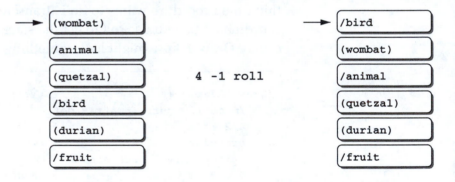

Compare this example with the example on page 241 to see the difference between a positive and negative value for *number_of_positions*. Note that *number_of_elements* **0 roll** does nothing, and a negative value for *number_of_elements* raises a **rangecheck** error.

Retrieve Element from Stack

index is a useful stack operator that retrieves an element from somewhere lower on the stack and pushes a copy of that element onto the top of the stack. The format of **index** is

n **index**

where n is the number of the element you wish to retrieve, counting from the top of the stack. The top element on the stack is element number 0 (zero).[†] **2 index** has this before and after picture.

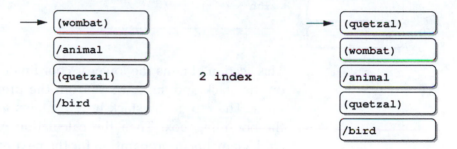

Element number 2, counting from 0, was retrieved from its position on the stack and pushed onto the top of the stack.

Here's a practical example using **index** to manipulate elements of the stack. When you do **pathbbox**, the stack contains the coordinates of the lower-left corner of the path and the upper-right corner of the path. For instance, after you execute the code below, the stack looks like the diagram to the left.

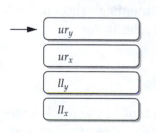

```
%!PS
/inch { 72 mul } def        %   define inch procedure
4.25 inch 5.5 inch          %   center of circle
4 inch                      %   radius of circle
0 360 arc                   %   complete 360° circle
pathbbox                    %   get path bounding box
```

[†] Note that **0 index** is the same as **dup**.

Frequently, what you really want—instead of the coordinates of the lower-left corner (ll_x, ll_y) and the upper-right corner of the bounding box (ur_x, ur_y)—are the coordinates of the lower-left corner and the width and height of the path. You can use **index** to obtain the results you want. The next two stack diagrams show the results as you do the calculations.

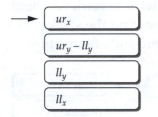

```
2 index             %   get lower y coordinate
sub                 %   compute height
exch                %   prepare for next calculation
```

This section obtains the lower y coordinate from a lower position on the stack and subtracts it from the previous top-of-stack element. The top of the stack now contains $ur_y - ll_y$—the height of the bounding box. Then the calculation exchanges the top two stack elements in preparation for the next part of the computation, which finds the width of the bounding box.

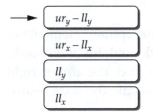

```
3 index             %   get lower x coordinate
sub                 %   compute width
exch                %   rearrange
```

Finally, the stack ends up with the four elements as shown, with the lower-left coordinate and the width and height.

Copy Top n Elements of Stack

Whereas **dup** simply duplicates the top element of the stack, **copy** duplicates n elements. **copy** has two different forms, and its behavior differs depending on which form you use. The first form shown here is the simple form.

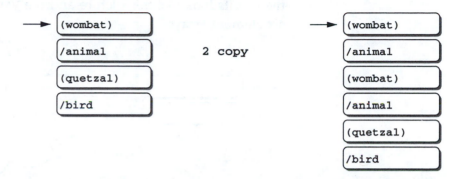

This form of **copy** is like a glorified form of **dup**. Elements of the stack are copied, and if the object on the stack is a composite object, all that gets copied is a reference to the object. The other form of copy actually copies the values of composite objects. The general syntax of this form is

$object_1$ $object_2$ **copy**

where $object_1$ and $object_2$ can be strings, arrays, or dictionaries. In PostScript Level 2, $object_1$ and $object_2$ can be graphics states. In this form of **copy**, $object_1$ and $object_2$ must be the same type of object. Therefore, you can't copy a dictionary into a string, for instance. Suppose the stack contains a reference to an array. The operand stack looks like this picture and the VM "cloud" holds the array, which is six elements long.

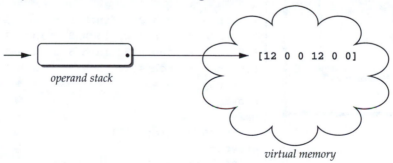

If you now do

```
dup
6 array copy
```

the results look like this picture and the VM "cloud" contains two six-element arrays.

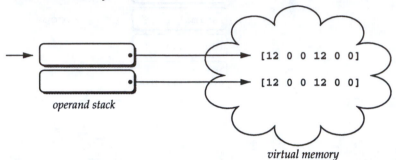

operand stack

virtual memory

This form of **copy** copies only one level deep. If an element of a composite object is itself a composite object, you can, if you wish, apply **copy** recursively to get all the sub-elements.

Clear Stack Down to Mark

cleartomark performs as its name implies—it clears the operand stack down to and including a **mark** object. Here's a practical application of **cleartomark**.

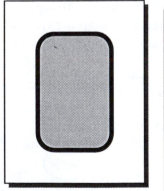

```
%!PS
/inch { 72 mul } def                    %   define inch procedure
4.25 inch 9 inch moveto                 %   set initial point
                                        %   draw four line/arc combinations
2    inch 9 inch 2     inch 5.5 inch 1 inch arcto
2    inch 2 inch 4.25 inch 2    inch 1 inch arcto
6.5 inch 2 inch 6.5   inch 5.5 inch 1 inch arcto
6.5 inch 9 inch 4.25 inch 9    inch 1 inch arcto
16 { pop } repeat                       %   clear debris from stack
closepath                               %   finish the shape
gsave                                   %   push graphics state
    0.90 setgray fill                   %   fill with light gray
grestore                                %   pop graphics state
0.125 inch setlinewidth stroke          %   stroke with fat line
showpage                                %   display page
```

arcto leaves four numbers on the stack.[†] In general, you don't need the four numbers, so you have to pop them off the stack.

The interesting line of code in this example is the line reading **16 {pop} repeat**. You can pop the numbers off the stack in a variety of ways, but another, possibly more succinct, way of doing this job would be to use a combination of **mark** and **cleartomark**.

```
%!PS
/inch { 72 mul } def                % define inch procedure
mark
4.25 inch 9 inch moveto             % set initial point
                                    % draw four line/arc combinations
2    inch 9 inch 2    inch 5.5 inch 1 inch arcto
2    inch 2 inch 4.25 inch 2    inch 1 inch arcto
6.5 inch 2 inch 6.5  inch 5.5 inch 1 inch arcto
6.5 inch 9 inch 4.25 inch 9    inch 1 inch arcto
cleartomark                         % clear debris from stack
closepath                           % finish the shape
gsave                               % push graphics state
0.90 setgray fill                   % fill with light gray
grestore                            % pop graphics state
0.125 inch setlinewidth stroke      % stroke with fat line
showpage                            % display page
```

mark pushes a **mark** *object* onto the operand stack. Then the code goes through various gyrations, ending with a **cleartomark**, which pops the stack down to and including the **mark** object.

Generally, you should always be aware of the contents of the stack, so you can easily use **pop** to remove extraneous stack elements. Use **cleartomark** when you aren't sure what's on the stack, such as when you're including Encapsulated PostScript into your application. **cleartomark** is a useful way to leave a clean stack after an included Encapsulated PostScript program. Your

---

† *Connect Arc to Path Segment* in Chapter 7 on pages 296–300 contains a thorough discussion of **arcto**.

application can start with a **mark** instruction. Then, after the Encapsulated PostScript program, you can execute **cleartomark** to clear the stack to where it was at the beginning of the Encapsulated PostScript program. You can read (a little) more about Encapsulated PostScript in Chapter 14.

Count Elements on Stack

count counts the number of elements on the operand stack and pushes the result onto the top of the operand stack.

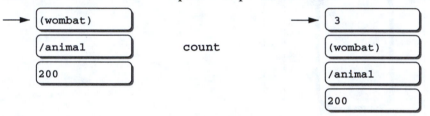

When would you use **count**? One very good use for **count** is when you're debugging new PostScript procedures. We got a little carried away with our stack manipulation and needed to know if the stack was clear of extraneous data at the end of the procedure.

Trigonometric Operators

PostScript is such a powerful graphics language that one would be surprised if PostScript did not supply trigonometric functions to support the graphics operators. PostScript provides the trigonometric functions **sin** and **cos** to compute the sine and cosine of an angle, and **atan** to compute the arctangent of an angle.

Arguments to **sin** and **cos** are angles measured in degrees, and **atan** returns its result in degrees. This is somewhat different from most other languages' trigonometric functions, which demand operand values in radians. If you really want to work in radians, define a procedure to convert radians to degrees. This definition makes a welcome change from **inch**.

```
/radian { 57.2957795 mul } def
```

where $57.2957795 = \dfrac{360}{2 \times \pi}$.

Here's a small example using **sin** and **cos** to draw a starburst of lines around the center of the page.

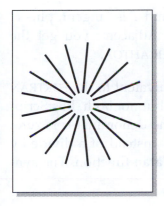

```
%!PS
/inch { 72 mul } def                          %   define inch procedure
/smallrad   50 def                            %   inner radius
/largerad  270 def                            %   outer radius
/points     17 def                            %   number of points on circle
/angle 360 points div def                     %   angle between lines
4.25 inch 5.5 inch translate                  %   place origin in center of page
0 1 points {                                  %   start for loop
   angle mul                                  %   compute angle for this point
   dup                                        %   make a copy
   sin exch cos                               %   compute sine and cosine
   2 copy                                     %   make copies of sine and cosine
   smallrad mul exch smallrad mul moveto
   largerad mul exch largerad mul lineto
} for                                         %   end for loop
8 setlinewidth                                %   set fat line width
stroke                                        %   paint all the lines
showpage                                      %   display page
```

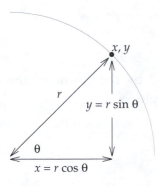

$x = r \cos \theta$

$y = r \sin \theta$

Sines and cosines become quite easy when you look at the picture. (x, y) is a point on the circumference of a circle. This picture shows only a quarter of the circle. If you draw a radius r from the center of the circle to the point (x, y), the line is inclined at some angle θ to the horizontal x axis. Basic trigonometry tells us x and y. The value of x is $r \times \cos \theta$, and the value of y is $r \times \sin \theta$.

Those who need mnemonics to remember elementary trigonometrical relationships might recall SOHCAHTOA. Anyway, the fundamental trigonometrical formulas are

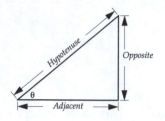

$$Sine\ \theta = \frac{Opposite}{Hypotenuse}$$

$$Cosine\ \theta = \frac{Adjacent}{Hypotenuse}$$

$$Tangent\ \theta = \frac{Opposite}{Adjacent}$$

So if you remember *S* is sine, *C* is cosine, and *T* is tangent, plus *H* is Hypotenuse, *O* is Opposite, and *A* is Adjacent, you get the mnemonic SOH, CAH, and TOA, to make SOHCAHTOA.

The PostScript **atan** function is roughly equivalent to the FORTRAN **atan2**. Either operand to **atan** can be zero, but not both. PostScript **atan** deals correctly with the case where the denominator is zero, leading to the correct value of 90° or 180° instead of a divide by zero error as would occur in the FORTRAN **atan** function. The syntax of the three trigonometric operators is

```
angle sin
angle cos
x y atan
```

where **sin** returns the sine of *angle,* **cos** returns the cosine of *angle,* and **atan** returns the angle whose tangent point is *x, y.* With these three operators you can easily define procedures to compute the other trigonometric functions. This procedure computes the tangent of an angle.

```
/tan {                              %   stack = angle
  dup sin exch cos div
} def
```

tan calculates the sine of the angle divided by the cosine of the angle, thus computing the tangent of the angle.

Relational and Boolean Operators

In *Control Flow—Conditionals* on pages 235–237 earlier in this chapter you read about **if** and **ifelse** control flow operators. Both **if** and **ifelse** require a Boolean value as a first operand to determine if a procedure should be executed. This section discusses the PostScript operators that generate Boolean values.

Comparison Operators

Let's begin with **eq** and **ne**, and their companion operators **le**, **lt**, **gt**, and **ge**. These operators are known as *relational* operators. They each require two operands and return either **true** or **false** depending on whether the stated relation is satisfied. This table defines the relational operators.

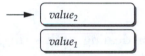

Stack prior to executing any relational operator.

			RELATIONAL OPERATORS
	RELATION		RETURNS **true** IF
$value_1$	$value_2$	eq	$value_1$ is equal to $value_2$
$value_1$	$value_2$	ne	$value_1$ is not equal to $value_2$
$value_1$	$value_2$	gt	$value_1$ is greater than $value_2$
$value_1$	$value_2$	ge	$value_1$ is greater than or equal to $value_2$
$value_1$	$value_2$	lt	$value_1$ is less than $value_2$
$value_1$	$value_2$	le	$value_1$ is less than or equal to $value_2$

The order of the operands is the same in postfix notation as it is in infix notation. Write the expression first in infix notation **a < b**. Then "translate" it into PostScript by placing the operands on the stack in left to right order before the operator: **a b lt**.

These relational operators can compare either numerical data or string data, but both operands must be of the same type. A **typecheck** error is generated if both operands are not the same type. For numerical data, the numerical values are compared. For string data, the strings are compared character by character to determine the relationship. For a string compare, each character of the string is converted to an integer, which is its ASCII value.

Logical Operators

Besides the comparison operators mentioned above, PostScript also supports four logical operators—**and**, **or**, **xor**, and **not**. **not** is easy. It returns **true** if its single operand is **false** and **false** if its single operand is **true**. The remaining logical operators are covered in this table.

TRUTH TABLE FOR LOGICAL OPERATORS				
OPERANDS		**and**	**or**	**xor**
false	false	false	false	false
false	true	false	true	true
true	false	false	true	true
true	true	true	false	false

String Operations

PostScript provides a set of operators for dealing with strings and arrays and, in some cases, for dealing with dictionaries. This section discusses operations you can perform with strings. You create string values on the stack simply by mentioning their literal value, like this example.

→ Snowbird

```
(Snowbird)
```

which places a string value on the operand stack. You can create a string object in the current dictionary with

```
/SkiAt (Snowbird) def
```

You can create a string object of a specified size like this example

```
100 string def
```

which places a string value of 100 eight-bit characters on the top of the operand stack. Finally, you create a named string object of a specified size in the current dictionary with

```
/name 100 string def
```

Getting an Element from a String

Now that you've created some string objects, what kinds of things can you do with strings? You fetch a single element (eight-bit character) out of a string using **get**.

```
(glop) 2 get
```

This example fetches the letter "o" out of the string and leaves the integer value of the "o" on the top of the operand stack. This picture illustrates the operand stack before and after **get**.

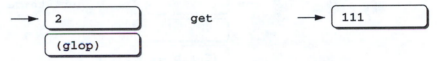

get extracts the integer value of the element from the string—you don't get a one-character substring left on the top of the stack. If you want a one-character substring, use **getinterval** instead. Note indexing in strings starts at zero, just as for arrays.

Putting an Element into a String

You put a single eight-bit character into a string using **put**. Here's a rather contrived example using **put**.

Flipping and flopping.

```
%!PS
/inch { 72 mul } def              %  define inch procedure
/Palatino-Roman findfont          %  choose font
3 inch scalefont setfont
/MyString (flip) def              %  define string
1.0 inch 6.5 inch moveto          %  set current point
MyString show                     %  show string
MyString 2 111 put                %  put new character
2.5 inch 4.5 inch moveto          %  set current point
1 -1 scale                        %  invert coordinate system
MyString show                     %  show string
showpage                          %  display page
```

As with **get**, the character is specified using its integer value. **put** does not leave any results on the operand stack.

Getting a Substring from a String

Notice **get** and **put** dealt with single characters from a string. The single characters are eight-bit integer values. PostScript also has operators to deal with substrings, or parts of strings.

getinterval obtains a substring of a string. Here is what it looks like both in PostScript code and on the stack

```
(Caribbean) 5 4 getinterval
```

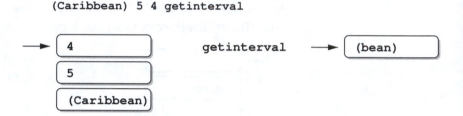

getinterval extracts four characters from the string, starting at character position 5, and leaves the new string **(bean)** on the top of the stack. Indexing begins from 0, just as with **get** and **put**.

Here's a practical example using **getinterval** in the process of obtaining information about fonts on our NeXT Computer.

Times-Bold.font/Times-Bold
Times-BoldItalic.font/Times-BoldItalic
Times-Italic.font/Times-Italic
Times-Roman.font/Times-Roman

Some names of fonts.

```
%!PS
/inch { 72 mul } def            %   define inch procedure
/Palatino-Italic findfont       %   choose font
48 scalefont setfont
/top 9 inch def                 %   y location for first string
/junk 256 string def            %   place holder
11 inch 0 translate             %   landscape page
90 rotate
(%font%Times*) {                %   match all Times fonts
    0.25 inch top moveto        %   set current point
    dup                         %   copy string
    6 exch length 6 sub         %   compute interval
    getinterval                 %   get substring
    show                        %   show it
    /top top 1.5 inch sub def   %   move y position
} junk filenameforall           %   loop on all files
showpage                        %   display page
```

This example uses an operator with which you are not yet familiar—**filenameforall**. All you need to know for this example is that **filenameforall** finds all the fonts in the Times family, then loops for each font and executes a procedure.

Inside the procedure of this example, the strings all have the form **%font%Times**. **getinterval** removes **%font%** and displays the rest of the font name. The lines

```
dup
6 exch length 6 sub
getinterval
```

do the trick. The **length 6 sub** computes the number of characters trailing the first six. So, **getinterval** starts with the sixth character and gets all the characters until the end of the string. **show** displays the substring returned by **getinterval**.

Putting a Substring into a String

putinterval is the complementary operator to **getinterval**. **putinterval** inserts a substring into a string. This example changes **Pantomime** to **Palm Tree**. We'd like to be on a tropical island, sipping mai tais under a palm tree about now. Ah, but we digress.

Tools you need to work with PostScript.

```
%!PS
/inch { 72 mul } def              %   define inch procedure
/Palatino-Roman findfont          %   choose font
1.5 inch scalefont setfont
/MyString (Pantomime) def         %   define string
0.5 inch 9.0 inch moveto          %   set current point
MyString show                     %   show string
MyString 2 (lm Tre) putinterval   %   change string
1.0 inch 1.0 inch moveto          %   set current point
MyString show                     %   show string
showpage                          %   display page
```

Like **put**, **putinterval** doesn't push results on the operand stack.

Using forall to Traverse Strings

You can use **forall** to work your way through a string, one character at a time. For each element (character) in the string, **forall** pushes that character onto the top of the operand stack.

The next program at the top of the following page is an example to work through the lowercase alphabet and print the integer values of the characters.

a = 97	b = 98
c = 99	d = 100
e = 101	f = 102
g = 103	h = 104
i = 105	j = 106
k = 107	l = 108
m = 109	n = 110
o = 111	p = 112
q = 113	r = 114
s = 115	t = 116
u = 117	v = 118
w = 119	x = 120
y = 121	z = 122

Character values using **forall**.

```
%!PS
/inch { 72 mul } def                    %    define inch procedure
/Palatino-Roman findfont 48 scalefont setfont
/top 10 inch def                        %    position of top line
/left 1 inch def                        %    position of left margin
/switch true def                        %    for switching margin
(abcdefghijklmnopqrstuvwxyz)            %    lowercase alphabet on stack
{                                       %    start forall loop
    dup                                 %    need copy of value
    1 string                            %    need one-character string
    dup                                 %    need copy for later
    0 4 -1 roll                         %    get parameters in right order
    put                                 %    put integer value in string
    left top moveto                     %    set current point
    show                                %    image character
    ( = ) show                          %    image equals sign
    10 string cvs                       %    convert integer value to string
    show                                %    show integer value
    switch {                            %    decide where to place margin
        /left 5 inch def                %    move margin to middle of page
        /switch false def               %    set up for next time
    } {
        /left 1 inch def                %    restore margin
        /top top 56 sub def             %    decrement line position
        /switch true def                %    set up for next time
    } ifelse
} forall                                %    end forall loop
showpage                                %    display page
```

Relational Operators With Strings

Relational operators for numerical values on page 251 work equally well for string values. The situation is slightly more complex for string values, however. Let's look at a procedure that uses the **gt** (greater than) relational operator to implement a simple bubble sort.

```
/bubble {                           %   stack = unsorted array
  /Array exch def                   %   remember array
  0 1 Array length 2 sub {          %   loop through array
    -1 0 {                          %   and again
      /i exch def                   %   define loop variable
      Array i 2 getinterval         %   get array with two strings
      aload pop                     %   get two strings
      2 copy                        %   copy them
      gt {                          %   is one greater
         exch 2 array astore        %   put strings in small array
         Array exch i exch          %   swap them
         putinterval
      } { pop pop } ifelse          %   otherwise clean up stack
    } for
  } for
  Array                             %   return sorted array
} def
```

On the next page is the bubble sort in action, sorting a list of wines (including bubbly!) into order. When **gt** is called, two neighboring strings are on the operand stack. **gt** returns **true** if the first string is greater than the second, and **false** otherwise. What does it mean for a string to be greater than another string? As you see from the example, $string_1$ is greater than $string_2$ if $string_1$ alphabetically follows $string_2$.

Cabernet
Cabernet Sauvignon
Champagne
Chardonnay
Chianti
Gamay
Merlot
Pinot Noir
Zinfandel

List of wines sorted into
ascending order.

```
%!PS
/inch { 72 mul } def                        %   define inch procedure
/Palatino-Roman findfont                    %   choose font
0.75 inch scalefont setfont
/base 9.5 inch def                          %   y location of first wine
[
    (Chardonnay)     (Cabernet)
    (Cabernet Sauvignon)
    (Chianti)     (Merlot)
    (Pinot Noir)     (Champagne)
    (Gamay)     (Zinfandel)
]                                           %   define array of strings
bubble                                      %   sort the array
{
    0.5 inch base moveto                    %   set current point
    show                                    %   show string
    /base base 1 inch sub def               %   move y position
} forall                                    %   for all strings in the array
showpage                                    %   display page
```

Notice the relative location of **Cabernet** and **Cabernet Sauvignon**. **Cabernet Sauvignon** is considered "greater than" **Cabernet** because it contains more characters. **lt** (less than) reverses the sense of the compare from **gt** (greater than) and returns **true** when the first string is less than the second.

To implement a descending sort, change **gt** to **lt** in the preceding bubble sort procedure. Now the wines will be sorted in reverse order. The bubble sort could be even more clever and change the sense of the sort based on a second operand. Here's the procedure definition for a bi-directional bubble sort, and the example on the next page illustrates the bi-directional bubble sort in action, using a procedure containing **lt** (less than) as the comparison criterion.

```
/bibubble {                              %  stack = unsorted array operator
  /compare exch def                      %  remember operator
  /Array exch def                        %  remember array
  0 1 Array length 2 sub {               %  loop through array
    -1 0 {                               %  and again
      /i exch def                        %  define loop variable
      Array i 2 getinterval              %  get array with two strings
      aload pop                          %  get two strings
      2 copy                             %  copy them
      compare {                          %  compare them
        exch 2 array astore              %  put strings in small array
        Array exch i exch                %  swap them
        putinterval
      } { pop pop } ifelse               %  otherwise clean up stack
    } for
  } for
  Array                                  %  return sorted array
} def
```

Zinfandel
Pinot Noir
Merlot
Gamay
Chianti
Chardonnay
Champagne
Cabernet Sauvignon
Cabernet

List of wines sorted into descending order.

```
%!PS
/inch { 72 mul } def                     %  define inch procedure
/Palatino-Roman findfont                 %  choose font
0.75 inch scalefont setfont
/base 9.5 inch def                       %  y location of first wine
[
    (Chardonnay)     (Cabernet)
    (Cabernet Sauvignon)
    (Chianti)     (Merlot)
    (Pinot Noir)     (Champagne)
    (Gamay)     (Zinfandel)
]                                        %  define array of strings
{ lt } bibubble                          %  sort in descending order
{
    0.5 inch base moveto                 %  set current point
    show                                 %  show string
    /base base 1.0 inch sub def          %  move y position
} forall                                 %  for all strings in the array
showpage                                 %  display page
```

Now you understand what it means for strings to be less than or greater than one another, but what does it mean for strings to be equal? To discover if strings are equal use the **eq** relational operator. **eq** returns **true** if

❑ the two strings are of equal length, and

❑ the two strings have exactly the same contents

eq returns **false** if

❑ the two strings are of unequal length, or

❑ the two strings are of equal length but have unequal contents

The next example decides what to do based on the weather.

Go To Beach

```
%!PS
/inch { 72 mul } def                    %   define inch procedure
/Palatino-Roman findfont                %   choose font
1.0 inch scalefont setfont              %   various weather conditions
/Piraeus (Sunny) def
/Seattle (Raining) def
/Aruba (Windy) def
/London (Foggy) def
/LosAngeles (Smoggy) def
/Bangkok (Humid) def
/Today (Windy) def                      %   today's weather
0.75 inch 5.5 inch moveto               %   ah, what to do
Today Piraeus eq Today Aruba eq or
{ (Go To Beach) show }
{ (Go To Cafe) show } ifelse
showpage                                %   display page
```

In the example, **Today** is exactly the same as **Aruba** so you can go to the beach. Had **Today** been **Wind, Winds,** or anything other than **Windy** or **Sunny,** you'd have to go to the cafe instead. You can determine the behavior of **ne** (not equal), **ge** (greater than or equal to), and **le** (less than or equal to) from that of **eq, gt,** and **lt.**

6 Line Weights and Line Styles

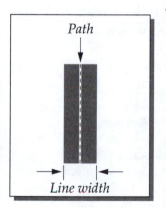

Path

Line width

Y ou were introduced to line width (often called *line weight*) in earlier chapters. This chapter continues with the exposition of line widths and also covers other aspects of line styles such as line joins, line caps, miter limits, and dashed line styles.

A PostScript job starts with a preset line width of one point, so that when you use the **stroke** operator to stroke a path, any line that gets stroked is one point wide. Before you use a **stroke** operator to stroke a path, you can set the width at which you wish the line to be drawn.

Non-uniform Scaling of Thick Lines

W hat happens to the width of a line in a non-uniformly scaled coordinate system is not immediately obvious. As it happens, line widths get scaled along with everything else—the PostScript transformation model is quite consistent. Here is an example of a square stroked with a fat line. But the coordinate system was scaled prior to stroking the path.

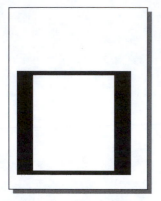

Non-uniformly scaled lines.

```
%!PS
/inch { 72 mul } def          % define inch procedure
1 inch 1 inch moveto          % set current point
6 inch 0 rlineto              % bottom of square
0 6 inch rlineto              % right side of square
-6 inch 0 rlineto             % top of square
closepath                     % complete the path
0.25 inch setlinewidth        % set fat line width
4 1 scale                     % scale coordinate system
stroke                        % paint the outline the page
showpage                      % display page
```

As you see, the line width along the *x* axis is fatter than the line width along the *y* axis. This aspect of scaling the line width becomes especially important when you draw curved path segments. Suppose you draw an ellipse stroked with a fat line.

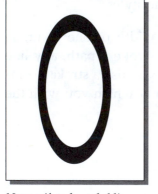

Non-uniformly scaled lines.

```
%!PS
/inch { 72 mul } def          % define inch procedure
newpath                       % start new path
4.25 inch 5.5 inch translate  % translate to middle of page
1 2 scale                     % scale for ellipse
0 0 2 inch 0 360 arc          % draw circle in scaled system
closepath                     % finish the shape
0.5 inch setlinewidth         % set fat line width
stroke                        % stroke the path
showpage                      % display page
```

You can see the slightly unexpected result—the weight of the line is scaled along with everything else. Although somewhat surprising, this is perfectly consistent with the PostScript imaging model. But it may not be what you actually want unless you're playing with fancy calligraphic effects.

The temptation is to fix this problem by doing the **scale** operation to scale the coordinate system, and then "resetting" the scaling, by possibly doing something like the following:

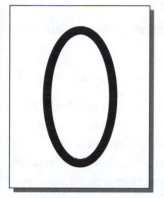

Uniformly scaled lines.

```
%!PS
/inch { 72 mul } def                    %  define inch procedure
newpath                                 %  start new path
4.25 inch 5.5 inch translate            %  translate to middle of page
1 2 scale                               %  scale for ellipse
0 0 2 inch 0 360 arc                    %  draw in scaled coordinate system
closepath                               %  finish the shape
1 0.5 scale                             %  reset scaling
0.5 inch setlinewidth                   %  set fat line width
stroke                                  %  stroke the path
showpage                                %  display page
```

This is not the correct way to go about the job, however. The way to get the line width stroked uniformly around the curve is to remember the CTM, establish the path in the scaled coordinate system, then restore the CTM that was in effect before the scaling took place. Here's some new code alongside the results.

Uniformly scaled lines with path constructed in a non-uniformly scaled coordinate system.

```
%!PS
/inch { 72 mul } def                    %  define inch procedure
/Draw_Ellipse {                         %  x y xr yr
    /m matrix currentmatrix def         %  remember CTM
    4 2 roll translate scale            %  scale coordinate system
    0 0 1 0 360 arc                     %  draw circle in scaled coordinates
    closepath                           %  finish the shape
    m setmatrix                         %  restore CTM
} def
4.25 inch 5.5 inch 2 inch 4 inch Draw_Ellipse
1.0 inch setlinewidth                   %  set fat line width
stroke                                  %  stroke the path
showpage                                %  display page
```

Minimum Line Width

PostScript accepts a line width of zero as an argument to the **set-linewidth** operator. The result of

```
0 setlinewidth                          %    bad—device-dependent!
```

is the thinnest possible line the imaging device can render. On a 300 dots per inch laser printer, the thinnest line is one pixel wide, which is $\frac{1}{300}$ inch wide. Such a line width may well be quite acceptable to you, but asking for a thin line in this way makes your PostScript document device-dependent. Some printing devices can't print a one-pixel line at all. The typesetter used to typeset this book prints lines so fine they are virtually invisible. The moral of the story is, do not use **0 setlinewidth** as a quick hack to get minimum line width. If you really want a line $\frac{1}{300}$ inch wide, use **0.24 setlinewidth** (0.24 points is $\frac{1}{300}$ inch).

Line Caps

Line *caps* refer to the way in which the ends of lines are "finished" when they are stroked. A line can be "finished" in one of three ways. Two of these line caps project the end of the line outside the path that you have established.

❑ *butt cap*—the stroke is squared off at the end of the path. Also called *chopped* by some applications

❑ *round cap*—the stroke is finished with a rounded end

❑ *square cap*—the stroke is finished with a squared off end

The type of line cap is established in the graphics state by the **set-linecap** operator. The argument to **setlinecap** determines the type of line cap.

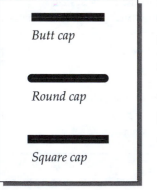

Butt cap

Round cap

Square cap

LINECAP VALUE	TYPE OF LINE CAP
0 setlinecap	Butt cap (default)
1 setlinecap	Round cap
2 setlinecap	Square cap

Butt Line Caps

Butt caps are the simplest form of line caps. Line ends are finished square to the endpoints of the path; the ends do not extend past the endpoints.[†] Butt caps are the preset value of line caps. You set butt caps with a **0 setlinecap** instruction.

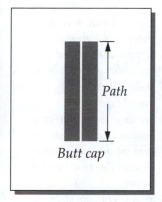

Path

Butt cap

```
%!PS
/inch { 72 mul } def              %   define inch procedure
4.25 inch 3.0 inch moveto         %   move to initial point
4.25 inch 9.0 inch lineto         %   draw a line segment
gsave                             %   remember graphics state
    2 inch setlinewidth           %   make line fat
    0 setlinecap                  %   butt caps
    0.50 setgray stroke           %   stroke with medium gray
grestore                          %   restore graphics state
gsave                             %   remember graphics state
    0.125 inch setlinewidth       %   thinner line to show path
    1.0 setgray stroke            %   stroke with white
grestore                          %   restore graphics state
showpage                          %   display page
```

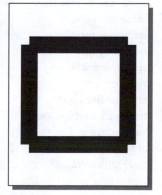

Butt caps chop off the ends of lines.

```
%!PS
/inch { 72 mul } def              %   define inch procedure
1.25 inch 2.5 inch moveto         %   set current point
7.25 inch 2.5 inch lineto         %   add line segment
7.25 inch 2.5 inch moveto         %   set current point
7.25 inch 8.5 inch lineto         %   add line segment
7.25 inch 8.5 inch moveto         %   set current point
1.25 inch 8.5 inch lineto         %   add line segment
1.25 inch 8.5 inch moveto         %   set current point
1.25 inch 2.5 inch lineto         %   add line segment
1 inch setlinewidth               %   fat line width
stroke                            %   paint the path
showpage                          %   display page
```

[†] Butt caps are also called *chopped line caps* by some applications.

Round Line Caps

Round caps draw a rounded end at the endpoints of the path, with a radius of half the current line width.

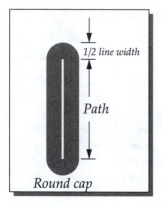

1/2 line width

Path

Round cap

```
%!PS
/inch { 72 mul } def                    %   define inch procedure
4.25 inch 3.0 inch moveto               %   move to initial point
4.25 inch 9.0 inch lineto               %   draw a line segment
gsave                                   %   remember graphics state
    2 inch setlinewidth                 %   make line fat
    1 setlinecap                        %   round caps
    0.50 setgray stroke                 %   stroke with medium gray
grestore                                %   restore graphics state
gsave                                   %   remember graphics state
    0.125 inch setlinewidth             %   thinner line to show path
    1.0 setgray stroke                  %   stroke with white
grestore                                %   restore graphics state
showpage                                %   display page
```

Round caps stick beyond ends of lines.

```
%!PS
/inch { 72 mul } def                          %   define inch procedure
4.25 inch 1 inch moveto                       %   set current point
4.25 inch 10 inch lineto                      %   add line segment
stroke                                        %   stroke the path
2 inch setlinewidth                           %   set fat line width
4.25 inch 5.5 inch 3 inch 270 90 arc          %   draw arc
1 setlinecap                                  %   set round line caps
0.5 setgray stroke                            %   stroke with medium gray
4.25 inch 5.5 inch 3 inch 270 90 arc          %   draw arc again
0 setlinecap                                  %   set butt line caps
0.0 setgray stroke                            %   stroke with black
showpage                                      %   display page
```

This example of round line caps illustrates a well-known optical illusion—the semi-circular caps give a kind of "dumbbell" appearance to the ends. Doctor Peter Karow of URW covers this phenonemon in *Digital Formats for Typefaces* and discusses using *clothoid curves* instead of round line caps to avoid the illusion.

Square Line Caps

Square caps draw squared-off ends at the ends of the path. The extent of the squared-off section is half the current line width.

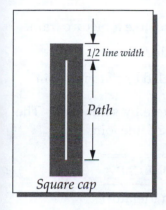

Square cap

```
%!PS
/inch { 72 mul } def            % define inch procedure
4.25 inch 3.0 inch moveto       % move to initial point
4.25 inch 9.0 inch lineto       % draw a line segment
gsave                           % remember graphics state
    2 inch setlinewidth         % make line fat
    2 setlinecap                % square caps
    0.50 setgray                % 50% gray color
    stroke                      % stroke the path
grestore                        % restore graphics state
gsave                           % remember graphics state
    0.125 inch setlinewidth     % thinner line to show path
    1.0 setgray                 % draw it in white
    stroke                      % stroke the path
grestore                        % restore graphics state
showpage                        % display page
```

square caps project beyond ends of lines.

```
%!PS
/inch { 72 mul } def            % define inch procedure
1 inch 2 inch moveto            % set current point
4.25 inch 9 inch lineto         % add line segment
4.25 inch 9 inch moveto         % set current point
7.5 inch 2 inch lineto          % add line segment
7.5 inch 2 inch moveto          % set current point
1 inch 2 inch lineto            % add line segment
2 setlinecap                    % set square caps
1 inch setlinewidth             % fat line width
stroke                          % paint the path
showpage                        % display page
```

Line Joins

Line joins refer to the way in which ends of lines are joined or connected when they meet at an angle. Lines can be joined in one of three ways.

Mitered

Rounded

Beveled

❏ *mitered join*—lines are joined with a mitre, like a picture frame

❏ *round join*—lines are joined with a rounded corner

❏ *beveled join*—lines are joined with a beveled or flattened join

The type of line join is set in the graphics state by **setlinejoin**. The argument to **setlinejoin** determines the type of line join.

LINECAP VALUE	TYPE OF LINE CAP
0 setlinejoin	Mitered join (default)
1 setlinejoin	Round join
2 setlinejoin	Beveled join

Mitered Line Joins

Mitered joins are joined in the manner of a picture frame such that the corner joins at a sharp angle.

*Mitered
line join*

```
%!PS
/inch { 72 mul } def              % define inch procedure
1.5 inch 1 inch moveto            % move to initial point
4.25 inch 7 inch lineto           % draw left leg
7.0 inch 1 inch lineto            % draw right leg
gsave                             % push graphics state
    2 inch setlinewidth           % set fat line width
    0 setlinejoin                 % mitered line join
    0.50 setgray stroke           % stroke with medium gray
grestore                          % pop graphics state
gsave                             % push graphics state
    1 setlinejoin                 % round line join
    0.125 inch setlinewidth       % thin line width to show path
    1.0 setgray stroke            % draw path in white
grestore                          % pop graphics state
showpage                          % display page
```

Line segments that meet at very sharp angles and with mitered line joins can potentially produce a long "spike."

```
%!PS
/inch { 72 mul } def                       % define inch procedure
3.0 inch 1 inch moveto                     % move to initial point
4.25 inch 7 inch lineto                    % draw left leg
5.5 inch 1 inch lineto                     % draw right leg
gsave                                      % push graphics state
    1.5 inch setlinewidth                  % set fat line width
    0 setlinejoin                          % mitered line join
    0.50 setgray stroke                    % stroke with medium gray
grestore                                   % pop graphics state
gsave                                      % push graphics state
    1 setlinejoin                          % round line join
    0.125 inch setlinewidth                % thin line width to show path
    1.0 setgray stroke                     % draw path in white
grestore                                   % pop graphics state
showpage                                   % display page
```

You can prevent these weird looking "spikes" on mitered joins by using the **setmiterlimit** operator. With judicious use of **setmiterlimit**, the PostScript interpreter converts mitered joins smaller than specified angles to beveled joins. **setmiterlimit** is described later in this chapter.

Round Line Joins

Round joins produce a rounded corner at the line joins.

Round line join

```
%!PS
/inch { 72 mul } def                    % define inch procedure
1.5 inch 1 inch moveto                  % move to initial point
4.25 inch 8 inch lineto                 % draw left leg
7.0 inch 1 inch lineto                  % draw right leg
gsave                                   % push graphics state
    2 inch setlinewidth                 % set fat line width
    1 setlinejoin                       % rounded line join
    0.50 setgray stroke                 % draw line in gray
grestore                                % pop graphics state
gsave                                   % push graphics state
    1 setlinejoin                       % round line join
    0.125 inch setlinewidth             % thin line width to show path
    1.0 setgray stroke                  % draw path in white
grestore                                % pop graphics state
showpage                                % display page
```

Round line joins round off corners.

```
%!PS
/inch { 72 mul } def                    % define inch procedure
1 inch 2 inch moveto                    % set current point
4.25 inch 9 inch lineto                 % add line segment
7.5 inch 2 inch lineto                  % add another line segment
closepath                               % finish the shape
1 setlinejoin                           % set round line joins
1 inch setlinewidth                     % fat line width
stroke                                  % paint the path
showpage                                % display page
```

Beveled Line Joins

Beveled joins draw a beveled end at the place where the line segments meet. The next picture and code example illustrate beveled line joins.

*Beveled
line join*

```
%!PS
/inch { 72 mul } def              %   define inch procedure
1.5 inch 1 inch moveto            %   move to initial point
4.25 inch 8 inch lineto           %   draw left leg
7.0 inch 1 inch lineto            %   draw right leg
gsave                             %   push graphics state
    2 inch setlinewidth           %   set fat line width
    2 setlinejoin                 %   beveled line join
    0.50 setgray                  %   gray shade
    stroke                        %   stroke the path
grestore                          %   pop graphics state
gsave                             %   push graphics state
    1 setlinejoin                 %   round line join
    0.125 inch setlinewidth       %   thin line width to show path
    1.0 setgray                   %   draw path in white
    stroke                        %   stroke the path
grestore                          %   pop graphics state
showpage                          %   display page
```

The *PostScript Language Reference Manual* states that beveled line joins are actually stroked by stroking the lines with butt line caps, and then filling in the "notch" that's left over. This picture illustrates the process.

```
%!PS
/inch { 72 mul } def          %  define inch procedure
1.0 inch 2.0 inch moveto      %  move to initial point
4.25 inch 8 inch lineto       %  draw left leg
7.5 inch 2.0 inch lineto      %  draw right leg
2.0 inch setlinewidth         %  set fat line width
2 setlinejoin                 %  mitered line join
0.50 setgray                  %  gray shade
stroke                        %  stroke the path
showpage                      %  display page
```

Miter Limits

Closely related to the line join is the *miter limit*. The miter limit[†] has nothing to do with Bishop's headgear but refers to the control you can impose on how mitered line joins behave when the lines meet at sharp angles.

When thick lines with mitered line joins meet at small angles, the point of the join gets longer, until you eventually end up with unacceptably long "spikes." These examples illustrate what happens when the angle between the lines gets smaller—the "spike" gets longer until it looks completely ridiculous, and finally, the interpreter cuts off the "spike" and converts it to a bevel join.

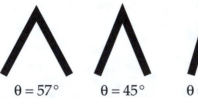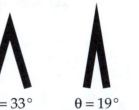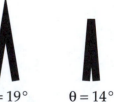

θ = 57°   θ = 45°   θ = 33°   θ = 19°   θ = 14°

This next diagram illustrates miter length and line width for two fat lines joining at an angle. The actual path is illustrated by the

---

† or mitre limit, depending where you live.

white line in the center of the fat lines. The miter length is the distance from the inside point of the line join to the top of the point. The angle θ is the angle between the lines of the path.

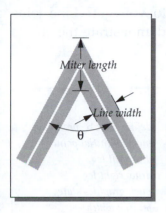

```
%!PS
/inch { 72 mul } def          %    define inch procedure
1 inch 2 inch moveto          %    set initial point
4.25 inch 8 inch lineto       %    left leg of path
7.5 inch 2 inch lineto        %    right leg of path
1.5 inch setlinewidth         %    set fat line width
0.75 setgray stroke           %    paint the path
showpage                      %    display page
```

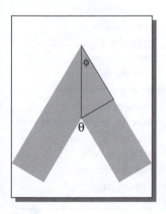

This diagram shows the relationship between the miter length and the line width. You can construct a right-angled triangle that occupies half the intersection of the lines. The angle θ is the angle between the lines of the path, and the angle φ is the "half angle"—that is, $\frac{\theta}{2}$. You can see that the half angle φ is the interior angle of this constructed triangle. The hypotenuse of the triangle is the miter length. The opposite side of the triangle is the line width. By simple trigonometry you can see that

$$\frac{line\ width}{miter\ length} = \sin\phi$$

More importantly, you can turn this equation around so that given the half angle φ and the line width, you can compute what the miter length will be

$$miter\ length = \frac{line\ width}{\sin\phi}$$

So far you've seen line width versus miter length and how they're related to the angle between the lines. Where does the miter limit come in? The miter limit determines an angle at which the mitered line join gets converted to a beveled line join, so that the spike gets cut off to a nice square end.

Interactions Between Line Caps and Line Joins

How do line caps and line joins interact? If you set round line caps and mitered line joins, what do you get? Line joins override line caps. This code and picture demonstrate the effects of mitered line join with rounded line caps.

Rounded line caps with mitered line joins.

```
%!PS
/inch { 72 mul } def              %   define inch procedure
1.5 inch 1.5 inch moveto          %   move to initial point
4.25 inch 8 inch lineto           %   draw left leg
7.0 inch 1.5 inch lineto          %   draw right leg
gsave                             %   push graphics state
    2.0 inch setlinewidth         %   fat line width
    0 setlinejoin                 %   mitered line join
    1 setlinecap                  %   rounded line cap
    0.50 setgray                  %   gray shade
    stroke                        %   stroke the path
grestore                          %   pop graphics state
gsave                             %   push graphics state
    1 setlinecap                  %   rounded line cap
    0.125 inch setlinewidth       %   thin line width to show path
    1.0 setgray                   %   draw path in white
    stroke                        %   stroke the path
grestore                          %   pop graphics state
showpage                          %   display page
```

Dashed Line Styles

One of the services PostScript offers is *dash patterns* to use for stroking lines. You set dash patterns using the **setdash** operator, and with judicious use of the patterns combined with line caps, you get dotted lines for free.

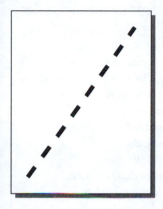

```
%!PS
/inch { 72 mul } def                        %   define inch procedure
1 inch 1 inch moveto                        %   set current point
7.5 inch 10 inch lineto                     %   line across page
[ 0.75 inch  0.75 inch ] 0  setdash  %   dash pattern
0.25 inch setlinewidth                      %   fat line width
stroke                                      %   paint the path
showpage                                    %   display page
```

This is basic **setdash**. It draws a diagonal line across the page with ¾-inch dashes spaced every ¾ inch. The first argument—the array of values—specifies the dashes and spaces. The second argument is an offset, which you will see shortly. **setdash** can be more complex than this example. Here is a variation with pairs of dashes separated by a wider gap.

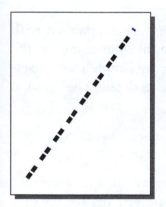

```
%!PS
/inch { 72 mul } def                        %   define inch procedure
1 inch 1 inch moveto                        %   set current point
7.5 inch 10 inch lineto                     %   line across page
                                            %   set dash pattern
[0.375 inch  0.125 inch  0.375 inch  0.5 inch] 0 setdash
0.25 inch setlinewidth                      %   fat line width
stroke                                      %   paint the path
showpage                                    %   display page
```

You can set dash patterns for lines anywhere—this example is chosen to illustrate that dashes "go around corners."

```
%!PS
/inch { 72 mul } def                    %   define inch procedure
4.25 inch 2 inch moveto                 %   set current point
                                        %   draw four arc/line combinations
6.5 inch 2 inch 6.5 inch 5.5 inch 1 inch arcto
6.5 inch 9 inch 4.25 inch 9 inch 1 inch arcto
2 inch 9 inch 2 inch 5.5 inch 1 inch arcto
2 inch 2 inch 4.25 inch 2 inch 1 inch arcto
closepath                               %   finish the shape
16 { pop } repeat                       %   remove dross from stack
gsave                                   %   push graphics state
  0.50 setgray fill                     %   fill with medium gray
grestore                                %   pop graphics state
[ 0.5 inch  0.25 inch ] 0 setdash       %   set dash pattern
0.25 inch setlinewidth                  %   fat line width
stroke                                  %   paint the path
showpage                                %   display page
```

Note also that the gaps are really gaps—they are not painted with white but are left free of paint, so that the fill color comes to the edge of the path. Now that you've seen some simple uses of **setdash**, you need to see the operator in more detail. The general form of **setdash** looks like this:

$$[\; on_1 \; off_1 \quad on_2 \; off_2 \quad \cdots \quad on_n \; off_n \;] \quad offset \quad \texttt{setdash}$$

setdash has only two parameters—an array of on_n and off_n values, and an *offset* value. Each on_n represents the length of a dash. Each off_n represents the length of a gap between dashes. Finally, the *offset* parameter determines the distance into the dash pattern that the first dash will start. Think of the offset as a kind of "phase" parameter that selects the starting point in the pattern.

Dashed Line Styles with Line Caps

How do the different line caps interact with dashed lines? Suppose you draw a dashed line across the page. Here is the picture and the code to draw the line.

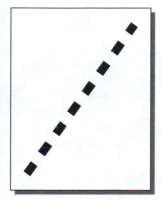

```
%!PS
/inch { 72 mul } def              %  define inch procedure
1 inch 1 inch moveto              %  set current point
7.5 inch 10 inch lineto           %  draw line across page
0.5 inch setlinewidth             %  fat line width
[ 0.75 inch  0.75 inch ] 0 setdash  %  dash pattern
stroke                            %  paint the path
showpage                          %  display page
```

This fragment of PostScript code draws a line from one inch above and to the right of the origin to one inch below and to the left of the upper-right corner of a sheet of 8½-by-11-inch paper.

In the absence of any information to the contrary, the preset line cap is the butt cap. The dashed line you see is what you specified. What happens if you specify a different line cap?

```
%!PS
/inch { 72 mul } def              %  define inch procedure
1 inch 1 inch moveto              %  set current point
7.5 inch 10 inch lineto           %  draw line across page
[ 0.75 inch 0.75 inch ] 0 setdash  %  dash pattern
0.5 inch setlinewidth             %  fat line width
1 setlinecap                      %  round line caps
stroke                            %  paint the path
showpage                          %  display page
```

Dashed lines with rounded line caps.

The line reading **1 setlinecap** sets rounded line caps for the **stroke** operator. Notice how the rounded ends of the line segments protrude, so that the gaps between the dashes are smaller. This behavior of line caps in conjunction with dashed lines is perfectly consistent with the behavior of stroked lines.

You can use this effect of round line caps with dashed line styles to draw dotted lines. You get dotted lines by specifying a dash length of zero and a space length of whatever you want the gap between dots to be. Here's an ellipse with a necklace of round dots painted around its circumference. The definition of the **ellipse** procedure appears at the top of page 316.

Dotted lines around a path. The dots aren't uniformly finished.

```
%!PS
/inch { 72 mul } def                    %  define inch procedure
4.25 inch 5.5 inch 3 inch 4 inch ellipse
gsave                                   %  push graphics state
  0.50 setgray fill                     %  fill with medium gray
grestore                                %  pop graphics state
[ 0 0.75 inch ] 0 setdash               %  set dash pattern
0.25 inch setlinewidth                  %  set fat line width
1 setlinecap stroke                     %  round line caps
showpage                                %  display page
```

Notice from the picture that the dots aren't spaced evenly at the East point of the ellipse. **setdash** lays out the marks and spaces of the dash pattern in precisely the way you asked for it. PostScript makes no attempt to divine your intentions—so if you wish the marks and spaces to be evenly spread around a perimeter, you (or your application) must perform the computations to determine the mark-to-space ratio. Here's an example to compute the size of the spaces to lay dots evenly around a circle.

Dotted lines around a path with spacing computed correctly.

```
%!PS
/inch { 72 mul } def                              %  define inch procedure
4.25 inch 5.5 inch 3 inch 0 360 arc               %  draw circle
closepath                                         %  finish the shape
gsave                                             %  push graphics state
  0.50 setgray fill                               %  fill with medium gray
grestore                                          %  pop graphics state
[ 0 3 inch 2 3.14159 mul mul 0.5 inch div ] 0 setdash
0.25 inch setlinewidth                            %  set fat line width
1 setlinecap                                      %  round line caps
stroke                                            %  paint the path
showpage                                          %  display page
```

The computation **3 inch 2 3.14159 mul mul** is $c = 2 \cdot \pi \cdot r$, which computes the circumference of the circle c from its radius r.

Tricks of the Trade

When you're developing new PostScript program fragments, you'll often wish for a handy tool to get an idea of where things are landing on the page. A grid of dots is useful to see where things are. Here is a quick grid generator, combining rounded line caps and dashed line styles, as you saw in previous examples.

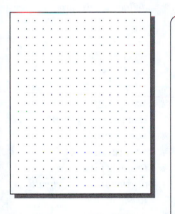

```
%!PS
/inch { 72 mul } def          %   define inch procedure
/gap 0.5 inch def             %   define the grid size
1 setlinecap                  %   rounded line caps
4 setlinewidth                %   4 point radius circles
[ 0 gap ] 0 setdash           %   0 length mark; gap length space
gap gap 8.0 inch {            %   start for loop
    0.0 moveto                %   march across page
    0.0 11.0 inch rlineto     %   draw path up page
    stroke                    %   stroke path
} for                         %   end for loop
showpage                      %   display page
```

The preceding PostScript program effectively uses a trick to get a grid of dots across the page. You set a dashed pattern where the "on" parts of the dashes are *zero* length. By using a fat line width and rounded line caps, you get filled circles drawn every **gap** interval along the line. Then all that remains to be done is to draw a bunch of lines (vertical lines in this case) across the page. The dash pattern machinery takes care of most of the work for you.

Here's one possible answer to a frequently asked question—how to obtain squared-off dashed lines with round caps at the ends of the lines. The PostScript code is fairly simple.

First you draw the line you want using **setdash** and **stroke**. Follow that by placing what Adobe calls a "degenerate line segment" at the start and end of the line. "Degenerate" doesn't mean the line segments are dissembling but means a zero-length line segment. The zero-length line effectively creates a placeholder for the round line cap to draw a circular blob in the right place. You have to ensure that your dashed pattern is such that the dashes actually come all the way to the ends of the lines for this trick to work.

```
%!PS
/inch { 72 mul } def                          %   define inch procedure
/LineStart { 1 inch      1 inch } def
/LineEnd   { 7.5 inch 10 inch } def
LineStart moveto                              %   set current point
LineEnd lineto                                %   add line segment
1 inch setlinewidth                           %   fat line width
[ 1.25 inch 0.75 inch ] 0 setdash             %   dash pattern
0 setlinecap                                  %   chopped off line caps
stroke                                        %   paint path
[] 0 setdash                                  %   remove dash pattern
LineStart moveto                              %   to start of line
LineStart lineto                              %   degenerate line segment
LineEnd moveto                                %   to end of line
LineEnd lineto                                %   degenerate line segment
1 setlinecap                                  %   round line caps
stroke                                        %   paint degenerate lines
showpage                                      %   display page
```

Fat Dashed Lines on Circular Paths

Using **setdash** with fat line widths on arcs may not necessarily get you what you want.

```
%!PS
/inch { 72 mul } def                    % define inch procedure
4.25 inch 5.5 inch 3 inch 0 180 arc    % add arc segment to path
2.0 inch setlinewidth                   % set fat line width
[ 0.75 inch 0.75 inch ] 0 setdash      % dash pattern
stroke                                  % stroke the path
showpage                                % display page
```

You see that the "dashes" are in fact wedge shaped. This may or may not be the result you want. If you do want to obtain dashes of uniform width spaced around a circular path, you need to draw individual lines, like this.

```
%!PS
/inch { 72 mul } def                    % define inch procedure
4.25 inch 5.5 inch translate           % origin to middle of page
0 1 11 {                                % start a for loop
    pop                                 % discard unwanted value
    30 rotate                           % rotate coordinate system
    2 inch 0 moveto                     % set current point
    4 inch 0 lineto                     % add line segment to path
} for                                   % end for loop
0.75 inch setlinewidth                  % set fat line width
stroke                                  % stroke the path
showpage                                % display page
```

7 Arcs and Curves

On a cloth untrue

With a twisted cue

And *elliptical* billiard balls.

Gilbert and Sullivan—*The Mikado*

PostScript would be boring if you could draw only straight lines and rectangles. To make PostScript interesting, you need to be able to draw arcs, circles, ellipses, and other nice curvy shapes. The first part of this chapter discusses PostScript operators for drawing arcs of circles. The second part of this chapter discusses PostScript operators for drawing curves. PostScript has no specific operators for drawing circles or ellipses. What PostScript *does* have are operators to draw *arcs*. When you think of a circle, you realize it's just an arc that extends 360 degrees. So, that's what you can use in PostScript to draw circles—the **arc** operator. To draw a four-inch radius green beginner skier's circle in the middle of the page, you can use this PostScript program.

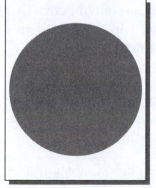

Beginner skier's circle. See color plate I.

```
%!PS
/inch { 72 mul } def            % define inch procedure
newpath                         % initialize path
4.25 inch 5.5 inch              % x y coordinates of center of circle
4.0 inch                        % radius of circle
0 360 arc                       % start and end angles and draw
closepath                       % finish circle
0.0 1.0 0.0 setrgbcolor         % set green color
fill                            % fill the circle
showpage                        % display page
```

arc requires five operands, and its general syntax looks like this:

$$x_{center} \quad y_{center} \quad radius \quad angle_{start} \quad angle_{end} \quad \textbf{arc}$$

where x_{center} and y_{center} are the coordinates of the center of the arc, *radius* is the radius of the circle, $angle_{start}$ is the angle from the horizontal axis to the beginning of the arc, and $angle_{end}$ is the angle from the horizontal axis to the end of the arc. The picture shows the **arc** operator and its operands in detail. The first end point of the arc starts at the point

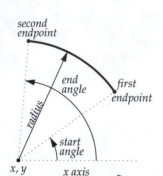

$$x_{first} = x_{center} + radius \cdot \cos angle_{start}$$

$$y_{first} = y_{center} + radius \cdot \sin angle_{start}$$

Operation of basic arc.

The arc segment is drawn to the second end point at the point

$$x_{second} = x_{center} + radius \cdot \cos angle_{end}$$

$$y_{second} = y_{center} + radius \cdot \sin angle_{end}$$

You'll notice the current point does not need to be defined when you draw an arc. All the parameters of the arc—center, radius, and angles—are specified as arguments to **arc**. If a current point *is* defined, however, a straight line segment is drawn from the current point to the first end point of the arc, as shown here. This behavior may or may not be precisely what you want, and this topic is covered in more detail later in this chapter.

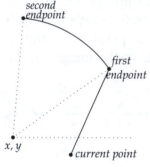

Behavior of arc with defined current point.

Angles are always measured counterclockwise from the horizontal axis, and arcs drawn with **arc** are drawn in the counterclockwise direction. To draw clockwise arcs, use **arcn**, described in *Clockwise Circles and Arcs* on pages 285–288 in this chapter.

The sequence *x y radius* **0 360 arc** is a useful cliché that should be remembered as "draw a circle."

Closing the Path When Drawing Circles

Note that **closepath** is *very* important when you wish to stroke a complete 360° circle with a fat line. If you don't use **closepath**, the circle isn't stroked properly, but you end up with a "notch" that isn't quite filled in. This picture illustrates the situation.

Incorrectly drawn arc because of missing **closepath**.

```
%!PS
/inch { 72 mul } def         %   define inch procedure
4.25 inch 5.5 inch           %   center of circle
2.75 inch                    %   radius of circle
45 405 arc                   %   complete 360° arc
                             %   note no closepath
2.75 inch setlinewidth       %   fat line width
stroke                       %   paint path
showpage                     %   display page
```

The arc was drawn between 45° and 405° to show the notch a little better. **closepath** was deliberately omitted from this example and you see there's a funny-looking region that isn't quite filled in. The moral of this tale is always use **closepath** when you really want a completely stroked circle.

You may have noticed three other PostScript operators related to arcs—**arcto**, **arct**, and **arcn**. **arcn** draws arcs clockwise around the circle, whereas **arc** draws arcs counterclockwise around the circle. **arcn** is described in the next section. **arcto** and **arct** are more complex operators for connecting arcs to line segments and are described in detail in *Connect Arc to Path Segment* on pages 296–300 in this chapter.

Clockwise Circles and Arcs

Whereas **arc** draws arcs counterclockwise in user space, **arcn** draws arcs *clockwise* in user space. At first sight, you might think **arcn** is redundant. But you need **arcn** to deal with winding number rules, which you read about in *Filling Rules* on pages 59–63 in Chapter 2. First of all, let's see **arcn** in action. Let's draw the simple beginner skier's circle using **arcn** instead of **arc**.

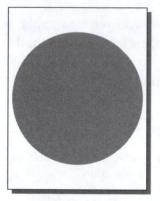

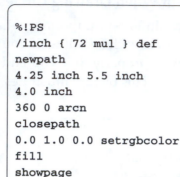

```
%!PS
/inch { 72 mul } def          %   define inch procedure
newpath                       %   initialize path
4.25 inch 5.5 inch            %   x y coordinates of center of circle
4.0 inch                      %   radius of circle
360 0 arcn                    %   start and end angle and draw
closepath                     %   finish circle
0.0 1.0 0.0 setrgbcolor       %   set green color
fill                          %   fill the circle
showpage                      %   display page
```

Circle drawn in clockwise direction.

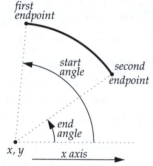

Operation of reverse arc.

This doesn't look that different from the circle you just saw, but it's there to illustrate that **arcn** is subtly different from **arc**.

arcn requires the same five operands as does **arc**, with one very important difference you should notice from the preceding code and diagram. When you use **arc** to draw a circle, you draw from $angle_{start} = 0°$ to $angle_{end} = 360°$. But when you use **arcn**, you must reverse the order of the angles. To draw a circle using **arcn**, you must set $angle_{start} = 360°$ and $angle_{end} = 0°$. The best way to see the difference between **arc** and **arcn** is to see two samples that draw arcs of circles. Here is a 90° arc drawn using **arc**.

```
%!PS
/inch { 72 mul } def          %   define inch procedure
newpath                       %   initialize path
4.25 inch 5.5 inch            %   x y coordinates of center of arc
3.5 inch                      %   radius of arc
0 90 arc                      %   start and end angle and draw
1.0 inch setlinewidth         %   fat line width
stroke                        %   fill the arc
showpage                      %   display page
```

90° arc drawn counterclockwise.

That arc is drawn as you'd expect. $angle_{start} = 0°$ and $angle_{end} = 90°$ and the arc is drawn counterclockwise so it extends a quarter of the full circle. Now let's see use **arcn** instead of **arc**.

```
%!PS
/inch { 72 mul } def        %   define inch procedure
newpath                     %   initialize path
4.25 inch 5.5 inch          %   x y coordinates of center of arc
3.5 inch                    %   radius of arc
0 90 arcn                   %   start and end angle and draw
1.0 inch setlinewidth       %   fat line width
stroke                      %   fill the arc
showpage                    %   display page
```

90° arc drawn clockwise.

The arc is drawn from $angle_{start} = 0°$ to $angle_{end} = 90°$, but in the clockwise direction. The lesson of this story is that angles are always measured around the clock (so to speak) in the counterclockwise direction. Angles do not go around the other way when you use **arcn**. To obtain a 90° arc using **arcn** you must reverse the order of $angle_{start}$ and $angle_{end}$.

```
%!PS
/inch { 72 mul } def        %   define inch procedure
newpath                     %   initialize path
4.25 inch 5.5 inch          %   x y coordinates of center of arc
3.5 inch                    %   radius of arc
90 0 arcn                   %   start and end angle and draw
1.0 inch setlinewidth       %   fat line width
stroke                      %   fill the arc
showpage                    %   display page
```

90° arc drawn clockwise with reversed angles.

Now, once again, why do you even need **arcn**? To answer that question let's use a combination of **arc** and **arcn** to draw a large toroidal shape.

```
%!PS
/inch { 72 mul } def                  %  define inch procedure
newpath                               %  initialize path
4.25 inch 5.5 inch                    %  x y coordinates of center of circle
4.0 inch                              %  radius of circle
0 360 arc                             %  start and end angle and draw
closepath                             %  finish circle
4.25 inch 5.5 inch                    %  x y coordinates of center of circle
2.0 inch                              %  radius of circle
360 0 arcn                            %  start and end angle and draw
closepath                             %  finish circle
AstroidLeaf setpattern                %  fancy pattern fill
fill                                  %  fill with pattern
showpage                              %  display page
```

Toroidal shape taking advantage of winding number fill rule.

The standard **fill** operation uses the winding number rule discussed on pages 59–63 in Chapter 2. The winding number rule requires that paths be drawn in opposite directions so **fill** will produce the correct results for such a shape. Here's what happens if you use only **arc** to draw both circles.

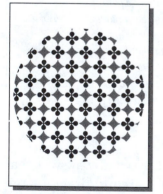

```
%!PS
/inch { 72 mul } def                  %  define inch procedure
newpath                               %  initialize path
4.25 inch 5.5 inch                    %  x y coordinates of center of circle
4.0 inch                              %  radius of circle
0 360 arc                             %  start and end angle and draw
closepath                             %  finish circle
4.25 inch 5.5 inch                    %  x y coordinates of center of circle
2.0 inch                              %  radius of circle
0 360 arc                             %  start and end angle and draw
closepath                             %  finish circle
AstroidLeaf setpattern                %  fancy pattern fill
fill                                  %  fill with pattern
showpage                              %  display page
```

"Toroidal" shape not working.

Variations on Drawing Arcs

PostScript **arc** operators have a "feature" that is sometimes useful and sometimes annoying. You may have noticed that the current point does not have to be set before executing either **arc** or **arcn**. These two operators require an (x, y) position to indicate the center point of the curve.

The next six examples show different behaviors of **arc** used in different forms, with and without a current point established before drawing the arc. Our first example shows the simplest arc—a 360° arc to form a circle.

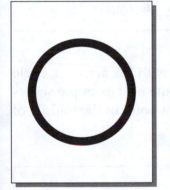

```
%!PS
/inch { 72 mul } def                    %   define inch procedure
newpath                                 %   ensure new path
4.25 inch 5.5 inch 3 inch 0 360 arc
closepath                               %   finish circle
0.5 inch setlinewidth                   %   fat line width
stroke                                  %   paint outline
showpage                                %   display page
```

Simplest stroked circle.

The second example shows the same 360° arc drawn to form a circle, but this time you can establish the current point in the middle of the page using **moveto**.

```
%!PS
/inch { 72 mul } def                    %   define inch procedure
newpath                                 %   ensure new path
4.25 inch 5.5 inch moveto
4.25 inch 5.5 inch 3 inch 0 360 arc
closepath                               %   finish circle
0.5 inch setlinewidth                   %   fat line width
stroke                                  %   paint outline
showpage                                %   display page
```

Current point defined.

A line is drawn from the center of the circle to the starting point of the arc, as defined in the PostScript language. You need to be certain this is in fact the behavior you really want when you're drawing arcs. Some applications have this wrong. Our next example is a partial arc, drawn between 20° and 290°.

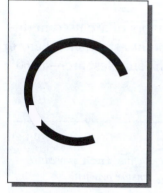

Basic partial arc.

```
%!PS
/inch { 72 mul } def                % define inch procedure
newpath                             % ensure new path
4.25 inch 5.5 inch 3 inch 20 290 arc
0.5 inch setlinewidth               % fat line width
stroke                              % paint outline
showpage                            % display page
```

This arc looks just the way it ought to, with an arc of a circle drawn between two endpoints. However, the next example shows what happens when you establish a current point in the middle of the page prior to creating the arc.

Partial arc with defined current point.

```
%!PS
/inch { 72 mul } def                % define inch procedure
newpath                             % ensure new path
4.25 inch 5.5 inch moveto
4.25 inch 5.5 inch 3 inch 20 290 arc
0.5 inch setlinewidth               % fat line width
stroke                              % paint outline
showpage                            % display page
```

Once again, a line is drawn from the current point—the middle of the page—to the starting point of the arc.

The next two examples are similar to the previous two, but with an explicit **closepath** before **stroke** is applied to the paths.

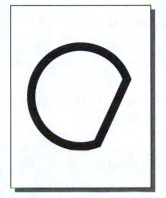

```
%!PS
/inch { 72 mul } def              %   define inch procedure
newpath                           %   ensure new path
4.25 inch 5.5 inch 3 inch 20 290 arc
closepath                         %   finish circle
0.5 inch setlinewidth             %   fat line width
stroke                            %   paint outline
showpage                          %   display page
```

Partial arc with closed path.

closepath does what you would expect; it draws a line segment from the endpoint of the path back to the starting point of the path. Our last example uses **closepath** just as the preceding example but once again establishes the current point in the middle of the page using **moveto** prior to creating the path.

```
%!PS
/inch { 72 mul } def              %   define inch procedure
newpath                           %   ensure new path
4.25 inch 5.5 inch moveto
4.25 inch 5.5 inch 3 inch 20 290 arc
closepath                         %   finish circle
0.5 inch setlinewidth             %   fat line width
stroke                            %   paint outline
showpage                          %   display page
```

Partial arc, defined current point, and closed path.

As you see, when the current point is set before drawing the arc, a line is drawn from the original current point to the starting point. When the current point is not set before drawing the arc, you get just the arc. The other variable in the preceding two arcs is **closepath**. If the current point is set before the **arc** operator is executed, the current point and the line drawn from there to the starting point are considered to be part of the continuous path. Thus, when the interpreter encounters **closepath**, a line is drawn from the last point on the arc to the original starting point.

Pie Charts

This behavior of **arc** is useful for drawing pie charts.

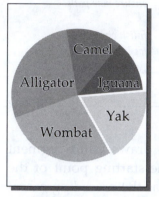

Delicious pies.

```
%!PS
/inch { 72 mul } def                              %   define inch procedure
4.25 inch 5.5 inch moveto                         %   Iguana Pie
4.25 inch 5.5 inch 4 inch 5 50 arc
closepath 0.50 setgray fill
4.25 inch 5.5 inch moveto                         %   Camel Pie
4.25 inch 5.5 inch 4 inch 50 100 arc
closepath 0.60 setgray fill
4.25 inch 5.5 inch moveto                         %   Alligator Pie
4.25 inch 5.5 inch 4 inch 100 200 arc
closepath 0.70 setgray fill
4.25 inch 5.5 inch moveto                         %   Wombat Pie
4.25 inch 5.5 inch 4 inch 200 300 arc
closepath 0.80 setgray fill
4.25 inch 16 add 5.5 inch 8 sub moveto %   Yak Pie
4.25 inch 16 add 5.5 inch 8 sub 4 inch 300 365 arc
closepath 0.90 setgray fill
showpage                                          %   display page
```

Notice the use of the **16 add** and **8 sub** operations in the last arc. They push the final pie segment out a little.

PAC-MAN

Finally, establishing the current point and finishing with a **closepath** is an easy way to draw pac-man figures, as you see in the picture on the next page.

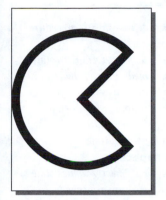

```
%!PS
/inch { 72 mul } def            % define inch procedure
newpath                         % ensure new path
4.25 inch 5.5 inch moveto
4.25 inch 5.5 inch 4 inch 45 315 arc
closepath                       % finish the shape
0.5 inch setlinewidth           % fat line width
stroke                          % paint outline
showpage                        % display page
```

This "feature" of arcs using a current point if one is defined can lead to unexpected results. Here's a couple of circles drawn as two disjoint subpaths and filled and stroked.

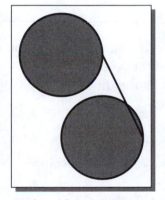

Circles with gratuitous line.

```
/inch { 72 mul } def                % define inch procedure
3 inch 8 inch 2.5 inch 0 360 arc closepath
5.5 inch 3 inch 2.5 inch 0 360 arc closepath
gsave                               % remember graphics state
    0.50 setgray                    % medium gray shade
    fill                            % fill shapes
grestore                            % restore graphics state
8 setlinewidth                      % fat line width
stroke                              % paint outline
showpage                            % display page
```

There are at least two ways around this problem. One easy way is to draw the circles as separate paths, filling and stroking each as you go. That way you start a new path for each circle.

Separate paths—no complimentary line this time.

```
/inch { 72 mul } def                    %  define inch procedure
3 inch 8 inch 2.5 inch 0 360 arc closepath
gsave                                   %  remember graphics state
    0.50 setgray                        %  medium gray shade
    fill                                %  fill shapes
grestore                                %  restore graphics state
8 setlinewidth                          %  fat line width
stroke                                  %  paint outline
5.5 inch 3 inch 2.5 inch 0 360 arc closepath
gsave                                   %  remember graphics state
    0.50 setgray                        %  medium gray shade
    fill                                %  fill shapes
grestore                                %  restore graphics state
8 setlinewidth                          %  fat line width
stroke                                  %  paint outline
showpage                                %  display page
```

Another approach, if you really must use disjoint subpaths for arcs, is to set the current point at the start of the second and subsequent arcs. That way, you get a degenerate subpath consisting of a single point at the starting point of the arc.

*Circles drawn using **moveto** trick—it works, but is it art?*

```
/inch { 72 mul } def                    %  define inch procedure
3 inch 8 inch 2.5 inch 0 360 arc closepath
8.0 inch 3 inch moveto                  %  set current point
5.5 inch 3 inch 2.5 inch 0 360 arc closepath
gsave                                   %  remember graphics state
    0.50 setgray                        %  medium gray shade
    fill                                %  fill shapes
grestore                                %  restore graphics state
8 setlinewidth                          %  fat line width
stroke                                  %  paint outline
```

To use this approach, you need to compute the start point of the arc. You're probably better off using the separate subpaths approach if possible.

Arcs Greater Than 360 Degrees

You saw earlier that a 360° arc draws a circle

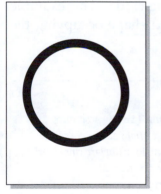

```
%!PS
/inch { 72 mul } def          %   define inch procedure
newpath                       %   initialize path
4.25 inch 5.5 inch            %   x y coordinates of center of circle
3.0 inch                      %   radius of circle
0 360 arc                     %   start and end angles and draw
closepath                     %   finish circle
0.5 inch setlinewidth         %   fat line width
stroke                        %   paint outline
showpage                      %   display page
```

Basic circle.

An interesting question is what do you get if you ask for an arc whose total angles are greater than 360°? The results can be different depending on the specific PostScript interpreter involved.

Adobe PostScript interpreters give you a full circle

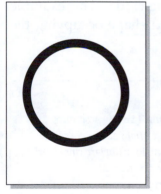

```
%!PS
/inch { 72 mul } def          %   define inch procedure
4.25 inch 5.5                 %   coordinates of center
3 inch                        %   radius
0 405 arc                     %   draw more than circle
0.5 inch setlinewidth         %   fat line width
stroke                        %   paint outline
showpage                      %   display page
```

Adobe PostScript.

Other interpreters we've investigated differ in their interpretation and compute the angles modulo 360° and give you a truncated segment of an arc

"Brand X" PostScript interpreters.

```
%!PS
/inch { 72 mul } def            % define inch procedure
4.25 inch 5.5 inch              % coordinates of center
3 inch                          % radius
0 405 arc                       % draw more than circle
0.5 inch setlinewidth           % fat line width
stroke                          % paint outline
showpage                        % display page
```

Connect Arc to Path Segment

The **arcto** operator is a somewhat more complex version of **arc** and **arcn** discussed earlier. A popular example for **arcto** is to construct round cornered boxes (like playing cards). This example uses **arcto** to construct a giant playing card shape occupying the middle of the page.

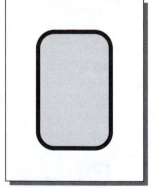

Playing card.

```
%!PS
/inch { 72 mul } def                         % define inch procedure
4.25 inch 9 inch moveto                       % set initial point
                                              % draw four line/arc combinations
2   inch 9 inch 2    inch 5.5 inch 1 inch arcto
2   inch 2 inch 4.25 inch 2    inch 1 inch arcto
6.5 inch 2 inch 6.5  inch 5.5 inch 1 inch arcto
6.5 inch 9 inch 4.25 inch 9    inch 1 inch arcto
16 { pop } repeat                             % clear debris from stack
closepath                                     % finish the shape
gsave                                         % push graphics state
0.90 setgray fill                             % fill with light gray
grestore                                      % pop graphics state
0.25 inch setlinewidth stroke                 % stroke with fat line
showpage                                      % display page
```

Something to note is the **16 {pop} repeat** sequence. Each **arcto** leaves four numbers on the operand stack. You don't often need the four numbers, but you must **pop** them to leave the operand stack clear of extraneous debris. Also notice the explicit **closepath** in the example. This is one of those times when **closepath** is really needed. Let's omit **closepath** and see what happens.

Playing card—shape not closed.

```
%!PS
/inch { 72 mul } def              %  define inch procedure
4.25 inch 9 inch moveto           %  set initial point
                                  %  draw four line/arc combinations
2    inch 9 inch 2    inch 5.5 inch 1 inch arcto
2    inch 2 inch 4.25 inch 2    inch 1 inch arcto
6.5 inch 2 inch 6.5  inch 5.5 inch 1 inch arcto
6.5 inch 9 inch 4.25 inch 9    inch 1 inch arcto
16 { pop } repeat                 %  clear debris from stack
gsave                             %  push graphics state
0.90 setgray fill                 %  fill with light gray
grestore                          %  pop graphics state
0.25 inch setlinewidth stroke     %  stroke with fat line
showpage                          %  display page
```

There's a gap in the last path segment. The path starts at (4.25 inch, 9 inch) in the middle of the page. Had the path started at (5.5 inch, 10 inch) there would not have been a gap. However, this slightly failed example does show the behavior of **arcto**. You see the behavior better from this figure that looks like a futuristic archway, in the example at the top of the next page.

Star Trek door.

```
%!PS
/inch { 72 mul } def              %   define inch procedure
7.5 inch 1 inch moveto            %   set initial point
4.25 inch 10 inch                 %   first direction point
1 inch 1 inch                     %   second direction point
1 inch                            %   radius
arcto                             %   add arc segment to path
4 { pop } repeat                  %   clear jetsam from stack
1 inch 1 inch lineto              %   draw left leg
closepath                         %   finish the shape
gsave                             %   push graphics state
  0.95 setgray fill               %   fill with light gray
grestore                          %   pop graphics state
0.25 inch setlinewidth            %   set fat line width
stroke                            %   stroke the path
showpage                          %   display page
```

That's the entire figure. But here's the state of the line and arc if you stop the path after **arcto**.

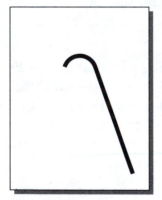

Star Trek door under construction.

```
%!PS
/inch { 72 mul } def              %   define inch procedure
7.5 inch 1 inch moveto            %   set initial point
4.25 inch 10 inch                 %   first direction point
1 inch 1 inch                     %   second direction point
1 inch                            %   radius
arcto                             %   add arc segment to path
4 { pop } repeat                  %   clear jetsam from stack
0.25 inch setlinewidth            %   set fat line width
stroke                            %   stroke the path
showpage                          %   display page
```

Now you see **arcto** really does what its name implies. It draws an arc in the direction of the final point but not to that point. This behavior of **arcto**—drawing parts of arcs between lines—provides the means to construct what are called *fillets* in the drawing trade (and they have nothing to do with steaks). Here's what an **arcto** looks like with the points filled in for illustration.

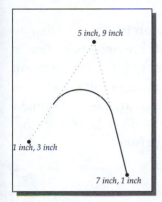

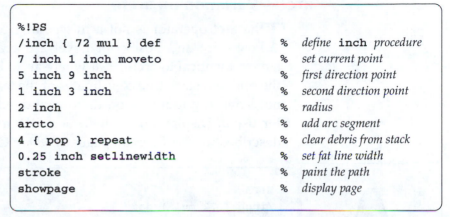

Operation of **arcto**.

```
%!PS
/inch { 72 mul } def          %   define inch procedure
7 inch 1 inch moveto          %   set current point
5 inch 9 inch                 %   first direction point
1 inch 3 inch                 %   second direction point
2 inch                        %   radius
arcto                         %   add arc segment
4 { pop } repeat              %   clear debris from stack
0.25 inch setlinewidth        %   set fat line width
stroke                        %   paint the path
showpage                      %   display page
```

If **arcto** draws an arc only in the direction of the final point (x_2, y_2) but not actually *to* the final point (x_2, y_2), where does the arc actually stop? Good question! It stops at the second tangent point, (xt_1, yt_1) in the diagram.

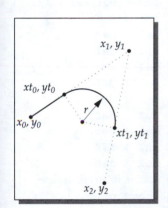

The first tangent point is at the point labeled (xt_0, yt_0). This point represents the place where the arc joins the line from (x_0, y_0) to (x_1, y_1). The arc leaves the line at the point (xt_0, yt_0) and continues around to the point (xt_1, yt_1), in the direction of (x_2, y_2).

To find the center of the circle, you construct one line perpendicular to the line from (x_0, y_0) to (x_1, y_1), and another line perpendicular to the line from (x_1, y_1) to (x_2, y_2). The point where the two perpendiculars cross is the center of the circle.

Clearing the Stack After arco

You read on page 297 in this chapter that **arcto** leaves four numbers on the stack—the coordinates of the two tangent points. Any PostScript program you write using **arcto** must remove the tangent points from the stack if you don't need them.

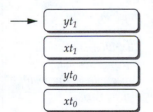

State of operand stack after **arcto**.

You can clear the stack in a variety of ways. You could use four separate **pop** operators, or a **4 {pop} repeat** sequence. Another way to clear the stack is to use a **mark** and **cleartomark** combination. **cleartomark** was discussed in *Clear Stack Down to Mark* on pages 246–248 in Chapter 5.

arct—Variation on arcto

The **arct** operator is not a misspelling of **arcto**—it's a Display PostScript and PostScript Level 2 operator whose behavior is almost identical to **arcto**. But where **arcto** leaves four numbers on the operand stack (the coordinates of the tangent points), **arct** does not leave any numbers on the operand stack. **arct** was designed for use in Display PostScript where it can be used in user paths, described in *User Paths* on pages 81–89 in Chapter 2.

Weird, almost geometric amoeba shape drawn with **arct**.

```
%!PS
/inch { 72 mul } def                    %  define inch procedure
/Outer 5 inch def                       %  outer ring of points
/Inner 2 inch def                       %  inner ring of points
/P1 { Outer  18 cos mul   Outer  18 sin mul } def
/P2 { Outer  90 cos mul   Outer  90 sin mul } def
/P3 { Outer 162 cos mul   Outer 162 sin mul } def
/P4 { Outer 234 cos mul   Outer 234 sin mul } def
/P5 { Outer 306 cos mul   Outer 306 sin mul } def
/I1 { Inner  54 cos mul   Inner  54 sin mul } def
/I2 { Inner 126 cos mul   Inner 126 sin mul } def
/I3 { Inner 198 cos mul   Inner 198 sin mul } def
/I4 { Inner 270 cos mul   Inner 270 sin mul } def
/I5 { Inner 342 cos mul   Inner 342 sin mul } def
4.25 inch 5.5 inch translate            %  origin in middle of page
3 inch 31.5 cos mul 3 inch 31.5 sin mul moveto
                                        %  draw series of lines and arcs
I1 P2 0.5 inch arct     P2 I2 0.5 inch arct
I2 P3 0.5 inch arct     P3 I3 0.5 inch arct
I3 P4 0.5 inch arct     P4 I4 0.5 inch arct
I4 P5 0.5 inch arct     P5 I5 0.5 inch arct
I5 P1 0.5 inch arct     P1 I1 0.5 inch arct
closepath                               %  finish the shape
gsave                                   %  push graphics state
  0.50 setgray fill                     %  fill with medium gray
grestore                                %  pop graphics state
0.25 inch setlinewidth stroke           %  stroke with fat line width
showpage                                %  display page
```

arct doesn't leave tangent points on the operand stack, so you can use **arct** just as you would use **arcto**, but you don't need to fiddle with **pop** or other mechanisms to clear the stack.

Curves

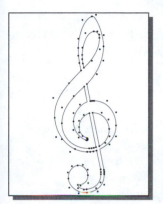

A figure composed of Bézier curves, with Bézier control points visible.

The first part of this chapter concentrated on arcs and variations of arcs constructed using **arc**, **arcn**, and **arcto**. And by scaling the coordinate system in a nonuniform manner, you saw how to generate ellipses and elliptical arcs. There comes a point in graphical displays where the kinds of shapes you can draw using parts of circles and parts of ellipses can't meet the needs of the task.

For example, if you delve into the design of letterforms, you'll see that beautiful designs rely heavily on splines for their pleasing curves. Early (Renaissance) type designers attempted to design letterforms based on mathematical formulas. Unfortunately, these designs were not very successful because the designers restricted themselves to "ruler and compass" constructions. Ruler and compass constructions can represent only second order equations of the form $y = a\,x^2 + b\,x + c$.

Whatever the reasons, second order equations can't accurately render all the subtleties of letterforms. For æsthetically pleasing character outlines, third order or cubic equations are needed.[†] The types of curves that do the job are known as *splines*, or, more accurately, *cubic splines*.

Splines are from a family of curves sometimes known in the drafting trade as "French curves." Various forms of cubic splines are B-splines, beta-splines, and Bézier splines. PostScript uses Bézier splines as the basis for curve drawing functions. Bézier splines are used extensively in interactive computer-aided design (CAD) systems—their control points can be dragged around and their shapes changed in a very intuitive fashion. Now you will see some PostScript Bézier splines in action.

---

† although several companies, URW Corporation in particular, insist they have successfully drawn character outlines by piecing together partial arcs of circles of different curvatures

Add Bézier Curve to Current Path

Here is a small example using **curveto** to draw a heart in the middle of the page. This example calls the **DrawHeart** procedure, which is defined after this code and picture.

A heart drawn with two Bézier curves.

```
%!PS
/inch { 72 mul } def                    %   define inch procedure
4.25 inch 1 inch translate              %   set origin
8 inch DrawHeart                        %   draw heart shape
1.0 0.0 0.5 setrgbcolor fill            %   fill with nice pink
showpage                                %   display page
```

Here is the procedure definition for **DrawHeart**.

```
%!PS
/DrawHeart {                            %   stack = size
   /size exch def                       %   define size temporarily
   /offset size 4 div def               %   define offset temporarily
   0 0 moveto                           %   first end point
   size size                            %   first Bézier control point
   offset size offset add               %   second Bézier control point
   0 size                               %   second end point
   curveto                              %   draw Bézier curve
   offset neg size offset add           %   first Bézier control point
   size neg size                        %   second Bézier control point
   0 0                                  %   second end point
   curveto                              %   draw Bézier curve
} def
```

The general syntax of **curveto** is

$$x_1 \quad y_1 \quad x_2 \quad y_2 \quad x_3 \quad y_3 \qquad \text{curveto}$$

where (x_1, y_1) and (x_2, y_2) are the Bézier control points, and (x_3, y_3) is the final end point. (x_0, y_0) is implied by the current point. **curveto** is yet another path operator where the current point must be established prior to using the operator; otherwise a **nocurrentpoint** error is raised.

A Bézier curve segment is defined by four points. Two of the points, (x_0, y_0) and (x_3, y_3), are the end points of the Bézier curve shown in the diagram. The other two points, (x_1, y_1) and (x_2, y_2), are known as the control points.

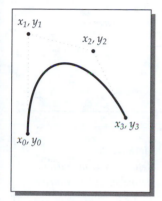

Bézier curve with control points highlighted.

```
%!PS
/inch { 72 mul } def              %   define inch procedure
/P0 { 1.0 inch 1.0 inch } def     %   first end point
/P1 { 1.0 inch 7.0 inch } def     %   first control point
/P2 { 5.0 inch 6.0 inch } def     %   second control point
/P3 { 7.0 inch 2.0 inch } def     %   second end point
P0 moveto P1 P2 P3 curveto        %   draw Bézier curve
0.125 inch setlinewidth           %   fat line width
stroke                            %   stroke the path
showpage                          %   display page
```

Notice how procedures are used to define the end points and control points. The Bézier curve starts at (x_0, y_0) and ends at (x_3, y_3). The Bézier curve does not actually pass through the control points (x_1, y_1) and (x_2, y_2). Instead, the control points determine the "enthusiasm" or "velocity" at which the curve leaves and approaches the endpoints. The control points effectively control the shape of the Bézier curve.

Relative Bézier Curves

Just as with **rmoveto** and **rlineto**, the relative form of **curveto**, appropriately called **rcurveto**, has arguments that are offsets from the current point. Its general syntax is

$$\delta x_1 \quad \delta y_1 \quad \delta x_2 \quad \delta y_2 \quad \delta x_3 \quad \delta y_3 \quad \text{rcurveto}$$

where the various δx_n and δy_n are the relative positions. Here's our heart figure again using **rcurveto**, instead of **curveto**. The example calls on the **RelativeHeart** procedure, which is defined after the example.

Using relative Bézier curves instead of absolute.

```
%!PS
/inch { 72 mul } def                    % define inch procedure
4.25 inch 1 inch translate              % set origin
8 inch RelativeHeart                     % draw the shape
1.0 0.0 0.5 setrgbcolor fill            % fill with nice pink
showpage                                 % display page
```

Here is the definition for **RelativeHeart**.

```
%!PS
/RelativeHeart {                                      % stack = size
  /size exch def                                      % define size temporarily
  /offset size 4 div def                              % define offset temporarily
  0 0 moveto                                          % first end point
  size size  offset size offset add  0 size   rcurveto
  offset neg offset  size neg 0  0 size neg   rcurveto
} def
```

Here's a diagram of the relative Bézier curve with its control points highlighted.

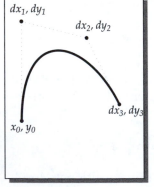

Bézier curve with control points highlighted.

```
%!PS
/inch { 72 mul } def                    % define inch procedure
/P0 { 1.0 inch 1.0 inch } def          % first end point
/P1 { 0.0 inch 6.0 inch } def          % first control point
/P2 { 4.0 inch 5.0 inch } def          % second control point
/P3 { 6.0 inch 1.0 inch } def          % second end point
P0 moveto P1 P2 P3 rcurveto            % draw relative Bézier curve
0.125 inch setlinewidth                 % fat line width
stroke                                   % stroke the path
showpage                                 % display page
```

More About Bézier Curves

What are Bézier curves? Bézier curves, or Bézier splines, are just one kind of curve from a family technically known as *Bernstein polynomials*. Bézier curves were first defined by Dr. Pierre Bézier when he worked for the Renault automobile company in the 1970s.

You can make substantial changes to the shape of the Bézier curve by altering the placement of the two intermediate control points. In this example, the control points are above and below the curve.

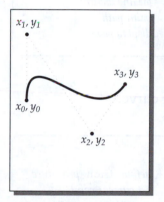

Changing the position of the control points.

```
%!PS
/inch { 72 mul } def              % define inch procedure
/P0 { 1.0 inch 3.0 inch } def     % first end point
/P1 { 1.0 inch 7.0 inch } def     % first control point
/P2 { 5.0 inch 1.0 inch } def     % second control point
/P3 { 7.0 inch 4.0 inch } def     % second end point
P0 moveto P1 P2 P3 curveto        % draw Bézier curve
0.125 inch setlinewidth           % fat line width
stroke                            % stroke the path
showpage                          % display page
```

Finally, you can create Bézier curves that contain "knots" by placing the intermediate control points "backward," as shown here.

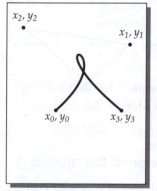

Creating knots in Bézier curves.

```
%!PS
/inch { 72 mul } def              % define inch procedure
/P0 { 3.0 inch 2.0 inch } def     % first end point
/P1 { 7.5 inch 6.0 inch } def     % first control point
/P2 { 1.0 inch 7.0 inch } def     % second control point
/P3 { 7.0 inch 2.0 inch } def     % second end point
P0 moveto P1 P2 P3 curveto        % draw Bézier curve
0.125 inch setlinewidth           % fat line width
stroke                            % stroke the path
showpage                          % display page
```

Incidentally, **arc** is really a PostScript "convenience" operator. Arcs are constructed using Bézier curves internally in the PostScript interpreter. Here's a 90° arc stroked with a fat line. The Bézier control points for this arc are marked with small dots.

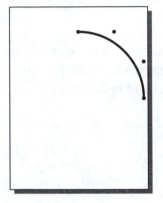

```
%!PS
/inch { 72 mul } def          %   define inch procedure
4.25 inch 5.5 inch            %   center of circle
4 inch                        %   radius of circle
0 90 arc                      %   complete 360° arc
0.125 inch setlinewidth       %   fat line width
stroke                        %   paint path
showpage                      %   display page
```

You can get the same picture using a Bézier curve.

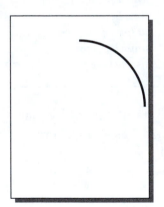

```
%!PS
/inch { 72 mul } def          %   define inch procedure
8.25 inch 5.5 inch moveto     %   set current point
8.25 inch 7.708 inch          %   first Bézier control point
6.458 inch 9.5 inch           %   second Bézier control point
4.25 inch 9.5 inch            %   end point of Bézier curve
curveto                       %   draw Bézier curve
0.125 inch setlinewidth       %   fat line width
stroke                        %   paint path
showpage                      %   display page
```

The numbers 7.708 inch and 6.458 inch are related to the radius of the arc. In this case, *radius* = 4 inches. The center of the arc is at (4.25 inch, 5.5 inch), so $\frac{7.708 - 5.5}{4} = 0.552$, and $\frac{6.458 - 4.25}{4} = 0.552$. This factor of 0.552 represents the "magic number" you can use to obtain the coordinates of the Bézier control points. A 90° arc can be represented by a Bézier curve in this way to within an error of $\frac{radius}{3600}$.

Convex Hull

Another little snippet of Bézier theory is that no matter what the shape of the Bézier curve, it is always enclosed by the convex quadrilateral defined by the four control points, as this diagram and code segment illustrate.

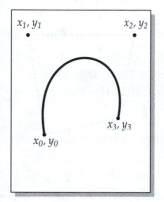

Convex hull.

```
%!PS
/inch { 72 mul } def                    % define inch procedure
/P0 { 2.0 inch 1.0 inch } def           % first end point
/P1 { 1.0 inch 7.0 inch } def           % first control point
/P2 { 7.5 inch 7.0 inch } def           % second control point
/P3 { 6.5 inch 2.0 inch } def           % second end point
P0 moveto P1 P2 P3 curveto              % draw Bézier curve
0.125 inch setlinewidth                 % fat line width
stroke                                  % stroke the path
showpage                                % display page
```

The quadrilateral that encloses the Bézier curve is known as the *convex hull* and is covered at length in *Computational Geometry* by Michael Shamos.

Joining Bézier Curve Segments

Even Bézier curves can't represent every possible curve you might want to draw. You'd end up with higher and higher order polynomials and the computations would become too complicated. But you can get as close an approximation as you want by joining sections of Bézier curves together.

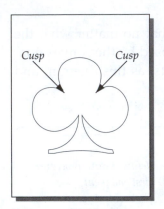

Bézier curves with cusps.

Sections of Bézier curves that join together should fit smoothly without *cusps*—unless of course you actually want cusps.

Bézier curves joined with no regard to the smoothness of the join (the end point of one segment joined to the start of the next segment) are said to have *zero-order continuity*. To join two Bézier curves with zero order continuity, make the last point of one curve the first point of the next curve. In PostScript, this is easy because the last point of one curve is the current point, so you just specify the next three points for the Bézier curve and add another Bézier segment to the path. Our preceding heart was one example of two Bézier segments with zero order continuity; the two curves joined at the top of the heart but formed a cusp.

The next picture and code show two independent Bézier segments constructed by independent sets of **moveto** and **curveto** operations. The control points of the first curve are labeled (x_{10}, y_{10}) through (x_{13}, y_{13}), and the control points of the second curve are labeled (x_{20}, y_{20}) through (x_{23}, y_{23}). The control points are indicated by small dots.

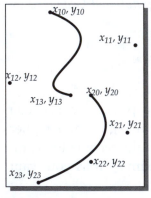

Independent Bézier curve segments.

```
%!PS
/inch { 72 mul } def              %  define inch procedure
/P10 { 2.75 inch 10.5 inch } def  %  Bézier points for first curve
/P11 { 8.0 inch 8.5 inch } def
/P12 { 0.25 inch 6.25 inch } def
/P13 { 4.0 inch 5.5 inch } def
/P20 { 5.25 inch 5.5 inch } def   %  Bézier points for second curve
/P21 { 7.5 inch 3.25 inch } def
/P22 { 5.25 inch 1.5 inch } def
/P23 { 2.0 inch 0.25 inch } def
P10 moveto                        %  current point for first curve
P11 P12 P13 curveto               %  draw Bézier segment
0.125 inch setlinewidth           %  fat line width
stroke                            %  paint path
P20 moveto                        %  current point for second curve
P21 P22 P23 curveto               %  draw Bézier segment
0.125 inch setlinewidth           %  fat line width
stroke                            %  paint path
showpage                          %  display page
```

You can join the curves into one continuous curve by making the last point of one curve congruent with the first point of the next curve segment. That is, make (x_{13}, y_{13}) congruent with (x_{20}, y_{20}). The following picture and code show two Bézier segments joined with zero order continuity.

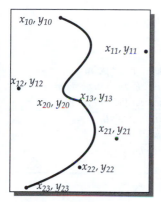

Bézier curves joined with zero order continuity.

```
%!PS
/inch { 72 mul } def            %   define inch procedure
/P10 { 3.0 inch 10.5 inch } def %   Bézier points for first curve
/P11 { 8.25 inch 8.5 inch } def
/P12 { 0.5 inch 6.25 inch } def
/P13 { 4.25 inch 5.5 inch } def
/P21 { 6.5 inch 3.25 inch } def %   Bézier points for second curve
/P22 { 4.25 inch 1.5 inch } def
/P23 { 1.0 inch 0.25 inch } def
P10 moveto                      %   set current point
P11 P12 P13 curveto             %   first Bézier curve segment
P21 P22 P23 curveto             %   second Bézier curve segment
0.125 inch setlinewidth         %   fat line width
stroke                          %   paint path
showpage                        %   display page
```

Zero order continuity is not necessarily always what you want. The points meet, but they don't flow smoothly into each other. To obtain Bézier curves flowing smoothly from one to the next with no kinks, you need *first order continuity*. How do you obtain this feature?

To get first order continuity in connected Bézier segments you must satisfy two conditions. Not only must the last point of one curve be congruent with the first point of the next curve—$(x_{13}, y_{13}) = (x_{20}, y_{20})$ in our preceding example—but the tangent lines at the meeting point of the two curves must lie along the same straight line. Here are the code and picture from the preceding example, but with the control points adjusted to make the curves meet with first order continuity.

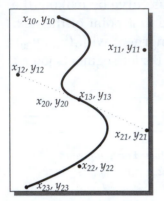

Bézier curves joined with first order continuity.

```
%!PS
/inch { 72 mul } def                        %   define inch procedure
/P10 { 3.0 inch 10.5 inch } def             %   Bézier points for first curve
/P11 { 8.25 inch 8.5 inch } def
/P12 { 0.5 inch 7.0 inch } def
/P13 { 4.25 inch 5.5 inch } def
/P21 { 8.375 inch 3.65 inch } def           %   Bézier points for second curve
/P22 { 4.25 inch 1.5 inch } def
/P23 { 1.0 inch 0.25 inch } def
P10 moveto                                  %   set current point
P11 P12 P13 curveto                         %   first Bézier curve segment
P21 P22 P23 curveto                         %   second Bézier curve segment
0.125 inch setlinewidth                     %   fat line width
stroke                                      %   paint path
showpage                                    %   display page
```

The diagram also includes a straight line drawn from (x_{12}, y_{12}) through (x_{13}, y_{13}) to (x_{20}, y_{20}), and you can see how the two curves now meet smoothly at the point where they join.

Composing a mental image of what Bézier curves will look like given their control points is not easy unless you've looked at a lot of them. Some people are able to imagine what an equation "looks like" after lots of practice. A better way to become visually facile with Bézier curves is to explore one of the excellent illustration packages available for Macintosh and NeXT computers, such as Adobe Illustrator or Aldus Freehand, or any one of a number of font design tools. Adobe Illustrator enables you to grab hold of the control points and drag them around, and you can see the shape of the Bézier curve changing in front of your eyes. Half an hour spent with one of these software packages brings you a visual understanding you can't get in weeks of playing with cubic parametric equations.

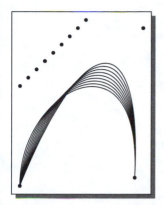

A family of Bézier curves.

```
%!PS
/inch { 72 mul } def              %   define inch procedure
/P0 { 0.5 inch 0.5 inch } def     %   initial control points
/P1 { 0.5 inch 6.5 inch } def
/P2 { 8.0 inch 10.0 inch } def
/P3 { 7.5 inch 1.0 inch } def
0 1 8 {                           %   start for loop
    0.5 inch mul dup              %   compute δx and δy
    P0 moveto                     %   set current point
    P1 4 1 roll add 3 1 roll add  %   add δx and δy
    2 copy                        %   copy for later
    P2 P3 curveto                 %   add Bézier segment
    stroke                        %   paint the path
    8 0 360 arc fill              %   show variable control point
} for                             %   end for loop
P0 8 0 360 arc closepath fill     %   show initial point
P2 8 0 360 arc closepath fill     %   show fixed control point
P3 8 0 360 arc closepath fill     %   show final point
showpage                          %   display page
```

This diagram shows a collection of Bézier curves drawn with the initial and final points (x_0, y_0) and (x_3, y_3) and the second control point (x_2, y_2) all fixed, while the first control point (x_1, y_1) varies by marching it across the page by half an inch in x and y. You can get a feel for how the first control point (x_1, y_1) "pulls" the shape of the Bézier around the path.

Notes for Application Developers

What do zero order continuity and first order continuity have to do with life? Well, if you are an application developer providing Bézier curves as one of the features in an interactive drawing application, you may need to offer these choices to your users. Adobe Illustrator, for example, draws connected curves with first order continuity as a standard option, so curves are connected smoothly. Adobe Illustrator offers options for changing the continuity aspects of connected curves with the "Convert Anchor Point" option.

8 Clipping

For "Is" and "Is-Not" though *with* Rule and Line
And "Up-and-Down" *without*, I could define,
　　　I yet in all I only cared to know,
Was never deep in anything but—Wine.

Ohmar Khayyám—*The Rubáiyat*

Clipping to obtain intersecting shapes.

In addition to stroking or filling a path, as you saw earlier, you can also use a path to *clip*. The best way to think of a clipping region is as a stencil through which images are poured. Images poured inside the clipping area appear on the final output. Images poured outside the clipping area disappear.

This picture is the familiar Borromean Rings—any two of the rings are separate, but the presence of the third ring locks them all. To obtain such intersecting figures with PostScript, you must use clipping.

Suppose you want to fill a square with slanted lines. The brute force way to do this is to compute the endpoints of each line—a tedious, iterative process that would be unportable and difficult to debug. Calculating endpoints of the lines is relatively easy when the figure is simple and regular, like a square, circle, or ellipse. But when a figure is irregular, the computations become unbearable. So use the capabilities of the PostScript interpreter to do the clipping for you. First, here's the definition of a procedure to draw the square, plus some code to show its use.

313

```
%!PS
/DrawSquare {                        %   stack = side
    newpath                          %   initialize the path
    0 0 moveto                       %   set initial point
    dup 0 rlineto                    %   bottom of square
    dup 0 exch rlineto               %   right side of square
    neg 0 rlineto                    %   top of square
    closepath                        %   close the shape
} def
/inch { 72 mul } def                 %   define inch procedure
1.25 inch 2.5 inch translate         %   translate to correct position
6 inch DrawSquare                    %   draw square path
0.0 0.0 1.0 setrgbcolor              %   blue color
fill                                 %   fill square with blue
showpage                             %   display page
```

*Just a straightforward
square.*

Here's the code for the square filled with slanted lines.

```
%!PS
/inch { 72 mul } def                 %   define inch procedure
1.25 inch 2.5 inch translate         %   translate to correct position
6 inch DrawSquare                    %   draw square path
clip                                 %   use as clipping area
newpath                              %   initialize the path
0 1 6 -3 sub 2 mul {                 %   start for loop
    0.5 inch mul 3 inch sub          %   y coordinate
    0 exch                           %   x coordinate
    moveto                           %   set current point
    6 inch 3 inch rlineto            %   add line segment to path
} for
stroke                               %   stroke all the diagonal lines
showpage                             %   display page
```

*Diagonal lines clipped to
square area.*

You can see that using clipping requires very little effort. The example uses the box as the clipping path, then draws slanted lines outside the boundaries of the box. The interpreter takes care of calculating the edges of the box.

Note the **newpath** right after the **clip**. Why is **newpath** here? The answer is simple. Whereas **stroke** and **fill** clear out the current path, **clip** does not clear the current path.[†] This simple facet of the behavior of **clip** has fooled many PostScript programmers, experts as well as novices. Your authors have had to fix more than one piece of knuckleheaded PostScript where **newpath** operators were needed and had been omitted.

Just as **fill** has an **eofill** counterpart that uses even-odd filling rules, so **clip** has an **eoclip** counterpart that uses the even-odd rule instead of the winding number rule. Here's a "sunburst" of lines radiating around the center of the page.

Sunburst of lines radiating from center of page.

```
%!PS
/inch { 72 mul } def          %   define inch procedure
4.25 inch 5.5 inch translate  %   origin to center of page
0 1 72 {                      %   start for loop
        1 inch 0 moveto       %   set current point
        3.125 inch 0 rlineto  %   add line segment to path
        5 rotate              %   rotate coordinate system
} for                         %   end for loop
stroke                        %   stroke the lines
showpage                      %   display page
```

The next illustration is the same sunburst clipped through a shape consisting of two intersecting ellipses.

The next block of code is the procedure definition for the ellipse.

---

† but **rectclip**, discussed on pages 327–328 in this chapter, does clear the path.

```
%!PS
/inch { 72 mul } def                      %    define inch procedure
/ellipse {                                %    stack = x y width height
    matrix currentmatrix def              %    save CTM
    4 2 roll translate                    %    origin to center of ellipse
    scale                                 %    scale for ellipse
    0 0 1 0 360 arc                        %    draw 360° arc
    closepath                             %    finish shape
    setmatrix                             %    restore previous matrix
} def
```

Here's the sunburst clipped through the intersecting ellipses using the standard winding number rule for clipping.

Sunburst clipped using winding number rule.

```
%!PS
/inch { 72 mul } def                             %  define inch procedure
4.25 inch 5.5 inch 4 inch 2 inch DrawEllipse
4.25 inch 5.5 inch 2 inch 4 inch DrawEllipse
clip                                             %  add to clipping path
newpath                                          %  start a new path
4.25 inch 5.5 inch translate                     %  origin to center of page
0 1 72 {                                         %  start for loop
    1 inch 0 moveto                              %  set current point
    3.125 inch 0 rlineto                         %  add line segment to path
    5 rotate                                     %  rotate coordinate system
} for                                            %  end for loop
stroke                                           %  stroke the lines
showpage                                         %  display page
```

Here's the same sunburst clipped through the same two intersecting ellipses, this time using **eoclip** to compute the clipping region.

Sunburst clipped using even-odd rule.

```
%!PS
/inch { 72 mul } def                          %  define inch procedure
4.25 inch 5.5 inch 4 inch 2 inch DrawEllipse
4.25 inch 5.5 inch 2 inch 4 inch DrawEllipse
eoclip                                        %  add to clipping path
newpath                                       %  start a new path
4.25 inch 5.5 inch translate                  %  origin to center of page
0 1 72 {                                       %  start for loop
    1 inch 0 moveto                           %  set current point
    5 inch 0 rlineto                          %  add line segment to path
    5 rotate                                  %  rotate coordinate system
} for                                         %  end for loop
stroke                                        %  stroke the lines
showpage                                      %  display page
```

Clipping really comes into its own when you want to intersect sections of different shapes with each other. Rather than computing the intersection points yourself, you let the PostScript interpreter's graphics machinery compute the intersections for you. After all, that's what the PostScript interpreter was designed to do.

Here's a picture of a pentagonal star (a pentagram) clipped through a pentagon. The pentagon acts like a sheet of translucent glass through which the pentagonal star can be seen, somewhat dimly. This is the code that generated the figure.

Pentagram clipped through a pentagon.

```
%!PS
/inch { 72 mul } def                      %  define inch procedure
4.25 inch 5.5 inch translate              %  move to middle of page
pentagram 0.0 setgray fill                %  draw black pentagram
pentagon 0.9 setgray fill                 %  draw light gray pentagon
pentagon clip                             %  make pentagon clipping region
pentagram 0.5 setgray fill                %  draw darker gray pentagram
pentagon 0.0 setgray stroke               %  draw borders of pentagon
showpage                                  %  display page
```

The example uses two procedures—**pentagram** draws the pentagonal star and **pentagon** draws the pentagonal shape. Their definitions are a little further along so as not to clutter the code with definitions at this point. The important thing is how the definitions are used.

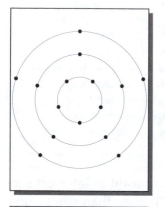

The two shapes in the example (the pentagram and the pentagon) are drawn within three circumscribing circles. An inner and outer circle define the limits of the pentagram. An intermediate circle defines the limits of the pentagon. Just in case you're wondering where all the funny numbers and angles come from, the picture shows the circumscribing circles and the points for the two pentagonal shapes used in the clipping example.

Here's the code to draw the pentagram, followed immediately by the code to draw the pentagon.

```
%!PS
/inch { 72 mul } def                    %  define inch procedure
/outer_rad 4.125 inch def
/inner_rad 1.375 inch def
/pentagram {
    newpath
    outer_rad  18 cos mul outer_rad  18 sin mul moveto
    inner_rad  54 cos mul inner_rad  54 sin mul lineto
    outer_rad  90 cos mul outer_rad  90 sin mul lineto
    inner_rad 126 cos mul inner_rad 126 sin mul lineto
    outer_rad 162 cos mul outer_rad 162 sin mul lineto
    inner_rad 198 cos mul inner_rad 198 sin mul lineto
    outer_rad 234 cos mul outer_rad 234 sin mul lineto
    inner_rad 270 cos mul inner_rad 270 sin mul lineto
    outer_rad 306 cos mul outer_rad 306 sin mul lineto
    inner_rad 342 cos mul inner_rad 342 sin mul lineto
    closepath
} def
4.25 inch 5.5 inch translate
pentagram 0.50 setgray fill
showpage                                %  display page
```

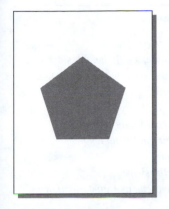

```
%!PS
/inch { 72 mul } def                    %   define inch procedure
/middle_rad 2.75 inch def
/pentagon {
    newpath
    middle_rad  18 cos mul middle_rad  18 sin mul moveto
    middle_rad  90 cos mul middle_rad  90 sin mul lineto
    middle_rad 162 cos mul middle_rad 162 sin mul lineto
    middle_rad 234 cos mul middle_rad 234 sin mul lineto
    middle_rad 306 cos mul middle_rad 306 sin mul lineto
    closepath
} def
4.25 inch 5.5 inch translate
pentagon 0.50 setgray fill
showpage                                %   display page
```

The color version of this picture is in plate XIV.

Here's another example of clipping. Hark back to the first picture on page 1 in Chapter 1 and you'll remember this picture of a large letter **Z** sticking through an elliptical "window pane." The part of the letter "behind" the window pane is shaded, giving the impression of looking at the letter through a translucent window. Translucency is a widely used technique in graphic design to provide illusions of depth.

The next few pictures and accompanying code samples show you how this effect is achieved using PostScript clipping areas and opaque paint imaging model. You build the picture in layers. To get this example started, you need some definitions. First is a procedure to draw a closed elliptical path, followed by some definitions for positions and sizes of the elements in the picture.

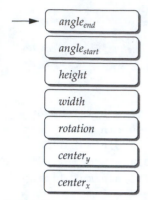

$angle_{end}$ ←
$angle_{start}$
height
width
rotation
$center_y$
$center_x$

*Operand stack prior to call on **EllipticalArc**.*

```
%!PS
/inch { 72 mul } def          %  three barleycorns
/EllipticalArc {              %  x, y, angle, width, height, start, end
    matrix currentmatrix      %  remember current transformation
    8 1 roll                  %  put matrix on bottom
    7 5 roll translate        %  set origin
    5 4 roll rotate           %  rotate coordinate system
    4 2 roll scale            %  scale for width and height
    0 0 1 5 3 roll arc        %  draw arc
    closepath                 %  finish the shape
    setmatrix                 %  restore previous transformation
} def
/EllipseCenter { 4.25 inch 5.5 inch } def
/EllipseRotation 15 def
/EllipseWidth 3.75 inch def
/EllipseHeight 5.375 inch def
/CharacterOrigin { -0.84 inch 1.75 inch } def
/CharacterScale 13.75 inch def
```

EllipticalArc draws a closed elliptical arc between two specified angles. Here's **EllipticalArc** used to draw a partial elliptical arc.

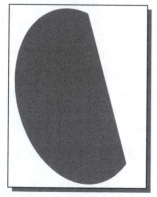

Partial elliptical arc.

```
%!PS
/inch { 72 mul } def                %  define inch procedure
EllipseCenter EllipseRotation       %  center and angle
EllipseWidth EllipseHeight          %  width and height
60 300 EllipticalArc                %  elliptical arc
0.50 setgray fill                   %  fill with medium gray
showpage                            %  display page
```

Now that you have the definitions and an example of their use, here are the layers of the drawing. The first layer is just a letter **Z** from ZapfChancery-MediumItalic, scaled so characters are 13¾ inches high. At this scale, only one letter fits on a page, but that's fine for this example. **show** the letter **Z** on the page. The code uses positions and sizes you already defined.

Large Z.

```
%!PS
/inch { 72 mul } def            % define inch procedure
/ZapfChancery-MediumItalic findfont  % find the required font
CharacterScale scalefont         % scale to required size
setfont                         % make it the current font
0.0 setgray                     % set color black
CharacterOrigin moveto          % set current point
(Z) show                        % image large character
showpage                        % display page
```

Now that the large **Z** is in place you're ready to lay down the next layer—the elliptical sheet of glass. Use **EllipticalArc** defined previously. The elliptical sheet of glass is filled with 90 percent gray—a very light gray in the PostScript model. The first picture on page 321 has the opaque sheet of glass covering the letter.

The next two layers of the picture are the interesting ones. For the next layer, you use the left half of the ellipse as a clipping region and pour a second occurrence of the large letter **Z** through it to give the impression that part of the letter **Z** is "sticking through" the sheet. The second picture on page 322 shows the results of the letter **Z** "sticking through" the left half of the clipping region.

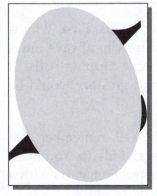

Large Z obscured by ellipse.

```
%!PS
/inch { 72 mul } def                % define inch procedure
/ZapfChancery-MediumItalic findfont  % find the required font
CharacterScale scalefont             % scale to required size
setfont                             % make it the current font
0.0 setgray                         % set color black
CharacterOrigin moveto              % set current point
(Z) show                            % image large character
newpath                             % start new path
EllipseCenter EllipseRotation        % center and angle
EllipseWidth EllipseHeight           % width and height
0 360 EllipticalArc                  % complete 360° arc
0.90 setgray fill                    % fill with light gray
showpage                            % display page
```

Large Z sticks through left side.

```
%!PS
/inch { 72 mul } def                    %  define inch procedure
/ZapfChancery-MediumItalic findfont     %  find the required font
CharacterScale scalefont                %  scale to required size
setfont                                 %  make it the current font
0.0 setgray                             %  set color black
CharacterOrigin moveto                  %  set current point
(Z) show                                %  image large character
newpath                                 %  start new path
EllipseCenter EllipseRotation           %  center and angle
EllipseWidth EllipseHeight              %  width and height
0 360 EllipticalArc                     %  complete 360° arc
0.90 setgray fill                       %  fill with light gray
gsave                                   %  remember graphics state
    EllipseCenter EllipseRotation       %  center and angle
    EllipseWidth EllipseHeight          %  width and height
    90 270 EllipticalArc                %  left 180° arc
    clip                                %  make clipping region
    newpath                             %  start new path
    0.0 setgray                         %  set color black
    CharacterOrigin moveto              %  set current point
    (Z) show                            %  image large character
grestore                                %  restore graphics state
showpage                                %  display page
```

This section of code contains two interesting points. First, why is the code in a **gsave** and **grestore** pair? Because **clip** always intersects the path you just created with the current clipping path. If you didn't put the clip code inside **gsave** and **grestore**, you'd be stuck with the smaller clipping path.

And why is there a **newpath** after the **clip**? Well, remember that **clip** doesn't clear the current path like **stroke** and **fill** do. You must use **newpath** so the next part of the path construction starts with a clean slate. Now you're ready for the last step.

Large Z sticks through left side and you see through the right side.

```
%!PS
/inch { 72 mul } def                          %   define inch procedure
/ZapfChancery-MediumItalic findfont           %   find the required font
CharacterScale scalefont                      %   scale to required size
setfont                                       %   make it the current font
0.0 setgray                                   %   set color black
CharacterOrigin moveto                        %   set current point
(Z) show                                      %   image large character
newpath                                       %   start new path
EllipseCenter EllipseRotation                 %   center and angle
EllipseWidth EllipseHeight                    %   width and height
0 360 EllipticalArc                           %   complete 360° arc
0.90 setgray fill                             %   fill with light gray
gsave                                         %   remember graphics state
    EllipseCenter EllipseRotation             %   center and angle
    EllipseWidth EllipseHeight                %   width and height
    90 270 EllipticalArc                      %   left 180° arc
    clip                                      %   make clipping region
    newpath                                   %   start new path
    0.0 setgray                               %   set color black
    CharacterOrigin moveto                    %   set current point
    (Z) show                                  %   image large character
grestore                                      %   restore graphics state
gsave                                         %   remember graphics state
    EllipseCenter EllipseRotation             %   center and angle
    EllipseWidth EllipseHeight                %   width and height
    270 90 EllipticalArc                      %   right 180° arc
    clip                                      %   make clipping region
    newpath                                   %   start new path
    0.70 setgray                              %   medium gray shade
    CharacterOrigin moveto                    %   set current point
    (Z) show                                  %   image large character
grestore                                      %   restore graphics state
showpage                                      %   display page
```

With the **Z** sticking through the elliptical sheet, the final layer involves the right half of the ellipse this time. Another letter **Z** is poured through it, with the letter painted in a slightly darker shade of gray than that of the ellipse, producing the illusion you can partially "see through" the elliptical pane.

Once again, the code lives inside a **gsave** and **grestore** pair. This step is not strictly necessary in this example, because this was the last layer in this drawing, but it's a good habit to get into. Just as before, **clip** is followed by **newpath** to clear the current path.

Intersecting Paths

Books on PostScript state that **clip** and **eoclip**

"intersect the current path with the current clipping path to produce a new clipping path."

What does "intersect" mean? These diagrams illustrate the process of intersecting one clipping path with another clipping path.

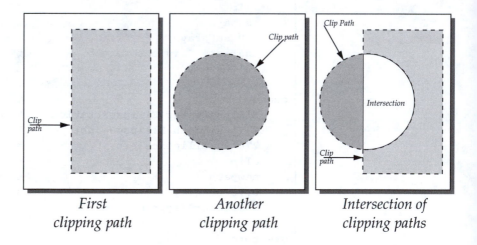

| *First* | *Another* | *Intersection of* |
| *clipping path* | *clipping path* | *clipping paths* |

As you see from the progression of the three diagrams, when the second clipping path is intersected with the first clipping path, the intersection of the two paths forms a third, smaller, clipping path. There is no way to expand the size of the current clipping path, except by using **initclip** to restore the original clipping path for the device, or by using **gsave** and **grestore** to "remember" previous values of the clipping path.

Having established a smaller clipping path as shown in the diagrams, here's what happens when you draw using that path as a clipping region.

Drawing through inter-sected clipping areas.

```
%!PS
/inch { 72 mul } def              %  define inch procedure
3 inch 1 inch moveto              %  set current point
5 inch 0 inch rlineto             %  bottom of rectangle
0 inch 9 inch rlineto             %  right side of rectangle
-5 inch 0 inch rlineto            %  top of rectangle
closepath                         %  finish the shape
clip                              %  make it the clipping path
newpath                           %  clear current path
3.25 inch 5.5 inch 3 inch 0 360 arc  %  add circle to path
closepath                         %  finish the shape
clip                              %  make smaller clipping path
newpath                           %  clear current path
9 inch setlinewidth               %  very fat line width
0 0 moveto                        %  set current point
8.5 inch 11 inch lineto           %  draw line across page
[ 0.25 inch 0.25 inch ] 0 setdash  %  set dashed pattern
0.00 setgray                      %  black color
stroke                            %  paint the path
0 0 moveto                        %  set current point
8.5 inch 11 inch lineto           %  draw line across page
[ 0.25 inch 0.25 inch ] 0.25 inch setdash
0.50 setgray                      %  medium gray color
stroke                            %  paint the path
showpage                          %  display page
```

Initial Clipping Area

When a PostScript job starts, the clipping region is all of device space. What constitutes all of device space depends on the specific device you are using. In the United States, the "standard" paper size is 8½-by-11-inches. However, mechanical limitations of specific printing engines usually result in a smaller imageable area than the actual size of the paper. An 8½-by-11-inch sheet of paper is 612×792 PostScript points, so the bounding box of the paper is $ll_x = 0$, $ll_y = 0$, $ur_x = 612$, and $ur_y = 792$.

Ghostscript, for example, reports the imageable area as $ll_x = 0$, $ll_y = 0$, $ur_x = 611.52$, and $ur_y = 792$. In other words, Ghostscript uses almost all the possible area.

But, as an example, our LaserWriter II–NTX reports its clipping area (its imageable area) as $ll_x = 14.16$, $ll_y = 7.92$, $ur_x = 597.6$, and $ur_y = 784.32$. This means in practice that ink can't go all the way to the very edge of the printed page—what printers call a "bleed." Here is a PostScript program to show the clipping area of paper from our printers, with the picture you get from the printer.

llx = 14.16   lly = 7.92

urx = 597.6   ury = 784.32

Initial clipping region of printer.

```
%!PS
/inch { 72 mul } def                              %   define inch procedure
clippath                                          %   get clipping path
0.9 setgray                                       %   light gray fill color
fill                                              %   fill the path
clippath                                          %   get clipping path again
8 setlinewidth                                    %   set nice fat line width
0.0 setgray                                       %   black color
stroke                                            %   stroke the path
clippath                                          %   get clipping path again
pathbbox                                          %   get path bounding box
/Palatino-Roman findfont 48 scalefont setfont
4.25 inch 4.00 inch moveto                        %   display upper right y
(ury = ) show (          ) cvs show
0.50 inch 4.00 inch moveto                        %   display upper right x
(urx = ) show (          ) cvs show
4.25 inch 6.00 inch moveto                        %   display lower right y
(lly = ) show (          ) cvs show
0.50 inch 6.00 inch moveto                        %   display lower right x
(llx = ) show (          ) cvs show
showpage                                          %   display page
```

Mechanical limitations of specific printing engines determine the actual imageable area that the printer can print. These values vary from one printer to another, so consult your printer manual for precise details on the imageable area available to you. If you're writing application software to generate PostScript, you should not assume a specific printing device, or, for that matter even assume the generated PostScript will be printed at all. Assuming PostScript programs will print on specific printing devices has led to some less portable PostScript.

Clipping with Rectangles

Rectangle operators—specifically **rectstroke** and **rectfill**—were covered on pages 65–81 in Chapter 2. This discussion covers *clipping* with rectangles. Use **rectclip** when you need rectangular regions for clipping—a common requirement in window systems and graphical user interfaces. There's not a whole lot to say about **rectclip**—it operates in much the same manner as the other rectangle operators. Here's an example.

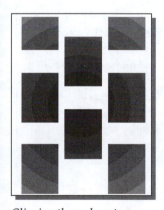

Clipping through rectangles.

```
%!PS
/inch { 72 mul } def                       %  define inch procedure
[                                          %  list of rectangles
    0.625 inch 8.8 inch 2.25 inch 2 inch
    3.25 inch 6.6 inch 2.25 inch 3 inch
    5.875 inch 8.8 inch 2.25 inch 2 inch
    0.625 inch 4.4 inch 2.25 inch 3 inch
    5.875 inch 4.4 inch 2.25 inch 3 inch
    3.25 inch 2.2 inch 2.25 inch 3 inch
    0.625 inch 0.1 inch 2.25 inch 3 inch
    5.875 inch 0.1 inch 2.25 inch 3 inch
] rectclip                                 %  clip to rectangles
newpath                                    %  ensure new path
4.25 inch 5.5 inch translate               %  origin to center of page
10 -1 1 {                                  %  start for loop
    dup                                    %  save copy for later
    1 inch mul                             %  radius of circle
    0 0 3 2 roll 0 360 arc                 %  draw circle
    closepath                              %  finish circle
    1 sub 0.1 mul setgray                  %  set gray shade
    fill                                   %  fill circle
} bind for                                 %  end for loop
showpage                                   %  display page
```

This code sets up a bunch of rectangles as a clipping region and then draws a collection of concentric circles, in the manner of a target, which get clipped to the rectangles you established prior. Note that **rectclip** clears the current path, as if you'd done a **newpath**, in contrast to **clip** and **eoclip**, where you must perform an explicit **newpath** to clear the existing current path.

Stroking a Path

The **strokepath** operator replaces the current path with a new path consisting of the outline of the shape you would get if you were to **stroke** the current path. What does this mean? Let's look at a very simple example.

Path stroked with fat line.

```
%!PS
/inch { 72 mul } def            %   define inch procedure
4.25 inch 1 inch moveto         %   set current point
4.25 inch 10 inch lineto        %   add line segment to path
4 inch setlinewidth             %   set fat line width
0.50 setgray                    %   set gray shade
stroke                          %   stroke the path
showpage                        %   display page
```

Well, in and of itself, this is nothing really remarkable. This example simply draws a fat line down the middle of the page. However, let's modify the example a little and see what happens if you use **strokepath** in combination with **stroke**.

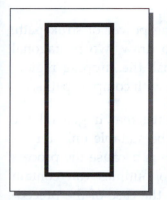

```
%!PS
/inch { 72 mul } def          %   define inch procedure
4.25 inch 1 inch moveto       %   set current point
4.25 inch 10 inch lineto      %   add line segment to path
4 inch setlinewidth           %   set fat line width
strokepath                    %   replace current path
0.25 inch setlinewidth        %   set line width
stroke                        %   stroke the path
showpage                      %   display page
```

Path stroked after
strokepath.

Again, nothing very remarkable, but the real power of **strokepath** comes in when you use the path obtained as a clipping path. Let's see this in action now with a more complicated example.

```
%!PS
/inch { 72 mul } def              %   define inch procedure
/side 3.5 inch def                %   define length of side
/m matrix currentmatrix def       %   remember the CTM
2.25 inch 2.5 inch translate      %   translate to first point
newpath                           %   start a new path
0 0 moveto                        %   set current point
side 0 rlineto                    %   add line segment to path
1 1 3 {                           %   start for loop
    side 0 translate              %   set new origin
    72 rotate                     %   rotate coordinate system
    side 0 rlineto                %   add line segment to path
} for                             %   end for loop
closepath                         %   close the shape
1.5 inch setlinewidth             %   set fat line width
strokepath                        %   replace current path
clip                              %   use it as a clipping path
m setmatrix                       %   restore CTM
newpath                           %   start new path
4.25 inch 1 inch moveto           %   set current point
4.25 inch 10 inch lineto          %   add line segment
8 inch setlinewidth               %   set very fat line width
[ 0.25 inch 0.25 inch ] 0 setdash %   set dash pattern
stroke                            %   stroke the line
showpage                          %   display page
```

strokepath *used to estab-*
lish complex clip path.

Filling Areas

The preceding example demonstrates the power of **strokepath**. Without **strokepath** you would have to draw two pentagonal shapes—an inner and an outer, to establish the clipping region. **strokepath** greatly eases the job of clipping with complex paths.

The *PostScript Language Reference Manual* states that, in general, the path returned by **strokepath** will usually be suitable only for filling or clipping and not for stroking. This is because the process that **strokepath** uses to convert paths to outlines can contain disconnected or overlapping subpaths. In the case of the preceding shape, filling the path would look the same as if you had stroked the path with a fat line. But watch out for **eofill**—here's what happens in this case, because of intersecting subpaths.

```
%!PS
/inch { 72 mul } def          % define inch procedure
/side 3.5 inch def            % define length of side
2.25 inch 2.5 inch translate  % translate to first point
newpath                       % start a new path
0 0 moveto                    % set current point
side 0 rlineto                % add line segment to path
1 1 3 {                       % start for loop
    side 0 translate          % set new origin
    72 rotate                 % rotate coordinate system
    side 0 rlineto            % add line segment to path
} for                         % end for loop
closepath                     % close the shape
1.5 inch setlinewidth         % set fat line width
strokepath                    % replace current path
eofill                        % fill the shape
showpage                      % display page
```

As you see, there are "holes" because of the intersecting paths. The size and shape of the holes will vary from interpreter to interpreter, as each interpreter may calculate shapes differently. The other major use for **strokepath** is to obtain paths from character outlines to use as clipping areas for patterned text. You saw some examples of this in Chapter 3.

Obtaining Path Bounding Box

You know you can do many different operations on a path you have constructed. You have seen **fill** and **stroke** and **clip**. Here's something else you can do—use **pathbbox** to obtain the *bounding box* of a path. Here's a fairly simple example to show **pathbbox** in action. Let's draw a shape first. This shape is a seven-pointed star—a heptagram—drawn with one continuous set of line segments, then filled. This code example simply calls a **DrawHeptagram** procedure (defined later) to draw the path.

```
%!PS
/inch { 72 mul } def              % define inch procedure
4.25 inch 5.5 inch translate      % origin to middle of page
DrawHeptagram                     % draw the shape
0.50 setgray                      % set medium gray color
eofill                            % fill the shape
showpage                          % display page
```

Here is the PostScript procedure to draw the heptagram.

```
%!PS
/DrawHeptagram {
    3 inch 0 inch moveto          % set initial point
    3 3 18 {                      % set up for loop
        360 7 div mul             % angle for seven points
        dup                       % need copy
        cos 3 inch mul            % compute x coordinate
        exch sin 3 inch mul       % compute y coordinate
        lineto                    % add line segment to path
    } for                         % end for loop
    closepath                     % close the path
} def
```

So far so good. This is a nice, simple shape with which to illustrate the bounding box of a path. Let's extend the preceding example so that in addition to drawing the shape, you obtain its bounding box and stroke the path so obtained.

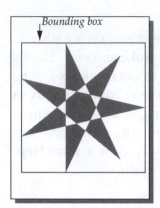

Bounding box

```
%!PS
/inch { 72 mul } def            %   define inch procedure
4.25 inch 5.5 inch translate    %   origin to middle of page
DrawHeptagram                   %   draw the shape
gsave                           %   push graphics state
    0.50 setgray eofill         %   fill with medium gray
grestore                        %   pop graphics state
pathbbox                        %   get path bounding box
newpath                         %   start a new path
4 2 roll 2 copy moveto          %   set current point
dup 4 index exch lineto         %   bottom of box
4 2 roll dup 3 1 roll lineto    %   right side of box
2 index exch lineto             %   top of box
pop pop                         %   discard unwanted stack values
closepath                       %   close the path medium gray
stroke                          %   stroke the box
showpage                        %   display page
```

pathbbox places the coordinates of the shape's bounding rectangle on the stack. Then the rectangle is drawn with some stack manipulation. This is easy—the bounding box of a shape like this one is a rectangle that encloses the shape. The same is true for an ellipse, for instance.

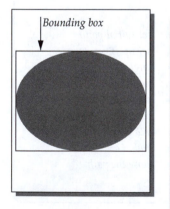

Bounding box

```
%!PS
/inch { 72 mul } def            %   define inch procedure
4.25 inch 5.5 inch translate    %   origin to middle of page
0 0 4 inch 3 inch DrawEllipse   %   draw ellipse
gsave                           %   push graphics state
    0.50 setgray eofill         %   fill with medium gray
grestore                        %   pop graphics state
pathbbox                        %   get path bounding box
newpath                         %   start a new path
4 2 roll 2 copy moveto          %   set current point
dup 4 index exch lineto         %   bottom of box
4 2 roll dup 3 1 roll lineto    %   right side of box
2 index exch lineto             %   top of box
pop pop                         %   discard unwanted stack values
closepath                       %   close the path medium gray
stroke                          %   stroke the box
showpage                        %   display page
```

However, you can end up with a situation where the points of a path are way outside the borders of the shape. This usually arises when you are drawing Bézier curves. The control points of the Bézier are outside the area actually enclosed by the shape itself. But in fact you can get the same situation using **arcto** because arcs are drawn as Bézier curves

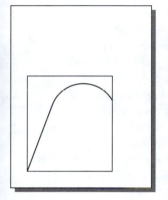

```
%!PS
/inch { 72 mul } def                   %  define inch procedure
1 inch 1 inch moveto                   %  set current point
                                       %  do arcto
4 inch 9 inch 8 inch 2 inch 2 inch arcto
4 { pop } repeat                       %  clear unwanted flotsam
gsave                                  %  push graphics state
    4 setlinewidth                     %  set fatter line width
    stroke                             %  stroke the path
grestore                               %  pop graphics state
pathbbox                               %  get path bounding box
newpath                                %  start a new path
4 2 roll 2 copy moveto                 %  set current point
dup 4 index exch lineto                %  bottom of box
4 2 roll dup 3 1 roll lineto           %  right side of box
2 index exch lineto                    %  top of box
pop pop                                %  discard unwanted stack values
closepath                              %  close the path medium gray
stroke                                 %  stroke the box
showpage                               %  display page
```

You see that the top of the bounding box is actually some distance above the shape outlined by the **arcto**. You can get the same effect from drawing Bézier curves. Here's an example showing a Bézier curve and its bounding box. The two intermediate control points are marked with circles to show where they are and why they affect the bounding box the way they do.

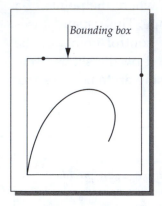

Bounding box

```
%!PS
/inch { 72 mul } def              %   define inch procedure
1 inch 1 inch moveto              %   set current point
2 inch 8 inch                     %   first control point
8 inch 7 inch                     %   second control point
6 inch 3 inch curveto             %   draw Bézier
gsave                             %   push graphics state
    4 setlinewidth                %   set fatter line width
    stroke                        %   stroke the path
grestore                          %   pop graphics state
pathbbox                          %   get path bounding box
newpath                           %   start a new path
4 2 roll 2 copy moveto            %   set current point
dup 4 index exch lineto           %   bottom of box
4 2 roll dup 3 1 roll lineto      %   right side of box
2 index exch lineto               %   top of box
pop pop                           %   discard unwanted stack values
closepath                         %   close the path medium gray
stroke                            %   stroke the box
showpage                          %   display page
```

The effect of the bounding box being outside the actual shape is particularly acute when drawing Bézier curves. The effect shows up a lot when obtaining the bounding box of character outlines, because character outlines of many fonts use Bézier curves to describe the shapes of the characters. Chapter 3 included discussions of **pathbbox** in conjunction with **charpath**.

Flattening Path for Accurate Bounding Boxes

In the previous section describing **pathbbox**, you saw how to obtain the bounding box for a path. You also saw minor problems that arise when the bounding box doesn't coincide with the shape, usually because the points that describe the shape lie outside the shape. This is particularly true of Bézier curves but can also show up in other circumstances.

To obtain a correct bounding box for a path, you need to ensure that control points are as close to the actual shape as possible. You obtain this by using **flattenpath**. Here's the previous example of the Bézier curve but with **flattenpath** added to make the path bounding box close to the actual drawn shape.

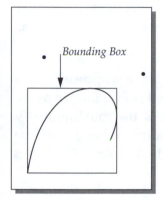

Bounding Box

```
%!PS
/inch { 72 mul } def          %   define inch procedure
1 inch 1 inch moveto          %   set current point
2 inch 8 inch                 %   first control point
8 inch 7 inch                 %   second control point
6 inch 3 inch curveto         %   draw Bézier
gsave                         %   push graphics state
    4 setlinewidth            %   set fatter line width
    stroke                    %   stroke the path
grestore                      %   pop graphics state
flattenpath                   %   flatten the path
pathbbox                      %   get path bounding box
newpath                       %   start a new path
4 2 roll 2 copy moveto        %   set current point
dup 4 index exch lineto       %   bottom of box
4 2 roll dup 3 1 roll lineto  %   right side of box
2 index exch lineto           %   top of box
pop pop                       %   discard unwanted stack values
closepath                     %   close the path medium gray
stroke                        %   stroke the box
showpage                      %   display page
```

Once again, Bézier control points are marked with dots. You see from the picture that the control points are outside the actual area of the shape. If there are too many elements in the path, **flattenpath** can **limitcheck**—even on paths that can be easily rendered.

Flatness Error Tolerance

Closely related to **flattenpath** in the preceding section is the **setflat** operator. In general, raster output devices don't draw curves; they only lay down dots in regular arrays. This means that when a raster output device renders curved path segments, it must do so by approximating the curves with many straight line segments. Most good raster devices have sufficiently high resolution to give a close approximation of the curves.

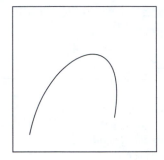

If you were to look at a curved path segment under very high magnification, you would see that the curve actually looks like this picture. What you see is that the raster output device can only approximate a curve with straight lines.

The precision to which the straight line segments approximate a curve segment is called the *error tolerance*, and is also known as the *flatness* in PostScript terminology. Flatness is the maximum distance of a point on the approximation from the related point on the curve. Flatness is measured in output device pixels, and so is quite device-dependent.

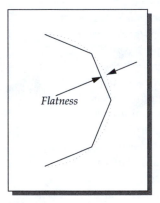

Flatness error tolerance.

The flatness parameter is a part of the graphics state. Normally, the PostScript interpreter sets up the flatness parameter such that you obtain the best possible approximation for that specific device. On our LaserWriter II-NTX, for instance, the preset flatness parameter is 1. This picture illustrates how the error tolerance differs from the exact curve.

Clipping Outside Clipping Region

You've seen how to use clipping to restrict a fill pattern to a specific area of the page. Suppose you have a shape with a fill pattern consuming almost the entire page. The example on the next page illustrates the idea.

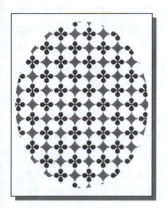

```
%!PS
/inch { 72 mul } def              %   define inch procedure
4.25 inch 5.5 inch 4 inch 5 inch DrawEllipse
AstroidLeaf setpattern            %   fancy pattern
fill                              %   fill the shape
showpage                          %   display page
```

This example is simple. There is no PostScript operator to draw an ellipse, by the way; **ellipse** is a procedure that has been defined.

Now you can use clipping to mask areas of the page into which you want to apply paint, while not placing paint on any other area of the page.

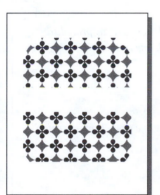

```
%!PS
/inch { 72 mul } def              %   define inch procedure
1 inch 2 inch moveto              %   define first clipping region
6.5 inch 0 rlineto
0 3 inch rlineto
-6.5 inch 0 rlineto
closepath
1 inch 6.5 inch moveto            %   define second clipping region
6.5 inch 0 rlineto
0 3 inch rlineto
-6.5 inch 0 rlineto
closepath eoclip
newpath                           %   start new path
4.25 inch 5.5 inch 4 inch 5 inch DrawEllipse
AstroidLeaf setpattern            %   fancy pattern
fill                              %   fill the shape
showpage                          %   display page
```

This example defines two rectangular clipping regions on the page. Now when you draw your ellipse, only the portions of the ellipse that lie within the clipping regions will be displayed.

PostScript supports the notion of clipping inside a clipping region. However, a frequently asked question is how to use the clipping region as a stencil so that the area outside the clipping region is filled, while the area inside the region is left untouched. You need to do something like the example shown on the next page.

The trick here is to start by defining a clipping region bigger than the physical page. The clipping region is twice the size of the 8½-by-11-inch page, just for illustration. You could make the clipping region any size you like as long as it's larger than the existing page. You define your smaller clipping regions just as before, but the clipping rules now make the two small clipping regions "outside" instead of "inside," and you get the effect you want.

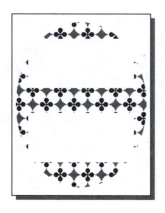

```
%!PS
/inch { 72 mul } def                    %  define inch procedure
-4.25 inch -5.5 inch moveto             %  define huge clipping region
17 inch 0 rlineto
0 22 inch rlineto
-17 inch 0 rlineto
closepath eoclip
1 inch 2 inch moveto                    %  define first clipping region
6.5 inch 0 rlineto
0 3 inch rlineto
-6.5 inch 0 rlineto
closepath eoclip
1 inch 6.5 inch moveto                  %  define second clipping region
6.5 inch 0 rlineto
0 3 inch rlineto
-6.5 inch 0 rlineto
closepath eoclip
newpath                                 %  start new path
4.25 inch 5.5 inch 4 inch 5 inch DrawEllipse
AstroidLeaf setpattern                  %  fancy pattern
fill                                    %  fill the shape
showpage                                %  display page
```

This topic comes up a lot, and quite frankly, we're baffled as to why anybody needs to do this. As far as we can tell, the requirement springs from wanting to lay down paint in the wrong order—that is, some application code is placing its drawing layers in the wrong sequence.

Playing Back a Path

Another important PostScript operation is **pathforall**—the ability to traverse around an existing path and read it back again. **pathforall** is designed to read back a path you have previously constructed. First, let's see **pathforall** in action. This example shows a very simple use of **pathforall** to give back the Bézier curves used to construct a circle. A minor surprise to PostScript newcomers is that arcs are converted to Bézier curves inside the interpreter. This code is minimal to show the flow—essential procedures are contained in following code segments.

```
594.0  396.0  moveto
594.0  554.976
464.976  684.0
306.0  684.0  curveto
147.024  684.0
17.9999  554.976
17.9999  396.0  curveto
17.9999  237.024
147.024  108.0
306.0  108.0  curveto
464.976  108.0
594.0  237.024
594.0  396.0  curveto
closepath
```

```
%!PS
/inch { 72 mul } def                        % define inch procedure
/top 10.5 inch def                          % define top margin
/junk 100 string def                        % temporary string for results
4.25 inch 5.5 inch                          % center of circle
4 inch                                      % radius of circle
0 360 arc                                   % draw a circle
closepath                                   % finish circle
/Courier-Bold findfont 36 scalefont setfont
   /movetoProc load                         % reads out moveto
   /linetoProc load                         % reads out lineto
   /curvetoProc load                        % reads out curveto
   /closepathProc load                      % reads out closepath
pathforall                                  % replay path
showpage                                    % display page
```

To understand what this code is about you need to know the syntax of **pathforall**. It is as follows:

```
{ moveto procedure }    { lineto procedure }
{ curveto procedure }   { closepath procedure } pathforall
```

As **pathforall** works its way through parts of a path, it calls one of four procedures for each kind of path segment. As you see in the syntax, a PostScript path has only four kinds of path segments: **moveto**, **lineto**, **curveto**, and **closepath**. You define these procedures to do anything you like, or nothing at all. When the **moveto**, **lineto**, or **curveto** procedures are called, the stack contains the appropriate parameters as if you were about to execute that specific operator.

What do the four procedures do? Here is the code of the procedures. **movetoProc** accepts an (x, y) coordinate pair on the stack and prints them out followed by "**moveto**".

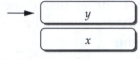

Stack at point when **moveto** *procedure is called.*

```
/movetoProc {                  %    reads out moveto
  newline                      %    start new line
  displayX displayY            %    display x and y coordinates
  space (moveto) show          %    this was a moveto
} def
```

linetoProc is basically the same as **movetoProc**—it accepts an (x, y) coordinate pair on the stack and prints them out followed by "**lineto**" instead of "**moveto**".

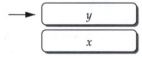

Stack at point when **lineto** *procedure is called.*

```
/linetoProc {                  %    reads out lineto
  newline                      %    start new line
  displayX displayY            %    display x and y coordinates
  space (lineto) show          %    this was a lineto
} def
```

curvetoProc is basically the same as **movetoProc** and **linetoProc**, except it must deal with three (x, y) coordinate pairs and print them out followed by "**curveto**".

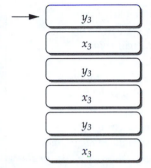

Stack at time when **curveto** *procedure is called.*

```
/curvetoProc {              % reads out curveto
  newline                   % start new line
  6 4 roll                  % first control point to top
  displayX displayY         % display x and y coordinates
  newline                   % start new line
  4 2 roll                  % second control point to top
  displayX displayY         % display x and y coordinates
  newline                   % start new line
  displayX displayY         % display x and y coordinates
  space (curveto) show      % this was a curveto
} def
```

closepathProc doesn't get any parameters—it just prints out the word "**closepath**".

```
/closepathProc {            % reads out closepath
  newline                   % start new line
  (closepath) show          % this was a closepath
} def
```

These four procedures are designed to print the coordinates of a path with their appropriate operators. The code isn't perfect because there's no provision for a path whose printout would be longer than a page. The preceding procedures call on several small utility functions to set the current point, adjust the current vertical position, and so on. Here are the utility procedures.

```
/newline {                          %   to start a new line
  /top top 40 sub def               %   move top margin down
  0.75 inch top moveto              %   set current point
} def
/space {                            %   space between numbers
  ( ) show                          %   show a space
} def
/displayX {                         %   display x coordinate
  exch                              %   x coordinate to top of stack
  junk cvs show                     %   display converted x coordinate
} def
/displayY {                         %   display y coordinate
  space                             %   space before y coordinate
  junk cvs show                     %   display converted y coordinate
} def
```

Seems like a lot of procedures for an apparently small example. But that's what procedures are for—they encapsulate portions of the job so you don't go crazy repeating code all over the place.

That's all there is in the example of **pathforall**, except for one thing. Why does the code read

```
/movetoProc load                    %   reads out moveto
/linetoProc load                    %   reads out lineto
/curvetoProc load                   %   reads out curveto
/closepathProc load                 %   reads out closepath
```

instead of just naming the procedures? If you omit the / signs and use the procedure names directly, the interpreter starts executing the procedures immediately. Errors will occur because the required values aren't on the stack.

Well, that just shows you how to construct the basic parameters for **pathforall**. Here's a more interesting example using **pathforall** to show a string of text around the outside of a circle.

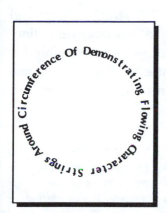

Really awful character spacing around periphery of circle—more work needed.

```
%!PS
/inch { 72 mul } def            %   define inch procedure
4.25 inch 5.5 inch              %   center of circle
3.5 inch                        %   radius of circle
90 450 arc                      %   draw a circle
closepath                       %   finish circle
reversepath                     %   reverse the order of the path
1 setflat flattenpath           %   reduce path to line segments
  /movetoProc load              %   reads out moveto
  /linetoProc load              %   reads out lineto
  /curvetoProc load             %   reads out curveto
  /closepathProc load           %   reads out closepath
pathforall                      %   replay path
showpage                        %   display page
1 setflat flattenpath
/Optima-Bold findfont 48 scalefont setfont
/showString
  (Demonstrating Flowing Character Strings
  Around Circumference Of Circle) def
  /movetoProc load              %   reads out moveto
  /linetoProc load              %   reads out lineto
  /curvetoProc load             %   reads out curveto
  /closepathProc load           %   reads out closepath
pathforall                      %   replay path
showpage                        %   display page
```

Let's analyze this code a section at a time. First you draw a circle. A slightly unusual thing about this circle is that the start angle is 90° and the end angle is 450°. That's because you want the text to start showing from the top of the circle, not from the right hand side. Had you drawn the circle in the regular fashion starting at 0° and ending at 360°, the text would start at the west side of the circle. The other slightly unusual part is the **reversepath**. It's there to get the segments of the path flowing left to right—the order in which you're accustomed to reading text. Had you read the path without **reversepath**, elements of the path would come from right to left and the text would go backward around the circle.

flattenpath turns the circle from Bézier curves into line segments. Following that, **pathforall** deals with the process of placing characters around the outside of the circle. The string to be placed around the periphery of the circle is defined as **showString**. **linetoProc**, defined in the following code sections, is responsible for pulling **showString** apart character by character. Now here come the procedures for **pathforall**. First there's **movetoProc**.

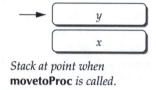

Stack at point when
movetoProc *is called.*

```
/movetoProc {                    %   reads out moveto
    /previousY exch def          %   remember y coordinate
    /previousX exch def          %   remember x coordinate
    /charNum 0 def               %   character index for string
} def
```

movetoProc should be called only once for this example. Its job is to set up the initial x and y coordinates so **linetoProc** can use them when it gets called. **movetoProc** also sets the initial value of the character index used for working through **showString**. The next block of code shows **linetoProc**.

linetoProc looks more complicated than it really is. **linetoProc** is responsible for pulling a character out of the show string every time it is called. **linetoProc** does this function in three stages. First, it calculates the angle by which to rotate the coordinate system to show the current character in the correct orientation. Second, **linetoProc** computes the length of the line segment on which the character will be shown, computes the correct position on the line segment, and shows the character there. Finally, the current x and y coordinates are copied into the previous x and y coordinates, ready for the next time **linetoProc** is called, and the character string index is updated, ready for the next character.

```
/linetoProc {                                   %  reads out lineto
  /currentY exch def                            %  current y coordinate
  /currentX exch def                            %  current x coordinate
                                                %  compute rotation angle
  currentY previousY sub                        %  compute δy
  currentX previousX sub                        %  compute δx
  atan                                          %  determine angle to rotate
  /angle exch def                               %  save angle
                                                %  compute hypotenuse
  currentX previousX sub dup mul                %  compute x²
  currentY previousY sub dup mul                %  compute y²
  add sqrt                                      %  compute √(x² + y²)
  /hypot exch def                               %  save for later
                                                %  image character
  gsave                                         %  remember graphics state
    previousX previousY translate               %  origin to start of line
    angle rotate                                %  rotate to correct angle
    showString charNum 1 getinterval %          %  get current character
    dup                                         %  make copy for show later
    stringwidth pop                             %  compute width of character
    hypot exch sub 2 div 0 moveto               %  set current point
    show                                        %  image character
  grestore                                      %  recall saved graphics state
                                                %  set up for next time around
  /previousX currentX def                       %  update y coordinate
  /previousY currentY def                       %  update x coordinate
  /charNum charNum 1 add def                    %  update character index
} def
```

The math comments read:

- compute x^2
- compute y^2
- compute $\sqrt{x^2 + y^2}$

curvetoProc and **closepathProc** do nothing. In theory, **curvetoProc** should never be called, because the **flattenpath** turns all Béziers into line segments. If you wish, you could introduce code into **curvetoProc** to print a warning something's wrong if it gets called.

```
/curvetoProc {                    %   reads out curveto
                                  %   should not be called
} def
/closepathProc {                  %   reads out closepath
                                  %   should do nothing
} def
```

In PostScript Level 1, you could not use **pathforall** on any path that contained the results of a **charpath**. You would get an **invalidaccess** error if you tried. PostScript Level 2 removed this restriction. Note that the *PostScript Language Reference Manual—Second Edition*, which covers PostScript Level 2, states the restriction is still in force, but Appendix **A** states the restriction has been lifted for "most fonts."

9 Images

For I dipt into the future, far as human eye could see,
Saw the Vision of the world, and all the wonder that would be;
Saw the heavens fill with commerce, argosies of magic sails,
Pilots of the purple twilight, dropping down with costly bales;

Alfred, Lord Tennyson

Previous chapters concentrated on analytical graphics and text—pictures represented by PostScript programs consisting of lines and curves. This chapter concentrates on images—pictures built from sampled data. Sampled data is simply a pattern of bits. A file of sampled data is often called a bitmap. Common sources of sampled bitmap data include scanned photographs and the output from "paint" programs.

Here is a character, printed large, from the Ryumin–Light font.[†] The character on the page is generated from outlines—lines and curves. This character was chosen for its pleasing asymmetry. Next, to illustrate images, the character was rendered so it occupied about 64×64 pixels, then "captured" from the screen. Screen capture usually generates some kind of a raster file format.[‡] You need to convert this raster file into a form of data suitable for the PostScript **image** operator. How you achieve this conversion depends on your computer system. In general, the printing dialog of your system applications can provide a means to capture the generated PostScript into a file that you can subsequently edit. The result of such a conversion is image data.

Large character converted from outlines.

---

† This character means "vermilion" or "cinnabar" or "red heart."

‡ Macintosh screen capture generates either MacPaint or PICT format files. NeXT screen capture generates TIFF.

Here is the same character, but this time rendered as an image instead of a series of PostScript drawing operations. Rendering characters as bitmaps, by the way, was the manner in which many printing languages did the job prior to PostScript.

Large character printed as a bitmap—note the "jaggies".

```
%!PS
/inch { 72 mul } def                        %  define inch procedure
/temp 16 string def                         %  string for temporary results
1.25 inch 2.5 inch translate                %  set origin
6 inch 6 inch scale                         %  scale image large
64 64 1                                     %  width, height, and depth
[ 64  0  0  64  0  0 ]                       %  image matrix
                                            %  image procedure
{ currentfile temp readhexstring pop }
image                                       %  image operation
FFFFFFFFFFFFFFFF FFFFFFFFFFFFFFFF           %  lines of data
FFFFFFF3FFFFFFFF FFFFFFF81FFFFFFF
            . . .
     28 lines of data omitted
            . . .
FFFFFFF83FFFFFFF FFFFFFF87FFFFFFF
FFFFFFFCFFFFFFFF FFFFFFFFFFFFFFFF
showpage                                    %  display page
```

The first thing you notice is that this image has the "jaggies"— you can see individual bits of the image. For this reason, you should really use images only where they are appropriate—for applications such as scanned photographs.

A Walk Through an Image

Now **image** can be pulled apart into its components. This discussion applies (with minor variations) to **imagemask**, described in *Image Masks* on page 355 in this chapter. To illustrate the various parts of **image**, let's use a somewhat smaller image—a screen dump of σ—the Greek letter *sigma*. This image is small enough that you can see all the bits in their entirety.

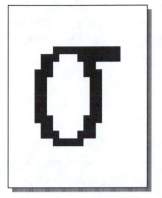

Small bitmapped character.

```
%!PS
/inch { 72 mul } def              %   define inch procedure
/sigma <
    F07F C71F CF9F 8F8F
    9FCF 9FCF 9FCF 9FCF
    9FCF 8F8F CF9F C701 F001
> def                             %   hexadecimal image string
1.25 inch 2.5 inch translate      %   set origin
6 inch 6 inch scale               %   scale image large
16  13  1                         %   width, height, depth
[ 16  0  0  13  0  0 ]            %   image matrix
{ sigma }                         %   image procedure
image                             %   image operation
showpage                          %   display page
```

This image of the letter σ happens to be 16 bits wide and 13 bits high. Generally, though, you talk about images in terms of the number of scan lines they contain. This image contains 13 scan lines, and each scan line contains 16 bits. Let's take a look at the general format of **image**. There are actually two different forms. The first form of **image** looks like this:

width   height   depth   [*matrix*]   { *image procedure* }   **image**

This is the only form of **image** PostScript Level 1 handles. This format is handled by PostScript Level 2 as well. Pulling apart the parameters to **image**, you can divide the parameters into three separate parcels. The three parcels are image size, image transformation matrix, and image data procedure. The next few pages describe these parts of **image** in greater detail. The other form of **image** looks like this:

```
%!PS
```
image_dictionary   **image**

This form of **image** was introduced with PostScript Level 2, and you'll see this form in action later on.

The first parcel is information to tell **image** the size of the image. This parcel is the width, height, and depth fields of the operation. In our example, *width* = 16, *height* = 13, and *depth* = 1. There are 13 scan lines of 16 bits each, and the image is monochrome (black and white). The image would be a gray scale image or a color image if *depth* were greater than one.

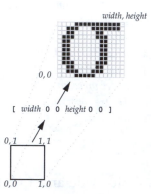

The second parcel is an image matrix. This matrix is just like a regular PostScript CTM. The image matrix specifies how the image will be mapped onto a one-unit square in the user coordinate system. This particular image matrix specifies the unit square of user space maps onto the corners of the image as shown in this sketch.

image is designed to be consistent with PostScript coordinate system models. Remember that user space is defined with the origin at the lower-left hand corner of the "page." Images are assumed to be in that orientation also. This means **image** expects to see the scan lines of the image data coming in bottom to top, left to right.

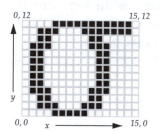

The image matrix also defines the order in which the bits of the image are arranged. Remember how the PostScript user coordinate system looks like the picture, with the origin at the lower-left corner. The image coordinate system has the same orientation. PostScript likes to see the bits of the image arranged in the fashion shown here.

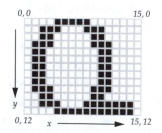

Most computer screens, though, arrange their coordinate system so (0, 0) is the upper-left corner of the screen instead of the lower-right. And most image-capturing facilities produce image data in the same orientation as the screen—top to bottom, left to right. This means the bits of our image are actually laid out as shown here. As well as the upside-down nature of computer systems, the color model of monochrome (black and white) screens differ from that of PostScript. The PostScript color model uses 0.0 to mean black and 1.0 to mean white. This is consistent with color, where 1.0 means fully saturated color, and 0.0 means no color, or black. Most computer systems, however, use a "1" pixel to mean black and a "0" pixel to mean white. In addition to computing an image transformation matrix to position and orient the image correctly, an application must also invert the sense of the bits.

So an image matrix of [*width* **0 0** *–height* **0 0**] tells **image** to map the data upside-down. This means the coordinate system is flipped vertically. Hence you must **translate** upward by the height of the image before rendering it. Your image matrix then looks like [*width* **0 0** *–height* **0** *height*].

Image matrices behave just like the CTM. You can transform images using shear as described in Chapter 4. Here's the leaning trilithon of Stonehenge.

Leaning trilithon because of skewed image matrix.

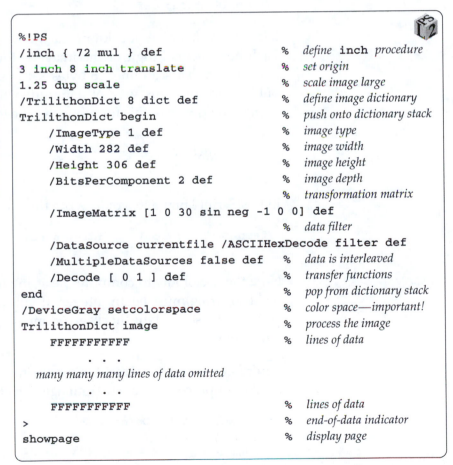

```
%!PS
/inch { 72 mul } def          %   define inch procedure
3 inch 8 inch translate       %   set origin
1.25 dup scale                %   scale image large
/TrilithonDict 8 dict def     %   define image dictionary
TrilithonDict begin           %   push onto dictionary stack
    /ImageType 1 def          %   image type
    /Width 282 def            %   image width
    /Height 306 def           %   image height
    /BitsPerComponent 2 def   %   image depth
                              %   transformation matrix
    /ImageMatrix [1 0 30 sin neg -1 0 0] def
                              %   data filter
    /DataSource currentfile /ASCIIHexDecode filter def
    /MultipleDataSources false def   %   data is interleaved
    /Decode [ 0 1 ] def       %   transfer functions
end                           %   pop from dictionary stack
/DeviceGray setcolorspace     %   color space—important!
TrilithonDict image           %   process the image
    FFFFFFFFFF                %   lines of data

        . . .
    many many many lines of data omitted
        . . .

    FFFFFFFFFF                %   lines of data
>                             %   end-of-data indicator
showpage                      %   display page
```

This image example uses the **image** operator with an image dictionary. You'll read about image dictionaries later in this chapter.

The third parcel of information is a procedure that delivers image data to the **image** operator. This specific example defines a hexadecimal string called **sigma**. The procedure that **image** calls references **sigma**, which places the string on the operand stack.

The example on page 348 shows the commonly used method of reading scan lines of the image one at a time using **readhexstring**. The definition of the string to hold the lines of the image was just a little cavalier. The definition was

```
/temp 16 string def
```

because in this case you know each scan line occupies 16 bytes. Each hexadecimal digit of the image is four bits. The image contains 64 bits per scan line. 16 bytes × 4 bits = 64 bits. This is fine, but a more rigorous way of computing the size of the required string would be like this for monochrome (one bit deep) images.

$$stringlength = \frac{(width + 7)}{8}$$

In PostScript language, you'd write this as

```
/temp  width  7  add  8  idiv  string  def
```

Note the use of **idiv** to compute the string length. The *length* argument to **string** must be an integer. If you used **div** instead of **idiv** you would see a **typecheck** error message from the PostScript interpreter.

You're now ready to parcel the whole image-processing job into a PostScript procedure called **DoImage**, which you call like this.

```
width   height   depth   DoImage
      lines of image
      lines of image
        .  .  .
      lines of image
      lines of image
```

Here's the definition of **DoImage**.

```
/DoImage {                          %   depth    height    width
   4 dict begin                     %   anonymous dictionary
     /depth exch def                %   define depth
     /height exch def               %   define height
     /width exch def                %   define width
                                    %   temporary string
     /temp width 7 add 8 idiv string def
     gsave                          %   save graphics state
        width height depth          %   image parameters
        [ width 0 0 height 0 0 ]    %   image matrix
                                    %   image procedure
        { currentfile temp readhexstring pop } bind
        image                       %   do image process
     grestore                       %   restore graphics state
   end                              %   pop anonymous dictionary
} def
```

And here's **DoImage** in action on the data from the example on page 348.

Image rendered using pack-aged image procedure.

```
%!PS
/inch { 72 mul } def                %   define inch procedure
1.25 inch 2.5 inch translate        %   set origin
6 inch dup scale                    %   scale image large
64 64 1 DoImage                     %   process image
FFFFFFFFFFFFFFFF FFFFFFFFFFFFFFFF    %   lines of data
FFFFFFF3FFFFFFFF FFFFFFF81FFFFFFF

         • • •
    28 lines of data omitted
         • • •

FFFFFFF83FFFFFFF FFFFFFF87FFFFFFF
FFFFFFFCFFFFFFFF FFFFFFFFFFFFFFFF
showpage                            %   display page
```

Image Data as Strings

Some of the examples so far have used **readhexstring** to read the image data from the current file. Reading image data with **readhexstring** is commonly understood and it works well for the general case. The examples with the small sigma character showed how you can "cheat" a little if your images are small ("small" will be defined in a moment). Let's use an example of a "small" image to show this alternative method in action. Here's a picture of a trilithon.

```
/inch { 72 mul } def                    %   define inch procedure
2 inch 8 inch translate                 %   set origin
1.25 dup scale                          %   scale image large
<                                       %   start of hexadecimal string
    FFFFFFFFFF                          %   lines of data
        . . .
  beelyuns and beelyuns and beelyuns of sagans of data omitted
        . . .
    FFFFFFFFFF                          %   lines of data
>                                       %   end of hexadecimal string
282 306 2                               %   width, height, depth
[1 0 0 -1 0 0]                          %   image matrix
{}                                      %   null procedure
image                                   %   image operation
showpage                                %   display page
```

Now the entire image is placed on the stack as a hexadecimal string and there's no need for **readhexstring**. But you have to be aware that using this method is limited, because there is a limit to the number of characters that can be placed in a single string. If the total number of bytes in your image exceeds the number of characters a string can hold, one of two things happen. Either you get a **limitcheck** error from the interpreter, in which case your PostScript job terminates, or the remaining bytes are discarded, and your image ends up looking rather strange. The picture shows the sailboat image from Chapter 1 and what happens to the image if the excess bytes are discarded.

Why use this method of placing image data on the stack? One very good reason is that your page description might want to render the same image several times. Replicating the image every time it is required considerably expands the PostScript file size.

Image Masks

Image on a background— white bits obscure background.

You have learned by now that the PostScript painting model is one of opaque paint. And paint laid down on the page obscures any paint previously laid down in the same place. Now you come to *masks*—a PostScript feature to partially skate around the opaque painting model. The reason to use masks is to apply paint at designated places on a background without disturbing the background. This picture illustrates why you need masks. You can use the previous character bitmap, but place the image on a light gray background.

```
%!PS
/inch { 72 mul } def              %   define inch procedure
0 0 moveto                        %   set current point
8.5 inch 0 rlineto                %   bottom of rectangle
0 11 inch rlineto                 %   right side
-8.5 inch 0 rlineto               %   top
closepath                         %   finish the shape
0.9 setgray fill                  %   light gray background
0.0 setgray                       %   reset color to black
/temp 16 string def               %   string for temporary results
1.25 inch 2.5 inch translate      %   set origin
6 inch 6 inch scale               %   scale image large
64 64 1                           %   width, height, depth
[ 64  0  0  64  0  0 ]            %   image matrix
{ currentfile temp readhexstring pop }%   image procedure
image                             %   image operation
FFFFFFFFFFFFFFFF FFFFFFFFFFFFFFFF %   lines of data
FFFFFFF3FFFFFFFF FFFFFFF81FFFFFFFF
          . . .
          . . .
FFFFFFF83FFFFFFF FFFFFFF87FFFFFFF
FFFFFFFCFFFFFFFF FFFFFFFFFFFFFFFF
showpage                          %   display page
```

The image overlays the gray background. Unfortunately, the white bits of the image obscure the gray background just the same as the black bits of the image. This effect is fine as long as that's what you want. But what if you want the image to look like this next picture? That's where **imagemask** comes into play.

Image mask on a background—only black bits draw.

```
%!PS
/inch { 72 mul } def                              %   define inch procedure
0 0 moveto                                        %   set current point
8.5 inch 0 rlineto                                %   bottom of rectangle
0 11 inch rlineto                                 %   right side
-8.5 inch 0 rlineto                               %   top
closepath                                         %   finish the shape
0.9 setgray fill                                  %   light gray background
0.0 setgray                                       %   reset color to black
/temp 16 string def                               %   string for temporary results
1.25 inch 2.5 inch translate                      %   set origin
6 inch 6 inch scale                               %   scale image large
64 64 false                                       %   width, height, and Boolean
[ 64  0  0  64  0  0 ]                             %   image matrix
                                                  %   imagemask procedure
{ currentfile temp readhexstring pop }
imagemask                                         %   imagemask operation
FFFFFFFFFFFFFFFF FFFFFFFFFFFFFFFF                 %   lines of data
FFFFFFF3FFFFFFFF FFFFFF81FFFFFFFF                 %   lines of data
            . . .
   28 lines of data omitted
            . . .
FFFFFFF83FFFFFFF FFFFFFF87FFFFFFF                 %   lines of data
FFFFFFFCFFFFFFFF FFFFFFFFFFFFFFFF                 %   lines of data
showpage                                          %   display page
```

The black bits of the image display the way you want them to, but the white bits of the image don't obscure the gray background. This is the key idea of masks. A mask itself doesn't apply any paint. The mask acts as a stencil through which a predefined color can be painted. If you've ever seen silk-screening in action you get the idea behind masks.

The preceding example poured black paint through the mask onto a gray background. But as you just read, the color that pours through the mask can be any color. Let's change the example again slightly to make the background a light gray and the image a darker gray.

Dark gray image mask on light gray background.

```
%!PS
/inch { 72 mul } def              %  define inch procedure
0 0 moveto                        %  set current point
8.5 inch 0 rlineto                %  bottom of rectangle
0 11 inch rlineto                 %  right side
-8.5 inch 0 rlineto               %  top
closepath                         %  finish the shape
0.9 setgray fill                  %  light gray background
0.5 setgray                       %  reset color to medium gray
/temp 16 string def               %  string for temporary results
1.25 inch 2.5 inch translate      %  set origin
6 inch 6 inch scale               %  scale image large
64 64 false                       %  width, height, and Boolean
[ 64  0  0  64  0  0 ]            %  image matrix
                                  %  imagemask procedure
{ currentfile temp readhexstring pop }
imagemask                         %  imagemask operation
FFFFFFFFFFFFFFFF FFFFFFFFFFFFFFFF
FFFFFFF3FFFFFFFF FFFFFFF81FFFFFFFF %  lines of data
          . . .
    28 lines of data omitted
          . . .
FFFFFFF83FFFFFFF FFFFFFF87FFFFFFF
FFFFFFFCFFFFFFFF FFFFFFFFFFFFFFFF
showpage                          %  display page
```

You can use the same scheme to obtain light gray images on a dark gray background.

Light gray image mask on dark gray background.

```
%!PS
/inch { 72 mul } def                % define inch procedure
0 0 moveto                          % set current point
8.5 inch 0 rlineto                  % bottom of rectangle
0 11 inch rlineto                   % right side
-8.5 inch 0 rlineto                 % top
closepath                           % finish the shape
0.4 setgray fill                    % dark gray background
0.9 setgray                         % set color to light gray
/temp 16 string def                 % string for temporary results
1.25 inch 2.5 inch translate        % set origin
6 inch 6 inch scale                 % scale image large
64 64 false                         % width, height, and Boolean
[ 64  0  0  64  0  0 ]              % image matrix
                                    % imagemask procedure
{ currentfile temp readhexstring pop }
imagemask                           % imagemask operation
FFFFFFFFFFFFFFFF FFFFFFFFFFFFFFFF   % lines of data
FFFFFFF3FFFFFFFF FFFFFFF81FFFFFFF

           . . .
           . . .

FFFFFFF83FFFFFFF FFFFFFF87FFFFFFF
FFFFFFFCFFFFFFFF FFFFFFFFFFFFFFFF
showpage                            % display page
```

The foreground and background colors don't have to be monochrome—black and white and shades of gray. You can establish any color you like to be painted using **imagemask**. Of course, to see the results in color you need a color printer or color display device. By changing the two **setgray** lines in the code, you can get colors. Two lines changed in the preceding example place a blue image on a light green background, and the color picture of this appears in plate XXX.

See plate XXX for the color version.

```
%!PS
/inch { 72 mul } def                % define inch procedure
0 0 moveto                          % set current point
8.5 inch 0 rlineto                  % bottom of rectangle
0 11 inch rlineto                   % right side
-8.5 inch 0 rlineto                 % top
closepath                           % finish the shape
0.0 0.5 0.0 setrgbcolor             % light green color
fill                                % fill background
0.0 0.0 0.5 setrgbcolor             % medium blue color
/temp 16 string def                 % string for temporary results
1.25 inch 2.5 inch translate        % set origin
6 inch 6 inch scale                 % scale image large
64 64 false                         % width, height, and Boolean
[ 64  0  0  64  0  0 ]              % image matrix
                                    % imagemask procedure
{ currentfile temp readhexstring pop }
imagemask                           % imagemask operation
FFFFFFFFFFFFFFFF FFFFFFFFFFFFFFFF   % lines of data
FFFFFFF3FFFFFFFF FFFFFFF81FFFFFFFF

           . . .
           . . .

FFFFFFF83FFFFFFF FFFFFFF87FFFFFFF
FFFFFFFCFFFFFFFF FFFFFFFFFFFFFFFF
showpage                            % display page
```

Image Dictionaries

PostScript Level 2 **image** and **imagemask** can accept a *dictionary* as an operand. An example appears on the next page.

This example is fairly straightforward. Items of note are the **/ImageType** key and the **/Decode** key. The **/ImageType** key is required for PostScript Level 2 image dictionaries. At the time of writing, only **/ImageType 1** is defined. The **/Decode** key specifies a transfer function in a device-independent fashion. In PostScript Level 1 you could get an inverted image by playing with the transfer function using **settransfer**, but doing so is device-dependent. In PostScript Level 2, you can change the order of the numbers in the **Decode** array to invert the image.

Using PostScript Level 2 image dictionary.

```
%!PS
/inch { 72 mul } def                % define inch procedure
/temp 16 string def                 % string for temporary results
/ShuImage 7 dict def                % define image dictionary
ShuImage begin                      % place on dictionary stack
    /ImageType 1 def                % required
    /Width 64 def                   % bits per scan line
    /Height 64 def                  % number of scan lines
    /BitsPerComponent 1 def         % depth of image
                                    % image matrix
    /ImageMatrix [ 64 0 0 64 0 0 ] def
    /DataSource { currentfile temp readhexstring pop } def
    /Decode [ 0 1 ] def             % transfer function
end                                 % remove from dictionary stack
1.25 inch 2.5 inch translate        % set origin
6 inch 6 inch scale                 % scale image large
ShuImage                            % image dictionary
image                               % image operation
FFFFFFFFFFFFFFFF FFFFFFFFFFFFFFFF   % lines of data
FFFFFFF3FFFFFFFF FFFFFFF81FFFFFFF
          . . .
     28 lines of data omitted
          . . .
FFFFFFF83FFFFFFF FFFFFFF87FFFFFFF
FFFFFFFCFFFFFFFF FFFFFFFFFFFFFFFF
showpage                            % display page
```

Here's an example of changing the order of the numbers in the **/Decode** array. This example also illustrates the use of << and >> syntax to introduce a transient dictionary for **image**.

Inverting colors through
/Decode *array.*

```
%!PS
/inch { 72 mul } def                        %  define inch procedure
/temp 16 string def                         %  string for temporary results
1.25 inch 2.5 inch translate                %  set origin
6 inch 6 inch scale                         %  scale image large
<<                                          %  start image dictionary
    /ImageType 1                            %  required
    /Width 64                               %  bits per scan line
    /Height 64                              %  number of scan lines
    /BitsPerComponent 1                     %  depth of image
                                            %  image matrix

    /ImageMatrix [ 64 0 0 64 0 0 ]
    /DataSource { currentfile temp readhexstring pop }
    /Decode [ 1 0 ]                         %  transfer function
>>                                          %  end image dictionary
image                                       %  image operation
FFFFFFFFFFFFFFFF FFFFFFFFFFFFFFFF           %  lines of data
FFFFFFF3FFFFFFFF FFFFFFF81FFFFFFF
                . . .
        28 lines of data omitted
                . . .
FFFFFFF83FFFFFFF FFFFFFF87FFFFFFF
FFFFFFFCFFFFFFFF FFFFFFFFFFFFFFFF
showpage                                    %  display page
```

Now you see an inverted image. You can play games with the
transfer function by changing the values of the lower and upper
numbers, in which case PostScript will map the values to the
range of the numbers you choose. Of course, with purely black
and white pixels, you don't exactly get a lot of interesting shades,
but this example illustrates the use. In the following example the
lower number is set to 0.25 and the upper number to 0.75 and you
see the shades of gray instead of just black and white.

Colors migrated towards gray.

```
%!PS
/inch { 72 mul } def                           % define inch procedure
/temp 16 string def                            % string for temporary results
/ShuImage 7 dict def                           % define image dictionary
ShuImage begin                                 % place on dictionary stack
    /ImageType 1 def                           % required
    /Width 64 def                              % bits per scan line
    /Height 64 def                             % number of scan lines
    /BitsPerComponent 1 def                    % depth of image
    /ImageMatrix [ 64 0 0 64 0 0 ] def%        image matrix
    /DataSource { currentfile temp readhexstring pop }
    /Decode [ 0.25 0.75 ] def                  % transfer function
end                                            % remove from dictionary stack
1.25 inch 2.5 inch translate                   % set origin
6 inch 6 inch scale                            % scale image large
ShuImage                                       % image dictionary
image                                          % image operation
FFFFFFFFFFFFFFFF FFFFFFFFFFFFFFFF              % lines of data
FFFFFFF3FFFFFFFF FFFFFFF81FFFFFFF

        . . .
    28 lines of data omitted
        . . .

FFFFFFF83FFFFFFF FFFFFFF87FFFFFFF
FFFFFFFCFFFFFFFF FFFFFFFFFFFFFFFF
showpage                                       % display page
```

Color Images

Early in the evolution of PostScript, color printing devices appeared on the market. PostScript operators were added to deal with color. **colorimage** was one of these operators. Where **image**, described earlier in this chapter, was designed for monochrome and gray scale images, **colorimage**, as its name implies, was designed to deal with color images. PostScript Level 2 versions of **image** have gone beyond **colorimage** in their ability to deal with color spaces, and **colorimage** remains for backward compatibility with earlier printers. For this reason, **colorimage** lacks the capability to accept an image dictionary as an operand.

The general syntax of **colorimage** is as follows:

$$width \quad height \quad bits\_per\_component \quad image\ matrix$$
$$data\_source_0 \quad data\_source_1 \quad ... \quad data\_source_{n-1}$$
$$multiple\_flag \quad number\_of\_components \quad \texttt{colorimage}$$

Examples following are marked PostScript Level 2 but in fact, **colorimage** was around before PostScript Level 2—you might think of it as being PostScript Level "one-and-a-half." The use of **image** to do color images is definitely a PostScript Level 2 feature. Here's **colorimage** used to image a Mandelbrot figure on the page.

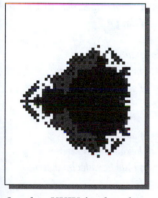

See plate XXIX for the color version.

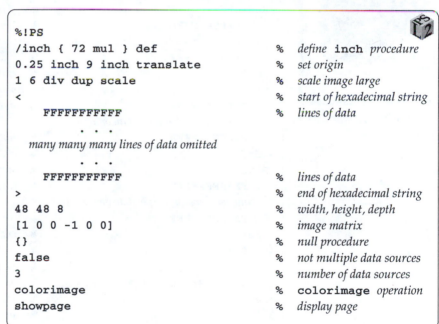

```
%!PS
/inch { 72 mul } def                  %    define inch procedure
0.25 inch 9 inch translate            %    set origin
1 6 div dup scale                     %    scale image large
<                                     %    start of hexadecimal string
    FFFFFFFFFFFF                      %    lines of data

          . . .
  many many many lines of data omitted
          . . .

    FFFFFFFFFFFF                      %    lines of data
>                                     %    end of hexadecimal string
48 48 8                               %    width, height, depth
[1 0 0 -1 0 0]                        %    image matrix
{}                                    %    null procedure
false                                 %    not multiple data sources
3                                     %    number of data sources
colorimage                            %    colorimage operation
showpage                              %    display page
```

Red	Green	Blue
Red	Green	Blue
Red	Green	Blue
Red	Green	Blue
Red	Green	Blue
Red	Green	Blue

Interleaved color image data—one data source.

This version of **colorimage** has only one data source and three color components. The color model is RGB, and because the multiple data sources Boolean is **false**, the data is already "weaved" or interleaved. This means the data comes in as three-byte triplets of a byte of red color, a byte of green color, and a byte of blue color.

Let's see the same example with three separate data sources.

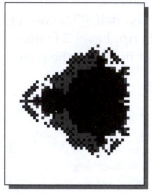

Color image—separate data sources.

```
%!PS
/inch { 72 mul } def                    %   define inch procedure
0.25 inch 9 inch translate              %   set origin
1 6 div dup scale                       %   scale image large
/Red <                                  %   start of red hexadecimal string
    FFFFFFFFFF                          %   lines of data
many many many lines of data omitted
    FFFFFFFFFF                          %   lines of data
> def                                   %   end of hexadecimal string
/Green <                                %   start of green hexadecimal string
    FFFFFFFFFF                          %   lines of data
many many many lines of data omitted
    FFFFFFFFFF                          %   lines of data
> def                                   %   end of hexadecimal string
/Blue <                                 %   start of blue hexadecimal string
    FFFFFFFFFF                          %   lines of data
many many many lines of data omitted
    FFFFFFFFFF                          %   lines of data
> def                                   %   end of hexadecimal string
48 48 8                                 %   width, height, depth
[1 0 0 -1 0 0]                          %   image matrix
{ Red } { Green } { Blue }              %   data procedures
true                                    %   multiple data sources
3                                       %   number of data sources
colorimage                              %   colorimage operation
showpage                                %   display page
```

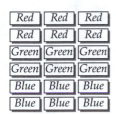

Non-interleaved color image data—three separate data sources.

This version of **colorimage** has three data sources and three color components. The color model is RGB, and because the multiple data sources Boolean is **true**, the data is in three separate sources.

Just as with **image** and **imagemask**, you can pull the parameters of **colorimage** apart into three separate bundles—image size, image transformation matrix, and image data procedures.

The various data source procedures are related to the *multi* parameter to **colorimage**. *multi* is a Boolean specifying how **colorimage** obtains data from the data sources. If *multi* is **false**, there is only one source of data—*data_source*$_0$. This data source contains all the color components already interleaved. If *multi* is **true**, there are multiple sources of data—*data_source*$_0$ through *data_source*$_{n-1}$. These data sources each contain one of the color components. The number of data sources is determined by the *number_of_components* parameter, described later.

The term "data sources" is used now. In PostScript Level 1, the data source was a procedure that delivered the data. In PostScript Level 2, the data sources can be procedures, strings, or filtered files. If there is more than one data source to **colorimage**, all the sources must be of the same type—you can't mix, say, procedures and filtered files in the same execution of **colorimage**.

The *number_of_components* parameter to **colorimage** specifies which color model is used to render the image. *number_of_components* can have the value **1**, **3**, or **4**.

number_of_components = 1 means this image has only one color component. That component is gray, so calling it a "color component" is stretching the truth a little. In this model, **colorimage** behaves precisely like **image**. In PostScript Level 2 terms, the image is rendered according to **/DeviceGray** color space.

number_of_components = 3 means the samples of the image consist of red, green, and blue components. The image is rendered according to **/DeviceRGB** color space.

number_of_components = 4 means the samples of the image consist of cyan, magenta, yellow, and black components. The image is rendered according to **/DeviceCMYK** color space.

These examples showed the data coming in as hexadecimal strings. If the data comes in as part of the current file, you can use the same method to read data as for monochrome images. That is,

```
{ currentfile tempstring readhexstring pop }
```

to read the data. For color images with multiple data sources, you need as many procedures as there are components in the color image. For this RGB color image, you need three procedures:

```
{ currentfile redstring readhexstring pop }
{ currentfile greenstring readhexstring pop }
{ currentfile bluestring readhexstring pop }
```

and, very important indeed—your color data procedures must use distinct strings for each color. If you try to reuse the red string, say, for the green data, some of your red data could get lost.

PostScript Level 2 Color Images

PostScript Level 2 color images can be imaged using the **image** operator in its dictionary form. **colorimage** doesn't accept the alternative form where the image parameters are packaged into an image dictionary. So instead of using **colorimage**, which is becoming outdated, you can use the one-operand form of **image** to process color images. Here's the Mandelbrot example again, this time using **image** with an image dictionary.

*Color image using PostScript Level 2 **image** operator.*

```
%!PS
/inch { 72 mul } def                        % define inch procedure
0.25 inch 9 inch translate                  % set origin
1 6 div dup scale                           % scale image large
/MandelDict 8 dict def                       % define image dictionary
MandelDict begin                             % push onto dictionary stack
    /ImageType 1 def                         % image type
    /Width 48 def                            % image width
    /Height 48 def                           % image height
    /BitsPerComponent 8 def                  % image depth
                                             % transformation matrix
    /ImageMatrix [1 0 0 -1 0 0] def
                                             % data filter
    /DataSource currentfile /ASCIIHexDecode filter def
    /MultipleDataSources false def           % data is interleaved
    /Decode [ 0 1 0 1 0 1 ] def              % transfer functions
end                                          % remove from dictionary stack
/DeviceRGB setcolorspace                     % color space—important!
MandelDict image                             % process the image
    FFFFFFFFFF                               % lines of data

        . . .
    many many many lines of data omitted
        . . .

    FFFFFFFFFF                               % lines of data
showpage                                     % display page
```

This example defines an image dictionary as in previous examples, but you should note a few items. First, notice the use of a filter to read the data. Filters are a PostScript Level 2 feature and you'll read more about them later in this chapter. Most important is the line to set the color space to **/DeviceRGB**. Where the old **colorimage** explicitly specified the number of color components, the new **image** interprets the color data according to the current color space. You must set the current color space before calling **image**. If you don't, you get a **typecheck** error from the PostScript interpreter. You must also ensure the current color space is set correctly, otherwise your images won't look right—a RGB image interpreted in CMYK color space is probably not what you want.

Images with Filters

PostScript Level 2 provides a variety of *filters* useful in conjunction with images. Here's **image** using **ASCIIHexDecode** filter as a data source.

Image using PostScript Level 2 data filter.

```
%!PS
/inch { 72 mul } def                    % define inch procedure
/temp 16 string def                     % string for temporary results
1.25 inch 2.5 inch translate            % set origin
6 inch 6 inch scale                     % scale image large
<<                                      % start image dictionary
    /ImageType 1                        % required
    /Width 64                           % bits per scan line
    /Height 64                          % number of scan lines
    /BitsPerComponent 1                 % depth of image
    /ImageMatrix [ 64 0 0 64 0 0 ]      % image matrix
    /DataSource currentfile /ASCIIHexDecode filter
    /Decode [ 0 1 ]                     % transfer function
>>                                      % end image dictionary
image                                   % image operation
FFFFFFFFFFFFFFFF FFFFFFFFFFFFFFFF       % lines of data
FFFFFFF3FFFFFFFF FFFFFFF81FFFFFFF
            . . .
    28 lines of data omitted
            . . .
FFFFFFF83FFFFFFF FFFFFFF87FFFFFFF
FFFFFFFCFFFFFFFF FFFFFFFFFFFFFFFF
>                                       % end-of-data marker
showpage                                % display page
```

This example changes the canonical methods of using

```
{ currentfile temp readhexstring pop }
```

to read data from the current file. PostScript Level 2 generalizes the notion of data sources, which are handy for images and other areas of the language. Notice the new line reading

```
/DataSource currentfile /ASCIIHexDecode filter
```

This line identifies the current file as the source of data, and the data is to be filtered through the **/ASCIIHexDecode** filter. Also notice the > character appearing at the end of the hexadecimal data. This character is an end-of-data (EOD) indicator for **/ASCIIHexDecode**. Different filters have different end-of-data markers.

Another popular filter is **/ASCII85Decode**.

Image using PostScript Level 2 data filter.

```
%!PS
/inch { 72 mul } def                    %   define inch procedure
/temp 16 string def                     %   string for temporary results
1.25 inch 2.5 inch translate            %   set origin
6 inch 6 inch scale                     %   scale image large
<<                                      %   start image dictionary
     /ImageType 1                       %   required
     /Width 64                          %   bits per scan line
     /Height 64                         %   number of scan lines
     /BitsPerComponent 1                %   depth of image
     /ImageMatrix [ 64 0 0 64 0 0 ]     %   image matrix
     /DataSource currentfile /ASCII85Decode filter
     /Decode [ 0 1 ]                    %   transfer function
>>                                      %   end image dictionary
image                                   %   image operation
s8W-!s8W-!s8W,ss8W-!s8W,oJ,fQKs8W,o5QCc'
s8W,o5QCc's8W,o5QCc's8W,o5QCc'n,NF_5QCc'
                . . .
   12 lines of data omitted
                . . .
s8N2rJ,fQKs8NW)5QCc's8RTD+92B@s8W,o+92B@
s8W,o+92B@s8W,js8W-!s8W-!s8W-!s8W-!
~>                                      %   end-of-data marker
showpage                                %   display page
```

Notice that the end-of-data marker is different for base 85 encoding. An advantage of this encoding scheme is that the data is readable[†] seven-bit ASCII, and the data file can be compressed to around ⅝ the size of a hexadecimal encoded file.

---

† well, kind of readable.

/ASCII85Decode uses an encoding scheme that packs 32 bits into five ASCII bytes, using base 85 encoding. This filtering scheme is similar to the popular **btoa** and **atob** utilities found on many systems. The preceding example was the familiar character again, with its data source encoded in base 85 instead of hexadecimal.

Filters are a general PostScript Level 2 facility for reading from data sources and writing to data targets, with transformations on the data performed on the fly. The source or target of a filter can in fact be another filter. Here's the general syntax of using a filter for decoding a file.

```
%!PS
```
datasource   *filtername*   `filter`

You've seen the notion of filters used with image data, because images have been a common requirement for data compression in the past. But, in fact, you can use filters anywhere you wish to deal with data sources and destinations.

10 Fonts

They scratch with their pens in the mould of their graves,
  And the ink and the anguish start.
For the Devil mutters behind the leaves,
  "It's pretty, but is it Art?"

Rudyard Kipling—*The Conundrum of the Workshops*

Palatino Regular
❖❖■❊☉❀▼▲
Bookman
小 林 剣
Optima Regular
Ηελλας Σ √ ∂ ∞
New Century
Zapf Chancery

Typefaces come in a variety of shapes and sizes.

You've seen that PostScript is built on a foundation of a few simple but powerful graphics and text operators. You read about graphics and text operators in Chapters 2 through 4 and in 6 through 9. This chapter leads you into another building block in the PostScript foundation—facilities to create or enhance fonts. Let's delve now into issues of fonts, typefaces, and letterforms.

Typefaces and letterforms have been an important aspect of visual communication for hundreds of years and continue to be so. Letterforms impart tone and style to a document. The visual effects of a document are the means of calling attention to the content of a document without overwhelming or distracting attention from the message the document is supposed to convey. Traditionally, the letterforms of a typeface are gathered together into collections called *fonts*. *An Overview Of Fonts* on pages 406–408 in this chapter discusses the nature of fonts.

PostScript fonts provide great flexibility—each character is represented as a small PostScript program. PostScript fonts are stored as *outlines*—collections of lines, arcs, and curves. The PostScript interpreter converts outlines to rasters (bits) dynamically. This dynamic conversion means users can print characters at any size, scale, and orientation. Unlike previous technologies, users don't need to install each size of each font to the printer—the bitmaps are generated dynamically at the required size and orientation. The following sections lead you through the process of creating your own PostScript Type 3 fonts.

Introducing User-defined Fonts

Meandering through PostScript literature you've probably heard of *user-defined fonts* and *Type 3 fonts*, and may have wondered what these terms mean. You may also have come across the term *Type 1 fonts*. The terms user-defined fonts and Type 3 fonts actually refer to the same thing—fonts any PostScript programmer can create and use. Fonts that are readable as PostScript code. Fonts that can be created and edited using a simple text editor. Type 3 fonts, like other PostScript font types, are simply PostScript dictionaries that conform to specific conventions and are registered with the font machinery. They contain specific key-value pairs that give information to the font engine about the font as a whole: its bounding box, its transformation matrix, and information about individual characters.

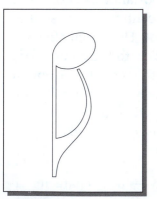

Outline of character described by lines and Bézier curves.

The primary difference between PostScript Type 3 fonts and Type 1 fonts is the way character programs are stored. Character definitions in a user-defined font are just a series of PostScript operators and operands that define a path—or many subpaths—that, when stroked or filled, display the character. When you look at the source of a Type 3 font you can read the PostScript code and figure out how each character is formed. You could, if you wished, encrypt your Type 3 fonts against causal prying, in the same way Type 1 fonts are encrypted.

Type 1 fonts, on the other hand, are written to a much stricter syntax than normal PostScript programs. Character outlines are the heart of a Type 1 font. Type 1 fonts contain specialized "hints" to direct the font interpreter how to place pixels so the characters look good at low resolutions and small sizes. The character outlines are encoded for compactness and usually encrypted against casual prying. Type 1 fonts can be created by hand only with considerable difficulty. They are generally created using font creation and editing software. You really need a specialized font editor to do a good job of creating Type 1 fonts. This chapter does not attempt to educate you on building Adobe Type 1 fonts. Details of Adobe Type 1 fonts are covered in *Adobe Type 1 Font Format*, published by Adobe Systems. This chapter concentrates on how to create Type 3 or user-defined fonts.

In theory, creating Type 3 fonts should be a thing of the past. These days, almost every reasonable computer system has software to design fonts in Adobe Type 1 format, and sometimes in a variety of other formats. Clever software packages are available to create special effects with characters. If you have the design skills,[†] you can open your own font house with a personal computer and font design software ranging in price from hundreds of dollars to hundreds of thousands of dollars, depending on how critical your eye is versus the thickness of your wallet.

Theory aside, the time comes when you need to look inside font programs, or you want to make a quick and dirty modification to a Type 1 font program, or you need to create a Type 3 font for some fast prototyping so you can check things, or other reasons nobody has thought of yet.

Creating a User-defined Font

Let's start by creating a minimal but complete user-defined font—otherwise known as a Type 3 font. This font has only four characters since it's for illustration. The components of this font will, however, be used in further examples. This example leads you step by step through the component parts of the font and the dictionaries you need to create to make a font. Our example font is called **Card-Suits** and consists of the shapes of the "spots" in a deck of cards.

---

† or even if you don't...

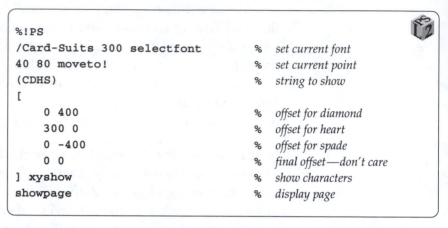

```
%!PS
/Card-Suits 300 selectfont          %   set current font
40 80 moveto!                       %   set current point
(CDHS)                              %   string to show
[
    0  400                          %   offset for diamond
    300  0                          %   offset for heart
    0  -400                         %   offset for spade
    0  0                            %   final offset—don't care
] xyshow                            %   show characters
showpage                            %   display page
```

A minimal font with just four characters.

Notice **xyshow**—a PostScript Level 2 operator. To run this example on a PostScript Level 1 device you have to change the code to use straightforward **show** operators. Also notice the code uses **selectfont** to set the current font in the graphics state. **selectfont** works just as well on a user-defined font as on a Type 1 font.

How is a PostScript font constructed? A PostScript font is a dictionary that contains various elements. Some of the elements within the font dictionary are themselves other dictionaries and you'll see these different dictionaries as the font develops. The "top level" dictionary—known as the font dictionary—is the object you get when you perform a **findfont**. So the first thing you must do when building a font is to create a dictionary.

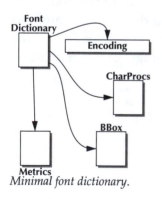

Minimal font dictionary.

The diagram shows the basic structure of just about the simplest PostScript font. The top level font dictionary contains three dictionaries, among other items. The **CharProcs** dictionary contains PostScript procedures to draw the shapes of the characters. **Encoding** is a PostScript array that provides mapping from character codes to names of PostScript procedures in **CharProcs**. **Metrics** is a dictionary of character displacements, and **BBox** is a dictionary of character bounding boxes. The top level dictionary contains other items you will read about later. The most important of these other items are **BuildChar** and, in PostScript Level 2, **BuildGlyph**—procedures that interface the font machinery to the font's PostScript procedures for drawing the shapes.

Card-Suits is constructed in parts, starting with the top level font dictionary. This dictionary contains, at a minimum, the name of the font, information about the characteristics of the font, and a **CharProcs** dictionary of PostScript procedures to draw individual characters. You construct a PostScript font in three stages:

❑   create the top level font dictionary
❑   fill in the pieces
❑   define the font

Here goes with the top level font dictionary.

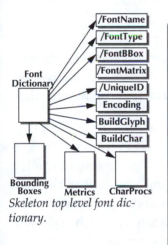

Skeleton top level font dictionary.

```
%!PS
12 dict                           %   create font dictionary
begin                             %   font dictionary on dictionary stack
    /FontName /Card-Suits def     %   name of font—optional
    /FontType 3 def               %   user-defined font
                                  %   overall font bounding box
    /FontBBox [ -20 -30 870 830 ] def
                                  %   font transformation matrix
    /FontMatrix [ 0.001 0 0 0.001 0 0 ] def
    /Encoding 256 array def       %   encoding vector
    . . .                         %   fill in encoding
    /BoundingBoxes 5 dict def     %   bounding box information
    . . .                         %   fill in character bounding boxes
    /Metrics 5 dict def           %   character width information
    . . .                         %   fill in character bounding boxes
    /UniqueID 1 def               %   unique ID for font
    /CharProcs 5 dict def         %   character building procedures
    . . .                         %   fill in character outline procedures
    /BuildGlyph {                 %   Optional for Level 2
        . . .                     %   fill in BuildGlyph procedure
    } def
    /BuildChar {                  %   Required for Level 1
        . . .                     %   fill in BuildChar procedure
    } def
    currentdict                   %   font dictionary to operand stack
end                               %   pop font from dictionary stack
/Card-Suits exch definefont       %   define the font
pop                               %   pop font dictionary off operand stack
```

This is about the minimal amount of code to fit into the top level font dictionary of a Type 3 base font. Optional entries that can appear in the font dictionary are discussed later in this chapter. The dictionary should be one element larger than you actually need. When you eventually define the font, **definefont** needs one element in the dictionary into which it will store a unique identification for the font under the name **/FID**. The preceding code is only a skeleton of the code to construct a font. The following pages describe each entry in detail and give the steps to fill them in correctly. Let's now go through the pieces one by one.

Font Name

The first entry is, conventionally, the name of the font, accessed through the **/FontName** key. This font is called **/Cards-Suits**—the same name as the name supplied to **definefont** when the time comes to define the font.

As it happens, **/FontName** is not required at all in the font dictionary. The name by which PostScript programs locate fonts from the font directory is the name given at the time you define the font using **definefont**. Watch out for PostScript code that assumes the existence of a **/FontName** key in a font dictionary. Such code will fail when it runs on fonts without the **/FontName** key.

Font Type

Next, and very important, is **/FontType**. **/FontType** is required in the top level font dictionary and it tells the PostScript interpreter about the structure of the font. There are several different proprietary encrypted font formats. **/FontType 1** is reserved to mean this is a font defined according to the Adobe special encoded font format in *Adobe Type 1 Font Format*, published by Adobe Systems.

In addition, **/FontType 0** is a composite font, which you will read about in *Composite Fonts* on pages 416–429 in this chapter.

/FontType 3 means the font is a user-defined font. User-defined fonts are built of unencrypted PostScript code that includes character drawing procedures to draw the shapes of the glyphs.

"What happened to **/FontType 2**?" is a common question. **/FontType 2** doesn't exist, although there was a wonderful April Fools' joke once to the effect that **/FontType 2** was an Adobe Systems project to design a "stroked Courier" font.

Font Matrix

/FontMatrix is the transformation matrix that transforms from the character coordinate system to the user coordinate system.

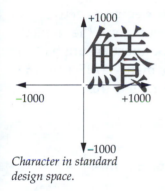

Character in standard design space.

By convention, Type 1 font characters are created in a coordinate system whose coordinates range from −1000 to +1000 in x and y. Most characters are designed so their coordinates are positive, but the character coordinate system provides for negative numbers. This figure shows a character[†] in its correct place in the character coordinate system. Parts of the character actually extend into $-y$ coordinates. The **FontMatrix** of

```
/FontMatrix  [ 0.001  0  0  0.001  0  0 ]  def
```

is designed to scale characters from the 1000×1000 unit character coordinate system into a unit square in the user coordinate system. When you do **scalefont**, **selectfont**, or **makefont**, this matrix gets modified to transform the character coordinate system into the user coordinate system according to the scale factors or matrix provided in the PostScript program. Books on PostScript recommend that you design fonts in a character coordinate system using a 1000-units convention. This convention exists because the Type 1 **CharStrings** interpreter can represent numbers only as integers (although fractional numbers can be obtained by computations). Numbers between −1131 and +1131 can be represented in a compact form. Thus the convention arose to use 1000×1000-unit coordinate systems to design characters.

---

† This is the character for "lawyer."

Font Bounding Box

llx, lly

Overall font bounding box.

FontBBox in the top level font dictionary is a four-element array that defines the bounding box for the entire font. The font bounding box array is in the form [ll_x ll_y ur_x ur_y], where ll_x and ll_y are the coordinates of the lower-left corner of the bounding box, and ur_x and ur_y are the coordinates of the upper-right corner. Notice that this method of specifying the corners of the box is quite different from rectangle operators, which specify rectangles by a corner and a width and height. The font bounding box is the rectangle that would enclose the outline of all the characters in the font if they were imaged on top of one another, as in this diagram.

You can make all four elements of **FontBBox** equal to zero if you wish, in which case the PostScript interpreter ignores the contents. If you make any of the entries non-zero, you must ensure that the entries are accurate. For historical reasons, many PostScript fonts store **FontBBox** as an executable array, looking like this:

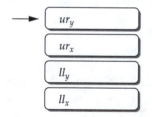

Operand stack after
FontBBox *when* **FontBBox**
is an executable array.

/FontBBox   { ll_x ll_y ur_x ur_y }   def

instead of as a regular array of four numbers, like this:

/FontBBox   [ll_x ll_y ur_x ur_y]   def

In general, you will want the four numbers on the operand stack when you need the font bounding box, so just mentioning it by name will place the four values of the bounding box onto the operand stack, as shown. If your program actually wants the font bounding box as an array, you must access it explicitly using **get** or **load**, instead of implicitly by just mentioning its name:

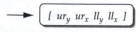

Operand stack after
/FontBBox get.

/FontBBox get

Filling in the Encoding Vector

Next you need to deal with **Encoding**. **Encoding** is a 256-element array of literal names that maps between integer character codes and the name of character procedures in **CharProcs**, as you see in the picture. The integer character code in the **show** string indexes into **Encoding**, where the name of the procedure in **CharProcs** is found. For **Card-Suits**, **Encoding** looks like this.

From **show** *string through* **Encoding** *to* **CharProcs**.

```
/Encoding 256 array def          %  define encoding vector
0 1 255 {                        %  for 256 characters
    Encoding exch /.notdef put   %  make not defined entry
} for
Encoding (C) 0 get /Club put     %  fill in name for Club
Encoding (D) 0 get /Diamond put  %  fill in name for Diamond
Encoding (H) 0 get /Heart put    %  fill in name for Heart
Encoding (S) 0 get /Spade put    %  fill in name for Spade
```

Encoding is filled with code-to-character mappings in two stages. Stage one fills all of **Encoding** with the name **/.notdef**, ensuring that any character outside the set of characters you created maps to a "do nothing" procedure. You'll create **/.notdef** in the character drawing procedures later. The second stage inserts the four character names into **Encoding**. The construct

```
Encoding (C) 0 get /Club put     %  fill in name for Club
```

obtains the integer value for the letter "C." You could code the ASCII value "67" because that's where the letter "C" lives in the ASCII character set, but the approach used is more indicative of what's going on and doesn't depend on your knowing the numbers for the ASCII characters. The same method is used to obtain the character positions for the other three letters.

This scheme of going through **Encoding** to get to the character procedure may seem somewhat indirect; however, dissociating the code for a character from the name of its procedure provides great flexibility when dealing with systems that map character codes to glyphs in different ways. You'll see more detail about changing encoding in *Font Encoding* on page 433 in this chapter. **Encoding** is even more important for composite fonts, which you'll read about in *Composite Fonts* on pages 416–429 in this chapter.

Character Bounding Boxes

Each character in **CharProcs** can have a corresponding set of data that are the bounding box data for that character. In **FontBBox**, the font bounding box is the box that encloses all characters in the font. Character bounding boxes are the boxes for individual characters. If the bounding boxes are the same for all characters in the font, you can set them in the call to **setcachedevice**. In this example, each character has a different bounding box, so the information is stored in a dictionary in the font. Here's the code to fill in the **BoundingBoxes** dictionary for this font.

Width, bounding box, and side bearings.

```
BoundingBoxes begin                    %  put on dictionary stack
    /.notdef [    0     0    0     0 ] def
    /Club    [    0     0  870  830 ] def
    /Diamond [    0   -30  640  840 ] def
    /Heart   [  -20   -20  780  850 ] def
    /Spade   [    0     0  680  850 ] def
end                                    %  remove from dictionary stack
```

The bounding box for a character is not the same as its width—the bounding box is the rectangle that encloses the shape of the character, whereas the width includes some extra space on either side of the character. These extra spaces on either side of a character are called *side bearings*. The width value for a character is the number defined in the **/Metrics** dictionary.

Character Metrics

In addition to character bounding boxes, each character in **Char-Procs** can have a corresponding item of data that consists of the *character metrics* for that specific character. You can set up the character metrics for characters at the time you call **setcachedevice** or **setcharwidth**, or you can define character metrics as specific numbers for each character. Here's the code to fill in the **Metrics** dictionary for this font.

```
Metrics begin                        %   put on dictionary stack
     /.notdef    0 def
     /Club     870 def
     /Diamond 640 def
     /Heart    780 def
     /Spade    680 def
end                                  %   remove from dictionary stack
```

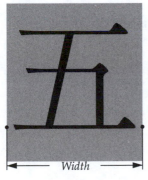

Character width.

The numbers in this particular **Metrics** dictionary are the ur_x values from the **BoundingBoxes** dictionary, plus a little extra displacement so the characters don't render on top of each other. Character metrics could be composed of both x and y displacements or could be composed of only y displacements. In this example, x displacements only are used.

The diagram shows the width of the character. The left dot represents the current point prior to a **show** of the character. The right dot shows the position of the current point after the character is imaged. Notice the small amount of space on either side of the character so successive characters in a string won't be jammed together. Note that character metrics are optional. The widths of characters are actually set by **setcachedevice**, discussed later, but the character metrics override the widths set by **setcachedevice**.

Unique ID for Fonts

Another important item in the font dictionary is **/UniqueID**, for keeping track of the font cache. Suppose you have two fonts, **Font-One** and **Font-Two**. If they both have the same **/UniqueID**, the font machinery will confuse them if you use both fonts in the same job. Suppose you show the character "**A**" from **Font-One**, and immediately after, switch to **Font-Two** and try to image the character "**A**" from **Font-Two**. You'll actually get the character "**A**" from **Font-One** again—the character comes out of the font cache, from whatever font that character was built from first.

Character Outline Definitions

Probably the most important part of your font program is the collection of PostScript procedures to draw the glyphs for the characters in the font. You place the character procedures in a dictionary that is, in turn, contained in the main font dictionary.

In a Type 1 font, this dictionary of character procedures must be called **CharStrings**. In Type 3 user-defined fonts, you can call this dictionary just about anything you like. This dictionary is called **CharProcs**, as in examples from other books and articles.

Before you get into **CharProcs** proper, you'll see the definitions of the procedures to draw the outlines of all four shapes. Each procedure is followed by a small piece of code to position and display the actual character so you can see what it looks like.

Outline for **/Club**.

```
%!PS
/Club {
    690 580 moveto    660 580 620 560 590 550 curveto
    610 590 620 630 620 660 curveto
    630 770 530 830 430 830 curveto
    330 830 240 780 240 670 curveto
    240 640 250 590 280 550 curveto
    250 560 210 570 180 570 curveto
    80 570 0 510 10 360 curveto
    20 260 110 190 200 190 curveto
    270 190 360 230 420 330 curveto
    420 120 280 40 150 30 curveto
    150 0 lineto    200 0 lineto
    340 30 540 30 680 0 curveto
    730 0 lineto    720 30 lineto
    530 40 450 210 450 330 curveto
    510 230 590 180 660 180 curveto
    760 180 850 260 860 370 curveto
    870 470 790 580 690 580 curveto
    closepath
} def
50 100 translate          %   move origin
0.625 dup scale           %   scale to fit page
Club fill                 %   draw and fill club
showpage                  %   display page
```

Outline for **/Diamond**.

```
%!PS
/Diamond {
    320 840 moveto    0 420 lineto
    320 -30 lineto
    640 420 lineto
    320 840 lineto
    closepath
} def
50 100 translate          %   move origin
0.625 dup scale           %   scale to fit page
Diamond    fill           %   draw and fill diamond
showpage                  %   display page
```

*Outline for /***Heart***.*

```
%!PS
/Heart {
    570 850 moveto    490 850 400 800 380 690 curveto
    350 800 260 850 180 850 curveto
    80 850 -20 750 0 610 curveto
    20 480 270 270 370 -20 curveto
    460 260 690 400 750 610 curveto
    780 750 670 850 570 850 curveto
    closepath
} def
50 100 translate              %   move origin
0.625 dup scale               %   scale to fit page
Heart     fill                %   draw and fill heart
showpage                      %   display page
```

*Outline for /***Spade***.*

```
%!PS
/Spade {
    340 850 moveto    320 660 0 470 0 350 curveto
    0 250 80 190 160 190 curveto
    210 190 280 220 330 300 curveto
    330 80 190 40 70 30 curveto
    60 0 lineto    110 0 lineto
    250 30 430 30 580 0 curveto
    620 0 lineto    620 30 lineto
    390 50 360 180 360 300 curveto
    390 220 460 190 520 190 curveto
    600 190 680 250 680 340 curveto
    680 490 390 620 340 850 curveto
    closepath
} def
50 100 translate              %   move origin
0.625 dup scale               %   scale to fit page
Spade     fill                %   draw and fill spade
showpage                      %   display page
```

Having defined the subsidiary procedures that go inside **Char-Procs**, here's how to fill in **CharProcs**.

```
CharProcs begin              %   place on dictionary stack
    /.notdef {               %   do nothing procedure
    } def
    /Club {                  %   definition of Club
    } def
                             %   use preceding Club definition
    /Diamond {               %   definition of Diamond
                             %   use preceding Diamond definition
    } def
    /Heart {                 %   definition of Heart
                             %   use preceding Heart definition
    } def
    /Spade {                 %   definition of Spade
                             %   use preceding Spade definition
    } def
end                          %   removed from dictionary stack
```

BuildGlyph and BuildChar Procedures

After the character outline procedures, other important parts of a PostScript font program are procedures to provide an interface between the character drawing procedures and the font machinery of the PostScript interpreter. Type 1 fonts have a rigorously defined structure and there is always a **CharStrings** dictionary from which the name of the character can be found. Type 3 fonts, on the other hand, do not necessarily conform to the structure of Type 1 fonts. The equivalent of **CharStrings** may be called something else. Ours are called **CharProcs**, like many examples in other PostScript books.

The interface between your character outline procedures and the font machinery differs from PostScript Level 1 to PostScript Level 2. The PostScript Level 2 situation is discussed first, followed by the PostScript Level 1 method, and how to make sure the two levels are compatible.

PostScript Level 1 fonts need a procedure called **BuildChar** to provide the font interface. PostScript Level 2 likes to see an optional procedure called **BuildGlyph**. PostScript Level 2 font machinery calls **BuildGlyph** if it's defined in your font dictionary, and calls **BuildChar** if there's no **BuildGlyph**.

PostScript Level 2 introduced a new text operator called **glyphshow**. **show**-related operators use a character code to obtain the name of the required character through **Encoding**. But **glyphshow** expects the name of the character directly. In PostScript Level 2, the name of the character is obtained from the **Encoding**, and the name and the font dictionary are passed to **BuildGlyph**. To support **glyphshow** for Type 3 fonts, you should have a procedure called **BuildGlyph** in your font dictionary. Here's the definition of **BuildGlyph** for this font.

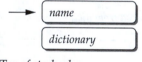

Top of stack when
BuildGlyph *is called.*

```
/BuildGlyph {                    %   stack = dictionary   name
    exch                         %   font dictionary to top
    begin                        %   put on dictionary stack
        dup                      %   need copy of character name
        Metrics                  %   metrics dictionary on stack
        exch get                 %   obtain x displacement
        0                        %   y displacement is zero
        2 index                  %   character name to stack top
        BoundingBoxes            %   bounding box dictionary on stack
        exch get aload pop       %   bounding box data onto stack
        setcachedevice           %   tell font machinery about it
        CharProcs exch get       %   get character drawing procedure
        exec                     %   execute drawing procedure
        fill                     %   fill shape
    end                          %   remove font dictionary
} def                            %   end of BuildGlyph
```

When **BuildGlyph** is called, the stack contains the font dictionary and the name of the character to be imaged. Let's go step by step through this code so you understand what's going on. The first step is to make the font dictionary the current dictionary so you can get things from it. This is a convenience, because you could achieve the same results by shuffling the stack.

Now the top of the operand stack holds the name of the character to be imaged. You will need this name to get the character metrics from the **Metrics** dictionary. You'll also need this name to get the character bounding box data from the **BoundingBoxes** dictionary. You'll need this name one last time to get the character drawing procedure from the **CharProcs** dictionary. **dup** makes a copy of the character name. You use that name to extract the character metrics out of the **Metrics** dictionary. Remember the **Metrics** dictionary only contains x displacement values. You push a **0** onto the stack for the y displacement. The sequence of **exch get exec** for the **BoundingBoxes** data executes the procedures stored there to push the four bounding box values onto the stack. Now you're ready to call **setcachedevice**.

Now you have six items—character metrics and bounding box— with which to call **setcachedevice**. The first two arguments to **setcachedevice** define the width of the character in x and y. These are really *displacement* values to position the origin of the next character. For most Western-style fonts x is non-zero and y is zero. The last four parameters to **setcachedevice** define the bounding box for the character—this information defines clipping boundaries for the bits in the font cache. A possible alternative to **setcachedevice** is **setcharwidth**, discussed in more detail on pages 412–415 in this chapter. What does **setcachedevice** do? Well, first you must understand that for a given character at a given size, **BuildGlyph** or **BuildChar** are called only when the outlines for specific character are to be converted to bits. In some circumstances, **BuildGlyph** or **BuildChar** may be called only once. **setcachedevice** is used within the context of **BuildGlyph** or **Build-Char** to move bounding box and displacement information about the character into the font cache.

Next, you obtain the character drawing procedure from the **Char-Procs** dictionary. The character outline procedure from **CharProcs** is on the top of the operand stack, so you can execute it to draw the outline of the character. Finally, in the case of our character definitions, you **fill** the outline drawn by the procedure.

ur_y

ur_x

ll_y

ll_x

$disp_y$

$disp_x$

Operand stack before call to **setcachedevice**.

must call **setcachedevice** from within **BuildGlyph**. You must call **setcachedevice** before any graphics operators are called. **setcachedevice** can be executed only with the **BuildGlyph** (or **BuildChar**) procedure of a Type 3 font.

For PostScript Level 1 you define a procedure called **BuildChar**. Let's fill in details of **BuildChar** for the font you're building.

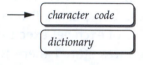

*Top of stack when **Build-Char** is called.*

```
/BuildChar {                        %   stack = dictionary  code
    exch                            %   font dictionary to top of stack
    begin                           %   dictionary to dictionary stack
        Encoding exch get           %   get character name
        dup                         %   need copy of character name
        Metrics                     %   metrics dictionary on stack
        exch get                    %   obtain x displacement
        0                           %   y displacement to stack
        2 index                     %   character name to stack top
        BoundingBoxes               %   bounding box dictionary on stack
        exch get aload pop          %   get bounding box data
        setcachedevice              %   tell font machinery about it
        CharProcs exch get          %   get character drawing procedure
        exec                        %   execute drawing procedure
        fill                        %   fill shape
    end                             %   remove font dictionary
} def                               %   end of BuildGlyph
```

You see there's hardly any difference between **BuildGlyph** and **BuildChar**. **BuildChar** adds one line of code to the **BuildGlyph** sequence. The extra line of code uses the integer character code to obtain the character name from **Encoding**. From then on, **Build-Char** looks just like **BuildGlyph**.

If you're building new Type 3 fonts to run on older PostScript Level 1 interpreters that don't know about **BuildGlyph**, define your **BuildGlyph** procedure as you would normally, then define your **BuildChar** procedure like this.

```
/BuildChar {                    %   stack = dictionary  code
    1 index /Encoding get       %   encoding vector to operand stack
    exch get                    %   character name from encoding
    1 index /BuildGlyph get     %   BuildGlyph procedure to stack
    exec                        %   execute BuildGlyph
} def                           %   end of definition
```

Defining the Font

Now your font dictionary is full with its required key-value pairs—font type, font matrix, font bounding box, **BuildGlyph** and **BuildChar** procedures, and drawing routines for each character in the font. The final thing you must do before you can use the font is define the font so it's usable by the font machinery.

```
    currentdict        %   current dictionary to operand stack
end                    %   pop current dictionary
/Card-Suits exch       %   set up font name and dictionary
definefont             %   font definition to font directory
pop                    %   remove font dictionary from operand stack
```

*Top of stack when **definefont** is called.*

definefont takes two operands—the font name and the font dictionary. This font's name is "**Card-Suits**", and the font dictionary is the one you just created. **definefont** checks that the font is well-formed and contains all required key-value pairs. It then registers the font with the font machinery under the key "**Card-Suits**". In PostScript Level 1 devices, this information is stored into a system level font directory called **FontDirectory** and, as mentioned previously, **definefont** adds a key-value pair to your font dictionary. This item is the unique ID for the font—**/FID**.

Note that **definefont** makes the font dictionary *read-only*. Older PostScript interpreters did not make the defined font read-only, and unfortunately, some applications created PostScript that inadvertently took advantage of this. When the error was fixed in newer interpreters, some generated PostScript stopped working.

When **definefont** has defined the font and placed it in the font directory, your font dictionary is left on the operand stack. You usually don't need the font dictionary for any other purpose, so you can **pop** it from the operand stack. Later in this chapter you can read about the PostScript Level 2 **undefinefont** operator to remove a font dictionary from the font directory.

Using Your User-defined Font

Now that you've defined your font, you'll want to use it to image characters. A user-defined font behaves just like any other font, so you can go ahead and use "**Card-Suits**" like any built-in font.

Using your user-defined font.

```
%!PS
/Card-Suits findfont                    % find required font
120 scalefont                           % scale to required size
setfont                                 % make it current font
/Radius 200 def                         % define radius of circle
/Letters [                              % define card letters
    (C) (D) (H) (S)
] def
300 400 translate                       % origin to center of page
0 1 11 {                                % start for loop
    4 mod                               % normalize to modulo 4
    0 Radius moveto                     % set current point
    Letters exch get                    % get current show string
    show                                % image character
    30 rotate                           % rotate coordinate system
} for                                   % end for loop
showpage                                % display page
```

This code is a loop to place characters at 30° around the perimeter of a circle. The characters are slightly offset because their origins are at the left side of the character instead of in the middle.

A Playing Cards Font

The next font definition is much larger and more complex, but it is used as the basis for building a composite font later. This font continues the theme of playing card spots, but now you get to define a font that actually draws cards. Once again, you start with the top level font dictionary.

This font dictionary differs somewhat from the **Card-Suits** font defined earlier. The font dictionary does not contain a **/Metrics** dictionary, nor does it contain any character bounding boxes. The reason is this font is a fixed-width font—all the characters are the same size. Also notice that **CharProcs** has room for 23 elements—there will be many more definitions in **CharProcs** for this font, because the individual character procedures use several subprocedures and definitions to construct the cards.

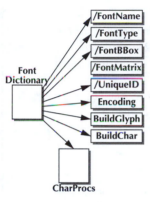

Skeleton font dictionary for playing cards font.

```
%!PS
12 dict                               %   create font dictionary
begin                                 %   font dictionary on dictionary stack
  /FontName /Spades-Suit def          %   name of font—optional
  /FontType 3 def                     %   user-defined font
                                      %   overall font bounding box
  /FontBBox [ 50 50 950 750 ] def
                                      %   font transformation matrix
  /FontMatrix [ 0.001 0 0 0.001 0 0 ] def
  /Encoding 256 array def             %   encoding vector
    . . .                             %   fill in encoding
  /UniqueID 1 def                     %   unique ID for font
  /CharProcs 23 dict def              %   character building procedures
    . . .                             %   fill in character outline procedures
  /BuildGlyph {                       %   Optional for Level 2
    . . .                             %   fill in BuildGlyph procedure
  } def
  /BuildChar {                        %   Required for Level 1
    . . .                             %   fill in BuildChar procedure
  } def
  currentdict                         %   font dictionary to operand stack
end                                   %   pop font from dictionary stack
/Spades-Suit exch definefont          %   define the font
pop                                   %   pop font dictionary from operand stack
```

First, fill in the name of the font. This font is called **/Spades-Suit**—the same name supplied to **definefont** when the time comes to define the font. **/FontType** is 3 to indicate this is a user-defined font. And once again, **/FontMatrix** is set up so characters are defined in a 1000-unit coordinate system.

Encoding for **Spades-Suit** looks something like this:

```
/Encoding 256 array def            %   define encoding vector
0 1 255 {                          %   for 256 characters
    Encoding exch /.notdef put     %   make not defined entry
} for
(0) 0 get                          %   find code for "0"
Encoding exch                      %   get Encoding
[
  /Ten /.notdef /Two /Three /Four
  /Five /Six /Seven /Eight /Nine
]
putinterval                        %   insert ten names
(A) 0 get                          %   find code for "A"
Encoding exch                      %   get Encoding
/Ace put                           %   Insert /Ace
```

After filling in **/Encoding** with **/.notdef** names as before, the second stage inserts ten character names into **Encoding**, starting at the character position whose code is "0", and then puts the code for the ace into character "A".

Each character in this card font has the same bounding box because all the characters have the same width and height. In this example, characters are drawn 650 units wide within a width of 750 units, meaning there are 50 units on each side of each card. Similarly, cards are 900 units high centered in a 1000-unit field. In this font, the character bounding boxes are the same as the overall font bounding box.

As in **Card-Suits**, important parts of your font are PostScript procedures to draw the glyphs. Before you get into character procedures proper, here's the definition of the spade character—the procedure to draw the shape used to fill in each card.

New spade character.

```
%!PS
/CardShape {
    40 -490 moveto
    -90 -470 -180 -380 -180 -250 curveto
    -150 -290 -100 -340 -30 -340 curveto
     40 -340 90 -290 90 -220 curveto
     90 -130 20 -80 -190 200 curveto
    -410 -90 -470 -140 -470 -220 curveto
    -470 -290 -410 -340 -340 -340 curveto
    -270 -340 -220 -290 -190 -250 curveto
    -190 -380 -290 -480 -410 -480 curveto
    -410 -490 lineto
    -260 -470 -110 -470 40 -490 curveto closepath
} def
300 400 translate          %   origin to center of page
0.5 dup scale              %   scale to fit on page
CardShape fill             %   draw spade outline and fill
showpage                   %   display page
```

This definition of spade is not the same spade character defined in **Card-Suits**. This spade has been redefined in a coordinate system with (0, 0) at the middle of the character, so drawing procedures using this shape can easily position the origin to the middle of the shape instead of accounting for offsets from the origin. This character definition is called **CardShape** for a very good reason, which you will see later when you get to composite fonts.

The definition of **CardShape** lives in the main font dictionary. The definitions of all other pieces for drawing specific cards live in **CharProcs**.

Here is the skeleton of **CharProcs**, showing the ten character procedures, an extra procedure called **/.notdef**, and some procedures called by the actual card drawing procedures. The full code of **CharProcs** appears on pages 397–405.

```
/CharProcs 23 dict def              %   create dictionary
CharProcs begin                     %   put on dictionary stack
    /.notdef { } def                %   very important!!!
    /NineTen      {  internal procedure    } def
    /CardOutline  {  draws card outline    } def
    /PutSmall     {  puts spots at corners } def
    /Ace          {  code to draw  Ace     } def
    /Two          {  code to draw  Two     } def
    /Three        {  code to draw  Three   } def
    /Four         {  code to draw  Four    } def
    /Five         {  code to draw  Five    } def
    /Six          {  code to draw  Six     } def
    /Seven        {  code to draw  Seven   } def
    /Eight        {  code to draw  Eight   } def
    /Nine         {  code to draw  Nine    } def
    /Ten          {  code to draw  Ten     } def
end                                 %   remove from dictionary stack
```

After the character outline procedures, you need to define the **BuildGlyph** and **BuildChar** procedures to interface between character drawing procedures and the font machinery. Here's **BuildGlyph** for this font.

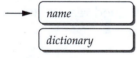

name

dictionary

Top of stack when **BuildGlyph** *is called.*

```
/BuildGlyph {                          %   stack = dictionary   name
  exch                                 %   font dictionary to top
  begin                                %   put on dictionary stack
    dup /.notdef eq {                  %   if /.notdef
      0 0 0 0 0 0 setcachedevice       %   zero size character
    } {
      CharProcs exch get               %   get character procedure
      750 0                            %   width and height
      0 0 750 1000                     %   bounding box
      setcachedevice                   %   tell font machinery
    } ifelse
    CharProcs begin                    %   put on dictionary stack
      exec                             %   execute character procedure
    end                                %   remove CharProcs
  end                                  %   remove font dictionary
} def                                  %   end of BuildGlyph
```

When **BuildGlyph** is called, the stack contains the font dictionary and the name of the character to be imaged. The first step is to make the font dictionary the current dictionary so you can get things from it. The first half of **ifelse** deals with **/.notdef** characters. In this case, **setcachedevice** is called with zeros everywhere to tell the font machinery this is a zero-sized character.

The other leg of **ifelse** deals with regular characters you want to image. The procedure to be executed later is obtained from **Char-Procs**. Now the character metrics—width and height—are pushed on the stack. The x displacement is 750, and the y displacement is 0—a common situation for Western character sets.

Metrics are specified explicitly in this example because you know the font is working in a fixed-width character system. Following the character metrics, you need to supply bounding box information to **setcachedevice**. Once again, this is a fixed-size font, so each character has the same size bounding box.

The final part of the job is to put the **Charprocs** dictionary on the dictionary stack so the definitions of characters are available. The character outline procedure from **CharProcs** is on the top of the operand stack, so you can execute it to draw the outline of the character. After that, remove **CharProcs** and the font dictionary from the dictionary stack, and **BuildGlyph** is finished.

Now the font dictionary is filled in with all the required information, and you're ready to define the font.

```
     currentdict           %   current dictionary to operand stack
end                        %   pop current dictionary
/Spades-Suit exch          %   set up font name and dictionary
definefont                 %   font definition to font directory
pop                        %   remove font dictionary from operand stack
```

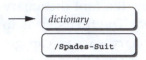

Top of stack when **define-font** *is called.*

When **definefont** has defined the font and placed it in the font directory, your font dictionary is left on the operand stack. You usually don't need the font dictionary for any other purpose, so you can **pop** it from the operand stack.

For PostScript Level 1, you define a procedure called **BuildChar**. Let's fill in the details of **BuildChar** for the font you're building.

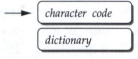

Top of stack when **Build-Char** *is called.*

```
/BuildChar {                        %  stack = dictionary   code
  exch                              %  font dictionary to top
  begin                             %  put on dictionary stack
    Encoding                        %  get encoding vector
    exch                            %  swap with character code
    get                             %  get character name
    dup /.notdef eq {               %  if /.notdef
      0 0 0 0 0 0 setcachedevice    %  zero size character
    } {
      CharProcs exch get            %  get character procedure
      750 0                         %  width and height
      0 0 750 1000                  %  bounding box
      setcachedevice                %  tell font machinery
    } ifelse
    CharProcs begin                 %  put on dictionary stack
      exec                          %  execute character procedure
    end                             %  remove CharProcs
  end                               %  remove font dictionary
} def                               %  end BuildChar
```

Once more, there's hardly any difference between **BuildGlyph** and **BuildChar**, other than one line of code that uses the integer character code to obtain the character name from **Encoding**.

Using Your Spades Suit Font

Once again, you'll want to use your defined font. So here's a short PostScript program to show the characters from **Spades-Suit**.

Using the spades playing cards suit.

```
%!PS
/CardChar [ (A) (2) (3) (4) (5) (6) (7) (8) (9) (0) ] def
/Spades-Suit findfont                 %   find required font
150 scalefont                         %   scale to required size
setfont                               %   make it current font
250 320 translate                     %   move origin for showing
0 1 9 {                               %   start for loop
    dup                               %   copy multiplier
    360 10 div mul neg 54 add         %   compute angle
    dup                               %   copy angle
    cos 220 mul                       %   compute x position
    exch sin 300 mul                  %   compute y position
    moveto                            %   set current point
    CardChar exch get                 %   get character to image
    show                              %   show that character
} for                                 %   end loop
showpage                              %   display page
```

This example is a **for** loop that images each of the ten cards around the periphery of an ellipse. The sine and cosine calculations position the characters every 36° around the clock. Now that you've seen the top level parts of this font, here are the detailed procedures you can use to fill in the remainder.

Detailed Character Procedures

You already saw the definition for the spade character on page 393. Now here is the detailed definition of **CharProcs**. First you define **Charprocs**. In addition to eleven slots for character procedures, it has other entries for definitions of the size of the various pieces. Here's the beginning of **Charprocs**.

```
/Charprocs 23 dict def              %   define dictionary
Charprocs begin                     %   place on dictionary stack
  /CardWidth   650 def
  /CardHeight 900 def
  /LeftEdge 700 CardWidth sub 2 div def
  /RightEdge LeftEdge CardWidth add def
  /BottomEdge 1000 CardHeight sub 2 div def
  /TopEdge BottomEdge CardHeight add def
  /VertMiddle 500 def
  /HorMiddle 350 def
  /Radius 72 def                    %   radius for corners
```

The next part of **CharProcs** is a procedure to place the small suit shapes at the upper-left corner and lower-left corner of the card outline. You need this procedure definition to draw the card outline—the subject of the next item of code.

```
/PutSmall {                         %   define procedure
  gsave                             %   remember graphics state
    LeftEdge TopEdge translate      %   set origin
    0.100 dup scale                 %   scale small
    500 -500 translate              %   move origin to middle
    CardShape fill                  %   fill the shape
  grestore                          %   restore graphics state
  gsave                             %   remember graphics state
    RightEdge BottomEdge translate  %   set origin
    0.100 dup scale                 %   scale small
    -500 500 translate              %   move origin to middle
    1 -1 scale                      %   flip coordinate system
    CardShape fill                  %   fill the shape
  grestore                          %   restore graphics state
} def                               %   end of definition
```

This is a procedure to draw the outline of a card and call **PutSmall** to place the small shapes in their correct places on the card.

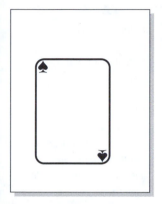

Basic card outline.

```
/CardOutline {                              %   define outline procedure
  mark                                      %   push mark for later cleanup
  HorMiddle BottomEdge moveto               %   set current point
  RightEdge BottomEdge RightEdge VertMiddle Radius arcto
  RightEdge TopEdge HorMiddle TopEdge Radius arcto
  LeftEdge TopEdge LeftEdge VertMiddle Radius arcto
  LeftEdge BottomEdge HorMiddle BottomEdge Radius arcto
  closepath 16 setlinewidth stroke          %   finish shape
  closepath 16 setlinewidth stroke          %   fat line width
  closepath 16 setlinewidth stroke          %   paint outline
  cleartomark                               %   remove jetsam from stack
  PutSmall                                  %   place spots at corners
} def                                       %   end of definition
100 100 translate
0.5 dup scale
CardOutline
showpage                                    %   display page
```

Next comes procedure definitions for each card. This is the **/Ace**.

```
/Ace {                                      %   define Ace procedure
  CardOutline                               %   draw outline of card
  HorMiddle VertMiddle translate            %   origin to center of card
  0.75 dup scale                            %   set scale factor
  CardShape fill                            %   fill CardShape outline
} def
```

Ace card from Spade font.

```
%!PS
/Spades-Suit findfont 600 scalefont setfont
80 80 moveto                                %   set current point
(A) show                                    %   show Ace
showpage                                    %   display page
```

Now comes the definition for the **/Two**. The **/Two** consists of two calls on **CardShape** to create the two spots, one at the top of the card and the other upside-down at the bottom of the card.

Two card from Spade font.

```
/Two {                          %   define two procedure
  CardOutline                   %   draw outline of card
  gsave                         %   remember graphics state
    HorMiddle                   %   x position
    TopEdge 160 sub             %   y position
    translate                   %   set origin
    0.20 dup scale              %   set scale factor
    CardShape fill              %   draw and fill CardShape
  grestore                      %   restore graphics state
  gsave                         %   remember graphics state
    HorMiddle                   %   x position
    BottomEdge 160 add          %   y position
    translate                   %   set origin
    0.20 dup neg scale          %   set scale for upside-down
    CardShape fill              %   draw and fill CardShape
  grestore                      %   restore graphics state
} def
```

The definition for **/Three** is simple—it's the **/Two** with an extra spot in the middle of the card.

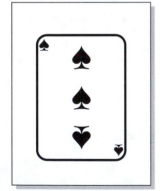

Three card from Spade font.

```
/Three {                        %   define Three procedure
  Two                           %   execute Two definition
  gsave                         %   remember graphics state
    HorMiddle                   %   x position
    VertMiddle                  %   y position
    translate                   %   set origin
    0.20 dup scale              %   set scale factor
    CardShape fill              %   draw and fill CardShape
  grestore                      %   restore graphics state
} def
```

/Four provides the basis for the rest of the cards. Here's the definition of **/Four**—it places the spots at each corner of the card.

Four card from Spade font.

```
/Four {                                    % define Four procedure
  CardOutline                              % draw outline of card
  gsave                                    % remember graphics state
    LeftEdge CardWidth 4 div add           % x position
    TopEdge 160 sub translate              % y position
    0.20 dup scale                         % set scale factor
    CardShape fill                         % draw and fill CardShape
  grestore                                 % restore graphics state
  gsave                                    % remember graphics state
    RightEdge CardWidth 4 div sub          % x position
    TopEdge 160 sub translate              % y position
    0.20 dup scale                         % set scale factor
    CardShape fill                         % draw and fill CardShape
  grestore                                 % restore graphics state
  gsave                                    % remember graphics state
    LeftEdge CardWidth 4 div add           % x position
    BottomEdge 160 add translate           % y position
    0.20 dup neg scale                     % set scale factor
    CardShape fill                         % draw and fill CardShape
  grestore                                 % restore graphics state
  gsave                                    % remember graphics state
    LeftEdge CardWidth 4 div 3 mul add%    x position
    BottomEdge 160 add translate           % y position
    0.20 dup neg scale                     % set scale factor
    CardShape fill                         % draw and fill CardShape
  grestore                                 % restore graphics state
} def
```

The definition for **/Five** is as simple as that for **/Three**—it's the **/Four** with an extra spot in the middle of the card.

Five card from Spade font.

```
/Five {                           %   define Three procedure
  Four                            %   execute Four definition
  gsave                           %   remember graphics state
    HorMiddle                     %   x position
    VertMiddle                    %   y position
    translate                     %   set origin
    0.20 dup scale                %   set scale factor
    CardShape fill                %   draw and fill CardShape
  grestore                        %   restore graphics state
} def
```

The definition for **/Six** is also simple—a **/Four** with two extra spots.

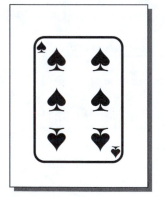

Six card from Spade font.

```
/Six {                            %   define Six procedure
  Four                            %   execute Four definition
  gsave                           %   remember graphics state
    LeftEdge CardWidth 4 div add  %   x position
    VertMiddle                    %   y position
    translate                     %   set origin
    0.20 dup scale                %   set scale factor
    CardShape fill                %   draw and fill CardShape
  grestore                        %   restore graphics state
  gsave                           %   remember graphics state
    RightEdge CardWidth 4 div sub %   x position
    VertMiddle                    %   y position
    translate                     %   set origin
    0.20 dup scale                %   set scale factor
    CardShape fill                %   draw and fill CardShape
  grestore                        %   restore graphics state
} def
```

/Seven is **/Six** with an extra spot.

```
/Seven {                                  %   define Seven procedure
  Six                                     %   execute Six definition
  gsave                                   %   remember graphics state
    HorMiddle                             %   x position
    TopEdge CardHeight 3 div sub          %   y position
    translate                             %   set origin
    0.20 dup scale                        %   set scale factor
    CardShape fill                        %   draw and fill CardShape
  grestore                                %   restore graphics state
} def
```

Seven card from Spade font.

Similarly, **/Eight** is **/Seven** with an extra spot.

```
/Eight {                                  %   define Eight procedure
  Seven                                   %   execute Seven definition
  gsave                                   %   remember graphics state
    HorMiddle                             %   x position
    BottomEdge CardHeight 3 div add       %   y position
    translate                             %   set origin
    0.20 dup neg scale                    %   set scale factor
    CardShape fill                        %   draw and fill CardShape
  grestore                                %   restore graphics state
} def
```

Eight card from Spade font.

/Nine and **/Ten** are slightly more complicated. They both contain **/Four,** with four extra spots squeezed into the space between the corner spots. **/Nine** has one spot in the middle of this configuration and **/Ten** has two spots in the middle. **/Nine** and **/Ten** use a procedure called **/NineTen** to do most of the layout.

```
/NineTen {                                % define NineTen procedure
  Four                                    % execute Four definition
  gsave                                   % remember graphics state
    LeftEdge CardWidth 4 div add          % x position
    TopEdge 350 sub                       % y position
    translate                             % set origin
    0.20 dup scale                        % set scale factor
    CardShape fill                        % draw and fill CardShape
  grestore                                % restore graphics state
  gsave                                   % remember graphics state
    RightEdge CardWidth 4 div sub         % x position
    TopEdge 350 sub                       % y position
    translate                             % set origin
    0.20 dup scale                        % set scale factor
    CardShape fill                        % draw and fill CardShape
  grestore                                % restore graphics state
  gsave                                   % remember graphics state
    LeftEdge CardWidth 4 div add          % x position
    BottomEdge 350 add                    % y position
    translate                             % set origin
    0.20 dup neg scale                    % set scale factor
    CardShape fill                        % draw and fill CardShape
  grestore                                % restore graphics state
  gsave                                   % remember graphics state
    RightEdge CardWidth 4 div sub         % x position
    BottomEdge 350 add                    % y position
    translate                             % set origin
    0.20 dup neg scale                    % set scale factor
    CardShape fill                        % draw and fill CardShape
  grestore                                % restore graphics state
} def
```

Now **Nine** uses **NineTen** and inserts one extra spot.

Nine card from Spade font.

```
/Nine {                              %   define Nine procedure
  NineTen                            %   execute NineTen definition
  gsave                              %   remember graphics state
    HorMiddle VertMiddle translate   %   translate for middle spot
    0.20 dup scale                   %   set scale factor
    CardShape fill                   %   draw and fill CardShape
  grestore                           %   restore graphics state
} def
```

Finally, **Ten** uses **NineTen** and inserts two extra spots.

Ten card from Spade font.

```
/Ten {                               %   define Ten procedure
  NineTen                            %   execute NineTen definition
  gsave                              %   remember graphics state
    HorMiddle                        %   x position
    TopEdge CardHeight 4 div sub     %   y position
    translate                        %   translate for middle spot
    0.20 dup scale                   %   set scale factor
    CardShape fill                   %   draw and fill CardShape
  grestore                           %   restore graphics state
  gsave                              %   remember graphics state
    HorMiddle                        %   x position
    BottomEdge CardHeight 4 div add  %   y position
    translate                        %   translate for middle spot
    0.20 dup neg scale               %   set scale factor
    CardShape fill                   %   draw and fill CardShape
  grestore                           %   restore graphics state
} def
```

That's the complete **CharProcs** for this font full of spades. Unlike many books, the definitions for the clubs, diamonds, and hearts are not "left as an exercise for the reader" but are defined and used in *Extending the Playing Cards Font to a Composite Font* on pages 421–429 in this chapter.

Overview of Fonts

Now you've seen two complete Type 3 fonts built from start to finish. Let's delve into some ideas behind fonts—where they come from, why things are the way they are in the PostScript universe, and how life was before PostScript fonts came along. Although the question was addressed briefly in Chapter 3, this chapter expands on the question of what, precisely, is a font? The answer needs to be cleared up for PostScript terminology, because the definition of font differs depending on which authorities you listen to and the antiquity of the literature you read.

Palatino Roman	*Palatino Italic*
Palatino Bold	***Palatino Bold Italic***

Optima Roman	*Optima Oblique*
Optima Bold	***Bold Oblique***

Font families.

Briefly, a font is a specific variation on the design of a typeface, within what is called a *font family*. This book is typeset in Palatino. The Palatino font family has four variations—the regular Palatino you are reading, Palatino Italic, Palatino Bold, and Palatino Bold Italic. Optima is the other font family used in this book. Within the Optima family you see Optima Regular, Optima Oblique, Optima Bold, and Optima Bold Oblique. **Optima Bold** is used for headings in this book and for PostScript operators in running text. Many font families have these four variations of regular, Italic, bold, and bold Italic.

Some font families are more complex. Adobe Garamond, for example, has regular, Italic, bold, bold Italic, semibold, and semibold Italic. Adobe Garamond also includes an "expert" set of expert regular, bold, italic, bold italic, semibold, semibold italic, alternate regular, alternate italic, and Titling Capitals.

Historically, a font meant a specific variation of a font family—Palatino Bold, for example—designed for a specific size, such as twelve points. PostScript brought the notion of *scalable* fonts to the marketplace. A PostScript font is a collection of outlines for the specific characters. A PostScript font is not designed for a specific size. Instead, you ask for the size of the characters when you select the font. The PostScript font interpreter scales the outline of the font to the size you requested. PostScript Type 1 fonts contain "hints" that tell the font interpreter how to make characters look good at various sizes and resolutions. Scalable outline typefaces have led to changes in the definition of the term *font*. The use of *font* to include one typeface (specific shape and weight) in all sizes (or no specific size) has become common. This definition is probably typographically less precise, but it reflects how people actually use the terms nowadays.

FontInfo Dictionary

FontInfo is an optional dictionary in an Adobe font. Please note "optional." Far too many PostScript programs, both examples and those generated by applications, assume **FontInfo** exists. PostScript programs that assume **FontInfo** exists are doomed to be unportable across different implementations of PostScript interpreters. Fonts do not have to contain a **FontInfo** dictionary, but if they do, they should at least contain useful and correct information. Regrettably, some implementations don't fill in the fields correctly. Here is a brief (but not necessarily all-inclusive) description of what goes in **FontInfo**.

/FullName is the full name of the font. You'll see names like "Adobe Garamond Expert Semibold Italic" as the full name of a specific font that is part of the Adobe Garamond font family.

/FamilyName specifies the font family to which this font belongs. Palatino Roman, Palatino Italic, Palatino Bold, and Palatino Bold Italic, for example, are all members of the Palatino font family.

/Weight indicates the relative weight of the characters in the font. Values for **/Weight** include **Bold** for fonts such as Adobe Garamond Bold and Adobe Garamond Bold Italic. You will see values such as **Regular** or **Medium** for fonts such as Adobe Garamond Italic, Palatino Italic, and Palatino. **Semibold** appears in semibold fonts such as Adobe Garamond Expert Semibold. **Light** appears in fonts designated as "light," such as Garamond Light. **Titling** is specified for fonts such as Adobe Garamond Titling Capitals.

/isFixedPitch is a Boolean value that indicates if this font is a fixed-pitch font. `Courier` and `Bold Courier`, the fonts used for code listings in this book, have **/isFixedPitch** set **true**. Palatino-Roman is a proportional font, thus **/isFixedPitch** is **false**. Your **Card-Suits** font would have **/isFixedPitch** set **false**, whereas your **Spades-Suit** font would have **/isFixedPitch** set **true**.

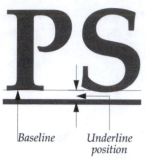

Baseline   *Underline position*

Underline position.

/**UnderlinePosition** specifies where underlines should be drawn relative to the character. /**UnderlinePosition** is given in character coordinate system units. /**UnderlineThickness** specifies the line width to be used for underlining. /**UnderlineThickness** is also specified in character coordinate system units.

Some implementations have defined both /**UnderlinePosition** and /**UnderlineThickness** but have inserted incorrect values. Your application must always be prepared for fonts that do not contain a /**FontInfo** dictionary at all, or fonts that contain /**FontInfo** but do not contain /**UnderlinePosition** or /**UnderlineThickness**, or fonts that define them but get them wrong. In such cases your application code must be able to take a fallback position and generate reasonable numbers based on the size of the font.

A Derived Font with Color

This next example builds from scratch another user-defined font. The first example in this chapter was self-contained. This font uses two other fonts as part of its definition. It references existing fonts but contains all the elements of a user-defined font. This font is called /**ScrabbleTiles**.[†]

Basic Scrabble font.

```
%!PS
/ScrabbleTiles findfont              %   obtain required font
70 scalefont setfont                 %   scale and make current
30 0 translate                       %   set origin
0 350 moveto (SCRABBLE) show         %   show tiles
                                     %   show other tiles
0 630 moveto (F) show     0 560 moveto (O) show
0 490 moveto (N) show     0 420 moveto (T) show
420 490 moveto (T) show   420 420 moveto (I) show
420 280 moveto (E) show   420 210 moveto (S) show
showpage                             %   display page
```

---

† Scrabble is a trademark of Selchow and Righter.

This example illustrates **setcharwidth** instead of **setcachedevice**. Here's the dictionary definition that starts our font.

```
%!PS
12 dict                                 %   create dictionary
begin                                   %   place on dictionary stack
    /FontName /ScrabbleTiles def        %   name of font
    /LanguageLevel 2 def                %   uses Level 2 features
    /TileSize 950 def                   %   size of tile
    /FontType 3 def                     %   user-defined font
                                        %   font transformation matrix
    /FontMatrix [ 0.001 0 0 0.001 0 0 ] def
                                        %   font bounding box
    /FontBBox [0 0 TileSize TileSize] def
    /Encoding 256 array def             %   encoding vector
    . . .                               %   fill in encoding
    /DrawTile {                         %   procedure to draw tiles
    . . .                               %   fill in procedure
    } def
    /CharProcs 27 dict def              %   character drawing procedures
    CharProcs begin                     %   place on dictionary stack
    . . .                               %   fill in character procedures
    end                                 %   remove from dictionary stack
    /BuildGlyph {                       %   optional for Level 2
    . . .                               %   fill in Glyph procedure
    } def
    /BuildChar {                        %   required for Level 1
    . . .                               %   fill in Character procedure
    } def
    currentdict                         %   font to operand stack
end                                     %   remove from dictionary stack
/ScrabbleTiles                          %   name of font
exch                                    %   get in correct order
definefont                              %   define the font
pop                                     %   remove font dictionary
```

The font dictionary is created with eleven elements. **definefont** will supply the twelfth. Once again, **/FontType** must be 3 because you're building a user-defined font. The **/FontMatrix** for this font follows the "standard" convention that maps 1000 character space units to one user space unit. The bounding box for this example is easy. Each character contains a visible tile drawn slightly smaller than the 950×950-unit bounding box defined by **TileSize**. Also notice the use of **LanguageLevel** in this font. This key is a PostScript Level 2 feature to tell the font machinery (in this example) that PostScript Level 2 features **rectstroke** and **rectfill** are being used. You can use the rectangle emulation code from *Emulating Level 2 Rectangle Operators* in Chapter 2 to run this code on PostScript Level 1 printers.

Filling in **Encoding** is easy. Our example defines only upper-case letters—each drawing routine is named after its corresponding letter. Undefined characters are named **/.notdef**, as before.

```
/Encoding 256 array def          %    define encoding vector
0 1 255 {
    Encoding exch /.notdef put
} for
Encoding 65 [
    /A /B /C /D /E
    /F /G /H /I /J
    /K /L /M /N /O
    /P /Q /R /S /T
    /U /V /W /X /Y /Z
] putinterval
```

Now you've finished the housekeeping for your font and must get down to the business of drawing the font. Here is the definition of **DrawTile**, which draws the outline of a tile.

Each character consists of a tile with a large letter centered in the middle of the tile and small number in the lower-right corner. You can write a procedure to draw all tiles based on two parameters—the character and the number. Now let's look at just one character:

```
/M { (3) (M) DrawTile } def
```

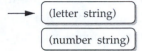

Top of stack when **DrawTile** *is called.*

```
/TileSize 950 def              %   define size of tile
/DrawTile {                    %   stack = number   letter
    0.6666 setgray             %   do gray drawing first
    0 0 TileSize TileSize rectfill
    1.0 setgray                %   then white
    0 0 30 TileSize rectfill
    0 TileSize 30 sub TileSize 30 rectfill
    0.0 setgray                %   then black
                               %   image large letter
    /Optima findfont 700 scalefont setfont
    200 300 moveto show
    0 0 TileSize TileSize rectstroke
    0 0 TileSize 20 rectfill
    TileSize 20 sub 0 20 TileSize rectfill
                               %   image small number
    /Palatino-Bold findfont 180 scalefont setfont
    dup length                 %   decide on placement
    2 eq {
        720 70 moveto show     %   two character number
    } {
        800 70 moveto show     %   one character number
    } ifelse
    0.3333 setgray             %   then dark gray
    20 20 TileSize 40 sub 20 rectfill
    TileSize 40 sub 20 20 TileSize 40 sub rectfill
} def
```

You define a routine that calls **DrawTile** with two parameters— one-character strings that are the numbers and letters to go on the Scrabble tile. What does **DrawTile** do? First, you're borrowing character outlines from Optima and Palatino-Roman. You scale Optima to 700 units, because you're working within a 1000×1000- unit drawing area that contains only one character. You want the letter to fill much of the Scrabble tile. Finally, place the scrabble value in the lower-right corner of the tile.

The final entry in the font dictionary is **CharProcs**, which contains
the character definitions. You must have one entry per character.
As before, you must have a **/.notdef** so the font machinery knows
what to do for undefined characters. Here is **CharProcs**.

```
/CharProcs 27 dict def              %   define dictionary
CharProcs begin                     %   put on dictionary stack
/.notdef {} def
/A {  (1) (A) DrawTile } def  /B {  (2) (B) DrawTile } def
/C {  (3) (C) DrawTile } def  /D {  (3) (D) DrawTile } def
/E {  (1) (E) DrawTile } def  /F {  (3) (F) DrawTile } def
/G {  (4) (G) DrawTile } def  /H {  (3) (H) DrawTile } def
/I {  (1) (I) DrawTile } def  /J {  (8) (J) DrawTile } def
/K {  (4) (K) DrawTile } def  /L {  (1) (L) DrawTile } def
/M {  (3) (M) DrawTile } def  /N {  (1) (N) DrawTile } def
/O {  (1) (O) DrawTile } def  /P {  (3) (P) DrawTile } def
/Q { (10) (Q) DrawTile } def  /R {  (1) (R) DrawTile } def
/S {  (1) (S) DrawTile } def  /T {  (1) (T) DrawTile } def
/U {  (1) (U) DrawTile } def  /V {  (4) (V) DrawTile } def
/W {  (3) (W) DrawTile } def  /X {  (8) (X) DrawTile } def
/Y {  (3) (Y) DrawTile } def  /Z { (10) (Z) DrawTile } def
end                                 %   remove from dictionary stack
```

Using setcharwidth

As before, you now get the procedure definitions for **BuildGlyph**
and **BuildChar**.

```
/BuildGlyph {
    exch                            %   font dictionary to top of stack
    begin                           %   place on dictionary stack
        CharProcs                   %   character procedures dictionary
        exch                        %   character name to top of stack
        get                         %   get character drawing procedure
        1000 0 setcharwidth         %   set character width information
        exec                        %   execute drawing procedure
    end                             %   remove font dictionary
} def
```

Now here's the definition of the backward-compatibility version of **BuildChar**.

```
/BuildChar {                % for compatibility
    1 index                 % font dictionary to top of stack
    /Encoding get           % get encoding vector
    exch                    % character code to top of stack
    get                     % get character name
    1 index                 % font dictionary to top of stack
    /BuildGlyph get         % get character interface procedure
    exec                    % execute it
} def
```

In the **/Card-Suits** and **/Spades-Suit** fonts, character drawing procedures called **setcachedevice** to pass width and bounding box information to the font machinery. **ScrabbleTiles** can't use **setcachedevice**. Why? Because when you use **setcachedevice**, you cannot use **setgray**, **sethsbcolor**, **setrgbcolor**, **settransfer**, or **image**. The font cache can't store color information. If you try using, say, **setgray** within the scope of **BuildGlyph** or **BuildChar**, you'll see an **undefined** message indicating that **setgray** is at fault. None of these operators are defined when you enter the scope of **BuildGlyph**. That's where **setcharwidth** comes in. Use **setcharwidth** when you want a font to have its own color information.

Note a crucial difference between **setcachedevice** and **setcharwidth**. **setcharwidth** requires only two operands—the x and y displacements of the character. This information is used for the same purpose as it was used with **setcachedevice**—to determine the origin of the next character in the string. The bounding box information is not required; that information is used only to determine cache space required to store the character and the bounding box of the font image moved into the cache.

Using ScrabbleTiles Font

Here's some PostScript code to use the font you created.

Complete Scrabble alphabet.

```
%!PS
/inch { 72 mul } def                    %   define inch procedure
/fontSize 100 def                       %   define size of characters
/ScrabbleTiles findfont                 %   find font
fontSize scalefont                      %   scale to size
setfont                                 %   set in graphics state
/scrabblebet [                          %   define alphabet
        (A) (B) (C) (D) (E)
        (F) (G) (H) (I) (J)
        (K) (L) (M) (N) (O)
        (P) (Q) (R) (S) (T)
        (U) (V) (W) (X) (Y) (Z)
] def
/row 0 def                              %   define initial row
/col 0 def                              %   define initial column
/h_gap 8.5 inch 5 fontSize mul sub 6 div def
/v_gap 11 inch 6 fontSize mul sub 7 div def
scrabblebet {                           %   work through alphabet
    col h_gap mul                       %   compute x coordinate
    col fontSize mul add
    h_gap add
    row v_gap mul                       %   compute y coordinate
    row fontSize mul add
    v_gap add fontSize add
    11 inch exch sub
    moveto                              %   set current point
    show                                %   show character
    col 4 eq {                          %   adjust row and column positions
        /col 0 def                      %   reset column position
        /row row 1 add def              %   increment row position
    } {
        /col col 1 add def              %   increment column position
    } ifelse
} forall                                %   end loop
showpage                                %   display page
```

Including color or gray scales in your font means you must consider two trade-offs. First, **setcharwidth** foregoes the use (and, consequently, the benefits) of the font cache. As a matter of fact, **setcharwidth** specifically tells the font machinery this character is not to go in the font cache. Rendering characters will be slower on pages dense with text.

Then you must consider that your font now contains its own color. Any color directives set outside the font will not affect characters drawn from this font. Color information in a font is unusual. A font is normally one opaque color—the user's current color setting. The outline is visible and the area within the bounding box is transparent. **ScrabbleTiles** shows there may be special cases when you really want fonts to contain color information, and that's when to use **setcharwidth** instead of **setcachedevice**.

Undefining a Font

Postscript Level 2 introduced a new font operator to remove a font dictionary from the font directory. The new operator is called **undefinefont** and is the counterpart to **definefont**, described earlier in the context of constructing a new font.

You call **undefinefont** like this:

fontname   `undefinefont`

undefinefont removes the named font from the font directory. The exact status of the removed font dictionary depends on how you defined it in the first place. If you created the original font dictionary as a named object in another dictionary prior to **definefont**, you can get that dictionary back into the font directory by making it the subject of another **definefont**. If you created the original font dictionary as an "anonymous" dictionary, it is gone forever.

Composite Fonts

Ryumin Light

Composite fonts are a PostScript Level 2 feature to cater to demands for large character sets—character sets with more than 256 characters. A standard PostScript Level 1 font—known as a *base font*—can deal with only 256 characters. While 256 characters are usually adequate for English and most European languages,[†] this scheme fails completely for some Asian languages.

Composite fonts were created in part to meet the needs of the marketplace for Asian languages. Countries that base their writing system on Chinese ideographic characters need to deal with very large character sets of potentially more than 50,000 characters. The core character set used in Japanese computer publishing systems is around 8,000 characters. Japan has two script alphabets, Hiragana and Katakana, plus Kanji characters borrowed from Chinese. Korea has a native Hangul script, plus Hanja characters borrowed from Chinese. Of course, you can use composite fonts for purposes other than typesetting Asian character sets.

Descendant fonts in a composite font may be any kind of font—Type 1, Type 3, or even another (Type 0) composite font. Characters in a composite font can select different base fonts. Composite fonts were an early extension to the basic PostScript language. To accommodate Chinese-style characters, several limits of the PostScript interpreter had to be raised beyond standard limits. For example, the standard PostScript interpreter has a limit of 1500 elements in a path. Some of the more complex Chinese-style characters have many more than 1500 path elements, so the path limit had to be raised.

---

† Some European languages demand more diacritical marks than can be provided in 256 characters.

Composite Font Encoding

Let's review the mapping method used in a regular base font. The font dictionary of a base font contains an **Encoding** vector and a **CharStrings** dictionary. A character extracted from a **show** string selects the name of a procedure from the **Encoding** vector. The procedure with that name is found in the **CharStrings** dictionary, and from there the procedure is executed to convert the outline description of the character into bits.

The encoding for a composite font is more complex. A composite font is, in fact, a font of fonts. The **Encoding** vector of a composite font contains indexes into an array called **FDepVector**, which is an array of font dictionaries. Going from a **show** string is a two-part (sometimes more than two-part) process. In 8/8 mapping, for instance, each character is represented by sixteen bits. The first eight bits of the character selects a font dictionary from **FDepVector**. For the purposes of this example, the font dictionary just found is assumed to be a regular base font. The second eight bits of the **show** string then finds the required character from the base font in the regular fashion.

Mapping from character to outline in a composite font.

Font Mapping Method

With the advent of composite fonts, the font machinery was extended to include a *font mapping method*. The actual index computed to look up the **Encoding** vector is determined by the composite font's mapping method. The font dictionary for a composite font contains an entry called **FMapType**—an integer that specifies the mapping method. Early implementations of composite fonts (in PostScript printers such as the LaserWriter IINTX-J) provided five mapping methods. PostScript Level 2 composite fonts provide *seven* mapping methods. Make sure you know if your printer supports full PostScript Level 2 composite fonts. *Double escape mapping* and *shift mapping* methods are supported only in Level 2. The *PostScript Language Reference Manual, Second Edition*, supplies a full description of composite fonts and their mapping methods. One mapping method used in our examples is *escape code mapping*, and you'll see this in action later in this section.

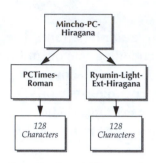

Organization of 1/7 mapped font.

A very simple mapping method is called 1/7 mapping. A single byte is extracted from the **show** string, just as for a regular base font. The most significant bit is the font number and the least significant seven bits are the character code from that font. Mincho-PC-Hiragana and Mincho-PC-Katakana are real world examples of fonts that use 1/7 mapping. Both fonts have two base fonts. Font 0 in both cases is PCTimes-Roman—a font that uses only 96 of the possible 128 characters. Font 1 is Hiragana or Katakana, respectively. These fonts are ideal for applications that mix Roman and Hiragana or Roman and Katakana.

9/7 mapping splits a sixteen-bit code into a nine-bit font number that selects one of a possible 512 fonts and the lower seven bits select a character from the font. "8/8 mapping" splits a sixteen-bit code into an eight-bit font number and the lower eight bits selects the character.

There has been much confusion over the nature of composite fonts. One reference uses "composite fonts" when they really mean a derived font, as in the Scrabble example—a font which uses another font as part of its definition. Yet another reference use "composite" fonts when they really mean what are called *composite characters*—characters built from two or more glyphs from the same font. Be aware of these confusions in terminology. Composite fonts are as described in the *PostScript Language Reference Manual*, second edition, and in this book.

Building a New Composite Font

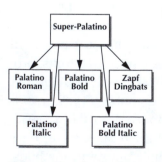

Organization of super font.

To show composite fonts in action, let's build a new "superfont" from existing base fonts. Later you'll extend the spades playing card suit to make a composite font of all four suits. But first, let's build a new font called **Super-Palatino** from base fonts consisting of Palatino-Roman (the regular Palatino typeface), *Palatino-Italic*, **Palatino-Bold**, and ***Palatino-BoldItalic***. Let's throw in Zapf Dingbats for good measure.

What font mapping method would you use for a "superfont"? You'd probably want to use map type 3—escape code mapping. You don't want 1/7 mapping because you're using five fonts and

1/7 mapping can select only one of two fonts. Plus, seven bits of character code gets you only 128 characters, and both Palatino and Zapf Dingbats use almost all 256 entries in the font. 9/7 mapping is also not useful for most of the same reasons. 8/8 mapping is not suitable either, because **show** would require two bytes for every character. Therefore, escape code mapping is a good choice. Here is the code to create an escape-mapped composite font.

```
%!PS
12 dict                                 %   create font dictionary
begin                                   %   put on dictionary stack
    /FontName /Super-Palatino def       %   name of font
    /FontType 0 def                     %   0 = composite font
    /WMode 0 def                        %   0 = horizontal writing mode
    /FontMatrix matrix def              %   dummy matrix
    /Encoding [ 0 1 2 3 4 ] def         %   simple encoding—five fonts
    /FMapType 3 def                     %   3 = escape mapping
    /EscChar 255 def                    %   use 255 as escape character
    /FDepVector [                       %   define descendant fonts
        /Palatino-Roman findfont
        /Palatino-Italic findfont
        /Palatino-Bold findfont
        /Palatino-BoldItalic findfont
        /ZapfDingbats findfont
    ] def                               %   descendant fonts
    FontName                            %   name of font on stack
    currentdict                         %   current dictionary on stack
end                                     %   pop font off dictionary stack
definefont                              %   define the font
pop                                     %   remove font dictionary
```

The value of the escape character was defined explicitly. If you leave out the **EscChar** entry when defining a font with map type 3, **definefont** adds the entry and defines the escape code to be 255. Now that you have defined **Super-Palatino**, let's see it in action.

Palatino Regular

Palatino Italic

Palatino Bold

Palatino Bold Italic

✳❂▢✳ ✦✳■✳❂✦▼▲

Results of using super font.

```
%!PS
/inch { 72 mul } def              %  define inch procedure
/Super-Palatino findfont          %  find required font
56 scalefont                      %  scale to required size
setfont                           %  set in graphics state
0.5 inch 9 inch moveto (\377\000Palatino Regular) show
0.5 inch 7 inch moveto (\377\001Palatino Italic) show
0.5 inch 5 inch moveto (\377\002Palatino Bold) show
0.5 inch 3 inch moveto (\377\003Palatino Bold Italic) show
0.5 inch 1 inch moveto (\377\004Zapf Dingbats) show
showpage                          %  display page
```

In each case, the escape character (the value **\377**, which is the octal number for 255) indicates to the font machinery that the next byte contains the number of the descendant font to use for imaging following characters. You see that accessing descendant fonts of the composite font is quite concise. Life gets even more concise when you mix descendant fonts within a single **show** string. Let's modify the basic **show** example from page 92 in Chapter 3.

Showing text from an escape mapped font.

```
%!PS
/Super-Palatino findfont          %  find required font
160 scalefont                     %  scale to required size
setfont                           %  set in graphics state
100 40 moveto                     %  set current point
52 rotate                         %  rotate coordinate system
(Po\377\001st\377\002Sc\377\003ri\377\004pt) show
showpage                          %  display page
```

If you just show a string without specifying a descendant font, the string is shown using the first font in the list of descendant fonts.

Extending the Playing Cards Font to a Composite Font

Now you get to extend the spades suit you defined back on pages 373–405. The first thing to do is to create three new base fonts, one each for clubs, diamonds, and hearts. First comes the definitions for the spots.

Diamond and definition.

```
%!PS
/Diamond {
    0 405 moveto      -320 -15 lineto
    0 -465 lineto      320 -15 lineto
    0 405 lineto      closepath
} def
300 400 translate
0.5 dup scale Diamond fill
showpage                            %    display page
```

Club and definition.

```
%!PS
%!PS
/Club {
    255 165 moveto     225 165 185 145 155 135 curveto
    175 175 185 215 185 245 curveto
    195 355 95 415 -5 415 curveto
    -105 415 -195 365 -195 255 curveto
    -195 225 -185 175 -155 135 curveto
    -185 145 -225 155 -255 155 curveto
    -355 155 -435 95 -425 -55 curveto
    -415 -155 -325 -225 -235 -225 curveto
    -165 -225 -75 -185 -15 -85 curveto
    -15 -295 -155 -375 -285 -385 curveto
    -285 -415 lineto     -235 -415 lineto
    -95 -385 105 -385 245 -415 curveto
    295 -415 lineto     285 -385 lineto
    95 -375 15 -205 15 -85 curveto
    75 -185 155 -235 225 -235 curveto
    325 -235 415 -155 425 -45 curveto
    435 55 355 165 255 165 curveto     closepath
} def
300 400 translate
0.5 dup scale  Club fill
showpage                            %    display page
```

Heart and definition.

```
%!PS
/Heart {
    170 415 moveto     90 415 0 365 -20 255 curveto
    -50 365 -140 415 -220 415 curveto
    -320 415 -420 315 -400 175 curveto
    -380 45 -130 -165 -30 -455 curveto
    60 -175 290 -35 350 175 curveto
    380 315 270 415 170 415 curveto     closepath
} def
300 400 translate
0.5 dup scale  Heart fill
showpage                             %   display page
```

You've seen definitions for each shape. Now let's modify the original **/Spades-Suit** font for each of the other three suit, then make a top-level root font called **Playing-Cards**, which will use each suit as one of its base fonts. Here's how **/Spades-Suit** was modified to become a base font for the playing cards font.

```
%!PS
12 dict                             %   dictionary for base font
dup                                 %   make copy for later
begin                               %   place on dictionary stack
/FontName /Spades-Suit def          %   define name
/FontType 3 def                     %   user-defined font
/FontMatrix [ 0.001 0 0 0.001 0 0 ] def%   1000-unit system
/FontBBox [ 0 0 0 0 ] def           %   overall font bounding box
/Encoding 256 array def             %   encoding
0 1 255 {                           %   fill with /.notdef
  Encoding exch /.notdef put
} for
(0) 0 get                           %   get position of character "0"
Encoding exch                       %   get encoding
[                                   %   ten characters
  /Ten /.notdef /Two /Three /Four
  /Five /Six /Seven
  /Eight /Nine
] putinterval                       %   fill in character codes
(A) 0 get                           %   get position of "A"
Encoding exch                       %   get encoding
/Ace put                            %   put name for  /Ace
```

```
/Metrics 10 dict def              %   define Metrics dictionary
/UniqueID 4 def                   %   ensure unique ID
/CardShape {                      %   shape definition for spade
  . . .
  . . .                           %   use previous definition
  . . .
} def                             %   end of shape definition
/BuildChar {                      %   interface procedure
  rootfont /RootBuildChar get     %   get root font interface procedure
  exec                            %   execute it
} def                             %   end of interface procedure
end                               %   remove from dictionary stack
/Spades-Suit exch                 %   name of font
definefont                        %   define this base font
pop                               %   remove extraneous dictionary
```

You see how the definition of **/Spades-Suit** has shrunk dramatically. All the main definitions now appear in the top level font for the composite font. Also notice how **BuildChar** for this font has shrunk. The definitions for the other three suits follow this same basic template, with the names of the fonts being changed, and the definition for the shape procedure being different. Here's the basic outline of the top level **Playing-Cards** font.

```
%!PS
14 dict                           %   define dictionary
begin                             %   place on dictionary stack
  /FontName /Playing-Cards def    %   define name
  /FontType 0 def                 %   0 = composite font
  /WMode 0 def                    %   0 = horizontal
  /FontMatrix matrix def          %   dummy matrix
  /Encoding [ 0 1 2 3 ] def       %   four base fonts
  /FMapType 3 def                 %   3 = escape code mapping
  /EscChar 255 def                %   escape character
  /FDepVector [                   %   define base fonts
    /Clubs-Suit findfont
    /Diamonds-Suit findfont
    /Hearts-Suit findfont
    /Spades-Suit findfont
  ] def
  /RootBuildChar {                %   stack = code  dictionary
```

```
    exch begin                          %  place on dictionary stack
       Encoding exch get                %  get character name
                                        %  establish metrics
       dup /.notdef eq {
         0 0 0 0 0 0 setcachedevice
       } {
         750 0 0 0 750 1000 setcachedevice
       } ifelse
       rootfont /CharProcs get          %  get this font's CharProcs
       exch get                         %  get character procedure
       rootfont /CharProcs get          %  get this font's CharProcs
       begin                            %  place on dictionary stack
          exec                          %  execute drawing procedure
       end                              %  remove from dictionary stack
    end                                 %  remove from dictionary stack
  } def                                 %  end of interface procedure
  /CharProcs 23 dict def                %  character building procedures
  /CharProcs begin                      %  place on dictionary stack
     . . .                              %  fill in character procedures
  end                                   %  remove from dictionary stack
  FontName                              %  get font name
  currentdict                           %  get this dictionary
end                                     %  remove from dictionary stack
definefont                              %  define the font
pop                                     %  remove extraneous dictionary
```

CharProcs are not shown here because it's the code from the original **/Spades-Suit** font just moved into the root font.

Using Your Composite Playing Cards Font

Finally, just as in the other fonts you've created, here's some code to show the playing cards from the composite font.

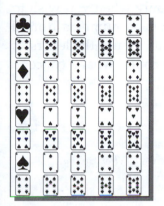

Complete set of cards from composite cards font.

```
%!PS
/inch { 72 mul } def                              %  define inch procedure
/h_pos 8.5 inch 5 div def                         %  horizontal positions
/v_pos 11 inch 8 div def                          %  vertical positions
/Playing-Cards findfont                           %  find required font
v_pos scalefont                                   %  scale to required size
setfont                                           %  make it current font
/CardCodes [                                       %  card codes for positions
   (\377\000A) (\377\0002) (\377\0003) (\377\0004) (\377\0005)
   (\377\0006) (\377\0007) (\377\0008) (\377\0009) (\377\0000)
   (\377\001A) (\377\0012) (\377\0013) (\377\0014) (\377\0015)
   (\377\0016) (\377\0017) (\377\0018) (\377\0019) (\377\0010)
   (\377\002A) (\377\0022) (\377\0023) (\377\0024) (\377\0025)
   (\377\0026) (\377\0027) (\377\0028) (\377\0029) (\377\0020)
   (\377\003A) (\377\0032) (\377\0033) (\377\0034) (\377\0035)
   (\377\0036) (\377\0037) (\377\0038) (\377\0039) (\377\0030)
] def
0.25 inch 0 translate                             %  set origin initially
0 1 7 {                                            %  iterate over rows
    /row exch def
    0 1 4 {                                        %  iterate over columns
        /col exch def
        col h_pos mul                             %  compute x coordinate
        11 inch v_pos sub row v_pos mul sub          %  compute y coordinate
        moveto                                    %  set current point
        row 5 mul col add                         %  compute card number
        CardCodes exch get                        %  get the show string
        show                                      %  image the card
    } for                                         %  end column loop
} for                                             %  end row loop
showpage                                          %  display page
```

Modifying the Font Mapping

As an example of different font mapping methods, let's modify the root font of the playing cards to change the font mapping from **FMapType 3** (escape code mapping) to **FMapType 2** (8/8 mapping). In this mapping type, you have to supply every character as a sixteen-bit code, whereas using escape code mapping you supply the escape code and the font number only when you wish to change fonts. Instead of supplying the suits as numbers from 0 through 3, let's change this example so you can use the letters **C**, **D**, **H**, and **S** for the suit codes—mnemonic codes, what a concept. Here's the new outline of the font.

```
%!PS
14 dict                              %   define dictionary
begin                                %   place on dictionary stack
  /FontName /Playing-Cards def       %   define name
  /FontType 0 def                    %   0 = composite font
  /WMode 0 def                       %   0 = horizontal
  /FontMatrix matrix def             %   dummy matrix
  /Encoding 256 array def            %   256 element encoding array
    0 1 255 {                        %   fill with reference to empty font
        Encoding exch 0 put
    } for
  Encoding (C) 0 get 1 put           %   font 1 at "C"
  Encoding (D) 0 get 2 put           %   font 2 at "D"
  Encoding (H) 0 get 3 put           %   font 3 at "H"
  Encoding (S) 0 get 4 put           %   font 4 at "S"
  /FMapType 2 def                    %   2 = 8/8 mapping
  /FDepVector [                      %   define base fonts
    /EmptyFont findfont
    /Clubs-Suit findfont
    /Diamonds-Suit findfont
    /Hearts-Suit findfont
    /Spades-Suit findfont
  ] def
  /RootBuildChar {                   %   stack = code  dictionary
    exch begin                       %   place on dictionary stack
      Encoding exch get              %   get character name
      dup /.notdef eq {
        0 0 0 0 0 0 setcachedevice
      } {
        750 0 0 0 750 1000 setcachedevice    %   establish metrics
      } ifelse
      rootfont /CharProcs get        %   get this font's CharProcs
      exch get                       %   get character procedure
      rootfont /CharProcs get        %   get this font's CharProcs
      begin                          %   place on dictionary stack
        exec                         %   execute drawing procedure
```

```
        end                         %   remove from dictionary stack
      end                           %   remove from dictionary stack
    } def                           %   end of interface procedure
    /CharProcs 23 dict def          %   character building procedures
    /CharProcs begin                %   place on dictionary stack
        . . .                       %   fill in character outline procedures
    end                             %   remove from dictionary stack
    FontName                        %   get font name
    currentdict                     %   get this dictionary
  end                               %   remove from dictionary stack
definefont                          %   define the font
pop                                 %   remove extraneous dictionary
```

This font definition introduces a couple of new twists. The codes for the base fonts are scattered sparsely throughout the encoding. What do you do for those positions where no valid font exists? You need to point to a dummy font, called **/EmptyFont**. The definition of **/EmptyFont** follows the next example showing the use of the 8/8 mapped composite cards font.

The next example shows the picture of the complete font with the code to display the characters. You see that in this specific example, the encoding to get fonts and characters is quite different from the escape-mapped font used in the preceding example. The codes to select the suits are indicative of their names, rather than "names" like **001**.

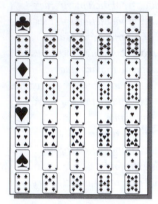

Complete set of cards from composite cards font.

```
%!PS
/inch { 72 mul } def                    %   define inch procedure
/h_pos 8.5 inch 5 div def               %   horizontal positions
/v_pos 11 inch 8 div def                %   vertical positions
/Playing-Cards findfont                 %   find required font
v_pos scalefont                         %   scale to required size
setfont                                 %   make it current font
/CardCodes [                            %   card codes for positions
   (CA)  (C2)  (C3)  (C4)  (C5)
   (C6)  (C7)  (C8)  (C9)  (C0)
   (DA)  (D2)  (D3)  (D4)  (D5)
   (D6)  (D7)  (D8)  (D9)  (D0)
   (HA)  (H2)  (H3)  (H4)  (H5)
   (H6)  (H7)  (H8)  (H9)  (H0)
   (SA)  (S2)  (S3)  (S4)  (S5)
   (S6)  (S7)  (S8)  (S9)  (S0)
] def
0.25 inch 0 translate                   %   set origin initially
0 1 7 {                                 %   iterate over rows
    /row exch def
    0 1 4 {                             %   iterate over columns
        /col exch def
        col h_pos mul                   %   compute x coordinate
        11 inch v_pos sub row v_pos mul sub %  compute y coordinate
        moveto                          %   set current point
        row 5 mul col add               %   compute card number
        CardCodes exch get              %   get the show string
        show                            %   image the card
    } for                               %   end column loop
} for                                   %   end row loop
showpage                                %   display page
```

Here's the definition of **EmptyFont**, as promised.

```
%!PS
9 dict                                    %  create nine-element dictionary
dup                                       %  make copy on stack
begin                                     %  push on dictionary stack
  /FontName /EmptyFont def                %  name of font
  /FontType 3 def                         %  3 = user-defined font
  /FontMatrix [ 0 0 0 0 0 0 ] def         %  dummy matrix
  /FontBBox [ 0 0 0 0 ] def               %  dummy bounding box
  /Encoding 256 array def                 %  define encoding
  0 1 255 {                               %  fill with null character names
     Encoding exch /.notdef put
  } for
  /BuildGlyph {                           %  minimal BuildGlyph
     pop pop                              %  get rid of name and dictionary
  } def
  /UniqueID 1 def                         %  dummy unique ID
end                                       %  remove dictionary
/EmptyFont exch definefont pop            %  define the font
```

Multiple Master Fonts

*M*ultiple *master fonts* are a new Adobe font technology announced in 1991 and first became available in 1992. Multiple master fonts are "beyond PostScript Level 2," in the sense they came after the announcement of PostScript Level 2, but in fact multiple master fonts can be used in PostScript Level 1 interpreters with appropriate PostScript emulation procedures.

The principles of multiple master fonts go back a long way, to the days of metal typefaces. In traditional metal typefaces, each style of a typeface was designed slightly different for each specific size.

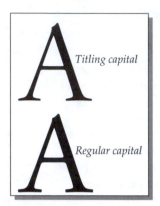

Titling capitals versus regular capitals.

If you look at a complete font family, such as Adobe Garamond, you'll see that the letters of the "titling capitals" are quite different in design from the capital letters in the regular typeface. Notice in the picture that the line weights of the letter "A" titling capital are more slender than those of the regular capital letter. Notice the more delicate serifs and the thinner crossbar. These subtle changes to line weights are required because the eye perceives weights and relationships differently at large sizes than at small sizes. Small letters tend to have thicker line weights, while larger letters are designed with thinner stems.

With the advent of digital type, some of the old techniques of typefaces designed for specific sizes were lost for a while. The principles behind multiple master fonts are based on ideas implemented in the mid-1970s by Peter Karow and others at URW, Donald Knuth's METAFONT, developed in the late 1970s and early 1980s, also developed the idea of mutable fonts, though Knuth's approach was different from the Adobe approach. Multiple master typefaces bring some of the old technology back again.

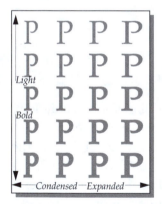

A two-axis multiple master font.

A multiple master font can be seen as a multi-dimensional space where each dimension or axis is defined by at least two "polar" font forms. The "interpolants" along that axis are fonts produced by linear interpolation between the two poles. The illustration shows the concepts of a two-axis multiple master font. One axis varies between condensed and expanded. The other axis goes from light to bold. With the appropriate user interfaces and new PostScript font operators, you can interpolate an essentially unlimited number of variations of a single typeface from the one multiple master font.

The two-axis multiple master font shown is a two-dimensional space. Multiple master fonts can have more than two design axes, leading to higher dimensional spaces. Optical scaling, for instance, is another axis, with designs for small sizes at one pole and large sizes at another pole. Multiple masters can handle at least a three-dimensional space—eight fonts, and possibly a four-dimensional space—sixteen fonts. Your choices for design axes can be interesting—some experimental typefaces have design axes going from serif to sans-serif.

You don't normally use a multiple master font directly. First of all, application writers should provide an interface to choose interpolation points along the various axes of the master. Then, what gets created is a *font instance*—a new font is created from the master font, and you then use that new font. The new font instance is created using the new **makeblendedfont** operator.

Myriad was Adobes' first commercial multiple master font—a two-axis design, the two axes being weight (from light to black) and width (from condensed to expanded). Their next multiple master design was Minion—a three-axis font, the axes being weight, width, and optical size.

Creating A Font Instance

Here's an example of creating and using a font instance from the Myriad multiple master font.

Extra black character from a multiple master font instance .

```
%!PS
/MyriadMM findfont            % find master font
[ 0.0  0.0  0.0  1.0 ]        % weight vector for extra black
makeblendedfont               % create new font instance
begin                         % push on dictionary stack
    /FontName /ExtraBlack def % new name
    currentdict               % font dictionary to operand stack
end                           % remove from dictionary stack
/ExtraBlack exch              % new name
definefont                    % define the font
pop                           % remove from operand stack
/ExtraBlack findfont          % find the new font
800 scalefont                 % scale it very big
setfont                       % make current font
50 100 moveto                 % set current point
(Z) show                      % show character
showpage                      % display page
```

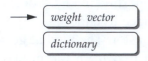

Operand stack prior to call
on **makeblendedfont**.

All the work is done here by the new **makeblendedfont** operator. The *weight vector* is an array of numbers which must sum to 1.0.[†] The number of elements in the weight vector is equal to the number of master designs. In this particular two-axis font, there are four master designs—one at each "corner" of the design space. Elements in the weight vector determine the amount that each master design contributes to the final blend. If the values of the numbers in the weight vector do not sum to 1.0 you get a **rangecheck** error.

The weight vector chosen for the example represents an extreme value. It chooses the black and extended endpoint of the design axes. By adjusting the values in the weight vector, you can roam around all over the design space of the font.

This example chose an arbitrary name of **/ExtraBlack** for the new font instance. In practice, Adobe have suggested a naming convention for font instances derived from multiple master fonts and you should follow their suggestions whenever possible.

The picture shows five font instances created from the Myriad multiple master font. The four corners represent the extremes of the design space. The character in the middle was obtained using a weight vector of [**0.25 0.25 0.25 0.25**], thereby blending a font which falls in the middle of the design space.

Instances of Myriad multiple master font.
1—*light condensed*
2—*light expanded*
3—*normal*
4—*black condensed*
5—*black expanded*

We don't go into the design of multiple master fonts in this book, one major reason being that a multiple master font must be a Type 1 font, and this chapter concentrates on Type 3 fonts. You have already read how to design several fonts, including composite fonts. A multiple master font is much more complex. For instance, in addition to the overall font bounding box, each of the polar fonts has its own separate bounding box. The font dictionaries are much more complicated, with many more entries. A new **makeblendedfont** operator is required to interpolate between the master fonts along the various design axes.

---

† This is known as a *barycentric* coordinate system.

Making a multiple master font is a big design job. A three-dimensional multiple master font—one Roman and one Italic—means two separate fonts, each one with eight master designs. That comes to sixteen different typefaces just for the ends of the design axes. Adobe Systems' Minion font is such a typeface. At 256 characters per font, you have to design 4096 characters. Designing a multiple master font creates font production problems of the magnitude of Asian character sets. A multiple master Asian font would be a truly Gargantuan design job.

Font Encoding

A PostScript base font contains an encoding vector—an array of 256 names that map character codes to names of procedures to draw the specified characters. The encoding of the top level (root) font of a composite font maps numbers to other fonts, until you eventually get to a base font, where once again the encoding vector maps character codes to names of procedures.

There's a fundamental difference between character set and encoding. The character set is the collection of shapes. Encoding maps character codes—numerical values to the procedures that draw the shapes that comprise the character set. The names in **Encoding** can be any names you wish as long as you name the character procedures to match. Most regular fonts, of course, have names like **/A**, **/B**, **/C**, and so on, because those names match nicely the actual characters you see on Western style keyboards. Other characters get names like **dollar** and **asterisk**.

	Carta Castle
	Sonata one28noteup
	Ryumin-Light r46.c23
	Zapf Dingbats a3

Characters and their names.

Some fonts don't have standard names like **a**, **b**, **c**, and so on. **Carta**, for example, is a font of cartographic symbols with names like **wintersports**, **marina**, and **pagoda**, to match the specific symbols. **Sonata**—musical symbols—has names like **serpent**, **trillo-finno**, and **tremeloshort**. **Zapf Dingbats** has its own special encoding. Characters are called **a**nnn. Characters in the base fonts of Ryumin-Light, for another example, are called **c**nnn.

A common misconception is that PostScript fonts are limited to 256 characters, because there's room for only 256 names in the **/Encoding** vector. This notion is incorrect. The **/CharStrings** or **/CharProcs** (or whatever you call it) dictionary of a PostScript font can have as many character definitions as you like. The snag is you can get at only 256 characters at a time. To get at all the characters, you must create new fonts with different **/Encoding** vectors.

To inject a note of humor into this otherwise boring situation, Adobe encoding uses the names *guillemotleft* for the « signs and *guillemotright* for the » signs—sometimes called "continental quotes" because they're widely used in France and Germany to quote material the way the English language uses " and " printer's quotes. In fact, a *guillemot* is a bird—a Northern pelagic avian.[†] The names for « and » should be *guillemetleft* and *guillemetright*, but it's too late to change now.

Re-encoding a Font

Re-encoding a font is the process of changing the order of the names in the encoding vector. That is, you change the mapping between character codes and glyph names. The question arises, why would you want to re-encode a font?

One reason to re-encode fonts comes from differences in keyboard layouts between computer systems. Adobe created mappings from character codes to glyph names according to what they defined as "Adobe Standard Encoding." Macintosh keyboards, for example, map character codes to glyphs different from Adobe Encoding. When you generate PostScript from Macintosh applications, you must re-encode **Encoding**.

Another need for re-encoding a font comes from a class of UNIX-based applications that can handle only those characters whose codes lie in the range 0–127. Such applications can't access the

---

† the Arctic's answer to the penguin.

characters in the upper range of the font encoding—character positions 128–255.

When building your own font, you can elect to use the Adobe standard encoding vector, accessed through the **StandardEncoding** operator, which places the Adobe standard encoding vector on the operand stack. When you're defining the encoding vector for a font, you get Adobe standard encoding by coding:

```
/Encoding StandardEncoding def
```

For a long time, North America could get away with a character set of about 96 characters. European countries, on the other hand, use many more accented characters, and the precise set of accented characters varies between countries.

To alleviate some of the confusion, the International Standards Organization—ISO for short—created a character encoding standard called ISO Latin 1. This character set provides access to all the accented characters. Prior to PostScript Level 2, you had to provide your own ISO Latin 1 encoding vector. PostScript Level 2 provides a new **ISOLatin1Encoding** operator analogous to **StandardEncoding**, which pushes the ISO Latin 1 encoding vector onto the operand stack. To get ISO Latin 1 encoding, you can code:

```
/Encoding ISOLatin1Encoding def
```

IBM PC-style computers use a character encoding different from the standard Adobe encoding. What's more, different applications encode their fonts differently. Usually, when you buy fonts for the PC, you get a set of charts telling you which keys to type to obtain specific characters. Most of the variations occur in the "upper" half of the character set, where all the accented characters live.

Re-encoding a font is a simple process. You have to define a new font. You can't change definitions in the existing font, because a defined font in the font directory is read-only. Besides, redefining printer-resident fonts is anti-social and annoys other users. The re-encoding process makes a copy of the existing font dictionary and defines everything anew in the copy, except for the font ID. The font ID field is filled in by **definefont**.

This next example, though somewhat frivolous, leads you through the basic steps of re-encoding a font. First, you see a procedure definition called **ReencodeFont**. Here's the procedure definition plus a picture of the stack contents prior to calling the procedure.

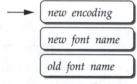

new encoding

new font name

old font name

Stack contents prior to call to **ReencodeFont***.*

```
/ReencodeFont {                    %   font newfont array
    3 2 roll                       %   font name to top of stack
    findfont                       %   find old font
    dup                            %   need copy of font dictionary
    length dict                    %   create new dictionary
    begin                          %   push onto dictionary stack
    {                              %   begin forall loop
        1 index /FID ne {          %   if not FID
            def                    %   define in new dictionary
        } {
            pop pop                %   remove name and value
        } ifelse
    } forall                       %   end forall loop
    /Encoding exch def             %   define new encoding
    /FontName exch def             %   define new font name
    FontName                       %   get new font name
    currentdict                    %   get new font dictionary
    end                            %   remove from dictionary stack
    definefont                     %   define new font
    pop                            %   remove font dictionary
} def                              %   end of definition
```

Having redefined the font, the example at the top of the next page shows how to call on **ReencodeFont** font to install a new encoding vector. This frivolous example reverses the order of all the letters—the simplest form of substitution cipher. The example then uses the new font in a parody of the basic text show example from page 92 in Chapter 3.

Showing **PostScript!** *with a reversed* **/Encoding** *vector.*

```
%!PS
StandardEncoding              %  get standard encoding vector
256 array                     %  create new array
copy                          %  copy old encoding into it
/ReverseEncoding exch def     %  define in current dictionary
ReverseEncoding 65            %  starting at letter "A"
[
    /Z /Y /X /W /V /U /T /S /R /Q /P /O /N
    /M /L /K /J /I /H /G /F /E /D /C /B /A
] putinterval                 %  put reverse upper-case alphabet
ReverseEncoding 97            %  starting at letter "a"
[
    /z /y /x /w /v /u /t /s /r /q /p /o /n
    /m /l /k /j /i /h /g /f /e /d /c /b /a
] putinterval                 %  put reverse lower-case alphabet
/Palatino-Roman               %  old font name
/Palatino-Roman-Reverse       %  new font name
ReverseEncoding               %  new encoding vector
ReencodeFont                  %  re-encode the font
/Palatino-Roman-Reverse findfont %  find reversed font
145 scalefont                 %  scale to required size
setfont                       %  make current font
100 40 moveto                 %  set current point
52 rotate                     %  rotate coordinate system
(PostScript!) show            %  show reversed string
showpage                      %  display page
```

The two **putinterval** instructions insert reversed upper-case and lower-case alphabets into the array created, then calls on **ReencodeFont** to create a new font with the new encoding. Then the new font is used to show a string of characters across the page.

Sensible Re-encoding

Application writers should note that if you must re-encode fonts, be sure to re-encode each font only once, in the setup section of the prolog of your PostScript programs. One application we studied re-encoded each font every time the font was called for in the body of the generated PostScript.

Font Metrics Files

Applications dealing with text need to determine information about the actual characters PostScript will place on the final output. If an application displays text on the screen as an approximation of what that text will look like on paper, the application must have knowledge of how to place the characters relative to one another. The specific information that the applications require are called *font metrics*, and in the case of PostScript fonts supplied by Adobe Systems, the font metrics data are known as *Adobe Font Metrics*, abbreviated to AFM. So when you hear people talking about AFM files, you know they're referring to Adobe Font Metrics Files. AFM files have had two major extensions. One extension caters to composite fonts. Such metrics files are called ACFM (Adobe Composite Font Metrics) files. The second extension covers multiple master fonts, and these metrics files are called AMFM (Adobe Multiple Font Metrics) files.

So just what are font metrics? The simplest form of font metrics you could have would contain just the widths of the individual characters in a font. In practice, sophisticated text layout software wants to know more than just the character widths. AFM files contain a collection of information about a font and the characters in the font. The main collections of data are:

❑ general data about the font

❑ metrics for each character in the font

❑ kerning data—there can be both track kerning information and pairwise kerning information

❑ composite character data

In addition, composite font metrics contain data specific to each base font (also called descendant fonts). Multiple master font metrics files contain data specifying how many design axes are in the font, plus data about each master design in the font.

The most important data for an application are the character metrics section. In principle, applications can do without the kerning data and composite data, but a page layout or text formatting application which doesn't kern characters is not taken seriously.

Kerning Data

Kerning refers to the process of moving characters closer together to improve the appearance of printed text, and incidentally, to pack more text into a given space. Adobe Font Metrics files can contain sections detailing *track kerning*, to specify how to increase or decrease distance between all characters, and a section describing *kerning pairs*, specifying which pairs of characters should be kerned, and by how much they should be kerned. If kerning is too tight, readability suffers, In addition, if kerning is too loose as in the first line, readability can also deteriorate.

Pair kerning concentrates on adjusting spacing between selected pairs of characters. Candidates for pair kerning are letter combinations like "V" and "o'—the "o" can be moved closer to the "V" so that the "o" is tucked in under the diagonal stroke of the "V".

This example shows the word VAT printed in the Palatino bold font, using combinations of **show** and **rmoveto**. The top line is kerned according to the kerning pair data from the AFM file for this font. The bottom line is not kerned—characters are just imaged using regular **show**.

Unkerned string on bottom and kerned string on top.

```
%!PS
/inch { 72 mul } def                        %   define inch procedure
/DesignSize 1000 def                         %   character design space
/PointSize 3.5 inch def                      %   size for character
/ScaleFactor PointSize DesignSize div def
/Palatino-Bold findfont                      %   find required font
PointSize scalefont                          %   scale to required size
setfont                                      %   make current font
0.25 inch 2 inch moveto                      %   set current point
(VAT) show                                   %   image unkerned string
0.25 inch 7 inch moveto                      %   set current point
(V) show                                     %   image kerned string
-129 ScaleFactor mul 0 rmoveto               %   adjust current point
(A) show                                     %   image "A"
-92 ScaleFactor mul 0 rmoveto                %   adjust current point
(T) show                                     %   image "T"
showpage                                     %   display page
```

kerning distance

Kerning distance needed to take up slack.

In the kerned version, characters are imaged one at a time. The current point is adjusted backward by the amount of the kerning data. The top line shows the relationship between the end of the first character, the **V**, and the origin of the second character, the **A**. Because there is so much overhang between **V** and **A**, you can take advantage of their shapes to kern them close to each other.

The bottom line in the picture shows the kerning distance used in the examples. Note that the kerning distance is relatively large.

Notice the motions you went through in the preceding example to set the new current point. This is where PostScript Level 2 and Display PostScript **xshow** comes into play. You can write the kerned version much more succinctly using **xshow**.

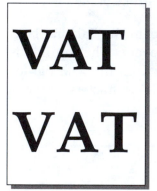

Kerned string using **xshow**.

```
%!PS
/inch { 72 mul } def                    % define inch procedure
/DesignSize 1000 def                    % character design space
/PointSize 3.5 inch def                 % size for character
/ScaleFactor PointSize DesignSize div def
/Palatino-Bold findfont                 % find required font
PointSize scalefont                     % scale to required size
setfont                                 % make current font
                                        % image unkerned string
0 2 inch moveto                         % set current point
(VAT) show                              % image string
                                        % image kerned string
0 7 inch moveto                         % set current point
(VAT)                                   % string to image
[
    778 129 sub ScaleFactor mul         % tweaks for first character
    778  92 sub ScaleFactor mul         % tweaks for second character
    667 ScaleFactor mul                 % width for last character
] xshow
showpage                                % display page
```

This example uses **xshow**. There's no need for **xyshow** in this case because the *y* displacements of the characters are zero.

Where pair kerning concentrates on specific pairs of characters, track kerning adjusts the space between all characters uniformly. You saw examples of these adjusments in the variations on **show** in Chapter 3. Here's an example of track kerning in action.

Kerning Spread

Kerning None

Kerning Light

Kerning Medium

Kerning Tight

Track kerning from none to tight.

```
%!PS
/inch { 72 mul } def              % define inch procedure
/Palatino-Roman findfont          % find required font
1.125 inch scalefont              % scale to required size
setfont                           % make current font
/BaseLine 9 inch def              % initial y position
/KernValues [                     % values to adjust characters
    { 2  0 }                      % positive—spread characters
    { 0  0 }                      % neutral—no kerning
    { -2 0 }                      % negative—mild kerning
    { -4 0 }                      % negative—medium kerning
    { -6 0 }                      % negative—tight kerning
] def                             % end of kern definition
0                                 % index to access kern values
[                                 % strings to kern
    (Kerning Spread)
    (Kerning None)
    (Kerning Light)
    (Kerning Medium)
    (Kerning Tight)
]
{                                 % start forall loop
    0.25 inch BaseLine moveto     % set current point
    KernValues 2 index get exec   % get kern values onto stack
    3 2 roll                      % rearrange for ashow
    ashow                         % show with adjustments
    /BaseLine BaseLine 2 inch sub def  % decrement y position
    1 add                         % increment array index
} forall                          % traverse array of strings
showpage                          % display page
```

Composite Characters

Composite characters are single printed characters made up of two or more characters from a font. Composite characters have been and are often confused with composite fonts, but they have nothing to do with each other. This picture and code illustrates a composite character from the Optima font. The character is the A ring, frequently used to denote Angstrom units.

```
%!PS
/inch { 72 mul } def                    %  define inch procedure
/DesignSize 1000 def                    %  character design space
/PointSize 10 inch def                  %  size for character
/ScaleFactor PointSize DesignSize div def
/Optima findfont                        %  find required font
PointSize scalefont                     %  scale to required size
setfont                                 %  make current font
1 inch 1 inch translate                 %  position origin
0 0 moveto                              %  set current point
(A) show                                %  show "A" character
147 ScaleFactor mul                     %  compute x position
206 ScaleFactor mul                     %  compute y position
moveto                                  %  set current point
(312) show                              %  show ring character
showpage                                %  display page
```

The numbers 147 and 206 in the example come from the AFM file for this font (Optima) indicating the relative displacement in character coordinate system units.

11 Patterns

Shapes of all Sorts and Sizes, great and small,
That stood along the floor and by the wall;
      And some loquacious Vessels were; and some
Listen'd perhaps, but never talked at all.

Ohmar Khayyám—*The Rubáiyát*

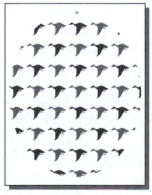

Area filled with repeating pattern.

Patterns were introduced in PostScript Level 2 as a part of the new PostScript graphics capabilities. So far you've seen how to fill an area or stroke the outline of a path with gray shades or colors. Chapter 13 contains a more detailed discussion of color and color spaces. This chapter leads you through a new type of "color," called a *pattern color space*. You've seen several examples of patterns in use throughout the book. Look at page 39 in Chapter 1 for just one example. This chapter describes how to create patterns for use as a "color."

Patterns come from the frequent need to tile an area with a repeating shape. PostScript Level 1 provides neither a good way to describe a repeating pattern nor a good way to tile an area with a pattern. Tiling an area with a pattern in PostScript Level 1 usually involves one of two methods. One method uses the halftone machinery through the **setscreen** operator to define patterns locked to device space (not to user space). Making patterns using the halftone machinery is not a satisfactory solution, because the resulting patterns are device-dependent and, more importantly, because halftoning works only on devices that support halftoning. The second method of obtaining patterns in PostScript Level 1 involves creating a font to represent the pattern. Indeed,

PostScript Level 1 emulation of patterns use exactly this method. The problem of using a font as a pattern is that the PostScript program has to take care of all the gory details of computing how many characters from the font pattern are needed to correctly tile the area. A lot of complex information needs to be kept around to keep track of the position of the pattern's origin.

PostScript Level 2 provides a pattern color space to establish repeating patterns as the current color. Operators such as **fill**, **stroke**, and **show** apply "paint" by tiling a graphic called a *pattern cell* at fixed intervals in x and y to cover the areas to be painted.

You define the contents of a pattern—its visual appearance—using PostScript procedures that can include arbitrary graphics, text, and images. The pattern cell need not be rectangular, and the spacing of tiles can differ from the size of the pattern cell.

Patterns may be colored or uncolored. Colored patterns provide for specifying colors in the pattern. Uncolored patterns can be used as a mask to paint a color defined in some other color space.

Note that all examples in this chapter are specific to PostScript Level 2, so you need a PostScript Level 2 device on which to construct these examples.

Overview of Creating and Using Patterns

Creating and using PostScript Level 2 patterns is somewhat analogous to creating and using fonts. The process is slightly different, because patterns are more flexible. You create and use patterns in four stages. The *PostScript Language Reference Manual* uses rather flowery language to describe the steps of creating and using patterns. The four steps are *create*, *instantiate*, *select*, and *paint*. Some of the mystery is removed from these processes in sections to follow.

A prototype pattern cell.

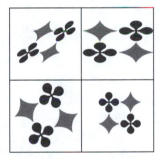

Four different instances of a pattern cell.

Shape filled with pattern.

Create. The first step in creating patterns is building the prototype. The main item in a pattern prototype is the PostScript procedure to draw the pattern. The picture on the left shows the prototype of a pattern cell. You've see this particular pattern in other parts of the book. Its name is **AstroidLeaf**, and its definition appears on pages 458–461 in this chapter. The analogous notion from a font is the PostScript procedure to draw one character of the font. There is more to a pattern than the PostScript procedure to draw the shape—just as there's more to a font than the PostScript procedures to draw the characters. You will see all the parts of a pattern in the following section.

Instantiate. Once you have created a pattern prototype, you can build any number of instances of the pattern using that prototype. What is an instance? An instance of a pattern is roughly analogous to what happens when you use **scalefont** or **makefont** on a font—you get a specific transformed version of the font prototype. The picture at left shows the previous pattern cell, scaled and transformed to a different orientation. You can create any number of unique instances of a pattern from the same prototype. Each instance can be given a name and retrieved using that name.

Select. Selecting the instance of a pattern involves setting that specific instance as the current color in the color space. This step is like **setfont** to establish a transformed font prototype as the current font in the graphics state. Use **setcolorspace** with **setcolor**, or use **setpattern** as a "convenience" operator.

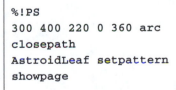

```
%!PS
300 400 220 0 360 arc          %  draw circle
closepath                      %  finish circle
AstroidLeaf setpattern         %  fancy pattern fill
showpage                       %  display page
```

Paint. Finally, painting with the pattern instance from the pattern color space lays down a mosaic of your pattern on the page. Painting with a pattern is similar to showing characters from a font.

The picture shows a circle filled with an astroid and cloverleaf pattern. You can use any PostScript painting operators with patterns—**fill**, **stroke**, **show**, **imagemask**, and so on.

Creating a Pattern Prototype

Creating a pattern in PostScript Level 2 is a simple process. A pattern is a dictionary with specific key-value pairs, so creating one is very much like filling out a form. Of course, there is the creative work that must be done to dream up a pattern and design it. And there is also the work of writing the PostScript code to describe the pattern. However, by following some guidelines and learning the possibilities for patterns, you will be able to quickly and easily produce your own.

To start defining patterns, let's define a very simple shape—a heart composed of precisely two Bézier curves. You will use this shape in more complex examples as you go. Here's the picture and the code that generated the shape.

Prototype pattern.

```
%!PS
/middle { 306 396 } def                 %  define middle of page
/Heart {
    0 0 moveto                          %  set current point
    500 500   125 625   0 500  curveto %  right side of heart
    -125 625  -500 500  0 0    curveto %  left side of heart
} def
middle translate                        %  place origin
0.75 dup scale                          %  scale smaller
Heart                                   %  draw heart shape
0.50 setgray                            %  medium gray shade
fill                                    %  fill heart shape
showpage                                %  display page
```

You can use this simple shape as the basis for your very first pattern, a basic no-frills pattern indeed. Here's the code to define the heart pattern.

```
%!PS
/OneHeartProto 8 dict def          %  define dictionary for pattern
OneHeartProto begin                %  push onto dictionary stack
  /PatternType 1 def               %  required—must be 1
  /PaintType 1 def                 %  colored pattern
  /TilingType 1 def                %  device grid adjustment
  /BBox [ -253 0 253 545 ] def     %  bounding box
  /XStep 1000 def                  %  size of cell in x dimension
  /YStep 1000 def                  %  size of cell in y dimension
  /PaintProc {                     %  define the paint procedure
    pop                            %  remove pattern dictionary
    0 0 moveto                     %  set current point
    500 500  125 625 0 500  curveto  %  right side of heart
    -125 625 -500 500  0 0  curveto  %  left side of heart
    0.50 setgray fill              %  fill with medium gray
  } def
end                                %  pop from dictionary stack
```

The code here represents the first step in creating and using patterns. This code sample builds a prototype pattern dictionary. For the moment you can ignore most of the entries. The important entry is **/PaintProc**.

Instantiating a Pattern

The next step is to instantiate the pattern whose prototype was just defined. You can also use the term making an instance of the pattern. What does this mean? Well, the pattern prototype you just created will create a shape roughly 506×545 points (about 7 by 7¾ inches) if imaged at full scale. Chances are a pattern this size is bigger than any shape you want to paint with it, so it won't "tile" very well. You really want to scale it smaller. So let's do that in this code—instantiate the pattern

```
%!PS
OneHeartProto                      %   pattern dictionary to operand stack
[ 0.04 0 0 0.04 0 0 ]              %   transformation matrix
makepattern                        %   make an instance of the pattern
/SmallHeart exch def               %   stash the instantiated pattern
```

The matrix operand, with scale factors of **0.04** for x and y, scales the pattern prototype to around 20 points. This example just scales the pattern, but the parameter to **makepattern** is a PostScript transformation matrix, which means you can apply any other transformation you like, such as rotation, translation, or shear.

Selecting and Painting with a Pattern

The final steps in using a pattern are to set the current "color" to the instance of the pattern you'd stashed away, and then use that "color" to paint a shape. Let's do those two steps together.

Large letter filled with pattern.

```
%!PS
/Palatino-Bold findfont            %   get required font
720 scalefont                      %   scale to required size
setfont                            %   make current font
20 240 moveto                      %   set current point
SmallHeart setpattern              %   use the instantiated pattern
(Q) show                           %   image large letter full of hearts
20 240 moveto
0.0 setgray                        %   set black color
(Q) false charpath                 %   get character outline
4 setlinewidth                     %   fatter line width
stroke                             %   stroke the outline
showpage                           %   display page
```

A Walk Through the Pattern Dictionary

Now that you've seen the basic steps, let's revisit the code sequence where you defined the prototype pattern. A prototype pattern lives in a dictionary, a concept with which you are familiar by this time. A pattern dictionary can have all kinds of parameters, and the example is one of the simplest. Here's the code of the heart pattern again so you don't need to refer to it.

```
%!PS
/OneHeartProto 8 dict def          %  define dictionary for pattern
OneHeartProto begin                %  push onto dictionary stack
    /PatternType 1 def             %  required—must be 1
    /PaintType 1 def               %  colored pattern
    /TilingType 1 def              %  controls device grid adjustment
    /BBox [ -253 0 253 545 ] def   %  bounding box
    /XStep 1000 def                %  size of cell in x dimension
    /YStep 1000 def                %  size of cell in y dimension
    /PaintProc {                   %  define the paint procedure
      pop                          %  don't need the pattern dictionary
      0 0 moveto                   %  set current point
      500 500   125 625 0 500   curveto
      -125 625 -500 500   0 0   curveto
      0.50 setgray fill            %  fill with medium gray
    } def
end                                %  pop from dictionary stack
```

Pattern Type

/PatternType is required. In the current implementation of PostScript, **/PatternType** must always be **1**. **/PatternType** is included for expandability, much like **/FontType** in a font dictionary. Currently only one type of pattern—type 1—is defined. There is room for future extensions to the pattern mechanisms.

Painting Type

/PaintType specifies the source of color for the pattern. A **/Paint-Type** of **1**, as in this example, indicates a colored pattern. "Colored" in this context means the pattern supplies its own color, which can be shades of gray or scanned images as well as color. Later, you'll see patterns with a **/PaintType** of **2**. Such patterns don't supply their own colors, but the color is supplied by the calling program at the time the pattern is used.

Tiling Type

/TilingType defines how the pattern will be adjusted to device space when the pattern is laid out on the display surface. **/TilingType** basically determines what to do when the pattern must be adjusted to fit to device coordinates. **/TilingType 1** means that **makepattern** may distort the pattern slightly to make it fit to the device grid. Unless your requirements are stringent, **/TilingType 1** is a reasonable choice because the distortion is only ever one device pixel and you won't see this at high resolutions. **/TilingType 2** will fit the pattern to device coordinates without any of the warping implied by **/TilingType 1**, but the spacing between cells could vary by up to one device pixel. **/TilingType 3** gives you constant spacing with a fast tiling algorithm that may warp the pattern even more than **/TilingType 1**. Use **/TilingType 3** when you aren't concerned about small distortions in the pattern.

Bounding Box

Bounding box for heart figure after flattening path.

/BBox is the bounding box for the pattern prototype.[†] This bounding box is similar in concept to the bounding box for a character in a font. The dimensions of the bounding box are in the coordinate system of the pattern prototype. This heart shape was designed in

---

† The *Technically Speaking* column of the May 1992 issue of IEEE *Spectrum* magazine suggested **bbox** as an abbreviation for "breadbox," a possible standard unit of measure used in phrases like "...bigger than a breadbox but smaller than an elephant..." The **BBox** you see here and in form dictionaries is not related to breadboxes.

a 1000×1000 points coordinate system—similar to that for designing fonts. When defining the bounding box for a pattern prototype, make sure you get the bounding box derived after the path has been flattened. The figure here shows the bounding box for the heart shape after the path has been flattened.

Bounding box for heart figure without flattening path.

If you don't get a correct bounding box by flattening the path first, the pattern machinery in the PostScript interpreter can be misled into making incorrect clipping decisions. Our heart shape is a good example, because its Bézier control points lie well outside its bounding box. The figure shows the bounding box from an unflattened path, with the control points highlighted as dots.

Step Amounts

/XStep and **/YStep** control the spacing or pitch between successive copies of the pattern cell when it is painting the page. These two values are independent of the pattern cell bounding box.

Pattern with very tight x and y steps.

In our first example, **/XStep** and **/YStep** were both 1000 units—the same dimensions as the coordinate system of the pattern cell. The actual painted figure measures around 506×545 points. In the original example, the painted shapes were spread sparsely across the area to be painted. By changing the values of **/XStep** and **/YStep** you can get your pattern cells to overlap. The effect of overlapping cells in this particular example is that the painted part of the cells becomes more densely packed. This figure shows the effect of changing **/XStep** and **/YStep** to 600 units—the hearts are packed more densely in the painted shape. These pictures show the differences up close.

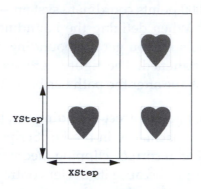

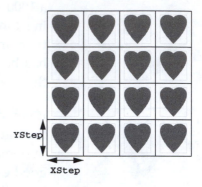

Sparsely packed pattern.
XStep *and* **YStep** *set to 1000 units*

Densely packed pattern.
XStep *and* **YStep** *set to 600 units*

Painting Procedure

/PaintProc is the important component of the prototype pattern. **/PaintProc** is the actual PostScript code that generates the shape of the pattern. In our prototype example, **/PaintProc** looks like this.

```
/PaintProc {                        %   define the paint procedure
  pop                               %   don't need pattern dictionary
  0 0 moveto                        %   set current point
  500 500  125 625 0 500   curveto  %   right side of heart
  -125 625 -500 500  0 0   curveto  %   left side of heart
  0.50 setgray fill                 %   fill with medium gray
} def
```

You can put just about anything into the **/PaintProc**, with certain exceptions, to be covered later. What's important is that when **/PaintProc** is called, the operand stack contains a copy of the dictionary in which **/PaintProc** was originally defined. The dictionary is passed to the paint procedure so the pattern dictionary can contain definitions to be used by the paint procedure. You will see this aspect in action a little later.

This particular **/PaintProc** is simple enough that it doesn't need anything defined in the enclosing pattern dictionary, so your paint procedure can simply **pop** the pattern dictionary off the operand stack.

Uncolored Patterns

You saw the basic notions of patterns in the previous section. You started with a simple shape and built repeating patterns from it. The pattern created previously used a **/PaintType** of **1**, which means that the pattern is a colored pattern. The color (or shades of gray) used to fill the shapes of the pattern are specified as a part of the pattern's paint procedure.

Now for a different type of pattern. An uncolored pattern has a **/PaintType** of **2**, meaning the pattern itself has no inherent color associated with its shapes. The color with which the pattern will be filled is supplied as a parameter when the pattern is established in the color space.

Let's see this in action by building a pattern dictionary as before. Use a different shape this time—the heart is getting boring.

This pattern uses an outline of a duck as a pattern. The code to generate the pattern dictionary appears on the next page. Some of the code for the duck is omitted here; the complete code for the outline of the duck appears on page 458.

The steps to create a pattern prototype for an uncolored pattern are essentially the same as those for a colored pattern, except for one major difference. **/PaintType** must be set equal to **2** to indicate an uncolored pattern.

```
%!PS
/OneDuckProto 12 dict def               %   define dictionary for pattern
OneDuckProto begin                      %   push onto dictionary stack
  /PatternType 1 def                    %   required—must be 1
  /PaintType 2 def                      %   uncolored pattern
  /TilingType 1 def                     %   controls grid adjustment
  /BBox [ 30 87 933 713 ] def           %   bounding box for shape
  /XStep 1000 def                       %   increment in x dimension
  /YStep 1000 def                       %   increment in y dimension
  /ProtoDuck {                          %   start definition
    677 505 moveto
    673 538 762 498 819 500 curveto
    . . .                               %   parts of duck omitted
    781 455 779 465 767 465 curveto
    745 465 712 460 680 469 curveto
  } def                                 %   end of shape definition
  /PaintProc {                          %   pattern dictionary on stack
    begin                               %   push onto dictionary stack
      ProtoDuck   fill                  %   draw the outline and fill it
    end                                 %   pop off dictionary stack
  } def                                 %   end of paint procedure
end                                     %   pop off dictionary stack
```

Instantiating this pattern is essentially the same process as instantiating a colored pattern.

```
OneDuckProto                            %   pattern dictionary to operand stack
[ 0.1 0 0 0.1 0 0 ]                     %   transformation matrix
makepattern                             %   make an instance of the pattern
/SmallDuck exch def                     %   stash the instantiated pattern
```

Painting with an Uncolored Pattern

Painting with an uncolored pattern is more involved than painting with a colored pattern, which supplies its color from its paint procedure. You instantiate an uncolored pattern in the same way as a colored pattern. But when the time comes to paint with the uncolored pattern, where does the color come from? You must supply the color as an extra parameter to **setcolor**.

```
%!PS
/inch { 72 mul } def                % define inch procedure
4.25 inch 5.5 inch 4 inch 5 inch DrawEllipse
gsave                               % remember graphics state
  0.50 setgray                      % medium gray shade
  fill                              % fill shape
grestore                            % restore graphics state
[
    /Pattern
    /DeviceGray
] setcolorspace                     % color space is pattern
1.0 SmallDuck setcolor              % use the instantiated pattern
fill                                % fill full of ducks
showpage                            % display page
```

This example consists of two parts—one is simple and the other needs explaining. The simple part is the first part, which draws an ellipse in the center of the page and fills it with medium gray. The second part is similar to our example of filling a space with a pattern, except this time, **setcolor** needs an extra parameter in addition to the name of the pattern dictionary. Recall that our pattern is an uncolored pattern—its fill color must be supplied at the time the pattern is set into color space. This example supplied a value of **1.0** to indicate the pattern should be filled with white when it is painted. The result is shown in the picture—a gray ellipse filled with white ducks.

All well and good. "But," you say, "Could I not have done this with a colored pattern just as easily?" We're glad you asked. Let's see the uncolored pattern in action again. This time you'll use it twice in a row, with a different color on each invocation.

Painting with uncolored patterns.

```
%!PS
/inch { 72 mul } def                        %   define inch procedure
4.25 inch 7.5 inch 3 inch 0 360 arc
closepath                                   %   finish circle
gsave                                       %   push graphics state
  0.90 setgray                              %   set light gray color
  fill                                      %   fill circle
grestore                                    %   pop graphics state
[
    /Pattern
    /DeviceGray
] setcolorspace                             %   color space is pattern
0.1 SmallDuck setcolor                      %   dark gray and ducks pattern
fill                                        %   fill full of dark ducks
4.25 inch 3.5 inch 3 inch 0 360 arc
closepath                                   %   finish circle
gsave                                       %   push graphics state
  0.10 setgray                              %   set dark gray color
  fill                                      %   fill circle
grestore                                    %   pop graphics state
0.9 SmallDuck setcolor                      %   light gray and ducks pattern
fill                                        %   fill full of light ducks
showpage                                    %   display page
```

The main lines of interest in this example are those with the **setcolor** instructions. The previous **setcolorspace** instruction was set with an array of two color spaces—a pattern color space and a gray scale color space. Now, each time you call **setcolor**, you must provide it with two parameters. The first parameter is the shade of gray you wish to use and the second parameter is the pattern to be painted in that specific shade of gray.

You can use essentially the same code to paint the outline and patterns, but this time in real color. The changes are fairly minimal.

See plate XVII for the color version.

```
%!PS
/inch { 72 mul } def              %   define inch procedure
4.25 inch 7.5 inch 3 inch 0 360 arc
closepath                         %   finish circle
gsave                             %   push graphics state
   0.0 0.5 0.0 setrgbcolor        %   medium green color
   fill                           %   fill circle
grestore                          %   pop graphics state
[
    /Pattern
    /DeviceRGB
] setcolorspace                   %   color space is pattern
0.0 0.0 0.5 SmallDuck setcolor    %   medium blue and ducks pattern
fill                              %   fill with medium blue ducks
4.25 inch 3.5 inch 3 inch 0 360 arc
closepath                         %   finish circle
gsave                             %   push graphics state
   0.0 0.0 0.5 setrgbcolor        %   medium blue color
   fill                           %   fill circle
grestore                          %   pop graphics state
0.0 0.5 0.0 SmallDuck setcolor    %   medium green and ducks pattern
fill                              %   fill with medium green ducks
showpage                          %   display page
```

This example is similar to the previous example, which used shades of gray, but this example first paints blue ducks on a green background, followed by green ducks on a blue background.

Patterns can be treated like fonts and can be downloaded onto a printer when the printer is powered on, or can be stored on the printer's mass storage device. Everyone with access to that printer then has access to pattern resources as well as font resources.

Here's the PostScript outline of the duck used as patterns earlier in the chapter.

Quack! Quack!.

```
%!PS
/Duck {
    700 500 moveto    700 540 760 500 820 500 curveto
    870 500 880 540 930 560 curveto
    830 570 710 700 570 700 curveto
    510 700 410 630 340 630 curveto
    280 630 230 710 190 710 curveto
    120 710 110 620 40 630 curveto
    30 630 30 610 40 610 curveto
    100 600 80 600 120 600 curveto
    250 630 280 610 300 580 curveto
    320 540 400 530 400 400 curveto
    400 200 380 140 350 90 curveto
    400 120 520 190 550 270 curveto
    570 320 640 450 670 450 curveto
    740 460 710 460 680 470 curveto
    closepath
} def
```

The **AstroidLeaf** pattern cell used in many examples in this book is a pattern cell made of two shapes painted in different shades of gray. The first shape is a cloverleaf. Here's its definition.

```
%!PS
/CloverLeaf {
    /OneLeaf {
    10 0 rlineto    10 110 110 100 110 220 rcurveto
    0 70 -60 120 -130 120 rcurveto
    -70 0 -130 -50 -130 -120 rcurveto
    0 -110 110 -120 120 -220 rcurveto
    closepath
    -20 -10 rmoveto
    } def
    400 400 moveto
    OneLeaf
    90 rotate OneLeaf
    90 rotate OneLeaf
    90 rotate OneLeaf
} def
```

Here's the cloverleaf shape when you draw its path and fill it.

Basic cloverleaf shape.

```
%!PS
0 144 translate              %   set origin for shape
0.8 dup scale                %   scale to fit on page
CloverLeaf                   %   draw cloverleaf shape
0.25 setgray                 %   dark gray shade
fill                         %   fill shape
showpage                     %   display page
```

That's the first part of the pattern cell. Now you get to the other part, the astroid shape. Here's the definition of the astroid.

```
%!PS
/Astroid {
    410 10 moveto
    0 220 180 390 380 380 rcurveto
    20 10 20 10 0 20 rcurveto
    90 rotate
    0 220 180 390 380 380 rcurveto
    20 10 20 10 0 20 rcurveto
    90 rotate
    0 220 180 390 380 380 rcurveto
    20 10 20 10 0 20 rcurveto
    90 rotate
    0 220 180 390 380 380 rcurveto
    20 10 20 10 0 20 rcurveto
} def
```

And here's what the astroid shape looks like when you draw its path and fill it.

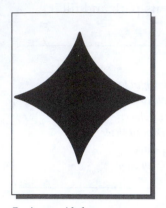

Basic astroid shape.

```
%!PS
-18 144 translate          %  set origin for shape
0.8 dup scale              %  scale to fit on page
Astroid                    %  draw astroid shape
0.25 setgray               %  dark gray shade
fill                       %  fill shape
showpage                   %  display page
```

The preceding two shapes are the components of the pattern cell you're about to see. This astroid and leaf pattern cell is used in many examples throughout this book. The shapes are designed in a 1000×1000-unit character coordinate system. For examples in this book, the pattern cells were designed in an 8½-by-8½-inch square so they could be easily designed on a page.

Here is what the astroid and cloverleaf pattern cell looks like when it's filled in.

AstroidLeaf *pattern cell.*

```
%!PS
-18 90 translate           %  set origin for shape
AstroidLeaf                %  draw AstroidLeaf shape
showpage                   %  display page
```

```
%!PS
/AstroidLeaf {                          %  start definition of cell
  gsave                                 %  remember graphics state
    0 8 translate                       %  lower-left portion
    0.4 dup scale                       %  scale to required size
    CloverLeaf                          %  draw cloverleaf shape
    0.25 setgray fill                   %  fill with dark gray shade
  grestore                              %  restore graphics state
  gsave                                 %  remember graphics state
    306 8 translate                     %  lower-right portion
    0.4 dup scale                       %  scale to required size
    Astroid                             %  draw astroid shape
    0.50 setgray fill                   %  fill with medium gray shade
  grestore                              %  restore graphics state
  gsave                                 %  remember graphics state
    0 306 8 add translate               %  upper-left portion
    0.4 dup scale                       %  scale to required size
    Astroid                             %  draw astroid shape
    0.50 setgray fill                   %  fill with medium gray shade
  grestore                              %  restore graphics state
  gsave                                 %  remember graphics state
    306 306 8 add translate             %  upper-right portion
    0.4 dup scale                       %  scale to required size
    CloverLeaf                          %  draw cloverleaf shape
    0.25 setgray fill                   %  fill with dark gray shade
  grestore                              %  restore graphics state
} def                                   %  end of definition
```

12 Forms

In the beginning was the void,
    and the Earth was without forms.

Undiscovered version of the Book of Genesis 1:1

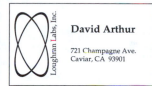

David Arthur

721 Champagne Ave.
Caviar, CA 93901

Forms were introduced in PostScript Level 2 as a part of the new PostScript graphics capabilities. According to one market survey conducted in 1990, the worldwide forms market has become an eight billion dollar business. The traditional idea of a "form" is, of course, something a bureaucrat asks you to fill in when you really want an answer to a question. But besides this notion of "forms," other examples include letterhead, stationery, overhead presentation backgrounds, labels, and envelopes. Where patterns, described in Chapter 11, are descriptions of images used to tile regions of a page, forms are descriptions of arbitrary graphics, text, and images that can be painted multiple times on each of several pages, or can be painted at several different locations on a single page. Forms depart from the traditional PostScript approach of providing you with basic tools to place graphics and text on a page or on the screen. Rather, forms belong in the realm of advanced tools for a specialized job.

Forms provide you with a simple and efficient means of reproducing the common skeletal framework of your image many times. Of course, in PostScript Level 1, you can easily emulate forms—just define a procedure that images the same picture each time. The potential disadvantage of this approach is that it is subject to performance problems. The image must be transmitted to the interpreter and processed each time you wish to use it.

The major advantage of PostScript Level 2 forms is that a form is cached and can be used multiple times very efficiently. You define a form once, transmit it once and interpret it once—its representation stays cached between each use. Subsequent invocations of the form are imaged from the cache, saving both transmission time and interpretation time.

Overview of Creating and Using Forms

Creating and using forms in PostScript Level 2 is very simple and somewhat analogous to creating fonts or patterns in Level 2, although creating and using forms requires fewer steps. To create and use a form, you need to

❑   build a prototype

❑   create a form dictionary

❑   use **execform** to image the form

❑   fill in the form

The first two steps create the form; the last two steps use the form.

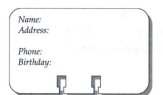

Build a prototype. The first step in building a form is to build a prototype. The main item in the prototype is the procedures to draw the picture. This picture shows a form prototype. This particular prototype implements the outline of a Rolodex® card and some titles. The outline and titles will be imaged many times. The personal information filled in later varies from card to card and is not part of the form. The procedure to draw the form is analogous to the procedure to draw a character from a font.

Often, building a prototype for a form requires little thought. A PostScript procedure or set of procedures will present itself as a candidate for a form; the same image is rendered many times. If you have PostScript code that is a candidate for a form, you've already built a form prototype. On other occasions, you need to produce the PostScript code for the prototype either by hand or with the help of an application.

Create a form dictionary. As with fonts and patterns, a form is a PostScript dictionary that conforms to guidelines and contains specific elements to give information about the form to the interpreter. Step two of creating and using a form is to create such a dictionary. Form dictionaries are modest, containing few elements. *A Walk Through the Form Dictionary* on pages 470–474 in this chapter discusses each element in detail. You should define the form dictionary in the current dictionary so you can refer to the form by name when you use it. The form dictionary must contain one extra, empty element for use by the PostScript interpreter.

Image the form. The first two steps create the form. This step uses the form. You use **execform** to image the form on the current page. **execform** selects the form (either by executing the PostScript instructions in the form dictionary directly or by getting the image from the cache) and images the form. The first time the interpreter images any form, the interpreter verifies that the dictionary is correct and contains all the necessary elements. The interpreter then images the form and saves the results in the form cache for subsequent rendering.

Name:	Richard Campione
Address:	50 Hulahupa Court
	Hanamaulu, HI 09876
Phone:	(415) 767–2676
Birthday:	29 Dec 63

Fill in the form. The final step of using a form is to fill in the variable information, provided there is any. For the Rolodex card, this means putting a name and other information onto the card in the appropriate slots. This picture shows such a card.

The primary benefit of forms is they're cached. This same benefit leads to a slight disadvantage—PostScript forms cannot directly support filling in a form. The PostScript interpreter images forms at unpredictable times, and sometimes not at all—the interpreter copies the bits from a cache. You can't rely on the environment in which the form is executed or even that the form will be executed. Therefore, you can't image variable information directly in the form. You must write PostScript instructions outside the framework of the form dictionary to place variable information within the form. However, you can use the power of the PostScript dictionary mechanisms and still maintain code modularity. You can put into your form dictionary definitions that contain positions and sizes of variable objects. The domino example on pages 479–483 in this chapter demonstrates maintaining code modularity while filling in a form.

Build a Form Prototype

Company logos are good candidates for forms—they appear on everything from mailing labels to business cards and letterhead. Logos are often printed in different sizes and at different orientations. The business card on page 463 at the beginning of this chapter shows the company logo for the prestigious Loughran Laboratories, Inc. Let's make the logo into a form by first creating a prototype.

```
%!PS
/inch { 72 mul } def                     %  define inch procedure
/ellipse {                               %  stack = rotation angle
    gsave
        rotate                           %  rotate user space
        1.0 0.4 scale                    %  scale y axis
        0 0 4.0 inch 0 360 arc stroke    %  draw ellipse
    grestore
} def
gsave                                    %  save graphics state
    20 setlinewidth                      %  fat line width
    4.25 inch 3.25 inch translate        %  translate to center
    20 ellipse 160 ellipse               %  two ellipses
grestore                                 %  undo translate
/Palatino-Roman findfont                 %  choose font
64 scalefont setfont
0.5 inch 0.3 inch moveto                 %  set current point
(Loughran Labs, Inc.) show               %  show name
showpage                                 %  display page
```

Basically, this PostScript program draws the same ellipse at two different rotations and places the company name beneath them. Notice that the line width of the ellipse is scaled along with the ellipse to give an illusion of electrons spinning about the nucleus. This series of PostScript instructions can be bundled together into a PostScript procedure that becomes the form prototype.

Create a Form Dictionary

A PostScript form is a dictionary. To create a form dictionary from a prototype is quite simple. Create a named PostScript dictionary; that is, define the form dictionary in the current dictionary as a key-value pair. Then insert the prototype procedure into the dictionary along with some other elements. The procedure to draw the form shape must be named **PaintProc**. Here's a form dictionary implementing the Loughran Labs logo form.

Loughran Labs, Inc.

```
%!PS
/inch { 72 mul } def                          %   the dreaded inch
/LoughranForm 6 dict def                       %   define dictionary for form
LoughranForm begin                             %   push onto dictionary stack
  /FormType 1 def                              %   Required—must be 1
  /BBox [0 0 8.3 inch 5.5 inch] def            %   bounding box
  /Matrix [1 0 0 1 0 0] def                    %   transformation matrix
  /ellipse {                                   %   stack = rotation angle
    gsave
      rotate                                   %   rotate user space
      1.0 0.4 scale                            %   scale y axis
      0 0 4.0 inch 0 360 arc stroke            %   draw ellipse
    grestore
  } def
  /PaintProc {                                 %   define paint procedure
    begin                                      %   push form dictionary
      gsave                                    %   save graphics state
        20 setlinewidth                        %   fat line width
        4.25 inch 3.25 inch translate %        %   translate to center
        20 ellipse 160 ellipse                 %   two ellipses
      grestore                                 %   undo translate
      /Palatino-Roman 64 selectfont            %   choose font
      0.5 inch 0.3 inch moveto                 %   set current point
      (Loughran Labs, Inc.) show               %   show name
    end
  } def
end
```

As you see, a form dictionary contains few entries. For now you can safely ignore details of the form dictionary—each element of a form dictionary is covered in detail in *A Walk Through the Form*

Dictionary on pages 470–474 in this chapter. Notice that the PostScript instructions to draw the logo have been bundled together into a PostScript procedure named **PaintProc**.

Image the Form

Imaging your form requires one PostScript operator—**execform**. This code shows **execform** and the picture shows the results.

Loughran Labs, Inc.

```
%!PS
/inch { 72 mul } def            % define inch procedure
LoughranForm execform           % execute the form
showpage                        % display page
```

The results are not surprising—the form produced exactly the same picture as the prototype you started with. The advantage is that the image is now cached and next time the logo is imaged it will not be interpreted again; the results will be copied from the cache.

Forms, like other graphics, are affected by the CTM. By altering the CTM you can change the results of executing a form. This example displays the Loughran Labs logo at a smaller scale and 90° rotation—useful for business cards.

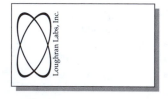

```
%!PS
/inch { 72 mul } def            % the dreaded inch procedure
BusinessCardOutline             % draw outline
1.2 inch 0.15 inch translate    % translate to new position
90 rotate                       % turn image sideways
0.2 dup scale                   % smaller scale
LoughranForm execform           % draw logo
showpage                        % display page
```

Note **execform** selects the form and images it as well. This means transformations to user space must be performed before **execform**.

Modifications to the graphics state affect the caching of forms. The same form imaged in the same graphics state is rendered from the cache. If user space has been scaled or rotated, the form must be interpreted again. In general, translations in user space don't affect form caching. Regardless, the behavior of form caching in the PostScript interpreter is not guaranteed.

Here's the code for the **BusinessCardOutline** procedure used in the preceding examples. You can substitute **rectfill** or **rectstroke** for **DrawRect fill** and **DrawRect stroke**, respectively, if you have a Level 2 PostScript interpreter.

```
%!PS
/inch { 72 mul } def              %  define inch procedure
/DrawRect {                       %  stack = x y width height
  4 2 roll moveto 1 index 0 rlineto
  0 exch rlineto neg 0 rlineto
  closepath
} def
/BusinessCardOutline {
  0.66666 setgray                 %  drop shadow
  8 -8 3.5 inch 2.0 inch DrawRect fill
  1 setgray                       %  white background
  0 0 3.5 inch 2.0 inch DrawRect fill
  0 setgray
  1 setlinewidth                  %  outline of card
  0 0 3.5 inch 2.0 inch DrawRect stroke
} def
```

Fill in the Form

The final step in using your form is to overlay the information that changes from instance to instance on top of the imaged form. Let's make a business card for David Arthur. Besides his name, the address is also considered variable because Loughran Labs, Inc. have many offices around the world.

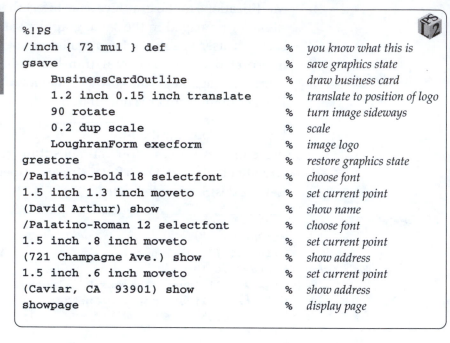

```
%!PS
/inch { 72 mul } def                        %   you know what this is
gsave                                       %   save graphics state
    BusinessCardOutline                     %   draw business card
    1.2 inch 0.15 inch translate            %   translate to position of logo
    90 rotate                               %   turn image sideways
    0.2 dup scale                           %   scale
    LoughranForm execform                   %   image logo
grestore                                    %   restore graphics state
/Palatino-Bold 18 selectfont                %   choose font
1.5 inch 1.3 inch moveto                    %   set current point
(David Arthur) show                         %   show name
/Palatino-Roman 12 selectfont               %   choose font
1.5 inch .8 inch moveto                     %   set current point
(721 Champagne Ave.) show                   %   show address
1.5 inch .6 inch moveto                     %   set current point
(Caviar, CA  93901) show                    %   show address
showpage                                    %   display page
```

Notice that simple PostScript instructions render the variable information. You have to rely on your knowledge of the form to place the information in the right spot. Let's investigate the contents of the form dictionary in detail.

A Walk Through the Form Dictionary

By now, you should be quite familiar with the basic steps required for creating a form. Let's step through the elements of the form dictionary using the Loughran Labs' logo dictionary created in the preceding section. This particular dictionary is quite simple, and, really, form dictionaries don't get much more complex. Here it is again for your convenience.

```
%!PS
/inch { 72 mul } def                              %   the dreaded inch
/LoughranForm 6 dict def                          %   define dictionary for form
LoughranForm begin                                %   push onto dictionary stack
  /FormType 1 def                                 %   Required—must be 1
  /BBox [0 0 8.3 inch 5.5 inch] def               %   bounding box
  /Matrix [1 0 0 1 0 0] def                        %   transformation matrix
  /ellipse {                                      %   stack = rotation angle
    gsave
      rotate                                      %   rotate user space
      1.0 0.4 scale                               %   scale y axis
      0 0 4.0 inch 0 360 arc stroke               %   draw ellipse
    grestore
  } def
  /PaintProc {                                    %   define paint procedure
    begin                                         %   push form dictionary
      gsave                                       %   save graphics state
        20 setlinewidth                           %   fat line width
        4.25 inch 3.25 inch translate %   translate to center
        20 ellipse 160 ellipse                    %   two ellipses
      grestore                                    %   undo translate
      /Palatino-Roman 64 selectfont               %   choose font
      0.5 inch 0.3 inch moveto                    %   set current point
      (Loughran Labs, Inc.) show                  %   show name
    end
  } def
end
```

FormType

The first element in the dictionary is **/FormType**. This entry is required in all form dictionaries and must be 1 in the current (1992) implementation of PostScript. **/FormType** is included for future extensions to the form mechanism, much like **/FontType** in a font dictionary and **/PatternType** in a pattern dictionary. Currently only one type of form is available—type 1.

BBox

/BBox is a required element in a form dictionary and is the bounding box for the form prototype. This bounding box is similar in concept to that of a character in a font or the bounding box for a pattern prototype. The dimensions of the bounding box are in the coordinate system of the form prototype. In this particular example, the coordinate system of the form prototype is the same as user space, although that's not required. When the form is rendered, it is clipped to the boundaries of its bounding box. If the bounding box is incorrect, you may lose portions of your image.

You can use two methods to figure out the bounding box of a path—either "guesstimate" the bounding box (as was done here with trial and error), or calculate it precisely using the techniques shown in *Flattening Path for Accurate Bounding Boxes* on page 334 in Chapter 8. The picture shows the bounding for each ellipse individually. It was easier to "eyeball" the shape and guess the bounding box than to figure out the composite bounding box for both ellipses and the company name.

Matrix

/Matrix is required in all form dictionaries. **/Matrix** defines the relationship between form space and user space. This matrix is concatenated with the CTM before the form is executed. The matrix used in the logo form example

```
/Matrix [1 0 0 1 0 0] def
```

is the *identity* matrix—the coordinate system of the form corresponds exactly to user space.

PaintProc

/PaintProc is the most interesting entry in a form dictionary and is required. The paint procedure is the heart of the form. **/PaintProc** is the PostScript procedure to draw the form. In the logo example, **/PaintProc** looks like this.

```
%!PS
/PaintProc {                                   %   define paint procedure
  begin                                        %   push form dictionary
    gsave                                      %   save graphics state
      20 setlinewidth                          %   set line width
        4.25 inch 3.25 inch translate %        translate to center
        20 ellipse 160 ellipse                 %   two ellipses
    grestore                                   %   undo translate
    /Palatino-Roman 64 selectfont              %   choose font
    0.5 inch 0.3 inch moveto                   %   set current point
    (Loughran Labs, Inc.) show                 %   show name
  end                                          %   pop form dictionary
} def
```

You can put just about anything into **/PaintProc**, with certain exceptions. *Embedded Forms* on pages 474–478 in this chapter covers these exceptions in detail.

What's important to know is that when **/PaintProc** is called, the operand stack contains a copy of the dictionary in which **/PaintProc** was originally defined. You can define variables or procedures within the form dictionary that **/PaintProc** can use, such as **ellipse** shown in the example. To get at the definitions in the form dictionary, **/PaintProc** pushes the form dictionary onto the dictionary stack with **begin**. The last instruction in **/PaintProc** pops the form dictionary from the dictionary stack with **end**. If your form is simple and requires no extra definitions, remember to **pop** the form dictionary off the operand stack.

Other Form Dictionary Entries

/FormType, **/BBox**, **/Matrix**, and **/PaintProc** are all required entries in a Type 1 form dictionary. There are two other possible entries as well—**/Implementation** and **/XUID**.

The PostScript interpreter adds **/Implementation** to the dictionary when **execform** is called. The type and value of this entry is implementation-dependent. In general, you needn't be concerned with **/Implementation** except to make room for it when creating your forms dictionary.

The final element of a form dictionary is optional. **/XUID** is an *extended unique identifier*. In short, an extended unique identifier is an array whose components uniquely identify a PostScript object. The components of the array consist of an organizational ID and an object ID. An extended unique identifier should be properly constructed. See the *PostScript Language Reference Manual*, Second Edition, for more information about constructing **/XUID**s. You should not put an **/XUID** entry in a form generated dynamically by application programs.

You now know basically everything there is to know about forms. Forms are simple in both concept and design. This chapter goes on to delve a bit deeper and to give a few more hints about implementing forms in PostScript Level 2.

Embedded Forms

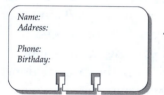

As mentioned before, forms must conform to certain guidelines. These guidelines serve to keep the form from interfering with the environment in which it was called.

The paint procedure for the form should avoid operators that are unsuitable for Encapsulated PostScript files (see the *PostScript Language Reference Manual*, Second Edition, for more information) including **copypage**, **showpage**, or any device setup operators.

Other than removing its dictionary from the operand stack, **/PaintProc** should leave the environment in which it was invoked unchanged. **execform** saves the graphics state before **/PaintProc** is called and restores the graphics state afterwards. The paint procedure should have no side-effects other than painting the form.

The paint procedure should rely on information only within the form dictionary; it should not depend on being called in any specific environment. **PaintProc** is invoked by the interpreter at unpredictable times.

PaintProc should produce the same effects each time it's called. The appearance of the form depends only on the graphics state. These restrictions make sense when you consider that one form can be embedded within another (or within anything else for that matter).

The Rolodex card shown on page 474 was actually created with two forms—one embedded inside the other. The first form implements the outline of the card. The second form implements the titles of the card. Let's first look at **TitleForm**, which draws the titles on the card.

Name:
Address:

Phone:
Birthday:

```
%!PS
/TitlesForm 5 dict def              %   define form dictionary
TitlesForm begin                    %   push form dictionary
  /FormType 1 def                   %   Required—must be 1
  /BBox [0 0 3.6 inch 2.2 inch] def %   bounding box
  /Matrix [1 0 0 1 0 0] def         %   transformation matrix
  /PaintProc {                      %   define paint procedure
    pop                             %   pop form dictionary
    /Palatino-Italic 18 selectfont  %   choose font & draw titles
    0.25 inch 2.1 inch moveto (Name:) show
    0.25 inch 1.8 inch moveto (Address:) show
    0.25 inch 1.2 inch moveto (Phone:) show
    0.25 inch 0.9 inch moveto (Birthday:) show
  } def
end
```

There's nothing complicated about this form. The form just places words in specific positions on the current page using **moveto** and **show**. Now look on the following page to see the form for imaging the Rolodex card outline.

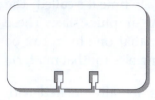

```
%!PS
/RolodexForm 7 dict def            %   define form dictionary
RolodexForm begin                  %   push form dictionary
/FormType 1 def                    %   Required—must be 1
/BBox [0 0 4 inch 7 add 2.5 inch] def %  bounding box
/Matrix [1 0 0 1 0 0] def          %   transformation matrix
/insertNotch {                     %   draw notches
  ...details omitted...
} def
/DrawBox {                         %   draw card outline
  ...details omitted...
} def
/PaintProc {                       %   define paint procedure
  begin                            %   push form dictionary
    gsave
      7 -7 translate
      DrawBox 0.6666 setgray fill  %   drop shadow
    grestore
    DrawBox 1 setgray fill         %   white background
    DrawBox 0 setgray stroke       %   black outline
  end
} def
end
```

Note the extra elements in the form dictionary. The paint procedure needed two PostScript procedures, **InsertNotch** and **DrawBox**. Those procedures must be defined inside the form dictionary, because the paint procedure can't rely on anything from the calling environment—not even procedures defined in **userdict**. The paint procedure gains access to the procedures defined in the form dictionary by pushing the form dictionary onto the dictionary stack with **begin**. In this way, the paint procedure can call **DrawBox**, which, in turn, can call **InsertNotch**. Here are the complete procedure definitions for **DrawBox** and **InsertNotch**.

```
/insertNotch {                          %   draw notches
    0 0.1875 inch rlineto -0.0625 inch 0 rlineto
    0 0.3125 inch rlineto 0.25 inch 0 rlineto
    0 -.3125 inch rlineto -.0625 inch 0 rlineto
    0 -.1875 inch rlineto
} def
/DrawBox {                              %   draw card outline
    1.4357 inch 7 moveto insertNotch
    2.4357 inch 7 lineto insertNotch
    4 inch 7 4 inch 2.5 inch 25 arcto
    4 inch 2.5 inch 0 2.5 inch 25 arcto
    0 2.5 inch 0 7 25 arcto
    0 7 4 inch 7 25 arcto
    closepath
} def
```

Now let's change **RolodexForm** so **TitleForm** is embedded within it.

These are the modifications to the Rolodex form:

❏ first, the size of the RolodexForm dictionary was increased by one to make space for one more element—the form dictionary of the embedded form

❏ second, the embedded form was folded into the **RolodexForm** dictionary

❏ finally, the paint procedure of the card outline form executes **TitleForm** with **execform**

The results appear in the next picture, with the code alongside.

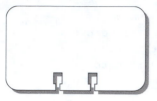

```
%!PS
/RolodexForm 8 dict def                          %   define form dictionary
RolodexForm begin                                %   push form dictionary
/FormType 1 def                                  %   Required—must be 1
/BBox [0 0 4 inch 7 add 2.5 inch] def            %   bounding box
/Matrix [1 0 0 1 0 0] def                        %   transformation matrix
/TitlesForm 5 dict def                           %   embedded form dictionary
TitlesForm begin                                 %   push form dictionary
  /FormType 1 def                                %   Required—must be 1
  /BBox [0 0 3.6 inch 2.2 inch] def              %   bounding box
  /Matrix [1 0 0 1 0 0] def                      %   transformation matrix
  /PaintProc {                                   %   define paint procedure
    ...details omitted...
  } def
end
/insertNotch {                                   %   draw notches in card
  ...details omitted...
} def
/DrawBox {                                       %   draw outline of card
  ...details omitted...
} def
/PaintProc {                                     %   define paint procedure
  begin                                          %   push form dictionary
    gsave
      7 -7 translate
      DrawBox 0.6666 setgray fill                %   drop shadow
    grestore
    DrawBox 1 setgray fill                       %   white background
    DrawBox 0 setgray stroke                     %   black outline
    TitleForm execform                           %   execute embedded form
  end
} def
end
```

Emulating Forms in PostScript Level 1

According to the *PostScript Language Reference Manual, Second Edition*, you can use the following PostScript procedure to emulate **execform** in your Level 1 interpreter.

Stack contents before call to **execform**.

```
/execform {
    gsave                              %   save graphics state
        dup /Matrix get concat %   concatenate form matrix with CTM
        dup /BBox get aload pop
        exch 3 index sub
        exch 2 index sub
        rectclip                       %   clip to bounding box
        dup /PaintProc get
        exec                           %   execute paint procedure
    grestore                           %   restore graphics state
} def
```

This code is a little suspicious, because **rectclip** in the procedure is, in fact, a Display PostScript and PostScript Level 2 operator. Other than this minor detail, the code fragment has been used successfully to emulate **execform** by also defining a procedure to emulate **rectclip**. See *Emulating Level 2 Rectangle Operators* on pages 74–81 in Chapter 2 for emulation of **rectclip**.

The **execform** procedure emulates the PostScript Level 2 **execform** in five steps:

- ❏ saving the graphics state
- ❏ concatenating the form's transformation matrix with the CTM
- ❏ clipping to the extent of the form's bounding box
- ❏ executing **PaintProc** with the form dictionary as an operand
- ❏ restoring the graphics state

Let's create a new form to image domino tiles and use that form to walk through the emulation of **execform.** The following program defines a form to draw domino tiles.

```
%!PS
/inch { 72 mul } def                        % define inch procedure
/DominoForm 12 dict def                      % define form dictionary
DominoForm begin                             % push form dictionary
  /FormType 1 def                            % form type = 1
  /BBox [-18  -18   518   1018] def           % bounding box
  /Matrix [0.001 0 0 0.001 0 0] def           % transformation matrix
  /DrawBox {                                 % stack = width height
    ...details omitted...
  } def
  /topBaseline 500 def
  /center 250 def
  /adj 125 def
  /PlaceSpot {
    ...details omitted...
  } def
  /PaintProc {                               % define paint procedure
    ...details omitted...
  } def
end                                          % end forms dictionary
```

That's the framework for the form dictionary. Here's the code to implement **DrawBox**.

```
%!PS
/DrawBox {                                   % stack = width height
    /height exch def                         % define height
    /width exch def                          % define width
    150 0 moveto                             % set current point
    width 0 width height 85 arcto            % draw four rounded corners
    width height 0 height 85 arcto
    0 height 0 0 85 arcto
    0 0 height 0 85 arcto
    closepath                                % finish the shape
    16 { pop } repeat                        % garbage collect
} def
```

Here's the code for **PlaceSpot**.

```
%!PS
/PlaceSpot {                        %  stack = δx δy
    adj mul center add              %  calculate y position
    exch                            %  x on top
    adj mul center add              %  calculate x position
    exch                            %  y on top
    25 0 360 arc closepath fill     %  draw spot
} def
```

And finally, here's the code to implement **PaintProc**, the most important procedure.

```
%!PS
/PaintProc {
    begin                               %  push form dictionary
        0.5 inch setlinewidth           %  fat line width
        500 500 DrawBox stroke          %  draw bottom half
        gsave                           %  save graphics state
            0 500 translate             %  position for top half
            500 500 DrawBox stroke      %  draw top half
        grestore                        %  restore graphics state
    end                                 %  pop form dictionary
} def
```

On the next page, we see the form in action. And before getting back to the subject of emulating **execform**, we'll take a look at a nifty feature of this form.

We stated previously that PostScript forms don't directly support placing variable information atop the form. However, this form uses the dictionary mechanism to maintain code modularity.

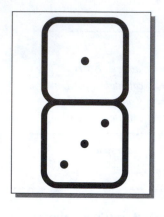

```
%!PS
/inch { 72 mul } def              %  define inch procedure
2 inch 0.5 inch translate         %  position for huge domino
10 inch 10 inch scale             %  scale for 10 inch domino
DominoForm execform               %  image the form
DominoForm begin                  %  push form dictionary
    Matrix concat                 %  get into form space
    0 0 PlaceSpot                 %  center spot
    -1 -1 PlaceSpot               %  lower spot
    1 1 PlaceSpot                 %  upper spot
    0 topBaseline translate       %  position for upper half
    0 0 PlaceSpot                 %  center spot
end                               %  push form dictionary
showpage                          %  display page
```

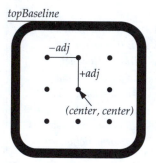

topBaseline

center, adj, topBaseline, and PlaceSpot are defined within the form dictionary, and all these PostScript objects work together to place variable information—the spots on the domino—on the form. center is the x and y location on the domino for the center dot. adj is the displacement in both the x and y directions to position the other spots. topBaseline is the location of the bottom edge of the top half of the domino. Finally, PlaceSpot draws a spot on the domino in the right location depending on two parameters.

To draw the spots, the example program images the form, pushes the form dictionary onto the stack, and calls PlaceSpot multiple times. The values of center, adj, and topBaseline are meaningful only within form space. So the program concatenates the form matrix with the CTM, transforming user space into form space, before calling PlaceSpot. This step is unnecessary if form space and user space coincide and the form matrix is the identity matrix.

Now back to the subject at hand—emulation. Let's watch the emulation procedure in action when imaging this huge domino. As with execform, the form dictionary is passed to the emulation version of execform, which uses the contents of the dictionary to set up the graphics state before imaging the form.

A form must have no effects on the state of the interpreter. The emulation of **execform** ensures that the form doesn't modify the interpreter state by enclosing the execution of the form within **gsave** and **grestore**. So the first step in the emulation code is **gsave**.

The next step

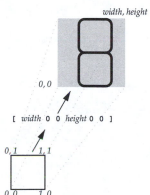

```
dup /Matrix get concat
```

concatenates the form's transformation matrix with the CTM. The domino tile is designed in a 1000×1000-unit coordinate system. In form space, the domino is about 1000 units tall and 500 units wide. The form's transformation matrix

```
[ .001 0 0 .001 0 0 ]
```

scales the 1000×1000 domino into a one-unit square in user space. Subsequent **scale** operations produce a domino exactly the height of the y scale factor. That is, **2 inch 2 inch scale** creates a domino two inches tall and one inch wide. Of course, any other transformations in the CTM affect the form image as well.

Next, the emulation procedure clips to the extent of the form's bounding box. The bounding box is specified in form space— however, the previous **concat** operation translated the bounding box into user space. The picture illustrates the clipping region of the domino.

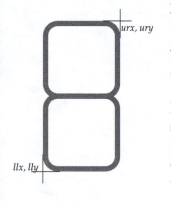

Finally, **execform** pushes the form dictionary onto the operand stack, retrieves **PaintProc** from the form dictionary, and executes **PaintProc**. Just before returning to the main PostScript program, **execform** restores the graphics state to its condition before the call to **execform**.

13 Color and Halftones

They may crush cinnabar,
  yet they do not take away its color;
One may burn a fragrant herb,
  yet it will not destroy the scent.

Admiral Yamamoto—*quoting Confucius*

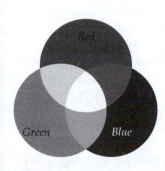

Additive (RGB) color model—see color plate III.

Color—it's a complicated subject, full of mystery and specialized jargon. This chapter contains three distinct sections that attempt to unravel some of the complications of color technology. After a brief overview of the color models supported by the PostScript language, the first section provides a detailed discussion of each color model and its related PostScript operators. Included in this discussion are CIE (Commission Internationale de l'Eclairage) color specification and color separations. The second section focuses on issues revolving around the use of color in PostScript programs. The third and final section discusses halftoning for both monochrome and color images.

Overview of Color Models

Color (like brightness) is a physiological sensation and as such cannot be directly measured, nor described. Color models allow the color formation process to be described and predicted. The link between a color model and perceived color remains human perception, which is complex and dependent on a number of physical, psychological, and physiological factors beyond the control of a printer or computer screen.

485

The PostScript language adopted several color models from the printing, television and scientific communities, that you use to specify the *current color* in the graphics state. Gray scale, RGB, and HSB color models supported by PostScript Level 1 together with CMYK supported by PostScript Level 2[†] can be grouped into a category of color models known as *Device Color Spaces*. Device color spaces map directly to the capabilities of output devices. In addition to device color spaces, PostScript Level 2 also supports pattern color spaces, separations, and CIE color specification. All PostScript color spaces except patterns are covered in this chapter. Chapter 11—*Patterns*—is dedicated to pattern color spaces.

Gray Scale—use this color model to specify shades of gray. You have already seen many examples of gray scale throughout this book. Gray scale is particularly useful for devices with no color capability such as low end printers or monochrome devices. For more information see *Gray Color Model* on pages 488–491.

RGB is the Red–Green–Blue color model. Other colors are derived from combinations of the three *primary colors*. RGB is an *additive* color model, typically used in applications where light is generated, such as computer screens. *RGB Color Model* on pages 491–495 covers RGB in detail.

HSB is the Hue–Saturation–Brightness color model. When specifying colors in HSB, first you specify the actual color (or hue). Then you lighten or darken it with the brightness component and purify the color with the saturation component. HSB is not so much a separate color model as a different way of thinking about RGB. HSB is the color model used in television sets. For more information see *HSB Color Model* on pages 495–499.

CMYK is the Cyan-Magenta-Yellow-blacK color model, and has four primary colors. CMYK is a *subtractive* color model, typically used in applications where light is reflected, such as printing. CMYK is covered in *CMYK Color Model* on pages 499–503.

---

† Some PostScript Level 1 devices support the CMYK color model, which did not officially become part of the PostScript language until Level 2.

CIE is the *Commission Internationale de l'Eclairage*—the organization that developed this color specification standard. Use this color space to specify colors in a manner related to visual perception rather than to specific traits of output devices. See *CIE Color Specification* on pages 504–512 for more information.

And finally, the separation color space. During traditional printing each process color is printed on a separate plate. These plates are known as *separations*. PostScript Level 2 separation color spaces allow you to create paths and apply tint to one color plate or any combination of plates. Read *Separations* on pages 512–517.

Ensuing sections discuss these color models in detail, and describes PostScript operators that apply to each color model.

Additive and Subtractive Color

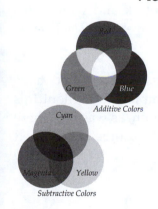

Additive Colors

Subtractive Colors

Additive (RGB) and subtractive (CMYK) color models—see color plate XI.

To fully understand color models you need to understand the difference between additive and subtractive color models. The scenario where different colors are added together to create new colors is known as *additive color mixing*. A second scheme, called *subtractive color mixing*, applies to the scenario where light is subtracted or absorbed to create new colors.

The additive color scheme comes into play when your eye looks directly at light emitted from its source, not at light that is reflected off an object. In the world of additive colors, red, green, and blue are the primary colors. Primary colors are those colors from which all other colors can be derived. Red, green, and blue phosphors in a computer monitor enable us to create a large range of colors (but not all visible colors). Light is added from each of the three sources in varying amounts to produce the desired color. Since light is being added together to produce a desired color, this color scheme is called additive. When all colors are added together in the additive model the result is white.

The subtractive color scheme comes into play when the eye sees light reflected off an object. The object absorbs some light waves and reflects others. The color you see is that of the reflected light waves. The primary colors of subtractive color mixing are cyan, magenta, and yellow, each of which are combinations of the primary colors of additive color mixing. Cyan contains both blue and green, so cyan paint reflects blue and green light, and absorbs red light. Thus, you see a blend of blue and green—cyan. This process subtracted out red light—thus the name *subtractive* color mixing. Although subtractive color models are primarily used for printing or painting, think of subtractive color mixing in terms of light absorption rather than ink mixing.

Gray Color Model

Many devices can display or print only black and white images. If your printer or display device can't handle color, PostScript simulates colors using gray tones. So you may want to specify your "colors" in gray tones to start with. Depending on the device, some grays can be directly displayed on the screen or paper, but more likely will be simulated using patterns of black and white. This simulation of grays is called *halftoning* and is covered in *Halftones* at the end of this chapter.

To specify colors in the gray spectrum use **setgray**. You have already seen **setgray** in action in many examples throughout this book. You can use grays to give an image depth, as was done here with this pyramid. You can imagine a "light source" positioned somewhere off to the right of the pyramid.

*Gray scale pyramid drawn using **setgray**.*

```
%!PS
/inch { 72 mul } def                % define inch procedure
4.0 inch 10.0 inch moveto 1.0 inch 2.0 inch lineto
5.5 inch 1.5 inch lineto closepath
gsave 0.333 setgray fill            % current gray = 33 percent white
grestore 0.0 setgray stroke         % current gray = black
4.0 inch 10.0 inch moveto 7.5 inch 3.0 inch lineto
5.5 inch 1.5 inch lineto closepath
gsave 0.667 setgray fill            % current gray = 66 percent white
grestore 0.0 setgray stroke         % current gray = black
showpage                            % display page
```

Use **setgray** to specify a shade of gray as the current color. **setgray**'s general syntax is

percent_white `setgray`

Operand stack before call to **setgray**.

where *percent_white* indicates the percentage of white found in the resultant gray. A value of 0.0 is black, and a value of 1.0 is white.

In the example, shades of gray are used to give the image a three-dimensional feel. **0.333 setgray** means set the current color to 33 percent gray, which could be more black than white or vice versa, depending on your viewpoint. So, remember the operand to **setgray** specifies the percent white found in the result. Therefore, **0.333 setgray** is 33 percent white—a relatively dark gray.

Many people think the PostScript gray model is "backwards." A graphic artist will tell you 70 percent gray is darker than 30 percent gray. However, the PostScript model is consistent with color models where 0.0 (no color) is black and 1.0 (all color) is white, and is also consistent with the model used in image processing.

Gray Device Space

Unfortunately, **setgray** isn't the entire story. In PostScript Level 1, you always worked directly with color models using operators such as **setgray**. Now color models are better understood and PostScript Level 2 redefined color in the PostScript interpreter. Color models are abstract notions of concrete *device spaces*. The underlying device space mechanism is now accessible to PostScript programs. You can choose to work at the lower level of the PostScript device space, or you can work at the abstract level of color models. Specifying colors in PostScript Level 2 actually requires two steps:

❑ specify the color space with **setcolorspace**, and, then,

❑ specify the current color within that color space with **setcolor**

In PostScript Level 2 **setgray** is a "convenience" operator taking care of both steps for you, where in PostScript Level 1 it was the only way to set the current gray. Let's rewrite the pyramid example using **setcolorspace** and **setcolor** instead of **setgray**.

Gray scale pyramid drawn using **setcolorspace**.

```
%!PS
/inch { 72 mul } def                % define inch procedure
4.0 inch 10.0 inch moveto 1.0 inch 2.0 inch lineto
5.5 inch 1.5 inch lineto closepath
/DeviceGray setcolorspace           % set color space
gsave 0.333 setcolor fill           % current gray = 33 percent white
grestore 0.0 setcolor stroke        % current gray = black
4.0 inch 10.0 inch moveto 7.5 inch 3.0 inch lineto
5.5 inch 1.5 inch lineto closepath
gsave 0.667 setcolor fill           % current gray = 66 percent white
grestore 0.0 setcolor stroke        % current gray = black
showpage                            % display page
```

Notice you only need set the color space once. The color space is installed from the time **setcolorspace** is called until you change it again. There are two forms of **setcolorspace**. The preceding example uses the simple form of **setcolorspace**, which is

color space **setcolorspace**

Operand stack before call to **setcolorspace**.

where *color space* is the name of the device space. In the example, the color space is set to **/DeviceGray**—the one of three available device color spaces in PostScript Level 2. The other two device spaces are **/DeviceCMYK**, for use with the CMYK color model, and **/DeviceRGB**, used with both RGB and HSB.

The number of operands to **setcolor** vary depending on the current color space and are interpreted according to that color space. In the example, the color space is **/DeviceGray**, so **setcolor** requires one operand—the gray component of the color—the same operand required by **setgray**. When the color space is set to **/DeviceGray**, the value of the single operand passed to **setcolor** must be a floating point number between 0.0 (black) and 1.0 (white). As with **setgray**, the number represents the percentage of white in the color.

gray `setcolor`

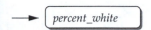

Operand stack before call to **setcolor** *with* **/Devi-ceGray**.

There is no real reason to specify colors using **setcolorspace** and **setcolor**. Deal directly with color models using the shorthand operators and leave details of the output device to the interpreter.

RGB Color Model

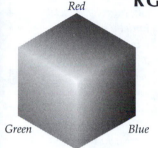

Red

Green   *Blue*

The RGB *color cube.*

The RGB model is based on additive color mixing. Using the RGB color model, new colors are specified by adding colors from a three-color palette of red, green, and blue. A variety of visible colors can be created with blends of different quantities of the three primary colors. Notice we're careful to say a variety of visible colors—RGB cannot produce the full visible spectrum. We'll get to that a bit later. You can visualize the RGB color model as a "color cube" whose edges are parallel to the red, green, and blue "axes" with black at one corner and white at the opposite corner. Refer to color plate IV for the color version of the RGB color cube.

RGB relates directly to physical capabilities of computer screens. Color screens typically have three light guns—one each of red, green, and blue. Specifying colors in the RGB color model tells the computer screen exactly which guns to turn on and the intensity at which to turn them on. Color models like RGB whose primaries correspond to inks or phosphors of physical devices are called *Device Color Models* or *Device Color Spaces*.

To specify individual colors in RGB, use **setrgbcolor**. The logo in the next picture contains several colored bands over which white initials are superimposed. The colors in the logo were set using the RGB color model. Here's the PostScript program to implement the colorful logo.

See color plate XIII.

```
%!PS
/inch { 72 mul } def                          % define inch procedure
/Colors [ [ 1.0 0.0 0.0 ]                      % current color = red
    [ 1.0 0.5 0.0 ]                            % current color = orange
    [ 1.0 1.0 0.0 ]                            % current color = yellow
    [ 0.0 1.0 0.0 ]                            % current color = green
    [ 0.0 0.0 1.0 ]                            % current color = blue
    [ 0.5 0.0 1.0 ]                            % current color = indigo
    [ 0.5 0.0 0.5 ] ] def                      % current color = violet
/YPos 1.5 inch def                             % initial y position
/YInc 1.2 inch def                             % y increment
0 1 6 {                                         % draw 7 rectangles
    Colors exch get                           % get color values from array
    aload pop setrgbcolor                      % set current color
    0.5 inch YPos                             % lower-left corner
    7.5 inch 1.0 inch DrawRect fill           % fill rectangle
    /YPos YPos YInc add def                    % increment y
} for
/Palatino-Roman findfont                       % choose font
4.0 inch scalefont setfont
1.0 1.0 1.0 setrgbcolor                         % set color to white
2.15 inch 0.15 inch moveto                      % position current point
45 rotate (ELM) show                            % rotate and show characters
showpage                                         % display page
```

This program calls procedure **DrawRect**, which requires four arguments—the *x* and *y* position of the lower-left corner of the rectangle, and the width and height of the rectangle. Here's the procedure definition for **DrawRect**. If you have a Level 2 device, you can replace **DrawRect fill** with **rectfill**.

```
/DrawRect {                                    % stack = x y width height
    4 2 roll moveto                           % move to x, y
    1 index 0 rlineto                          % bottom edge
    0 exch rlineto                             % right edge
    neg 0 rlineto                              % top edge
    closepath                                  % close rectangle
} def
```

Let's examine the use of **setrgbcolor** in this program. Ignore the PostScript instructions immediately preceding the call to **setrgbcolor** for now. Those instructions extract three values from the **Colors** array—the red, blue, and green operands for **setrgbcolor**. The general syntax of **setrgbcolor** is

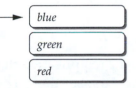

Operand stack before call to **setrgbcolor**.

```
red  green  blue  setrgbcolor
```

where *red*, *green*, and *blue* are the amounts of red, green, and blue light contributing to the resulting color. By varying the amounts of red, green, and blue you can change the resultant color. Operands to **setrgbcolor** must be in the range from 0.0 to 1.0, where 0.0 is no contribution to the resulting color, and 1.0 is 100 percent contribution.

Let's examine a couple of the color combinations from the example and find out what the values of the operands actually mean. The red band—the lowest one appearing in the logo—was created with these RGB values and this **DrawRect** instruction:

```
1.0 0.0 0.0 setrgbcolor
0.5 inch YPos 7.5 inch 1.0 inch DrawRect fill
```

The first operand to **setrgbcolor** represents red. The value 1.0 indicates that red appears in the resultant color at maximum intensity. The other two operands, green and blue, are 0.0 and contribute no color to the resultant color. The result is pure red at full intensity. These values establish the color for the orange band:

```
1.0 0.5 0.0 setrgbcolor
0.5 inch YPos 7.5 inch 1.0 inch DrawRect fill
```

Red is present at full intensity, green at half intensity, and blue is not present at all—producing orange. Examine the other colors used in the example and make sure you understand the mixtures. At the end of the logo example letters in white are superimposed over the colored bands, the current color is set to white with the following instruction:

```
1.0 1.0 1.0 setrgbcolor
```

Notice white consists of all colors at their maximum intensity. This is because the RGB color model is an additive model. This PostScript instruction

```
0.0 0.0 0.0 setrgbcolor
```

produces black, because the absence of color produces black.

RGB Device Space

As with the gray color model, PostScript Level 2 requires two steps to set the current color in the graphics state. First set the current color space with **setcolorspace**, then set the current color within that space with **setcolor**. Let's rewrite the logo example using **setcolorspace** and **setcolor** instead of **setrgbcolor**. Modifications are highlighted so that you can locate them more easily.

```
%!PS
/inch { 72 mul } def                         %   define inch procedure
/DeviceRGB setcolorspace                     %   set color model
/Colors [ { 1.0 0.0 0.0 }                    %   current color = red
  { 1.0 0.5 0.0 }        { 1.0 1.0 0.0 } %   orange / yellow
  { 0.0 1.0 0.0 }        { 0.0 0.0 1.0 } %   green / blue
  { 0.5 0.0 1.0 }        { 0.5 0.0 0.5 } %   indigo / violet
] def
/YPos 1.5 inch def                           %   initial y position
/YInc 1.2 inch def                           %   y increment
0 1 6 {                                       %   draw 7 rectangles
  Colors exch get                            %   get color values from array
  exec setcolor                              %   set current color
  0.5 inch YPos                              %   lower-left corner
  7.5 inch 1.0 inch DrawRect fill            %   fill rectangle
  /YPos YPos YInc add def                    %   increment y
} for
/Palatino-Roman findfont                     %   choose font
4 inch scalefont setfont
1.0 1.0 1.0 setcolor                          %   set color to white
2.15 inch 0.15 inch moveto                   %   position current point
45 rotate (ELM) show                         %   rotate and show characters
showpage                                     %   display page
```

In the example, the current color space is set to **/DeviceRGB**—the name of the device space in PostScript Level 2 for setting colors using red, green, and blue. **/DeviceRGB** is also used with HSB.

When the color space is **/DeviceRGB**, **setcolor** requires three operands—the red, green, and blue components of the color. These are the same operands required by **setrgbcolor**. The syntax of **setcolor** when **/DeviceRGB** is the current color space is:

red   green   blue `setcolor`

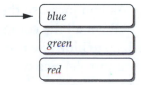

Operand stack before call to **setcolor** *with* **/DeviceRGB**.

There is no real reason to specify colors using **setcolorspace** and **setcolor**. Deal directly with color models using the shorthand operators and leave details of the output device to the interpreter.

HSB Color Model

Another highly useful color model is the HSB color model. HSB specifies colors using hue, saturation, and brightness components. The HSB color model is one of a number of closely related "subjective" color models—the others are Hue-Saturation-Value and Hue-Lightness-Saturation. These are subtly different from HSB, but not enough to worry about here. HSB is subjective because it provides a more natural way to specify colors corresponding to descriptions like "pale bluish-green," not because it is any less precise than specifying a color in RGB.

Typically, people facile with computers prefer the RGB color model because it is closely related to the output device. Graphic artists prefer the HSB color model because, after the initial strain of memorizing numbers for useful colors, you can easily lighten a color, make it lighter or more intense with the saturation and brightness components.

The HSB color cone.

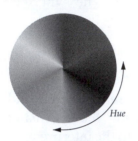

Hue

Brightness

Saturation

As mentioned previously, you can visualize the RGB color model as a "color cube." By contrast, a popular way to visualize the HSB color model is as a cone. Black is at the apex, white is at the center of the base and the primary colors are arranged around the circumference of the base. See color plate VI for the color version of the HSB color cone.

Hue is measured around the circumference of the cone and tells you the dominant color (sometimes called tone). Hues are identified by name, such as purple, orange, or blue. As you increase the hue component of a color from 0.0 to 1.0 you will get all the colors of the rainbow. PostScript rainbows start at red, go to blue like normal rainbows, and then go back to red again via purple! See color plate VII for the color version of the hue diagram.

Brightness is measured along the vertical axis of the cone. Think of brightness as related to the shade of the color. Brightness values near 0.0 correspond to the darkest shades, and values near 1.0 correspond to the lightest shades. Changing the brightness component allows you to lighten or darken a color without affecting the perceived tint. See color plate X for the color version of the brightness diagram.

Saturation is how far from the central axis of the cone toward the surface you will find a color. Saturation corresponds to the intensity or purity of the color. Low values of saturation, near the axis, give very pale colors, while high values give more intense colors. Decreasing saturation is like adding more water when painting with watercolors. Increasing saturation is like adding more paint. See color plate IX for the color version of the Saturation diagram.

Visualizing HSB as a cone shows one important feature of the model; if the brightness component is zero, you get black regardless of the hue and saturation components. In fact, as you decrease brightness, you will find that varying the saturation has less effect on the quality of the color you see, because you tend to perceive darker shades as more muted even if they are saturated (you see brown instead of yellow, and so on).

Let's borrow an example from page 320 in Chapter 8 and add colors using the HSB color model. Only part of the PostScript program is listed here—the procedure and constant definitions are listed in Chapter 8.

Blue Z clipped through elliptical sheet—see color plate XIV.

```
%!PS
/inch { 72 mul } def                    %  define inch procedure
/ZapfChancery-MediumItalic findfont
CharacterScale scalefont setfont        %  choose font
0.667 1.0 1.0 sethsbcolor                %  current color = blue
CharacterOrigin moveto (Z) show
newpath EllipseCenter EllipseRotation
EllipseWidth EllipseHeight
0 360 EllipticalArc
0.333 0.5 1.0 sethsbcolor fill          %  current color = light green
newpath gsave
    EllipseCenter EllipseRotation
    EllipseWidth EllipseHeight
    90 270 EllipticalArc
    clip newpath
    0.667 1.0 1.0 sethsbcolor           %  current color = blue
    CharacterOrigin moveto (Z) show
grestore
newpath gsave
    EllipseCenter EllipseRotation
    EllipseWidth EllipseHeight
    270 90 EllipticalArc
    clip newpath
    0.45 1.0 1.0 sethsbcolor            %  current color = bluish green
    CharacterOrigin moveto (Z) show
grestore
showpage                                %  display page
```

Refer to color plate XIV for the full-color picture of this example. The general syntax of **sethsbcolor** is

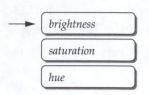

Operand stack before call to **sethsbcolor**.

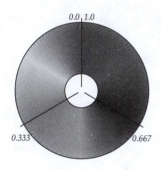

See color plate VII.

hue saturation brightness `sethsbcolor`

where *hue*, *saturation*, and *brightness* are the hue, saturation and brightness components of the resultant color. Each component must be in the range of 0.0 to 1.0. Let's dissect a couple of the **sethsbcolor** instructions in the listing to see what the values mean for each component. The first color used in the example is blue.

```
0.667 1.0 1.0 sethsbcolor
```

The first operand to **sethsbcolor** is the hue component. The picture illustrates color assignments for hue. Colors are assigned a hue value between 0.0 and 1.0, as follows: 0.0 is red, 0.333 (one third) is green, 0.667 (two thirds) is blue, and 1.0 is back to red. When placed in a circle, 0.0 and 1.0 end up being next to each other, so you can understand why both 0.0 and 1.0 are red. Colors halfway between these four values (0.167 [one sixth], 0.5, and 0.833 [five sixths]) are mixtures of the adjacent primary colors. For example, at 0.5 you find *cyan*—the color created by mixing equal amounts of green and blue. HSB is directly related to RGB, as the hue is based on mixing red, green, and blue. Therefore, HSB is also an additive color model.

In the example, the next color used is light green. Light green is created by reducing the saturation of pure green. In the example, light green is half saturated and is coded as follows:

```
0.333 0.5 1.0 sethsbcolor
```

Saturation indicates the "pureness" of the color specified with hue. A saturation of 0.0 yields white, and a saturation of 1.0 yields the purest rendition of the hue the device can render. Brightness is the brightness of the color specified by the hue and saturation. A brightness of 0.0 yields black, and a brightness of 1.0 yields the brightest possible rendition of that color. Experimenting with saturation and brightness values in the previous example will give you a good feel for the effects of those components.

HSB Device Space

Because HSB is just another way of thinking about RGB, in PostScript Level 2 the HSB color model is specified within the **/DeviceRGB** color space. **sethsbcolor** is the only PostScript operator to specify the current color using the HSB color model. You may not use a combination of **setcolorspace** and **setcolor** while working with the HSB color model. For example, if you tried

```
/DeviceRGB setcolorspace
hue  saturation  brightness  setcolor
```

you won't get the results you expected. **setcolor** interprets its operands according to the device space. Since HSB and RGB share a color space, **setcolor** will interpret hue as the red component, saturation as the green, and brightness as the blue.

CMYK Color Model

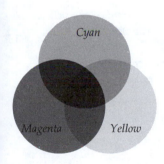

See color plate V.

The CMYK color model is, in part, the color model you learned in primary school, with either a plastic color wheel or finger paints. As a child you learned the three primary colors—blue, red, and yellow. Well, your first-grade teacher lied to you; they are really cyan, magenta, and yellow. Perhaps primary school teachers think children can't handle colors with strange names like magenta. PostScript Level 2 added the CMYK color model to its repertoire.

You will also notice that black has become one of the primary "colors." Theoretically, you can mix equal quantities of cyan, magenta, and yellow to create black. However, nature isn't so cooperative, and what you really get is muddy brown. Black was added to the color model to compensate. CMYK is typically used for printing or painting applications. When you print your color PostScript image and take your separations to a printing house, you'll find that just about every printer uses a CMYK color model. The important thing about the CMYK color model is that it is a subtractive color model, unlike RGB and HSB, which are additive color models. CMYK is subtractive because the semi-transparent printing inks absorb light instead of generating light.

In honor of the Olympics, the next example shows you how to draw the interlinked Olympic rings using the CMYK color model to set the current color. Let's look at the first half of the program.

First half of Olympic circles.

```
%!PS
/inch { 72 mul } def                    %   define inch procedure
0.25 inch setlinewidth
       %   draw upper left portion of top rings from right to left
       %   draw upper right portion of bottom rings from right to left
newpath
0.0 1.0 1.0 0.0 setcmykcolor            %   current color = red
6.5 inch 5.5 inch 1.0 inch 45 225 arc stroke
newpath
1.0 0.0 1.0 0.0 setcmykcolor            %   current color = green
5.25 inch 4.5 inch 1.0 inch -45 135 arc stroke
newpath
0.0 0.0 0.0 1.0 setcmykcolor            %   current color = black
4.0 inch 5.5 inch 1.0 inch 45 225 arc stroke
newpath
0.0 0.0 1.0 0.0 setcmykcolor            %   current color = yellow
2.75 inch 4.5 inch 1.0 inch -45 135 arc stroke
newpath
1.0 1.0 0.0 0.0 setcmykcolor            %   current color = blue
1.5 inch 5.5 inch 1.0 inch 45 225 arc stroke
```

The syntax of **setcmykcolor** is

cyan magenta yellow black `setcmykcolor`

Operand stack before call to
setcmykcolor.

where *cyan*, *magenta*, *yellow*, and *black* are the cyan, magenta, yellow, and black components of the resultant color. Each operand is a value from 0.0 to 1.0 and indicates the amount of ink present. 0.0 means no ink and the color absorbs no light. 1.0 indicates maximum ink and the color absorbs all the light it can. The first color created in the example is red. Red is created from equal mixtures of yellow and magenta. In the example, the maximum amount of both colors is used. Thus to create red in the CMYK color model, the PostScript instruction is

```
0.0 1.0 1.0 0.0 setcmykcolor
```

Neither cyan nor black contributes to the color red. Examine the other **setcmykcolor** instructions in the example, and make sure you understand the mixtures. Oh yes—here's the second half of the program to complete the Olympic circles. The margin picture shows the final result of both halves of the program.

Second half of Olympic circles. See color plate XII.

```
%    draw lower-right portion of top rings from left to right
%    draw lower-left portion of bottom rings from left to right
newpath
1.0 1.0 0.0 0.0 setcmykcolor            %   current color = blue
1.5 inch 5.5 inch 1.0 inch 225 45 arc stroke
newpath
0.0 0.0 1.0 0.0 setcmykcolor            %   current color = yellow
2.75 inch 4.5 inch 1.0 inch 135 -45 arc stroke
newpath
0.0 0.0 0.0 1.0 setcmykcolor            %   current color = black
4.0 inch 5.5 inch 1.0 inch 225 45 arc stroke
newpath
1.0 0.0 1.0 0.0 setcmykcolor            %   current color = green
5.25 inch 4.5 inch 1.0 inch 135 -45 arc stroke
newpath
0.0 1.0 1.0 0.0 setcmykcolor            %   current color = red
6.5 inch 5.5 inch 1.0 inch 225 45 arc stroke
showpage                                %   display page
```

CMYK Device Space

/DeviceCMYK is the PostScript Level 2 device that corresponds to this color model. Let's rewrite the Olympic rings using **setcolorspace** and **setcolor** to specify the colors. When you use **setcolor** with **/DeviceRGB**, **setcolor** requires three operands. But now the color space is set to **/DeviceCMYK** and **setcolor** requires four operands—the same operands required by **setcmykcolor**. As with **setcmykcolor** the values passed to **setcolor** are floating point values from 0.0 to 1.0. These values indicate the amount of ink for each color component—cyan, magenta, yellow, and black—where

0.0 is no ink (absorbs no light) and 1.0 is maximum ink (absorbs all the light that it can).

```
%!PS
/inch { 72 mul } def                      %  define inch procedure
0.25 inch setlinewidth
/DeviceCMYK setcolorspace                  %  set color space
    %  draw upper left portion of top rings from right to left
    %  draw upper right portion of bottom rings from right to left
newpath
0.0 1.0 1.0 0.0 setcolor                   %  current color = red
6.5 inch 5.5 inch 1.0 inch 45 225 arc stroke
newpath
1.0 0.0 1.0 0.0 setcolor                   %  current color = green
5.25 inch 4.5 inch 1.0 inch -45 135 arc stroke
newpath
0.0 0.0 0.0 1.0 setcolor                   %  current color = black
4 inch 5.5 inch 1.0 inch 45 225 arc stroke
newpath
0.0 0.0 1.0 0.0 setcolor                   %  current color = yellow
2.75 inch 4.5 inch 1.0 inch -45 135 arc stroke
newpath
1.0 1.0 0.0 0.0 setcolor                   %  current color = blue
1.5 inch 5.5 inch 1.0 inch 45 225 arc stroke
    %  draw lower-right portion of top rings from left to right
    %  draw lower-left portion of bottom rings from left to right
newpath
1.0 1.0 0.0 0.0 setcolor                   %  current color = blue
1.5 inch 5.5 inch 1.0 inch 225 45 arc stroke
newpath
0.0 0.0 1.0 0.0 setcolor                   %  current color = yellow
2.75 inch 4.5 inch 1.0 inch 135 -45 arc stroke
newpath
0.0 0.0 0.0 1.0 setcolor                   %  current color = black
4.0 inch 5.5 inch 1.0 inch 225 45 arc stroke
newpath
1.0 0.0 1.0 0.0 setcolor                   %  current color = green
5.25 inch 4.5 inch 1.0 inch 135 -45 arc stroke
newpath
0.0 1.0 1.0 0.0 setcolor                   %  current color = red
6.5 inch 5.5 inch 1.0 inch 225 45 arc stroke
showpage                                   %  display page
```

Again, you are encouraged to use the color model operators to enforce abstraction away from physical devices.

Converting Between Device Color Spaces

Once you specify the current color using a device color model, you can use any of several different PostScript operators to request the current color from the PostScript interpreter. By specifying color in one device color space, and retrieving it in another, you convert between device color spaces. Converting between CIE color spaces is more complicated and is covered in the *PostScript Language Reference Manual*, Second Edition. Five PostScript operators return the current color:

❑ **currentcolor** returns the current color specified in the current color space

❑ **currentrgbcolor** returns the current color specified in the RGB color model

❑ **currenthsbcolor** returns the current color specified in HSB

❑ **currentcmykcolor** returns the current color specified in the CMYK color model

❑ **currentgray** returns the current color specified in gray scale

Suppose you set the current color to red using the RGB color model as shown here:

```
1.0 0.0 0.0 setrgbcolor
```

You can request the current color with any of the above operators regardless of the device space used to specify the color. The PostScript interpreter converts the color from the current color space to the requested color space—results are different depending on the operator you use. For example, suppose you asked for the current color using

```
currentcmykcolor
```

after using the **setrgbcolor** instruction just previous.

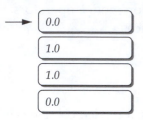

Operand stack after call to **currentcmykcolor**.

The results are placed on the stack as shown in the picture. The topmost element is the black component, the second element is the yellow component, and so on to the bottom of the stack.

The conversions performed by the interpreter vary depending on the participating color spaces and are discussed in excruciating detail in the *PostScript Language Reference Manual*, Second Edition.

CIE Color Specification

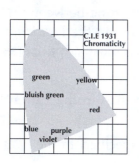

Color chromaticity.

PostScript Level 2 introduced support for CIE color specification. CIE is an acronym for *Commission Internationale de l'Eclairage*—an international standards body for color. In 1931, the Commission introduced a new method for specifying color. Rather than specifying colors relative to the capabilities of specific devices such as monitors or printing presses, the CIE came up with a scheme related to human color perception.

The human eye has three different kinds of color-sensitive receptors (in addition to a set that responds only to brightness). These are sensitive to light in three different areas of the spectrum. The three receptors are most sensitive to red, green, and blue light. Unfortunately, the responses are "smeared out"—for example, the red receptors also respond quite well to green.[†]

This new color model works well until you try to match an arbitrary real-world color on a computer monitor. You can try varying amounts of red, green, and blue until colors match. Unfortunately, because of the smearing of your eyes' sensitivity to color, you will find many natural colors you can't match. The colors may appear to be the right tint, but perhaps too bright, and you'll want to add a negative amount of red, for example. These colors just can't be displayed on a monitor—they're said to be outside the monitor's *color gamut*. No matter how you choose the three primary colors for your monitor, you can't display certain colors.

---

† which explains why the most common form of color blindness is the inability to distinguish red and green—the chemicals in red and green receptors are very similar.

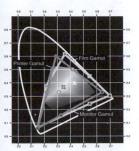

Device gamuts. See plate XV for the color version.

As the picture illustrates, color film can reproduce more colors than a monitor, but still not as many as you can see. Printers can reproduce some colors monitors cannot reproduce, and monitors can reproduce some colors printers cannot reproduce.

In 1931, the CIE introduced a color space based on three hypothetical primaries, X, Y, and Z, which are to some extent based on spectral responses of the three color receptors in your eyes. These primaries don't correspond to any physical colors you can generate with lights or phosphors, but they have a very useful property that lets you describe any color you can see (and many more besides) with positive values for all three. The CIE specified that the Y coordinate should encode the brightness of the image and X and Z encode the color information. Pure white has the XYZ coordinates (1.0, 1.0, 1.0).[†]

Transforming a color specification from the CIE primaries to a different set of primaries is a simple linear transformation and requires just a few multiplications and additions. You can even compensate for the fact that different monitor manufacturers use slightly different phosphors, which emit slightly different colors. For this reason, XYZ is often called a device-independent color space, since the component values of a particular color are unambiguous. The difficult bits happen when you transform a color from XYZ to RGB and discover that the color you get cannot be displayed on your monitor or printer. PostScript provides a mechanism for dealing with this, in the form of **setcolorrendering**. Fortunately, you don't have to worry about this operator—your printer's or monitor's manufacturer handles the situation.

Incidentally, you'd only use CIE based colors when writing applications. Specifying colors this way is sufficiently non-intuitive, compared to say RGB, that you're unlikely to ever do it by hand.

---

† This is, in fact, the sort of white found only in soap powder advertisements, and most colors you think of as white (especially on your computer monitor) actually have a reddish or bluish tint.

CIE Based Color Spaces

PostScript Level 2 added support for color based on CIE's XYZ color space. This section shows you the practicalities of setting up a CIE based color space and specifying colors in that space.

As with other PostScript color spaces, the first thing you must do is set the color space in the graphics state with **setcolorspace**. You specify a new CIE based color space (whose primaries are named arbitrarily A, B, and C) as a two-stage transformation of CIE's XYZ color space. In this way, PostScript lumps together support for a number of different but related color spaces under the single CIEBasedABC color space.[†] The *PostScript Language Reference Manual*, Second Edition, lists a number of possible standard spaces supported by **CIEBasedABC**—original XYZ, L*a*b*, YIQ, and YUV. The last two spaces are important for video applications, as they are the color spaces used for NTSC and PAL television signals, respectively. The relationship between these color spaces and CIE's XYZ color space is well-defined and out of the scope of this chapter. Tabular data defining the color-matching functions for CIE's XYZ are in a number of texts including *Color Science: Concepts and Methods, Quantitative Data and Formulae*, published by John Wiley & Sons.

You should note there are some device-independent color spaces that cannot be mapped into **CIEBasedABC**. Two you might come across are L*u*v*, (derived from another CIE-created standard), and TekHVC, a new standard created by Tektronix and supported by various other manufacturers as well as the MIT X Consortium.

So, how does PostScript Level 2 support all these different color spaces? When you set **CIEBasedABC** color space, you pass a dictionary to **setcolorspace**, which describes how to map from your color space to XYZ color space. This mapping is defined by two *warp functions* and two matrix multiplications. The following

---

† There is another space, **CIEBasedA**, for monochrome applications. This bears the same relationship to **CIEBasedABC** as to **DeviceGray** does **DeviceRGB**, so we will not discuss it further here.

illustrations show how A is mapped to X, B is mapped to Y, and C is mapped to Z.

$$A \longrightarrow \boxed{} \longrightarrow L_a\ L_b\ L_c \longrightarrow \boxed{} \longrightarrow X_a\ X_b\ X_c \longrightarrow X$$

$$B \longrightarrow \boxed{} \longrightarrow M_a\ M_b\ M_c \longrightarrow \boxed{} \longrightarrow Y_a\ Y_b\ Y_c \longrightarrow Y$$

$$C \longrightarrow \boxed{} \longrightarrow N_a\ N_b\ N_c \longrightarrow \boxed{} \longrightarrow Z_a\ Z_b\ Z_c \longrightarrow Z$$

The transformation is carried out in two identical stages, which allows you to map to an intermediate color space (represented by components L, M, and N) before mapping to XYZ. The letters A, B, C, L, M, and N do not have any special significance—they simply denote components in your own color spaces. Each stage of the transformation consists of a warping stage, which allows you to apply a non-linear transformation to each component of the stage individually, followed by a linear transformation that transforms from one set of components to another.

Let's see a concrete example—a Rubik's Cube™—and let's use a simple XYZ-based color space. First, you have to define a dictionary with the data for the color space components:

```
%!PS
/CIEColors 3 dict def                              %   color space dictionary
CIEColors begin                                    %   make current
  /WhitePoint [0.981 1 1.184 ] def                 %   White point
  /RangeABC   [0 0.981 0 1 0 1.184 ] def           %   Primary Range
  /RangeLMN   [0 0.981 0 1 0 1.184 ] def           %   Intermediate Range
end                                                %   end dictionary
```

What do the entries in the dictionary mean? The most important is **WhitePoint**. You must specify a white point every time you set a **CIE** based color space. You may also set a black point, but this is less important for most applications. The white point gives the XYZ coordinates of the color that represents white in the source image. Normally, you would get the XYZ coordinates for your colors from some kind of color database or color service—for example, from the Pantone® color matching system.

Choosing the white point.

In real life you choose the white point appropriate to your application. Normally, the white point is the brightest white you expect to appear. However, some finesse may be appropriate. For example, if you have a picture that includes "glows" or "highlights," you may find these have a brightness greater than the "maximum" of 1.0. You have two alternatives—leave the white point alone, in which case the glows will appear as saturated highlights—or increase the brightness of the white point. This will have the effect of darkening the overall picture, reproducing the glows correctly as "whiter than white."

Choosing the black point.

The black point, if you supply it, gives the XYZ coordinates of the darkest color in the picture. If you don't give a value, the default of (0.0 0.0 0.0) is usually good enough. If you do adjust the white point or the black point to enhance a particular picture, you must use consistent values for all the pictures in the same job.

The *PostScript Language Reference Manual*, Second Edition, talks about adjusting the black and white points in the color rendering dictionary. The color rendering dictionary should not normally be changed, so adjusting the black and white points there is not a good idea.

Choosing the **RangeABC** and **RangeLMN** entries.

The **RangeABC** and **RangeLMN** entries set the minimum and maximum allowed values for color components. Values outside these ranges are clamped to the minimum or maximum value. This is often called color "clipping." The component values should not be clipped until the later stages of color mapping and the color cannot be reproduced on the monitor or printer. In the example **RangeABC** runs from (0.0 0.0 0.0) to the white point.

Normally, you want to clip colors as late in the transformation process as possible (ideally immediately before the final transformation to RGB or CMYK). So why have the intermediate range entries at all? The intermediate ranges enable PostScript to do a better job. Converting a color is a potentially expensive operation, if you blindly carry out all the calculations. The usual trick is simply to build lots of lookup tables. However, there are two problems with doing this for **CIEBasedABC** colors. First, all device components usually depend on all the XYZ components—the transformation is not *separable*. This means we are not just talking about lookup tables but large 3D matrices. Secondly, the component values are not restricted to the range 0.0 to 1.0, so just building a table that splits the range 0 to 1 into 256 slots is no good either. In order to get reasonable results, PostScript must know the possible ranges of component values at key points in the pipeline.

Now, let's put all this newly specified color space to work drawing an unsolved Rubik's Cube. First, here are some definitions used by the main PostScript program.

```
%!PS
/inch { 72 mul } def            %   define inch procedure
/side 1.33333 inch def          %   edge of small squares
/x_squash { 30 cos } def        %   for isometric projection
/y_shear { 30 sin } def         %   for isometric projection

/square {                       %   stack = side
  0 0 moveto                    %   set current point
  dup 0 rlineto                 %   bottom of square
  dup 0 exch rlineto            %   right side of square
  neg 0 rlineto                 %   top of square
  closepath                     %   finish the shape
} def                           %   define procedure
```

The **/square** procedure is used to draw a side of the cube. On the next page appears **/littleSquare**, the procedure to draw individual squares on the face of the cube.

```
%!PS
/littleSquare {
  [
    /CIEBasedABC
    CIEColors
  ] setcolorspace    %   set color space
  aload pop setcolor            %   set current color
  side square fill              %   fill small square
  side square                   %   small square
  0 setgray                     %   black for outline
  stroke                        %   paint outline
} def
```

It is inside **/littleSquare** that the CIE color is set, once for each little square. This more complicated form of **setcolorspace** in **littleSquare** requires an array operand whose first element is the name of the color space.

array `setcolorspace`

Stack before call to **setcolorspace**.

For CIE-based color spaces this value can be either **/CIEBasedABC** for color applications, or **/CIEBasedA** for monochrome applications. The second element in the array in the example is a color space dictionary. The color space dictionary describes the new color space as it relates to PostScript CIE's XYZ color space.

Finally, here's the procedure to draw a row of squares across the face of the cube.

```
%!PS
/Row {
  gsave                          %   save graphics state
    0 exch side mul translate    %   move to position
    littleSquare                 %   right most square
    side 0 translate             %   move to position
    littleSquare                 %   middle square
    side 0 translate             %   move to position
    littleSquare                 %   left most square
  grestore                       %   restore graphics state
} def
```

On the next page is the main portion of the PostScript program and the CIE color specifications to generate the picture. Each section sandwiched between **gsave** and **grestore** draws one side of the square—first establishing a skewed coordinate system, then drawing three rows of small colored squares. Coordinates specified in each color array **green**, **blue**, and so on, are used as operands to **setcolor** (which is hidden away in **littleSquare**).

```
%!PS
0.10 inch setlinewidth                          %   establish line width
4.25 inch 1 inch translate                      %   translate graphics state

/green   [ 0.149 0.234 0.106 ] def              %   CIE color = green
/orange  [ 0.386 0.311 0.066 ] def              %   CIE color = orange
/yellow  [ 0.614 0.644 0.112 ] def              %   CIE color = yellow
/blue    [ 0.05  0.035 0.183 ] def              %   CIE color = blue
/white   [ 0.981 1     1.184 ] def              %   CIE color = white
/red     [ 0.176 0.102 0.048 ] def              %   CIE color = red

gsave                                           %   right side of cube
   [ x_squash  y_shear  0  1  0  0 ] concat
   orange green green 0 Row                      %   bottom row
   green yellow green 1 Row                      %   middle row
   orange orange blue 2 Row                      %   top row
grestore
gsave                                           %   left side of cube
   [ x_squash neg  y_shear  0  1  0  0 ] concat
   yellow yellow white 0 Row                     %   bottom row
   red white red 1 Row                           %   middle row
   blue yellow orange 2 Row                      %   top row
grestore
gsave                                           %   top side of cube
   0 3 side mul translate
   [ x_squash y_shear x_squash neg y_shear 0  0 ] concat
   blue red red 0 Row                            %   bottom row
   blue orange green 1 Row                        %   middle row
   blue yellow yellow 2 Row                       %   top row
grestore
showpage                                        %   display page
```

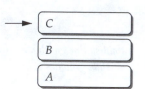

→

C

B

A

Stack before call to **setcolor** *in a* **CIEBasedABC** *color space.*

The syntax of **setcolor** when referring to a color (not monochrome) CIE color space is

    A B C `setcolor`

The particular values in the color arrays come from the XYZ color space. The large horseshoe shape in the color gamut diagram on page 505 shows the plane of XYZ color space where $X + Y + Z = 1$.

Separations

Traditionally, color images are produced with separations. Each primary color or process color is printed on a separate page—a *separation*. During the printing process, all separations were combined onto one page, producing a full color picture. Here's an example you've seen before that uses several colors.

```
%!PS
/inch { 72 mul } def                       %   define inch procedure
/Colors [
   { 1.0 0.0 0.0 }                         %   red
   { 1.0 0.5 0.0 }    { 1.0 1.0 0.0 }      %   orange / yellow
   { 0.0 1.0 0.0 }    { 0.0 0.0 1.0 }      %   green / blue
   { 0.5 0.0 1.0 }    { 0.5 0.0 0.5 }      %   indigo / violet
] def
/YPos 1.5 inch def                         %   initial y position
/YInc 1.2 inch def                         %   y increment
0 1 6 {                                     %   draw 7 rectangles
   Colors exch get exec setrgbcolor        %   set color values from array
   0.5 inch YPos                           %   lower-left corner
   7.5 inch 1.0 inch DrawRect fill         %   fill rectangle
   /YPos YPos YInc add def                 %   increment y
} for
/Palatino-Roman findfont                   %   choose font
4 inch scalefont setfont
1 1 1 setrgbcolor                          %   set color to white
2.15 inch 0.15 inch moveto                 %   position currentpoint
45 rotate (ELM) show                       %   rotate and show characters
showpage                                   %   display page
```

Notice the use of executable arrays to hold the color values and **exec** to get the values onto the operand stack.

Here are the cyan, magenta, and yellow separations for the preceding picture. Black contributes no color to the picture.

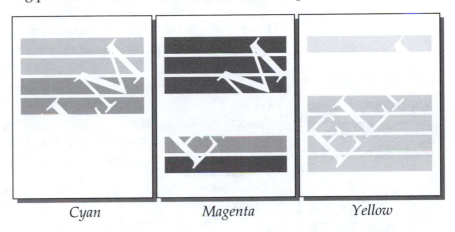

| Cyan | Magenta | Yellow |

When printed together on a single page, the colors from each separation blend where they overlap, creating new colors. Traditionally, creating separations was done by professionals at a color separation house. The advantage to this process was that professionals did the work and had gained much expertise in the area of separating artwork. The disadvantage was that all too often changes had to be made. And, typically, changes made at the last minute were extremely expensive.

With the advent of PostScript, inexpensive scanners, and desktop publishing software, more and more designers are now producing their own separations. In this case, last minute changes to the separations can be made easily and inexpensively. However, the designer must now become an expert at separating artwork. Most PostScript devices don't support separations; all process colors are printed together on a single page. However, the designer can use applications such as Adobe Separator or similar utilities to transform a full color PostScript image into its separations. You can use Adobe Separator to produce separations on any device, not only expensive devices designed for the job.

PostScript Level 2 goes a step further and turns separations into independent color spaces. You can apply tint to any separation without affecting the others or you can paint all of them at once. Now you can create separations within PostScript code without relying on post-processing applications.

This picture is the magenta separation for the ELM logo example. Here's the PostScript code used to generate the separation.

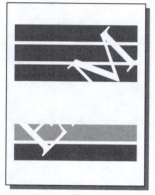

Magenta separation for color logo.

```
%!PS
/inch { 72 mul } def                          %   define inch procedure
/Colors [ 1.0 0.5 0.0 0.0 1.0 1.0 1.0 ] def
[
  /Separation                                 %   name of color space
  (Magenta)                                   %   name of separation
  /DeviceCMYK                                 %   alternate color space
  { 0.0 exch 0.0 0.0 }                        %   transformation to alternate
] setcolorspace                               %   set color space
/YPos 1.5 inch def                            %   initial y position
/YInc 1.2 inch def                            %   y increment
0 1 6 {                                       %   draw 7 rectangles
  Colors exch get setcolor                    %   set current color
  0.5 inch YPos                               %   lower-left corner
  7.5 inch 1.0 inch DrawRect fill             %   fill rectangle
  /YPos YPos YInc add def                     %   increment y
} for
/Palatino-Roman findfont                      %   choose font
4 inch scalefont setfont
1 1 1 setrgbcolor                             %   set color to white
2.15 inch 1.15 inch moveto                    %   set current point
45 rotate (ELM) show                          %   rotate and show characters
showpage                                      %   display page
```

The **Colors** array contains seven values; one tint for each rectangle. These values are passed to **setcolor**. A value of 0.0 indicates no color. A value of 1.0 indicates pure color. The next instruction in the program is the interesting part.

```
[
    /Separation                   %   name of color space
    (Magenta)                     %   name of separation
    /DeviceCMYK                   %   alternate color space
    { 0.0 exch 0.0 0.0 }          %   transformation to alternate color space
] setcolorspace                   %   set color space
```

This new form of **setcolorspace** requires an array with four elements and sets the current color space to the separation indicated. Let's look at each value of the array.

The first value is always **/Separation** when specifying a separation color space. The second value is the name of the separation. For convenience, the PostScript interpreter assigns the names **Cyan**, **Magenta**, **Yellow**, and **Black** to correspond to the primary colors of the CMYK color model. The PostScript interpreter also assigns **Red**, **Green**, and **Blue** to correspond to the primary colors of the RGB color model. If you specify **All**, subsequent painting operators will apply tints to all separations produced by the device. If you specify **None**, tint will be applied to no separation.

The third element of the array operand to **setcolorspace** indicates the *alternative color space* to the separation requested. If the device cannot produce the requested separation, the colors are rendered in the alternative color space. The alternative color space can be any of the device color spaces or any CIE-based color space, but it can not be a pattern or indexed color space. The example specifies **/DeviceCMYK** as its alternate color space.

The final element is a PostScript procedure known as the *tint transform*. If the device cannot produce the requested separation, the interpreter uses the tint transform to convert colors from the requested separation space into the alternative color space. The example transforms the color with this procedure:

```
{ 0.0 exch 0.0 0.0 }
```

When transforming the tint to the alternative color space, this procedure supplies the tint as the magenta component of a CMYK color. That makes sense since the example is writing only magenta to the separation. More complex tints (fuchsia, for example) require more complicated transformations. The alternative color space and tint transform elements are ignored if the device can produce the separation you requested.

Separations for Spot Color

You are not limited to producing separations that correspond to the primary colors of existing color spaces. Separations are named, and you can create your own separations to implement *spot color* or to apply special colorants such as metallic or fluorescent inks. Spot color is often used in publications for highlighting chapter headings, section headings, or titles. Here's a sample page from a newsletter for the travel group "Warp Tours," which specializes in travel tours that cover all the sights of a city in a single day. This newsletter uses spot color for its title.

See color plate XIX.

```
%!PS
/inch { 72 mul } def                    % define inch procedure
[ /Separation                           % separation color space
  (WarpedPurple)                        % separation for spot color
  /DeviceGray                           % alternate color space
  { 0.0 sub } ] setcolorspace           % reverse polarity from device gray
1.0 setcolor                            % set full tint
/Palatino-Roman findfont                % choose font
72 scalefont setfont
4.25 inch 9.75 inch                     % location for text
(Warp Tours, Inc.) center_show          % show text
0.5 inch 6.25 inch                      % x position for globe
4.82 inch 2.75 inch                     % y position for globe
DrawRect stroke                         % outline for globe
5 setlinewidth                          % set line width
0.5 inch 9.5 inch moveto
8.0 inch 9.5 inch lineto stroke         % draw underline
0.75 setgray                            % new separation
                                        % show text rectangles
0.5 inch 0.5 inch 2.16 inch 5.5 inch DrawRect fill
3.16 inch 0.5 inch 2.16 inch 5.5 inch DrawRect fill
5.82 inch 0.5 inch 2.16 inch 8.5 inch DrawRect fill
showpage                                % display page
```

The gray rectangles represent areas to be filled with text. This example uses two separations. The first separation contains the elements of the newsletter to be printed in spot color. The second separation contains the remaining elements to be printed in the main color of the newsletter—black for most publications. Here are the separations when printed on individual pages. Refer to color plate XIX for the color versions of these separations.

Spot Color

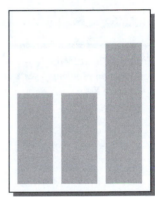

Black

Color Issues

Now you can specify colors in PostScript using any of several color models. The next several subsections talk about issues to consider when generating color images.

Trapping

Undoubtedly you have seen printed material looking like the picture on the next page. The solid yellow heart doesn't line up with the hole in the background, nor does the magenta outline line up with the yellow heart beneath. Both pieces of the shape are out of place. Objects often get out of place because four-color presses can shift between separations, even during a single job.

Figure without trapping—registration problems. See color plate XXI.

```
%!PS
/inch { 72 mul } def                    %   define inch procedure
1.0 0.0 0.0 0.0 setcmykcolor            %   cyan background
0.5 inch 0.0 inch 7.5 inch 9.0 inch DrawRect fill
4.25 inch 4.5 inch translate            %   white hole in background
0.0 0.0 0.0 0.0 setcmykcolor
Heart fill
0.0 0.0 1.0 0.0 setcmykcolor            %   yellow heart
Heart fill
0.0 1.0 0.0 0.0 setcmykcolor            %   magenta heart outline
15.0 setlinewidth Heart stroke
showpage                                %   display page
```

You can prevent this from happening to your artwork by using a technique called *trapping*. In the picture, the solid yellow heart is exactly big enough to fill the hole in the cyan background. And the outline of the heart is just big enough to cover the solid heart beneath it. Even the slightest shift in the press can cause registration problems when objects are the exact size required. You solve this by creating an object slightly larger than it needs to be. In this way, objects overlap slightly, preventing registration problems. The overlap is known as *trap*. You can have two types of trap—*spread trap* and *choke trap*. In spread traps, the object overlaps the background. In choke traps, the background overlaps the object. In general, you should trap lighter colors over darker colors and consider not trapping overlapping objects if they share 20 percent or more of any process color.

This program uses two traps to fix the registration problems of the first picture. First, the hole in the background is smaller than the yellow heart. This creates a choke trap; the cyan background chokes the yellow heart. Second, the line width for the magenta outline of the heart is 0.75 PostScript points wider (taking into account the scale factor). This creates a spread trap; the outline spreads over the background and the yellow heart. The overlap should be anywhere from 0.3 to 1.0 printer points.

Figure with trapping. See color plate XXII.

```
%!PS
/inch { 72 mul } def              %  define inch procedure
1.0 0.0 0.0 0.0 setcmykcolor      %  cyan background
0.5 inch 0.0 inch 7.5 inch 9.0 inch DrawRect fill
gsave
   4.25 inch 4.5 inch translate   %  heartshaped hole
   0.7 0.7 scale                  %  spread trap
   0.0 0.0 0.0 0.0 setcmykcolor
   Heart fill
grestore
gsave
   4.25 inch 4.5 inch translate   %  yellow heart
   0.75 0.75 scale
   0.0 0.0 1.0 0.0 setcmykcolor
   Heart fill
grestore
gsave
   4.25 inch 4.5 inch translate   %  magenta outline
   0.75 0.75 scale
   0.0 1.0 0.0 0.0 setcmykcolor
   16.0 setlinewidth              %  choke trap
   Heart stroke
grestore
showpage                          %  display page
```

Overprinting

An opaque imaging model is fundamental to PostScript. When two objects overlap, the last object created overlays any objects created previously. The two objects in this next picture overlap. The yellow circle partially covers the magenta square. The intersecting area of the two objects is yellow, the color of the top object.

No overprinting.

```
%!PS
/inch { 72 mul } def              %  define inch procedure
0.0 1.0 0.0 0.0 setcmykcolor      %  draw magenta square
0.5 inch 1.0 inch 6.5 inch 6.5 inch DrawRect fill
0.0 0.0 1.0 0.0 setcmykcolor      %  draw yellow circle
5.0 inch 7.0 inch moveto
5.0 inch 7.0 inch 3.0 inch 0 360 arc fill
showpage                          %  display page
```

The color renditions of the preceding picture and the following separations are found in color plate XXV. The color separations for this picture are shown on the next page.

Notice that part of the square in the magenta separation has been "knocked out". This is exactly the result desired. When the final picture is printed, the yellow circle obscures the corner of the magenta square. Notice also there is no cyan component.

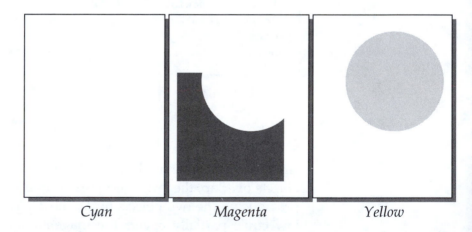

Cyan   Magenta   Yellow

Sometimes you *want* the overlapping colors to blend. The printing business calls this *overprinting*—the yellow circle overprints the magenta square, the colors blend, and the intersection is colored red. PostScript Level 2 added the **setoverprint** operator so you can specify whether underlying objects blend with overlay objects. **setoverprint** takes effect only when a device is creating separations. Here's the same example with overprinting on.

```
%!PS
/inch { 72 mul } def              %   define inch procedure
true setoverprint                 %   turn overprinting on
0.0 1.0 0.0 0.0 setcmykcolor      %   draw magenta square
0.5 inch 1.0 inch 6.5 inch 6.5 inch DrawRect fill
0.0 0.0 1.0 0.0 setcmykcolor      %   draw yellow circle
5.0 inch 7.0 inch moveto
5.0 inch 7.0 inch 3.0 inch 0 360 arc fill
showpage                          %   display page
```

Overprinting.

The syntax of **setoverprint** is

Boolean **setoverprint**

where *Boolean* is either **true**, indicating underlying objects blend with overlay objects, or **false**, indicating overlay objects obscure underlying objects. The color renditions of the preceding picture and the following separations are found in color plate XXVI. The separations for the preceding example with overprinting turned on are shown here.

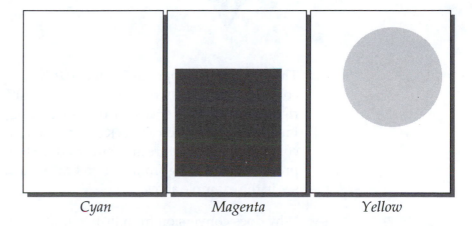

Cyan   Magenta   Yellow

In the magenta separation, the entire square is present. When printed, the colors for the overlapping areas blend to create red. Use **currentoverprint** to get the current value of the overprint attribute in the graphics state. The preset value of overprint is **false**.

A final word on **setoverprint**: it is device-dependent and works only on devices that support separations. So you are better off avoiding **setoverprint** altogether and writing your PostScript without it. Use clipping and **setcmykcolor** for the device-independent results you want.

Undercolor Removal and Black Generation

The two pictures below appear to be the same. However, if you look closely you'll notice the colors on the left are somewhat muddied and the colors on the right are purer and clearer. The difference is particularly noticeable in the darker colors. Refer to color plates XXIII and XXIV.

The PostScript program for the left-hand picture specified the colors using the RGB color model. The PostScript program for the right-hand picture specified the colors using CMYK. When both images are printed on a CMYK device such as a four-color press, the colors in the left picture are converted to CMYK during the printing process. Converting from RGB to CMYK can muddy colors as you see in the example above.

Why does conversion from RGB to CMYK cause problems? For the same reason the K (black) component was added to the CMYK color model in the first place—inks and paints contain impurities that muddy colors mixed from cyan, magenta, and yellow. The K component was introduced to the CMY color model so blacks and grays could be created with black ink instead of mixtures of cyan, magenta, and yellow. When doing a simple conversion from RGB to CMY, the K component is not computed. So any black or dark colors are created with a cyan, magenta, and yellow mixture, which can be muddied.

Traditional printing uses two techniques during color conversion to produce purer colors—*Black Generation* and *Undercolor Removal*. PostScript Level 2 provides both techniques. Let's see the PostScript conversion process. First, the PostScript interpreter uses these equations as basic conversions from RGB to CMY.

$$cyan = 1.0 - red$$

$$magenta = 1.0 - green$$

$$yellow = 1.0 - blue$$

Second, the interpreter calculates the black component of the color. The amount of black is based on the smallest of the cyan, magenta, or yellow components. For example, suppose $cyan = 0.15$, $magenta = 0.75$, and $yellow = 0.5$. 0.15 is the smallest of the three color components. 0.15 is not the black component, but the interpreter looks up the amount of black in a table using 0.15 as the index. Computing the black component in this manner is called *Black Generation* or *Gray Component Replacement* (GCR).

The third step in the conversion of RGB colors to CMYK colors is called *Undercolor Removal*. So far, the PostScript interpreter has converted the base color to CMY, then added a black component. Now the blackness of the resulting color receives two more "contributions"—once with the pure black component, and again with the mixture of cyan, magenta, and yellow. To get a true conversion of the original RGB color, the mixed black must be removed. So the final step of conversion is to remove some each of cyan, magenta, and yellow.

In general, the conversions performed by the PostScript interpreter produce accurate results. The built-in tables and conversions are tuned for each class of device. But sometimes a specific printer or imagesetter needs fine-tuning. PostScript Level 2 gives control over black generation and undercolor removal during color conversion. Both black generation and undercolor removal are PostScript procedures and are part of the graphics state.

In PostScript Level 2, you can write your own black generation and undercolor removal procedures using two new PostScript operators—**setblackgeneration** and **setundercolorremoval**.

The next two examples on page 525 uses these new operators to draw a fan of colors. Each example uses a **fanBlade** procedure to draw an individual blade. Here's the definition of **fanBlade**.

```
/fanBlade {
  0 0 moveto               %   set current point
  0 inch 9 inch lineto     %   first side
  1.5 inch 0 inch rlineto  %   top side
  closepath                %   finish the shape
  fill                     %   fill with current color
} def
```

The first program specifies its colors in the RGB color model, ignoring conversion issues altogether.

Fan of colors without undercolor removal and black generation.

```
%!PS
/inch { 72 mul } def                       %   define inch procedure
/Colors [ { 1.0 0.0 0.0 }                  %   red
  { 1.0 0.5 0.0 }     { 1.0 1.0 0.0 } %   orange / yellow
  { 0.0 1.0 0.0 }     { 0.0 0.0 1.0 } %   green / blue
  { 0.5 0.0 1.0 }     { 0.5 0.0 0.5 } %   indigo / violet
] def
4.25 inch 1 inch translate                 %   adjust user space
33 rotate
0 1 6 {
  Colors exch get exec setrgbcolor    %   set color components
  fanBlade                            %   draw fan blade
  -9 rotate                           %   rotate for next fan blade
} for
showpage                                   %   display page
```

Notice that the colors are specified using **setrgbcolor**. When these colors are rendered on a CMYK device, the colors are converted to CMYK. The next example compensates for the color conversion using **setblackgeneration** and **setundercolorremoval**.

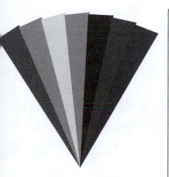

Fan of colors with under-color removal and black gen-eration.

```
%!PS
/inch { 72 mul } def                        %   define inch procedure
{ .06 add } setblackgeneration              %   generate black component
{ .06 add 3 div } setundercolorremoval %   remove mixed black
/Colors [ { 1.0 0.0 0.0 }                   %   red
    { 1.0 0.5 0.0 }      { 1.0 1.0 0.0 }    %   orange / yellow
    { 0.0 1.0 0.0 }      { 0.0 0.0 1.0 }    %   green / blue
    { 0.5 0.0 1.0 }      { 0.5 0.0 0.5 }    %   indigo / violet
] def
4.25 inch 1 inch translate
33 rotate
0 1 6 {
    Colors exch get exec setrgbcolor        %   set color components
    fanBlade                                %   draw fan blade
    -9 rotate                               %   rotate for next fan blade
} for
showpage                                    %   display page
```

This listing contains two new instructions. Here's the first.

```
{ .06 add } setblackgeneration
```

setblackgeneration sets the black generation component of the graphics state, a PostScript procedure to calculate the black component of a CMYK color during conversion. The black generation procedure is called unpredictably and must run without any side-effects, except for removing its operand from the operand stack.

Black

Stack before call to black generation procedure.

The black generation procedure is called with a single operand k, where k is between 0.0 and 1.0 and represents the amount of black in the color. The procedure returns a value between 0.0 and 1.0, which is the final black component. The black generation procedure can either return its operand and accept the conversion from the PostScript interpreter or make adjustments to the black component by adding to or subtracting from its operand. The example adds a small amount to the black component. The next line of interest is the following:

```
{ .06 add 3 div } setundercolorremoval
```

setundercolorremoval sets the undercolor removal component of the current graphics state, a PostScript procedure to adjust the cyan, magenta, and yellow components of a CMYK color during conversion. As with the black generation procedure, the undercolor removal procedure is called unpredictably and must run without any side effects, except for removing its operand from the operand stack. The undercolor removal procedure is called with a single operand k, where k is between 0.0 and 1.0 and represents the amount of black in the color.

The undercolor removal procedure returns a value to be subtracted from each of the cyan, magenta, and yellow components of the final color. If the undercolor removal procedure returns 0.0, no adjustment is made. A positive result removes color and a negative result adds color. The example removes one-third the amount of black added to the black component during the black generation phase of conversion.

Both black generation and undercolor removal are device-dependent computations and should not be used in page descriptions intended to be device-independent. The application can easily perform its own conversions from RGB to CMYK, obviating the need for black generation and under color removal on the final output device.

Stack before call to under color removal procedure.

Halftones

Well, that's a lot of color theory and practice. Displaying colors (and gray scales) on color monitors and printing on color printers can give you reasonable output that will look more or less like you wanted it to. As we discussed earlier, color gamuts differ from device to device, and an entire industry has grown up around issues of color matching and color calibration.

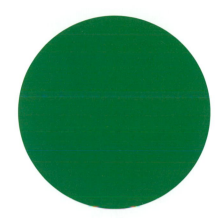

PLATE I

**kier's Beginner's Circle created using
GB color model**. See Chapter 7 for
stScript code to generate this picture.

PLATE II

**Skier's Intermediate Square created
using RGB color model**. See *The
PostScript Painting Model* in Chapter 2
for PostScript to generate this picture.

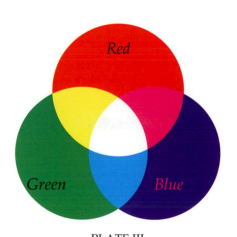

PLATE III

**B color model—colors add to pro-
ce white**. See *RGB Color Model* in
apter 13 for information on using the
B color model.

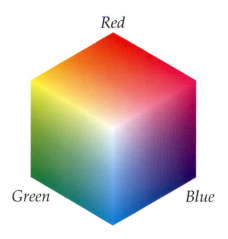

PLATE IV

**RGB color cube is the popular way to
visualize this color model**. See *RGB
Color Model* in Chapter 13 for information on using the RGB color model.

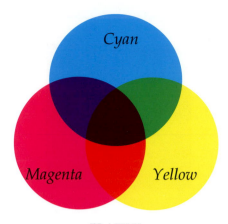

PLATE V

CMYK color model—colors subtract to produce black. See *CMYK Color Model* in Chapter 13.

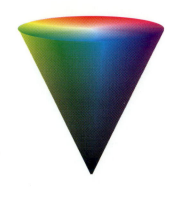

PLATE VI

HSB color cone is the popular way t visualize this color model. See *HS Color Model* in Chapter 13.

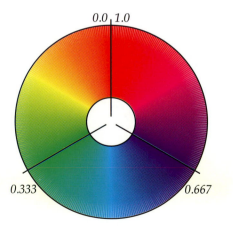

PLATE VII

Hue component values of HSB color model. See *HSB Color Model* in Chapter 13 for further details.

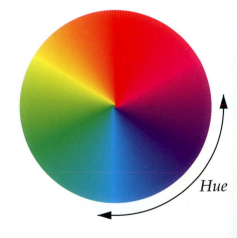

PLATE VIII

Hue component of HSB color space See *HSB Color Model* in Chapter 13.

PLATE IX
Saturation component of HSB color space.
See *HSB Color Model* in Chapter 13.

PLATE X
Brightness component of HSB color space.
See *HSB Color Model* in Chapter 13.

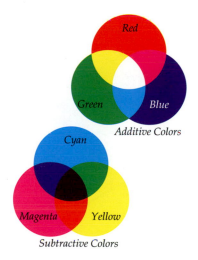

PLATE XI
Additive (RGB) and subtractive (CMYK) color models. See *Additive and Subtractive Color* in Chapter 13.

PLATE XII
Olympic circles drawn using CMYK color model. See *CMYK Color Model* in Chapter 13.

PLATE XIII
Color logo using RGB color model.
See *RGB Color Model* in Chapter 13.

PLATE XIV
HSB color model version of clipping **shape through a translucent sheet**. See *HSB Color Model* in Chapter 13.

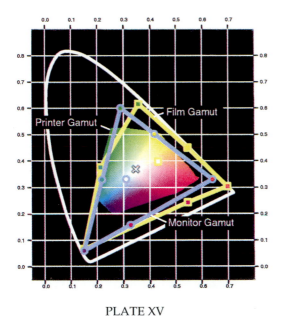

PLATE XV
CIE-based color models—color gamut **diagram**. See *CIE Color Specification* in Chapter 13 for more information.

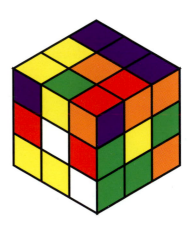

PLATE XVI
Rubik's Cube drawn using CIE color **model**. See *CIE Color Specification in* Chapter 13.

PLATE XVII

Intrinsically uncolored pattern with color added using PostScript Level 2 pattern color space. See *Uncolored Patterns* in Chapter 11.

PLATE XVIII

Separations from PostScript Level 2 separation color space. See *Separations* in Chapter 13.

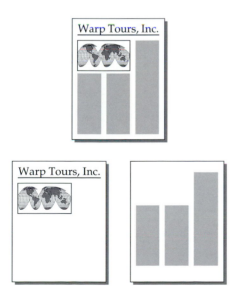

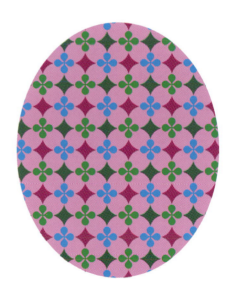

PLATE XX

Colored pattern fill using PostScript Level 2 pattern color space. Chapter 11 has details of colored patterns.

PLATE XIX

Separations for spot color.
See *Separations* in Chapter 13.

PLATE XXI

Press misregistration problems when shapes are not trapped. See *Trapping* in Chapter 13.

PLATE XXII

Trapping compensates for possible misregistered press. See *Trapping* in Chapter 13.

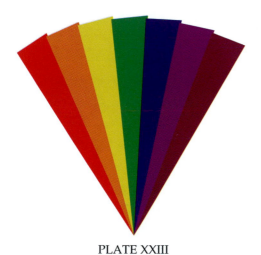

PLATE XXIII

Color fan without undercolor removal. See *Undercolor Removal and Black Generation* in Chapter 13 for more information.

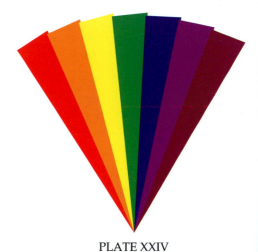

PLATE XXIV

Color fan with undercolor removal. See *Undercolor Removal and Black Generation* in Chapter 13 for more information.

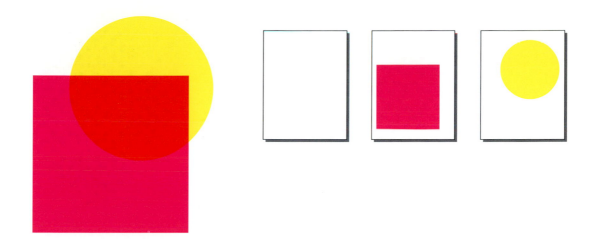

PLATE XXV

Composite image and its separations with overprinting.
See *Overprinting* in Chapter 13 for information on overprinting in PostScript Level 2.

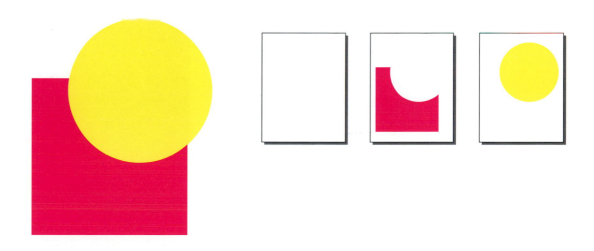

PLATE XXVI

Composite image and its separations with no overprinting.
See *Overprinting* in Chapter 13 for information on overprinting in PostScript Level 2.

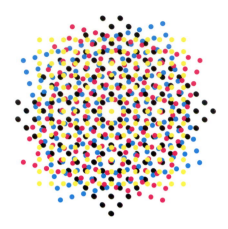

PLATE XXVII

Rosette patterns formed by halftone screens aligned at correct angles. See *Choosing an Angle for Color Halftone Screens* in Chapter 13.

PLATE XXVIII

Moiré patterns formed when halftone screen angles are incorrect. See *Choosing an Angle for Color Halftone Screens in* Chapter 13.

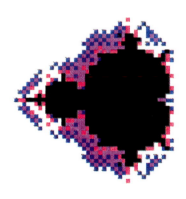

PLATE XXIX

Color image rendered by PostScript Level 2 colorimage or image operators. See *Color Images* in Chapter 9.

PLATE XXX

Image mask can place colored image on colored backgrounds. See *Image Masks* in Chapter 9.

Now cranking out twenty color printouts of your super slide presentation designed to induce the venture capitalists to part with a sufficiently large quantity of simoleons to fund your venture is one thing. Cranking out 100,000 copies of your annual report in glorious six-color process after your venture is wildly successful is another. At some point or another, you have to get your color output actually printed on a real printing press, and that's when all the fun starts. Amazingly enough, newcomers to this subject need to be educated (usually the hard way) that printing presses only print one color at a time. To get them to print arbitrary blends of colors, you must use *process color*. And process color means halftoning.

If you look through a magnifying glass at a color picture in a magazine or a newspaper, you'll see that the picture is not a continuous blend of ink, but is instead built from thousands of tiny dots. This is because lithography can only print or not print—it can't support a continuous tone. Continuous tones are simulated through the tiny dots. The dots are small enough so when you view the picture from a normal distance you cannot distinguish them as individual dots—rather, you perceive a single color covering the area. The process of simulating colors (or in fact shades of gray) with tiny dots is known as *halftoning*. Typically, in color halftoning, the tiny dots are cyan, magenta, yellow, and black. The size of the colored dots as they relate to one another determines the color you perceive. For example, the larger the cyan dot (as compared to magenta, yellow, and black), the more cyan is contained in the perceived color.

Preset halftone screen.

In addition to colors being simulated with tiny dots, shades of gray are also simulated with halftone screens. In gray halftoning, the dots are all black. The dot size determines the gray level your eyes perceive—the larger the dot, the darker the gray shade appears to be. The golf club uses gray halftoning to trick you into seeing shades of gray.

Halftone Screens in PostScript

Each PostScript device is shipped with preset halftoning algorithms. In fact, this is an area where many vendors are adding value above and beyond what Adobe provides. Halftoning was not officially part of the language until PostScript Level 2 added operators so programs can modify preset halftoning behavior. Some PostScript Level 1 interpreters also supported user-defined halftoning in the form of **setscreen**. With **setscreen**, you can specify a single halftone screen in the same manner as traditional printing—in terms of *frequency*, *angle*, and *spot function*. Angle, frequency and spot function are defined in the next section.

Halftoning in PostScript Level 2 provides a new paradigm for specifying halftones using halftone dictionaries. With halftone dictionaries you can specify halftones using frequency, angle, and spot function (as in Level 1), or you can specify halftones using *threshold arrays*. PostScript Level 2 also allows you to specify multiple halftone screens; typically, one for every process color, whereas PostScript Level 1 limited you to a single halftone screen. Of course, for backward compatibility, PostScript Level 2 supports PostScript Level 1 **setscreen**.

Setting Halftone Screens Using setscreen

Let's use **setscreen** to introduce the terms *frequency*, *angle*, and *spot function*. The next several pages define these terms in greater detail and discuss important issues to consider for each component when you design your own halftone screens.

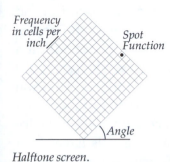

Frequency in cells per inch

Spot Function

Angle

Halftone screen.

setscreen requires three operands—the halftone frequency, the angle of the halftone screen, and the spot function, respectively. The syntax of **setscreen** is

frequency   angle   { spot_function } **setscreen**

where *frequency* is a number representing the number of halftone cells per inch. *Angle* is another number representing the halftone angle in degrees. *spot_function* is a PostScript procedure to define the shape of the halftone dots.

The next picture illustrates the three components of a halftone screen. Notice how the elements interact with one another. Frequency is not measured on the horizontal; frequency is actually measured along the angle of the halftone screen. The first row shows 25 percent black imaged with frequencies ranging from 10 cells per inch to 130 cells per inch. The second array shows the same gray imaged with angles ranging from 0° to 90°. The final array shows 50 percent gray using four different spot functions.

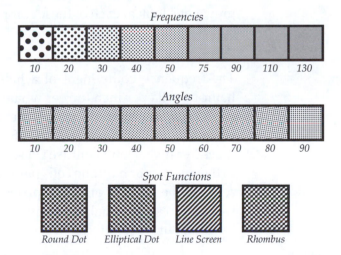

Frequencies

10   20   30   40   50   75   90   110   130

Angles

10   20   30   40   50   60   70   80   90

Spot Functions

Round Dot   *Elliptical Dot*   *Line Screen*   *Rhombus*

So, how do halftone screens relate to the tiny dots that simulate colors or gray tones? The term *halftone screen* refers to the imaginary screen through which ink is poured (or through which pixels are illuminated) to simulate new colors. Imagine that the next picture magnifies a section of the golf club you saw on page 527. You see the detail of the halftone screen.

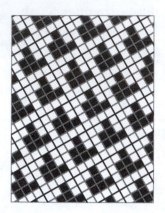

Halftone screens are composed of *halftone cells*—the large squares in the picture. All halftone cells in a given screen are identical and contain a group of device pixels—the small squares outlined in gray. When simulating a gray tone, some device pixels within a halftone cell are turned on and some are left off. All halftone cells darken the same pixels so the perceived color is uniform. The ratio of black pixels to white pixels determines the shade of perceived gray. The halftone cells in the picture each contain sixteen device pixels (four on a side). In the picture, all halftone cells have six of the sixteen pixels darkened, resulting in 37.5 percent gray.[†]

So now you ask, "How do all these halftone cells and device pixels relate to **setscreen**"? You control the number of halftone cells per inch with the frequency argument to **setscreen**. The halftone frequency and the resolution of the output device determine the number of device pixels within each halftone cell. The angle argument to **setscreen** determines the angle at which the halftone screen is positioned over the output device. The spot function determines how many and which device pixels are darkened for any shade of gray. Let's look at each of these components.

Frequency

The frequency component of a halftone screen is the number of halftone cells per inch (or per whatever your units are). In Europe, you encounter the term *mesh* instead of frequency. You may also encounter the acronym LPI to refer to frequency. LPI stands for Lines Per Inch. Don't confuse LPI with DPI (dots per inch). LPI refers to the number of halftone cells per inch in a halftone screen, and DPI refers to the number of device pixels per inch on a device. Here are two pictures using halftone screens with the same angle and spot function but with different frequencies.

---

† In real life, the numbers can get slightly more complicated. Your eye perceives gray levels as a sinusoidal function, not as a linear function. In addition, artifacts called *tonal jumps* complicate life still more.

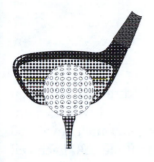

```
30                              %   frequency = 30
0                               %   angle = 0°
{                               %   spot function
    dup mul exch dup mul add 1 exch sub
} setscreen                     %   set halftone
```

Ignore the PostScript instructions between the braces for now—we'll get to them later. The first operand to **setscreen** is the frequency of the halftone screen. This image uses **setscreen** to establish a halftone screen with 30 lines per inch, while the next picture uses a frequency of 50 lines per inch.

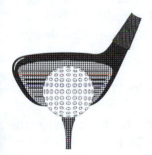

```
50                              %   frequency = 50
0                               %   angle = 0°
{                               %   spot function
    dup mul exch dup mul add 1 exch sub
} setscreen                     %   set halftone
```

You see that the size of the halftone dots are smaller and closer together in the second golf club. Overall, the simulation of the various shades of gray is more convincing with the higher frequency than with the lower frequency. However, that is not always the case. The final result of any frequency depends on other factors as well, such as the resolution of the output device and the number of gray tones you wish to produce.

Choosing a Frequency

In both color and gray halftoning, three factors influence the size of halftone cells:

❑ frequency

❑ the resolution of the output device

❑ the number of gray tones you wish to produce

When choosing a frequency for your halftone screen, you must balance all three factors to produce the most effectively sized halftone dots. Mathematically, the relationship between the three factors can be expressed as follows:

$$\frac{resolution}{frequency} = pixels\ per\ side\ of\ halftone\ cell$$

$$number\ of\ grays = (pixels\ per\ side\ of\ halftone\ cell)^2 + 1$$

The same halftone screen can produce radically different results on devices with different resolutions. Let's look at real world examples for two different resolutions. On a 300 dots-per-inch device, 60 halftone cells per inch give you a 5×5 pixel halftone cell. Each cell can produce 26 shades of gray (5×5)+1. On a 1200-dots-per-inch device, the same 60 halftone cells per inch gives you a 20×20 pixel halftone cell. Potentially, each cell can produce 401 shades of gray (20×20)+1 (except that PostScript Level 1 had a limit of 256 shades of gray). As you see, a 1200 dpi Linotronic produces significantly different results than a 300 dpi device.

For a given resolution, decreasing frequency increases the size of the halftone cells and increases the number of producible gray tones. Smaller frequencies produce larger halftone dots. For example, on a 300 dpi device using a frequency of 10 halftone cells per inch, each halftone cell is composed of 30 device pixels per side. This produces 901 levels of gray, but it is overkill and you pay for it with loss of resolution. This gray ramp varies shades of gray from black to white.

The dots are large enough so you can distinguish them from one another and see a pattern. Instead of simulating a shade of gray with tiny dots, the area has been effectively tiled with a pattern.[†]

For any given resolution, as you increase frequency, you decrease the size of the halftone cells and reduce the number of producible gray tones. Higher frequencies produce smaller halftone dots and limit the number of grays you can produce. This gray ramp varies

---

† and, indeed, this is how some people emulated patterns in PostScript Level 1. This method of pattern emulation is device dependent and runs out of memory quickly.

shades of gray from black to white; but the frequency is so high you get only two shades—black and white.

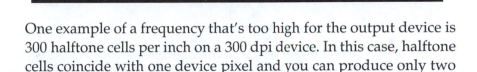

One example of a frequency that's too high for the output device is 300 halftone cells per inch on a 300 dpi device. In this case, halftone cells coincide with one device pixel and you can produce only two colors, black and white, as in the preceding picture.

In general, you should strive for halftone cells with four to eight device pixels per side (17 to 65 gray levels). Fewer than 17 gray levels produce banding effects—you can see the transitions or jumps between the levels. Large halftone cells producing more than 65 gray tones is a waste as the eye can't detect the difference.

Angle

The angle element of the halftone screen defines the angle at which the halftone screen is placed over device space. Angle is expressed in degrees and represents the orientation of the screen relative to the horizontal axis of device space. Here are two pictures using halftone screens with the same frequency and spot function, but with different angles.

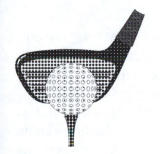

```
30                                        %  frequency = 30
0                                         %  angle = 0°
{                                         %  spot function
        dup mul exch dup mul add 1 exch sub
} setscreen                               %  set halftone
```

Again, ignore the PostScript instructions between the braces. The second operand to **setscreen** is the angle of the halftone screen. This image uses **setscreen** to establish a halftone screen with a halftone angle of 0°, while the angle is 30° for the next picture.

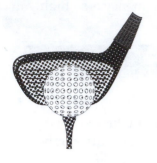

```
30                                          %   frequency = 30
30                                          %   angle = 30°
{                                           %   spot function
         dup mul exch dup mul add 1 exch sub
} setscreen                                 %   set halftone
```

You can see that the halftone dots in each image fall along a line at the angle of the halftone screen. The screen angle in no way affects the angle of rotation of user space. Halftone screens are set in device space, not in user space. You can't change the screen angle by using **rotate**. As such, **setscreen** is device-dependent.

Choosing an Angle for Gray Halftone Screens

Halftone cells are physically square.[†] So, for most spot functions, rotating a halftone cell by 0° is effectively the same as rotating it 90°, or 180°, etc. Thus, the only effective angles for a halftone screen are between 0° and 89°.

When choosing an angle for your gray halftone screen, you should generally avoid using an angle of 0° and, consequently, 90°. Halftone cells positioned at an angle of 0° are readily detectable. An angle of 0° is a viable option for color halftone screens. But more about that in the next section.

In traditional printing, halftone screens are set at 30°, 45°, or 60°. The best halftone angle seems to be 45° because it's halfway between 0° and 90°. Sometimes halftone screens use 15° or 75° for the angle. However, as you see in the following gray ramps, these angles produce disturbing visual artifacts where the halftone dots meet horizontal and vertical lines. Try to choose a halftone angle that interacts well with the image and does not generate obvious patterns like these:

---

† You may think that means halftone cells have the same number of device pixels per side. However, with device resolutions such as 300 by 600 dpi becoming popular, that is not always the case.

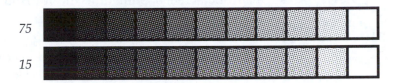

75

15

Rosettes. See color plate XXVII.

Choosing an Angle for Color Halftone Screens

In the case of color halftoning in PostScript Level 2, you specify four halftone screens—one for each process color (cyan, magenta, yellow, and black). You should choose a different angle for each screen so the halftone dots from one color don't completely cover the halftone dots of another. The picture shows four halftone screens overlaying one another at different angles. The dots form rosette patterns.

Theoretically, using angles 30° apart yields the best rosette patterns. The only effective angles are between 0° and 90° (and we need to set four halftone screens), so that's not possible. Typical screen angles used for traditional photomechanical screening are cyan at 15°, magenta at 75°, yellow at 0°, and black at 45°. Black is the darkest and most obtrusive color and is set at 45° where it's less distracting. Yellow is placed horizontally because it's the lightest color and less obtrusive at that angle than the other colors. Magenta and cyan are placed 30° on either side of black.

You can choose other angles when an image contains predominant colors. For example, when a picture contains a lot of fleshtones, set magenta instead of black at 45°. The color halftone screens in the preceding rosette picture uses the traditional angles.

Moiré patterns. See color plate XXVIII.

Rosette patterns are common in both traditional and electronic halftone screens. Sometime the four halftone screens interact and the rosette patterns become so obvious as to disturb the continuity of color in the picture. Disturbing visual patterns like these are called *moiré patterns*. The picture shows four halftone screens whose rosette patterns interact to produce moirés. Moiré patterns can be caused by the following conditions:

❑ badly chosen screen angles

❑ slight shifts of the printing machinery

❑ angle substitution by the halftoning machinery. See *Rational and Irrational Tangent Angles* for more information about why the halftoning machinery might substitute angles for you.

❑ patterns in the original image might interact with the rosette patterns of the halftone screens

PostScript-generated colors are highly susceptible to developing moiré patterns. Dark colors with a black component, such as purples and blues, are particularly susceptible. You can get around this by using lighter colors or by substituting a combination of cyan, magenta, and yellow for all or part of the black component. Of course, you have to balance this technique with undercolor removal and black generation to avoid producing muddy colors instead of the true color.

Rational and Irrational Tangent Angles

Previous notes on choosing halftone angles were general guidelines, but there's more to the story. Sometimes, the halftoning machinery doesn't produce exactly the screen you asked for. In fact some systems will give angles up to 15° different from the angle you requested! This section uses some basic trigonometry to describe why you don't always get the angles (and consequently the frequencies) exactly as you asked for them. The answer to this question has to do with *rational tangent angles* and *irrational tangent angles*. The first order of business is to define these terms. Let's start with *tangent*. This picture illustrates a typical angle θ. The tangent of θ is calculated

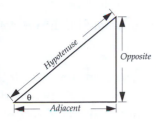

$$tangent\ \theta = \frac{Opposite}{Adjacent}$$

where *Opposite* and *Adjacent* are the lengths of the lines opposite and respectively adjacent to the angle θ. So much for tangent. Now for rational and irrational. According to *The Random House Dictionary of the English Language*, rational numbers are

"capable of being expressed exactly by a ratio of two integers."

Conversely, irrational numbers are

"incapable of being expressed exactly by a ratio of two integers."

So rational tangent angles are angles whose tangents can be expressed by the ratio of two integers, and irrational tangent angles are those whose tangents cannot be expressed by the ratio of two integers. Great. Where do halftone screens come in?

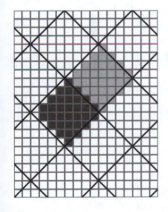

Halftone screens are placed over device space consisting of a regular grid of pixels. Halftone screens should intersect with device space consistently so halftone cells contain the same number of device pixels, as in this picture. Note the corner of each halftone cell corresponds exactly with the corner of a pixel, and each cell encompasses the same pattern of device pixels. Rational tangent angles produce halftone screens that ultimately intersect with device space in a consistent manner. So the halftone cells are identical and the rendering machinery can calculate one master cell and replicate it over device space. You're home free if you "accidentally" choose a rational tangent angle. The PostScript rendering machinery will give you the halftone screen you asked for.

Irrational tangent angles produce halftone screens that never intersect with device space consistently. So master cells cannot be computed and replicated consistently over device space. This unfortunate situation can be handled by the rendering machinery in two different ways, as follows:

❑ substitute the nearest rational tangent angle for the requested irrational tangent angle, and adjust the frequency accordingly

❑   use the irrational tangent angle, and calculate each halftone cell individually

The second method produces high quality results but requires lots of computation time. So, the halftoning machinery typically substitutes a rational tangent angle and adjusts the frequency accordingly. This is why you don't always get the angle and frequency you asked for.

Spot Function

The spot function is the essence of the halftone screen—it defines the shape of halftone dots. These two golf clubs use the same frequency and angle but different spot functions.

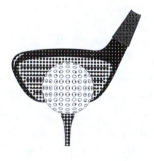

```
30                                          %   frequency = 30
0                                           %   angle = 0°
{                                           %   round dot
        dup mul exch dup mul add 1 exch sub
} setscreen                                 %   set halftone
```

This golf club uses a very common halftone shape—the round dot. If you look carefully at the image, you can clearly see that the halftone dots are tiny circles.

```
30                                          %   frequency = 30
0                                           %   angle = 0°
{                                           %   elliptical dot
        dup mul exch dup mul .7 mul add 1 exch sub
} setscreen                                 %   set halftone
```

This image uses an elliptical dot screen where each halftone dot is an ellipse. The spot function is the third operand to **setscreen** and is a PostScript procedure. The PostScript instructions between the braces are the instructions for the spot function. Let's look at how to construct spot functions for halftone screens.

A halftone cell has a coordinate system like that in the picture. Every device pixel has x and y coordinates such that x and y are between −1 and +1. The PostScript interpreter calls the spot function for every device pixel within a halftone cell. The spot function assigns a value between −1 and +1 to that device pixel. The spot function value for each pixel determines the order in which that device pixel will be darkened in relation to the other pixels within the halftone cell. As the desired gray approaches black, pixels are darkened according to their spot function value from highest to lowest. The specific value returned by the spot function is not important, but the value as it relates to other values is significant.

This picture shows the spot function values for a halftone cell containing sixteen device pixels. At 50 percent gray, half of the pixels are darkened. In this example, the pixels with a spot function value ≥ 0.4 will be darkened (eight pixels are darkened and eight are not). You notice there are several "ties"—many device pixels have the same value. When ties occur, the PostScript interpreter chooses the next pixel randomly, but consistently.

One consequence of this algorithm is that halftone dots grow in a consistent fashion. Let's use the sixteen-pixel halftone cell in the preceding picture as an example. Suppose you request 12.5 percent gray. The two pixels whose values are 0.8 are darkened. Now moving to 25 percent gray, the same two pixels are darkened, and the two with values of 0.6 are also darkened. Each pixel darkened for gray level j is also darkened for gray level $k > j$. This is known as a *growth sequence* and minimizes contouring effects.

Let's generate a very simple spot function. When the PostScript interpreter calls the spot function for a device pixel, it passes the (x, y) coordinate of that pixel to the spot function. A simple spot function could assign the x coordinate to the pixel. The picture shows the state of the operand stack when the spot function is called. To assign the x coordinate to the device pixel, **pop** the y coordinate from the stack. The following **setscreen** instruction sets the halftone screen for the Christmas ornament.

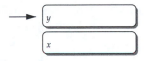

Contents of stack prior to call to spot function.

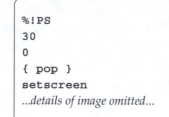

```
%!PS
30                        %   frequency
0                         %   angle
{ pop }                   %   spot function
setscreen                 %   set halftone screen
...details of image omitted...
```

1	.5	.5	1
1	.5	.5	1
1	.5	.5	1
1	.5	.5	1

This particular spot function implements a *line screen*—halftone dots are actually lines. Pixels further from the horizontal center of the halftone cell have larger x coordinates, thus larger spot function values, and are darkened first. The picture shows a halftone cell whose spot function values implement a line screen.

Choosing a Spot Function

The shape of a halftone dot is key to successful halftone screens. When you design halftone dots, you should ensure that the halftone shape is effective in the three ranges of gray:

❑ the very lightest shades of gray, sometimes known as *highlights*

❑ medium shades of gray, also known as *midtones*†—the shades in the region where adjoining halftone dots are large enough to begin touching. This phenomenon is known as *midtone shift*.

❑ the darkest shades of gray, also known as *shadows*

Halftone dot shapes should work well in all three ranges. Each range presents its own set of problems. This section looks at each range and looks at a few spot functions in each range.

First, the light grays—when halftone dots are very small. Some inks or papers don't hold up well for extremely tiny halftone dots and dots can "fall off" the page for very low percentage grays. Good halftone shapes help ink stick to the paper and improve the

---

† from whence came the name of an unknown popular music group.

chance of reproducing very light grays. Shapes with minimal edges do this job better than shapes with larger edges. These four squares all contain three percent black, but each uses a different halftone shape and a small frequency so you can easily see the halftone dots.

Very light grays

Round Dot   *Elliptical Dot*   *Line Screen*   *Rhombus*

What about medium gray shades? One tricky aspect of halftone dots is that, ultimately, they grow such that adjoining cells begin to touch. Sudden apparent visual changes—known as *tonal jumps*—occur when halftone dots join, and most halftone shapes join somewhere in the medium gray range. Each of the following squares contains 50 percent black using different halftone shapes. You can see in the rhombus shape how the tiny dots actually overlap significantly at the apexes and both circles and diamonds just barely join at 50 percent gray. Joining halftones dots such as these cause tonal jumps such as those to the left.

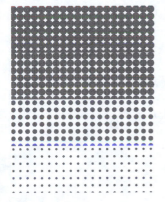

Major tonal jump in the third section when dots start touching.

Medium grays

Round Dot   *Elliptical Dot*   *Line Screen*   *Rhombus*

In darker shades of gray, halftone dots are large and may overlap. A good halftone shape resists *plugging*—the tendency for ink to flow into the areas between dots. Plugging occurs when halftone spots intrude on the open white spaces between dots. For dark grays, the shape of the halftone dots isn't nearly as important as the shape of the white spaces. Again, here are the four squares, each using a different halftone shape. The gray shade is 75 percent black.

Dark grays

Round Dot   Elliptical Dot   Line Screen   Rhombus

Let's talk about how different shapes work in each tonal region.

Light Grays

Let's compare a simple round halftone dot with a simple diamond dot in the very light gray shades. Here's the PostScript code to establish a halftone screen with a simple round halftone dot.

```
%!PS
30                                      %   frequency
0                                       %   angle
{                                       %   round dot spot function
   dup mul exch dup mul add 1 exch sub
} setscreen
...details of image omitted...
```

The spot function is based on the equation for a circle, $x^2 + y^2 = r^2$, thus producing round halftone dots. The next picture establishes a halftone screen with a simple diamond halftone dot—actually squares rotated by 45°.

```
%!PS
30                                      %   frequency
0                                       %   angle
                                        %   diamond dot spot function
{  abs exch abs add 2 div  } setscreen
...details of image omitted...
```

The spot function is the equation $\dfrac{\mathrm{abs}(x) + \mathrm{abs}(y)}{2}$

Which dot works better in light grays? The one with the smallest amount of edge. Which shape has the smallest perimeter? For ease of computing, start with a one-inch diameter (half-inch radius) circle. A diamond to produce the same shade of gray as the circle has the same area and is 0.886 inches on a side.[†] The circumference of the circle is $\pi d = 2\pi r$ because $r = \frac{1}{2}$. The perimeter of the square is $3.544 = x \times 4$. The circle has the smallest perimeter and works better in light grays. Of the common halftone shapes, the simple round dot is most compact and has the smallest edge. For pictures with lots of light gray, round dot halftones are a good choice.

Medium Grays

The circle and diamond dot shapes are symmetrical both horizontally and vertically. Shapes such as these join at four points simultaneously and produce significant jumps in perceived gray—sometimes as much as 5 percent. Both circles and diamonds join at 78 percent gray. The diamond dot has the disadvantage that a visible checkerboard pattern appears at the joining tone.

You can reduce the tonal jump by reducing the number of points that join simultaneously. Let's change the round dot into an elliptical dot and the diamond dot into a rhomboid dot by shortening one axis in relation to the other. Now the dots join first at two points, and then later at two other points. You've essentially turned one large tonal jump into two smaller, less noticeable jumps. Here's the PostScript code to establish a halftone screen with an elliptical halftone dot.

[†] *Area of circle* $= \pi r^2 = \pi \times 0.5^2 = 0.785$
Area of square $= 0.785 = x^2 = 0.886^2$

```
%!PS
30                              %   frequency
0                               %   angle
{                               %   ellipse dot spot function
   dup mul 0.7 mul exch dup mul add 1 exch sub
} setscreen
```
...details of image omitted...

This spot function is the same as the round dot, except the x axis is 30 percent smaller than the y axis. Now, one tonal jump occurs when the y axis meets, and a second when the x axis meets. Elliptical dots reduce problems of tonal jump somewhat, but they're generally not as good as round dots in any other way. Ellipses have more edge than circles and don't work so well in light grays.

Here's PostScript code to establish a halftone screen with a *rhomboid* halftone dot. Dots are still diamond shaped with one axis longer than the other.

```
%!PS
30                              %   frequency
0                               %   angle
{                               %   rhomboid dot spot function
   abs .7 mul exch abs add 2 div
} setscreen
```
...details of image omitted...

This function is the same as the diamond dot, except the x axis is 30 percent smaller than the y axis. As with the elliptical dot, one tonal jump occurs when the y axis meets, and second when the x axis meets. Rhombus dots work similarly to elliptical dots, reducing tonal jumps, but not doing so well in other areas.

The moral of the story is that both squares and circles work badly in medium grays. These halftone shapes produce noticeable tonal jumps because both shapes join in four places at the same gray level. You can skew the shape to avoid significant tonal jumps but doing so creates problems in other ranges.

Dark Grays

The white area for a round halftone dot is a cusped diamond with lots of edge and likely to fill with ink (plug). The white area for a diamond dot is also a diamond. As mentioned before, the diamond has a lot of edge and is also likely to fill with ink. The ellipse and the rhombus are worse, exaggerating the cuspy aspect for the white spaces of the round dot and the diamond dot.

What shapes do work well in dark grays? Shapes that form white areas with minimal edge. You learned in the diatribe about light grays that circles have the smallest edge of all halftone shapes. So what you really want for dark grays is an inverted round dot shape like this one.

```
%!PS
30                                          % frequency
0                                           % angle
{                                           % inverted round dot spot function
  dup mul exch dup mul add sqrt 2 sqrt div
} setscreen
...details of image omitted...
```

However, this shape has the same problems of the round dot in medium grays and has major problems with "dot loss" (ink not sticking to the paper) in light grays.

By now, you get the idea that *no* spot function works well in all ranges. That's true, but you can choose the best spot function for each range and create a *conditional spot function*, which changes shape depending on the shade of gray. The spot function could be a round dot in light grays, elliptical in medium grays, and an inverted round dot in dark grays.

For truly extensive coverage of halftoning issues, color screening, and just about anything else dealing with practical day-to-day details, we recommend *Desktop To Press*—a newsletter published by Peter Fink Communications. See the bibliography for further details of Peter's excellent newsletter.

Halftone Dictionaries

PostScript Level 2 expands your control over halftones through the dictionary mechanism. In PostScript Level 2 you use dictionaries and a new **sethalftone** operator to set halftone screens. Level 2 has several types of halftone dictionaries, the simplest form of which is directly related to **setscreen**. Type 1 halftone dictionaries allow you to define halftone screens using frequency, angle, and spot function, just like **setscreen**. This code segment sets a halftone screen with **setscreen**.

```
%!PS
30                                         %   frequency = 30
0                                          %   angle = 0°
{                                          %   round dot
  dup mul exch dup mul add 1 exch sub
} setscreen
```

This **setscreen** instruction defines a halftone screen with a frequency of 30 dots per inch, an angle of 0°, and a round dot spot function. Here's the same halftone screen using **sethalftone** and a Type 1 halftone dictionary. The ornament shows an image using the halftone dictionary.

```
%!PS
/Halftone 4 dict def                       %   define dictionary
Halftone begin
  /HalftoneType 1 def                      %   halftone dictionary type
  /Frequency 30 def                        %   frequency = 30
  /Angle 0 def                             %   angle = 0°
  /SpotFunction                            %   round dot
    { dup mul exch dup mul add 1 exch sub }
  def
end
Halftone sethalftone
```

To create a halftone dictionary, create a dictionary large enough for the number of elements you need and then define the required elements within the dictionary. Setting up a dictionary and defining variables and procedures within that dictionary are covered in Chapter 5. For this particular halftone screen you need only four elements. Let's look at each element of the halftone dictionary.

The **HalftoneType** element of a halftone dictionary is always required and must be a value indicating the halftone type supported by Level 2. You just met a Type 1 halftone dictionary. PostScript Level 2 supports five halftone dictionary types, as shown in this table.

HALFTONE TYPE	DESCRIPTION
1	defines a halftone screen using frequency, angle, and spot function; equivalent to using **setscreen**
2	defines four halftone screens, one for each primary color; defines halftone screens in terms of frequency, angle, and spot function
3	defines a halftone screen using a threshold array
4	defines four halftone screens, one for each primary color; defines halftone screens in terms of threshold arrays
5	defines an arbitrary number of halftone screens, one for each color component; defines halftone screens in terms of frequency, angle, and spot function

The other three elements of the halftone dictionary defined above are **Frequency**, **Angle**, and **SpotFunction**. As with **setscreen**, **Frequency** is a number representing the number of halftone cells per inch. See *Frequency* on pages 530–533 for information about what this value means and how to choose a frequency wisely. **Angle** is a number representing the angle at which the halftone screen is positioned over device space. See *Angle* on pages 533–538 for more information about issues surrounding angle choice. **SpotFunction** is a PostScript procedure defining the shape of halftone dots. See *Spot Function* on pages 538–545 for more information about how to write a spot function and how spot functions are called by the PostScript interpreter.

Frequency, Angle, and **SpotFunction** are required elements for a Type 1 halftone dictionary. A **typecheck** error occurs if any required elements are missing from a halftone dictionary.

Controlling Accurate Screens

The PostScript halftoning machinery may substitute a rational tangent angle for the irrational tangent angle you requested. Sometimes this angle substitution produces moiré patterns. Adobe developed *accurate screens* technology to address this issue.

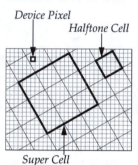

Device Pixel

Halftone Cell

Super Cell

Adobe accurate screen takes a new approach to laying halftone cells over device space. Previously, the corners of *every* halftone cell had to correspond exactly with the corner of a device pixel, essentially limiting the choice of angles. Accurate screens increase the choice of angles and consequently increase the accuracy of the angle achieved. Using accurate screens technology, the halftoning machinery constructs *supercells* consisting of many halftone cells. Now, only the corners of the supercells have to correspond with the corners of device pixels. The position of the individual halftone cell's corners no longer matters. This method of constructing halftone cells is known as the *supercell technique*. The picture illustrates a supercell that is three halftone cells on a side. Each supercell aligns with device pixels, but individual halftone cells do not. Supercells use rational tangent angles but create a large enough moiré period to be less objectionable.

By default, accurate screens are turned off in the PostScript interpreter. You must explicitly turn them on, if you wish to do so. You can turn on accurate screens only through the dictionary mechanism, not through **setscreen**. Simply add this element to your halftone dictionary:

```
/AccurateScreens true def
```

Accurate screens are precise but computationally expensive, so they are normally turned off. You can explicitly turn accurate screens on when specifying halftones via the halftone dictionary mechanism. You cannot use accurate screens with **setscreen**.

Color Halftone Dictionaries

PostScript Level 2 supports separate halftone screens for individual process colors. For example, you can create a halftone screen for each of cyan, magenta, yellow, and black for color imagesetters. Use Type 5 halftone dictionaries to specify one halftone per color or separation. The PostScript code in this example sets up a color halftone screen. Each color uses the same frequency and spot function but is set at a different angle.

```
/ColorHalftone 5 dict def
ColorHalftone begin
  /Cyan <<
    /HalftoneType 1              % halftone for cyan separation
    /Frequency 30
    /Angle 15
    /SpotFunction { dup mul exch dup mul add 1 exch sub }
  >> def
  /Magenta <<
    /HalftoneType 1              % halftone for magenta separation
    /Frequency 30
    /Angle 75
    /SpotFunction { dup mul exch dup mul add 1 exch sub }
  >> def
  /Yellow <<
    /HalftoneType 1              % halftone for yellow separation
    /Frequency 30
    /Angle 0
    /SpotFunction { dup mul exch dup mul add 1 exch sub }
  >> def
  /Default <<
    /HalftoneType 1
    /Frequency 30               % halftone for all others
    /Angle 45
    /SpotFunction { dup mul exch dup mul add 1 exch sub }
  >>
end
```

Elements of a Type 5 halftone dictionary are also halftone dictionaries (Type 1 or 3) known as *leaf dictionaries*. There's one leaf dictionary for each separation—spot colors as well as standard primary colors. The name of each separation screen (the key for the leaf dictionary in the main halftone dictionary) corresponds to the name of the separation. For more information about separation color spaces see *Separations* on pages 512–517 in this chapter.

This example provides a different halftone screen for cyan, magenta, and yellow, and a **/Default** halftone screen. **/Default** is required in a Type 5 halftone dictionary and is used for any separation for which a halftone screen is not provided. This example deliberately omitted a black halftone screen, knowing the default screen would be used in its stead.

This example uses PostScript Level 2 short-cut dictionary constructors << and >> to create each separation halftone dictionary.

Threshold Arrays

Besides specifying halftone screens with frequency, angle, and spot function, PostScript Level 2 added support for defining halftone screens via threshold arrays. Threshold arrays provide a higher degree of control over individual pixels in a halftone cell and you can specify rectangular halftone cells. Type 1 halftone dictionaries limit you to square halftone cells. This PostScript code creates a halftone screen with rectangular halftone cells.

```
%!PS
/ThresholdDict 4 dict def          %   define dictionary
/ThresholdDict begin               %   place on dictionary stack
    /HalftoneType 3 def            %   halftone type
    /Width 5 def                   %   width of halftone cell
    /Height 3 def                  %   height of halftone cell
    /Thresholds                    %   threshold array values
end                                %   pop from dictionary stack
```

Let's walk through this halftone dictionary to see exactly what's going on. Of course, the first element is **/HalftoneType**. A halftone dictionary of Type 3 means threshold arrays. **Width** and **Height** establish the width and height, respectively, of the halftone cell. In this example, the halftone cell is five device pixels wide and three pixels high—fifteen pixels per cell.

/**Thresholds** is the heart of a Type 3 halftone dictionary. **Thresholds** is an array containing *width* × *height* eight-bit numbers. Each number corresponds to a pixel within the halftone cell and indicates the gray value threshold at which the pixel is darkened. If the desired gray is less than the threshold value, the pixel is darkened. Otherwise, the pixel remains white. The eight-bit number 255 or FF_{16} corresponds to white and the eight-bit number 0 corresponds to black. The picture shows the halftone cell established by the code above. Notice that the origin of the halftone cell is the lower-left corner, and the threshold array is row major—that is, when filling up the array from the halftone cell, x varies faster than y. This particular threshold array darkens pixels from the center out, similar to a round dot spot function. The PostScript interpreter converts Type 1 halftone dictionaries into threshold arrays internally.

20	80	C0	A0	40
60	E0	F0	D0	50
30	90	B0	70	10

14 PostScript Nine to Five

'Tis all a Chequer-board of Nights and Days
Where Destiny with Men for Pieces plays;
     Hither and thither moves, and mates, and slays,
And one by one back in the Closet lays.

Ohmar Khayyám—*The Rubáiyát*

A variety of PostScript printers.

PostScript you've seen so far in this book has been fairly simple, covering different facets of the PostScript language. There's another side to PostScript, however, and that is the practical PostScript issues you deal with every day in connection with real printing devices and real applications. This chapter contains somewhat of a gallimaufry of issues that PostScript programmers and users alike should know about. Let's start with a very popular topic—listing fonts.

Obtaining a List of Fonts from the Printer

A frequent request in the PostScript community is how to obtain a list of fonts from the printer. Getting a list of fonts from your printer is a job of varying difficulty, depending on the specific system, resources (such as hard disks) attached to the printer, and other factors. The job is possible though, so let's start with a simple PostScript program to print a list of fonts currently resident in the PROM of your printer.

```
AvantGarde-BookOblique        Helvetica-Narrow-BoldOblique
NewCenturySchlbk-Roman        Helvetica-Bold
Times-BoldItalic              AvantGarde-Book
Helvetica-Oblique             Emulatorfont
Courier-Oblique               Helvetica-BoldOblique
NewCenturySchlbk-BoldItalic   Times-Italic
NewCenturySchlbk-Italic       AvantGarde-Demi
Palatino-Italic               Bookman-Demi
Bookman-LightItalic           Helvetica-Narrow
Helvetica-Narrow-Oblique      Bookman-Light
Helvetica                     Courier
Palatino-Bold                 Palatino-Roman
NewCenturySchlbk-Bold         Courier-BoldOblique
Times-Bold                    Times-Roman
Courier-Bold                  Helvetica-Narrow-Bold
ZapfChancery-MediumItalic     Palatino-BoldItalic
Bookman-DemiItalic            AvantGarde-DemiOblique
Symbol
```

Fonts in font directory of
Apple LaserWriter IIg.

```
%!PS
/inch { 72 mul } def                                    % define inch procedure
/PrintSize 12 def                                       % point size for list
/Leading 14 def                                         % baseline leading
/TopMargin 10.5 inch def                                % initial top margin
/BottomTopMargin 0.5 inch def                           % final bottom margin
/LeftMargin 0.5 inch def                                % initial left margin
/Courier-Bold findfont                                  % find required font
PrintSize scalefont                                     % scale to required size
setfont                                                 % make it current font
/whichSide 0 def                                        % left or middle
/BaseLine TopMargin def                                 % set initial baseline position
/JunkString 256 string def                              % string for conversions
/ShowFontName {                                         % stack = name of font
  JunkString cvs                                        % convert font name to string
                                                        % set current point
  LeftMargin whichSide 4.25 inch mul add BaseLine moveto
  show                                                  % image name of font
  /whichSide 1 whichSide sub def                        % switch side or middle
  whichSide 0 eq {                                      % if starting a new line
    /BaseLine BaseLine Leading sub def
    BaseLine BottomTopMargin lt {                       % if baseline below bottom
      showpage                                          % display page
      /BaseLine TopMargin def                           % reset baseline
    } if
  } if
} def
FontDirectory                                           % font directory onto stack
{                                                       % start forall loop
  pop                                                   % discard font dictionary
  ShowFontName                                          % display name of font
} forall                                                % traverse font directory
showpage                                                % display page
```

That's the code to list the fonts. The picture on the next page illustrates the output you get from such a program.

```
AvantGarde-BookOblique          Helvetica-Narrow-BoldOblique
NewCenturySchlbk-Roman          Helvetica-Bold
Times-BoldItalic                AvantGarde-Book
Helvetica-Oblique               Emulatorfont
Courier-Oblique                 Helvetica-BoldOblique
NewCenturySchlbk-BoldItalic     Times-Italic
NewCenturySchlbk-Italic         AvantGarde-Demi
Palatino-Italic                 Bookman-Demi
Bookman-LightItalic             Helvetica-Narrow
Helvetica-Narrow-Oblique        Bookman-Light
Helvetica                       Courier
Palatino-Bold                   Palatino-Roman
NewCenturySchlbk-Bold           Courier-BoldOblique
Times-Bold                      Times-Roman
Courier-Bold                    Helvetica-Narrow-Bold
ZapfChancery-MediumItalic       Palatino-BoldItalic
Bookman-DemiItalic              AvantGarde-DemiOblique
Symbol
```

Fonts in font directory of Apple LaserWriter IIg.

Well, that's a list of fonts. A picture of a page full of words is not super exciting, so subsequent examples of listing fonts will revert to the standard miniature page models, and you'll need to use a magnifying glass to read the print, but the code examples are the important aspect anyway.

> font dictionary
>
> name of font

*State of stack after each iteration of **forall** on the font directory.*

This program uses **forall** to traverse the printer font directory. Remember, all defined fonts reside in the font directory. The **FontDirectory** instruction places the font directory, which is a dictionary, on the operand stack. The font directory associates names (such as **/Palatino-Roman**) with their font dictionaries. Remember that when you use **forall** to traverse a dictionary, the value is on the top of the stack and the key under it. In this case, font dictionary is not used for anything, so it's popped off the stack. The **forall** loop then uses **ShowFontName** to format and print the font name.

By the way, this program is a good example of one that does not obey document structuring conventions. The major sin committed by this program is that it computes when to perform **showpage**, instead of predetermining it and placing pages within document structuring comments, described later. Since this is a utility program and not particularly intended to be used cooperatively with other PostScript programs, this sin can be forgiven in this case.

In addition, the list is not in alphabetical order. It's in whatever order the keys in **FontDirectory** are ordered. So the next enhancement is to list the fonts alphabetically.

Getting the List in Alphabetical Order

Here's the preceding example, enhanced to list the fonts in alphabetical order. Sorting into alphabetical order is done using the bubble sort routine from page 257 in Chapter 5.

This program has a minor change from the preceding. The preceding example uses a predefined string called **JunkString** to format the font name each time around the loop. This example, places the string inside the loop in the form **256 string**... Why? Well, remember from Chapter 5 that strings are stored in VM and only a reference to the string is on the operand stack. If you used **Junk-String** each time around the loop, what would get put into the array each time would be a reference to **JunkString**. The end result would be an array of garbled strings, with names of fonts overlapping each other. Try it just for fun—seeing what happens when programs are wrong is always a good learning exercise.

```
AvantGarde-Book        AvantGarde-BookOblique
AvantGarde-Demi        AvantGarde-DemiOblique
Bookman-Demi           Bookman-DemiItalic
Bookman-Light          Bookman-LightItalic
Courier                Courier-Bold
Courier-BoldOblique    Courier-Oblique
Emulatorfont           Helvetica
Helvetica-Bold         Helvetica-BoldOblique
Helvetica-Narrow       Helvetica-Narrow-Bold
Helvetica-Narrow-BoldOblique Helvetica-Narrow-Oblique
Helvetica-Oblique      NewCenturySchlbk-Bold
NewCenturySchlbk-BoldItalic NewCenturySchlbk-Italic
NewCenturySchlbk-Roman Palatino-Bold
Palatino-BoldItalic    Palatino-Italic
Palatino-Roman         Symbol
Times-Bold             Times-BoldItalic
Times-Italic           Times-Roman
ZapfChancery-MediumItalic
```

Alphabetical list of fonts in font directory of Apple LaserWriter IIg.

```
%!PS
/inch { 72 mul } def                                    % define inch procedure
/PrintSize 12 def                                       % point size for list
/Leading 14 def                                         % baseline leading
/TopMargin 10.5 inch def                                % initial top margin
/BottomTopMargin 0.5 inch def                           % final bottom margin
/LeftMargin 0.5 inch def                                % initial left margin
/Courier-Bold findfont                                  % find required font
PrintSize scalefont                                     % scale to required size
setfont                                                 % make it current font
/whichSide 0 def                                        % left or middle
/BaseLine TopMargin def                                 % set initial baseline position
/ShowFontName {                                         % stack = name of font
  256 string cvs                                        % convert font name to string
                                                        % set current point
  LeftMargin whichSide 4.25 inch mul add BaseLine moveto
  show                                                  % image name of font
  /whichSide 1 whichSide sub def                        % switch side or middle
  whichSide 0 eq {                                      % if starting a new line
    /BaseLine BaseLine Leading sub def
    BaseLine BottomTopMargin lt {                       % if baseline below bottom
      showpage                                          % display page
      /BaseLine TopMargin def                           % reset baseline
    } if
  } if
} def
FontDirectory                                           % font directory onto stack
dup                                                     % make a copy
length                                                  % take its length
array /FontList exch def                                % make an array that long
0                                                       % set initial array index
{                                                       % start forall loop
    pop                                                 % discard font dictionary
    256 string cvs                                      % convert name to string
    FontList exch                                       % index FontList name
    2 index exch                                        % index FontList name index
    put                                                 % place font name into array
    1 add                                               % increment for next item
} forall                                                % traverse font directory
pop                                                     % discard array index
FontList                                                % get array of font names
bubble                                                  % sort in alphabetical order
{                                                       % start forall loop
    ShowFontName                                        % display name of font
} forall                                                % traverse font directory
showpage                                                % display page
```

Listing Font Samples

The preceding examples just provide you with a list of fonts but the names are printed in `Courier-Bold`. Another frill is to print the name of the font in its own font, as in *Palatino-Italic* and **Optima-Bold**. Of course, this method breaks very slightly when you pick a font like Σημβολ, where the name of the font is unclear from the printout. We can extend the frill with a crude check to see if this font has a non-standard encoding, and if so, print the name of the font in `Courier-Bold` followed by a sample of the font. Here's the next version of the font lister.

List of fonts in their own font.

```
%!PS
/inch { 72 mul } def                        %   define inch procedure
/PrintSize 12 def                           %   point size for list
/Leading 14 def                             %   baseline leading
/TopMargin 10.5 inch def                    %   initial top margin
/BottomTopMargin 0.5 inch def               %   final bottom margin
/LeftMargin 0.5 inch def                     %   initial left margin
/Courier-Bold findfont                      %   find required font
PrintSize scalefont                         %   scale to required size
setfont                                     %   make it current font
/whichSide 0 def                            %   left or middle
/BaseLine TopMargin def                     %   set initial baseline position
/ShowFontName {                             %   stack = name of font
  /SaveWorld save def                       %   snapshot of VM
  dup dup                                   %   need two copies of name
  findfont /Encoding get                    %   get font encoding vector
  (A) 0 get get                             %   get name stored at "A"
  LeftMargin whichSide 4.25 inch mul add BaseLine moveto
  /A eq {                                   %   if name is "/A"
    findfont PrintSize scalefont setfont
    256 string cvs                          %   convert name to string
    show                                    %   image name of font
  } {
    /Courier-Bold findfont PrintSize scalefont setfont
    256 string cvs                          %   convert name to string
    show ( ) show                           %   image name of font
    dup findfont PrintSize scalefont setfont
    256 string cvs                          %   convert name to string
    show                                    %   image name of font
  } ifelse
```

```
/whichSide 1 whichSide sub def          %   switch side or middle
whichSide 0 eq {                        %   if starting a new line
    /BaseLine BaseLine Leading sub def
    BaseLine BottomTopMargin lt {       %   if baseline below bottom
        showpage                        %   display page
        /BaseLine TopMargin def         %   reset baseline
    } if
} if
SaveWorld restore                       %   restore VM to prior
} def
FontDirectory                           %   font directory onto stack
{                                       %   start forall loop
    pop                                 %   discard font dictionary
    ShowFontName                        %   display name of font
} forall                                %   traverse font directory
showpage                                %   display page
```

The trick in this version is to get the name stored at position "A" from the encoding vector and check if the name stored there is "/A". If the name is "/A", you can assume that the encoding is standard, and go ahead and convert the name of the font to that font. But if the name is not "/A", you can assume that the font has some other encoding vector,[†] in which case you first print the name in **Courier-Bold**, followed by the sample of the name in its own font. This is a crude assumption, and it may well break down in the general case, but it works well for many fonts.

Another notable item about this font lister. Why is there a **save** and **restore** wrapped around the process of showing the font name? This is to guard against a frequently overlooked feature of the PostScript interpreter: **findfont** performs an implicit **definefont** to install the font you found in VM. Without the **save** and **restore** around the process, you could potentially fill up VM. Service bureaus typically have entire font libraries of more than a thousand fonts. Chinese and Japanese fonts, as another example, are composite fonts consisting of hundreds of base fonts.

---

† For example, Sonata codes the name **/quarternotedownB** at position "A".

Printing names of fonts in their own fonts works well for standard (base) fonts. This technique may not work properly with composite fonts—you have to know you're listing a composite font, and you have to take into account which mapping method the font uses. Let's use an example from *Modifying the Font Mapping* on pages 425–429 in Chapter 10. In that example, you made the formerly escape-code-mapped playing cards font into an 8/8 mapped font. Using that particular font, let's just try to print the name **Playing-Cards** in its own font.

```
%!PS
/Playing-Cards findfont          %   find the playing cards font
24 scalefont                     %   scale to required size
setfont                          %   make it the current font
50 400 moveto                    %   set current point
(Playing-Cards) show             %   (try to) images the name
showpage                         %   display page
```

This example fails with a **rangecheck** error, with **show** as the errant command. What happened? Well, the string **Playing-Cards** happens to be thirteen characters long, and an 8/8 mapped font requires an even number of bytes in the show string.

You could be more clever, then, and have your listing program check the length of the names and insert extra characters if needed. If you do so with this particular name and make a name like "**Playing-CardsX**", for instance, you will then get an empty page. Why? Because the characters needed to select the base fonts are **C**, **D**, **H**, and **S**, and the characters to select cards from a font range from **0** through **9**, plus **A**. No such combinations appear in this show string. The only one that comes close is the **Ca** combination—all that does is select an undefined character that does nothing.

Well, that displays the fonts from the printer's font directory. This program is not the end of the story, though. On a NeXT system using Display PostScript, **FontDirectory** gets you nothing. If you run this program under control of YAP, for example, you'll get a blank page. The Display PostScript system contains some of the foundations of PostScript Level 2, and system fonts are defined in a global font directory called **SharedFontDirectory**. So, if you change the line reading **FontDirectory** to **SharedFontDirectory**, you'll get the correct answer on a Display PostScript system.

Listing Fonts on the Printer's Hard Disk

This is still not the whole story. What about printers with attached mass storage devices? Let's look at the details of a LaserWriter II-NTX-J, II-NTX, or LaserWriter IIg with an attached hard disk. You place PostScript font programs on the hard disk by downloading them using vendor-supplied software. You could write PostScript to download a font to the printer's hard disk, but the process is error prone. You're safer using vendor-supplied software whenever possible.

By the way, file system formats vary from device to device. Original LaserWriter II-NTX and II-NTX-J file systems were reputed to be based on Apple II file system layouts. Newer LaserWriter models such as the LaserWriter IIf and IIg have file systems compatible with Macintosh HFS. Needless to say, this causes a problem upgrading from older devices to newer devices. You can't take your disk of fonts from your LaserWriter II-NTX and just plug it straight into your LaserWriter IIg.

Writing a useful font listing program to discover font names on external devices is extremely device dependent. You need to know the details of how devices store fonts and other files. Consult the supplementary manual for your specific printer to determine details. That said, here's a program that prints a list of the fonts on the hard disk of a LaserWriter. Much of the code is similar to previous examples. Changed sections are highlighted.

```
ZapfDingbats              Tekton-Oblique
Tekton-BoldOblique        Tekton-Bold
Tekton                    Sonata
SI000PIXymbols            Optima-Oblique
Optima-BoldOblique        Optima-Bold
Optima                    OneStrokeScriptPlain
Lucida-Italic             Lucida-BoldItalic
Lucida-Bold               Lucida
LGamePi-FrenchCards       LGamePi-EnglishCards
LGamePi-DiceDominoes      LGamePi-ChessDraughts
ItcEras-Ultra             ItcEras-Medium
ItcEras-Light             ItcEras-Demi
ItcEras-Book              ItcEras-Bold
GillSans-LightItalic      GillSans-Light
GillSans-Italic           GillSans-BoldItalic
GillSans-Bold             GillSans
Garamond-LightItalic      Garamond-Light
Garamond-BoldItalic       Garamond-Bold
Copperplate-TwentyNineBC  Copperplate-TwentyNineAB
Copperplate-ThirtyTwoBC   Copperplate-ThirtyTwoAB
Copperplate-ThirtyThreeBC Copperplate-ThirtyOneBC
Copperplate-ThirtyOneAB   Copperplate-ThirtyOneBC
Copperplate-ThirtyAB      Copperplate-ThirtyBC
BrushScript               Carta
AGaramond-Semibold        AGaramond-SemiboldItalic
AGaramond-Italic          AGaramond-Regular
AGaramond-Bold            AGaramond-BoldItalic
```

Fonts on hard disk attached to Apple LaserWriter IIg.

```
%!PS
/inch { 72 mul } def                % define inch procedure
/PrintSize 12 def                   % point size for list
/Leading 14 def                     % baseline leading
/TopMargin 10.5 inch def            % initial top margin
/BottomTopMargin 0.5 inch def       % final bottom margin
/LeftMargin 0.5 inch def            % initial left margin
/Template (fonts/*) def             % template string for matching
/Courier-Bold findfont              % find required font
PrintSize scalefont                 % scale to required size
setfont                             % make it current font
/whichSide 0 def                    % left or middle
/BaseLine TopMargin def             % set initial baseline position
/ShowFontName {                     % stack = name string
  (fonts/) search { pop pop } if    % extract font name
                                    % set current point

  LeftMargin whichSide 4.25 inch mul add BaseLine moveto
  show                              % image name of font
  /whichSide 1 whichSide sub def    % switch side or middle
  whichSide 0 eq {                  % if starting a new line
    /BaseLine BaseLine Leading sub def
    BaseLine BottomTopMargin lt {   % if baseline below bottom
      showpage                      % display page
      /BaseLine TopMargin def       % reset baseline
    } if
  } if
} def
Template                            % template string
{ ShowFontName }                    % procedure to execute
256 string                          % scratch string
filenameforall                      % traverse through file system
showpage                            % display page
```

This program is quite different from the previous one—it uses **filenameforall** to traverse files on the hard disk file system. In this particular system, fonts are stored on the hard disk in a **fonts** directory (*folder* in Macintosh vernacular). So all fonts have a name of the form **fonts/***fontname*. The syntax of **filenameforall** is

file name

State of stack after each iteration of **filenameforall** *on matched file names.*

template   { *procedure* }   *scratch*   `filenameforall`

where *template* is a character string providing the filenames to match against, *procedure* is a procedure to be executed for every file that **filenameforall** matches, and *scratch* is a junk string big enough to hold a matched filename.

filenameforall provides limited "wild-card" matching so you can match filenames against patterns. Specifically, ***** matches zero or more characters, so the template string used in this example is (**fonts/***) meaning "match any file whose name starts with the character string "**fonts/**" followed by any other string of characters." The **ShowFontName** procedure executed for every file is almost the same as the one in the previous example, but it accepts a string as a parameter instead of a name. The shenanigans at the start of **ShowFontName** aren't strictly needed, but they strip off the prefixed template string so you see only the actual filenames.

This example was marked as PostScript Level 2 but, in fact, **filenameforall** is another of those in-between operators that appeared prior to PostScript Level 2 to support printers with attached mass storage devices.

We stated previously that obtaining a listing of fonts from the file system is extremely system dependent. The preceding program doesn't work on a NeXT computer, for instance. Fonts on a NeXT are stored in the regular UNIX file system, possibly in more than one directory. To run this program on a NeXT system, you would have to specify the font device explicitly. The font device is identified by the name **%font%**, so your template and **ShowFontName** must change, because what you get back from **filenameforall** includes the name of the directory where the font lives as well as the font name. Here it is for our NeXT System.

```
Courier                        Courier-Bold
Courier-BoldOblique            Courier-Oblique
Helvetica                      Helvetica-Bold
Helvetica-BoldOblique          Helvetica-Oblique
Lexi                           Oblia
Symbol                         Times-Bold
Times-BoldItalic               Times-Italic
Times-Roman                    Garamond-Bold
Garamond-BoldItalic            Garamond-Light
Garamond-LightItalic           Optima-Bold
Optima-BoldOblique             Optima-Oblique
Optima                         Palatino-Bold
Palatino-BoldItalic            Palatino-Italic
Palatino-Roman                 ZapfChancery-MediumItalic
BrushScript                    ZapfDingbats
S2000PIXymbols                 Sonata
Carta                          LGamePi-ChessDraughts
LGamePi-DiceDominoes           LGamePi-EnglishCards
LGamePi-FrenchCards            OneStrokeScriptPlain
AGaramond-BoldItalic           AGaramond-Bold
AGaramond-Italic               AGaramond-Regular
AGaramond-SemiboldItalic       AGaramond-Semibold
Copperplate-ThirtyAB           Copperplate-ThirtyBC
Copperplate-ThirtyOneAB        Copperplate-ThirtyOneBC
Copperplate-ThirtyThreeBC      Copperplate-ThirtyTwoAB
Copperplate-ThirtyTwoBC        Copperplate-TwentyNineAB
Copperplate-TwentyNineBC       GillSans-BoldItalic
GillSans-Bold                  GillSans-Italic
GillSans                       Tekton-Bold
Tekton-BoldOblique             Tekton-Oblique
Tekton
```

Fonts on our NeXT computer.

`%!PS`	
`/inch { 72 mul } def`	% *define* **inch** *procedure*
`/PrintSize 12 def`	% *point size for list*
`/Leading 14 def`	% *baseline leading*
`/TopMargin 10.5 inch def`	% *initial top margin*
`/BottomTopMargin 0.5 inch def`	% *final bottom margin*
`/LeftMargin 0.5 inch def`	% *initial left margin*
`/Template (%font%*) def`	% *template string for matching*
`/Courier-Bold findfont`	% *find required font*
`PrintSize scalefont`	% *scale to required size*
`setfont`	% *make it current font*
`/whichSide 0 def`	% *left or middle*
`/BaseLine TopMargin def`	% *set initial baseline position*
`/ShowFontName {`	% *stack = name string*
`  (/) search { pop pop } if`	% *strip out font name*
	% *set current point*
`  LeftMargin whichSide 4.25 inch mul add BaseLine moveto`	
`  show`	% *image name of font*
`  /whichSide 1 whichSide sub def`	% *switch side or middle*
`  whichSide 0 eq {`	% *if starting a new line*
`    /BaseLine BaseLine Leading sub def`	
`    BaseLine BottomTopMargin lt {`	% *if baseline below bottom*
`      showpage`	% *display page*
`      /BaseLine TopMargin def`	% *reset baseline*
`    } if`	
`  } if`	
`} def`	
`Template`	% *template string*
`{ ShowFontName }`	% *procedure to execute*
`256 string`	% *scratch string*
`filenameforall`	% *traverse through file system*
`showpage`	% *display page*

For example, on the NeXT, the **Palatino-Roman** font lives in a directory called **Palatino-Roman.font**, so what would come back from **filenameforall** is

%font%Palatino-Roman.font/Palatino-Roman

The **search** operator looks for the **/** and the name of the font is assumed to be the string following the **/**.

Listing Fonts in PostScript Level 2

As you see from preceding discussions, obtaining lists of fonts from PostScript devices is system-dependent and device-dependent. PostScript Level 2 provides a more general method to obtain names of *resources*, which includes fonts but can include patterns and forms, among others. Here's the same program, yet again, this time using PostScript Level 2 **resourceforall**.

Fonts on our LaserWriter IIg—both ROM fonts and disk fonts.

```
%!PS
/inch { 72 mul } def                    % define inch procedure
/PrintSize 12 def                       % point size for list
/Leading 14 def                         % baseline leading
/TopMargin 10.5 inch def                % initial top margin
/BottomTopMargin 0.5 inch def           % final bottom margin
/LeftMargin 0.5 inch def                % initial left margin
/Courier-Bold findfont                  % find required font
PrintSize scalefont                     % scale to required size
setfont                                 % make it current font
/whichSide 0 def                        % left or middle
/BaseLine TopMargin def                 % set initial baseline position
/ShowFontName {                         % stack = name string
                                        % set current point
  LeftMargin whichSide 4.25 inch mul add BaseLine moveto
  show                                  % image name of font
  /whichSide 1 whichSide sub def        % switch side or middle
  whichSide 0 eq {                      % if starting a new line
    /BaseLine BaseLine Leading sub def
    BaseLine BottomTopMargin lt {       % if baseline below bottom
      showpage                          % display page
      /BaseLine TopMargin def           % reset baseline
    } if
  } if
} def
(*)                                     % template string
{ ShowFontName }                        % procedure to execute
256 string                              % scratch string
/Font                                   % resource category = /Font
resourceforall                          % traverse through resources
showpage                                % display page
```

This program shows all your fonts—from the memory-resident font directory, from the shared font directory, and from mass storage devices. Get your magnifying glass and you'll see that this list of fonts is the memory-resident fonts followed by the disk-resident fonts. **resourceforall** takes care of finding all resources of the specific named category.

Determining Printer Memory Usage

Related to listing and downloading fonts is the ability to check how much memory is available for new resources. If you're about to download a font—or find a font that's on the printer's mass storage device—you need to check ahead of time if there's enough room in VM for the font. You determine the amount of used and available memory with the **vmstatus** operator. Here's a PostScript program to print the values obtained from **vmstatus**.

Level = 2

Used = 25548

Maximum = 2121216

Printout of values returned from **vmstatus**.

```
%!PS
/inch { 72 mul } def                        %  define inch procedure
/Courier-Bold findfont 24 scalefont setfont
vmstatus                                     %  obtain VM status
1 inch 3 inch moveto                         %  set current point
(Maximum = ) show                            %  maximum available caption
16 string cvs show                           %  convert and show maximum
1 inch 5 inch moveto                         %  set current point
(Used = ) show                               %  memory used caption
16 string cvs show                           %  convert and show used
1 inch 7 inch moveto                         %  set current point
(Level = ) show                              %  save level caption
16 string cvs show                           %  convert and show save level
showpage                                     %  display page
```

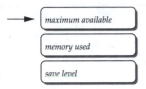

Stack contents after call to
vmstatus.

vmstatus reports three numbers, of which the maximum available memory is the most interesting. The listing above shows numbers returned from an Apple LaserWriter IIg with eight megabytes of RAM. The report indicates there are over two megabytes of RAM available for user programs to consume.

The amount of memory used increases, and, consequently the amount of memory available decreases, when you install resources into VM. When we install the playing cards composite font from chapter 10, the amount of memory used goes up over 50,000 bytes and the maximum amount decreases.

Listing Characters in a Font

After listing fonts from the printer, the next job is to obtain a list of characters in a font. The code to do this is listed out in sections. This first section just sets up some definitions.

List of characters from the Zapf Dingbats font.

```
%!PS
/inch { 72 mul } def              % define inch procedure
/WhatFont /ZapfDingbats def        % font to display
/DisplaySize 24 def                % size of displayed characters
/Left      0.75 inch   def         % left margin
/Right     8.25 inch   def         % right margin
/Top       9.50 inch   def         % top margin
/Bottom    0.50 inch   def         % bottom margin
/BoxWidth   Right Left sub 16 div def
/BoxHeight  Top Bottom sub 16 div def
/Glyph 1 string def                % string for one character
/ColString 1 string def            % column number
/RowString (00) def                % row base
/LowerHex (0123456789abcdef) def   % for translations
```

This next code section draws a grid of gray lines, places row and column addresses down the left side and across the top of the page, and shows the name of the font as a title.

Grid lines with row and columns addresses.

```
0.9 setgray                                      %   set light gray
0 1 16 {                                          %   draw grid of boxes
    dup BoxWidth mul Left add Bottom moveto
    dup BoxWidth mul Left add Top lineto
    dup BoxHeight mul Bottom add Left exch moveto
    dup BoxHeight mul Bottom add Right exch lineto
} for
stroke                                            %   stroke all the lines
0.0 setgray                                       %   back to black
/Courier findfont 16 scalefont setfont            %   font for addresses
0 1 15 {                                          %   place addresses
    /RowCol exch def
    RowCol BoxWidth mul BoxWidth 4 div add Left add
    Top 0.125 inch add moveto
    ColString dup 0 LowerHex RowCol get put show
    RowCol Top exch BoxHeight mul
    BoxHeight 3 div 2 mul add sub
    Left 0.5 inch sub exch moveto
    RowString dup 0 LowerHex RowCol get put show
} for
/Courier-Bold findfont                            %   font for title
DisplaySize scalefont                             %   scale to required size
setfont                                           %   make current font
WhatFont 128 string cvs dup                       %   convert name of font
stringwidth pop 8.5 inch exch sub 2 div %          center title
Top 0.75 inch add moveto show                     %   display title
```

Finally, this section of code does the work of imaging each character at its correct position in the grid.

Palatino Bold font listed on
grid.

```
WhatFont findfont                        %   get font to display
DisplaySize scalefont                    %   scale to required size
setfont                                  %   make current font
0 1 15 {                                 %   work down the rows
    /Row exch def
    0 1 15 {                             %   work across the columns
        /Col exch def
        Row 16 mul Col add               %   character number
        Glyph exch 0 exch put            %   insert that character
        Col BoxWidth mul BoxWidth 4 div add Left add
        Top Row BoxHeight mul BoxHeight 3 div 2 mul add sub
        moveto Glyph show                %   display glyph
    } for
} for
showpage                                 %   display page
```

Well, that's not too bad. But consider a couple of items. First, this
code only lists characters that are in the encoding vector for the
font. Characters can be defined in the font but not be present in the
encoding. If you wish to see all characters in a font, you must get
their names into the encoding.

Second and once again, this code can fail with composite fonts. Say
you apply this code to a composite font with escape-code mapping.
You start imaging characters from the first base font because you
didn't explicitly pick a font with an escape-character-font-number
sequence. All will go well until the character code you try to image
is the escape code. At this point, the font machinery wants another
byte to specify the number of the base font. But the show string is
only one byte long. Once more, the process fails with a **rangecheck**.
You need to be aware of the mapping method for this code to work
correctly with a composite font.

Listing Character Metrics from a Font

Listing the characters from a font is nice, but some users want more, more, more! The next job is to list more data about individual characters, including widths and bounding boxes. The next PostScript program prints data about an individual character. This picture shows one huge character on the page with its metrics data. In practice, you would want to place as many characters on a page as can be fitted comfortably without compromising readability. As before, the code is presented in sections, each section being a module in the larger piece. The first piece of code is definitions.

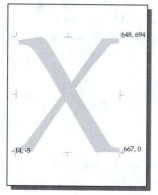

One character with its metrics data.

```
%!PS
/inch { 72 mul } def                    %  define inch procedure
/WhatFont   /Palatino-Roman def
/WhatCharacter  (X) def
/DesignSize 1000 def
/BoxSize 720 def
/ScaleFactor BoxSize DesignSize div def
/MarkLen 18   def
/HalfMarkLen MarkLen 2 div def
/TwoMarkLen MarkLen 2 mul def
/NoteSize 30 def
/Temp1 128 string def
/Temp2 128 string def
```

The next part of the code draws marks at the corners, and also draws marks at the midpoints. This code uses the definitions of **llx**, **lly**, **urx**, and **ury**, which are defined later down in the code at the time the character is processed.

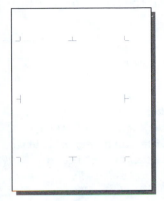

Character Bounding box marks.

```
/DrawBounds {
    /midx llx urx llx sub 2 div add def
    /midy lly ury lly sub 2 div add def
                                          %   lower-left marker
    llx 2 sub lly moveto MarkLen neg 0 rlineto
    llx lly 2 sub moveto 0 MarkLen neg rlineto
                                          %   lower-right marker
    urx 2 add lly moveto  MarkLen 0 rlineto
    urx lly 2 sub moveto 0 MarkLen neg rlineto
                                          %   upper-right marker
    urx 2 add ury moveto  MarkLen 0 rlineto
    urx ury 2 add moveto 0  MarkLen rlineto
                                          %   upper-left marker
    llx 2 sub ury moveto MarkLen neg 0 rlineto
    llx ury 2 add moveto 0  MarkLen rlineto
                                          %   bottom marker
    midx MarkLen sub lly moveto
    TwoMarkLen 0 rlineto
    midx lly moveto 0 MarkLen neg rlineto
                                          %   right marker
    urx midy MarkLen sub moveto
    0 TwoMarkLen rlineto
    urx midy moveto MarkLen 0 rlineto
                                          %   top marker
    midx MarkLen sub ury moveto
    TwoMarkLen 0 rlineto
    midx ury moveto 0 MarkLen rlineto
                                          %   right marker
    llx midy MarkLen sub moveto
    0 TwoMarkLen rlineto
    llx midy moveto MarkLen neg 0 rlineto
    stroke                       %   stroke all the lines
} def
```

This code draws the crosses for the origin and the character width.

Origin and character width marks.

```
/Cross {                                    %   stack = x y
    /YOrigin exch def
    /XOrigin exch def
    XOrigin 1 sub YOrigin moveto HalfMarkLen neg 0 rlineto
    XOrigin 1 add YOrigin moveto HalfMarkLen 0 rlineto
    XOrigin YOrigin 1 sub moveto 0 HalfMarkLen neg rlineto
    XOrigin YOrigin 1 add moveto 0 HalfMarkLen rlineto
    stroke                                  %   stroke all the lines
} def
```

This next section places the numbers for the bounding box and origin in their respective places around the character shape.

Values for origin, width, and bounding box.

```
/ShowCorners {
    /Palatino-Roman findfont NoteSize scalefont setfont
    LowerY Temp2 cvs
    LowerX Temp1 cvs
    llx 4 sub lly 4 sub moveto show (, ) show show
    UpperY Temp2 cvs
    UpperX Temp1 cvs
    urx 4 add ury 4 add moveto show (, ) show show
    YWidth Temp2 cvs
    XWidth Temp1 cvs
    XOrigin 4 add YOrigin 4 add moveto show (, ) show show
} def
```

Finally, the main part of the code pulls the other pieces together.

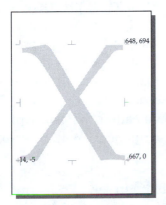

Complete character metrics listing.

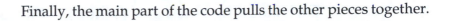

```
WhatFont findfont DesignSize scalefont setfont
                              %   get width of character
newpath 0 0 moveto WhatCharacter stringwidth
round cvi /YWidth exch def
round cvi /XWidth exch def

                              %   get bounding box
newpath 0 0 moveto WhatCharacter false charpath
flattenpath pathbbox
4 1 roll round cvi /UpperY exch def
4 1 roll round cvi /UpperX exch def
4 1 roll round cvi /LowerY exch def
4 1 roll round cvi /LowerX exch def
                              %   scale to display size

/ury UpperY ScaleFactor mul def
/urx UpperX ScaleFactor mul def
/lly LowerY ScaleFactor mul def
/llx LowerX ScaleFactor mul def
                              %   get font and scale
WhatFont findfont BoxSize scalefont setfont
gsave
    10 150 translate           %   set origin
    newpath 0 0 moveto         %   set current point
    0.90 setgray               %   light gray
    WhatCharacter show         %   show the character
    0.0 setgray                %   back to black
    0.25 setlinewidth          %   thin line width
    newpath 0 0 Cross          %   draw cross at origin
    XWidth ScaleFactor mul     %   draw cross at right side
    YWidth ScaleFactor mul Cross
    DrawBounds                 %   draw bounding boxes
    ShowCorners                %   fill in values
grestore
showpage                       %   display page
```

This code as described shows only one character. You can revamp this code and use some of the ideas from the previous example to show all characters in a font and create a new program that will show metrics for all characters.

Downloading Fonts and Other PostScript Programs

Downloading—this is a term you hear often. What precisely *is* downloading? In PostScript (indeed, in general computer) jargon, downloading is a fancy term for sending a PostScript program to a PostScript interpreter so that a PostScript job can use resources created or defined by the downloaded part. If you've typed any of the examples in this book and used a utility program[†] to send the file to your printer, you've "downloaded" a PostScript job. Downloading can be temporary or permanent, with "permanent" having a variety of interpretations.

A more specific use of "download" is the ability to send PostScript files to the printer and make the effect of those files available for subsequent PostScript jobs. The most common use of downloading in this context is to send font programs to the printer and store the fonts permanently, either in the printer's memory or on the printer's hard disk. Suppose you're operating a service bureau. Customers come in with a variety of PostScript jobs, all needing different fonts. Sending the fonts to the printer as part of every job consumes a lot of time, both in transmitting the fonts to the printer and in waiting for the printer to interpret and store the fonts. A much better scene is to send the fonts once and have them available all the time for every customer job.

PostScript *service bureaus* use downloading to install what are known as "prep files" in their imagesetters. PostScript documents usually consist of a *prolog* section followed by a *script* section, which is the pages to be printed. The script (pages) uses the procedures defined in the prolog section. A frequently used prolog can be extracted from a document and downloaded to the printing device as a permanent "prep file," saving the time required to install the prolog for subsequent jobs.

Another use for downloading is to install an *error handler* in the printer. As noted in Chapter 1, PostScript printers are taciturn

---

† such as Downloader on Macintosh or **psdown** on PC

about what made a job fail, so you'll want to install a PostScript program that reports on the causes of errors. You usually download an error handler once, right after you switch on the printer. The error handler stays resident in printer memory until you switch the printer off.

To gain a better understanding of downloading, think about some of the fonts you created and defined in Chapter 10. To print a PostScript job using a font that is not installed in the printer, you must send the definition of the font as an integral part of the job in which it's used. If you send a lot of jobs requiring this font, the time to transmit the font definition to the printer becomes excessive. What you'd like to do is transmit the font once. To better understand how downloading works, you now need to know about the PostScript *server* and the *server loop*.

The PostScript Server and the Server Loop

PostScript literature contains frequent references to this mysterious animal called the *server loop*. What is the server loop? When a PostScript printer is switched on, a PostScript procedure (whose name is the server loop) is placed on the execution stack. The server loop is reminiscent of old-style "batch processing" systems. The server loop performs several tasks, including the following tasks that affect downloading:

❑ taking a snapshot of the state of the PostScript interpreter environment before the job starts (using **save**)

❑ executing the job and calling the error handler if necessary[†]

❑ restoring the state of the PostScript interpreter environment after the job is complete (using **restore**)

---

† Error handling is environment-dependent and can be changed by the user. *Handling PostScript Errors* on pages 581–589 in this chapter contains a discussion on error handlers.

The **save** and **restore** bracket defeat naive attempts to install fonts and other resources. At the end of a PostScript job, the server restores the interpreter environment to its state at the beginning of the job. Anything you defined in VM are wiped away. To install resources permanently in printer memory, you must sidestep **save** and **restore** so your definitions remain across jobs. How you do this depends on whether you're in a PostScript Level 1 environment or a PostScript Level 2 environment.

PostScript Level 1 systems bypass the normal operation of the server loop with **exitserver**. Here's how to use **exitserver**:

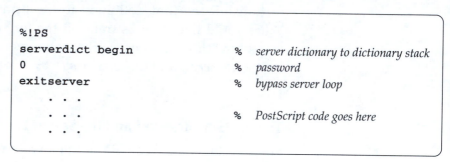

```
%!PS
serverdict begin          %   server dictionary to dictionary stack
0                         %   password
exitserver                %   bypass server loop
   . . .
   . . .                  %   PostScript code goes here
   . . .
```

If you have a means to monitor the communication line from the printer to the host computer, you will see the following message coming back from the printer:

```
%%[ exitserver: permanent state may be changed ]%%
```

exitserver is one of the fuzzy areas of PostScript. **exitserver** is not an "official" part of the PostScript language but most interpreters implement **exitserver** to meet the requirement of installing resources that can reside in printer memory for long periods. In PostScript Level 2, the recommended way to bypass the server loop is to use **startjob**, which is more flexible than **exitserver**.

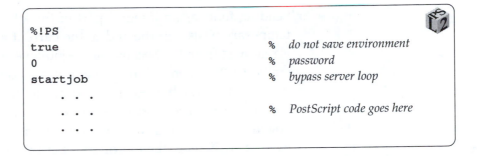

```
%!PS
true                              %   do not save environment
0                                 %   password
startjob                          %   bypass server loop
     . . .
     . . .                        %   PostScript code goes here
     . . .
```

One of the most common uses of downloading is to make fonts available for PostScript jobs. Why and when do you need to download a font to a PostScript printer? Simple—if your application software requests a font that is not present in the printer, you must download that font to make it available in the printer. How would you use **exitserver** or **startjob** to download a font? Various strategies deal with downloading. The strategy you use will depend to a large extent on the support your computer operating system provides for you.

One method is to send the font as an integral part of your current PostScript print job. The advantage of this approach is that you consume printer memory only for the duration of the job. The disadvantages are the time to transmit the font to the printer and the time the PostScript interpreter takes to interpret the font program and your PostScript print job.

There's another snag to this approach—a legal snag. PostScript font programs are licensed, not sold, and they're usually licensed for use with only one printer. If you include a PostScript font program as an integral part of your print job, you can't distribute that file. This is an oversimplified statement of the issue, and you need to make sure you're clear on licensing issues.

Macintosh print manager interrogates the printer to determine if the font is already resident and downloads the font only if required. UNIX systems, in general, don't have anything resembling a print manager, so you must employ a different approach.

Sending fonts as an integral part of the job downloads fonts on a temporary basis—at the end of the current job, the font definition is removed from VM because of the job-level **save** and **restore**. Generally, UNIX systems don't have a way to determine what fonts a PostScript print job needs nor a means to interrogate the printer to find out if fonts are already resident. This means that on many UNIX systems you must download fonts permanently. UNIX systems have a different flavor of PostScript support from that of Macintosh—if indeed "support" is the correct term. In general, UNIX systems print files through the aegis of a "spooler." The main thing to understand with respect to UNIX is that the spooler is not a print manager. The spooler does absolutely nothing to ensure that your PostScript documents print correctly. You, the user, must do font management and other resource management. Worse still, in a networked environment, you must coordinate with other users to make sure fonts are downloaded only when needed. Usually, UNIX spoolers have some intermediary process between the printer device and the spooler.

To describe PC-based systems *versus* PostScript, Adobe Systems probably said it as cogently as possible:

> *PC applications do not support fonts in a standard way. Font installation, selection, and downloading, vary by application.*

You can extrapolate to note that PC-based systems don't support *anything* in a "standard" way. Capabilities for downloading on PC-based systems vary widely. Some applications understand PostScript and do the appropriate printer management functions for you. Other applications are oblivious to PostScript and you must do more work. Adobe supplies the **psdown** and **pcsend** programs with PC font packages. **psdown** works with printers connected to serial (RS-232) ports, and **pcsend** is for printers connected to parallel ports. The two programs are similar; they are called *font downloaders* but, in fact, they can send arbitrary PostScript files to the printer, since a font is just another PostScript file. **psdown** and **pcsend** have four primary functions. The function of interest in this discussion is sending a PostScript file to the printer. They are "menu-driven" programs and simple, if somewhat clumsy.

Other font vendors may or may not supply a font downloader with their font packages. You need only one font downloader, not one per font package. So if you already have one, you don't need to keep buying more. You'd be wise to ask your dealer if the font package comes with a downloader before you shell out for a font package that is unusable on your PC.

PostScript Level 2 Resources

In previous chapters you saw fonts, patterns, forms, and halftone dictionaries. PostScript Level 2 introduced the notion of *resources*. A resource is a PostScript object that can be loaded into VM by name. PostScript resources are grouped into categories. In PostScript Level 1, the only "resource" was a font and fonts were not thought of as abstract resources. PostScript Level 2 has many categories of resources, including forms, fonts, patterns, and halftone screens. All resources within a single category are grouped into a name space and must have a unique name. But resources in different categories can share names. For example, you can have a form resource named *Scrabble* and a font resource named *Scrabble*. No collision occurs because forms and fonts are different categories of resources and are stored in different name spaces. You cannot have two forms (or two fonts) named *Scrabble*. The next few pages describe how to define, find, and use named resources. The examples used here build on the forms defined in Chapter 12 for illustration.

Defining a Named Resource

Use **defineresource** to install a form as a named resource in the PostScript interpreter. Here's how to install **Rolodex** form.

```
/Rolodex RolodexForm /Form defineresource
```

Now, for as long as your PostScript job is running, **RolodexForm** can be loaded into VM by name. The general syntax of **defineresource** is

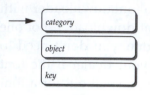

Stack contents before call to **defineresource**.

key object category `defineresource`

where *key* is the name associated with the resource—the Rolodex example uses the name **/Rolodex**. The name can be a string, a name, or any other PostScript object. However, be aware of the limitations of names on external storage devices. Using a font dictionary as the name of an object is quite legitimate PostScript, but an external file system may well insist on names of specific length with restricted syntax. Think of DOS, for instance, with its eight-character name limitations. *object* is the actual resource, which must be of the appropriate type for the category. In the case of forms, *object* must be a form dictionary. The example uses the form dictionary defining the Rolodex card. *category* indicates the category type for this resource. PostScript Level 2 has several categories of resources, including patterns, fonts, and halftone dictionaries. To specify a form resource, *category* must be **/Form**. *Category* is **/Font** for fonts, **/Pattern** for patterns, and so on.

Finding a Named Resource

Once you've installed your form as a named resource, you can load it by name into VM any time during the execution of the program. Use **findresource** to locate the resource you want. The general format of **findresource** is

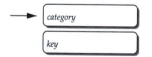

Stack contents before call to **findresource**.

key category `findresource`

where *key* is the name associated with the resource—the same name used to define the resource with **defineresource**. *category* is the category of the resource (as defined previously). To retrieve the Rolodex card resource, use **findresource** as follows:

```
/Rolodex /Form findresource
```

findresource locates the resource, loads it into VM, and places a reference to the resource on the operand stack.

Presumably you found the resource in order to use it. You could very well have found the resource and used it all in one instruction, as follows:

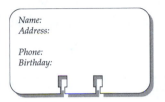

```
/Rolodex /Form findresource execform
```

Since **Rolodex** is a form resource, you use **execform** to image the form on the page.

You've just seen a quick overview of how to use forms as named resources. More complicated issues related to defining and using resources do exist, for example, defining resources in global VM or local VM and making those definitions persist beyond the boundaries of a single PostScript program. These issues are covered in detail in the *PostScript Language Reference Manual*, Second Edition.

Handling PostScript Errors

Everybody makes ~~mitsakes~~ ~~misteaks~~ mistakes. While writing this book we developed several thousand PostScript programs and made probably thirty thousand programming mistakes. With the help of good PostScript previewers (Ghostscript on a Sun-3/60 and YAP on the NeXT) and good error handlers for our printers, we were able to deal with problems quickly.

PostScript programs can fail to print for a variety of reasons. One reason might be that the program contains errors. Another possible reason is device characteristics that can print PostScript code fine on one device but will fail to print on another device. One of the design goals of Adobe was to develop a PostScript interpreter that could image anything you could describe *via* an arbitrary PostScript program. To a large degree, the implementors of PostScript achieved the design goals. However, due to limitations of specific devices and misunderstanding of PostScript issues by application writers, you can run into situations where something you describe will not print. Or, perhaps, a page description that prints fine on your Apple LaserWriter fails to image when you try to print it on a high-resolution typesetter.

Some PostScript devices have a two-way communication channel between the host computer and the printer. This means that you can send PostScript code down to the printer, and the printer can send messages back to the host. The following PostScript program contains an error. It would normally print a triangle as shown, but one line is incorrect.

```
%!PS
/inch { 72 mul } def          %   define inch procedure
1 inch 1 inch moveto          %   set current point
4.25 inch lineto              %   add line segment—MISTAKE
7.5 inch 1 inch lineto        %   add another line segment
closepath                     %   finish shape
1 inch setlinewidth           %   fat line width
stroke                        %   paint outline
showpage                      %   display page
```

Triangle that would be displayed except for error in PostScript program.

The line reading **4.25 inch lineto** is incorrect—the y coordinate is missing. When you run this program on a printer that can send messages back to the host computer, you see this message:

```
%%[Error: stackunderflow; OffendingCommand: lineto ]%%
```

You can do a remarkable amount of debugging with this small amount of information. Many PostScript errors are trivial. When your PostScript printer blinks its lights for a while and then doesn't print anything, what's the very first thing you should look for? Check for a missing **showpage**! If that's not the problem, read on to find out how to build an error handler.

A Basic Error Handler

Let's build a basic error handler. An error handler is a PostScript program that intercepts and displays the reason for errors in other PostScript programs. Error handlers can be as simple or as elaborate as you like, ranging from displaying only the PostScript instruction that caused the error, to complicated displays of the stacks. Let's start with the basics, to illustrate the methods by which PostScript deals with errors. This error handler provides about the same amount of information as the message from the printer to the host computer, as you just saw, but prints the message on the page instead. Let's start with the code.

```
%!PS
errordict begin                         %   error dictionary on dictionary stack
  /handleerror {                        %   define error handler
  systemdict begin                      %   systemdict on dictionary stack
    initgraphics                        %   restore original graphics state
                                        %   font for printout
    /Courier findfont 12 scalefont setfont
    72 720 moveto                       %   set current point
    (Postscript problem: ) show %   show error
    $error /errorname get
    =string cvs show
    72 700 moveto                       %   set current point
    (Command: ) show                    %   show command causing error
    $error /command get
    =string cvs show
    systemdict /showpage get exec%   display page
    end  %  systemdict                  %   remove systemdict
  } def                                 %   end of error handler
end                                     %   remove errordict
```

Under normal operation, your printer would not print anything, because the **lineto** instruction is incorrect. You tack this error handling code onto the front of your PostScript program and ship the whole thing to the printer. If you run the incorrect code example with the error handler code in front, your printer will print the page as shown. The scale is exaggerated so you can read the text.

This is a very simple error handler, but it contains a lot of detail about the workings of the PostScript error machinery. Let's dissect this program. First of all, when the PostScript interpreter detects an error, it looks in a special dictionary, called **errordict,** for the name of a procedure corresponding to that specific error condition. If you were to look inside **errordict** you'd see the names of the error

```
Postscript problem: stackunderflow
Command:  lineto
```

Results of PostScript error handler.

conditions, such as **undefined, typecheck,** and so on. An important procedure inside **errordict** is called **handleerror**.

All the preset error handlers function much the same. They record details of the error condition in a special system dictionary called **$error**, then execute **stop**. The preset error handlers don't print anything, although some printer error handlers may send a short message across the communication channel to the host computer.

The example program first places **errordict** on the top of the dictionary stack. Then it defines the error handling procedure (**/handleerror**), overriding the existing (**/handleerror**) procedure. The error handler obtains the Courier font for printing the errors.[†] Interesting parts of the error handler are the lines to obtain the name of the error (**/errorname**), the command causing the (**/command**) error from **$error**, and the use of the variable called **=string** for converting names to strings ready for printing. Some PostScript interpreters define **=string** in **systemdict**. **=string** is usually 128 bytes long and can be used as a scratch string for any purpose you wish. But be careful—some PostScript "clone" interpreters don't define **=string**, and programs depending on its existence are doomed to fail. You can use **where** to determine if **=string** is defined anywhere in your system. If **=string** is not present in your system, you can define it yourself. But what if the cause of the error is a lack of VM? In such a case, you're completely out of luck, because the memory required to report the error isn't there.

A More Complex Error Handler

The first version of the error handler gives you the same amount of information as the message from the printer. What you'd like to do next is print the contents of the operand stack at the time the error happened. So this next version of the error handler prints the error condition and PostScript instruction causing the error just as before, and now prints the contents of the operand stack in

---

† Courier is present in just about every PostScript interpreter. Substitute another font if Courier isn't present.

addition. When a PostScript error is trapped, the **$error** dictionary contains a snapshot of the operand stack, execution stack, and dictionary stack. All three stacks are recorded as arrays. In this error handler we're interested only in the operand stack. The code is written in two sections. The first section defines a collection of procedures for converting data types to strings. The second section is the error handler proper.

```
%!PS
$error /recordstacks true put                % Display PostScript
/SimpleErrorDict 20 dict def                 % define dictionary for types
SimpleErrorDict begin                        % place on dictionary stack
  /arraytype { pop (>> array <<) } def %    array procedure
  /booleantype { =string cvs } def           % Boolean procedure
  /conditiontype { pop (>> condition <<) } def
  /dicttype { pop (>> dictionary <<) } def
  /filetype { pop (>> file <<) } def
  /fonttype { pop (>> font ID <<) } def
  /gstatetype { pop (>> gstate <<) } def
  /integertype { =string cvs } def
  /locktype { pop (>> lock <<) } def
  /marktype { pop (>> mark <<) } def
  /nametype { pop (>> name <<) } def
  /nulltype { pop (>> null <<) } def
  /operatortype { pop (>> operator <<) } def
  /packedarraytype { pop (>> packed array <<) } def
  /realtype { =string cvs } def
  /savetype { pop (>> save object <<) } def
  /stringtype { } def                        % just print string
end                                          % pop from dictionary stack
/BaseLine 736 def                            % initial baseline
/NewLine {                                   % define new line procedure
  /BaseLine BaseLine 16 sub def              % decrement baseline
  72 BaseLine moveto                         % set current point
} def
/DisplayValue {                              % display based on type
  dup                                        % make copy of object
  type SimpleErrorDict exch get exec         % run conversion procedure
  show                                       % image converted object
  NewLine                                    % position to new line
} def
```

This version of the error handler is deliberately simple. Let's dissect it. This code is *very* system-dependent.

The first line is of interest if you're writing an error handler to run in the Display PostScript environment. Display PostScript does not normally record the contents of the stacks in the **$error** dictionary. You can control whether stacks are recorded by setting **/recordstacks** in **$error** to **true**. **/recordstacks** also exists in PostScript Level 2 interpreters.

The remaining definitions are simple. They depend on the way the **type** operator works. If you say **10 type**, you'll get the name **/integertype** on the stack because **10** is an integer. You can then use the name **/integertype** as a key to obtain a procedure to execute. Notice that the **/integertype** procedure simply converts the integer value to a string ready to show. Types such as **/arraytype** are not converted—they just leave a value like (>> **array** <<) on the stack and that is what is printed. Note that **/conditiontype**, **/gstatetype**, and **/locktype** are specific to Display PostScript.

Displaying the stack contents is slightly tricky because the way you display a given stack element depends on its type. Integers, reals, and Booleans are easy; just convert them to a string using **cvs**. But arrays, dictionaries, and other composite objects must be pulled apart piece by piece. Now on to the error handler.

Most of this new **handleerror** procedure is the same as the simple error handler. The addition is the code for printing the stack. The operand stack is stored as an array in **ostack** in the **$error** dictionary. This code uses **aload** to place each array element on the stack and leaves the original array as the top element of the stack. This is handy because you use the length of the array to control the **repeat** loop to print each element of the stack.

```
errordict begin                      %   error dictionary to dictionary stack
   /handleerror {                     %   define new handleerror
      systemdict begin                %   system dictionary to dictionary stack
         userdict begin               %   user dictionary to dictionary stack
            initgraphics              %   restore graphics state
            /Courier findfont 12 scalefont setfont
            NewLine                   %   start new line
            (PostScript problem: ) show%   show problem
            $error /errorname get
            =string cvs show
            NewLine
            (Command: ) show          %   show PostScript instruction
            $error /command get
            =string cvs show
            NewLine
            (Stack: ) show            %   show contents of stack
            NewLine                   %
            $error /ostack get        %   stack snapshot to stack
            aload                     %   spread contents onto stack
            length {                  %   get length for repeat count
               DisplayValue           %   display each stack element
            } repeat                  %   determined by length
            systemdict /showpage get%   get real showpage
            exec                      %   display page
         end  %  userdict            %   user dictionary off dictionary stack
      end  %  systemdict             %   system dictionary off dictionary stack
   } def                              %   end of handleerror procedure
end  %  errordict                     %   error dictionary off dictionary stack
```

Let's use this more complex error handler in conjunction with the flat triangle example from page 582 previously.

```
Postscript problem: stackunderflow
Command:  lineto
Stack:
306.0
```

```
%!PS
/inch { 72 mul } def          %   define inch procedure
1 inch 1 inch moveto          %   set current point
4.25 inch lineto              %   add line segment—MISTAKE
7.5 inch 1 inch lineto        %   add another line segment
closepath                     %   finish shape
1 inch setlinewidth           %   fat line width
stroke                        %   paint outline
showpage                      %   display page
```

*Results of more complex
PostScript error handler.*

You can make the printing procedures as elaborate as you wish. A common enhancement is to print the contents of arrays and dictionaries. Printing the contents of arrays may or may not be useful to you. There's a point at which receiving more data from the error handler doesn't really help. Like getting sixteen-Megabyte hexadecimal "core dumps" from your mainframe computer, printing the contents of all the stacks in detail may not necessarily provide helpful information—only data.

A Downloadable Error Handler

Tacking an error handler onto the front of every PostScript program you send to the printer could be tedious. You'd like to install the handler in the printer so it's there to trap errors whenever they occur. You can modify the error handler to download to your printer permanently to the printer's memory. So now you can add a section of code to the start of your error handler to define it in printer memory.

```
/SimpleErrorDict where {        %   look for error dictionary
    pop                         %   it's already defined
    (Error Handler already installed\n) print flush
    stop                        %   terminate this job
} {
    serverdict begin            %   server dictionary to dictionary stack
    0 exitserver                %   exit server loop
} ifelse
        . . .
            code of error handler follows
        . . .
```

This error handler will be installed in printer memory. Placing an error handler on the printer's hard disk can be even more useful, assuming you install it in memory from the disk startup file.

Generating PostScript Programs

If you're an application programmer intending to generate PostScript, you have a learning experience ahead of you. Let's say you write your drawing program or your page layout program in a modern language like Objective-C.[†] When you come to generate the PostScript, you're faced with a number of issues.

First, you need to learn another programming language— PostScript. And this book and others exhort you to learn to think in PostScript instead of writing C in a different dialect. Second, you need to learn how to generate "good" PostScript programs. Third, in addition to PostScript, you must learn another "language" known as *Document Structuring Conventions*. The burden of assimilating two new languages and new ways of thinking about them is no doubt one of the factors contributing to so much "bad" PostScript, but you must spend the time learning the conventions. By so doing, you will create PostScript documents that are

---

† Get serious—give up BASIC and FORTRAN.

interchangeable and device-independent. If you'll be spending significant time generating PostScript from your application, consider attending a "PostScript drivers" course, which teaches the concepts of generating good PostScript.

Let's start the discussion of generating PostScript by looking at a few goals of an application that will generate PostScript programs. You've probably heard the term *PostScript driver* mentioned a lot. Just what is a PostScript driver? In its simplest form, a PostScript driver is the part of your application[†] that turns the output from your application into a PostScript program suitable for sending to some device that can render the PostScript code.

The most basic objectives of generated PostScript are high quality output followed by good performance. High quality output means that the images produced by your PostScript code "look good." High quality coupled with good performance has a lot in common with the weather forecast—you want the generated PostScript to produce the highest quality output possible for the device, but you also want this output to be printed in less than tectonic timescales. To this end, you need to generate "good" PostScript that performs well on a variety of printing devices.

In addition to good-looking output produced in a reasonable amount of time, you must also address some slightly conflicting objectives, namely, what Adobe Systems calls *cooperative printing*, plus device-independence and support for device features.

What does "cooperative printing mean"? Primarily, it means generating PostScript programs that can be placed inside other PostScript programs. Cooperative printing also includes making no assumptions about the kind of device or PostScript environment (Encapsulated PostScript, for instance) on which the PostScript program will print.

---

† It could be a separate program to interpret your application file format and turn it into PostScript.

Device-independence means not assuming the existence of device features. This need conflicts with supporting device features. What kinds of features? Some printers support different paper sizes. Some support manual paper feeding. Other printers have power-driven envelope feeders, spindlers, folders, and mutilators. Some support multiple paper trays and double-sided printing. Some high-end imagesetters support different resolutions and the image-able area on which they can print differs depending on the resolution. Good PostScript programs use such features when available but never assume that those features are present.

Some objectives are handled by making use of PostScript *Document Structuring Conventions*—special PostScript comments that effectively impose a document control language on top of the PostScript graphics language. When used correctly, this control language can provide other useful capabilities, such as extracting specific pages from a document, printing pages two-up or four-up, and reverse-order printing.

Supporting device features can be handled by using PostScript *Printer Description Files*, which contain descriptions of device features, the means to query the device for the existence of those features, and methods to use those features, all in a device-independent fashion.

Structure of a PostScript Program

A complete and well constructed PostScript program consists of two separate sections—a prolog and a script. The prolog contains only definitions that will be used by the script. The script section is also sometimes called the *body*. The script contains the PostScript code to produce the images on the display surface, using definitions from the prolog.

The script can be further divided into a setup section, a pages section, and a trailer section. And each page can be broken down into page setup, page code, and end-of-page setup. Here is a small PostScript program to draw a diamond on the page. Document Structuring comments have been added to this program.

```
%!PS-Adobe-3.0
%%Pages: 1                          %   number of pages in document
%%EndComments                       %   end of comments section
%%BeginProlog                       %   start prolog section
/inch { 72 mul } def                %   define inch procedure
%%EndProlog                         %   end prolog section
%%Page: one 1                       %   start of page
%%BeginPageSetup                     %   start page setup section
/pageSave save def                  %   save state of VM
%%EndPageSetup                       %   end page setup section
4.25 inch 5.5 inch translate        %   origin to center of page
0.75 1 scale                        %   scale for diamond shape
45 rotate                           %   rotate to get diamond
-3 inch -3 inch moveto              %   set current point
3 inch -3 inch lineto               %   add line segment
3 inch 3 inch lineto                %   add another line segment
-3 inch 3 inch lineto               %   add another line segment
closepath                           %   finish the shape
gsave                               %   remember graphics state
    0.50 setgray                    %   medium gray
    fill                            %   fill
grestore                            %   restore graphics state
0.5 inch setlinewidth               %   fat line
0.0 setgray                         %   black
stroke                              %   paint outline of path
pageSave restore                    %   restore state of VM
showpage                            %   display page
%%EOF                               %   end of entire document
```

Lines beginning with **%%** are *Document Structuring Comments*. These comments impose another "language" on a document. The PostScript language determines what marks will be placed on the final printed page. The Document Structuring Comments say things about the structure of the document. For example, they tell print manager software where pages begin and end, what fonts are required for a document or a page, and other resources needed for this document. Let's go through this code briefly.

The first line, **%!PS-Adobe-3.0**, indicates that this is a PostScript document claiming to behave according to the Document

Structuring Conventions, revision 3.[†] The next line, which says %%**Pages: 1**, states that this document contains only one page. Your application software should know how many pages will be printed when generating the PostScript. The next line says this is the end of the comments section. You can have other information in the comments section, such as the name of the application that created the document (the %%**Creator:** comment), the name of the person who created the document (the %%**For:** comment), or the date and time the document was created (the %%**CreationDate:** comment).

The next important part of this document is the prolog section. The prolog is where you define all procedures and other definitions to be used by the pages of the document. The only item in the prolog of this example is the definition of the dreaded **inch**.

As part of the philosophy of keeping PostScript programs short and to the point, application writers need to be attentive to the contents of the prolog sections of generated PostScript programs. A square in the middle of a page can be drawn with about ten lines of PostScript code. For some reason, application programmers have discovered ways to carry this simple job to ridiculous extremes. Take another look at the program to draw a diamond on page 592 earlier in this chapter.

Even including Document Structuring Conventions, this picture was generated with only 28 lines of PostScript and could be even more compact. One drawing program we tested generated more than two hundred lines of prolog and epilog, boosting the total size of the file to over 7,000 characters. Another program emitted eleven hundred lines of prolog and epilog, raising the size of the file to 19,500 characters.

Try to emit procedure definitions only when they're needed. A PostScript figure consisting of a simple diamond on the page surely

---

† The Document Structuring Conventions have been through several revisions, and some of the later versions are slightly incompatible with earlier versions.

has no need for a complete library of definitions for ellipses, elliptical arcs, three kinds of cubic splines, two kinds of conic splines, and the proverbial partridge in the pear tree. Keep your prologs as short as they can be.

After the prolog, you can have an optional setup section. If you have a setup section, start it with %%**BeginSetup** and end it with %%**EndSetup**.

Finally, you get to the body or script of the document. Each page starts with a %%**Page:** comment. The %%**Page:** comment has two fields. The second field is easier to understand. It's the ordinal number of this page within the document. Pages are numbered from 1. The first field in the %%**Page:** comment is the page label. This can be anything you like. Books such as this one frequently have front matter (like the table of contents and the preface) with Roman numbered pages. Then, typically, the body pages of the document are numbered using Arabic numbers.

Pages in a PostScript document are usually considered the appropriate unit to enclose within a **save** and **restore** pair. Use **save** at the start of the page to take a snapshot of VM. Use **restore** at the end of the page, but *before* the **showpage**, to restore VM to the state it was in at the beginning of the page. The **save** in this example was done between %%**BeginPageSetup** and %%**EndPageSetup**. You do any other page setup functions within the setup section. **save** creates a save object, which is the snapshot of VM. The example defines this save object in the current dictionary. Then, at the end of the page, **restore** uses that save object to restore everything to a pristine state.

For a complete treatise on the Document Structuring Conventions, refer to the *PostScript Language Reference Manual*, Second Edition.

Encapsulated PostScript

Now to explore one of the major sources of confusion among PostScript users and programmers alike. Precisely what is Encapsulated PostScript? Instead of trying to provide a highly formal definition, let's approach Encapsulated PostScript from the viewpoint of how it's used. Take a look at these three pictures. The left-hand picture shows a page of text with a blank space in it, ready for an illustration (drawing, image, or whatever) to be dropped in. The middle picture is a PostScript drawing of a *geta* of Sushi. The right-hand picture shows the same page, but this time the *geta* of Sushi appears as a picture illustrating the text, a travel diary of a week of bliss and fine dining on the island of Kaua'i.

Page with space for picture.   *Encapsulated PostScript picture to be placed on page.*   *Encapsulated PostScript picture, correctly positioned and scaled.*

In a nutshell, this is what Encapsulated PostScript is about. The idea is to be able to drop PostScript illustrations onto pages of text or into other PostScript illustrations, and have them positioned and scaled appropriately. All the PostScript illustrations in this book are Encapsulated PostScript diagrams. What makes Encapsulated PostScript so special? What is the difference between a PostScript file and an Encapsulated PostScript file? Probably the most frequently asked question about PostScript is, "How do you convert PostScript to Encapsulated PostScript?" To explore these details, let's create a simple PostScript figure, much like many other PostScript examples you've seen throughout this book.

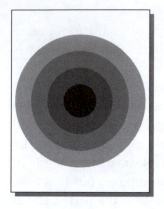

```
%!PS
/inch { 72 mul } def                    %  define inch define
1 inch setlinewidth                     %  fat line width
4.25 inch 5.5 inch 3.5 inch 0 360 arc closepath
0.66 setgray stroke                     %  stroke with light gray
4.25 inch 5.5 inch 2.5 inch 0 360 arc closepath
0.50 setgray stroke                     %  stroke with medium gray
4.25 inch 5.5 inch 1.5 inch 0 360 arc closepath
0.33 setgray stroke                     %  stroke with dark gray
4.25 inch 5.5 inch 0.5 inch 0 360 arc closepath
0.00 setgray stroke                     %  stroke with black
showpage                                %  fat line width
```

Now let's rewrite this PostScript code with correct Document Structuring Conventions. This will provide a look at what makes a file Encapsulated PostScript, and will continue with the ideas behind the Document Structuring Conventions.

```
%!PS-Adobe-3.0 EPSF-3.0                  %  DSC header
%%BoundingBox: 18 108 594 684            %  bounding box for figure
%%EndComments                            %  end of comment section
/inch { 72 mul } def                     %  define inch define
%%EndProlog                              %  bounding box for figure
1 inch setlinewidth                      %  fat line width
4.25 inch 5.5 inch 3.5 inch 0 360 arc closepath
0.66 setgray stroke                      %  stroke with light gray
4.25 inch 5.5 inch 2.5 inch 0 360 arc closepath
0.50 setgray stroke                      %  stroke with medium gray
4.25 inch 5.5 inch 1.5 inch 0 360 arc closepath
0.33 setgray stroke                      %  stroke with dark gray
4.25 inch 5.5 inch 0.5 inch 0 360 arc closepath
0.00 setgray stroke                      %  stroke with black
showpage                                 %  fat line width
%%EOF                                    %  end of file indicator
```

That's the same piece of code defined as an Encapsulated PostScript file. The important line is the one beginning with %%**BoundingBox**. The bounding box line defines the region of user space within which marks are made on the display surface. The format of the bounding box is

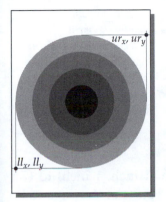

`%%BoundingBox:` ll_x ll_y ur_x ur_y

where ll_x and ll_y are the coordinates of the lower-left corner of the bounding box, and ur_x and ur_y are the coordinates of the upper-right corner of the bounding box. In this example, (ll_x, ll_y) are at $(18, 108)$ and (ur_x, ur_y) are at $(594, 684)$.

How do you determine the bounding box of a PostScript figure so you can add a **%%BoundingBox** comment? Ingenious methods have been devised to redefine PostScript path construction operators and determine the minimum and maximum values. One of the best methods is extremely simple—print the illustration and measure it with a ruler.

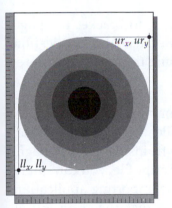

ll_x is the distance from the left edge of the paper to the left edge of the illustration. ll_y is the distance from the bottom edge of the paper to the bottom edge of the illustration. ur_x is the distance from the bottom edge of the paper to the right edge of the illustration. ur_y is the distance from the bottom edge of the paper to the top edge of the illustration. Convert the measurements into PostScript units and those are the values for your bounding box.

When you compute the bounding box, make sure you allow for fat lines. If you used **pathbbox** to compute the path, your path wouldn't take fat lines into consideration. This code and illustration shows the problem.

```
%!PS
/inch { 72 mul } def                  %   define inch procedure
1 inch 1 inch moveto                  %   set current point
4.25 inch 9 inch lineto               %   add line segment
7.5 inch 1 inch lineto                %   add another line segment
closepath                             %   finish the shape
1 inch setlinewidth                   %   fat line width
stroke                                %   paint outline of shape
showpage                              %   display page
```

Incorrect path because of fat line width.

Part of the path in this code extends from (1 inch, 1 inch) to (7.5 inch, 1 inch), but the fat line means that the parts of the page to be painted lie outside the path. If the importing application uses bounding box information to clip, parts of the picture will get clipped off.

Notice that an EPS document does not need to bracket the page inside a **save** and **restore** pair. Why? Because the application importing the EPS file is responsible for doing the **save** and **restore**, among other preparations.

An Encapsulated PostScript file should contain only one page. A multiple page Encapsulated PostScript file doesn't make sense, since it's supposed to be just a picture to fit inside another page. When you generate an Encapsulated PostScript file, you can safely place a **showpage** instruction in the file. The importing application is responsible for redefining **showpage** so that the page is not printed too soon.

The Encapsulated PostScript specification lists a set of operators you should not use inside Encapsulated PostScript files. Read Appendix H of the *PostScript Language Reference Manual*, Second Edition, to find out which operators are not permitted. In general, you shouldn't use those operators that would perturb the graphics environment of the surrounding PostScript.

Including Encapsulated PostScript Illustrations

Now that you've seen how to create Encapsulated PostScript files, how does your application go about including them and positioning them correctly? Here are some guidelines for including EPS files in documents. Applications generating EPS don't always do the job correctly. A multitude of sins have been committed in the name of Encapsulated PostScript, and some of the guidelines protect your importing program from incorrect EPS.

One pitfall of EPS is that the values supplied in the **%%Bounding-Box:** comment (ll_x, ll_y, ur_x, and ur_y) are all supposed to be integers. Some applications generate bounding boxes containing floating point numbers. If you're writing applications to import Encapsulated PostScript, be prepared for either integers or floating point values. For that matter, be prepared to parse the **%%BoundingBox:** in all upper case or all lower case,[†] and watch for a missing colon character in the statement.

Place a **save** and **restore** pair around the EPS file. Although EPS programs are not supposed to do their own **save** and **restore**, some do. There's a slight possibility this could cause some limits to be exceeded, so watch out for this when debugging.

Importing applications should redefine **showpage**, **erasepage**, and **copypage** as null procedures. Some experts recommend redefining **letter**, **legal**, and **a4** as null procedures also. These latter operators are page setup instructions and are peculiar to specific printers. PostScript programs that assume that these operators exist are inherently non-portable, and you should guard against them.

Set the graphics state to a known state. The EPS program should do this, but many don't, so include the following instructions in your PostScript program:

---

† To avoid the issue, convert it all to one case internally.

```
0 setgray                            %   gray scale = black
0 setlinecap                         %   butt line cap
1 setlinewidth                       %   one point lines
0 setlinejoin                        %   mitered line join
10 setmiterlimit
[] 0 setdash                         %   no dash patterns
/languagelevel where {               %   see if language level defined
    pop                              %   get rid of dictionary
    languagelevel 2 ge {             %   see if Level 2 or greater
        false setoverprint           %   no overprinting
        false setstrokeadjust        %   no stroke adjust
    } if
} if
newpath                              %   start new path
```

The **languagelevel** operator should be used as shown for compatibility between PostScript Level 1 and Level 2 printers.

Good EPS program define their own dictionaries for their own definitions. Unfortunately, there aren't enough "good" EPS programs out there, so push a copy of **userdict** onto the dictionary stack prior to importing the EPS file and remove the copy after the import. Also clear the operand stack prior to importing the EPS.

Place the EPS picture in the correct place on the page by following this four-step procedure:

❏   **translate** to the correct position on the page

❏   **rotate** if required

❏   **scale** if required

❏   **translate** again to get the lower-left corner of the EPS file's bounding box to the correct position

This last step is required because the lower-left corner of the bounding box is not necessarily at (0, 0). In fact, some applications generate EPS files with peculiar looking negative numbers in their bounding boxes.

Appendix H of the *PostScript Language Reference Manual*, Second Edition, recommends setting up a clipping path for the imported EPS file. You would normally expect the clipping path to be the same size as the picture specified by its bounding box. Clipping the picture may or may not give the results you expect. If the application generating the EPS was sloppy in computing its bounding box, as discussed previously, part of the picture may be clipped away.

The final aspects of EPS to be concerned about are preview sections and control characters. Preview sections are included in EPS files for benighted systems that can't render PostScript on the screen. The preview section provides a screen image to show the user a reasonable approximation of how the final result will look when printed.[†] Preview sections differ from system to system. Common formats are PICT, TIFF, and Windows Metafile. These three formats are binary images, so you must be prepared for EPS files that start with a binary header. Another preview format is an ASCII format called EPSI. When generating PostScript files for printing, be sure to strip out preview sections.

Dealing with control characters in EPS files is tricky. In theory, control characters shouldn't exist inside EPS files. In practice, especially in the PC arena, programmers inject control characters into EPS programs. The most common offender is Control-D. Willy-nilly stripping out control characters may cause problems because some PostScript documents include binary data that works for certain printers. Your importing application might want to check for Control-D at the very beginning and very end of the PostScript file (and Control_Z at the end also).

Conclusion

Well, that was a full fourteen chapters of PostScript, plus more than seven hundred illustrations—and, that's just a start. Like many aspects of education, learning PostScript and its related topics can be a continuous process rather than an event.

---

† kind of "What You See Is More Or Less What You Get."

Application developers dealing with PostScript issues are encouraged to read and re-read and thoroughly understand the conventions for document structuring and Encapsulated PostScript. If you're an application developer new to PostScript, we recommend strongly that you take a "drivers" course—the knowledge gained in such courses will pay off in good PostScript that performs well and cooperates with other PostScript. And now, all the best in your future dealings with PostScript.

Further Reading

I've got a little list.

I've got a little list.

Gilbert and Sullivan—The Mikado

PostScript Language Reference Manual—Second Edition

Adobe Systems, published by Addison-Wesley, 1990. *The PostScript Language Reference Manual*, Second Edition, describes PostScript Level 2, currently the new standard PostScript language. PostScript Level 2 is (at the time of writing—mid-1992) gradually emerging as the new PostScript standard and is subsuming PostScript Level 1, described in the *PostScript Language Reference Manual*.

PostScript Language Tutorial and Cookbook

Adobe Systems, published by Addison-Wesley, 1986. Commonly known as the "Blue Book," this book contains a variety of examples of usage of the PostScript language. The Blue Book is getting a little old now, given the advent of PostScript Level 2, but it still remains on the recommended reading list.

PostScript Language Program Design

Glenn Reid, formerly of Adobe Systems, and published by Addison-Wesley, 1988. Commonly known as "The Green Book," it focuses on well-designed PostScript programs.

Programming the Display PostScript System with NeXTstep

Adobe Systems, published by Addison-Wesley, 1992. *Programming the Display PostScript System with NeXTstep* is *the* premier reference for Display PostScript on NeXT systems. Sometimes called "the Purple Book," *Programming the Display PostScript System with NeXTstep* is recommended highly, whether or not you're programming NeXT systems. It is chock full of comparative studies on optimal ways to program in the time-critical context of display systems.

Adobe Type 1 Font Format—Version 1.1

Adobe Systems, published by Addison-Wesley, 1990. This book contains the specification for the Type 1 font format. In the tradition of naming books by the colors of their covers, this one has become known as "The White Book," or sometimes, "The Black and White Book." The Adobe Type 1 Font Format—Version 1.1 covers the latest (as of mid-1992) version of the Type 1 Font Format, and is the preferred version. A new version of this book is expected.

The Display PostScript System

Written and distributed by Adobe Systems. *The Display PostScript System* is a large collection of manuals describing the Display PostScript System in detail. Contact Adobe Systems Developer Support.

Thinking in PostScript

Glenn Reid, published by Addison-Wesley, 1990. *Thinking In PostScript* is a collection of hints and tips for application developers. Of particular value are areas explaining differences in "philosophy" between PostScript and other programming languages, with advice on how *not* to shoehorn PostScript into the Procrustean bed of already familiar languages.

Real World PostScript

Edited by Stephen Roth, published by Addison-Wesley, 1988. Subtitled "Tools and Techniques from PostScript Professionals, this book is a collection of case studies and essays from various practitioners of the Art of PostScript. It's sometimes called "The Orange Book." The authors of this book were all involved with PostScript in the days when people were going around asking "What is this PostScript stuff?" Even today, we can pick up this book and always find some new insight.

Learning PostScript—A Visual Approach
Ross Smith, published by Peachpit Press, 1990. An elementary text on PostScript. *Learning PostScript—A Visual Approach* is strongly recommended for its extensive use of "look and learn" graphics. Almost half the book is pictures—a laudable approach when the subject matter is graphics.

Graphic Design with PostScript
Gerard Kunkel, published by Scott, Foresman and Company, 1990. This book is written from the viewpoint of a real world graphic designer using PostScript to enhance the output from various publication and illustration packages. Gerard Kunkel's treatment of color issues is especially good, and you should read his book for that part alone.

Encapsulated PostScript
Peter Vollenweider, published by Prentice-Hall, 1990. Subtitled *Application Guide for the Macintosh and PC*, this book is a collection of information on Macintosh and PC applications, how they generate (often incompatible) versions of PostScript, and how to make them work together. The book is written from the practical day-to-day aspects of making software, computers, and printers play harmoniously.

Digital Typography
Richard Rubenstein, published by Addison-Wesley, 1988. Subtitled "An Introduction to Type and Composition for Computer System Design," this excellent book is a must for an introduction to digital typography, as well as covering some quite advanced topics. Highly recommended.

Computers and Typesetting
Donald Knuth, published by Addison-Wesley. *Computers and Typesetting* is a five-volume work on Knuth's widely acclaimed TEX document formatting system, METAFONT font design tools, and the Computer Modern typefaces. The complete five-volume set is published by Addison-Wesley, 1986.

The World of Digital Typesetting
John Seybold, published by Seybold Publications, 1984. This thoroughly useful book covers the history of typesetting from the beginning of writing through to the mid-1980s.

The TypEncyclopedia

Frank Romano, published by R. R. Bowker, 1984. This book is subtitled *A User's Guide to Better Typography*. Frank Romano is a recognized authority on type and typesetting, and he has a great sense of humor. His book is an easy—alphabetically ordered—quick reference for the language of type.

Digital Formats for Typefaces

Peter Karow, published by URW Verlag, 1987. Doctor Peter Karow is a partner of internationally renowned URW company, known for their IKARUS font editing system.

Graphics Gems

Andrew Glassner, published by Prentice Hall, 1990. A collection of short papers on graphics techniques. Highly recommended.

Computer Graphics, Principles and Practice—Second Edition

James Foley, Ph.D.., Andries van Dam, Ph.D.., Steven Feiner, Ph.D.., and John Hughes, Ph.D.., published by Addison-Wesley, 1990. A comprehensive book containing authoritative, up-to-date coverage of the quickly changing domain of computer graphics. Exhaustive coverage of subjects from 3-dimensional graphics to user interface design.

Mathematical Elements for Computer Graphics

David F. Rogers and J. Alan Adams, published by McGraw-Hill. A small book packed with information on graphics techniques. Includes algorithms written in BASIC, of all things.

Principles of Color Technology

Fred W. Billmeyer, Jr., and Max Saltzman, published by Inter-Science Publishers (a division of John Wiley & Sons). An excellent beginner's guide to the physics of colored light and the physiology of the human eye in relation to color.

Blue and Yellow Don't Make Green

Published by Rockport Publishers, 1989. Distributed by North Light Books, this book is written from the viewpoint of artists rather than publishers, but the author leads you through many of the mysteries of color mixing and tells you why what you learned in school was wrong.

Color Science: Concepts and Methods, Quantitative Data and Formulae

Published by John Wiley & Sons, this book contains the CIEXYZ color space specification among others.

Linotronic Imaging Handbook

James Cavuoto and Stephen Beale, published by Micro Publishing Press, 1990. This book goes well beyond run-of-the-mill 300-dots-per-inch laser printers and takes you into the realm of high-resolution imagesetters. The authors deal with gory details of color separation and lead you through the art of dealing with printing houses. Very highly recommended.

Getting It Printed

Mark Beach, Steve Shepro, and Ken Russon, and published by Coast to Coast Books, Portland, Oregon, 1986. The subtitle sums up the content: *How to work with printers and graphic arts services to assure quality, stay on schedule, and control costs.* If you deal with printers in any way, you need this book.

Desktop To Press

Subtitled *The Technical Information Newsletter for the PostScript Typesetting Community, Desktop To Press* is packed with information on the practical details of getting PostScript files from your desktop applications to the printing press. The publisher, Peter Fink, knows his stuff when it comes to separations and screening technology. Published by Peter Fink Communications, 120 Q Street NE, Washington, DC 20002.

Index

Disk Order Form

Source code (about thirteen thousand lines of PostScript) for many of the examples in this book is available on floppy diskette, for $20.00 per diskette. To order a source diskette, please fill in the information below.

Name ————————————————

DISKETTE FORMAT

Address ————————————————

❑ Mac 1.4Mb

————————————————

❑ NEXT 1.4Mb

————————————————

❑ DOS 1.4Mb

Cheque[†]

Make cheques for $20 per diskette payable to **Trilithon Software**

American Express
or
Visa
or
MasterCard

Card Number ————————————————

Expiration Date ————————————————

Signature ————————————————

Mail completed order to: TRILITHON SOFTWARE, TWO OHLONE, PORTOLA VALLEY, CALIFORNIA 94028

Telephone Orders: (415) 917–9201 during business hours in California.

FAX Orders: (415) 917–9202

Electronic Mail: `info@trilithon.com`

---

† "Checks" are also accepted.